SILCHESTER ROMAN TOWN:
THE INSULA IX TOWN LIFE PROJECT: VOLUME 2

SILCHESTER: CITY IN TRANSITION

THE MID-ROMAN OCCUPATION OF INSULA IX
c. A.D. 125–250/300

A REPORT ON EXCAVATIONS UNDERTAKEN SINCE 1997

SILCHESTER: CITY IN TRANSITION

THE MID-ROMAN OCCUPATION OF INSULA IX
c. A.D. 125–250/300

A REPORT ON EXCAVATIONS UNDERTAKEN SINCE 1997

BY

Michael Fulford and Amanda Clarke

With contributions by
Denise Allen, John R.L. Allen, Rowena Banerjea, Edward Besly, Joanna Bird,
Kate Clark, Samantha R. Cook, Nina Crummy, Petra Dark, Brenda Dickinson,
Kevin M. Hayward, Hella Eckardt, Claire Ingrem, Mary Lewis, Margaret Mathews,
Mark Robinson, Elizabeth Somerville, Jane Timby, Klare Tootell, Paul Tyers,
Peter Warry, Jacqui Watson, Sandie Williams

And an Appendix on 'The Iron Age and Roman Coins found at Silchester, as recorded
and catalogued by George Boon, 1951–54' by Dave Wythe

Illustrators: Margaret Mathews with Frances Taylor, Jane Timby and Brian Williams

Britannia Monograph Series
No. 25

Published by the Society for the Promotion of Roman Studies
Senate House Malet Street London WC1E 7HU
2011

BRITANNIA MONOGRAPH SERIES NO. 25

Published by the Society for the Promotion of Roman Studies
Senate House, Malet Street, London WC1E 7HU

This monograph was published with the aid of a grant from the University of Reading

British Library Catalogue in Publication Data
A catalogue record of this book is available from the British Library

ISBN   978 0 907764 37 3

Cover illustration: Aerial view of 'House 1' under excavation in 2002, from the south-west

Produced by Past Historic, Kings Stanley, Gloucestershire

Printed in Great Britain

CONTENTS

LIST OF FIGURES

LIST OF TABLES

ACKNOWLEDGEMENTS

This reporting of the archaeology of Insula IX in the second and third centuries A.D. relates back to fieldwork undertaken between the start of the project in 1997, when the remains of the town-houses reported here, which we now know date back to the early second century, began to come to light, and 2005 when the excavation of the last pits and wells of this phase of the project was completed.

The publication of *City in Transition*, as well as the continuation of the Silchester Insula IX Town Life Project, now in its fourteenth year, owes a great debt of gratitude to many organisations and individuals. First and foremost our University has provided both framework, through the Department of Archaeology and the School of Human and Environmental Sciences, of which the department is a member, and core resource, in underpinning both the undergraduate training experience, the Field School, at Silchester and the permanent staffing necessary both to manage that, and provide the essential underwriting and continuity of the post-excavation research. At the same time, without the support of the Hampshire County Council, the owner of the Roman town, and of English Heritage, who mediated the Scheduled Monument Consent granted by the Department of Culture, Media and Sport in 1997 and renewed in 2002 and 2007, the excavation could not have taken place.

The project has depended on grants from a number of organisations, academic, private and local authority, all of which are gratefully acknowledged here: first and foremost, The Arts and Humanities Research Council has been the principal supporter of the post-excavation programme (2005–8),[1] followed by The Leverhulme Trust, which awarded the first author a Major Research Fellowship (2004–7). Since 2005 The Calleva Foundation has provided continuous support for the project and, with The Headley Trust, has allowed us to develop a distinctive, scientific strand (Science@Silchester), led by Dr Sam Cook. Welcome annual support has also been provided by The Haverfield Bequest (University of Oxford), which has funded the conservation of our artefacts. The Arts and Humanities Research Council also supported the PhD studentship (2006–9) of Rowena Banerjea (Ch. 4).

In regard to the continuation of the excavation — the source of the data reported here — and its promotion to the wider public, Basingstoke and Deane Borough Council and The Hampshire County Council have, each year, generously provided us with the means to open the site to the public and maintain a visitor programme.

As funding has become ever more difficult, we are profoundly grateful to new supporters of the project, and of the Field School in particular. GML Ltd, along with The Englefield Charitable Trust, The Fishburn Family Trust, and The Horne Foundation have, since 2007, provided us with a level of support without which the Field School could not have been sustained. Through its sponsorship of villagers to take part, the Silchester Association has also provided much valued support to the Field School, while The Society for the Promotion of Roman Studies, through its imaginative bursary scheme, has also, each year, funded the participation of sixth-formers in the excavation. The engagement of local schools and colleges in the project owes a great deal to the pump-priming provided by a Heritage Lottery grant in 2004.

---

1   AHRC Grant reference: RGST/PID/120879/AID112201

Many individuals have been wonderful supporters of the project, in particular Nick and Biddy West of The Old Manor House, Silchester, who have assisted it in very many ways since its inception, not least through their warm hospitality each summer and in making generous space available in the barns for us to work on the finds and store equipment. They, and John Cook of Church Lane Farm, Silchester, also warmly generous in his support of the project, are among a growing group of supporters of the project, which Dudley Fishburn, member of the University's Council, has been instrumental in bringing together. Pre-eminent among these are Stephen Butt and Timothy Osborne and to them, but particularly to Dudley Fishburn and his wife, Victoria, we, and the University, owe an enormous debt of gratitude for their energetic support and enthusiasm for the project.

We thank Marilyn Tucker, former Mayor of Basingstoke and Deane, who has been a great supporter of the project throughout.

The Recreational Society, AWE, Aldermaston has been unfailingly generous every season in providing its sports club showers and facilities for the use of the participants in the excavation.

The tenancy of the County Council's estate at Silchester has moved from father to sons. We are grateful to the Best family for their understanding and support of the project throughout.

From Hampshire County Council we thank the late Alderman Dudley Keep, Chair of the County's Silchester Panel, Robin Edwards, Head of the County's Estate Practice, David Hopkins, County Archaeologist, David Allen, Keeper of Archaeology, and Kay Ainsworth, Hampshire County Museums Service. We also thank Dr Richard Massey, Inspector of Ancient Monuments, English Heritage, for his continued support and helpful facilitation of Scheduled Monument Consent for the project.

From the University of Reading we thank the Vice-Chancellor, Professor Gordon Marshall, and his predecessor, Professor Sir Roger Williams, for their unfailing support of the project since its inception, as well as that of the successive Heads of Archaeology: Professors Grenville Astill, Bob Chapman and Roberta Gilchrist; and the Heads of School, Professors Steven Mithen and Rob Potter, and acting Head of School, Stephen Northcliffe, through their various terms of office. Margaret Mathews is the principal illustrator of this volume, but she has also helped with each field season, not only with the planning, but also the interpretation of the excavation to visitors, not least with her richly imaginative reconstructions, some of which are presented in this report. Close, enthusiastic and energetic support of the excavation and post-excavation has been magnificently provided by the successive Silchester Project technicians: Dr Ruth Shaffrey (1998–2002), Klare Tootell (2002–9), who has contributed to this report, and, since 2008, Frances Taylor. We are grateful, too, to Sandie Williams, who, thanks to the AHRC funding, capably and enthusiastically looked after the needs of all our specialists and herself contributed to this report. We also thank Heather Browning, School Administrator, for her much appreciated help in many aspects of the organisation of the Field School. During the excavation seasons Ted Logan and Alan Absalom of the University's Facilities Management Directorate have provided much welcomed assistance with the logistics.

We warmly thank Mike Rains and the York Archaeological Trust, who have supported and developed our database, the IADB, from the inception of this project. Storing all the excavation and finds records in the IADB is an absolutely integral part of the Insula IX Town Life Project, and an essential foundation of, and tool for the post-excavation process. Through the OGHAM and VERA projects, generously supported by the JISC as part of their VRE (Virtual Research Environments) Programme, we have enhanced the ways in which we capture data in the field and engage the members of our research team in the use and development of the IADB. With JISC's assistance we have also experimented successfully with full, on-line publication in *Internet Archaeology*.

We are ever grateful to Dr Rachel Stewart who managed the Heritage Lottery-funded Access Project in 2004–5. She successfully set in place for future seasons the practice and procedure for the management and support of visitors, including the development of the Silchester website.

We remain indebted to Jean Chapman, who, with assistance from Serena Bartlett and Lorraine Mepham, and her husband, Chris, continued to cater for the very large numbers of students and other participants throughout the majority of seasons associated with this phase of the Town Life

Project, working heroically (and stoically) in far from ideal conditions on site. Following Jean's retirement at the end of the 2004 season, the role was shared by students and we thank Sarah Bell, Jude Haigh, Jessica Horniblow and Stuart Kennedy for their help in feeding the team.

To the roll call of supervisors and assistant supervisors acknowledged in *Life and Labour* we add and thank the following, who supported the project up to and including 2005: Edeltraud Aspoeck, Chris Ball, Meredith Carroll, Rob Cole, Jonathan Dicks, Jodie Ford, Ruth Hatfield, Sarah Henley, Dave Houghton, Tom Lyons, Jody Morris, Nick Pankhurst, Gareth Rees, Rebecca Rooney, Duncan Sayer, Rik Sayer, Adam Tinsley, Tamsin Turner and Dan Waterfall. An invaluable supervisor training scheme was set up in 2003 and we thank Kari Bower, Hannah Brown, Susan Brown, Anna Browne-Ribiero, Belinda Crerar, Helen Crossman, Elizabeth Jones, Georgina McHugh, Elizabeth Poulteney, Anthony Roach, Sue Taplin, Jeni Thurstan and Rebecca West for their support of the project.

We thank other key members of the on-site team: Dan Wheeler, Dave Houghton and Lucy Offord for their management of the planning; Darren Baker, Julie Cassidy, Liz Clark, Elise Fraser, Kay Rushton and Sandie Williams for looking after the finds processing, supported by Peter Davies, Oliver Hartree and John Hefferan, and under the attentive oversight of Hella Eckardt. We thank Nancy Fulford, Ann Griffin, Sean Keating and Klare Tootell for taking care of the processing of environmental samples with oversight by Dr Sam Cook assisted by Rowena Banerjea; Margaret Dixon and Mike Eckhoff for looking after the site photography; and Natalie Head, Kat Lund and Verity Murricaine for managing the visiting general public. Margaret James and Lyn Simmonds were invaluable administrative assistants during several excavation seasons, while Jon Tierney, site manager since 2002, proved indispensable in his support over many seasons in maintaining the infrastructure of the project.

We warmly thank all our contributors to this report. Together, their work has helped create a very rich and remarkable characterisation of life in Insula IX in the second and third centuries A.D. Claire Ingrem thanks Dale Serjeantson for her advice and Kate Clark for her assistance with the pathological bones reported in her chapter. Margaret Mathews thanks John Smith for helpful discussions of her interpretations of the Insula IX buildings and for his encouragement in the writing of her contribution, and Peter Warry for his helpful comments on roofing.

PREFACE

The Silchester Insula IX Roman Town Life Project began in 1997 with the objective of investigating in detail the structural and stratigraphic development of a substantial area of the Roman town from its origins in the late Iron Age to its demise in the fifth to seventh century A.D. and, at the same time, capturing the evidence for the changing life and occupations of the inhabitants. Insula IX, a block devoid of public buildings at the intersection of the main east–west and north–south streets of the town, and immediately to the north-west of the forum-basilica, was selected and an area of 3,025 square metres was identified for excavation in the northern part of the insula. The latter had been excavated in 1893–4 as part of the Society of Antiquaries' project to excavate the entirety of the Roman town at Silchester and its selection in 1997 was determined on the basis of the Victorian findings of larger town-houses and smaller buildings, probably houses-cum-workshops. Those early excavations proved to be limited to the exposure of the latest surviving phases of the masonry buildings identified by trial-trenching, leaving the majority of the stratigraphy untouched (Fulford and Clarke 2002). The quality of what has survived earlier excavation is indicated by the project completing its thirteenth season of excavation in the summer of 2009, reaching occupation of the mid-first century A.D.

City in Transition is the second 'monograph' report, following on from the publication of the fourth-century and later archaeology in *Life and Labour in Late Roman Silchester* (Fulford *et al.* 2006). This, in its turn, built on the publication of the Victorian excavations (Fulford and Clarke 2002) and the late/post-Roman Ogham stone and its context (Fulford *et al.* 2000). In addition, the development of the major town-house ('House 1') within the area under excavation was selected for electronic publication in *Internet Archaeology* (Clarke *et al.* 2007) to demonstrate the opportunities the electronic medium offers for presenting the complete underlying archive of the stratigraphic record, along with the conventional narrative of the structural and stratigraphic record and the reporting of the associated finds. This initiative built on the website publications linked to the publication of the Victorian archaeology in 2003 (www.silchester.reading.ac.uk/victorian) and of the late Roman archaeology in 2005 (www.silchester.reading.ac.uk/later).

In reporting all the archaeology across the excavation area of the period between the early second century and the mid/late third century *City in Transition* puts the relevant 'House 1' sequence in its wider context. There is inevitably some duplication with the electronic publication (Clarke *et al.* 2007), but the scale of the pottery and animal bone assemblages, in particular, is such that *City in Transition* only contains summaries of the previously reported material. To gain the full picture it is necessary to consult the electronic publication. Shaping the chronological scope and periodisation of the stratigraphic sequence for both the *Internet Archaeology* and *City in Transition* publications required an extensive, initial programme of spot dating using the coin and pottery evidence. This identified four periods of development of which *City in Transition* is concerned with two, Periods 3 and 4 (see below, Introduction). One exception made to this was to include a major assemblage of environmental evidence from a large latrine pit filled at the end of Period 2, *c.* A.D. 125 (see below, Robinson, Ch. 16 and Dark, Ch. 17).

While it is clear now from the ongoing excavation that Period 2 represents a radical departure from the preceding phase of occupation with the construction *de novo* of two new complexes of timber building, including the first, timber phase of the 'House 1' sequence, *City in Transition* reports only on the second and third phases of that development (Periods 3 and 4). The first phase of 'House 1', as first described in Clarke *et al.* (2007), will be further reported along with the rest of the Period 2 occupation in the next stage of 'final' reporting. A significant virtue of the *Internet Archaeology* publication is that it embraces the complete lifespan of an evolving household of one or more kin groups ('House 1') and their associated property through three phases of building, from the late first century A.D. until the final destruction of the house and associated re-allocation of space within the insula in the second half of the third century A.D.

The rationale for publishing fully while the excavation still continues downwards to the earliest Roman and late Iron Age levels, and thereby reversing the normal presentation of the archaeological sequence from earliest to latest, is pragmatic: the avoidance of the accumulation of a substantial backlog of unreported structures and stratigraphy with all their associated finds, both material and biological, and environmental data. At the same time there have been significant developments of methodology which have increased the volume and range of information arising from the project. Unlike *Life and Labour, City in Transition* has benefited from systematic research into soil chemistry (Cook, Ch. 3) and micromorphology (Banerjea, Ch. 4), both of which have made very significant contributions to the interpretation of the occupation and use of structures in the second and third centuries. In particular, these new directions of research have led to a completely different interpretation of one of the second-century timber buildings from that reported in Clarke *et al.* (2007). This new work highlights the general difficulties that the Insula IX project has had in the identification and interpretation of timber buildings in general since its inception. *City in Transition* presents the evidence for six timber buildings which were not recognised as such with any confidence during the excavation itself. To the interpretation of two of these geochemistry and soil micromorphology have made vital contributions. Without any doubt a wider application of these approaches would have contributed significantly to the recognition and interpretation of the other structures lacking clear and coherent evidence of structural features such as clay walls, posts or horizontally laid beams.

The reports on the geochemistry and soil micromorphology are presented immediately after the description of the structural and stratigraphic sequence. In presenting their data both contributors have required colour in order to illustrate their results satisfactorily. This has also chimed well with the need for as informative a presentation as possible of the complex structural evidence and its interpretation as standing buildings emerging from the excavation of Insula IX. Indeed, as prefigured in *Life and Labour,* Mathews' reconstructions extend beyond the buildings to their context within the insula, for which colour is, of course, essential. Thus, and representing a significant departure from the publication of *Life and Labour,* that of *City in Transition* makes significant use of colour. Colour is, of course, intrinsic to the archival database record of excavation and finds' images which, as with *Life and Labour,* are available electronically via www.silchester.reading.ac.uk/cit.

We are also very pleased to publish in Appendix 1 Dave Wythe's full list of Iron Age and Roman coins originally recorded and catalogued by George Boon, 1951–4.

Michael Fulford and Amanda Clarke
Department of Archaeology
University of Reading
November 2009

CHAPTER 1

INTRODUCTION

By Michael Fulford

The excavation of Insula IX, Silchester and the associated 'Town Life' project began in 1997. An area of 3,025m² covering the north-east of the insula was selected for total excavation of the archaeological sequence from the origins of the city in the late Iron Age to abandonment in the fifth to seventh century A.D. (FIG. 1). The reasons for investigating this particular area of *Calleva* are set out in Fulford *et al.* (2006, 4–7). The trench was bordered by the main, north–south street of the city on the eastern side, while a subsidiary, east–west street provided its northern boundary. The western and southern limits of the trench were essentially arbitrary, but their

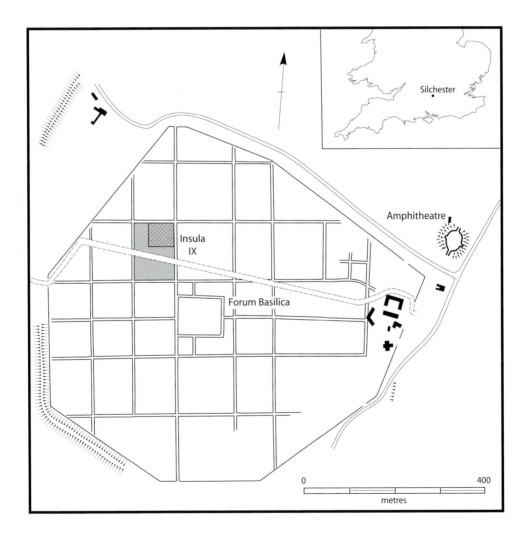

FIG. 1.   Silchester: simplified Roman town-plan showing location of Insula IX and excavation area, also with present-day buildings and lanes to north-west and south-east (black), and droveway (broken lines) across the walled area.

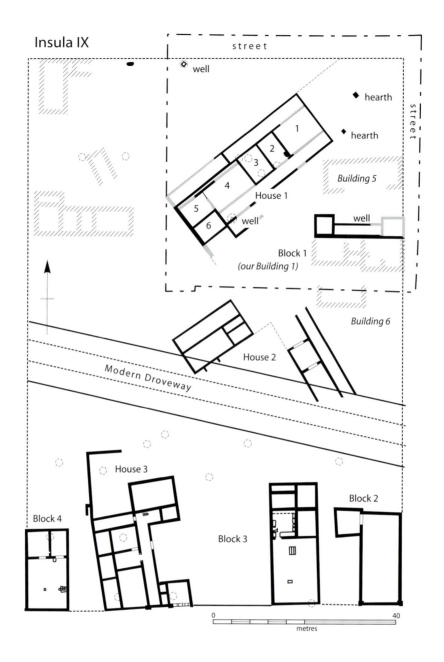

FIG. 2.   Insula IX showing the plan of 1893–4, buildings plotted from aerial photographs (shaded outlines) (after Bewley and Fulford 1996, folding plan), and the current area of excavation.

positioning ensured that they encapsulated the total area of both 'House 1', oriented north-east/south-west (and thus at a completely different orientation to that of the street grid), and Building 1, oriented east–west, as described by the original excavators of the insula in 1893–4 (Fox 1895) (FIG. 2). At the time of writing the excavation, now in its fourteenth year, has reached occupation spanning the mid-to-late first/early second centuries A.D.

   City in Transition represents the fifth stage in the programme of 'final' publication of this still on-going excavation, following on from the publication of the Victorian excavations (Clarke *et al.* 2001; Fulford and Clarke 2002) and of the later Roman and post-Roman occupation, including a re-analysis of the Ogham stone and its context (Fulford *et al.* 2000), the larger work published as *Life and Labour in Late Roman Silchester* (Clarke *et al.* 2005; Fulford *et al.* 2006). Both the reporting of 'Victorian' and 'Late Roman' archaeology linked conventional printed reports with websites which give access to the primary field and finds records. A completely digital publication of the succession of buildings which constituted the 'House 1' sequence, as the excavation revealed, ('The Development of an Urban Property') was published with the associated finds and environmental reports, also with live links back to the underlying database, in *Internet Archaeology* (Clarke *et al.* 2007).

The aim of *City in Transition* is to report the archaeology from the early to mid-second century through to the late third/beginning of fourth century A.D., which is the starting point for *Life and Labour* (Fulford *et al.* 2006). This phase of reporting is defined, on the one hand, by the construction of the first, masonry phase of 'House 1', which is represented by Early Roman Masonry Buildings 1 and 2, and, on the other, by the occupation which succeeded the abandonment of a suite of timber buildings occupying the south-eastern corner of the excavated area, which occurred around the second quarter of the second century. As with the reporting of the late Roman occupation, there is no single, definable horizon across the whole excavation area, but, just as the construction of the two masonry houses represents a distinct stage in the development of 'House 1', so, too, does the abandonment of the timber buildings in the south-east corner, even if the succeeding occupation is not, as we shall see, associated with clearly defined structures. The sequence embraced by *City in Transition* thus includes the Period 3 and 4 structures as defined in Clarke *et al.* (2007), and these periods are also retained for reporting the trench-wide occupation.

CONTEXT: INSULA IX AND SILCHESTER

The concept of *City in Transition* can be considered in a number of ways. In the local context of Insula IX and the excavated area, the period with which we are concerned takes the reporting and analysis of the occupation through to the moment of major replanning and redefinition of properties and property boundaries at the turn of the third and fourth centuries. Before that time the principal properties, Period 3 Masonry Buildings 1 and 2 and their successor, Period 4 Masonry Building 3, had been constructed on a north-east/south-west orientation, quite different to that of the street grid. By the end of the third/beginning of the fourth century, not only was Mid-Roman Building 3 completely demolished, but new buildings in masonry and timber along with their associated property boundaries had been constructed on a new orientation, the same as that of the street grid, which was itself aligned on the cardinal points (FIG. 3). Thus Insula IX in the fourth century had a very different character, at least in terms of layout and buildings, to that which it had had in the second and third centuries (FIG. 4). *City in Transition* will put flesh on those earlier structures by exploring their context within the insula and the nature of their associated occupation. In this way the report complements the *Internet Archaeology* publication with its focus on the 'House 1' structures alone (Clarke *et al.* 2007).

In the wider context of *Calleva* as a whole the time-span of *City in Transition* covers the period from the early second century, a time when the city, like the majority in the province, was apparently without defences. In fact we know comparatively little about the city at this time as so little has been subjected to modern, stratigraphic excavation, but, while it would not be prudent to imagine the plan of the city and its constituent buildings in the early second century as closely resembling that recovered by the Society of Antiquaries, it is reasonable to assume that most, if not the entirety, of the area contained by the later second-century defences was built up, but probably with a density of building not dissimilar to that found in Insula IX. However, such stratigraphic excavation as has been carried out reveals that the start of the Insula IX sequence reported here coincides with the construction of the forum-basilica in masonry and the repair of the amphitheatre in timber, both more or less, therefore, coincident with the construction of Period 3 Masonry Buildings 1 and 2, *c.* A.D. 125–150 (Fulford 1989a, 28–36; Fulford and Timby 2000, 58–68). By the end of the second century, however, the city, in common with the majority of the larger towns of Britain, had been provided with earthwork defences which were eventually replaced in their entirety in masonry by the late third century, *c.* A.D. 280 (Fulford 1984; Fulford *et al.* 1997). These excluded the amphitheatre, which itself was substantially refurbished in masonry in the early-to-mid-third century (Fulford 1989a, 37–56). The construction of our larger, Period 4 town-house, Masonry Building 3 (formerly House 1), though not closely dated,

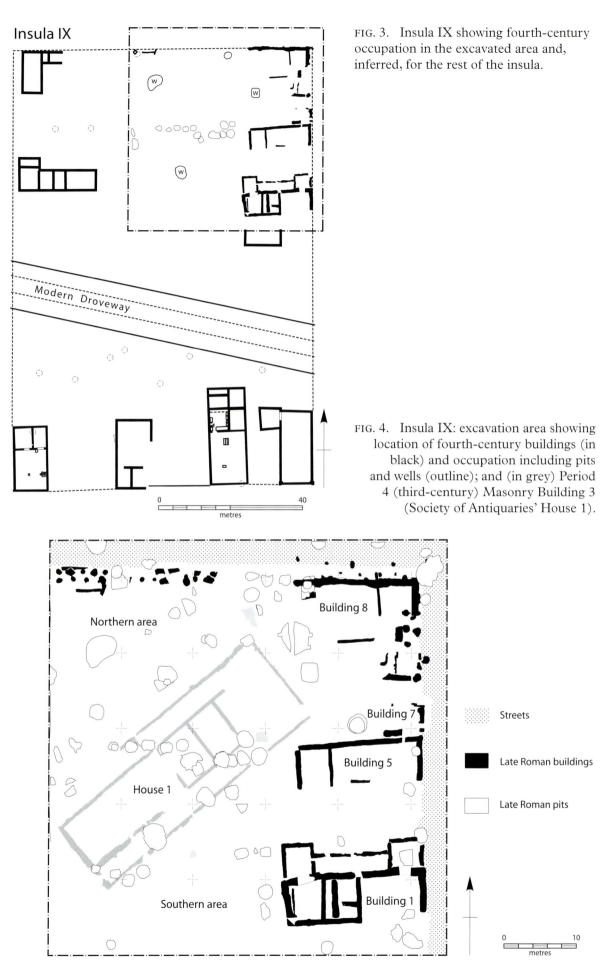

Insula IX

Modern Droveway

0   40
metres

FIG. 3. Insula IX showing fourth-century occupation in the excavated area and, inferred, for the rest of the insula.

FIG. 4. Insula IX: excavation area showing location of fourth-century buildings (in black) and occupation including pits and wells (outline); and (in grey) Period 4 (third-century) Masonry Building 3 (Society of Antiquaries' House 1).

Northern area

Building 8

Building 7

Building 5

House 1

Building 1

Southern area

Streets

Late Roman buildings

Late Roman pits

0   10
metres

is approximately contemporary with the earthwork phase of defences and the rebuilding of the amphitheatre.

At about the time of the rebuilding of the city walls in stone, *c.* A.D. 280, the great public space of the forum-basilica was given over to metalworking: copper alloy, pewter, iron-making and iron-working all being evidenced (Fulford and Timby 2000, 68–78). The major change of function indicated by the development of metalworking in the forum-basilica finds a parallel in the evidence for widespread change elsewhere across the city in the use of private space. In recalling that the end of the third century saw the demolition of the final phase of building on the 'House 1' site in Insula IX (our Period 4 Masonry Building 3), we should also note that there is evidence from other insulae, both close to Insula IX in the north-west quarter of the city and further to the south, of similar, radical change whereby houses oriented differently from the grain of the street grid were demolished and replaced by buildings which conformed to the orientation of the street grid (Fulford *et al.* 2006, 249–52). By focusing on the occupational evidence from Insula IX between the early second and the late third century, we have the possibility of gaining insights into the life and welfare of the occupants over some six generations, about 175 years in total. This *City in Transition* sequence thus spans two periods which saw coincident investment in both private and public building: the construction of residential housing and public buildings in masonry in the early second century; and the construction of new houses in the context of a larger urban reorganisation alongside the rebuilding in stone of the city defences in the late third century. However, the latter period also saw a significant change in the function of the forum-basilica.

CONTEXT: SOUTH-EASTERN BRITAIN

If we look beyond Silchester to other, neighbouring towns in Britain where archaeological investigation has shed light on this period, we can point to both parallel and divergent developments. Some of the best evidence derives from the immediate neighbours of London and Verulamium. The latter has a broadly similar history to Silchester in respect of the provision of defences, but Frere's work in Verulamium (1955–61) involved the excavation of a number of town-houses in advance of the widening of the modern road which bisected the city more or less along its central north-east/south-west axis. The results shed important light on the development of commercial and residential housing in the city. In particular, in terms of the histories of individual buildings, these findings contradicted those of the Wheelers who excavated in Verulamium in the 1930s (Frere 1972; 1983; Wheeler and Wheeler 1936). Instead of further evidence for a town much reduced by the perceived impact of the economic crisis of the third century, Frere demonstrated considerable vibrancy in the town in the second and third centuries, particularly in the context of the development of shops-cum-workshops and private housing. Nevertheless he also noted a change of tempo between the Antonine period and the late third century. Up to the destruction of an extensive area of the city by a major fire dated *c.* A.D. 155 (Frere 1983, 13, fig. 8), he recorded four successive phases of building and expansion among the twelve timber-built shops fronting Watling Street in Insula XIV between *c.* A.D. 75 and 155 (Frere 1972, 23–98). After the fire the frontage remained undeveloped until the late third century when six large masonry shops were constructed. Although the number of premises was less than in the mid-second century, the extent of the built-up area was closely comparable. However, he commented, 'Private dwellings had been small and plentiful: now they were large and correspondingly fewer. It appears that the curial class had at last come to town, but in doing so had changed the city's character to that of a residential, slightly sleepy, country town' (Frere 1983, 16).

In London, where the construction in stone of the landward circuit of the city walls took place as early as the beginning of the third century, but without an initial phase of earthwork defence, there is evidence between the early second and the late third century of both new developments and abandonments. In the case of the latter there is a record of the development of dark earths on the site of residential buildings and shops-cum-workshops demolished or abandoned in the second half of the second century (see Perring 1991, 76–89 ('The city in contraction')). On the other hand, there is also evidence for new investment in public building, such as the commemoration of the restoration of temples to Jupiter and to Isis, around the middle of the third century and the construction of the riverside section of the town walls shortly afterwards (see ibid., 90–105 ('The restoration of the city')). A little earlier, and certainly by the 240s, there had also been major reconstruction work on the waterfronts on the north bank of the river (Brigham and Hillam 1990, 138). In the second half of the third century there had also been significant demolitions, including two altars and a late Antonine or Severan monumental arch, whose remains were incorporated into the riverside section of the city wall (Perring 1991, 107–9). The forum-basilica was also largely demolished at the end of the third century (Brigham 1990, 82). In contrast to the evidence of public buildings, and as a consequence of the truncation of archaeological deposits by later development, much less has survived from London (and Southwark) to chart the pattern of development of private housing in the third century. In the same way that new shops were eventually constructed in masonry on the Watling Street frontage of Verulamium Insula XIV, similar developments may have taken place above or alongside London properties abandoned in the second half of the second century.

As more and more evidence comes to light, a strong sense of individuality emerges for each city. Nevertheless, in the sense that, through the loss of monumental architecture, including the amphitheatre (for a while) and the forum-basilica, London experienced more radical change in the third century than can be discerned at Verulamium, one is tempted to see a parallel with Silchester and the 'loss' of its forum-basilica. The truth is, however, that without modern research into its forum-basilica, we do not know the comparable situation in Verulamium. The problem of comparing urban histories is brought into sharper focus over the question of abandonment of commercial and residential properties in the later second and third centuries. How widespread was this phenomenon? On the face of the London evidence it would seem that there was significant abandonment, but this has to be tempered by our uncertainty over the extent of the loss, through truncation by subsequent medieval and modern development, of later Roman stratigraphy which might contain evidence of subsequent, new building. In the case of Verulamium, for example, it would appear that plots left vacant following the Antonine fire eventually saw rebuilding. In some cases this happened in the first half of the third, rather than the late second century, while in others there was significant delay, as in Insula XIV, where the street frontage was not apparently redeveloped for over a century, and in Insula XXVII the large courtyard house was not built until the late *fourth* century (Frere 1983, summarised pp. 14–15). Immediately beyond the boundaries of the city itself, it is the second half of the second century which saw the demise of the Verulamium-region pottery industry (Tyers 1996, 199–201).

While Frere contradicted the Wheelers' view of the effects of the third-century crisis on the city by drawing attention to the amount of development occurring throughout the third century, such that 'by the last quarter of the third century Verulamium possessed all the physical attributes of a first-class classical city' (1983, 19), he did not highlight the period between the late second and early third century when significant areas of the city remained derelict. In essence it is this period which could be regarded as the equivalent of the Wheelers' 'bombarded city' of A.D. 273 (Wheeler and Wheeler 1936, 28). Even if the immediate cause of, or trigger for, that dereliction may have been different in Verulamium to what it was in London, the fact remains that conditions were not such as to encourage rebuilding within two or three generations after the fire of *c.* A.D. 155. Perhaps the situation in the two cities, as far as commercial and residential building was concerned, was not so different between the later second and later third century? The more fundamental difference between London and Verulamium is that, in the case of the latter, we do have uninterrupted stratigraphic sequences which continue into the third and fourth centuries. The same is also true of Colchester where modern excavation has produced important sequences of development through the Roman period. Like Verulamium, there is evidence of uneven development, particularly in the century following the Boudiccan destruction, with some areas remaining open as cultivated spaces for long periods and, in one case, for most of the Roman period (P. Crummy 1992, 33). The period which sees the greatest density of occupation, including the development of large, courtyard-plan, town-houses, is, as evidenced by the excavations at Lion Walk and Culver Street, from about the middle of the second into the early third century, a period which coincides with the *floruit* of the Colchester pottery industry (P. Crummy 1984; 1992).

What is the situation at Silchester? Unfortunately, because of the lack of excavation of commercial and residential building in the town, our only source of modern, excavated evidence is Insula IX. Here we have an indication of a significant caesura in the latter part of the third century with the final abandonment of 'House 1' (here Period 4 Masonry Building 3) and its associated plot and the replanning and rebuilding in the insula (Fulford *et al.* 2006). As we have remarked above, there are indications of significant and comparable, major change elsewhere within the town at this time, but yet to be explored through modern excavation. The question is whether the extensive replanning, evidenced by the abandonment of properties not aligned with the street grid, was occasioned because properties had been abandoned for some time, and thus presented an opportunity for radical change, or for other, perhaps, political reasons. Consideration of the material evidence from Insula IX should allow us to address the question whether there was a significant period of abandonment before the rebuilding at the end of the third century. On the face of it, the evidence from Silchester, in terms of radical change, for the second half of the third century would seem to be different to that from London or Verulamium. It remains to be seen, however, how similar the record is for Silchester in comparison with London and Verulamium for the earlier period, the second half of the second century and the early third century.

These analyses of urban histories have to be seen against the context of a larger economic environment which was common to the cities of the South-East. In terms of the wider contacts as exemplified by the evidence of ceramics and material culture more generally, the second and third centuries saw major changes, particularly in relation to long-distance traffic. While the period from the A.D. 120s saw the influx of fine, sigillata tablewares from the workshops of Central Gaul and, to a lesser extent, from those situated in Eastern Gaul and on the Rhine, from early in the third century the traffic is almost entirely confined to that emanating from the latter region. The beginning of the third century also saw the end of the bulk importation of the olive-oil-carrying amphorae (Dressel 20) from the Guadalquivir valley in the province of Baetica, southern Spain. Officially-minted coin of the second and beginning of the third quarter of the third century is also rare — a possible symptom of a decline in the circulation of goods and money. Thus, with the exception of tableware imports from East Gaul and the Rhineland, there is little evidence of substantial long-distance trade between Britain and the rest of the Empire after the second decade of the third century (Fulford 1989b; 1991).

In southern Britain there are also some significant changes in the regional production and distribution of manufactured goods between the second and late third centuries. Our best source of evidence is, of course, pottery and it remains to be seen whether similar large-scale changes can be discerned in other industries. As far as Silchester and its immediate neighbours are concerned the period sees the demise in the second half of the second century of the Verulamium-region industry, which had been a significant source of kitchen and domestic wares from the third quarter of the first century A.D. Whether related or not to the fortunes of the former, this period sees the rise of the Colchester and Thames estuary (BB2) industries with decline at the end of the second/beginning of the third century. However, these have little impact on Silchester. On the other hand there are potteries which continued to develop significantly throughout the period and which, between them, account for the bulk of consumption at Silchester. These include the nearby Alice Holt industry which produced kitchen wares, the more distant, south-east Dorset cooking and kitchen ware (BB1) industry, and, to the north, the Oxfordshire industry, which produced mostly kitchen wares and mortaria in the second century and effectively replaced supplies from the Verulamium industry. Later, like the New Forest industry to the south, Oxfordshire developed capacity in the manufacture of table wares imitative of sigillata and other wares, from the middle decades of the third century (Tyers 1996). The latter, whether produced in the New Forest or Oxfordshire workshops (or further north in the Nene Valley), had almost completely replaced the range of table wares imported from East Gaul and the Rhineland. What can we conclude? For Silchester there appears to be consistency and stability in the local and regional sources of pottery through the second and third centuries, with the Verulamium-region industry being the only significant defaulter. With the loss of imported wares the regional sources become relatively and absolutely more important. If the ceramic evidence is seen as a proxy of economic activity more generally, it would seem to imply greater strength in the regional economy of central southern Britain in the second and third centuries.

The extent to which we can map economic and social behaviour from Insula IX between the second and the third century will depend on the incidence and scale of well-dated deposits and on the degree of continuity of occupation. However, with a methodology which embraces the integration of systematic and quantitatively-based analysis of environmental data provided principally by plant and faunal remains with a wide range of quantified material culture, including the evidence of activities such as metalworking, it should be possible to provide a richly-resourced picture of change over time. This in turn will offer a context in which to set the headline pattern of changes presented by the more conspicuous ceramic and numismatic evidence at a provincial level.

CHAPTER 2

THE EXCAVATION

By Amanda Clarke and Michael Fulford

INTRODUCTION

We have retained the chronology established in the publication of 'The Development of an Urban Property' [= 'House 1'] (Clarke *et al.* 2007) which defined four periods prior to the beginning of the late Roman sequence from *c.* A.D. 250/300, which is described and discussed in *Life and Labour* (Fulford *et al.* 2006, 18–19; 249–52):

Period 1: *c.* A.D. 40–50 – *c.* A.D. 70–80
Period 2: *c.* A.D. 70–80 – *c.* A.D. 125–150
Period 3: *c.* A.D. 125–150 – *c.* A.D. 200
Period 4: *c.* A.D. 200 – *c.* A.D. 250 [– *c.* A.D. 300]

Here we are reporting the occupation of Periods 3 and 4 only. The periods are defined on the basis of major structural changes on the 'House 1' site, a succession of buildings aligned north-east/south-west which occupied the larger part of the excavated area. The masonry building as first recorded and labelled 'House 1' in the excavation of Insula IX 1893–4 (Fox 1895) in fact proved to incorporate the remains of two earlier masonry buildings, our Masonry Buildings (MB) 1 and 2, which are assigned to our Period 3. With Mid-Roman Timber Building (MRTB) 1, these three structures replaced two timber buildings (ERTB 2–3), themselves attributed to our Period 2 of the later first and early second century (Clarke *et al.* 2007, p2_ertb2.htm; p2_ertb3.htm) (FIGS 5–6). There is evidence to suggest that ERTB 1 continued in use through Period 3. Period 4 saw the replacement of the Period 3 buildings with a single structure, our Masonry Building (MB) 3. The excavations are now (2008–9) showing that the Period 2 buildings underlying 'House 1' and their associated occupation represent major change over the underlying, pre-Flavian (Period 1) occupation and thus represent the first of three successive building phases occupying the same plot. Were the excavation of the Period 2 occupation completed, it and Periods 3 and 4 would make a logical grouping for publication, mirroring the focus of the *Internet Archaeology* report (Clarke *et al.* 2007). As it is, the complexity and quality of survival of Period 2 warrants publication in its own right.

Except for the occupation overlying the end of the Period 2 buildings in the south-east corner of the excavation area, these clear divisions in the sequence of buildings were not so neatly reflected in the stratigraphic sequence across the whole excavation area. Victorian excavation methodology had effectively isolated the stratigraphy inside the walls of the two periods of masonry buildings from that beyond. Thus, the establishment of trench-wide Periods 3 and 4 involved the identification of stratigraphy, with associated minor structures and negative features such as pits and wells, which shared a date-range contemporary with that of the successive phases of buildings. Inevitably it has not been possible to associate stratigraphy with each of Periods 3 and 4 across the entire excavation area. In establishing phasing across the excavation trench, first the dating of the fills of all significant pits and wells was established and this allowed these types of negative feature to be divided between Periods 3 and 4. Similarly an extensive area of complex stratigraphy which occupied the area to the south and south-east of the masonry buildings was also divided, but with no clear or absolute division, between contexts dated to

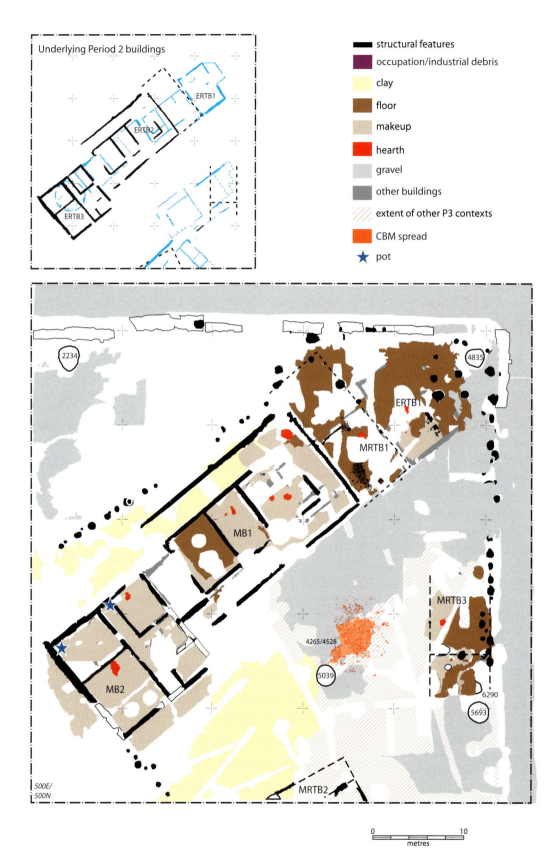

Underlying Period 2 buildings

ERTB1

ERTB2

ERTB3

■ structural features
■ occupation/industrial debris
☐ clay
■ floor
☐ makeup
■ hearth
☐ gravel
■ other buildings
▨ extent of other P3 contexts
■ CBM spread
★ pot

2234

ERTB1

MRTB1

4835

MB1

MRTB3

4265/4528

5039

6290

5693

MB2

500E/
500N

MRTB2

0   10
metres

FIG. 5.   Period 3: Masonry Buildings 1 and 2, Mid-Roman Timber Buildings 1–3, residual Early Roman Timber Building 1 and associated occupation, *c.* A.D. 125/50–*c.* A.D. 200; and (in inset plan) the underlying timber buildings of Period 2 shown in blue.

FIG. 6. Aerial view of the excavation of Insula IX from the south-west in 2002 showing MB 1 and MB 2 and associated occupation. Remains of late Roman pits and Victorian trenching are also visible.

Period 3 and those of Period 4. If the demolition of the Period 3 masonry buildings marked a clear, but probably brief break in occupation, this is not evident in the occupation represented by layers, pits and wells across the rest of the excavated area. With the exception of one Period 3 well in the north-west of the excavation trench, there was a lack of a clear second- and third-century occupational sequence both to the north-west and the south-west of 'House 1'. This report therefore concentrates on the second- and third-century occupation sequence and associated, possible structures to the south and east of 'House 1' and also, in Period 3, the structures between the north-east-facing wall of MB 1 and the intersection of the east–west and north–south streets.

PROPERTY BOUNDARIES (Object 500066) (FIGS 5 and 29–30)

An important question concerning the distribution of space across the insula and, more especially, the excavated area is the extent to which property boundaries can be defined around the actual buildings. In fact there are clear alignments of post-holes, for the most part flint-packed, running along the edges of the streets, particularly the eastern end of the east–west street and the majority of the length of the north–south street. More importantly, perhaps, there is evidence of a line of post-holes running almost parallel with the north-west-facing sides of the Periods 3 and 4 masonry buildings which then turns north to meet the post-holes towards the eastern end of the east–west street. These arrangements suggest the possibility of the excavation area containing the eastern end of a trapezoidal plot which extended west towards the north-west corner of the insula. One feature of this plot was that its northern boundary along the edge of the east–west street is only additionally defined by irregularly-placed posts parallel with the street.

A second plot, and one which embraces the larger area of the excavation, was that which contained the Period 3 and 4 houses. Its boundaries are clear on the northern and eastern sides in Period 3, but how far south did this property extend? While the flint-packed post-pits end at the point where large wells have been cut alongside the north–south street frontage, there is no evidence of a comparable return line of post-holes, running east–west or north-east/south-west (i.e. parallel with the houses) across the southern half of the excavation area. Does this mean that the southern boundary runs beyond the southern edge of the excavated area, and that all the occupation to the south and east of the Periods 3 and 4 buildings within the excavation trench is associated with the one property? The western boundary of the property is clear in Period 4 and is formed by a line of post-holes which extrapolates south-eastwards the line of the west wall of both Masonry Buildings 2 and 3 and runs up to the southern edge of the excavation trench (FIGS 29–30). It implies a third property extending to the south-west of the houses and then beyond the excavated area to the west and south. The direction of the western boundary south-east suggests that the southern boundary of the property associated with our houses does indeed lie beyond the southern limit of the excavation trench, perhaps extending up to the north-east corner of House 2 excavated in 1893 (FIG. 2). Assuming contemporaneity of House 2 with our Period 3 buildings and projecting its north-facing elevation to the north-east, we note that it coincides with the remains of our possible MRTB 2 (below, p. 33). Further extrapolation north-east takes us to the well 5693 and the slumped fills of 6290. This hypothetical line might mark the southern boundary of our 'House 1' property in Period 3, but there is no independent evidence, such as posts, to support it. So, while the lack of hard evidence for a southern boundary encourages us to suppose that the entirety of the area excavated to the south of the Period 3 and 4 'House 1' buildings belonged to them, we cannot be certain, particularly in the case of the south-eastern corner, until future excavation reveals evidence of a boundary. In this respect it is important to note that a line of small post-holes runs east–west from the north–south street to the south-east corner of Masonry Building 1/Masonry Building 3 (FIG. 29). If this was a major boundary it would suggest that the south-east-facing walls of the Periods 3 and 4 masonry buildings also represented the boundary of the property as a whole, though this seems unlikely, since the area occupied by the buildings and the property as a whole would then be one and the same. Other possibilities are that this boundary divided off the north-east corner of the insula to contain animals, or that it was sub-let, or that it was divided off as a completely independent entity from the rest of the property which contained the Period 3 and 4 houses. Precisely when this boundary was erected is not clear.

To conclude: the excavation trench embraces almost the entirety of one property which includes our succession of town-houses, as well as part of at least two other properties, one to the north of 'House 1' extending westwards to the north-west corner of the insula, the other extending to the south and west of the 'House 1' plot.

In presenting the second- and third-century archaeology of our excavation of Insula IX we give primacy to the built structures and then the occupation and activity to the south/south-east, all of which, as we have seen, may be associated with our buildings. Finally, for Period 3 only, we report the occupation to the north of the buildings, which, we believe, formed the rear part of a larger property which definitely extended west beyond the limits of our excavated area to front on to the north-west corner of the insula. There is no evidence to report of second- and third-century occupation associated with the property running beyond the excavation trench to the south-west.

PERIOD 3 (FIGS 5 and 7)

SUMMARY

The 'House 1' property in Period 3 included a row of two masonry buildings and one new timber building (MB 1–2; MRTB 1) aligned north-east/south-west and resting on the combined footprint of the two Period 2 timber buildings (ERTB 2–3). It appears that ERTB 1 was retained into Period 3. To the south-east there is evidence for occupation along the north–south street, and spreading westwards across the excavated area, associated with a possible, but not certain, built structure, MRTB 3. There is evidence for one deep pit, probably a well, 5693, adjacent

FIG. 7. Aerial view of MB 1 and 2 from the south-west in 2002. Remains of ERTB 1 and hearth 1433 visible to the north-east (top of photo). Late Roman pits and wells and Victorian trenching are also visible.

to the north–south street, which was filled by the mid-second century, and a further pit, 5039, which cut through the remains of one of the underlying Period 2 timber buildings, and was also filled by the mid-second century. A second possible timber building, MRTB 2, extended south beyond the limits of the excavation trench. In the northern part of the excavated area, the postulated backyard of a property occupying the north-west of the insula, there is evidence of a single well, 2234, of this date.

MASONRY BUILDING 1 (Object 50018) (FIGS 8–9)

Masonry Building 1 overlay the principal (town-house) building (ERTB 2) of Period 2 (Clarke *et al.* 2007, p.2_ertb2.htm). It was immediately adjacent to Mid-Roman Timber Building 1 to

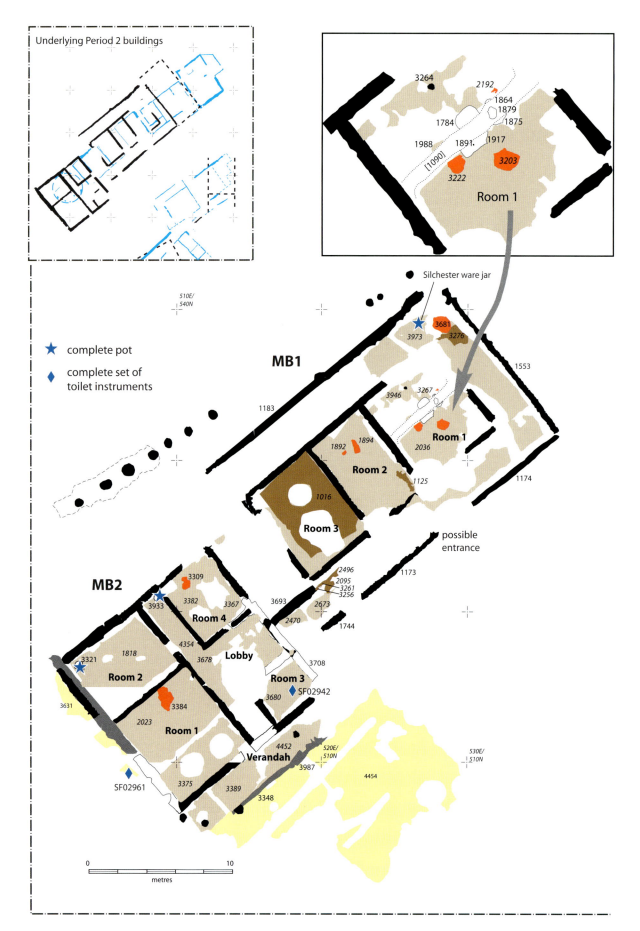

Underlying Period 2 buildings

complete pot

complete set of
toilet instruments

MB1

MB2

Room 1
Room 2
Room 3
Room 4
Lobby
Verandah

Silchester ware jar

possible
entrance

SF02942

SF02961

510E/540N

520E/510N

530E/510N

0   10
metres

FIG. 8. Period 3: Masonry Buildings 1 and 2 with detailed plan of MB 1, Room 1. The relationship with the underlying Period 2 buildings is shown in inset plan. For explanatory key, see FIG. 5. The findspots of the votive pots and complete sets of toilet instruments associated with MB 2 are indicated, as is the location of the large Silchester ware jar in MB 1.

FIG. 9. Period 3: view of foundations of MB 1 from the south-east after excavation of floor make-ups in Rooms 2 and 3; late Roman pits on east–west alignment in the foreground; traces of burning visible in Room 1 to the right (north-east). The scales are 2.0m long.

the north-east and no more than 4.0m distant from Masonry Building 2 to the south-west. It was of a row-plan type well known in Roman Britain (cf. Perring 2002, 64–5; Smith 1997, 46–64), comprising three rooms and surrounded by a corridor on at least three sides. With the exception of one, or, possibly, two limited areas, none of the original floors survived, the excavated surfaces being associated with make-ups. The surviving wall foundations of the core rooms of this house, some 0.5m in width and 0.3m in depth, were constructed of coursed flint with carefully knapped outer faces to create a more or less even, external surface to the walls. They and their associated, partly robbed-out, foundation trenches defined three rooms. This building was cut into by several late Roman pits (Objects 117 and 118) (Fulford *et al.* 2006, 37–40).

Room 1 to the north-east measured 7.0 by 7.0m, but was divided by a later intrusion, 1090, originally thought to be Victorian, but now re-interpreted as a wall inserted into the Period 4 building. Room 1 contained a gravel floor (3946/3267), topped by clay (2036/1988). Around the centre of the room is a group of three features, all of them shallow pits (1891/1917/1784 and 1875/1864/1879). Adjacent to these are two areas of burnt clay, one larger (3203), the other smaller (2192), and both interpreted as small hearths. A third feature was a shallow pit (3222), filled with ash and fragments of burnt ceramic tile and also interpreted as the remains of a hearth. All these features were set into the clay and gravel floor. Post-hole 3264 cut through gravel spread 3946 and may have been inserted for an internal structure of some kind. Lengths of wall foundation had been robbed out in the north-east and south-west corners prior to the construction of the successor, MB 3, house. An intrusive coin dating to A.D. 364–378 was excavated from one of the floor contexts of Room 1 (SF 01476). These gravel and clay surfaces overlay clay make-up (4111) which sealed ERTB 2 and contained the articulated foot bones of a roe deer, which might be interpreted as a foundation deposit (Ingrem 2007; below, Ch. 13).

The central room (Room 2) measured 7.0 by 4.0m with the vestigial remains of a tessellated floor (1125), probably the border to a mosaic, surviving in the east corner. The tesserae were of tile cubes, each with dimensions of *c.* 0.03m. Elsewhere the surface of the floor was a mixture of fine gravel with traces of mortar (4576, 3299, 1126), above layers of yellow clay (3659, 3288, 1912). On the northern side of the room there were patches of reddened, fire-hardened clay

FIG. 10.   Period 3: wall footings and nodular flint foundations of Room 3 of MB 1 cut by late Roman pits (excavated in 1893); view to south-east in 1997. The scales are each 2.0m in length.

(1892, 1894). Elevated concentrations of copper and strontium are recorded from this room (Cook, below, Ch. 3).

The third room (Room 3) measured 7.0 by 5.0m and was floored with nodular flint (1016) pressed into gravel and yellow clay (1905/3247) (FIG. 10). Towards the centre these had subsided into the fill of an underlying well which pre-dates the Period 2 ERTB 2. Whether the laying of the cobbles reflected an awareness of the need to counteract subsidence, or whether they related to a particular, intended function of the room is unclear. Together the three rooms provided an internal space of 112 square metres. There was no evidence of any thresholds to indicate how the rooms were accessed.

Corridor

Yellow clay, which had been employed in the foundations of the three rooms, also extended at the same level beyond to the outer walls which defined the corridor with a width of up to 3.0m on three sides. This clay also extended beyond the building along its north-west-facing side. The same, outer walls (1744, 1173, 1174, 1553, 1183) continued to serve the Period 4 town-house (MB 3) (below, pp. 35–9). It is not clear whether their surviving remains represented the original construction or a re-build of Period 4. They measured 0.44m in width with a depth of 0.2m, but their construction was of poorer quality than that of the walls of Rooms 1–3. Although in most cases the excavated foundations had two courses, these were quite roughly laid, with no evidence of the knapping to produce flush edges visible elsewhere in the walls of the core of the building. There was no clear evidence for an entry into the corridor from outside, but it is likely to have been around the middle of the south-east-facing elevation, perhaps opposite Room 2.

Whether the corridor continued around the south-west end of the house is not clear owing to the extent of late disturbance of this area (see below, Relationship, p. 21). There are traces of tile-tessellated and *opus signinum* flooring (2496, 3261, 2095, 2470, 3256, 2673), extending south-westwards along the south-east-facing corridor. However, at the southern end of this corridor, and appearing to block it, is a linear spread (3693) of ceramic tile on clay. It may have supported a wall, but its function is otherwise not clear. Apart from these remains, there was no further evidence with which to reconstruct the corridor and its floor, but, on the south-east-facing side it may have been open as a verandah. The north-east-facing corridor areas were covered with a mix of gravels, clay and silty sands, including one area of crushed ceramic building material reminiscent of a floor surface (3276), and a hearth (3681). If we assume that the corridor had originally been floored with a more durable surface, the hearth must belong late in the life of the building. An area of silting was also recorded in the south-east-facing corridor (1717, 1718, 1719).

The hearth 3681 is circular in plan, measuring 0.94m in diameter and 0.05m in depth. It contained several nails and a small quantity of hammerscale (Tootell, Ch. 11). In addition geochemical analysis of the associated soils gave high concentrations of strontium, copper, lead and zinc, as well as phosphorus (Cook, Ch. 3), probably indicating the working of copper alloys. Contexts associated with this hearth also produced measurable concentrations of gold, silver and tin (p. 59). Apart from being later than the underlying clay make-up, there is no independent evidence of date apart from a coin of Vespasian (A.D. 69–79) (SF 02740) from the corridor levelling-deposit (3989) and the remains of a large, flint-tempered, Silchester ware storage jar (SF 02377, p. 165, FIG. 76, No. 27) in later contexts 3259 and 3973, used here, secondarily perhaps, as a *clibanus* for cooking and/or, given its proximity to hearth 3681, a quenching vessel. This large jar lay on its side, the *in-situ* internal surface blackened (showing that it had been used on its side) and the surviving interior filled with sherds from its final collapse (FIGS 11–13). The latter showed no further, internal blackening which suggests the vessel functioned on its side in the latter part of its life. At the time of the construction of the house, Silchester ware had not been made for more than 50 years. Given that the corridor continued to be used in the Period 4 house, it is possible that the vessel belongs to this phase. In this case it may have been between one and two hundred years old at the time of its final breakage.

FIG. 11. Period 3: collapsed remains of Silchester ware storage jar in north-west-facing corridor of MB 1; remains of rim showing (left) and base (right) (= FIG. 76, No. 27). The scales are each 0.5m in length.

FIG. 12.   Period 3: Silchester ware storage jar after excavation of collapsed body; remains of rim (left) and of base (right); note blackening of internal surface (= FIG. 76, No. 27). The scale is 0.5m long.

FIG. 13.   Period 3: Silchester ware storage jar SF 2377 (= FIG. 76, No. 27) reconstructed. Height: 0.60m.

Finds

Given the lack of contexts associated with the occupation of the house and the uncertainty of the division between Period 3 and Period 4 occupation, it is difficult to distinguish finds which might be contemporary with the use of the building. Nevertheless, there are no metalwork finds of note from this phase and much of the glass and pottery is residual, but a flagon base with multiple, post-firing piercings (Timby 2007) and the remains of the large, flint-tempered storage jar, certainly associated with the life of the house, should be noted. Among the animal bone Ingrem (2007) notes the possibility that the three fragments of dog recovered from a clay make-up may belong to a single animal. Foetal/neonatal piglet bone was also recovered from a similar context. The roe deer foot bones from the levelling deposit sealing Period 2 ERTB 2 may represent a foundation deposit associated with construction of our Period 3 house.

Function of town-house MB 1

With its evidence of status represented by the traces of a tessellated floor, this building is interpreted as a small town-house. The central room, thus floored, probably served as the principal reception room of the house. Whether adjacent Room 1 to the north-east served as a workshop throughout its life is unclear; there is no evidence of a floor surface subsequently robbed out. Equally uncertain is the purpose of the third room and its distinctive, flint flooring. It is possible that potential subsidence into the underlying well was recognised at the outset and that this construction, with a mortared surface now lost, was to counteract its effects. Like Room 1, traces of tessellated flooring from the south-east-facing corridor provide the only clue as to whether the floors were originally finished with a laid surface of some kind. Apart from the presumed, secondary use of the corridor with the storage jar on its side acting as a possible cooking hearth, there is no clear evidence for a kitchen, although hearths were identified in Rooms 1 and 2 and in the corridor. It is possible that the kitchen function was provided by the adjacent MRTB 1 or the retained ERTB 1 (below, p. 22). Equally, it is not clear which room or rooms served as sleeping quarters.

None of the evidence for the *use* of the house can be independently or closely dated and, as there were no new floors or surfaces which could be associated with the successor, Period 4, MB 3 house, the make-ups associated with the Period 3 house merely provide a *terminus post quem* for the activities which took place upon them. Some of the evidence, therefore, may belong with the Period 4 house.

In addition to the hearths, or possible hearths, mentioned above in Room 1, we have also noted the evidence of heavy burning of the clay in the north-east corridor, which geochemical analysis indicated had probably been the location of copper alloy working (Cook *et al.* 2005; below, Ch. 3). Chapter 3 also reports wider evidence for the concentrations of metals in the areas of Rooms 1 and 2 and the adjacent corridor (including the presence of gold, silver and tin). Small quantities of hammerscale associated with hearth 3681 indicate some iron smithing (Tootell, below, Ch. 11).

Chronology

Both the samian and the coarse pottery suggest a Hadrianic *terminus post quem* of A.D. 125/150 with some intrusive coarse ware sherds dating as late as the third century (Timby 2007).

MASONRY BUILDING 2 (Object 50019) (FIGS 8 and 14)

Some 4.0m to the south-west of the surviving end-wall of MB 1, Masonry Building 2 (MB 2), square in plan and comprising four rooms with linking cross-corridor and possible entrance-hall space, was constructed on the same north-east/south-west orientation. No evidence survived of a threshold to indicate the entry point to the house. The outer wall contained the entirety of the underlying, Period 2, circular structure and, it has been suggested, replaced a timber-built, rectangular predecessor (Clarke *et al.* 2007, p2_ertb3.htm). Like MB 1, its foundations, which

FIG. 14.   Period 3: remains of MB 2 with its partly robbed foundations, from the south-east. The scales are each 2.0m in length.

had been extensively robbed prior to the construction of the successor, Period 4, house, were of coursed and knapped flint, measuring 0.6m wide and 0.35m in depth. The foundations of the south-west wall were deeper, perhaps to compensate for subsidence into an underlying pit or well, a potential problem perhaps evident at the time of construction.

The building was bisected by a corridor, just over 1.0m wide, on a north-west/south-east orientation. On its south-western side were two reception rooms, the larger (Room 1) measuring 6.0 by 7.0m, the smaller (Room 2) 6.0 by 5.0m. The latter produced a foundation deposit consisting of an almost complete (but fragmented at the time of excavation), small Silchester ware jar (SF 2039) from cut 3321, which was buried in the north-west corner of the room. A second foundation deposit, comprising a complete Alice Holt bead-rim jar (SF 2549) from cut 3933, was buried at the northern end of the corridor (FIG. 15) (Timby 2007, and below, p. 165, FIG. 76, Nos 30–1)). The Silchester ware jar would certainly have been residual by the early to mid-second century, while the Alice Holt jar was close to the end of its production life. These dates raise the possibility that the pots relate to the previous ERTB 3 (see discussion in Clarke *et al.* 2007, p2_ertb3.htm). However, we have noted the much older Silchester ware storage jar used during the life of MB 1 and a further foundation deposit consisting of two Alice Holt jars, one a bead-rimmed vessel identical to that described above, was recorded from beneath Period 3 MRTB 1 (below, p. 165).

On the north-east-facing side of the building were two smaller rooms, one in the south-east corner (Room 3), measuring 3.0 by 3.5m, the other in the north-west corner (Room 4), measuring 5.0 by 4.0m. Between these two rooms was a lobby area, opening into the corridor. While this may have served as an entrance-hall with the main door of the house opening onto MB 1, it is also possible that the corridor had doors opening out at each end.

Neither traces of thresholds nor of original flooring survived in any of the rooms. The exposed make-ups consisted of yellow clay 1818 (Room 2), 2023/3375 (Room 1), 3680 (Room 3),

FIG. 15.   Period 3: complete Alice Holt bead-rim jar SF 2549 (= FIG. 76, No. 31) in the foundations of MB 2. The scale is 0.2m long.

3382 (Room 4) and clay and gravel in the corridor (4354, 3678). In two rooms, close to their respective north-west walls, were patches of burnt clay suggestive of fireplaces or hearths: 3384 in Room 1 and 3309 in Room 4.

The stratigraphy associated with the exterior of the building outside the south-east-facing wall suggests the existence of a verandah, which closely follows the positions of the post-pads which we associate with ERTB 3 (Clarke *et al.* 2007, p2_ertb3.htm). These post-pads were subsequently covered by an extensive clay spread 4454 which acted as the construction level for MB 2. The verandah consisted of a shallow, rectangular cut (3345, 4460) which cut through 4454. It was *c.* 10m in length, *c.* 2m wide and up to 0.2m deep, and extended parallel with the south-east-facing walls of the house. This cut was filled with gravel (3389, 4452) and was edged on its south-east-facing side with a narrow beam-slot or possible 'drip gully' (3987, 3348).

The relationship between the houses (MB 1 and 2)

The facing end-walls of the two houses are only 4.0m apart. They cut the walls of Room 6 of the predecessor, Period 2, ERTB 2, which contained (non-functionally) re-used pieces of Bath limestone and evidence of a threshold in the centre of its south-east-facing side (Hayward 2007). These characteristics set this room apart from all the others of ERTB 2 and raise the question as to whether it had a special function which was in some way respected by the separate construction of the two successor houses, MB 1 and 2. If the corridor had returned around the south-west-facing side of MB 1 (and there is no trace of this), it would have left a gap of 1.0m between it and the adjacent end-wall of MB 2. This makes little sense. What then happened in the space between the two houses? One possibility is that the entire space was covered over with the roof of MB 1 continuing south-westwards supported by a combination of a continued outer, south-east-facing, corridor wall and the opposing walls of Room 3 of MB 1 and Room 4 of MB 2. This leaves the question of the outer corridor wall on the north-west-facing side of MB 1, since a linear spread of tile and flint (3693), measuring 3.5m in length and 0.75m in width and lying on a spread of clay oriented north-east/south-west, may be part of the wall foundation for a short length of wall linking Room 3 of MB 1 and the lobby of MB 2. However, it is slightly offset from the corner of Room 3 of MB 1 and it butts against the lobby of MB 2 where an entrance might be expected. Nevertheless it is difficult to resolve the end of MB 1 unless it was joined in some way to MB 2.

Finds

The recovery of two complete sets of toilet instruments (SF 02942; 02961) (for location see FIG. 8), which are rare as site finds, has suggested to Nina Crummy (2007) that their incorporation, like the burial of the two complete pots, in the make-ups of the building was deliberate and possibly votive in intent. With other finds it is difficult to isolate material which might have been contemporary with either the construction or the use of the building. However, among the animal bone, Ingrem (2007) notes the relatively high proportion of cattle from this house. Tootell notes the presence of very small quantities of iron-working slags, particularly from make-up 3367 in the corner of Room 4 (below, Ch. 11).

Function of town-house MB 2

Interpretation of function is hampered by the lack of surviving floor surfaces as well as more specific evidence of function, but it is suggested that the larger rooms, 1 and 2, served as reception rooms. Room 4 may have been a bedroom, while the smallest, and most isolated, room, 3, beside the entrance lobby might have provided accommodation for household slave(s). As with MB 1, there is no evidence for a dedicated kitchen space, and that function may have been served by MRTB 1 and retained ERTB 1 (below). While the foundations are more modest than those of MB 1, they were still capable of supporting an upper storey. However, given the overall dimensions of the house, it is unlikely that the roof was of single span, but rather divided, perhaps along the line of the corridor.

Chronology

The latest samian is Hadrianic/early Antonine, giving a *terminus post quem* of c. A.D. 125–150, but there is little second-century coarse ware.

MID-ROMAN TIMBER BUILDING 1 (MRTB 1) (FORMERLY ERTB 4) (Object 500078) (FIGS 16–17)

Between the north-east end of 'House 1' and the intersection of the north–south and east–west streets there is evidence of timber building extending over the north-east end of Period 2 ERTB 2 and the footprint of the Period 2 ERTB 1. When the development of buildings constituting 'House 1' was reported in *Internet Archaeology* (Clarke *et al.* 2007), the evidence was interpreted as the remains of a single timber building, ERTB 4. However, unlike its predecessor, no beam-slots had definitely been identified for the Period 3 building, whose existence was postulated on the spread of distinctive clay surfaces and the presence of hearths. The apparent size of the building coupled with the lack of structural evidence presented problems of reconstruction. How did the building work? Now we can introduce new evidence where the extent and character of the building is further informed by the results of geochemical, micromorphological and phytolith analyses (Cook, Banerjea, below, Chs 3–4).

Altogether the surfaces we have related to structure(s) define an area approximately trapezoidal in plan and extending over some 285 square metres. Two clear edges are defined, one to the

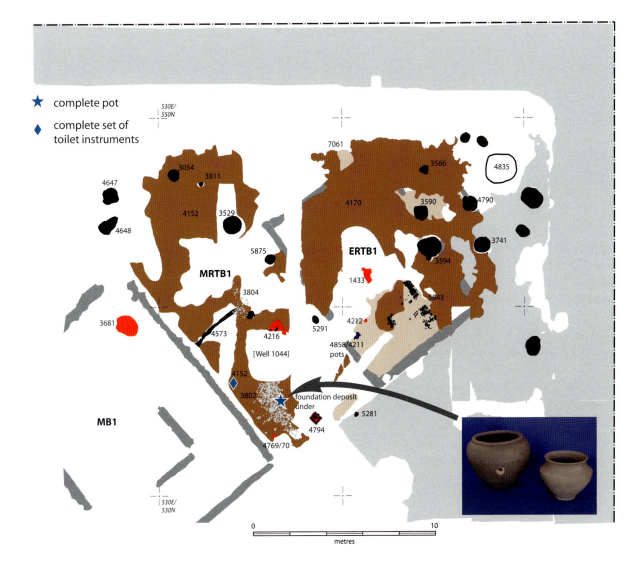

complete pot

complete set of toilet instruments

FIG. 16. Period 3: Mid-Roman Timber Building 1 and residual Early Roman Timber Building 1, and associated occupation in the north-east corner of the insula. For explanatory key see FIG. 5. The location of the two complete Alice Holt jars, SFs 3095 and 3096, is shown.

south-west, hard against the end-wall of MB 1, and one to the south-east against the line of the gravel deposits of an external lane or yard area (Object 500094). To the north and east the edges of the surfaces are irregular, finally limited by the streets and side-ditches. One major feature, the hearth 1433, appears to have been retained from the Period 2 building ERTB 1.

In determining the extent and character of the Period 3 timber building here two contemporary, locationally distinct and extensive spreads of clay, 4152 and 4170, provide the clues. Clay 4152 infilled the gap between MB 1 and the site of the earler, Period 2, building, ERTB 1. It contained a foundation deposit of two complete Alice Holt pottery jars, one of which was deliberately pierced, buried within it (FIG. 18) (Timby, below, Ch. 8, FIG. 76, Nos 28–9). Micromorphology suggests that this clay was a floor surface. Micromorphology of clay 4170, on the other hand, suggests that this spread of clay, located to the north of clay 4152, consisted of trample tracked in and out of a building, and it displayed the characteristics of an external surface (Banerjea, below, Ch. 4). The junction of these two spreads of clay was marked by a line of post-holes extending south-east to north-west (5291, 5875, 3529, 3811, 3054) and possibly turning west to meet with substantial post-hole 4648. This would define an area of *c.* 12 by 5m for the building, with its south-eastern extent marked by a hard line of gravel and a single post-hole, 5281. This building, which we now describe as Mid-Roman Timber Building 1 (see further below), was

FIG. 17.   Period 3: aerial view of Period 2–3 ERTB 1 retained into Period 3 and associated hearth 1433; view from south-west. The scales are each 2.0m in length.

divided into two, approximately equal halves by a beam-slot (4573), *c.* 0.3m in width, which was located running north-east some 3.0m from the south-west limit of 4152. MRTB 1 contained a hearth (4216), which consisted of layers of gravel and clay, interspersed with tile settings, and was cut by the late Roman well, 1044. It did not produce evidence of the same, sustained use as retained hearth 1433 (below, p. 25). Hearth 4216 was centrally located in the area to the south-east of beam-slot 4573/4556. In the southern corner of the south-east of MRTB 1 was a burnt clay spread (4769/4770) and a further hearth (4794) consisting of two broken tiles, which had been located by the Victorian excavators.

FIG. 18.   (a) The rims of two complete Alice Holt pots (SFs 3095; 3096) buried in the make-up associated with the construction of MB 1/MRTB 1 (for location, see FIG. 16); (b) the two vessels in the course of excavation (= FIG. 76, Nos 28–9). The scale in each photo is 0.5m long.

FIG. 19.   Period 2–3 ERTB 1: four fire-cracked tiles representing the surface of hearth 1433, from the south. The scales are, respectively, 0.5m and 1.0m long.

To the north-east of MRTB 1 was located spread 4170. The edges of this clay spread were ephemeral to the north-east and north-west, but bounded by the hard line of gravels to the south-east which ran up to the wall of ERTB 1. At right angles to this conjectured boundary was a line of fragmented tiles (5843), some 0.25–0.5m in width and extending 3.0m to the north-west. This could have served as the foundation for a cill-beam. Clay 4170 may have been the surface of a partly external area where animals tracked in and out of old ERTB 1. It is possible that the final stages of hearth 1433 (FIG. 19) continued in use in this area, possibly under a temporary cover as represented by cill-beam 5843, if not within the remains of the decaying ERTB 1. There is also some evidence for other small hearths in this semi-external area, for example burnt clay spread 4212. A cluster of post-holes (3741, 4790, 3586, 3590, 3594) in the northern corner in the area around cess-pit 4835 may be associated with a further structure here.

We should also note the rough surfacing, or hard standing, made up of fragmented tile (3802, 3804) running between the beam-slot 4573/4556 and the projected, south-west corner of the building. This possible path, which pre-dates the construction of MB 3, may relate to the demolition of MRTB 1. We should also recall that the deposits (4750, 4868) around the major hearth 1433 in this area, and extending to the south-west of it, were severely truncated by Victorian trenching in 1893. However, the remains of two pottery vessels (4858, 4211) were found lying on their sides within MRTB 1, in the area between hearths 1433 (4750) and 4212, one of Silchester ware, the other a grog-tempered storage jar.

There was no clear sealing layer over the Period 3 occupation, but spreads of silty gravel and occupation material continued to develop over the remains of the building. It remains possible, therefore, that there was continuation of use into Period 4. Much of the material associated with the earliest phases of the late Roman occupation contained high proportions of third-century pottery (Fulford *et al.* 2006).

Finds

Metalwork finds included both brooches and toilet instruments. Among the former, and contemporary with the occupation of the building, are a pennanular brooch (SF 02877) and two western, T-shaped brooches (SF 02985, 03256), while a complete toilet-set (SF 02079) from the clay sealing the remains of ERTB 1 and 2 is interpreted as a votive deposit. Other copper-alloy finds include a nail-cleaner, two tweezers, one possibly deposited as a votive, and a long-handled toilet spoon (Crummy 2007; and below, Ch. 6, FIG. 54, Nos 1–12). Given that the building and the area occupied by ERTB 1 contained occupation layers, the incidence of finds is greater than in the adjacent town-houses, which are largely represented by foundations and make-up layers. Among the ironwork, for example, there were almost 8kg of nails, representing about 70 per cent of all the nails from the Period 3 houses (Williams 2007). The glass assemblage, however, seems both relatively and absolutely very large, representing some 276 vessels, of which bottles (57) are the commonest form (D. Allen 2007; below, Ch. 7, Appendix 3). The pottery (the largest assemblage from the Period 3 houses) comprises a full range of material, including amphorae and table wares. Continental imports account for 8.3 per cent of the assemblage (Timby 2007). Among the animal bone the presence of several dog bones from a single context suggests the burial of a partial skeleton, while foetal/neonatal pig is also present. Contexts associated with this building include most of the examples of 'other taxa' recorded from this period as well as the principal domesticates (Ingrem 2007).

Although amounting to less than 1kg in weight, MRTB 1 and former ERTB 1 produced the largest quantity of slag of all the Period 3 buildings. This included a slag basin and other fragments of smelting slag, as well as a small amount of hammerscale, suggestive of iron forging, which was recovered from context 3532 (Tootell, below, Ch. 11).

Interpretation and function of the building

MRTB 1 is constructed in the space between MB 1 and the Period 2 building ERTB 1, and it uses the north-eastern (corridor) wall of MB 1 as its south-west-facing wall. It has a clay floor, a central partition and a small hearth, 4216. Its north-east wall consists of a line of wooden posts, suggesting that MRTB 1 was a small, single-storey, wooden lean-to against the end, corridor-wall of MB 1. To the north-east of MRTB 1 was another clay-surfaced area which contained the remains of the major hearth, 1433, which may still have been in use through Period 3. If this was the case, some kind of cover for it might have been expected. The proposed cill-beam 5843 might have provided the basis for this. However, the fact that MRTB 1 neatly occupies the space between the masonry town-house and the position of the Period 2 ERTB 1 implies that the latter was probably still standing, at least at the start of the period. The micromorphology suggests that, if this building continued in use, it became quite dilapidated, open to the weather and used for keeping animals. That ERTB 1 continued in domestic occupation for a while is also indicated by cess-pit 4835 situated right in the angle between the two streets, but respecting the footprint of the building. The pottery from this pit suggests that it was filled and therefore abandoned by about the middle of the second century. Formerly, as noted above, we have referred to the whole area to the north-east of MB 1 as ERTB 4, following the interpretation set out in Clarke *et al.* (2007). In fact, in the light of the new evidence set out here and in Chs 3 and 4, there is no case to support the existence of such a building and it would be more appropriate, as we have seen, to term the new building set between MB 1 and Period 2 ERTB 1 as Mid-Roman Timber Building 1 (MRTB 1).

The two, tiled hearths are a conspicuous feature of the building or buildings, one associated with clay spread 4152 (4216), the other with clay spread 4170 (and the final phase of 1433). Such hearths are not represented in either MB 1 or MB 2. Assuming all three buildings are connected, it can be suggested that MRTB 1 and, initially at least, ERTB 1 acted as a service building for one or both of the two adjacent town-houses where, for example, food and liquids were stored, prepared and cooked. The slag basin and hammerscale also suggest that there was a small amount of iron-making and iron-working, again perhaps on a scale only to serve domestic needs. The presence of domestic animals, indicated both by the foetal/neonatal pig remains and the micromorphology, suggests that the decaying ERTB 1 also served to accommodate animals. The development of the probable cooking-hearth (3681) in MB 1 may have coincided with the giving over of ERTB 1 to the accommodation of animals. Altogether these strands of evidence point to a multi-functional rather than specialised use for the building(s), or for MRTB 1 and the remaining space at the north-east corner of the insula formerly occupied by ERTB 1. Geochemically there is little to distinguish between the two spaces, but there are strong contrasts from the two combined with the results obtained from MB 1 and 2 (Cook, below, p. 56). Perversely, although sited at the junction of two streets close to the centre of the town, a potentially commercially advantageous position, the posts which flank the edge of the streets imply restricted, rather than open traffic, between the building and the streets. Indeed the cess-pit 4835 (below), situated right in the angle between the two streets and, presumably, at the rear of the building(s), suggests that MRTB 1 looked southwards, away from the streets and into the insula.

Although we are suggesting that the occupants of the building were subservient to those of the adjacent town-houses, the range and quantity of material culture and animal remains do not suggest poverty, unless the building accumulated material discarded (some perhaps only damaged) from the adjacent two houses. The question of the status of the occupants is brought into sharp focus by the relatively high proportion of imported pottery (15.6 per cent) from the assemblage in the cess-pit 4835 (Timby, below, Ch. 8). Perhaps the area occupied by the decayed or abandoned ERTB 1 was used as a midden by the two houses.

Chronology

In addition to the two, late first/early second-century, Alice Holt jars, a samian potter's stamp (SF 03164), dated to c. A.D. 100–120, was incorporated into the clay spread 4152. The latter also sealed the large cess-pit 5251/5354 which contained a pottery assemblage of late first/early second-century date. A further samian potter's stamp (SF 03079), of c. A.D. 120–145, was also recovered from the floors within the building (Timby 2007; below, Ch. 8).

The latest pottery from the occupation of the building includes samian and coarse wares of mid- or late Antonine date. A few contexts contain material which may date into the third century.

Pit 4835 (Object 500028) (FIGS 16 and 21)

A sub-rectangular, vertical-sided pit was cut into the angle between the two streets in the north-east corner of the insula adjacent to the former, Period 2, ERTB 1. It measured c. 2.0 by 2.0m with a depth of 1.75m. Above a basal layer of yellow clay (5923), the primary fills (5891, 5873, 5867), interspersed with a sealing layer of gravel (5886), were up to 1.0m in depth, black, organic-rich with much charcoal and contained a small quantity of pottery and animal bone, with less material in the gravel. The pit was sealed with a thick (0.5m deep) sealing layer of yellow clay (5821). The pottery assemblage includes some 15 per cent of continental imports including Central Gaulish samian of Hadrianic and Hadrianic-Antonine date, the latest dated material from the pit (Timby, below, Ch. 8). An almost complete grey ware dish was recovered from the lower fills (FIG. 76, No. 26), as well as the bases of two small grey ware jars (FIG. 20). Parts of two joiner's dogs were also recovered (Crummy, below, Ch. 6). Among the animal bones, cattle, in contrast with the finds from MRTB 1 and former ERTB 1, are the most numerous taxa. Remains of a dog skull were recovered from one of the basal fills. With its sealing layer of clay this pit is interpreted as the cess-pit contemporary with the early life of the MRTB 1 and the latter days of ERTB 1.

FIG. 20. Pit 4835 showing the bases of two grey ware jars resting on the bottom. The scale is 0.5m long.

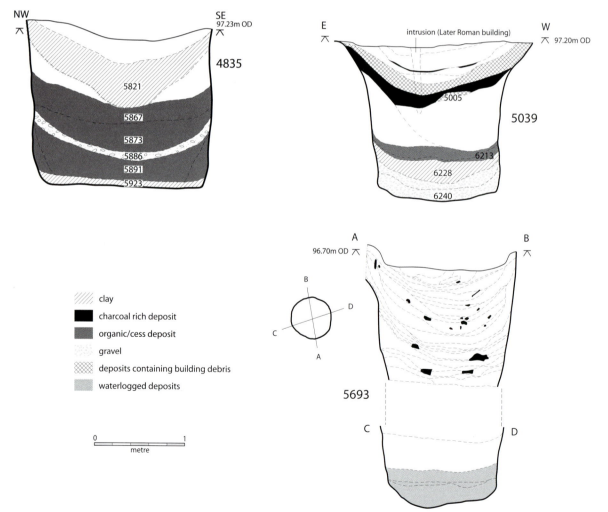

FIG. 21. Period 3: profiles of pits 4835 and 5039 and well 5693.

OCCUPATION TO THE SOUTH OF MB 1–2 AND MRTB 1: PITS AND WELLS (FIG. 22)

In addition to the spreads of occupation assigned to Period 3, extending southwards from the buildings described above, there was a single pit (5039) which was cut into one of the Period 2 buildings on the south-east of the excavated area and two wells, one of which was completely excavated (5693). Only the upper fills were excavated of the other (6290) as these contained slumped fills contemporary with the Period 3 occupation.

Pit 5039 (Object 500017) (FIGS 21 and 23)

Pit 5039 was circular in plan with a diameter of *c*. 2.0m at the top and *c*. 1.3m at the base, and

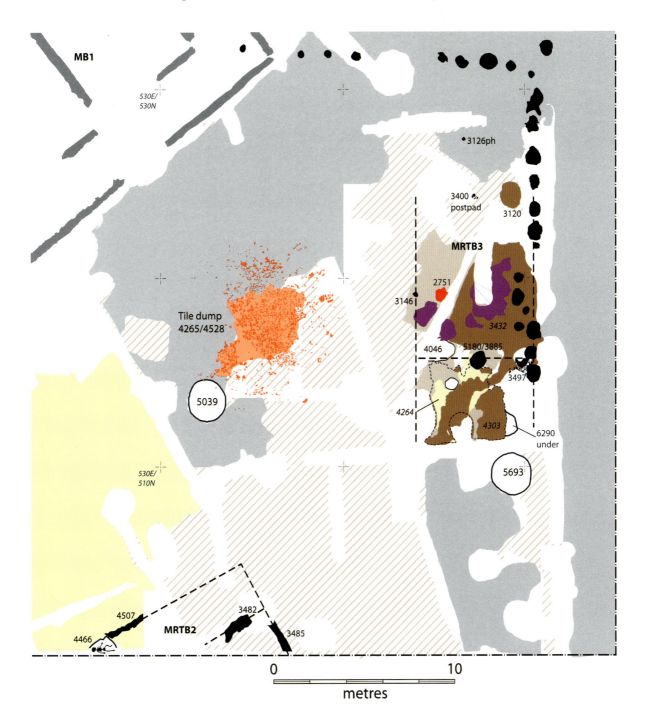

FIG. 22. Period 3: occupation south of Masonry Buildings 1 and 2 including Mid-Roman Timber Buildings 2 and 3, pit 5039, well 5693, and the tile dump. For explanatory key see FIG. 5.

FIG. 23. Period 3 pit 5039: (a) half-section of pit in course of excavation; (b) remains of large grey ware jar resting on the base of the pit. The scale is 0.2m long.

with a depth of 1.65m. It was filled with a series of deposits, for the most part horizontally laid, and none with a thickness greater than *c.* 0.2m. A clay layer (6228), laid towards the base of the pit, may have served to seal primary contents of cess. The basal layer (6240) contained the lower part of a large jar, while the upper fills contained more building material, including a dump of decayed wall-plaster from 5005. Over 200 ferrous, hammerscale flakes were recovered from samples taken from the lower fills 6213 and 6228. The pit contained a range of pottery, including a number of sherds of Gallic amphora, which accounted for about 6 per cent of the assemblage (by count), while imported material as a whole amounted to 10 per cent (by count) of the assemblage. The latest material is samian of Hadrianic date, suggesting that the pit was filled before the mid-second century (Timby, below, Ch. 8). Among the faunal remains, caprines (31 per cent) are the most numerous of the main domesticates, while other taxa account for almost a quarter of the assemblage. There were no significant small finds from this pit.

Though no mineralised plant remains were recovered, this pit is interpreted as having been dug as a cess-pit in the first instance. It is not clear to what building it relates and it is conspicuous as the only pit of its kind south of ERMB 1–2 and MRTB 1/ERTB 1 in Period 3. It also provides a clear *terminus ante quem* for the demolition of the underlying Period 2 building(s).

Well 5693 (Object 500035) (FIGS 21 and 24)

This well was dug close to the north–south street. It was sub-rectangular in plan at the surface with dimensions of *c.* 1.5m. It was dug with near-vertical sides to a depth of *c.* 2.5m below the Roman ground surface and was more circular in plan towards the base with a diameter at the bottom of 1.2m. The basal fills showed evidence of water-logging. Except for the latter which measured up to 0.3m in thickness, the remainder rarely exceeded 0.1m in depth. The character of the numerous contexts of clayey or sandy silts filling the well implies a long period of accumulation.

FIG. 24.   Period 3 well 5693: half-section. The horizontal scale is 1.0m long; the vertical scale is 2.0m long.

Pottery includes a range of continental imports accounting for 11 per cent of the assemblage by count, as well as regional imports amounting to some 4 per cent of the group. A decorated Central Gaulish Dr 37 from a middle fill provides a *terminus post quem* of *c.* A.D. 125–150 (Bird, below, Ch. 8, No. D2). In addition to fragments of a mirror, this well produced two joiner's dogs (Crummy, below, Ch. 6). Among the animal bone are the remains of two dogs from the basal fills of the well, one with evidence of skinning (Clark, below, Ch. 14).

Pit (well) 6290 (Object 701)

This pit — almost certainly originally dug as a well, or resulting from a succession of inter-cutting wells — has not yet been completely excavated. It is included in this report as its slumped, upper fills contained pottery the latest of which dates to *c.* A.D. 125–150, with one possibly later sherd. Like 5693, it is located close to the north–south street. At the surface it measures *c.* 1.4 by 1.25m in plan and it has been excavated to a depth of *c.* 1.5m below the contemporary Roman ground surface. The pit/well into which these deposits are slumping is obviously earlier than Period 3, and the slumped deposits should be considered as part of a major dumping and levelling episode in preparation for the Period 3 buildings sited here. These slumps are part of an effort to level up the uneven ground here, rather than consisting of later floors which have collapsed inwards. They consist of numerous clay deposits interleaved with silts, occupation material, gravel and domestic rubbish, including a significant dump (*c.* 1kg) of oysters in 5698 (Williams and Somerville below, Ch. 15). An important find from the same context was a complete, but very worn and broken, Brockley Hill mortarium of MATUGENUS, who operated between *c.* A.D. 90 and 120/5 (FIG. 77, No. 36). The uppermost fills consisted of levelling deposits of yellow-brown clay. Among the pottery, continental imports account for 8 per cent (by count) of the assemblage, while regional imports amount to *c.* 10 per cent (Timby, below, Ch. 8). Among a small number of small finds was a bone tube which may have formed part of a syrinx or pan-pipes (Crummy, below, Ch. 6, FIG. 56, No. 27).

The occupation south of MB 1–2 and MRTB 1: other contexts (Object 701) (FIG. 22)

Following the demolition of the Period 2 buildings in the south-east of the excavation trench the area was covered with gravel spreads and a very large dump of ceramic building material, mainly comprised of *imbrices* and *tegulae* (4265/4528) (Warry, below, Ch. 10) (FIG. 25). The latter may have derived from the demolition of the Period 2 buildings, and, as Warry observes, the mix of types of *tegulae* would imply they derived from more than one roof. We illustrate here sherds of a Libertus cup from this occupation (FIG. 26).

FIG. 25.   Period 3 tile dump (Object 701, context 4265); view to south-west. The scales are 2.0m in length.

FIG. 26.   Period 3 occupation: sherds of Libertus cup (= FIG. 74, D41).

MID-ROMAN TIMBER BUILDING 2 (FIG. 22)

Sealing the gravels and the dump of building material was an extensive lower silt horizon. Two beam-slots close to the southern edge of the excavation trench (FIG. 22) cut through the clay construction levels for MB 2. Parallel with beam-slot 4507, and oriented north-east/south-west, was a second slot, 3482, while a third, 3485, ran at right angles on a north-west/south-east alignment. The first two elements may have defined an outer corridor of a building which otherwise extended beyond the excavation area to the south-east. Together, these building fragments indicate a further period of construction in timber on the pre-street, north-east/south-west alignment around the mid-second century. Later than 4507 was the burial of a neonate (Lewis, below, Ch. 12). The neonate burial is set into a small pit 4466 which cuts through the beam-slot 4507. It is impossible to determine the date of this burial beyond noting that it cuts through the small building represented by beam-slot 4507.

To the north of MB 2 and overlying the lower silts was a spread of clay deposits which, in turn, was sealed by a further horizon of upper silts.

MID-ROMAN TIMBER BUILDING 3 (FIG. 22)

The latest Period 3 occupation in this area is represented by clay floors, post-holes and hearths alongside the north–south street, contemporary with the silts and gravels just described. As FIG. 22 shows, this occupation extends about 20m north from the well 5693 and about 8.0m west of the north–south street. From the evidence available it is not possible to define with any certainty or clarity an individual building or buildings within this area, though, on the grounds of the surface area of the contexts in question, it is possible to suggest either one, *c.* 20 by 8m, timber building, or two, each measuring *c.* 10 by 8m, and constructed parallel with the north–south street. Plausibly, we have a building with two phases, an earlier phase consisting of a clay floor (4303) and a substantial post-hole (5180) marking the northern limit of a small building, *c.* 5m square, located to the north of well 5693. This phase of occupation is then covered by a spread of clay (4264), perhaps to counteract slump into the Period 2 wells/pits below. A second phase of occupation then begins, consisting of clay floor (3432 and 3120), a re-instated post-hole (3885/5180), and further post-holes including 4046 with possible wall stub 3497. This area contained a hearth (2751) and small spreads of charcoal which may suggest some industrial activity. The new area of occupation extends the early building northwards to encompass an area *c.* 12m north–south by 5m east–west.

In summary, apart from the fragments of beam-slots relating to a building (MRTB 2) or buildings extending beyond the southern edge of the excavation trench, the only possible structures are those aligned with the north–south street and dating to the late second century. If we are right to interpret these contexts as the remains of buildings, they are the first within the excavation trench to be aligned with the Roman street grid. At least their east sides are parallel with the street, though there is a lack of definition of edge to the west and north. There are no pits or wells to associate with certainty with their occupation; those reported above having been filled no later than the mid-second century.

THE NORTHERN PROPERTY (FIG. 5)

The northern part of the excavated area is interpreted as the backyard of a building occupying the north-west corner of the insula. It is trapezoidal in plan, with evidence of fencing running alongside the east–west street which meets with the fencing described above which separated it from the larger property comprising MB 1 and 2.

Within this area there is only one cut feature which belongs to Period 3; this is the well 2234.

Well 2234 (Object 41016) (FIG. 27)

Well 2234 was located in the north-west corner of the excavation trench, adjacent to the east–west

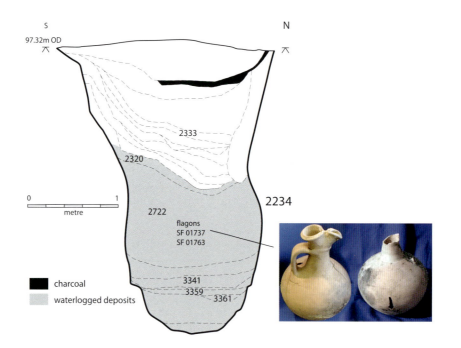

FIG. 27.   Period 3: profiles of well 2234 to the north of 'House 1', showing the findspots of the two Verulamium-region flagons SFs 01737 and 01763 (= FIG. 75, Nos 20–1)

street. It was roughly circular in plan with a diameter at the surface of *c.* 2.0m, narrowing to 1.2m at the base. It was *c.* 3.0m deep from the contemporary Roman ground surface. The basal fills of sand and gravel, *c.* 0.4m in depth, were largely sterile, but did contain some pottery and small fragments of wood, possibly derived from a wickerwork lining. Contexts associated with the main use-period of the well occupy the sequence between *c.* 1.6 and 2.1m in depth, from context 3361 and above to context 2722. Finds were more prolific, with a quantity of ceramic building material, from 3359; waterlogged plant remains were also recovered. One, almost complete, double-handed flagon was recovered from 3341 at a depth of *c.* 2.0m (FIG. 75, No. 19), while a further two, almost complete flagons were recovered a little higher up, from gravel fill 2722 (FIGS 28; 75, Nos 20–1). All were from the Verulamium region potteries. Timby (below, Ch. 8) comments that a minimum number of ten flagons was associated with the lower fills. Although context 2320 at a depth of 1.6m contained further waterlogged material, it seems to be the point

FIG. 28.   Period 3 well 2234: Verulamium-region ware flagon with pierced body (= FIG. 75, No. 20). The scale is 0.2m long.

from which use of the well as a source of water was abandoned and the pit accumulated rubbish. In particular, this deposit contained a significant quantity of animal bone, predominantly (and unusually for this period) cattle. Subsequent layers of gravel were interspersed with clay deposits. Above context 2333, above a depth of 1.0m, the upper fills contained some fourth-century material as well as residual, early Roman sherds.

Dating the use of this well is difficult. The flagon from the earliest context is not common and is dated provisionally to the later first/early second century. Similar dates are attached to the other two flagons, while material associated with the mid-depth use-contexts is assigned to the early second century (Timby, below, Ch. 8). It would appear that the well fell out of use *c.* A.D. 125, at the end of our Period 2, the start of Period 3. Consolidation of slumping fills continued into the fourth century. Overall the quantities of material from this feature were not great and there were few small finds (Crummy, below, Ch. 6)

PERIOD 4 (FIG. 29)

SUMMARY

The two town-houses, MB 1 and MB 2, were demolished and replaced with a single building, MB 3. There is no evidence to suggest the continuation in use of the Period 3 buildings in the north-east corner of the insula, MRTB 1 and ERTB 1. MRTB 2 and 3 were demolished and replaced with two, equally insubstantial, new timber buildings, MRTB 4 and 5, both of which were constructed on the line of the north–south street. Two successive wells (5735 and 1750) were sunk to the north of the southern building, MRTB 4, and a further four pits (2434, 2601, 3406 and 3102) were dug to its west. Other than cultivated soils and gravel spreads, there is no definable Period 4 occupation associated with the northern property.

MASONRY BUILDING 3 (Object 50046) (FIGS 30–31)

With the possible exception of the external, south-west, end wall and the internal walls separating Room 1 from Room 2 and the adjacent corridor, where the foundations survived, Masonry Building 2 was demolished to ground level and the remaining foundations, both of internal rooms and external walls, were extensively robbed out. This allowed the construction of a single, large house, which, in effect, represented an extension south-westwards of the footprint of MB 1. The only significant changes to the latter were the demolition and robbing of the foundations of the internal walls separating Room 1 from the corridor (1535). As we have seen above, these alterations may have taken place before the demolition of MB 2. To create the new building the north-west-facing wall (1015) of the internal wall line of MB 1 and the south-east-facing, outer wall of the corridor/verandah (1174) were both extended, cutting across the wall lines of the earlier MB 2. The new walls were also constructed of flint, their foundation trenches measuring 0.52m in width with a depth of 0.15m. A third element of the new building was a further, parallel wall, which extended the line of the south-east-facing, internal wall of MB 1. This was a shallower and wider structure, some 0.74m in width and 0.12m in depth, which re-used tile as well as flint in the foundations. The only outer wall-line to be retained was that at the south-west end. This showed indications of subsidence, particularly towards the northern end, and was almost certainly rebuilt. There was no certain evidence for the continuation south-westwards of the north-west-facing corridor/verandah of MB 1. A shallow trench (1257) which continued the line for a further 10.0m was found not to contain any flints when re-excavated in 1997–8. It is lightly shaded on the plan of Insula IX of 1893–4, which suggests that the Victorians found no flints either (Fox 1895, pl. xlv). Indeed it is possible that this extension was a creation of the excavators following the line of the outer wall 1183/1664. Altogether, measuring 36m in length by a maximum of 11m in width, the surface area of the new house amounted to some 396 square metres.

Apart from a continuous passage, probably a verandah rather than a closed corridor, running along the south-east-facing side of the house, the north-east-facing side and part of the north-

FIG. 29.   Period 4: Masonry Building 3, associated Mid-Roman Timber Buildings 4 and 5 and associated occupation, *c.* A.D. 200–*c.* A.D. 250/300.

west-facing side, the principal new element of the house was a large room (Room 4) to the south-west on the site of MB 2, measuring some 18m by 7m. Although we have noted that the foundations of the walls separating Room 1 from Room 2 and the adjacent corridor were not robbed out, it is highly unlikely that they were retained in MB 3 as they make little sense in terms of the plan of the new house. At the opposite end of the latter was the large, working space, perhaps already created by the demolition of the internal walls of Room 1. There is evidence for

FIG. 30. Period 4: Masonry Building 3 and adjacent occupation and post alignments. For explanatory key see FIG. 29.

FIG. 31.   Period 4: MB 3 viewed from the south-west in 2001 with foundations of Period 3 MB 2 also visible. The scales are 2.0m in length.

a shallow foundation trench (1090), running north-east/south-west and approximately dividing the new space into two equal halves. During excavation this was interpreted as a Victorian trench. However, its central location does suggest that this may well have been a structural element, presumably containing posts to hold up the roof, whose supports would otherwise have needed to span the full (11m) width of the building. Remains of one hearth to the east of 1090 (1802) and burnt areas (1544, 3231) in the original corridor space at the north-east end provide evidence for the continuation of metalworking in this part of the house. In particular, elevated concentrations of copper, zinc, lead, strontium and phosphorus are recorded from 1544, as well as from 3259, which overlies Period 3 hearth 3681 (Cook, below, Ch. 3). Elemental concentrations of gold and silver from 3259 suggest the possibility of the cupellation of precious metals as well as the working of copper alloy (Cook *et al.* 2005; below, Ch. 3) and iron (Tootell, below, Ch. 11). This end area of the house was roughly floored with clay spreads (2018/1047).

In the case of Rooms 2 and 3 (FIG. 32) we have no evidence to suggest that the flooring was different to what it was at the end of the life of MB 1, which is described above. Equally, there is no evidence when the floors were reduced to the state in which they were found in 1893 and 1997 and we must remain open to the possibility that this took place during the life of MB 3. No floor surfaces survived in the new Room 4, potentially the principal reception room of the house, other than of gravel. This might indicate original flooring of mortar, *opus signinum*, or of mosaic. Loose tesserae of dolomite cementstone, which might indicate a plain tessellated or even a mosaic floor, were found in association with 1757 at the south-west end of the building (Hayward 2007a; below, Ch. 9). Waste from the production of tesserae of this material was found in a number of contexts associated with MRTB 5 to the east of MB 3. Slag, including slag basins indicative of smelting, was recovered from make-up layers associated with Room 4.

Further evidence of alterations to the house is provided by a row of post-holes, equally spaced at 2m intervals, which ran the length of the north-west-facing corridor. These may have served both to help support the roof of the corridor and, possibly, to subdivide the internal space. Such interpretations may also account for the two post-holes in the north-east-facing end-corridor

FIG. 32. Period 4: MB 3. View to the north-west across the middle of the house (Rooms 2 and 3) cut by late Roman pits. The scales are, respectively, 1.0m (foreground) and 2.0m (centre) in length.

of the house. A further group of post-holes was recorded around the middle of the south-east-facing corridor (1947, 1949 and 2693).

No evidence survived to indicate the locations of doorways or thresholds. However, a gravelled path leading towards the middle of the south-east-facing elevation of the house suggests the approximate position of one external door (FIG. 33).

There is some evidence for the robbing of part of the south-east aisle-wall with the digging of a number of shallow, linear trenches (1911, 1777, 3920, 1753, 1241) at a later date.

Finds

The majority of glass and metal finds associated with the building appear to be residual from the first and second century (D. Allen 2007; below, Ch. 7; Crummy 2007; below, Ch. 6). Although the pottery assemblage is also dominated by residual material, there is an appreciable quantity of mid-to-late Antonine samian and later second- to third-century coarse wares (Timby 2007; below, Ch. 8). Material dating from the late third and fourth centuries derives from contexts which should be re-assigned to the late Roman occupation of the insula, after the demolition of the house in the second half of the third century. Two fragments of crucible are noted (J. Allen, below, Ch. 11).

Although there is a strong probability of a high residual element in the bone assemblage, the partial skeleton of an immature sheep, a group of small dog bones deriving from a partial skeleton, and the presence of foetal/neonatal caprine bones are probably contemporary with either construction or occupation of the building (Ingrem 2007; below, Ch. 13).

FIG. 33.   Period 4: Mid-Roman Timber Building 4 (with outline footprint of fourth-century Late Roman Building 1) and Building 5 (with outline footprint of Late Roman Building 5), and associated occupation, including wells 1750 and 5735 and pits 2434, 2601, 3102 and 3406. For key see FIG. 29.

Function of the building

With the exception of the burnt areas in 'Room 1' at the north-east end of the building and the associated geochemical evidence which indicates the continuation of metalworking from Period 3, there is little evidence with which to determine the function and status of the building. The house is one of the larger buildings in *Calleva* and so was presumably of considerable status. The latter was reflected in the continuous verandah along the south-east-facing elevation and the size of the possible reception Room 4. The plan recalls that of Perring's hall-type strip buildings, though in our case the hall is linked not to a strip building but to a row-type house (MB 1) (2002, 56–9, fig. 11). Unfortunately, there are no midden deposits which we can confidently associate with the building and thereby allow us to develop a fuller picture of occupation and status.

Chronology

Since the construction of the new walls of the Period 4 house involved cutting into the make-ups associated with the preceding period, there is little substantive evidence for the date of the construction of the new house. On the evidence of the latest pottery from Period 3, construction appears to date to around A.D. 200. We can be clearer, however, of the date of abandonment and demolition. Despite some superficial contexts with late Roman coins and/or pottery, which should be re-assigned to the late Roman occupation, the foundations of the house are cut by a number of pits, the earliest of which have contents which are datable to about the second half of the third century (Fulford *et al.* 2006, 14).

THE OCCUPATION SOUTH OF MASONRY BUILDING 3: PITS AND WELLS (Object 500017) (FIGS 33–34)

There are six, substantial, cut features associated with the Period 4 occupation. All are located in relatively close proximity to each other in the south-east corner of the excavation trench and

FIG. 34. Views of the south-eastern corner of the excavation trench: (a) showing location of Periods 3 and 4 pits and wells, and the excavated foundation trenches of Late Roman Building 1; (b) similar to (a), but at later stage of excavation showing wells 5693 and 5735 under excavation and post-holes flanking north–south street; some of the foundation trenches of Late Roman Building 1 are visible at the bottom of the photo. The scales in both photos are all 2.0m in length.

are probably to be associated with a predecessor to Late Roman Building 1 (below, p. 51). Two (1750 and 5735) definitely served as wells, two might have had this function (3102, 3406), while the remaining two were almost certainly dug as cess- or rubbish pits from the outset. Although the two adjacent pits 3102 and 3406 were of a comparable depth to others which more certainly served as wells, they only just reached the modern water-table and neither had evidence of waterlogged deposits.

Dating evidence from these pits and wells suggests a sequence for their fills. The earliest cut and subsequent fills would appear to be those associated with well 5735, followed by 1750 (of which only the earliest contexts were undisturbed), 2601 and 3102. The last seems earlier than its neighbour 3406 and the latest pit is 2434.

Well 5735 (Object 500037) (FIG. 35)

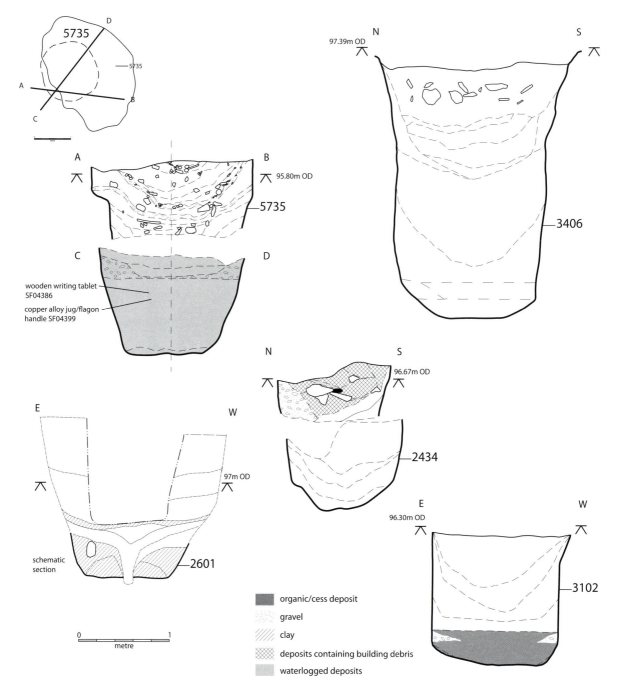

FIG. 35.   Period 4: profiles of associated pits 2434, 2601, 3102 and 3406 and well 5735.

Situated adjacent to the north–south street and beneath the foundations of Late Roman Building 1, well 5735 was succeeded chronologically by well 1750, located some 4m to the west. It was roughly circular in plan at the surface with a diameter of *c.* 1.65m, narrowing towards the base which had a diameter of 1.0m. The cut for this well, which had a depth of *c.* 2.1m, was defined at a low point relative to the contemporary Roman ground surface. The original depth would have been over 2m. The lower fills of gravel (6436) had a depth of 0.8m and were waterlogged. In addition to fragments of wood (but no surviving well lining) and plant remains, which included leaf fragments of box and holly (Robinson, below, Ch. 16), this context also contained a single-leaf writing-tablet of maple (FIG. 36) (Watson, below, p. 116, FIG. 60, No. 64) and part of a bucket handle. A further remarkable find from the lowest fills was the handle of a copper-alloy foot-handle jug (*Fusshenkelkrug*) (FIG. 37) (Crummy, below, Ch. 6, FIG. 60, No. 65). The well appears to have been filled with a succession of deposits of gravel and soil, each rarely more than 0.1m in thickness, with the upper layers containing relatively more soil, charcoal, ceramic building material, animal bone, pottery (with joining sherds from different layers), and other finds.

Among the pottery from the lowest contexts was a sherd of a South-East Dorset BB1 jar decorated with oblique lattice and dated to the early third century (p. 179). Further, possible, early third-century material from these lower contexts was found alongside pottery of mid to late Antonine date. Pottery more certainly attributed to the third century, two thirds (66 per cent)

FIG. 36. Writing-tablet of maple wood from well 5735 (FIG. 60, No. 64).

FIG. 37.   Copper-alloy handle of a *Fusshenkelkrug* from well 5735 (FIG. 60, No. 65).

of which was Dorset BB1, came from the upper contexts. From the well as a whole Dorset BB1 accounted for almost a quarter (23 per cent) of the pottery assemblage. In terms of function the assemblage includes a high proportion, almost one third (31 per cent), of vessels associated with drinking (beakers, cups and flagons) (Timby, below, Ch. 8).

Of the faunal remains from this well, cattle account for half of the sample, with dog, red deer, hare, rodent and goose all also represented (Ingrem, below, Ch. 13).

If the well was first dug at the beginning of the third century, it probably fell out of use before the end of the first quarter of that century when well 1750 was constructed.

Well 1750 (Object 500020) (FIGS 38–41)

This well was first excavated in 1893 when it was described as being 'of the usual timbered construction' (Fox 1895, 442). It was sealed beneath the foundations of Late Roman Building 1. The well pit measured *c.* 1.2 by 1.35m in plan at the surface and was dug to a depth of *c.* 4.8m below the Roman ground surface. At the base it contained a square lining of oak constructed within a sub-rectangular pit *c.* 1.3m square. The internal plan dimensions of the lining were *c.* 650 by 700mm and the structure survived to a height of 0.6m (two tiers of boards) above the oak base-plate. The latter comprised four, interlocking oak beams, each measuring *c.* 1.0 to 1.2m in length and 140 by 100mm in cross-section, above which rested the lining itself. While the

FIG. 38. The oak lining of well 1750 in the course of excavation. The scale is 0.5m long.

base-plate was left *in situ*, the surviving boards of the lining were lifted and recorded (FIG. 40). Attached securely to each other with mortise-and-tenon jointing, each of the four boards of the lowest tier measured *c.* 730 or 760mm by 260mm with a thickness of *c.* 50mm. Four struts, each *c.* 50 by 20mm in cross-section, cut diagonally into adjacent pairs of planks across each of the four corners, provided further strengthening at each tier of the lining. Only two, relatively poorly preserved planks with traces of the corner bracing survived of the upper tier. The western board of the upper tier had scored on its inside surface three vertical lines, perhaps representing the number III (FIG. 40).

Although excavated in 1893, the lowest fills, with a depth of 0.7m, were undisturbed and produced a small collection of pottery as well as faunal and waterlogged plant remains (Robinson, below, Ch. 16). The pottery included sherds of black-slipped Moselle ware of late second/ early third-century date, while the faunal assemblage was dominated by the remains of birds, accounting for almost half of the group (43 per cent). From the base of the cut (2767) for the well came twelve raven bones, including pairs of certain bones, several dog bones, including three articulating cervical vertebrae and a tibia with a well-healed fracture, and a tibia of a red deer (Ingrem, below, Ch. 13).

Although the timbers were examined by Dan Miles (Oxford Dendrochronology Laboratory) with a view to obtaining the dates of the felling of the wood, the growth rings could not be matched to master sequences. Subsequently, several radiocarbon determinations were obtained from one of the timbers from which it was deduced that the date of the outer ring of the sample should be 202–240 cal AD (Galimberti *et al.* 2004, 920–1). A date for the construction of the well in the first half of the third century fits with the postulated date for the abandonment of the neighbouring well 5735. A *terminus ante quem* for the abandonment of well 1750 is provided

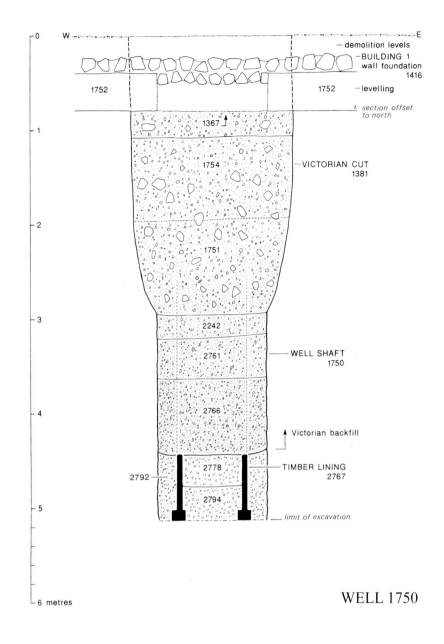

FIG. 39. Period 4: profile of well 1750. (*Drawn by B.Williams*)

by the construction of Late Roman Building 1 for which there is a *terminus post quem* of A.D. 287–293 provided by a coin of Carausius from the adjacent pit 2434 (below, and Fulford *et al.* 2006, 18–19).

Pit 2434 (Object 500031) (FIG. 35)

This pit was almost square, measuring 1.25 by 1.3m in plan, with vertical sides, a flattish base and a depth below the contemporary ground surface of *c.* 1.6m. The lowest fills included some mineralised plant remains (Robinson, below, Ch. 16) which suggest the pit was originally intended for cess. While the lower fills were of dark soil and gravel, the uppermost fill (2602) consisted of quantities of stone (flint), ceramic building material and clayey mortar dumped prior to the construction of Late Roman Building 1 whose foundations overlay the pit. This context also included an unworn coin of Carausius (A.D. 287–293) (SF 01612).

Among the finds (Crummy, below, Ch. 6) were three objects consistent with a late third-century date for the fill: a green glass, hexagonal bead, a bone hairpin with a globular head, and

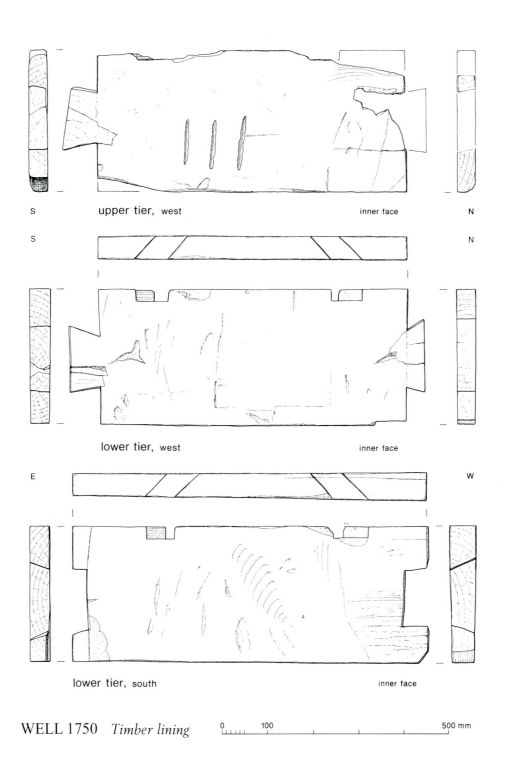

S   upper tier, west   inner face   N

S   N

lower tier, west   inner face

E   W

lower tier, south   inner face

WELL 1750   *Timber lining*   0   100   500 mm

FIG. 40. Period 4 well 1750: individual oak planks of timber lining. (*Drawn by B.Williams*)

a shale armlet with cable decoration. There were also the blade of a small saw and the remains of the sole of a shoe or a pair of soles. The glass included an almost complete, but fragmented example of a 'Mercury' bottle, a rare find in Britain (D. Allen, below, Ch. 7, FIG. 69, No. 74). The small assemblage of pottery included South-East Dorset BB1, Oxfordshire and New Forest wares dating to the second half of the third century (Timby, below, Ch. 8) and in which there is a high proportion (26 per cent) of drinking vessels (cups, mugs and beakers). Associated with the faunal assemblage, amongst which cattle predominate, there are significant proportions of wild

WELL 1750

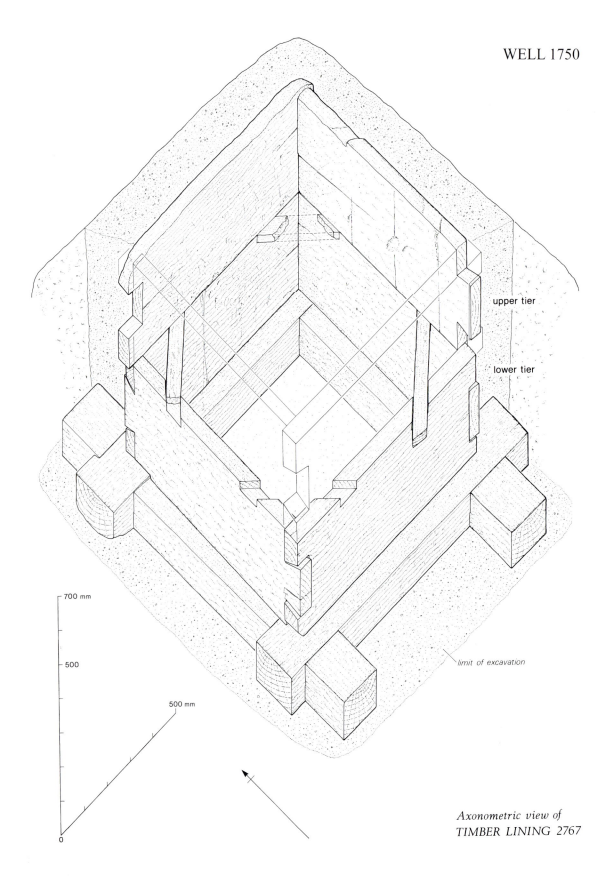

upper tier

lower tier

700 mm

500

500 mm

limit of excavation

0

Axonometric view of
TIMBER LINING 2767

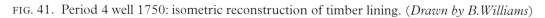

FIG. 41. Period 4 well 1750: isometric reconstruction of timber lining. (*Drawn by B.Williams*)

animals and birds other than galliform. These include three pieces of red deer antler and two partial badger skeletons (Ingrem, below, Ch. 13). There were also the remains of at least three dogs (Clark, below, Ch. 14).

Pit 2601 (Object 500032) (FIGS 35, 42–43)

This pit was sub-circular, measuring *c.* 2.2 by *c.* 1.65m in plan, with steeply sloping sides, a flat base and a depth below the contemporary Roman ground surface of *c.* 1.6m. It had been bisected by the foundation trench of the west wall of Late Roman Building 1. The basal layer (2781) of the pit was of clay into which numerous, small diameter, post-holes of uncertain function had been cut. Although no mineralised plant remains were recovered, it is assumed that this was primarily intended for cess. The primary and secondary fills were largely of dark soil and gravel, but there was no evidence of consolidating fills as with pit 2434.

The majority of the finds derive from the upper layers, among which there are several cross-joins between sherds from different contexts, suggesting rapid infill of the pit. The latest material from the relatively small assemblage of pottery includes Oxfordshire and South-East Dorset BB1 wares dating from after the mid-third century. Jars predominate in the assemblage and drinking vessels are not significantly represented (Timby, below, Ch. 8). The most outstanding find from the pit was a complete iron folding-knife or razor with an ivory handle in the form of two coupling dogs (FIG. 43) (Crummy, below, Ch. 6, FIG. 59, No. 56). This was associated with the remains of the partial skeleton of a young (24–36 weeks) dog which was probably deposited as a complete carcase. It was placed on the right side in a tightly curled up position with the muzzle tucked against the tarsal joints (Clark, below, Ch. 14). The possible ritual connotations of these associated finds are discussed further by Crummy and Eckardt (below, Chs 6 and 18). The remains of further dogs were also recovered from the same context, 2622. Of the other animal

FIG. 42. Period 4 pit 2601 in course of excavation. The scale is 1.0m long.

FIG. 43(a & b). Ivory-handled folding-knife or razor from pit 2601 (FIG. 59, No. 56).

and bird bones reported from this pit the occurrence of five raven bones probably deserves note (Ingrem, below, Ch. 13).

Pit/well 3102 (Object 500034) (FIG. 35)

This pit or well was subcircular in plan, measuring *c.* 2 by 1.8m in diameter at the surface and *c.* 1.4m towards the base. It had near-vertical sides, a flat base and a depth below the contemporary Roman ground surface of *c.* 2.75m. It was adjacent to pit/well 3406. The uppermost fill of this feature contained the foundations of a fourth-century mortared flint wall and is reported in Fulford *et al.* (2006, 37). Above primary fills of gravel, there was some evidence for a cess-like deposit (4040), although no mineralised plant remains were recovered from it. Finds occurred with increasing frequency in subsequent fills from 4030 and above. The pit was sealed with brown silty clay and gravel (3820), then a final capping of clayey gravel (3127) before contexts associated with the construction of the wall in the fourth century.

The majority of the finds were of pottery and animal bone, with very few individually accessioned artefacts: Crummy notes the occurrence of a pair of joiner's dogs and a rake prong (Ch. 6). A small unguent flask with a hole drilled through the side was recorded from 4030 (FIG. 81, No. 106). With the majority of the pottery from 3127 and below of Antonine/late Antonine date, the latest pottery appears to be South-East Dorset BB1 and of late second/early third-century date (Timby, below, Ch. 8). New Forest ware sherds dating from the later third century occurred in the capping layer 3127. Cattle remains dominate the animal bone assemblage with only a slight representation of wild species and birds.

Pit/well 3406 (Object 500033) (FIG. 35)

This pit or well was almost circular in plan, measuring *c.* 2.0m in diameter at the surface and *c.*1.65m towards the base. It had vertical sides, a flattish base and a depth below the contemporary ground surface of *c.* 2.8m. Although the well reached the modern water-table, no waterlogged finds were recovered from it. It was adjacent to pit/well 3102. The primary fills of slumped gravel, up to *c.* 1.5m from the base, contained few finds, but at a depth of *c.* 1.3m, from context 4044 and above, they were abundant. A third-century date, perhaps towards the middle of the century, for this and the middle fills is suggested by the typology and relative abundance of the South-East Dorset BB1 and other associated wares, particularly Oxfordshire ware (Timby, below, Ch. 8). Context 4044 also contained a complete Nene Valley colour-coated box-lid, most of a South-East Dorset BB1 jar and substantial parts of other jars (FIG. 81, Nos 93–102). The upper contexts of the well, particularly 3829 and 3821, contained quantities of ceramic building material and flints, presumably to consolidate the fill. Among these contexts were a few sherds of late third/fourth-century Hampshire grog-tempered pottery and the rim of a Spanish Almagro 50 amphora normally dated to the fourth century (below, p. 176, FIG. 81, No. 100).

The accessioned finds include some items of status: a silver-in-glass bead and a short length of gold wire threaded through a beryl (Crummy, below, Ch. 6, FIGS 59–60, Nos 57–63). There are also fragments of two shale vessels, bone hairpins, evidence for the disposal of footwear throughout the fill, and two probable bone tools of uncertain purpose. As with the adjacent pit 3102, cattle, including the remains of a partial skull, dominate the animal bone assemblage. Foetal dog and pig bone was present and there was a substantial representation of galliform bone (14 per cent) (Ingrem, below, Ch. 13). The remains of two further dogs are documented (Clark, below, Ch. 14).

THE OCCUPATION TO THE SOUTH OF MASONRY BUILDING 3: OTHER CONTEXTS (Object 700) (FIG. 33)

Mid-Roman Timber Building 4

In general terms the contexts and groups of contexts discussed below which, collectively, make up Object 700 are stratigraphically later than those described above as Object 701. Although the evidence is slight, the possibility of one, or two timber-framed buildings adjacent to, and parallel with the north–south street was discussed above (p. 33). In association with this succeeding, third-century phase, the evidence for structures is a little stronger. It has already been suggested above that the concentration of pits and wells in the south-east corner of the excavation trench reflects the existence of a building in close proximity. The existence of a hearth (2037), consisting of a spread of burnt clay, sandstone and chalk flints with a central area of burnt tiles measuring 3m east–west and 1.5m north–south, adds weight to this. Associated with it is occupation comprising clay floor 3911 and an overlying spread of occupation debris extending over an area of *c.* 10m (north–south) by 8m (east–west), parallel with, and adjacent to the north–south street, and immediately to the south of wells 1750 and 5735. Hearth 2037 was cut through by the foundation trench for the walls of Late Roman Building 1 and was located immediately to the west of sub-rectangular pit 3460, which had straight sides and measured 1.53m north–south and 1.76m east–west. It was over 1m deep. The fills of this pit contained some industrial waste and its close proximity to hearth 2037 suggests that these two features were closely associated. The northern and eastern limits of this occupation are truncated by the foundation trenches of Late Roman Building 1, the west by a Victorian trench. The southern edge seems to coincide with the edge of the excavation trench. If these spreads do coincide with the footprint of a building, for which no structural evidence in the form of beam-slots or post-holes survives, they do not entirely coincide with the footprint of Late Roman Building 1 whose outline is shown on FIGS 33–34 (Fulford *et al.* 2006, 18–26) (cf. the northern building, below). The position of the pits to the west perhaps marks the limits of an associated backyard of the building. Our Period 4 structure becomes Mid-Roman Timber Building 4.

Mid-Roman Timber Building 5

Thirteen metres to the north of the southern occupation, a rectangular area of gravel and mortar surfaces, measuring *c.* 12m by 4.5m, aligned east–west and fronting on the north–south street, seems to represent the ground-plan of a second, timber-framed building. In terms of its plan and extent this lies immediately beneath the footprint of the main room of Late Roman Building 5 and may be regarded as a direct predecessor (Fulford *et al.* 2006, 26–8) (FIG. 33). There are, however, no traces of associated beam-slots or post-holes, except on the eastern side fronting the street where four post-holes (6367, etc.) are recorded. Within the footprint of the proposed building there was evidence of a patchy surface and four, small, shallow pits interleaved with occupation deposits. The first, 2777, was sub-circular in plan, measuring *c.* 1.05m by 0.82m and with a depth of *c.* 0.1m. It contained a quantity of waste from the manufacture of Kimmeridge dolomite cementstone tesserae (Hayward, below, Ch. 9). Dolomite cementstone was the material of the commonest tesserae found in association with MB 3 (above, p. 38). Pit 2779, a close neighbour of pit 2777, was also sub-circular in plan with a diameter of *c.* 1.3m and a depth of 0.15m and was filled with dark soil with lenses of clay. Located immediately to the west of pit 2779 was a third pit (2643), measuring 1.7m east–west by 1.75m north–south, and with a depth of 0.25m. Nails, fragments of glass and dolomite cementstone tesserae were recovered from this pit. A fourth pit, 2769/2773, located in the eastern end of the proposed building, measured 1.3m square, with a depth of 0.2m. The surfaces within this structure were composed of gravels and clay silts and, like the shallow pits described above, contained nails and fragments of glass.

Of the other occupation to the west of our possible Period 4 buildings, represented by spreads of gravel and soils, we should particularly note the gravel path, *c.* 3.0m in width, which was traced running northwards from the southern edge of the excavation trench towards the Period 4 Masonry Building 3 (FIG. 33). This met a more extensive gravelled surface outside the south-east-facing frontage of MB 3. The area between these proposed Period 4 buildings and MB 3 was composed of spreads of compacted gravels, forming yards, hard-standings and small paths.

   The latest Period 4 contexts in the area to the south of MB 3 comprise make-ups associated, in particular, with the construction of Late Roman Building 1 and reported as Phase 1 in *Life and Labour* (Fulford *et al.* 2006, 18–19). These contexts included a range of occupational material, including a quantity of iron-smelting and iron-forging slags (Tootell, below, Ch. 11).

CHAPTER 3

THE GEOCHEMISTRY OF 'HOUSE 1' IN PERIODS 3 AND 4

By Samantha R. Cook

INTRODUCTION

Since 2002, in the context of the Insula IX project, a programme of soil material sampling has been undertaken with the aim of using simple geochemical analyses to complement and interrogate possible archaeological evidence for metalworking. The soil material analyses may also reveal areas of human activity (e.g. industrial activity or animal husbandry) for which there is no macroscopic archaeological evidence.

Residues can accumulate in soil from a great range of organic and inorganic materials used in food, clothing, buildings, household utensils and industrial activity as well as human and animal waste products, and many soils are capable of holding elements in relatively immobile forms (James 1999). Soil geochemical data can provide important information on activities within a given area, especially when interpretation has been difficult to determine from artefact data alone (e.g. Ball and Kelsey 1992; Lippi 1988). In previous archaeological studies elsewhere soil analysis has been used to distinguish different functions or land-use activities over a site and to aid identification and interpretation of settlement features (e.g. Aston and Gerrard 1999; Aston *et al.* 1998a).

The purpose of this study was, therefore, to use soil geochemical analyses to interrogate the archaeological evidence, particularly with reference to potential non-ferrous metalworking at the site. Effort was initially concentrated across the footprint of 'House 1' and the adjacent timber building MRTB 1/ERTB 1 (= former ERTB 4), where hearths and areas of burning had been observed, but where there was a notable absence of the commoner detritus of Romano-British precious metal and copper alloy working such as droplets, off-cuts, slags, crucible or mould fragments, as have been found previously at Silchester, but without supporting, associated evidence in the form of hearths, etc. for the precise location of activity (cf. Boon 1974, 272–7; Gowland 1900; Northover and Palk 2000; Richards 2000). In the course of the preparation of this excavation report, however, remains of crucibles have been identified among the ceramic material (J.R.L. Allen, below, Ch. 11) and of one unfinished copper-alloy artefact among the copper-alloy finds (Crummy, below, Ch. 6). Macroscopic and microscopic evidence for ferrous metalworking, however, in the form of hammer-scale and slag masses has been recovered across the excavation (J.R.L Allen below, Ch. 11; Tootell, below, Ch. 11). The question for the sequence of town-houses on the 'House 1' footprint was whether it would be possible to distinguish between a domestic or metalworking function for the associated hearths and burnt areas. To this end samples were taken and analysed using x-ray fluorescence spectroscopy (XRF). Initial results have already been published (Cook *et al.* 2005).

The trace metals (copper, zinc, lead) which were analysed were chosen on the basis of the information they would offer on possible metalworking at the site. During the Roman period habitual use was made of copper as an alloy with lead (Pb) and tin (Sn), with zinc (Zn) often occurring as an impurity. A variety of copper alloys were used in the Roman Empire, from traditional tin bronze to brass and combinations of these alloys, known by the modern term gunmetal (Cu, Zn and Sn) (Dungworth 1997a). Lead was often added to cast objects to decrease the melting point of the alloy and facilitate pouring (Dungworth 1997a).

Major elements were also investigated with special emphasis on strontium (Sr), calcium (Ca) and phosphorus (P) as indicators of human habitation. Phosphorus leaches from bones and organic tissues and concentrates in locations where organic materials were left to decay (Sarris *et al.* 2004). As phosphate phosphorus is relatively immobile and can be used to distinguish between living areas and middens, pits, stalls and pasture (see, for example, Bethell and Máté 1989; Conway 1983). Strontium and calcium can be an indication of bone deposition whether as rubbish disposal, ritual burial, or for use in cupellation.

METHODS

The samples were dried and disaggregated before being passed through a 1mm sieve, then ground and pressed into pellets for analysis by x-ray fluorescence (XRF) using a Philips PW1480 XRF with Philips X40 analytical software. All the material was clay-loam to sandy loam in character, in many cases with large (of several centimetres in size) flint pebbles. Samples were also taken from each of the major local lithologies, namely, the Silchester Gravels, the Bagshot Sands and the London Clay, to determine background elemental concentrations.

RESULTS

COPPER, ZINC, LEAD, STRONTIUM, CALCIUM AND PHOSPHORUS

Samples were taken from a variety of contexts within the 'House 1' footprint (Table 1), FIGS 44–45 show the concentrations of copper, zinc, lead and strontium found in samples taken from

TABLE I. ARCHAEOLOGICAL CONTEXTS SAMPLED FOR CHEMICAL ANALYSIS

	Context no.	Context description
Period 3 *c.* A.D. 125–150 – A.D. 200	1718	Occupation deposit
	3210	
	3281	NE aisle
	3375	Clay levelling deposit
	3385	
	3701	Hearth
	3707	Soft black charcoal with nails
	3709	Ash layer in hearth 3681
	3946	Levelling deposit
	4170	Large clay floor associated with large hearth 1433
	4189	Layer of burning on top of hearth 4216. Set in the house clay 4152 along with tiles. Above 4199
	4199	Chalk deposit from burning within hearth 4216 under layer of charcoal/silt (4189)
	4201	Soft, reddy brown/dark grey clayey silt, burnt clay on top of yellow clay (4202) and underneath CBM tile
	4210	Red burning of clay around hearth 4216
	4209	Yellow clay within hearth 4216
	4203	Gravel under hearth 4216
	4204	Clay between gravel layers within hearth 4216
	4205	Gravel layer under hearth 4216
	4207	Greyish clay under yellow clay (4204)
	4213	Hard, black charcoal, partially destroyed hearth probably associated with larger hearth
	7061	Clay levelling deposit

	Context no.	Context description
Period 4 c. A.D. 200–250	1544	Large hearth with nails
	4084	Levelling deposit
	3259	Levelling deposit NE aisle
	3282	Clay deposit in NE aisle

FIG. 44.   Concentrations (mg/kg dry weight) of copper, zinc, lead and strontium from Period 3 contexts.

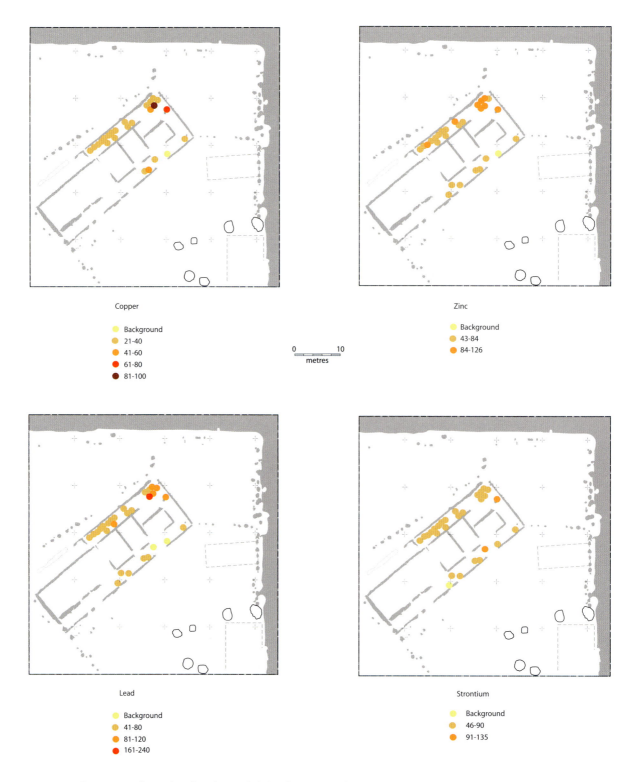

FIG. 45.   Concentrations (mg/kg dry weight) of copper, zinc, lead and strontium from Period 4 contexts.

Period 3 and 4 contexts respectively. The results have been ranked by concentrations relative to average background concentration (2 x background, 3 x background etc.); this allows an easy comparison of 'hot spot' locations, the darker reds corresponding to higher concentrations. Tables 2 and 3 show the 'hot-spot' concentrations of Ca and P in selected contexts.

Period 3

High concentrations of strontium were found in the contexts associated with ERTB 4, now redefined as MRTB 1 and an initially retained ERTB 1, to the north-east of the building at the junction of the north–south and east–west streets (FIG. 44). This area also has high concentrations of copper and zinc with scattered hot-spots of lead (FIG. 44). Notably elevated Zn, Cu and Sr concentrations are associated with hearth 4216, the smaller of the two hearths and located within MRTB 1 (FIG. 16). Relatively high phosphate concentrations (analysed as phosphate but recorded here corrected as elemental concentration) were also found in samples from context 4170 within ERTB 1 (approx 16 x background) and 7061 (FIGS 16 and 46). Unsurprisingly context 4199, a chalk deposit associated with hearth 4216, contains elevated concentrations of Ca (24.9mg/kg cf. 0.2mg/kg average background concentration) (FIG. 46). However, this sample also contains high concentrations of Zn.

The geochemical evidence presents a clear picture of elemental distribution for MB 1 with a combined 'hot spot' for Sr, Cu, Pb and Zn at the north-east corner (FIG. 44), which coincides with hearth 3681 (FIG. 8). Copper concentrations are also elevated in Room 2 with coincidently high concentrations of Sr (FIG. 44). High P concentrations are also recorded from context 3709 which is associated with hearth 3681 (Table 2).

TABLE 2. CONCENTRATIONS OF PHOSPHORUS AND CALCIUM FOUND IN PERIOD 3 CONTEXTS
(Concentration in mg/kg dry weight: only those contexts with concentrations significantly over background are shown here)

Context	Easting	Northing	P
7061	540.3	548	1.07
4170	543.089	536.942	1.00
3709	528.668	539.277	0.92
4170	541.886	547.9	0.79
1718	528.994	527.759	0.72
			Ca
4199	536.3	538.76	24.9
3375	524.900	527.793	6.49
3946	524.799	531.915	3.32
3946	524.882	532.706	2.76
3709	528.668	539.277	1.97

Period 4

The contexts which relate to Period 4 and MB 3 also contain elevated elemental concentrations (Cu, Zn, Pb and Sr) at one 'hot spot' location at the north-east end of the building (FIG. 45), coincident with hearth 1544 and context 3259 which overlies hearth 3681 (Period 3) (FIG. 30). Elevated P is also found in both context 1544 (a hearth) and context 4084 which runs along the south-east-facing corridor of the building (Table 3, FIG. 46).

TABLE 3. CONCENTRATIONS OF PHOSPHORUS AND CALCIUM FOUND IN PERIOD 4 CONTEXTS
(Concentration in mg/kg dry weight; only those contexts with concentrations significantly over background are shown here)

Context	Easting	Northing	P
1544	530.208	537.524	0.45
4084	527.568	526.933	0.35
			Ca
1544	530.208	537.524	1.15

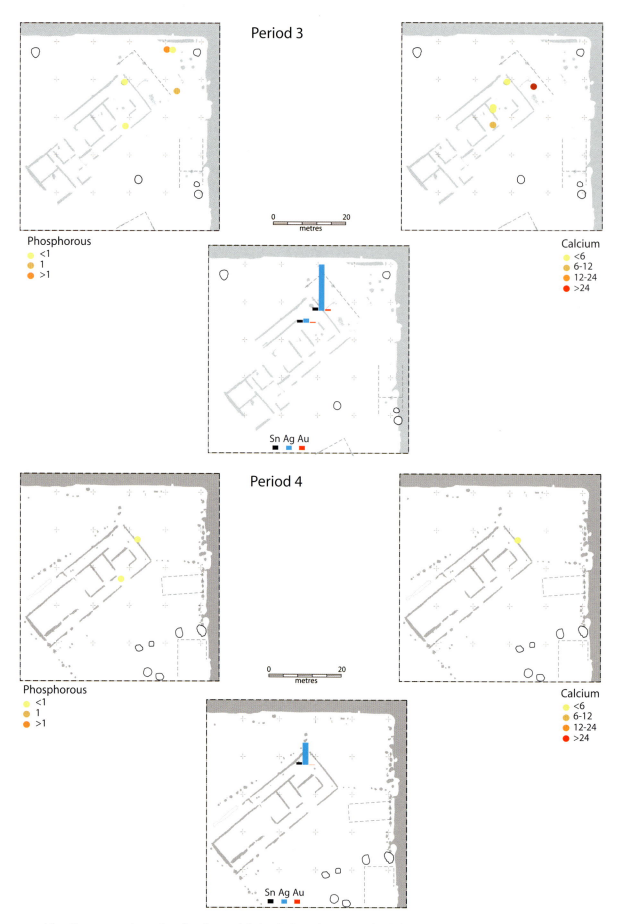

FIG. 46. Concentrations (mg/kg dry weight) of phosphorus and calcium, and of gold, silver and tin, from Periods 3 and 4.

GOLD, SILVER AND TIN

Of the samples taken for analysis using x-ray fluorescence three were also analysed for gold, silver and tin (Table 4). The low concentrations and tendency for gold, in particular, to exist as nuggets in soil meant that only those samples with high metals (Cu, Zn and Pb) were analysed for these elements. The analysis was carried out at the NERC ICP-MS facility at Kingston University.

Measurable concentrations of all three elements were found in three contexts (FIG. 46). From Period 3 elevated silver, tin and gold were found associated with contexts 3707 and 3281, which are associated with hearth 3681 (FIGS 8 and 46). Context 3259 (Period 4) also contained measurable concentrations of all three elements. This context overlies the Period 3 hearth (3681 and associated deposits) and it is, therefore, perhaps not surprising that this deposit also contains elevated levels of these metals.

TABLE 4. CONCENTRATIONS OF GOLD (AU), TIN (SN) AND SILVER (AG)

	Context			Ag	Sn	Au
Period 3	3707	528.102	539.090	6.15	90.14	3.41
	3281	524.102	536.036	6.31	9.53	2.40
Period 4						
	3259	527.458	538.356	5.81	52.94	0.68

DISCUSSION

PERIOD 3

MRTB 1: hearth 4216 (FIG. 16)

This suite of samples is associated with hearth 4216, a small hearth consisting of layers of gravel and clay interspersed with small tile-settings. Elevated Zn concentrations were found in these contexts, notably for contexts 4189, 4199, 4210 and 4213 (the distribution of these 'hot spots' is shown in FIG. 44). The micromorphology of 4189 shows that this context comprises reworked material, rubbish (including dung) and hearth debris (Banerjea, below, Ch. 4). The high Zn concentrations in this accumulation deposit may derive from zinc working, but are more likely to be a result of accumulated waste, both animal and hearth sweepings. This is further supported by the lack of other elevated metal concentrations as is seen for other hearths (e.g. context 3681).

Context 4199 is a chalky layer which is high in calcium. Micromorphological analysis (p. 72) suggests that this deposit was lime slurry used to level the floor once the small hearth was no longer in use. Since zinc is often enriched in carbonate deposits via substitution of the Zn^{+2} ion into the calcium carbonate mineral lattice, the elevated Zn observed here is therefore unlikely to be a result of metalworking activity. There is also considerable incorporation of domestic rubbish, such as animal bone, pottery sherds, charcoal, etc., from the above deposit via trampling, which supports the hypothesis that Zn enrichment has occurred via secondary deposition.

The group of samples from contexts which comprise floor surface 4152 (4201, 4202, 4209) and are associated with hearth 4216 do not contain elevated concentrations of Cu or Pb and only slightly elevated Zn. These results are certainly not indicative of any substantial metalworking activity. Indeed, the micromorphology (Banerjea, below, Ch. 4) indicates that, consistent with a domestic purpose, the area around hearth 4216 was kept clean.

Eastern side of ERTB 4 (= former ERTB 1): hearth 1433 (FIG. 16)

The samples taken from this area are associated with the larger of the two hearths (1433) and comprise contexts 4170, 5848 and 5870. Context 4170 contains high levels of strontium, copper and zinc spread across the entire floor surface of this building; this is consistent with the use of the industrial hearth for metalworking activity. Micromorphology has shown that this floor surface is made up of trampled deposits containing demolition debris and animal dung. The ubiquitous nature of these elements across the entire floor may suggest that this floor was not kept clean. Micromorphology has also revealed the presence of melted silica, ashes and fire-affected flint with an absence of wood charcoal. It is therefore likely that high temperatures were being employed during the lifetime of this hearth (Banerjea, below, Ch. 4). The presence of Sr is an indication of human activity as it is present in bones, whilst the high P levels recorded in two of the samples from this context relate to the deposition of animal and human waste as well as bones (Banerjea, below, Ch. 4, for more discussion on P accumulation). Context 5848 is also a trampled re-worked accumulation deposit and contains relatively high concentrations of Pb (160mg/kg cf. 30mg/kg background). The re-worked nature of this deposit and the presence of only elevated Pb precludes a definitive interpretation of this concentration as being evidence of metalworking.

The geochemical results for this building, ERTB 1, reinforce the evidence from micromorphology that suggests that animals were once kept here. The spread of elevated elemental concentrations in this area may suggest that the decaying building, ERTB 1, was also used as a low-status store-room or workshop whose floor was not regularly swept, allowing the accumulation of occupation debris. Indeed the remains of the building may have been used for the disposal of general household waste.

Town-house 1 (MB 1) (FIG. 8)

The most north-easterly of the combined lead, zinc and copper 'hot spots' within the walls of MB 1 coincides with the location of hearth 3681 in the corridor of the house. This feature was 0.94m in diameter with a shallow depth of 0.05m and a flat base. It was oriented north-east/ south-west and produced within it an ash layer which contained numerous iron nails and some iron-smithing slags. A layer of charcoal overlay the ash and a red-burnt clay layer measuring *c.* 1.28m in diameter covered the entire hearth. Adjacent to this were the trampled and fragmentary remains of a large, Silchester ware jar. On the basis of the nails, the slag and the interpretation of the pottery jar as a quenching vessel, this hearth had been provisionally interpreted as associated with iron-working (Clarke and Fulford 2002, 139). However, Timby (below, Ch. 8) speculates that the vessel may have been used for cooking.

Elevated gold, silver and tin concentrations were also found within this building, tin in particular showing elevated levels associated with the same hearth contexts as the other metals. This is not surprising as tin is frequently found in Roman alloys (54 per cent of alloys have more than 5 per cent tin) (Dungworth 1997a).

It is difficult to say, in the absence of *prima facie* evidence, with any certainty what type of metalworking activity was being carried out in the north-east corner of MB 1; however, the combination of metal 'hot-spots' in this location is good evidence that some industrial activity was indeed occurring during this period. The scarcity of iron-working slag and significant hammerscale (Tootell, below, Ch. 11) suggests that, although it is likely that this area was being used as a workshop, the industrial activity was light: the casting and working of non-ferrous metal rather than iron-working.

Elevated levels of metals recorded in Room 2 of MB 1 have no obvious association with a hearth. However, we can postulate that, as metalworking was occurring in the building, it may have had several working areas and metal sweepings, off-cuts, etc. are likely to have been distributed throughout the house.

Town-house 2 (MB 2) (FIG. 8)

The only 'hot-spot' which relates to this building occurs to the south-east of the building and is only seen for copper. Zinc levels are slightly elevated at approximately 3 x background. It is possible that these metal concentrations relate to sweepings from the building as they occur outside the building walls. Altogether this suggests a different emphasis of function for this building, domestic rather than industrial. It is noticeable that lead concentrations in particular are lower in this building compared with MB 1.

In summary, the area originally defined as ERTB 4, but now divided between a small, newly defined building MRTB 1 and the decaying remains of ERTB 1, also appears to have been divided in function. While the former was kept relatively clean, the latter appears to have been used for a variety of purposes including as a barn or byre, a workshop, and for the storage of household waste. MB 1 was the centre of metalworking activity and functioned as a workshop for at least part of its lifetime with a large hearth (3681) in the north-east aisle.

High phosphorus concentrations found in the charcoal layer of hearth 3681 (context 3709) may indicate the use of bones in cupellation, but it may also be a result of the presence of higher organic matter (food remains or wood from the fire), since P is known to accumulate where organic matter decays (Sarris *et al.* 2004). MB 2 had limited or no industrial or craft function and was more likely to have been devoted completely to domestic purposes.

PERIOD 4 (FIG. 30)

The elevated metal concentrations seen across the footprint of 'House 1' during Period 3 are not recorded by the time the two stone buildings (MB 1 and 2) become the one town-house (MB 3) in Period 4. Contexts from this period show elevated metal concentrations only in association with hearth 1544, the large industrial hearth from which there is associated evidence in the form of nails. The other observed 'hot-spot' locations sit directly above the Period 3 contexts associated with hearth 3681 in the corridor to the north-east of the building. It is possible that this represents continuity of the use of this hearth during Period 4.

Other than the activity situated in and around hearth 1544, the floors appear to have been swept clean, since in surrounding contexts and along the aisles of the building elemental concentrations are close to background levels. Only lead and copper show elevated concentrations similar to those seen in Period 3.

CONCLUSIONS AND SUMMARY

The value of the analysis of soils from archaeological sites is in the combination of their results with the archaeology to aid the interpretation of the use and evolution of space, particularly where function is ambiguous owing to the lack of finds.

In the case of Town-house 1 (MB 1) we clearly see evidence for human activity in Period 3 (*c.* A.D. 125/150–200) in the form of elevated metal concentrations in the corridor at the north-east corner. Whilst it is difficult to say with certainty what this 'hot-spot' represents, the coincidence of several metals at levels well above an average background concentration leads us to suggest that metalworking of some form was indeed being carried out in this building. The 'hot-spot' associated with the Period 4 context 3259 is difficult to interpret. It lies directly above hearth 3681 (Period 3) and, although it is possible that this location retained its industrial function into Period 4, we must also consider the possibility that this 'hot-spot' is a ghost or shadow of previous activity caused by re-working of underlying contexts. Certainly the industrial or craft activity in Period 4 is situated around hearth 1544, but metal levels are not as high as those for the Period 3 hearth 3681. This may indicate a change in function and usage to smaller-scale or less intensive craft activities.

The difficult interpretation of ERTB 4 = MRTB 1 and former ERTB 1 is aided using a combined approach with micromorphology where the geochemical evidence again shows human activity altering the chemistry of the deposits present. In this case the evidence comprises not only copper, lead and zinc (perhaps as a result of metalworking/industrial activity), but also the presence of elevated phosphate, suggesting animal husbandry. The elemental chemistry also allows us to differentiate between possible domestic use of the smaller hearth 4216 and the larger, possibly industrial (at least in part) hearth 1433. The most obvious difference between the town-houses and the location of the decaying ERTB 1 is the spread of elevated metal concentrations across the floor surfaces of the latter. The town-houses appear to have been kept much 'cleaner' whilst the spread of elevated metal concentrations in former ERTB 1 is possibly indicative of a re-worked or unkempt floor consistent with the micromorphological evidence and suggestive of multiple functions, including use for animal penning as well as for metalworking and the accumulation of household waste.

CHAPTER 4

MICROSCOPIC PERSPECTIVES ON THE USE OF PERIOD 3 MRTB 1/ERTB 1

By Rowena Banerjea

INTRODUCTION

The use of internal space is an under-studied area of Roman archaeology, particularly in relation to the structuring of activities and the changing use of space within structures (Goldberg and Macphail 2006, 239; Millett 2001, 64; Burnham et al. 2001, 73–4; MOLAS 2002, 34–5; Perring 1987, 147). Analysis of microscopic floor strata and occupation detritus aids interpretations of: (1) spatial organisation of the activities and households within the urban settlement; (2) temporal urban change in terms of (a) short-term changes in the life-history of the household and (b) long-term settlement change.

Microanalysis of archaeological deposits enables high resolution investigation of deposit colour, particle size, sorting, related distribution of coarse and fine fabric, the nature and properties of inclusions and their orientation and distribution, and the microstructure of the sedimentary matrix. These sedimentary properties facilitate interpretation of deposit origin, depositional events and human and animal activity, and post-depositional events and alterations (Courty *et al.* 1989; Schiffer 1987).

Since 2003, soil micromorphology samples have been taken from the floor and hearth areas within timber and earth-walled structures in Insula IX. Analysis of this material has contributed significantly to the interpretation of spatial and chronological variation in the use of internal space in the area to the north-east of MB 1. Originally interpreted as a single, roofed space (ERTB 4, referred to below as 'ERTB 4'), micromorphology (below) has played a major role in the re-interpretation of the area. As a result we are concerned now with two structures: a new MRTB 1 in Period 3 and a continuing ERTB 1 (see above Ch. 2, FIG. 16).

ARCHITECTURE AND STRATIGRAPHIC SEQUENCES IN THE FIELD

The structures under consideration directly overlie Period 2 ERTB 1 and part of ERTB 2 (FIGS 16 and 47). They include two hearths within the structure — the final phase of hearth 1433, which had four phases altogether and was first constructed for use in Period 2 ERTB 1, and a smaller hearth 4216 — and deposits that were presumed to be floor levels during excavation (4152, 4170, 5872, 5870). Unlike Period 2 ERTB 1, the successor structures did not have clearly defined edges and were thought to have floor surfaces (4152 and 5870), and occupation (5848 and 4170), spanning two rooms or separate spaces, with a hearth in each area: 4216 in the western side and 1433 in the eastern side. The separation of these two spaces was not confirmed during excavation due to the truncation of the area by Victorian trenches and later Roman building activities. The final phase of the larger hearth 1433 is associated with deposits 5870, 5848, 5872 and 4170. The smaller hearth 4216 is associated with deposits 4152=4201, 4202 and 4209, a chalk-like deposit 4199, and deposit 4189=3817. Deposit 4203 has been included as it may have formed during the abandonment of Period 2 ERTB 2, Room 2 or the construction of the successor MRTB 1.

Due to the absence of clearly defined parameters of the Period 3 structures between the north-east end of MB 1 and the intersection of the north–south and east–west streets, the possibility of lean-to-type construction, perhaps without solid walls and a substantial roof, will be tested. Some 'floors' may even be formed from lenses of compacted trampled sediment and occupation detritus, rather than deliberately constructed, mud floors. Deposit categories have been examined through micromorphological analysis to understand sediment origin, depositional and post-depositional formation processes.

The artefacts and macroscopic residues recovered during excavation suggest that the area formerly described as ERTB 4 (above, Ch. 2, p. 22) was a multi-functional space. To ascertain primary and changing use of space, the microscopic composition of inclusions will be examined in the context of microstratigraphic formation processes, to identify those artefacts and activity residues that were small enough to have escaped sweeping during the habitation stage of the building. While a building is in use it is assumed that it is cleaned and swept, with larger objects deposited elsewhere in features such as rubbish pits. Any larger artefacts and objects that are recovered during excavation are likely, therefore, to be associated with the abandonment stage of the building, perhaps where the space has been reused to dump rubbish (La Motta and Schiffer 1999).

METHODOLOGY

SITE SAMPLING

Soil micromorphology samples were collected from the area formerly described as ERTB 4 between the 2004 and 2006 excavation seasons. Samples collected during the 2004 and 2005 seasons were not taken using a clear strategy. These include samples from context 4170, which was interpreted as a large clay floor associated with hearth 1433, and the smaller hearth 4216. Samples from the latter were collected and recorded from an existing profile cut by a later Roman well (1044) which enabled retrieval of a chronological sequence pertaining to the use of ERTB 2 Room 2 and the successor building, now MRTB 1. The stratigraphic relationship between hearths 1433 and 4216 was unclear at the time of excavation. The strategy for sampling in 2006 took micromorphology samples from each floor and occupation deposit within the confines of Period 2 ERTB 1. Contexts 5872, 5848=5863 and 5870 are now known to be associated with Period 3.

Two samples were taken from 'clay floor' 4170 (<767> and <768>). Unfortunately it is only possible to locate these samples within a 5m by 5m area of the site (grid 29C) as the exact co-ordinates were not recorded during excavation. The remaining six micromorphology samples in this report have their precise location recorded. The location of deposit 5872 (<995>) is recorded in FIG. 47. Micromorphology samples of 'floors'/occupation surfaces 5870 (<953>) and 5848=5863 (<983>), and the 'floors'/ occupation surfaces associated with the latter stages of ERTB 1 (5921, 6014, 6022, 6024), were taken by creating a working section during excavation and noting location in plan. This strategy was employed to limit the amount of sections truncating the site in an area where stratigraphic relationships were already difficult to interpret.

Hearth 4216 was truncated by a later Roman well (1044), presenting a clear section through the feature and an opportunity to take soil micromorphology samples. Context 4189=3817 was initially interpreted as two separate deposits in the field. Context 3817 was interpreted as an accumulation deposit containing patches of charcoal sweepings and 4189 was interpreted as a layer of burning associated with the smaller hearth 4216. Micromorphology will challenge this interpretation as 4189 does not lie directly on the tile platform of hearth 4216 but is separated by a chalk-like deposit. Deposit 4189=3817 was the uppermost layer sampled comprising sample <666.3>. Sample <666.2> includes contexts 4199, 4201 and 4202, and sample <666.3> was taken from the material directly above <666.2>. Sample <666.1> was taken from floor 4209=4152 and represents a single deposit. Contexts 4201, 4202 and 4209 represent the same floor, 4152, and 4199 was interpreted in the field as a chalk deposit within the smaller hearth 4216. The location of these samples is shown on the section drawing FIG. 50.

All micromorphology samples are located on the multi-context plans exhibiting the: earlier deposits surrounding larger hearth 1433 (FIG. 47); later and contemporary deposits 4152, 4170 and 5870 (FIG. 48); and the later potential abandonment deposit 4189=3817 (FIG. 49).

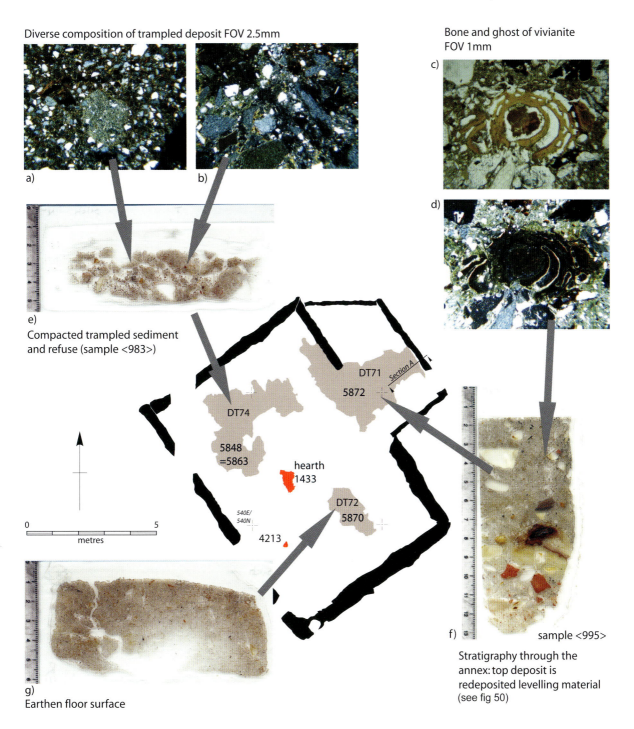

Diverse composition of trampled deposit FOV 2.5mm

a)

b)

Bone and ghost of vivianite
FOV 1mm

c)

d)

e)

Compacted trampled sediment
and refuse (sample <983>)

DT71
5872
Section A

DT74

5848
=5863

hearth
1433

540E/
540N

DT72
5870

4213

0 ————— 5
metres

f) sample <995>

Stratigraphy through the
annex: top deposit is
redeposited levelling material
(see fig 50)

g)
Earthen floor surface

FIG. 47. Period 3, Phase 1: contexts associated with a retained ERTB 1. (a) and (b) micropictographs showing diverse and 'unorientated' composition of trampled deposit 5848 = 5863; (c) plane-polarised light; FOV = field of view; (d) cross-polarised light; (e), (f), (g) scans of micromorphology slides.

LABORATORY METHODS AND ANALYSIS

Micromorphological thin-sections were prepared in the School of Human and Environmental Sciences, University of Reading. Dried monoliths were impregnated with epoxy resins and then cured overnight. Thin-sections were finished to a standard geological thickness of 30μm.

Micromorphological investigation was carried out using a Leica DMEP polarising microscope at magnifications of x40–x400 under plane-polarised light (PPL), cross-polarised light (XPL), and oblique incident light (OIL). Thin-section description was conducted using the criteria set out by Bullock *et al.* (1985) with reference to Courty *et al.* (1989) for the related distribution and microstructure, and Mackenzie and Adams (1994) for rock and mineral identification. The descriptions, inclusions and interpretations will be tabulated in a similar format to Matthews (2000) and Simpson (1998) and are available in digital format on the Silchester database (http://laws1.rdg.ac.uk/i3/index.htm). Digital images were taken using a Leica camera. Components are classed according to frequency categories set out in Table 5 (Bullock *et al.* 1985):

TABLE 5. CLASSIFICATION KEY FOR MICROMORPHOLOGICAL COMPONENTS

Frequency	Key in table
very dominant >70%	★★★★★★
dominant 50–70%	★★★★★
common 30–50%	★★★★
frequent 15–30%	★★★
few 5–15 %	★★
very few <5%	★

Post-depositional textural pedofeatures are classed according to abundance categories set out in Table 6 (Bullock *et al.* 1985):

TABLE 6. CLASSIFICATION KEY FOR POST-DEPOSITIONAL TEXTURAL PEDOFEATURES

Frequency	Key in table
very abundant >20%	●●●●●
abundant 10–20%	●●●●
many 5–10 %	●●●
occasional 2–5%	●●
rare <2%	●

RESULTS

Micromorphological results will be discussed as follows: deposit types; deposit components; and post-depositional alterations. In order to characterise types and the range of construction materials and accumulated occupation residues, microstratigraphic units/contexts have been classified into six deposit types and these will be discussed in turn (Table 7): 1. Sub-floor/Levelling material; 2. Constructed earthen floor; 3. Lime-plaster floor material; 4. Compacted trample; 5. Dump; 6. Accumulation. The distribution of the deposit types will be interpreted both spatially and chronologically in order to address the spatial organisation of the household and short-term changes in the life-history of the building. Deposit components for both off-site and on-site sediments will be discussed according to material type in the following order to characterise deposit origin and depositional events: particle size; rock and mineral; bioarchaeological remains; anthropogenic aggregates and micro-artefacts; and burnt and non-burnt components. These components are also documented and summarised in Tables 8 and 9. In order to investigate the post-depositional alterations to the sedimentary matrix, this chapter will examine traces of bioturbation, clay translocation, organic decay, chemical alteration, and neoformation of minerals. Examination of these specific post-depositional processes will provide evidence of biological reworking and stratigraphic integrity, preservation conditions, and the impact of activities and later use of space.

DESCRIPTION OF DEPOSIT TYPES

The sedimentary attributes discussed below are those that have been identified through soil micromorphological analysis and are considered to be significant for the categorisation of origin and deposition processes for the archaeological deposit types. The full micromorphological

TABLE 7. DEPOSIT TYPE CATEGORIES: MICROMORPHOLOGY DESCRIPTIONS OF THE SEDIMENT PROPERTIES

Deposit type number	Thin section sample number	Context number	Particle size	Sorting	Fine material	Groundmass	Colour	Related distribution	Microstructure	Inclusions: Orientation and Distribution
1	995	5872	Coarse sandy clay	Unsorted	Mineral	Crystallitic	PPL: orangey red-mid/dark brown. XPL: dark brown-reddy brown. OIL: orange-dark brown.	Linked and coated.	Channels and chambers 10%	Orientation: unorientated and unrelated. Distribution: random and unreferred.
	666.2	4201	Sandy clay loam	Unsorted	Mineral and organic	Crystallitic	PPL: dark red-brown XPL: orange/red-brown	Embedded and linked and coated	5% chambers. 5% channels and 5% vughs	Largely unorientated but some local orientation. Random and unreferred.
	666.2	4202	Sandy silt loam	Unsorted	Mineral and organic	Crystallitic	PPL: grey/dark brown XPL: yellow/red-brown.	Embedded and linked and coated	5% chambers, 20% channels and 10% vughs.	Locally orientated but some areas unorientated. Random and unreferred
2	666.1	4209	Loamy sand	Unsorted	Mineral and organic	Crystallitic	PPL: light/dark brown XPL: grey/yellow to red brown.	Embedded and linked and coated	10% chambers, 10% channels and 5% cracks.	Locally orientated. Random and unreferred.
	953	5870	Silty clay loam	Unsorted	Mineral	Crystallitic	PPL: yellow-mid brown. XPL: yellow-orangey brown. OIL: yellowish grey-orange.	Embedded and coated	Channels and chambers 20%	Orientation: unorientated and unrelated with some areas locally orientated clusters. Distribution: random and unreferred.
3	666.2	4199	Gravel sized chalk rock fragments with a finer material comprising a sandy loam	Unsorted	Mineral and organic	Crystallitic	PPL: grey/brown XPL: dark grey/brown	Intergrain aggregate and linked and coated.	5% channels, 5% spongy, 10% vughs and 10% cracks.	Unorientated, unrelated. Random and unreferred.

Deposit type number	Thin section sample number	Context number	Particle size	Sorting	Fine material	Groundmass	Colour	Related distribution	Microstructure	Inclusions: Orientation and Distribution
	768 (Z1)	4170 (a1)	Coarse sand-loamy sand	Unsorted	Mineral	Crystallitic	PPL: grey & dark brown XPL: pink & orange brown	Linked and coated but towards basal boundary coarser material embedded in ashes.	Channels and chambers 10%. Spongy 10%	Unorientated. Random and unreferred.
	768 (Z2)	4170 (a2)	Coarse sandy clay loam	Moderately sorted sand	Mineral	Crystallitic	PPL: yellow/dark brown. XPL: yellow/ reddy brown	Embedded and coated	Chambers 20%	Locally orientated quartz grains and flints. Referred and parallel distribution to basal boundary in places.
4	768 (Z3)	4170 (a3)	Loamy sand/ sandy clay loam	Unsorted	Mineral and ashes	Crystallitic	PPL: grey- pale brown. XPL: grey-gold (high order birefringence)	Intergrain aggregate, linked and coated and embedded in places.	Chambers 20%	
	767 (Z1)	4170 (b1)	Loamy sand	Poorly sorted/ Unsorted lenses	Mineral and organic	Crystallitic	PPL: light brown. XPL: grey-greenish grey	Embedded and coated	Channels and chambers 10%. Sub-horizontal cracks 5%.	Orientation: Unorientated and unrelated. Distribution: random and unreferred.
	767 (Z2)	4170 (b2)	Sandy clay loam	Unsorted	Mineral and organic	Crystallitic	PPL: light brown. XPL: dark brown.	Embedded and coated and linked and coated in places.	Chambers 10%	Orientation: Unorientated and unrelated. Distribution: random and unreferred.
	767 (Z3)	4170 (b3)	Loamy sand	Poorly sorted	Mineral and organic	Crystallitic	PPL: light brown. XPL: grey-greenish grey	Embedded and coated.		Orientation: Unorientated and unrelated. Distribution: random and unreferred.

767 (Z4)	4170 (b4)	Sandy clay loam	Unsorted	Mineral and organic	Crystallitic		Embedded and coated and linked and coated in places.		Orientation: Unorientated and unrelated. Distribution: random and unreferred.
4	5848= 5863	Loamy sand-sandy clay loam	Unsorted	Mineral	Crystallitic	PPL: grey-yellow-dark brown. XPL: grey, pale yellow, dark reddy brown. OIL: grey- orange-dark brown.	Embedded and linked and coated.	Planes 10%. Channels and chambers 20%.	Orientation: unorientated and unrelated. Distribution: random and unreferred.
5	666.3 / 4189	Coarse sandy loam with gravel sized inclusions	Largely unsorted-moderately sorted charcoal	Mineral and organic	Crystallitic	PPL: light/ orange brown. XPL: yellow/red brown.	Intergrain aggregate and linked and coated.	20% chambers, 10% channels and 10% cracks.	Unorientated. Random and unreferred.
6	666.2 / 4203	Coarse sandy loam with gravel sized inclusions	Unsorted	Mineral and organic	Crystallitic	PPL: light brown XPL: dark orange brown	Intergrain aggregate and linked and coated.	20% chambers and 5% channels.	Unorientated. Random and unreferred.

descriptions for each unit are grouped by deposit type listed in Table 7. The frequency of all inclusion categories and components for each unit are also grouped by deposit type and recorded in Table 8 and FIG. 51.

Deposit type 1: sub-floor/levelling

This deposit type category comprises context 5872=5340 (FIG. 47), and is the thickest deposit with a depth of 11.5cm. In origin, deposit type 1 (DT1) has a coarse sandy clay particle size comprising: phytoliths (<2%); unidentifiable charred wood (10%); calcitic ashes (5%); melted silica (<2%); phosphatised bone with vivianite formation, both burnt (2%) and un-burnt (5%); pottery (5%, 2.2cm); and plaster fragments (<2%). Rock fragments (flint 10%, chalk 2%) and minerals (quartz 15%, glauconite <2%, iron oxide 5%) are also present. The presence of glauconite is interesting as this mineral is absent from the deposit above, context 4170. Overall, the third highest frequency (74%) of anthropogenic inclusions occurs in this deposit type (FIG. 52). A greater frequency of plant remains, bioarchaeological residues and micro-artefacts occurs than in floor construction materials (DT1 and 2) (FIG. 51).

The anthropogenic detritus has been incorporated into the levelling material at the time of deposition. The massive bedding structure of the sedimentary matrix indicates that deposition took place in a single event. The fine material bridges and coats the coarse material (i.e. linked and coated related distribution) and is indicative of a dumping event (Matthews 1995). The unorientated and random distribution of the inclusions also supports this action. In addition, depositional units >10cm in thickness are characteristic of massive dumping (Goldberg and Macphail 2006).

Deposit type 2: constructed earthen floor

The units classified as deposit type 2 (DT2) represent the earliest laid floor in the western side of 'ERTB 4', contexts 4201, 4202, 4209=4152, samples <666.1 & 666.2>, and the earliest floor sampled in the eastern side of former ERTB 4, context 5870, sample <953> (FIG. 48). Contexts 4152 and 5870 have been constructed using similar construction fabrics and similar construction techniques. In origin, these deposits (4201, 4202, 4209) also exhibit a similar particle size to each other and to deposit 5870, ranging from silty clay loam to loamy sand size (Table 7). Both floor units predominantly consist of mineral components and a low frequency of bioarchaeological and micro-artefact inclusions (<20%), and context 4209 contains the lowest frequency of plant remains, bioarchaeological residues and micro-artefacts overall (10%) (FIG. 51). The diverse mineral component may highlight different source materials used to construct floors 4152 and 5870 (below, rock and mineral components, p. 76).

The unsorted, embedded nature of the deposits is indicative of a mud-plaster/deliberately laid floor (Matthews 1995); the coarse particles are embedded in the finer clay matrix as aggregates. Constructed earthen floors are distinguished by their embedded-related distribution: the coarser components of sand, gravel, pottery and plant remains have been added as temper and stabilisers and are embedded in the finer clay matrix. This is a similar process to that used in modern earth building for wall renders (Keefe 2005, 96–100; Norton 1997, 68). The inclusion of plant materials (exhibited as phytoliths and charred wood) is not strictly to stabilise, but to reduce cracking (Norton 1997, 31). The purpose of a stabiliser is to strengthen the soil and to reduce the erosion effects of surface water (Houben and Guillaud 1994, 75; Norton 1997, 27). The anthropogenic material, glass (5%) and daub (2%), may be the result of accidental inclusion at the time the floor was being prepared, and the greater amount of charred wood in 4201 may be a result of incorporation of falling fuel from the adjacent hearth.

Some of the trampled/compacted accumulation deposits (e.g. 4170, sample <768>, zone 2, and 5848) also have an embedded and linked-and-coated-related distribution. However, trampled/compacted accumulation deposits in 'ERTB 4' consist of a higher frequency and greater diversity of anthropogenic inclusions, and a higher ratio of coarse to fine material.

Context 4201 represents the baked surface of earthen floor 4202=4152 in the area directly adjacent to hearth 4216 (FIG. 48). The effects of combustion on the soils and sediments can

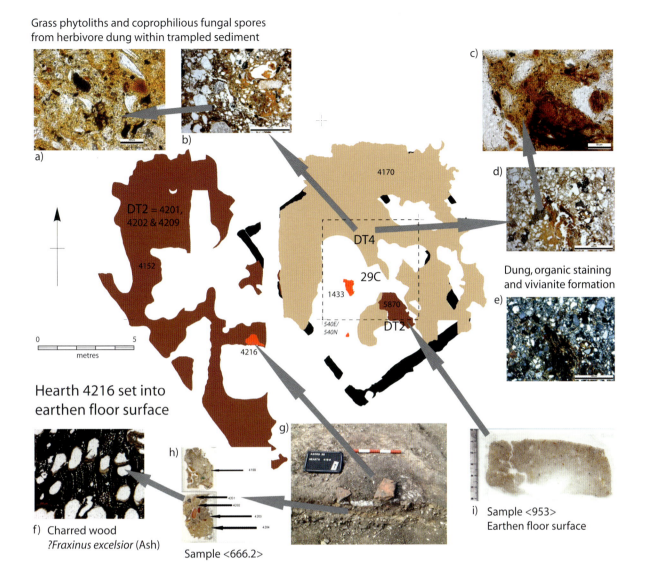

Grass phytoliths and coprophilious fungal spores
from herbivore dung within trampled sediment

a) b) c) d)

Dung, organic staining
and vivianite formation

e)

Hearth 4216 set into
earthen floor surface

f) Charred wood
    ?Fraxinus excelsior (Ash)

g) h)

Sample <666.2>

i) Sample <953>
    Earthen floor surface

FIG. 48.   Period 3, Phase 2: contexts associated with MRTB 1/ERTB 1 in decay. (a) Micropictograph showing grass phytoliths and coprophilious fungal spores within decaying herbivore dung (plane-polarised light = PPL); (b) dark brown lenses of herbivore dung and yellow vivianite (PPL); (c) as (a) (PPL); (d) as (b) (PPL); (e) as (d) (cross-polarised light = XPL); (f) micropictograph of charred wood (PPL x 200 magnification); (g) photograph of field section through hearth 4216 and floor layers below (see section in FIG. 50); (h) and (i) scans of micromorphology slides.

be key diagnostics in suggesting the type of hearth activity that was present (see Courty *et al.* 1989, 107–11). Courty *et al.* (1989, 107) state that alteration effects in most fires are mainly concentrated in the upper 10cm due to the rapid reduction in temperature with depth. For example, in fires reaching 500–700°C the temperature had dropped to 50°C at a depth of 5cm. However, Canti and Linford observed through experimentation that temperature reduction with depth was not so rapid, reducing by *c.* 50 per cent at a depth of 1cm and *c.* 75 per cent at a depth of 4cm (Canti and Linford 2000, 388–9). Comparative data from Courty *et al.* (1989) and Canti and Linford's burning experiments (Canti and Linford 2000) are not directly applicable to this research. Canti and Linford placed fires directly onto grass-covered exterior surfaces. In the case of deposit 4201 the tile platform is likely to have absorbed and radiated some of the heat as it sustained significant heat damage. Further burning experiments are required to investigate variables such as tile platforms, the duration of use, and the choice of fuel.

Deposit type 3: lime-plaster floor material

Deposit type 3 (DT3) classifies 4199, sample <666.2> which comprises a matrix of gravel-sized chalk fragments with a sandy loam material bridging the gaps (FIG. 48). The sandy loam material comprises quartz and feldspar minerals, charred wood, pottery fragments, and flints. The microstructure of the sedimentary matrix is spongy and vughy, indicating that water and air were trapped at the time of deposition. These characteristics would occur during the laying of a lime-slurry. Anthropogenic inclusions have been incorporated from the deposit above by trampling. Overall, jointly with context 4209, 4199 contains no anthropogenic bone and shell residues (FIG. 51), and the lowest frequency of anthropogenic inclusions (10%) (FIG. 52). Both these fabrics are architectural floor materials: 4209 is an earthen floor (DT2) and 4199 a lime-slurry floor covering. Within 'ERTB 4' floor construction fabrics contain lower frequencies of anthropogenic components than other deposit types.

Deposit type 4: compacted trample lenses

Deposit type 4 (DT4) categorises contexts 5848=5863 and 4170. Context 5848=5863, sample <983>, was located in grid square 29C in the eastern side of 'ERTB 4' and was the earliest layer from it (FIG. 47). Deposit 5848=5863 was interpreted during excavation as a clay layer comprising the house floor associated with the larger hearth 1433 and later revised as an accumulation deposit, probably formed during occupation. Context 5848=5863 is 3cm in thickness and has a massive bedding structure indicative of a single depositional event (Table 7). Before excavation, context 5848=5863 was thought to have a finer particle until rained on, and then the dominant sand component became clear.

Context 4170 was interpreted as a clay floor during excavation and is represented by two samples, <767> and <768>, both also within grid square 29C (FIG. 48). Both samples <767> and <768> from context 4170 have a laminated bedding structure and each lens has been assigned a zone number; zone 1 being the surface lens of trample. <767> comprises four zones (b1–4), and <768> comprises three (a1–3). The total thickness of the lenses comprising context 4170 ranges from 0.5cm to 6cm (Table 8). In origin, the lenses comprise generally coarse particle sizes ranging from sandy clay loam to coarse sand. The coarse fraction of DT4 comprises rock and mineral types such as flint, quartz, feldspar, mica and glauconite, and anthropogenic inclusions such as charred wood, dung, building materials, pottery, shell and bone. The fine material (<10μm) comprises quartz, phytoliths and spherical fungal spores.

The highest percentage of anthropogenic inclusions overall (85%) occurs within 4170 a1, and the fourth highest percentage (73%) occurs within 4170 a3 (FIG. 51). The greatest diversity and frequency of burnt material, including burnt flints, dung and building materials, occur within DT4 with similar frequencies to dumped deposits (deposit type 5) and accumulations of material (deposit type 6). There are six types of plant/organic remains: charred wood, charred plant tissue, ashes, phytoliths, melted silica, and dung (FIG. 51), and five types of micro-artefact and bioarchaeological residues: daub, earthen floor aggregate, sediment aggregate, bone, and oyster shell (FIG. 51).

The depositional history of DT4 is characterised by the following sedimentary attributes: sorting, related distribution, orientation and distribution of the inclusions (Table 7). Two depositional events, the debris from which has later been compacted through processes such as trampling, have been identified: (1) dumped hearth rake-out material, context (4170, a1 and a3); and (2) trampled dung and accumulated sediment (4170 a2, b1–4; 5848=5863).

DT4 ranges from unsorted to moderately sorted deposits. Deposits of anthropogenic residues may have accumulated by a range of anthropogenic and natural depositional pathways, and therefore result in the deposition of a range of particle sizes (i.e. an unsorted deposit). Lenses a2, b1 and b3 (4170), which are sorted to a greater extent, may indicate a larger component of sediment deposition by a natural force such as wind: (4170 a2) has a moderately sorted sand component which is locally orientated and (4170 b1) has poorly sorted and unsorted lenses within this micro-stratigraphic horizon.

Interestingly, lenses a2, b1 and b3 (4170) solely exhibit an embedded and coated related distribution unlike the remainder of units comprising DT4 which also exhibit an 'intergrain aggregate' and/or a 'linked and coated' related distribution. The embedding of coarse material within a matrix of finer material is most likely caused in this instance by post-depositional trampling, as also noted by Matthews (1995, 55). The linked and coated related distribution, where the coarse components are linked by bridges of finer material, and an inter-grain aggregate related distribution, where finer material in-fills voids between coarse components, are most likely caused by a depositional process which resulted in haphazard gravitational sorting where the finer material has fallen into the gaps between the coarser particles, and is most likely a depositional characteristic of discard (Matthews 1995, 60–1). The absence of a linked and coated related distribution in lenses a2, b1 and b3 (4170) may indicate that sediment accumulated *in situ* rather than being redeposited from elsewhere, perhaps with some sediment deposited by wind.

A degree of wind deposition of sediment may be most clearly demonstrated in a2 (4170), where the sand fraction (flint and quartz grains) is locally orientated, as well as being moderately sorted. These microfacies of sediment are interspersed with elongated, non-burnt, herbivore dung fragments that are orientated parallel to the basal boundary, a process that has most probably occurred by trampling. Thin lenses with strong parallel orientation and distribution of components generally suggest periodic accumulation and compaction over time (Goldberg and Macphail 2006). The predominant frequency of natural sediment in comparison to dung may either indicate that the dung was trampled in from areas adjacent to the building, by people or wandering animals, or that the area housed animals but was very well maintained. The bioarchaeological residues occur at the surface boundary with the lens 4170 a1 and ashes occur at the surface boundary with 4170 a1 and the basal boundary with 4170 a3. The bioarchaeological residues and ashes have been embedded and incorporated into lens 4170 a2, most probably by post-depositional trampling.

Inclusions throughout the other units comprising DT4 are unoriented, randomly distributed, and do not lay referred to any other components. These characteristics again indicate haphazard depositional processes.

Deposit type 5: dumped deposit including rake-out material

Deposit type 5 (DT5) describes context 4189, sample <666.3>, which has a very coarse particle size (coarse sandy loam with gravel-sized inclusions) (Tables 7–8; FIG. 49). In origin, 4189 comprises four types of micro-artefacts and bioarchaeological residues (FIG. 51): sediment aggregates, ceramic building material, pottery, and bone; and three types of plant remains (FIG. 51): charred wood, phytoliths, and pseudomorphic plant void, most probably resulting from a decayed root. Context 4189 contains the second highest frequency of anthropogenic inclusions overall (82%) (FIG. 52).

The depositional process is similar to DT4: the particles within 4189 are largely unsorted in size class, the deposit exhibits both an intergrain aggregate and linked and coated related distribution, and the inclusions are unorientated and unreferred with a random distribution. As discussed above in relation to DT4, these sedimentary properties are characteristic of a deposit of dumped material (Matthews 1995). The high frequency of charred wood (>20%) indicates that some of the material was most probably deposited during a rake-out episode of a hearth area. DT5 contains moderately sorted, relatively large fragments (0.8mm–0.8cm) in comparison with DT6; 4203 also containing >20 per cent charcoal, which is smaller in size (<1.25mm). Energy applied through the sweeping action selected and included larger fragments of charcoal within DT5 (4189) than in DT6 (4203), most probably due to the debris being in closer proximity to the hearth structure, possibly the hearth surface itself (see particle size, below, p. 76). However, deposit 4189 is not stratigraphically related to the tile platform below 4200, and 4189 and 4200 are separated by a lime-plaster floor, 4199. Therefore the material must originate from an area in close proximity to a hearth either elsewhere in 'ERTB 4' (possibly the larger hearth 1433), or from another building in the vicinity of 'ERTB 4'. It is not uncommon for dilapidated buildings to be reused as rubbish dumps in the post-abandonment period of their life-cycle (La Motta and Schiffer 1999).

There was no embedding of 4189, unlike DT4 where lenses of accumulated or dumped material had become compacted by trampling. The absence of compaction by trampling may indicate a low intensity of use/frequency of visitors to the area. This area may simply have been abandoned and used to dump material or sweepings.

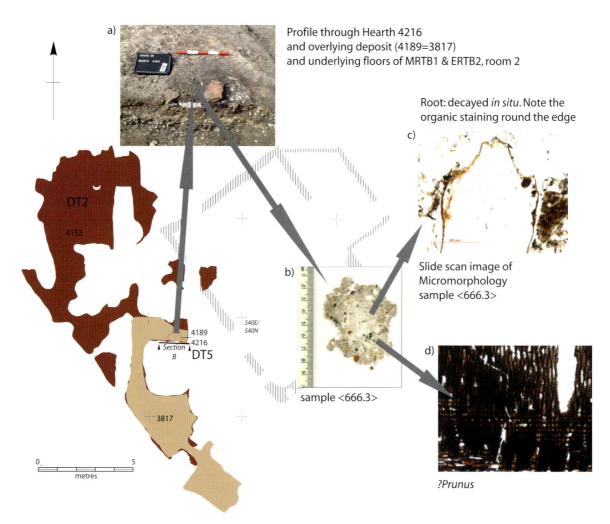

a) Profile through Hearth 4216 and overlying deposit (4189=3817) and underlying floors of MRTB1 & ERTB2, room 2

Root: decayed *in situ*. Note the organic staining round the edge

c)

Slide scan image of Micromorphology sample <666.3>

b)

sample <666.3>

d)

?*Prunus*

FIG. 49. Period 3, Phase 3: contexts associated with abandonment of hearth 4216 and the later life of MRTB 1. (a) Photograph of field section through hearth 4216 and overlying 'dumped' deposit 4189 = 3817 (see section in FIG. 50); (b) scan of micromorphology slide; (c) microphotograph of root (plane-polarised light = PPL); (d) micropictograph of charred wood, ? *prunus* (PPL).

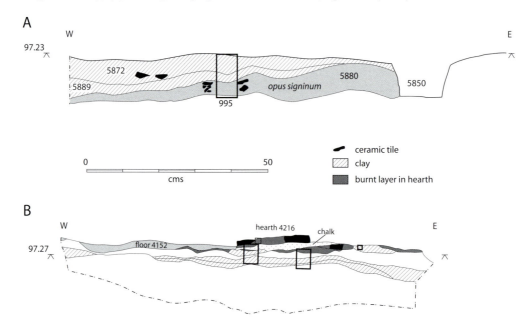

FIG. 50. (a) Profile of contexts associated with sample 995 and Phase 1 (FIG. 47); (b) profile of hearth 4216 and associated contexts of Phases 2 and 3 (FIGS 48–49).

Deposit type 6: accumulation deposit

Deposit type 6 (DT6) describes deposit 4203 and exhibits similar sedimentary attributes to DT5 (4189) (FIG. 48). In origin, DT6 contains the fifth highest frequency of anthropogenic inclusions overall (70%) (FIG. 52), comprising bone, pottery, charred wood, phytoliths and diatoms. Diatoms are associated with an isolated patch of graminaea ash which is mostly isotropic with a weak birefringence (Wattez and Courty 1987) and comprises grass phytoliths which may indicate a wetland, possibly a shallow lacustrine origin, for this plant material. Wetland grasses may be used in roofing materials (Letts 1999), or as rush flooring. Ethnographic data suggest that readily available assortments of plant material are sometimes used to thatch roofs and can weather around three years of use (Letts 1999). DT6 (4203) is heterogeneous, comprising isolated patches of material such as diatoms and grass phytoliths. Small fragments of charred wood (<1.25mm) are scattered throughout which may indicate that the charred wood originated from a room/area in which a hearth was located.

As discussed above in relation to compacted trampled lenses (DT4) and dumped material (DT5), the sorting, related distribution of the coarse and fine material, and orientation and distribution of the inclusions are all indicative of a deposit of dumped material (Matthews 1995). Unlike DT5, DT6 contains anthropogenic inclusions of a smaller size, and in isolated patches which may indicate that this material has accumulated after sweeping has removed the larger material. Similar to DT5, there was no embedding of 4203, unlike DT4 where lenses of accumulated or dumped material had become compacted by trampling. The absence of compaction by trampling may again indicate a low intensity of use/frequency of visitors to the area. This area may simply have been abandoned after accumulating sweepings.

OFF-SITE SURROUNDING NATURAL SEDIMENTS

This section discusses the sediments both underlying Silchester Roman town and sediments in the surrounding region. Understanding the underlying sediments enables a pre-site characterisation of the geology beneath the Roman town. Understanding both the local and regional sediments aids the interpretation of the depositional environment in terms of geology, types and range of potential sources of construction materials, and components within accumulated deposits.

Silchester Roman town is situated on the Lower Winter Hill Terrace of the Kennet valley (Jarvis 1968, 26), which overlies the Eocene London Clay formation. The natural sediment beneath the archaeology of the Roman town is not dissimilar to the C horizon of the Southampton soil series (Pale yellow, 2.5 YR 7/4, sandy gravel with flint pebbles and sub-angular flints) (Jarvis 1968, 63). Outcrops of the Eocene Bagshot Bed formation, younger in age than the London Clay, have also been located in the vicinity of the Roman amphitheatre. Both the London Clay and Bagshot Beds are of marine origin, and these sediments were deposited during the Ypresian cycle (spanning the period between 55.8 ± 0.2 Ma and 48.6 ± 0.2 Ma (million years ago)) when a lengthy phase of marine conditions prevailed in the Reading area (Jarvis 1968, 6). At its outcrop, the London Clay generally exhibits a brown weathered zone several feet thick. This colouration is probably a result of the oxidation of iron pyrites in the original deposit; otherwise the main facies of the London Clay is dark grey unmottled calcareous marine clay. Crystals of selenite (gypsum), present in the brown weathered zone of the London Clay, may provide initial sourcing indicators for construction fabrics in the Roman deposits at Silchester. Gypsum crystals do form through post-depositional processes in archaeological deposits but this usually occurs in semi-arid regions (Courty *et al.* 1989; Matthews 1995). Selenite crystals form through an evaporative process when sulphuric acid produced by the oxidation process is neutralised by reaction with calcium carbonate. The upper beds of the London Clay consist of mottled, non-calcareous fine sandy or silty clays (Jarvis 1968, 6).

The Bagshot Beds are mainly pale grey or yellow sands with seams of mottled grey plastic clay and mottled fine sandy clays. The sand component mainly comprises quartz and some mica, with scarce feldspar and flint grains (Jarvis 1968, 6–7). Further reading of Jarvis' report (1968, 7) provided an interesting description of the succeeding Bracklesham Beds which are mostly glauconitic sandy clays, bottle-green, yellow and strong brown in colour, with occasional seams of sand. The significance of the Bracklesham Beds in this report will be discussed further in the section on rock and mineral components below.

ON-SITE SEDIMENTS: ORIGIN AND COMPOSITION

This section discusses the origin and composition of on-site sediments in terms of: particle size to assess depositional pathways of materials; geological components to identify potential architectural source materials; bone and shell inclusions to identify potential food waste and processing; plant and organic components; anthropogenic aggregates and micro-artefacts to understand depositional pathways into occupation strata of architectural materials and activity by-products; and burnt and non-burnt components to identify choices of fuel and activities such as cooking.

Particle size

The particle sizes of deposits featured in this report range from silty clay loam to coarse sand and are predominantly unsorted and of anthropogenic origin and deposition (Table 8). However, deposit 4170 (FIG. 48) comprises occasional lenses of moderately and poorly sorted sand and may be partially wind-sorted. Deposit types 1, 3, 4, 5 and 6 fall in the coarser end of the particle size category range (coarse sandy loam to coarse sand), due to the addition of a diverse range of types and sizes of anthropogenic inclusions such as pottery fragments (0.3–2.2cm), bone (<0.7cm), and charred wood (<0.8cm).

Understanding regional off-site sediments and the interpretation of deposit type are central to understanding depositional pathways of anthropogenic inclusions on settlement sites. DT2, constructed earthen floor, encompasses contexts exhibiting a silty clay loam to loamy sand particle size which is similar to the surrounding London Clay, Bagshot Beds and Bracklesham Beds.

The way in which the coarse and fine particles relate to each other within the on-site sediments has enabled anthropogenic dumping processes to be identified as being responsible for the inclusion of hearth rake-out material, particularly in DT5. The particle size of the charred wood fragments in 'ERTB 4' (>0.5mm) indicates local fire influence. Experimental work on forest fires has demonstrated that smaller fragments (<0.5mm) are transported further away from the site of the fire (Ohlson and Tryterud 2000). However, fire size and location (inside/outside), anthropogenic depositional pathways and processes, and preservation are important variables to consider in associations between particle size and distribution on archaeological settlement sites. Charcoal fragments were also added to or present in materials selected for constructed earthen floors, DT2 (<5–30% of area). Deposit 4201 is the rubified (heat reddened) horizon of floor surface 4202 and 4209, and contained the greatest frequency of charred wood of all constructed earth floors (<30%). Deposits 4202 and 4209 contained significantly less charred wood (<5%). Charred material was incorporated into earthen architectural floor materials during construction. However, c. 25 per cent of the charred wood in deposit 4201 most probably originates from the use of hearth 4216, supported by the large size of some fragments (0.8cm) which are most likely primary residues.

Rock and mineral components

Flint and quartz are present in all deposit types (Table 8). Feldspar and mica are present in all deposit types with the exception of sub-floor levelling material (DT1). Isolated instances of rock and mineral components include: sandstone from specific samples in DT4 and 5; granite and chalk in DT3; and chalk only in DT1.

The range of rock and mineral components included within contexts 4201, 4202, and 4209=4152 (DT2) indicates that the Bagshot Beds may be a potential source material for this earthen floor. The sand component of the Bagshot Beds' sediment mainly comprises quartz and some mica, with scarce feldspar and flint grains (Jarvis 1968, 6–7). Glauconite, despite occurring in sub-floor material, constructed earthen floors and compacted trampled deposits (DT1, 2 and 4 respectively), only occurs in specific deposits from the eastern side of 'ERTB 4' (5872, 5870, 5848=5863) (FIG. 47). The presence of glauconite in earthen floor 5870 (DT2) may indicate a different source of construction material for this earthen floor than for floor 4152, such as the

Bracklesham Beds which are mostly glauconitic sandy clays (Jarvis 1968).

To summarise, earthen floor 4152 (FIG. 49), comprising quartz, mica and feldspar, has a similar mineral component to the Bagshot Beds, whereas floor 5870 (FIG. 47), comprising quartz, feldspar and glauconite, has a mineral component similar to the Bracklesham Beds. The absence of selenite (above, p. 75) from all deposit types within 'ERTB 4' suggests either that the London Clay may not have been utilised as a material for walling or flooring to construct this building, or that the crystals precipitated in episodes of wetting during manufacture (if crystals had dissolved through post-depositional wetting a pseudomorphic void would be expected in thin-section). The provenancing of these construction materials requires further research using X-Ray Diffraction.

Rock and mineral inclusions within deposits that have formed by anthropogenic disturbance processes, such as deposit types 1, 4, 5 and 6, may originate from eroded sediment from building materials, by natural processes such as wind and rain, and from pottery which may have been damaged or crushed by trampling. Rock or mineral types are largely similar to those included in the floor materials (DT2 and 3) which supports this argument.

Bone and shell inclusions

Bone and shell fragments are generally not as abundant in 'ERTB 4' as plant remains and micro-artefacts. Although bone and shell fragments occur in all deposit types, they are only present in half of the total number of contexts (8/16). Bone fragments are present in seven contexts, and fragments of oyster shell are present in two contexts (Table 8; FIG. 51). Bone and shell fragments occur infrequently (<5%) in constructed earthen floors, DT2 (Table 8; FIG. 51), and only occur in floor 4201, 4202, 4209=4152 on the western side of 'ERTB 4', now MRTB 1 (FIG. 49). Occurrence of bone in floor 4152 may be due to accidental incorporation at the time of construction. Oyster shell fragments only occur in two deposits comprising compacted trampled lenses, DT4, and not in any other deposit type. Bone and shell fragments have been incorporated into compacted trampled lenses, dumped and accumulated material (DT4, 5 and 6 respectively) through processes of anthropogenic disturbance: dumping, sweeping, and trampling.

Plant remains and organic components

The following plant and organic components occur within 'ERTB 4': herbivore dung, charred wood, charred plant tissue, calcitic ashes, phytoliths, melted silica, and plant pseudomorphic voids (Table 8; FIG. 51). Herbivore dung occurs fairly frequently in most compacted trampled lenses (DT4 (4170), lenses a1–3 and b1; FIGS 48 and 51) at concentrations of <15 per cent, which has particular spatial and chronological significance for the life-history of 'ERTB 4' (see discussion, below, p. 91). Charred wood occurs in all deposit types but is absent from some lenses of compacted trampled material (4170 lenses a1–3 and b3–4). Charred wood occurs at the greatest frequency in constructed earthen floor context 4201 (DT2), dumped deposit DT5, and accumulation deposit DT6 (FIG. 51): context 4201 (FIG. 48) is spatially and stratigraphically related to a hearth platform; DT5 is interpreted as including hearth rake-out material; and DT6 incorporates charred wood from sweepings. Interestingly, no charred wood is associated with 4170 a1 which contains high frequencies of ashes (<30%) and heat-affected flints (<50%) or with 4170 a2, in which the only occurrence of charred plant tissue is found along with calcitic ashes. This would indicate that within the rake-out material that was trampled into lenses 4170 a1 and a2, any wood that was primarily used as fuel may have been completely combusted.

Calcitic ashes occur in sub-floor levelling material DT1 and compacted trampled lenses DT4. DT1 is a redeposited spread used as sub-floor levelling material and the calcitic ashes were most probably accidentally incorporated along with the charred wood, melted silica, and phytoliths. In DT4 calcitic ashes only occur in sample <767> which encompasses 4170 a1–3. The greatest frequency of calcitic ashes (<30%) occurs in lens 4170 a1 and has been incorporated through the deposition of hearth rake-out material.

Phytoliths occur in very low frequencies in sub-floor levelling material and constructed earthen floors (DT1 and 2 respectively), and are fairly to moderately frequent in compacted trampled

TABLE 8. FREQUENCY OF ALL INCLUSION TYPES (see classification key in Table 5)

Deposit type number	Deposit type category	Context number	Thickness (cm)	Particle Size	Related distribution	Rock Fragments					Minerals				
						Flint	Heat affected flint	Sandstone	Granite	Chalk	Quartz	Mica	Glauconite	Feldspar	Iron Oxide
1	Sub-floor	5872	11.5	Coarse sandy clay	Linked and coated.	★★				★	★★★		★		★
2	Constructed earth floor	4201	0.5-1	Sandy clay loam	Embedded and linked and coated	★★★					★★★★	★		★★	
		4202	1.5	Sandy silt loam	Embedded and linked and coated	★★					★★★★	★		★★	
		4209	5	Loamy sand	Embedded and linked and coated	★					★★★★	★		★★	
		5870	4.5	Silty clay loam	Embedded and coated	★					★★★★		★★	★★	
3	Lime-plaster floor	4199	4	Gravel sized chalk rock fragments with a finer material comprising a sandy loam	Intergrain aggregate and linked and coated.	★★			★	★★★★★★	★★			★★	
4	Compacted trample	4170 a1	1-2	Coarse sand-loamy sand	Linked and coated but towards basal boundary coarser material embedded in ashes.	★★★★	★★★★				★★				
		4170 a2	1-2	Coarse sandy clay loam	Embedded and coated	★★					★★★★	★			
		4170 a3	0.5-2	Loamy sand/sandy clay loam	Intergrain aggregate, linked and coated and embedded in places.	★★★					★★★				
		4170 b1	6	Loamy sand	Embedded and coated	★★					★★★★				
		4170 b2	1	Sandy clay loam	Embedded and coated and linked and coated in places.	★★★★			★		★★★★				
		4170 b3	1.5	Loamy sand	Embedded and coated.						★★★★				
		4170 b4	1	Sandy clay loam	Embedded and coated and linked and coated in places.						★★★★				
		5848=5863	3	Loamy sand-sandy clay loam	Embedded and linked and coated.	★★					★★★	★	★	★	
5	Dump	4189	7	Coarse sandy loam with gravel sized inclusions	Intergrain aggregate and linked and coated.	★★		★			★★★	★		★★	
6	Accumulation	4203	2.8	Coarse sandy loam with gravel sized inclusions	Intergrain aggregate and linked and coated.	★★★					★★★	★		★★	

Building materials & Sediment aggregates					Micro-artefacts		Bioarchaeological			Organic/Plant remains							Micro-fossil	
CBM	Fired lime plaster	Daub	Earthen floor aggregate	Sediment aggregate	Pottery	Glass	Bone	Fish bone	Oyster shell	Dung	Charred wood	Charred plant tissue	Calcitic ashes	Phytolith	Melted silica	Plant pseudomorph	Spherical Fungal Spore	Diatom
	★				★★		★★				★★		★★	★	★			
					★★		★				★★★						★		
	★★			★	★						★							
								★			★							
		★				★★					★★			★				
					★						★							
		★		★						★★			★★★★		★			
		★★					★★		★★	★★		★★	★★					
		★★					★★			★★			★★	★★★	★		★★	
		★★								★★	★			★★			★	
											★★							
														★★			★	
														★★			★	
			★★		★★				★	★★								
★★				★	★		★★				★★★			★★★		★★	★	
					★		★★				★★★			★★				★

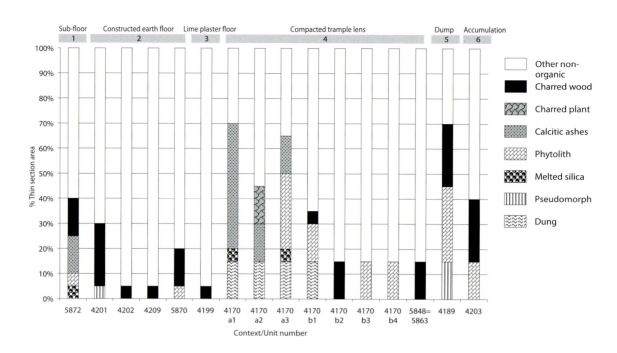

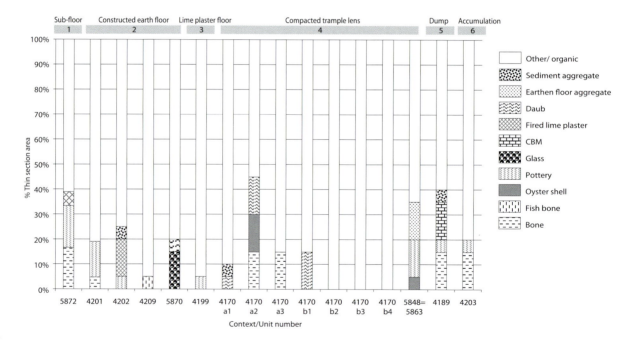

FIG. 51. (upper) Frequency of plant and organic remains in each context, grouped by deposit type; (lower) frequency of bioarchaeological and micro-artefact residues in each context, grouped by deposit type.

lenses, dumped rake-out, and accumulated material (DT4, 5 and 6 respectively), which would suggest differential depositional pathways for the inclusion of fresh plant material (grasses, herbaceous and arboreal leaves) throughout these deposit types. Significant quantities of fresh plant material are unlikely to have been incorporated into sub-floor levelling material (DT1) during the depositional event and, unless inclusion is accidental, charred wood rather than dung or straw seems to have been the preferred choice of vegetable stabiliser for constructed earthen floors (DT2). Phytoliths occur in association with diatoms in accumulation deposit 4203 (DT6) within an isolated patch of graminaea ash (FIG. 48). Interestingly, in compacted trampled deposit 4170 lenses a3 and b1 (DT4) (FIG. 48) phytoliths occur in association with dung and spherical fungal spores, and in compacted trampled deposit 4170 lenses b3 and b4 and dumped deposit 4189 (DT5) associated with spherical fungal spores only.

Anthropogenic aggregates and micro-artefacts

The following categories of anthropogenically modified aggregates are present in 'ERTB 4' (Tables 8–9; FIGS 51–52): ceramic building material (CBM); fired lime plaster; daub; earthen floor fragments; burnt earthen floor/oven wall; and burnt sediment aggregates. The micro-artefacts present in 'ERTB 4' are glass and pottery (Table 8; FIG. 51).

Building materials are present in several deposit categories (DT1, 2, 4, and 5) which demonstrates a diverse range of depositional pathways of materials within 'ERTB 4'. CBM has been incorporated into sweepings that form the dumped deposit rich in hearth rake-out material (DT5), context 4189 (FIG. 49). Fired lime plaster has been incorporated into both the dump of sub-floor levelling material DT1 and constructed earthen floor DT2, context 4152 (FIG. 48), perhaps as construction aggregate or through accidental inclusion. Daub fragments may also have been used as aggregate in constructed earthen floor DT2 and are present in compacted trample lenses DT4, most probably due to falling building debris becoming transported by feet, sweeping or wind. Fragments of earthen floor are also present in compacted trample lenses DT4, again transportation by feet or sweeping are potential depositional pathways. Burnt sediment aggregates occur as aggregate or by accidental incorporation in constructed earthen floors (DT2), and as burnt floor material swept from a hearth area and either transported by feet, sweeping or wind and compacted through trampling (DT4) or incorporated in the dump of material (DT5).

Pottery fragments occur in all deposit types, but glass only occurs in constructed earthen floors (DT2), context 5870 (FIG. 47). The potential depositional pathways of material for deposit types 1, 2, 4, and 5 have been discussed above, so will not be repeated. Pottery fragments within lime-plaster floors (DT3) occur in the coarse material that has been trampled into the lime-plaster floor from the deposit stratigraphically above. Sweeping is again a likely depositional pathway for the incorporation of pottery fragments into accumulated material (DT6).

Analysis of burnt and non-burnt components ('ERTB 4')

All inclusions are recorded in tabular form in Table 8, and in the following categories: burnt and non-burnt in Table 9. FIGS 51–52 record the comparative frequencies of plant/organic remains, bioarchaeological and micro-artefacts, and burnt residues. Comparative analysis of the frequencies of burnt and non-burnt residues within 'ERTB 4' will aid the interpretation of, and ascertain the presence and intensity of specific domestic and industrial activities, such as the cooking of food and metallurgy, as well as identifying the choices of materials for these activities through analysis of food remains and fuel type. A full discussion of the significant bioarchaeological components in relation to deposit type and spatial and chronological variations in the use of space is found in the discussion, below, p. 91, which provides insights into the structuring of activities within 'ERTB 4'.

Burnt components

Charred wood is the most frequently occurring component, present in all deposit types (FIGS 51–52). The vast majority of charred wood is unidentifiable; however, three fragments bear a strong likeness to *Prunus domestica* (radial section) (FIG. 49), *Quercus robur* (transversal section), context 4189 (DT5), and *Fraxinus excelsior* (transversal section), context 4201 (DT2) (FIG. 48) (Schweingruber 1990). As discussed above (p. 76), interpreting specific sedimentary attributes such as the related distribution of coarse and fine particles, and the orientation and distribution of inclusions, is central to understanding the processes by which the plant remains were deposited. DT5 represents a dumped deposit containing hearth rake-out material and deposition occurred during the temporary abandonment of this area of 'ERTB 4'. It is uncertain which hearth the

TABLE 9. FREQUENCY OF BURNT AND NON-BURNT BIOARCHAEOLOGICAL INCLUSIONS AND MICROARTEFACTS (see classification key in Table 5)

Deposit type number	Context number	Burnt										Microfossil			Non-burnt										
		Wood	Plant tissue	Dung: Charred	Melted silica	Calcitic ashes	Bone	Fish bone	Floor/Oven wall aggregate	Sediment aggregate	Burnt flint	Phytolith	Spherical Fungal Spore	Diatom	Dung	Plant pseudomorph	Oyster shell	Bone: unburnt	CBM	Fired lime plaster	Daub	Earthen floor aggregate	Pottery: Unidentified	Pottery: Samian	Glass
1	5872	★★			★	★★	★					★				★		★★		★			★★		
2	4201	★★★														★		★		★★			★★		
	4202	★																		★★			★	★	
	4209	★						★		★															
	5870	★★										★									★				★★
3	4199	★										★											★		
4	4170 a1			★★	★	★★★★				★	★★★★	★★★	★★		★★						★				
	4170 a2		★★	★★		★★	★★					★★	★		★★		★★				★★				
	4170 a3				★	★★												★★							
	4170 b1	★													★★						★★				
	4170 b2	★★										★★	★												
	4170 b3											★★	★												
	4170 b4								★																
	5848= 5863	★★															★					★★	★★		
5	4189	★★★								★		★★★	★			★★		★★	★★				★		
6	4203	★★★										★★		★		★★		★★	★★				★		

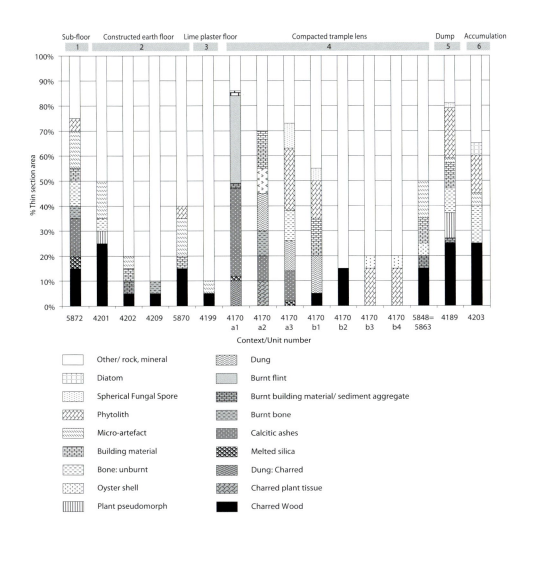

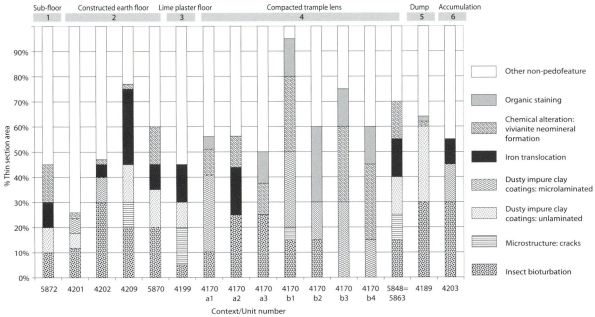

FIG. 52.   (upper) Frequency of burnt and unburnt micro-residues in each context grouped by deposit type; (lower) frequency of post-depositional alterations and pedofeatures in each deposit grouped by deposit type.

charred wood fragments originate from as there are several hearths in use elsewhere in 'ERTB 4' during this phase of use (see discussion, below, p. 91). However, context 4201 represents the upper, rubified, <1cm of constructed earthen floor 4152 (FIG. 48) and the charred wood is embedded in the surface of deposit 4201. Micromorphology sample <666.2> was taken adjacent to tile platform 4200 which forms the smaller hearth 4216 (FIG. 48). As discussed above, wood was certainly used on hearth 4216 and has been incorporated into 4201 (<30%). Although the 2-D species identification of the charred wood fragments is uncertain, it can be assumed that deciduous woods were a preferred choice of fuel within 'ERTB 4'. The rake-out material from context 4189 (FIG. 49) may originate from a hearth used for metallurgy. Oak is frequently used for the manufacture of charcoal for metallurgy, and fruit woods (*Prunus* sp.) burn adequately (Straker 2000). Roman smelting sites in the Weald demonstrated that different species may be used for different processes (Forbes 1964a, 22; 1964b, 106–7). Hearth 4216 may have been used as a heating installation. Ash is one of the best fuel woods with good heating properties (Straker 2000, 514).

As discussed above, charred dung is only present in compacted trampled lenses (DT4) and is specific to 4170 lens a1 (FIG. 48). Lens a1 predominantly comprises burnt flints (<50%) and calcitic ashes (<30%), with a low frequency of melted silica (<5%). The frequency of charred dung (<15%) is low compared to ashes; this is most probably because ash is almost always mixed with a minor amount of incompletely burnt organic matter (Courty *et al.* 1989, 106). The inclusion of burnt dung and the absence of charred wood in lens 4170 a1 (trampled, redeposited hearth rake-out) suggest either that dung may have been the preferred choice of fuel for whatever activity took place on the hearth, and/or that dung was burnt on the hearth as a disposal technique (see discussion, below).

Both calcitic ash and *graminaea* ash occur within 'ERTB 4'. Calcitic ash forms from the combustion of deciduous wood and the ash crystals exhibit a granular morphology and high birefringence (Wattez and Courty 1987, 679). Calcitic ash in 4170 a3 has been post-depositionally altered and is discussed below. When temperatures reach >600°C all organic matter is destroyed and ashes consist primarily of the whitish grey residue of silica (Courty *et al.* 1989, 106). *Graminaea* ash is mostly isotropic but with areas of weak birefringence (Wattez and Courty 1987, 680) and comprises grass phytoliths and also diatoms indicating the combustion of wetland grasses such as those patches within sweepings in accumulated material (DT6).

At very high temperatures phytoliths become melted and produce a glassy, non-birefringent silica residue (Courty *et al.* 1989, 107), exhibited in low frequencies (<5%) in sub-floor levelling material (DT1) and compacted trampled lenses (DT4). Inclusion of melted silica in DT1 most likely originates from incorporation, along with other burnt organic remains, into the material that was redeposited as sub-floor levelling. Melted silica occurs specifically in DT4, context 4170 lenses a1 and a3 (FIG. 48). In origin, lenses 4170 a1 and 3 are dumps of hearth rake-out material. The presence of melted silica indicates the combustion at >700–800°C of *Graminaea* material nearby (Matthews *et al.*1994), perhaps relating to the burning of herbivore dung indicated in 4170 a1.

The above analysis of burnt organic remains has suggested potential choices concerning selection of fuel within 'ERTB 4'. Analysis of the burnt bone and shell residues provides information relating to cooking practices and the disposal of food remains within 'ERTB 4'.

Burnt bone is infrequent in abundance and only present in sub-floor levelling material (DT1) and compacted trampled lenses (DT4). The only DT4 unit containing this component is context 4170 lens a2 (FIG. 48). A burnt fish bone/tooth is present in constructed earthen floor (DT2) context 4209=4152 (FIG. 48). These results may indicate either a very limited amount of meat cooking within 'ERTB 4' or careful maintenance of the structure and external discard of refuse. In fact bone residues in both sub-floor levelling (DT1) and constructed earthen floors (DT2) potentially derive from accidental incorporation into the construction material at the time of manufacture or, in the case of DT1, at the time of material acquisition. Food remains, including burnt bone and oyster shell, have been trampled into 4170 a2 from the above lens, 4170 a1. This suggests that the dump of hearth rake-out material 4170 a1 contains some remains from meat cooking (grilling or roasting to discolour the bone) and the preparation of oysters.

Other notable burnt sediment aggregates and rock types occur in compacted trampled lenses (DT4) context 4170 lens a1 and dumped deposit DT5. These are both deposits of dumped hearth rake-out material in which burnt sediment aggregates, perhaps fragments of burnt floor adjacent to the hearth, occur at a low frequency (<5%), and in 4170 lens a1 heat-affected flints are common (<50%), perhaps used as potboilers as microscopic cracks indicate that these flints are heat-shattered.

Non-burnt

The association of dung with grass phytoliths, and absence of bone fragments and other coprolite material, such as calcium phosphate nodules, suggest that the dung originates from herbivores, possibly foddered with hay. Only non-burnt dung occurs in association with phytoliths and fungal spores, suggesting that the phytoliths in compacted trampled lenses (DT4, context 4170) (FIG. 48) are the result of decaying grassy fodder ingested by the herbivores. However, the precise origin of the herbivore dung is uncertain: whether residual dung was trampled from a dung pile retained for use as fuel (such as ethnographic examples described by Hodder 1987 and Moore 1982) or from a nearby stabling/penning area is unclear.

Phytoliths are present in all deposit types, with the exception of lime-plaster floor DT3. In compacted trampled lenses (DT4) and dumped deposits (DT5) phytoliths are present in association with spherical fungal spore microfossils, with dung in DT4, and diatoms in DT6, suggesting a wetland origin of the grass phytolith material. Phytolith assemblages in DT4 and 5 comprise mainly grass phytoliths, <50μm and <20 per cent of inclusions; specific cell-types include: sinuous long-cells, smooth long-cells, rondels and dendritics, including sheets of multi-cells, with infrequent trichomes and plateys. Trichome phytoliths form in herbaceous plant species and platey phytoliths form in aboreal species. Phytoliths are present in constructed earthen floors (DT2) context 5870, but in low numbers, <2 per cent; the assemblage is also broken and fragmented with pieces only measuring <10μm.

Non-burnt bone occurs more frequently than burnt bone and in more deposit types. In deposit types 1, 4, 5 and 6 bone fragments were not burnt and their deposition may be due to some type of animal processing other than cooking, or boiling of meat rather than grilling or roasting. Non-burnt bone fragments in both sub-floor levelling material (DT1) and constructed earthen floors (DT2) may again originate from accidental incorporation during material acquisition/deposition.

POST-DEPOSITIONAL ALTERATIONS

The following post-depositional events have been identified in the deposits from 'ERTB 4' (Table 10; FIG. 52) and are classified using the key in Table 6: insect bioturbation; cracks, most probably the result of trampling, are visible in the microstructure of the sedimentary matrix; clay and iron translocation, of which both unlaminated and microlaminated dusty impure clay coatings occur; chemical alteration, which includes both vivianite neomineral formation and organic staining; and finally spherical fungal spores. Each post-depositional event is discussed in turn, in terms of the significance to the interpretation of each deposit type and depositional unit (context).

Insect bioturbation

Insect bioturbation is identified in thin-section by channels and chambers in the deposit's microstructure. Channels and chambers represent insect burrowing, worm and root action through the profile and potential reworking of the sedimentary matrix. Insect disturbance was visible during excavation and sampling of 'ERTB 4' by the occurrence of burrows through the sediment profile and actual insects. No earthworms were identified in this area of the site during excavation which is most probably due to acidic environmental conditions (below), which are unfavourable for earthworms. All deposit types and the vast majority of contexts are affected by insect bioturbation. Only 4170 b3 and 4 exhibit no reworking by biological activity. However, most channels are orientated horizontally doing little to modify the stratification and, where vertical channels do occur, no excremental pedofeatures are present within the channels, indicating minimal redistribution of organic and mineral particles (Courty et al. 1989).

TABLE IO. ABUNDANCE OF POST-DEPOSITIONAL ALTERATIONS AND PEDOFEATURES
(see classification key in Table 6)

Deposit type number	Context number	Microstructure effects		Translocation			Chemical alteration: vivianite neomineral formation	Organic staining
		Insect bioturbation	Cracks	Dusty impure clay coatings: unlaminated	Dusty impure clay coatings: microlaminated	Iron		
1	5872	●●●		●●●		●●●	●●●●	
2	4201	●●●		●●	●●		●	
	4202	●●●●●			●●●	●●	●	
	4209	●●●●	●●	●●●●		●●●●●	●	
	5870	●●●●		●●●●		●●●	●●●●	
3	4199	●●	●●●	●●●		●●●●		
4	4170 a1	●●●			●●●●●		●●●	●●
	4170 a2	●●●●				●●●●	●●●	
	4170 a3	●●●●					●●●	●●●
	4170 b1	●●●●	●●		●●●●●		●●●●●	●●●●
	4170 b2	●●●●			●●●●			●●●●●
	4170 b3				●●●●●		●●●●●	●●●●
	4170 b4				●●●●		●●●●●	●●●●
	5848= 5863	●●●●	●●●	●●●●		●●●●	●●●	
5	4189	●●●●●		●●●●●			●	●
6	4203	●●●●●			●●●●	●●●		

Trampling

Trampling effects play a prominent role in forming archaeological deposits through determination of passive, reactive and active zones in occupation floor materials and structural modifications to the sedimentary matrix (Gé et al. 1993). The effects of trampling on archaeological deposits depend on the intensity of trampling and the nature of the impact on surface sediment in terms of factors affecting penetrability such as: size and shape of particles; moisture content; chemical constituents; and vegetation (Schiffer 1987, 126). Within 'ERTB 4' the following micromorphological properties and observations associated with trampling formation processes have been identified (with reference to Gé et al. 1993): matrix bedding structure; embedding through compaction; sub-horizontal fissures (cracks) in the microstructure; and incorporation/transfer of anthropogenic material. Each property or observation will be discussed in turn with reference to the intensity and likelihood of potential trampling disturbance with specific reference to spatial context, and occurrence of other post-depositional events (Courty et al. 1989; Gifford 1978; Gifford-Gonzalez et al. 1985; Schiffer 1987), and penetrability of the floor material (Beckman and Smith 1973; Gifford 1978; Gifford-Gonzalez et al. 1985; Schiffer 1987, 129).

All deposit types have a 'massive' bedding structure representing single depositional events, with the exception of context 4170 (DT4) (FIG. 48). Context 4170 has a 'laminated' bedding structure whereby a series of lenses comprise each micromorphological sample, representing a series of depositional events. Sample <767> has four lenses and <768> three. Both samples from 4170 were taken from an area of 'ERTB 4' (grid 29C) prone to sediment accumulation and compaction, as well as chemical weathering (see below), perhaps suggesting that this locality either had a poor or no roof during occupation Phase 2 of 'ERTB 4'.

Trampling effects occur within 'ERTB 4' both as a formation process for DT4 as discussed above, and as post-depositional impact activity. The trampling formation processes are identifiable in thin-section by the presence of laminated bedding structure, specifically in regard to context 4170, and by an embedded related distribution formed both at the moment of sediment deposition and post-depositional compaction. Analysis of context 4170 showed a diverse series of depositional processes in which trampling played a key role both in actual sediment deposition and in post-depositional compaction. Micro-lenses of sediment interspersed with dung fragments orientated in a parallel fashion to the basal boundary were potentially deposited by either human or animal trampling as those identified at the cave site of Arene Candide (Wattez *et al.* 1989). Mechanical downward pressure would cause dung fragments to become horizontally compressed, meeting resistance from the compacted underlying sediment. Embedding is a term that describes the related distribution of the coarse and fine particles, whereby the coarser particles become embedded within a matrix of finer material, a process that can occur through compaction by mechanical pressure of trampling (Gé *et al.* 1993, 156). The degree of compaction or embedding can be dependent on two factors which are particle size and the nature of the substrate.

Lenses 4170 a1 and a3 have a particularly coarse particle size (coarse sand/loamy sand and loamy sand/sandy clay loam respectively) and a linked and coated related distribution with some embedding. The predominance of coarse particles means that the low frequency of finer material is only able to bridge the gaps between the coarser material, rather than forming a matrix in which material can become embedded, as well as allowing water percolation through the deposit, which induces chemical weathering and translocation of iron and clay particles (Courty *et al.* 1989), as discussed further below. Where compaction did occur within lenses 4170 a1 and a3, this has resulted in coarser material becoming embedded into areas of chemically weathered calcitic ashes, a process that is discussed further below (also see Courty *et al.* 1989, 113), or into the surface of the lens beneath, as was the case with 4170 a2.

Post-depositional compaction occurs in all contexts comprising DT4 (Table 7), and characteristics attesting an 'active floor zone' have been distinguished. An active floor zone is formed by the simultaneous actions of three elementary mechanisms: disaggregation, compaction, and addition of sedimentary materials (Gé *et al.* 1993, 155). Although each unit comprising DT4 exhibits these properties, the addition of sedimentary materials through trampling is usually/ may be derived from the underlying constructed floors. However, the units comprising DT4 form part of a complex stratigraphic sequence, whereby sediment may be incorporated from both underlying sub-floor levelling material (DT1) and other active zones, as well as by other depositional pathways discussed above (p. 73). Context 5848=5863, also DT4, stratigraphically underlies 4170, showing continuity of depositional processes characteristic of active floor zones, although potentially reflecting different use of space. Context 5848=5863 consists of a micro-aggregated, homogenised fabric as may be expected from an external area such as an open courtyard or street, whereas context 4170 consists of a regular microlaminated fabric often observed in stratigraphic sequences from rooms (Gé *et al.* 1993, 156) or an internal area. The stratigraphic relationships are as discussed further below.

Trampling effects in the form of sub-horizontal fissures (cracks) are observed in sediment microstructures from 'ERTB 4' in constructed earthen floors, lime-plaster flooring, and compacted trampled lenses (DT2, 3, and 4 respectively), but do not occur in all contexts (FIG. 52). Sub-horizontal fissures occur when the ground materials have a weak cohesion and are characterised by loosely packed grains (Gé *et al.* 1993, 157). Sub-horizontal fissures identified in context 4209=4152 (FIG. 48) occurred due to the weak consistency of the underlying deposit 4203 (DT6). Underlying deposit 4203 would have provided low resistance to downward pressure enabling these cracks/fissures to form.

The lime-plaster floor (DT3), context 4199, was laid over the severely heat-affected and cracked tile surface of hearth 4216, most probably to level the floor surface (FIG. 48). Trampling across the lime-plaster floor caused debris from the overlying dumped-deposit (DT5) to be reworked into the cracks of the reactive floor zone. Sub-horizontal fissures are found at the basal boundary with the underlying constructed earthen floor, context 4152 (DT2), indicating that this is an active zone of interaction associated with trampling (Gé *et al.* 1993, 153; Matthews 1995, 61).

Sub-horizontal fissures were identified in the microstructure of two units/contexts comprising the compacted trampled lenses (DT4): 5848=5863 and 4170 b1 (FIGS 47–48). Both contexts 5848=5863 and 4170 are characteristically similar to active zones of non-constructed occupation surfaces both within rooms and external areas from Tell sites (Gé *et al.* 1993, 156). Sub-horizontal fissures are clearly visible at an uneven, varying depth between 0.3cm and 1.0cm on the scan image of the micromorphology slide, sample <983> (5848=5863) (FIG. 47). Above and below the sub-horizontal fissure compacted microaggregated 'peds' form the deposit. The sediment comprising 4170 lens b1 may have accumulated through some natural processes as well as deposition of microlenses of dung through trampling as discussed above. Context 4170 b1 is the uppermost unit of sample <767> and generally the fissural microstructure is better expressed in the upper part of a laminated microfabric (Gé *et al.* 1993, 153) (FIG. 48). In this instance the reason is most likely due to more intensive trampling on 4170 lens b1, perhaps suggesting that the underlying laminations 4170 lenses b2–4 were rapidly laid down and therefore not subjected to prolonged trampling.

The final aspect of trampling effects on the microstratigraphic sequence discusses the incorporation and transfer of anthropogenic detritus both as a mechanical process of pressure (Gifford-Gonzalez *et al.* 1985), and of mechanical movement of material (Gé *et al.* 1993). The mechanical process of pressure must be considered in terms of penetrability of the floor material encompassing the following aspects: soil moisture, initial bulk density, and sediment texture (Beckman and Smith 1974; Gifford 1978; Gifford-Gonzalez *et al.* 1985; Schiffer 1987, 129). The mechanical movement of material concerns the transfer of occupation detritus and sediment from one area to another, allowing sediment in floor surfaces to become homogenised through churning which induces the collapse and internal reorganisation of the sample (Beckman and Smith 1974), and/or material, both micro-refuse and sediment, to become underlying deposits (Gé *et al.* 1993).

Two deposits/units show the incorporation of anthropogenic material from the stratigraphically overlying unit: 4199 (DT3) and 4170 lens a2 (DT4) (FIG. 48). Context 4199 is a lime-plaster floor that has undergone post-depositional chemical changes induced by weathering. The iron coating of voids indicates that the iron was in solution and therefore reducing conditions had occurred, and the loss of birefringence of the calcite crystals within the chalk indicates dissolution, induced by acidic conditions (Courty *et al.* 1989). The subsequent breakdown of the matrix of the lime-plaster floor made it more prone to trampling effects and the incorporation of sediment from the overlying dumped material, context 4189.

Context 4170 lens a2 forms part of a microstratigraphic sequence in which there are three lenses (FIG. 48). The overlying and underlying lenses a1 and a3 have a coarser particle size (loamy sand to coarse sand) than a2. The finer particle size of 4170 a2 (coarse sandy clay loam) led to increased strength in sediment consistency and consequently greater resistance to penetration of coarse material as demonstrated by trampling experiments by Gifford-Gonzalez *et al.* (1985). Food detritus became embedded at a depth of 1mm in lens 4170 a2 characterising this zone as 'reactive' (Gé *et al.* 1993, 153). On loose sandy substrates artefacts can migrate to a depth of 3–8cm, whereas the downward migration on a sandy silt loam substrate has been demonstrated to be minimal (Gifford-Gonzalez *et al.* 1985).

Clay translocation

Both unlaminated and microlaminated dusty impure clay coatings are present in the deposits from 'ERTB 4' (Table 10; FIG. 52) and provide supporting evidence for and interesting insights into spatial and chronological changes in the use of space within the structure, particularly concerning the number of contexts susceptible to chemical weathering. Translocation of clay and silty clay particles is influenced by factors related to water flow, chemical conditions, and energy and gravity. Movement can occur under any kind of climate, although temperate environments provide the best evidence, and through mixing and rotation of features in floor deposits (Courty *et al.* 1989).

Silty clay coatings that are poorly sorted, have a weak organisation, diffuse extinction and an absence of lamination (also termed dusty impure clay coatings) are indicative of turbulent hydraulic conditions (Courty *et al.* 1989). On an archaeological settlement the presence of dusty impure clay coatings can indicate anthropogenic disturbance processes such as trampling and dumping (Goldberg and Macphail 2006). Within 'ERTB 4', unlaminated dusty impure clay coatings are present in deposit types 1, 2, 3, 4 and 5, occurring very abundantly (>20%) in the dumped deposit category (DT5) and occasionally (2–5%) in the constructed earthen floor (DT2) beneath the tile surface of the smaller hearth 4216, context 4201=4152 (FIG. 48). There are variations in the distribution of dusty impure clay coatings within DT2, in particular within floor 4152=4201, 4202, and 4209. Context 4209 has around twice the amount of dusty impure clay coatings as 4201: 10–20 per cent in 4209 and 2–5 per cent in 4201. Context 4201 is protected by the tile platform, and therefore may have been protected from the disturbance effects that cause dusty impure clay coatings. Floor 5870 also has abundant (10–20%) dusty impure clay coatings, perhaps indicating similar levels of subsequent anthropogenic disturbance (FIG. 52; Table 10). In the case of floor 4209=4152 the coatings may originate from disturbance by the dumping of deposit 4189 under wet conditions. Context 4189 comprises rubbish, including dung, and hearth debris that was redeposited in this area, most probably in the post-abandonment phase (see La Motta and Schiffer 1999). Abandoned buildings often have failing roofs that leak water. Floor 5870 may have been subjected to later disturbance by animal or human trampling.

Dusty impure clay coatings within lime-plaster floor material (DT3) are included within material trampled in from the above dumped deposit 4189 and their presence within compacted trampled deposit 5848=5863 (DT4) is not surprising as this deposit was formed through trampling processes. Dusty impure clay coatings are, however, absent from the overlying trample 4170, in favour of microlaminated coatings that are discussed below.

Well-sorted, fine-textured laminated clay coatings can form easily in any kind of soil or sediment when surface run-off infiltrates into the subsurface through illuviation processes. Microlaminated clay/silty clay coatings exhibiting regular lamination and high birefringence indicate good orientation of fine particles as a result of slow aqueous deposition under calm conditions (Courty et al. 1989). Within 'ERTB 4', in constructed earthen floors, compacted trampled lenses and dumped deposits (DT 2, 4 and 6), fine microlaminated silty clay coatings of regular thickness occur around coarse grains and within pores, signifying that the particles were slowly deposited from weakly mobile water of capillary origin (Courty et al. 1989). Capillary action is responsible for moving groundwater from wet areas of soil/sediment to dry areas.

The area of 'ERTB 4' that is most affected by processes of water percolation is grid square 29C from which samples <767> and <768> were taken, representing context 4170, DT4 (FIG. 48). Here, dusty impure microlaminated clay coatings range from abundant (10–20%) to very abundant (>20%) in frequency. Sample <767>, comprising context 4170 lenses b1–4, is more affected than sample <768>, as every lens shows signs of clay dispersal through water percolation. In the area of smaller hearth 4216, contexts 4201 and 4202=4152 (DT2) (FIG. 48) have occasional (2–5%) to many (5–10%) dusty impure microlaminated clay coatings, which may relate to the use of water on the hearth or rain percolation from a poor roof in the post-abandonment phase of the building. The latter may also explain the abundant (10–20%), dusty impure microlaminated clay coatings in context 4203 (DT6), and so support the suggestion that this deposit relates to the abandonment of the previous structure, ERTB 2, Room 2.

Iron translocation

All deposit types within 'ERTB 4' exhibit free iron (i.e. iron that is capable of being moved) and signs that it is mobile, such as coatings of voids and coarse inclusions (Table 10; FIG. 52). Free iron is highly mobile only when present in the ferrous state which occurs under anaerobic conditions (Courty et al. 1989, 179).

Iron coatings (1st order red) are absent from dumped deposit (DT5) context 4189, despite occurring in the context stratigraphically below, lime-plaster floor 4199 (DT3) (FIG. 48). There are also abundant (10–20%) iron (1st order red), strongly orientated coatings both laminating voids and in an unlaminated form in the lime-plaster floor (DT3). Any iron present in 4189 may have leached into the lime-plaster floor deposit below. The poor preservation of the bone recovered from 4189 during excavation suggests acidic conditions that mobilise iron. The lime deposit potentially would have neutralised the pH, preventing the iron from staying in solution.

Ferrous iron is absent from compacted trampled deposit (DT4) context 4170, with the exception of lens a2. Here conditions were highly reduced which resulted in the formation of secondary ferrous phosphate (see below) (Courty et al. 1989).

Dissolution of ashes

In temperate climates and acidic environments the survival of ashy material and its recognition is problematic (Courty *et al.* 1989). Calcitic ashes are present in only two contexts within 'ERTB 4': an isolated patch in sub-floor levelling material 5872 (DT1) (FIG. 47) and compacted trampled lenses 4170 a1–3 (DT4) (FIG. 48). The ashes within 4170 a3 are cemented and greenish which can be caused when ashes become colonised by algae, lichens and mosses (Courty *et al.* 1989). This is again indicative of damp conditions within the area of 'ERTB 4' designated to grid square 29C.

Vivianite neomineral formation

Vivianite is an iron-phosphate mineral and in occupation deposits is a product of organophosphate solutions either from ash, bone, dung, cess or liquid waste (Courty *et al.* 1989). Vivianite is present both in solution, exhibited as coatings of voids and coarse material, and as needle-like crystal formations within void spaces within DT1–5 in 'ERTB 4' (Table 10; FIGS 47–48, 52).

There is a clear spatial division of the presence of vivianite within 'ERTB 4' and it occurs most frequently in the eastern side, abundant (10–20%) to very abundantly (>20%), in association with dung-trampled lenses, comprising sample <767>, context 4170, and ash-dominant lenses, comprising sample <768>, also context 4170. The deposits stratigraphically below (5872, 5848=5863 and 5870), have many (5–10%) to abundant (10–20%) vivianite crystals and coatings, suggesting leaching through the profile. Phosphatisation is rare (<2%) in the western side of 'ERTB 4'.

Organic staining

The degradation of organic matter and the complex relationships that exist between the different components within each soil ecosystem are broadly known as humification processes. Darkening in colour, known as organic staining, is observed in thin-section from the decomposition of organic matter. However, the precise chemistry of the organic substances cannot be identified by thin-section analysis alone. Humic and fulvic acids are classified through chemical extraction (Courty *et al.* 1989).

Organic staining occurs in compacted trampled lenses (DT4) context 4170 (FIG. 48), and less frequently (<2%) in dumped deposit (DT5) context 4189 (FIGS 49, 52; Table 10). Organic staining in context 4170 occurs in the form of coatings and is closely associated with dung, phytoliths, spherical spores, and vivianite. These links suggest that the organic staining in DT4 (4170) originates from the dissolution of herbivore dung. Organic staining in DT5 occurs along the edge of a pseudomorphic plant void, which indicates that the plant, possibly a root, decayed *in situ*.

Spherical fungal spores

Spherical fungal spores, 5–10 μm in diameter, are only found in compacted trampled lenses (DT4) and dumped deposits (DT5), and are associated with grass phytoliths and phosphate/vivianite coatings and crystals (DT4 and 5), and dung lenses and/or organic staining, and/or phosphate/vivianite coatings and crystals (DT4 only) (FIG. 48). The inclusion of grass phytoliths and spores in DT5 may suggest the redeposition and decay of grass-rich herbivore dung, which has caused minor post-depositional phosphatisation of the deposit (<2%). Smooth spherical spores (5–10 μm) are characteristic of sporangiospores from coprophilious fungus which particularly favours herbivore dung. Dung from omnivores or carnivores is usually broken down by bacteria rather than fungi (Bell 1983). Unfortunately random distribution of individual fungal spores, without containment in the sporangium does not facilitate identification of fungus species. However, potential coprophilious fungi include zygomycetes, fungus imperfecti, basidiomycetes and ascomycetes (Bell 1983). Coprophilious fungal spores are ingested by grazing herbivores and are able to pass through the gut unharmed and are then discharged in faeces. The spores then germinate to produce new fungus (Bell 1983). It is unlikely that the spores present in DT4 were deposited in faeces. Coprophilious fungi, particularly the final colonisers, break down the dung by exploiting the sugars in the dung, consuming the cellulose and disposing of the lignin (Bell 1983, 17). The co-occurrence of spores with phytoliths and organic staining suggests that the dung has been broken down.

SUMMARY OF PRESERVATION CONDITIONS

Anaerobic conditions occur in the local environment of 'ERTB 4', particularly in the eastern side, and have been identified by translocation of free iron in the ferrous state and the neoformation of vivianite which requires highly reducing conditions. This has led to the preservation of both charred and non-burnt dung but not faecal spherulites which are calcitic and require alkaline conditions. Clay translocation in the eastern side demonstrates that water has percolated through the profile adding to anaerobic conditions when it became trapped. Cemented greenish ashes are also evidence of damp conditions through the colonisation of the vicinity by algae, lichens and mosses.

DISCUSSION

SPATIAL VARIATION WITHIN 'ERTB 4'

Use of space: chronological and spatial changes

Soil micromorphology has augmented the identification of three phases of use within 'ERTB 4' attributed to chronological changes in specific activities within the structure. Specific stages in the life-cycle of 'ERTB 4' (as discussed by La Motta and Schiffer 1999) have been identified through formation and classification of deposit types (Table 7), and analysis of post-depositional events (Table 10; FIG. 52): habitation, structural decline, reuse, abandonment, and post-abandonment refuse deposition. The following activities and impact activities have been defined and classified as deposit types, and identified by activity by-products from types and depositional pathways of plant remains, bioarchaeological remains and micro-artefacts (Tables 8–9; FIGS 51–52): herbivore stabling, food cooking, heating, dumping, burning, and trampling. Phasing derived from the Harris matrix augmented with microstratigraphic analysis has enabled identification of an interesting sequence of events within 'ERTB 4'. The key deposits for each phase of use are located on scale plans of 'ERTB 4' (FIGS 47–49).

The life-cycle of 'ERTB 4': use-phase 1

FIG. 47 shows the earliest phase of 'ERTB 4' and is a stage of habitation, structural decline, and modification: habitation is demonstrated by the construction of floors and the formation of occupation deposits; structural decline of the structure is demonstrated by compaction and chemical weathering of occupation deposits, perhaps in a damp area such as a doorway or area covered by poor roofing; and modification of the structure is suggested by the disuse of the smaller hearth 4216.

The abandonment of preceding ERTB 2, Room 2, in the western side of 'ERTB 4' can also be attributed to this phase, and is characterised by a build-up of accumulated sweepings (context 4203 (DT6), FIG. 48), including ashes from the burning of wetland grasses (Table 8; FIG. 51). Context 4203 exhibits abundant (10–20%) microlaminated dusty impure clay coatings (Table 10; FIG. 52) (unlike deposits stratigraphically above, earthen floor 4152, and, below, earthen floor of ERTB 2 Room 2, which is beyond the scope of this report), indicating that water percolated through this unit depositing silty clay particles which lined voids and coarse particles. Rainwater entering from a failing roof may be a potential source of the water percolation. The ashes of wetland grasses may originate from the disposal by burning of old roofing materials. Letts' ethnographic research into the use of thatch highlighted that a range of plant materials can be used for roofing thatch, and often materials of convenience are used. Thatched roofs can often be temporary structures, efficient for only a couple of years before being replaced (Letts 1999; Letts pers. comm.).

The walls of the rectangular structure are clear at this stage and are re-used from the preceding building, ERTB 1, as is the central hearth which has been resurfaced. There is a chronological difference in the potential source of construction materials used in earth building materials from phase 1 and phase 2. Glauconite, despite occurring in sub-floor material, constructed earthen floors and compacted trampled deposits (DT1, 2 and 4, respectively) only occurs in specific deposits from the eastern side of 'ERTB 4' and only in phase 1 (contexts 5872, 5870, 5848=5863) (FIG. 47). The presence of glauconite in 5870 (DT2) may indicate a different source of construction material for this earthen floor than for floor 4152 (FIG. 48), occurring in phase 2, such as the Bracklesham Beds which are mostly glauconitic sandy clays (Jarvis 1968). Constructed earthen floor 4152 comprises quartz, mica and feldspar and has a similar mineral component to the Bagshot Beds, whereas floor 5870 comprises quartz, feldspar and glauconite and has a mineral component similar to the Bracklesham Beds.

Within the rectangular structure of retained ERTB 1, there is a clear north/south division of architectural space, both in terms of different deposit types and post-depositional chemical weathering: in the northern end compacted trample (DT4) context 5848=5863 and sub-floor levelling, constructed from redeposited sediment and refuse (DT1), context 5872 (Table 8; FIG. 51). A constructed earth floor (DT2) context 5870 is laid in the southern end and shows no transformation of the sedimentary matrix by trampling. However, there are many (5–10%) unlaminated dusty impure clay coatings (Table 10; FIG. 52) demonstrating that some disturbance took place. The formation by mechanical compaction of accumulated sediment and anthropogenic debris, including aggregates of earthen floor (Table 8; FIG. 51), in the north of the structure indicates that this area was damp and prone to intensive trampling, perhaps identifying a potential entrance to the structure.

Unlike floor 5870, unlaminated dusty impure clay coatings in context 5848=5863 are abundant (10–20%) (Table 10; FIG. 52), suggesting disturbance by trampling took place under wetter conditions. The deposition of redeposited sediment and refuse including bone (DT1) in context 5872 was not used as sub-floor levelling for an aesthetically pleasing floor surface such as context 5870, instead animals trampled across this deposit (see below). The later use of 'ERTB 4' for animals is likely to have caused the translocation of iron-phosphate, and neoformation of vivianite in contexts 5848=5863, 5870 and 5872 (Table 10; FIG. 52). Clay coatings in deposits from phase 1 are not laminated, suggesting that water was not leaking into the building at this stage and so percolating through the sediment.

The life-cycle of 'ERTB 4': use-phase 2

FIG. 48 shows the enlargement of 'ERTB 4' and that the building has encroached on the area that was formerly ERTB 2 Room 2 to create MRTB 1. There are no clearly defined parameters for 'ERTB 4' at this stage, other than a small wall foundation. However, some walls of ERTB 1 could still have been in use. Hearth 4216 is used during this phase and it is also possible that larger hearth 1433 continued to be used and it is discussed below with regard to specific activities within 'ERTB 4'.

During this phase of the life-cycle of 'ERTB 4' habitation and re-use stages have been identified with a clear east/west division of architectural space and activities within the structure (MRTB 1 and ERTB 1). These differences relate to deposit types and post-depositional chemical alterations, as well as variations in classifications of micro-refuse/activity by-products. Constructed earthen floors (DT2) contexts 4201, 4202, 4209=4152 and 5870 are present in the western side of 'ERTB 4' (= MRTB 1). Examination of the stratigraphic relationships indicates that it is possible that floor 5870 continued in use during this phase of 'ERTB 4'. There is an interesting spatial variation of unlaminated dusty impure clay coatings within the western side of 'ERTB 4'. Both constructed earthen floors 4209=4152 and 5870 exhibit around twice the amount (10–20%) of unlaminated dusty impure clay coatings as 4201, 4202=4152 (2–15%) (Table 10). The reason for this observation may be due to contexts 4201 and 4202 being protected from disturbance by trampling by the tile platform of hearth 4216.

In the eastern side of 'ERTB 4' (= decaying ERTB 1) an extensive spread of compacted lenses of sediment, herbivore dung, food residues and hearth rake-out (Tables 8–9; FIG. 51), context 4170 (DT4), was formed by trampling processes, most probably both human and animal as herbivore dung is present. The east/west division of space within 'ERTB 4' also represents an internal/external, or internal/semi-external division of space, identified by the comparative frequencies of microlaminated dusty impure clay coatings (Table 10). In the eastern side of

'ERTB 4' (= decaying ERTB 1), microlaminated dusty impure clay coatings are either very abundant (>20%) or abundant (10–20%), with several microlaminations indicative of repeated episodes of water percolation, and occur over a relatively large distance, in both samples <767> and <768>, from context 4170.

In the western side of 'ERTB 4' (= MRTB 1) no microlaminated dusty impure clay coatings are present in samples <953>, from floor 5870, or <666.1>, from floor 4209=4152. Few (2–5%) to many (5–10%) microlaminated dusty impure clay coatings are present in sample <666.2>, contexts 4201, 4202=4152, a comparatively lower frequency than in context 4170 from the eastern side of 'ERTB 4' (= ERTB 1) (Table 10). These samples are taken from directly adjacent to the hearth and therefore the water percolation that induced the translocation of silty clay particles may originate from water spillage from cooking on the hearth, or quenching the fire, or perhaps from the laying of DT3, the lime-plaster floor covering. The former and latter suggestions are preferred due to the infrequency of the microlaminated dusty impure clay coatings and minimal microlaminae around voids.

The repeated water percolation in the eastern side of 'ERTB 4' (= ERTB 1) may indicate that the area covered by the compacted trampled lenses, context 4170, either had no roof or a very poor roof, suggesting, perhaps, that this area was simply designed as a lean-to for animal shelter. Examination of the plan shows the trample, context 4170, to encroach into the main building in a possible doorway area, around hearth 1433. The notion of an animal shelter may be supported by the east/west spatial comparisons in frequency of iron translocation, phosphate and vivianite coatings and crystals, and organic staining (Table 10), and phytoliths (Table 8; FIG. 51) within 'ERTB 4'. Constructed earthen floor 4152 (DT2) exhibits few (<2%) vivianite coatings and crystals and no organic staining. Constructed earthen floor 5870 (DT2) exhibits no organic staining and abundant (10–20%) vivianite coatings and crystals, which may be due to its closer proximity to the animal activity in the eastern side. Animals may have wandered into the building and deposited liquid waste on the floor. Iron is more abundant in DT2 than in context 4170 (DT4). This may be due to the iron that was present in context 4170 transforming into vivianite, an iron-phosphate mineral, under reduced conditions.

In the eastern side of 'ERTB 4', sample <767>, context 4170 (DT4) exhibited high levels of neoformation of vivianite (>20%) within microfacies comprising grass phytoliths and organic staining in the form of coatings, representing horizons of decayed herbivore dung. These microfacies have been identified in lenses b1, b3 and b4, and are absent from b2 which may indicate a short period when animals were absent from this space. Spherical spores, 5–10 µm in diameter, are present in association with the dung in all zones from samples <767> and <768>. All zones containing dung in both <767> and <768>, context 4170, show a dominant proportion of grass phytoliths in association with spores. Microfacies in <767> contain long smooth, sinuous long, rondel and dendritic grass phytoliths. Phytoliths associated with dung within <768> comprise mainly grass phytoliths, specifically sinuous long-cells, smooth long-cells and dendritics, including sheets of multi-cells, with occasional trichomes and plateys. No bone and coprolite material is identified within the dung, clearly indicating that the animal ingested a purely vegetarian, grass-based diet characteristic of a herbivore (e.g. cow, sheep and goat), rather than an omnivorous diet such as that of a pig or human. Faecal spherulites are often found in deposits from herbivore stables but were most likely dissolved due to the acidic environmental conditions of the sediments.

The life-cycle of 'ERTB 4': use-phase 3

FIG. 49 shows the abandonment of hearth 4216 and post-abandonment deposition of refuse, context 4189=3817 (DT5), within the western side of 'ERTB 4' (= MRTB 1), which was later covered over by a tile path. Within the eastern side of 'ERTB 4' (= ERTB 1) deposits identified during excavation have not been microstratigraphically analysed.

In the western side of 'ERTB 4', once the tile platform of hearth 4216 became badly burnt and cracked, the hearth fell out of use. A lime plaster, context 4199 (DT3), was poured over the tile surface to conceal it and/or to level the floor. This action indicates the abandonment of this specific area for use as a fireplace and also, potentially, a change of use of space and internal architectural layout. The patchiness in the choices of floor-fabric materials suggests that the rationale for this depositional activity was not aesthetically driven and may provide further evidence for changing use of internal space and potential abandonment of the area.

Context 4189 (DT5) is a dump of sweepings and refuse, dominated in composition by hearth rake-out material. This context is one unit that comprises the post-abandonment deposit, context 3817. During excavation context 3817 was characterised as an occupation deposit comprising charcoal dumps and material such as bone, iron nails, ceramic building material and pottery. Deposits stratigraphically above, such as the tile path, take on a very different character representing different living conditions as building techniques become more masonry orientated.

SPECIFIC ACTIVITIES WITHIN 'ERTB 4'

Activity-related microscopic debris from the eastern side of 'ERTB 4' is more frequent in thin-sections from the compacted trampled lenses comprising 4170 (DT4) (FIG. 48). The evidence for high burning temperatures, burnt dung, non-burnt dung, and food residues, including burnt and non-burnt bone (Table 9; FIG. 52), support the idea of a multi-functional use of space during the deposition of the lenses of trample forming context 4170. From the diagnostic debris within the compacted trample lenses (DT4) the following activities are represented either within 'ERTB 4' or in close proximity to the structure: herbivore stabling, food cooking, and industrial activities such as metallurgy.

The inclusion of non-burnt dung, organic staining and phytoliths within the highly phosphatised trampled lenses indicates that animals were being kept and foddered using hay, perhaps over winter. Foddering using hay is demonstrated by the predominance of grass leaf and culm phytoliths in the dung, and sheets of dendritic husk phytoliths may indicate the disposal of cereal processing waste from the building in animal fodder, a phenomenon also suggested by Robinson (below, Ch. 16). The low level of phytoliths from herbaceous species suggests that animals were not grazing in fields, and so infrequently digesting herbs at the time the dung was deposited. The absence of dung from 4170 lens b2, sample <767>, indicates a period when animals were not housed in this space, and may have temporarily been in the surrounding fields.

It is likely that some cooking took place on nearby hearth 1433. Microscopic food residues (oyster shell and burnt bone) were trampled into 4170 a2 from dumped hearth rake-out material, 4170 a1. For bone to change colour due to burning, temperatures in excess of 400°C must be attained (Courty *et al.* 1989). Therefore, it is likely that the burnt bone originated from the grilling or roasting of meat, whereby the meat was placed directly on the heat source. The presence of microscopic non-burnt bone fragments in 4170 a3 may suggest several possible activities took place such as: pre-cooking butchery; boiling of meat rather than grilling/roasting; or bone-working crafts.

It is likely that the final phase of hearth 1433 was still in use while the trampled lenses in samples <768> and <767> accumulated. Sample <768> exhibited burnt and heat-affected inclusions throughout all three lenses of trample. In particular the inclusions in 4170 a1 were comparable to hearth rake-out material, comprising 72 per cent of the total inclusions. Specific residues associated with industrial activities, such as hammerscale and slag from metallurgy, have not been identified in 'ERTB 4' using soil micromorphology (see Tootell, below, Ch. 11). However, the heat-affected flints, calcitic ashes and the absence of charcoal and melted silica within the probable rake-out material are all indicative of burning temperatures >650°C on the nearby hearth (Courty *et al.* 1989). High burning temperatures on a hearth must be attained for most industrial activities and the evidence for burning temperatures from hearth 1433 are not high enough to clearly indicate bronze- or iron-working (which require temperatures >1000°C). However, on the basis of temperature, it is possible that other activities such as lead-working could have taken place as the melting point of lead is 400°C.

The presence of charred dung suggests that this material may have been used as fuel. Using the hearth simply to dispose of animal dung would seem wasteful but cannot be entirely disregarded as a possible explanation for the presence of burnt dung.

The use of dung as an excellent fuel in industry is documented ethnographically in Andean pottery production (Sillar 2000). All herbivore dung has a compact porous structure that, when dry, burns steadily, completely and evenly without a too-vigorous flame. Dung ash advantageously retains its structure after combustion which acts as an insulator making it an appropriate fuel for firings without a permanent hearth/kiln/furnace structure. Temperatures attained using dung can occasionally reach 1000°C, but this remains dependent on natural and cultural factors such as species type and husbandry practices, whereby the dung may be mixed with other materials by trampling, or compacted, or may or may not be affected by rain (Sillar 2000).

There is no activity-related microscopic detritus, with the exception of charred wood, directly associated with the use of hearth 4216, in the western side of 'ERTB 4' (FIG. 49). Those fragments that were identified most closely resembled characteristics of *Fraxinus excelsior*. Despite the absence of diagnostic, activity-related sediment characteristics and detritus, in comparison with deposits from the eastern side of 'ERTB 4', the following conclusions and observations have been made:

1 Temperatures on hearth 4216 were high enough to badly burn and crack the tile platform and to cause rubification of the mud-plaster floor below to an extent of 1cm, despite the tile absorbing some of the heat. However, this phenomenon may also result from prolonged firing;

2 Context 4209 (DT2) lies *c.* 0.5m east of the hearth's platform and has not been affected by the incorporation of charred wood. This indicates that the area around the hearth was kept clean during use, which has prevented debris accumulating other than directly adjacent to the platform;

3 There are no deposits comprising compacted lenses of trample (DT4) in the vicinity of hearth 4216;

4 The area of the mud-plaster floor 4152 that was not protected by the tile platform of hearth 4216 exhibited abundant (10–20%) dusty impure clay coatings, which may originate from water percolation through later dumped debris (DT5). These clay coatings are not as frequent nor microlaminated as those exhibited in the eastern side of 'ERTB 4' and may indicate that the western side of the building was covered by a more substantial roof. The comparison certainly indicates that there was a greater level of disturbance in the eastern side (= ERTB 1) of the building than in the western side (MRTB 1). The higher frequency of microlamination in the coatings from the eastern side indicates the effects of repeated weathering episodes.

5 There are minimal (<2%) phosphate coatings and vivianite crystals in the western side 'ERTB 4' (= MRTB 1), in the deposits around hearth 4216, unlike deposits such as sample <767>, context 4170, in the eastern side.

The above listed observations highlight the clear spatial division in use of architectural space, largely through distribution of deposit type categories, frequencies of occupation detritus, and post-depositional events and alterations. During use-phase 2 the western area of 'ERTB 4' (= MRTB 1), until its deliberate abandonment in phase 3, exhibits a character more suited to living quarters: there is a more substantial roof, no compacted lenses of trample, less build up of occupation detritus suggesting regular cleaning, and no characteristics of animal stabling.

CONCLUSIONS

It has been ascertained through micromorphological analysis that 'ERTB 4' was a dynamic structure in terms of depositional history, depositional processes, and use of space. Despite the absence of clearly defined parameters to the building, micromorphology shows clear distinctions in deposit types and activity residues between the eastern and western side of the structure, such that two separate buildings are proposed: MRTB 1 and a retained ERTB 1. Damp, anaerobic conditions have been identified on the eastern side, i.e. in ERTB 1, which very much supports the hypothesis that this part of the structure may have been a lean-to, perhaps without walls and a substantial roof.

CHAPTER 5

THE COINS A.D. 117–260

By Edward Besly

This report covers the coins of the period A.D. 117–260, corresponding to Periods 6–12 of Reece's scheme for the recording of Romano-British coin finds (Reece 1991), and of Periods 3 and 4 of Insula IX. Details of the individual coins are recorded on the IADB and the accompanying Schedule below therefore provides a summary of reigns and types — an approach similar to that in *Life and Labour* … (Fulford *et al.* 2006), but with the addition of references to *The Roman Imperial Coinage* (*RIC*), where these could be determined.

Coins of this period generally appear on Romano-British sites in smaller numbers than those of either the preceding or following periods and Insula IX is no exception: only 54 coins have been found (38 during the excavations and 16 from metal-detector searches of the topsoil) — a rate of unrecovered loss across the site of less than one coin every two years (FIG. 53a). This perhaps reflects the nature of the coinage of the day — which was either of high value and therefore carefully sought (silver denarii) or of large size (the sestertii, dupondii and asses) and therefore the easier to find if dropped than the small low-value coins of the later empire — as well perhaps as conditions on the ground during this time (FIG. 53b). The period covered is somewhat artificial in that coins of the Flavian emperors (A.D. 69–96), of Nerva (A.D. 96–98) and of Trajan (A.D. 98–117) — Reece's Periods 4–5 — will have formed an important element of the currency throughout the period A.D. 117–260 and worn examples from the site will add to the record of coin loss during that time. Over half of the post-A.D. 117 coins covered here are themselves in worn or even extremely worn condition (see Table 11), suggesting they were lost, perhaps, during the later part of the period (FIG. 53c); the last 80 years (A.D. 180–260) are represented by only ten coins, eight of them denarii.

Nevertheless, and in spite of the small numbers involved, one feature does appear to stand out: the reign of Antoninus Pius accounts for nearly half of the identifiable coins of A.D. 117–260 (46 per cent) and 39 per cent of the whole group, if the uncertain (mainly worn) coins are included, where Reece's British background figures suggest an average of 23 per cent, with the two towns cited, Cirencester and St Albans, giving figures of 20 and 23 per cent respectively (Reece 2002, 145). What is more, fourteen (two-thirds) of the Antonine coins from Insula IX and two of the five coins from the following reign are unworn or only slightly worn. (Of the eight coins of

TABLE 11. SILCHESTER INSULA IX COINS, A.D. 117–260: STATES OF WEAR, BY PERIOD

Period	Unworn	Slightly worn	Worn	Well worn
6: 117–138	-	1	4	3
7: 138–161	8	6	7	-
8: 161–180	1	1	2	1
9: 180–192	-	-	1	-
10: 193–222	3	2	-	-
11: 222–238	-	1	1	-
12: 238–260	-	-	-	-
Uncertain	-	-	-	8
Totals	**12**	**11**	**15**	**12**

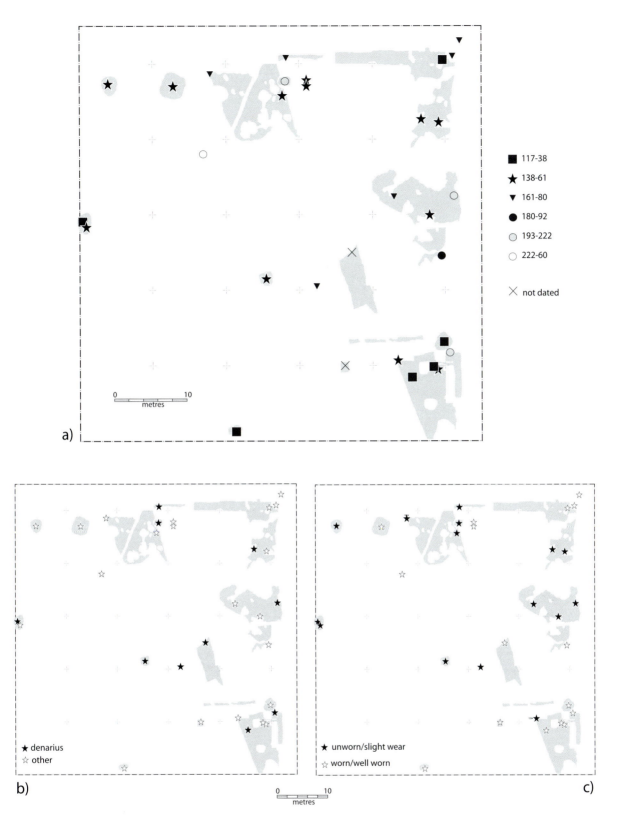

FIG. 53.   (a) The distribution of all coins dating between A.D. 117 and 260; (b) as (a), but denarii distinguished from the rest; (c) as (a), but worn/well-worn coins distinguished from those unworn or with slight wear.

Hadrian that are sufficiently well preserved, seven are worn or heavily worn.) It would appear that the middle years of the second century may have seen a minor peak in coin loss on the site, though as found many of these coins were no longer in their original deposition contexts, because of later activity. If this were the case, it would point up the extremely low rate of loss on the site during the remainder of the period A.D. 117–260. (The usual caveats about small samples and the subjective nature of assessment of wear in often poorly-preserved specimens should of course be borne in mind.)

The fact that so much of the second-century *aes* coinage found in Britain is so worn when lost may simply reflect long circulation in a self-contained and already adequately-supplied province; it has, however, crossed my mind to wonder whether there was indeed formal supply in the third century, but comprising old coins already well-circulated before being sent to Britain. Whether this could be demonstrated is another question. Be that as it may, *aes* of the period A.D. 200–260 is unusual in Britain, presumably introduced by informal mechanisms such as trade or by individual travellers; it is represented here by a single coin of Severus Alexander, struck in A.D. 223 but already somewhat worn when lost.

Archaeologically speaking, none of the 54 coins is both relatively unworn and from contexts dating to Periods 3 and 4, the 'City in Transition' period. All have been recovered either from post-A.D. 250 contexts in which they were plainly residual, or from unstratified contexts. The distribution plot shows that the majority were lost within about 10m of either street (FIG. 53); the lack of association, even residually, with the footprint of 'House 1' is striking. There is a notable cluster on the site of Late Roman Building 1 in the south-east corner of the trench, also the location of third-century MRTB 4.

Five coins, all denarii, are forgeries (10 per cent of the total, or one in three of the denarii); no counterfeit *aes* coins, whether cast or struck, have been recovered.

CONSOLIDATED SUMMARY LIST OF COINS, A.D. 117–260

All regular issues were struck at the mint of Rome. Irregular issues are listed under the issue period of their prototypes.

Period 6: Hadrian, A.D. 117–138 (9)

Hadrian: denarii, 2 (*RIC* 40a, 175); sestertii, 3 (*RIC* 631; uncertain); dupondii, 2 (*RIC* 557; uncertain); dp/as, 2 (uncertain)

Period 7: Reign of Antoninus Pius, A.D. 138–161 (21)

Antoninus Pius (12): denarii, 2 (*RIC* 260; obverse brockage); sestertii, 5 (*RIC* 635a, 776, 840, 855; uncertain); dupondii, 4 (*RIC* 602?, 688/809, 809, 937var.); as, 1 (*RIC* 934 [Britannia type])
Marcus Aurelius Caesar (5): denarius, 1 (*RIC* 446); sestertii, 3 (*RIC* 1232b, 1242a, 1352b); dp/as, 1 (*RIC* 1352)
Diva Faustina I (2): denarius, 1 (*RIC* 344); dp/as, 1 (*RIC* 1176)
Faustina II (2): dp/as, 2 (*RIC* 1409?; uncertain)

Period 8: Reign of Marcus Aurelius, A.D. 161–180 (5)

Marcus Aurelius (2): denarius, 1 (*RIC* cf. 35); dupondius, 1 (*RIC* 937)
Lucius Verus (1): sestertius, 1 (*RIC* 1342-7)
Faustina II (1): dp/as, 1 (uncertain)
Irregular (1): denarius of 'Lucius Verus' (struck in base metal)

Period 9: Reign of Commodus, A.D. 181–192 (1)

Crispina (1): dp/as, 1 (*RIC* 679)

Period 10: A.D. 193–222 (7)

Julia Domna (2): denarii, 2 (*RIC* 576, 580)
Elagabalus (2): denarii, 2 (*RIC* 161; uncertain fragment)
Irregular (3): denarius of 'Septimius Severus', 1 (cast); denarii of 'Caracalla', 2 (plated; struck
    in base metal)

Period 11: A.D. 222–238 (2)

Severus Alexander (1): as, 1 (*RIC* 403)
Julia Mamaea (1): denarius, 1 (*RIC* 360)

Period 12: A.D. 238–260

No coins

Uncertain, Periods 6–12 (9)

Regular coins: sestertius, 1; asses, 3; dp/as, 4
Irregular coin: denarius, 1 (plated)

CHAPTER 6

THE SMALL FINDS

By Nina Crummy

With a contribution on the wooden writing-tablet by Jacqui Watson

INTRODUCTION

In an urban setting, assemblages of small finds made and used in southern Britain from the early/mid-second century to the late third century A.D. are rarely defined in terms of close date ranges; they are simply 'Roman'. The chief distinction between such assemblages and those of the early and late Roman periods quite simply lies in the absence of artefacts belonging to either the first or fourth century. Remarkably few objects can be defined as specifically second-century, and even fewer as specifically third-century. In the north of Britain, chronology is more clearly defined by changes in military equipment, including brooches, but in the south of Britain small finds over this period add little to the dating evidence available from ceramics and coins.

It was hoped that the situation could be clarified by the Insula IX project, with marked differences being revealed between the artefacts of Period 3 and those of Period 4, but such has not been the case. There are certainly second- to third-century artefacts present in Period 3, and some third- to fourth-century ones in Period 4, but these are few in number. A high proportion of early Roman material is present in both Period 3 and Period 4, as it was in the late Roman assemblage from Insula IX (Crummy 2006a, 122) and also in the overlying ploughsoil, giving a misleading overall impression of a first- and second-century body of material, with only a limited number of later finds present.

The small finds from the various context groups (Objects) that have been used to chart the changing pattern of land use in Insula IX are briefly catalogued in a series of tables in Appendix 2. They are summarised below by Object and, where appropriate, context, with detailed descriptions reserved for artefacts of particular interest, either in terms of site context or the wider provincial or inter-provincial context. The discussion at the end of this chapter presents the material by functional group, and seeks to establish how the Insula IX material might be used to mark the shifts between early to mid, and mid to late Roman small finds assemblages, even when blurred by the presence of residual material.

CATALOGUE

PERIOD 3 TIMBER BUILDINGS MRTB 1/ERTB 1 [= ERTB 4] (Object 50037)
(Appendix 2, Table 27)

Object 50037 produced a comparatively high proportion of dress accessories and other small personalia, much of which may be debris directly associated with the occupation of the building. Among them is a T-shaped brooch with a lozenge-shaped expansion in the middle of the bow set with enamel, dated from the late first century into the middle of the second century (FIG. 54, No. 1, SF 2985). This is Hull's Type 122, a western form made in the lower Severn area, perhaps in the Mendips. Ten examples were among the large group of brooches offered as votives at the shrine on Nor'nour, Isles of Scilly (Hull 1968, fig. 13, 37–46; forthcoming, Type 122; Hattat 1987, 109–10, fig. 38, 918–19).

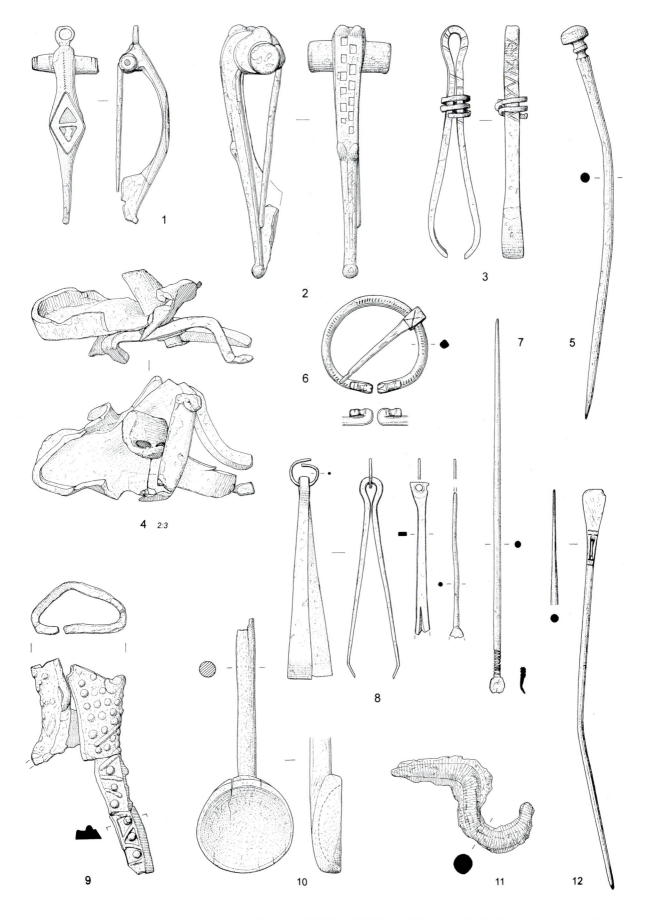

FIG. 54. Small finds: Period 3 timber buildings MRTB 1/ERTB 1 (Object 50037). Scale 1:1 except No. 4 (2:3) and No. 11 (1:2). (*Drawn by Brian Williams*)

A second western T-shaped brooch with the same date range and possibly from the same source came from a floor level in Object 50037. Belonging to Hull's Type 110, it has an enamelled panel on the upper bow, above small leaf-like side mouldings (FIG. 54, No. 2, SF 3256). From the same context came copper-alloy tweezers with a sliding clip made of coiled wire around the blades (FIG. 54, No. 3, SF 3484), an ivory peg (in very poor condition), and a crude lead candelabrum, made by slotting a tripod candlestick through the base of an open lamp, effectively converting the latter into a drip tray (FIG. 54, No. 4, SF 3037). The poor condition of the object (both elements are crushed) implies that it may have gone out of use some time before being deposited. Lead tripod candlesticks have an eastern and largely southern distribution and are often decorated with a relief geometric pattern, with most thus decorated coming from late Roman contexts, although there is one from an Antonine context at Carlisle and see below for a second example from Object 50037 (Eckardt 2002, 149–50, 339; Major and Eddy 1986), whereas the Silchester candlestick is plain and of earlier date. Lead open lamps are more widely found, although none was recorded from Silchester by Eckardt (2002, 331–3).

A large group of artefacts came from the latest phase of the building. Several predate its construction and are presumably residual. They include a Nauheim derivative brooch dated to *c*. A.D. 43–80/5, along with a frit melon bead that had probably gone out of use about the time the building was constructed. These two pieces, therefore, call into question the direct association with Object 50037 of other personalia and household equipment from the same context. Among the former is a complete hairpin of Cool's Group 6 (1990, 157), which dates to the later first and second century (FIG. 54, No. 5, SF 2860), and a penannular brooch with cast moulded terminals and small nicks on the upper face of the hoop (FIG. 54, No. 6, SF 2877) belonging to Fowler's Type D2, examples of which mainly come from southern Britain; the form probably dates to the second century (Fowler 1960, 152, 176). Other dress accessories are a copper-alloy finger-ring, a possible second one of iron, and an iron strap-plate, which may be from a harness strap instead of a belt. Toilet instruments from the group include a complete long-handled toilet spoon (FIG. 54, No. 7, SF 2576), used for extracting small quantities of scented unguents or cosmetics from toilet flasks or in medical procedures (Jackson 1986, 128, fig. 4, 28), a plain nail-cleaner and tweezers, and a complete toilet set held by a wire suspension loop, again of plain undated form (FIG. 54, No. 8, SF 2079). The toilet set came from a layer associated with the construction of MB 1, and may be a votive deposit.

Domestic equipment from this group of contexts consists of a second, damaged, tripod candlestick with geometric relief decoration (FIG. 54, No. 9, SF 2421) and a round-bowled bone spoon, a form belonging primarily to the first and second centuries (FIG. 54, No. 10, SF 2767), while a small pottery counter may have been used as a game counter or as a lid. Among the fittings are a wall-hook (FIG. 54, No. 11, SF 2660) and the bit from an L-shaped lift-key, and other finds include the point from an iron stylus and a copper-alloy needle with spatulate head (FIG. 54, No. 12, SF 2477). The very narrow eye of this needle, coupled with the width of the head, with the one pointing to the use of fine thread and the other to the use of fabric of coarse weave (Crummy 1983, 65), calls into question its use for sewing. The occurrence of styli of identical form but lacking the eye, e.g. at Wilcote, Oxon. (Hands 1993, fig. 26, 13; 1998, fig. 20, 57–60), suggests either that the Wilcote styli are unfinished needles, or that objects such as SF 2477 may have been dual-purpose items of writing equipment, with the eraser and point of a stylus for writing on wax, but an eye that allowed it to be used to sew together separate sheets of papyrus or other loose-leaf writing material.

PERIOD 3 MASONRY BUILDING 1 (Object 50018) (Appendix 2, Table 28)

Deposits predating the construction of Object 50018 contained two complete brooches, a Nauheim derivative (FIG. 55, No. 13, SF 3913) and a Colchester B derivative (FIG. 55, No. 14, SF 3933), the former dating to *c*. A.D. 43–80/5 and the latter to A.D. 50–70, and also a complete iron knife of an early Roman type with integral handle (FIG. 55, No. 15, SF 3717), a form represented in mid-first century A.D. contexts at Hod Hill but not present in Late Iron Age assemblages (Manning 1985, 113). These three objects provide a *terminus post quem* for MB

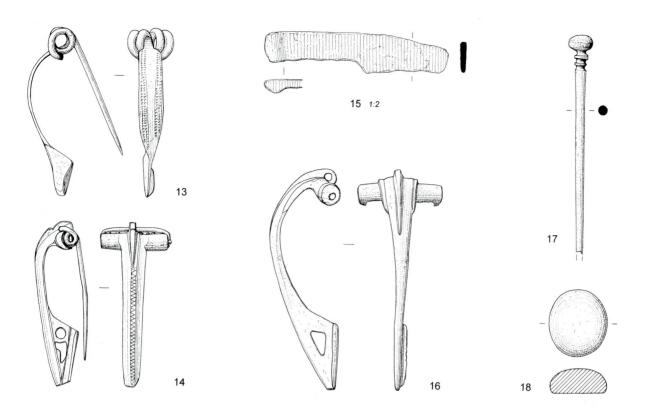

FIG. 55. Small finds: Period 3 Masonry Building 1 (Object 50018). Scale 1:1 except No. 15 (1:2). (*Drawn by Brian Williams*)

1, and, given their intact condition, may be deliberately placed foundation deposits, or perhaps termination deposits for an earlier building.

From contexts associated with the walls of MB 1 came a pottery counter, a fragment of a pottery spindlewhorl, a copper-alloy Polden Hill brooch (FIG. 55, No. 16, SF 2486) and a copper-alloy hairpin of Cool's Group 6 (FIG. 55, No. 17, SF 2487). The hairpin dates from the mid-first century to the mid-second century and is also represented in Object 50037. The brooch is Flavian, slightly later than those from the construction deposits but still earlier than the start date of Period 3.

The floor levels in the building produced mainly scrap fragments, including the foot of a Late Iron Age Langton Down brooch. Exceptions are a second pottery counter and a glass counter (FIG. 55, No. 18, SF 2313). Glass counters are usually found intact and are often represented in urban assemblages, a reflection of the popularity of gambling and of board games played in leisure hours. Several other glass counters have been found in Period 3 and 4 contexts.

PERIOD 3 MASONRY BUILDING 2 (Object 50019) (Appendix 2, Table 29)

A feature of the artefacts from Object 50019 is that a substantial proportion are intact, or nearly so, and many of these complete pieces appear from their contexts to have been deliberately buried. Such an interpretation needs to be approached with care given the finds-rich nature of Roman deposits, and condition at time of burial is not always a reliable criterion for deliberate deposition.

Three complete or near-complete brooches in Object 50019 all predate the building's construction by several decades. Although they would fall into the group of complete artefacts and so may be deliberate placements, there is a lengthy period between their well defined period of use and the date of their burial, making them more likely to be residual. One associated context contained a complete Colchester brooch, a late pre-Roman Iron Age type made from *c.* A.D. 10 to 40/3, with most in use at the Conquest deposited by *c.* A.D. 50 (FIG. 56, No. 19, SF 2786).

From another such context came part of a Nauheim derivative brooch with narrow wire bow, an imported type that first appeared *c*. A.D. 43 and was in use until at least *c*. A.D. 80/5 (FIG. 56, No. 20, SF 3133). (Corney's dating (2000, 337) for similar brooches on the Silchester forum-basilica site is much too broad.) Although the appearance of the type was linked to the Conquest, the high numbers on settlements in Britain implies use by civilians. A brooch in floor 1818 is a Hod Hill with small lugs at the top of the bow, which has a date-range of A.D. 43 to *c*. A.D. 60/5 (FIG. 56, No. 21, SF 2269). Hod Hills were much used by Roman military personnel, and this particular form (Hull Type 63) also occurs at sites such as Hod Hill, Cirencester, Richborough and Colchester, as well as on the forum-basilica site at Silchester (Corney 2000, fig. 153, 63, 67). The length of the foot on this example is shorter than is usual compared to that of the bow. Other brooches are represented only by small fragments. That a Late Iron Age brooch and two early Roman period brooches were curated for many decades to be deposited well into the second century seems unlikely, and these items can probably be discounted as deliberate deposits unless the date of construction of MB 2 has been set too late.

Other dress accessories from Object 50019 are a fragment of a turquoise frit melon bead and a copper-alloy hairpin, both from floor levels. The bead is another artefact introduced at the Conquest, generally occurring in mid to late first-century contexts and there is some doubt that in Britain they continued in use into the early years of the second century. The hairpin (FIG. 56, No. 22, SF 2642) has a globular head above a series of mouldings, with a depression in the top of the head that probably originally held a small piece of coloured glass. This feature links it to Cool's Group 21, dated to the second to third centuries (1990, 170), but the mouldings at the top of the shaft are not typical of that form. The shaft has been bent almost at a right angle near the top, a characteristic of deliberately mutilated votive deposits, and the possibility that this is an *ex voto* is high; it may relate to a nearby temple or shrine rather than MB 2 (*see* Discussion).

Toilet instruments are particularly well-represented in Object 50019, with one complete toilet set coming from a floor level (FIG. 56, No. 23, SF 2942), another from a wall context (FIG. 56, No. 24, SF 2961), and a tweezers fragment from a post-hole. The end of the ear-scoop on FIG. 56, No. 24, SF 2961 is missing, but such damage is common on these instruments and is likely to be a result of the decay of the extremely thin metal of the scoop during burial rather than of wear. Reviews of toilet instruments from London and Colchester have highlighted a marked distinction between votive deposition of complete toilet sets and the discarding of worn fragmentary instruments in ordinary domestic contexts (Crummy 2006b, 65; Crummy with Pohl 2008, 18–19). This implies that all complete sets that do not come from burials or ritual foci require careful scrutiny of their contexts to determine whether or not they may be formal offerings. As both sets from Object 50019 come from construction contexts, both could well be deliberate foundation deposits, in which case they probably date to close to the time of their burial, although neither can be closely dated on typological features. On neither set does the nail-cleaner belong to one of the regional types established during recent studies of small toilet instruments (Crummy and Eckardt 2003; Eckardt and Crummy 2008), thereby falling into the large number of toilet instruments with no distinguishing features that cannot be grouped into a formal typological system, although the bellied blade on FIG. 56, No. 23, SF 2942 is characteristic of a number of nail-cleaners from southern Britain (Eckardt and Crummy 2008, 122).

Of the remaining items from Object 50019, an iron needle from a post-hole is a comparatively rare survival. Although such objects were probably common in the Romano-British period, they would be difficult to identify without the use of X-radiography. An iron mason's trowel from a wall context represents not only a particularly apposite context for such a tool, but also another unusual survival and another possible deliberate deposit (FIG. 56, No. 25, SF 3140). In form, with rounded shoulders to the blade and integral offset tang, it matches an example from Colchester (Crummy 1983, fig. 115, 2975).

PERIOD 3 NORTHERN PITS (Object 500029) (Appendix 2, Table 32)

The northern pits contained few small finds. Parts of two iron joiner's dogs were found in cess-pit 4835 (Object 50028). Like the examples in the south-eastern pits 5693 (Period 3) and 3102

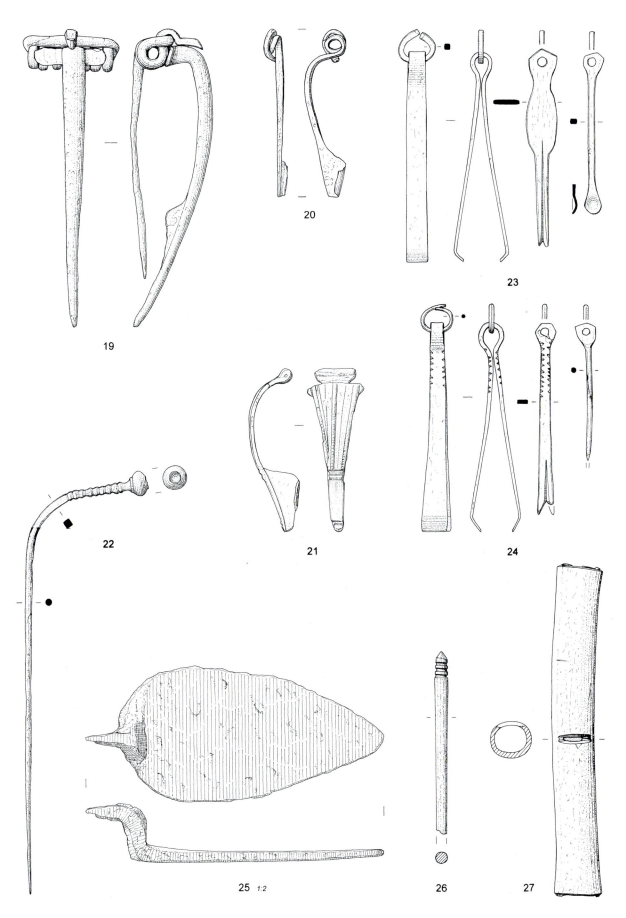

FIG. 56.   Small finds: Period 3 Masonry Building 2 (Object 50019) and south-eastern pits (Object 500017). Scale 1:1 except No. 25 (1:2). (*Drawn by Brian Williams*)

(Period 4), they may relate to the cess-pit's construction, perhaps coming from timber braces or lining, or from a wooden lid. Finds from well 2234 (Object 41016) included part of an iron stylus, a tile counter and a pottery counter. None of the objects can be closely dated.

PERIOD 3 SOUTH-EASTERN PITS (Object 500017) (Appendix 2, Table 31)

Pit 5039 (Object 44008)

The pit contained only small pieces of scrap that cannot be closely dated.

Pit 5693 (Object 500035)

Pit 5693 included two small fragments of a high-tin bronze mirror, probably from one of the mirror types imported into Britain from the second half of the first century from the Continent, especially from the workshops at Nijmegen (Lloyd-Morgan 1981, introduction p. x). The pit also held two joiner's dogs which may have come from timberwork lining or covering the pit. More were found in other negative features: two in Period 3 cess-pit 4835 (above), one in Period 4 well 5735, and three in Period 4 pit 3102.

'Pit' 6290 (Object 500036)

Among the finds from the slump into pit 6290, post-dating its primary fill, was part of an early Roman hairpin (FIG. 56, No. 26, SF 3806), a glass counter, and a bone tube cut from a bird ulna, which is naturally hollow (FIG. 56, No. 27, SF 3935). The tube may have been used as a bobbin. A small slit has been cut through one side of the bone at the midpoint. Both the surface of the tube and the sides of the slit are well polished. Similar tubes lacking the central slit have been found in medieval contexts at York and other towns. Their use is uncertain, but one possibility is that groups were set into a wooden stock to form a syrinx, or set of pan-pipes (MacGregor *et al.* 1999, 1977); this may be the case with the Silchester ulna, although a finger-stop is not used on the tubes of a syrinx as the different notes are achieved by varying the lengths of the pipes and there is no break in the polish at either end or on the sides that would be present had it been just one of a bundle of bound tubes.

PERIOD 3 OCCUPATION (Object 701) (Appendix 2, Table 33)

The assemblage from the sequence of layers and features comprising Object 701 is here briefly described in the chronological sequence of the contexts.

The Period 3 dumps and gravels, including the dump of ceramic building materials, principally contained dress and toilet accessories, with some household equipment and a single piece of cavalry harness.

In Object 701 there is a marked paucity of iron objects compared to several of the Period 3 pit groups described above (Object 500017). Dated dress accessories include two Nauheim derivative brooches of *c.* A.D. 43–80/5 (FIG. 57, Nos 28–9, SFs 3072 and 3450), a type represented in contexts associated with the Period 3 buildings (see above), and one example of each early form of bone hairpin, Types 1 and 2, with the plain tapering shafts characteristic of the period from the mid-first century into the second century. A nail-cleaner and tweezers (FIG 57, Nos 30–1, SFs 3066 and 3067) from context 4270 may both have belonged to the same set; although neither is of a form that can be unequivocally dated to the first century, in this context they are most likely to belong to the Claudian-Flavian period of mass production of this type of toilet equipment (Crummy and Eckardt 2003, 61; Eckardt and Crummy 2008, 62–5). A fragment of a round-bowled spoon (FIG. 57, No. 32, SF 3052) is one of several present in this mid-Roman assemblage, many of which come from secondary contexts and may be of mid to late first-century date. A small phalera from cavalry harness with traces of tinning on the surface is characteristic of the first century; it too may date to as early as the Claudian period (FIG. 57, No. 33, SF 3474).

The silt horizon that lay above the dumps and gravels contained many similar items, such as a

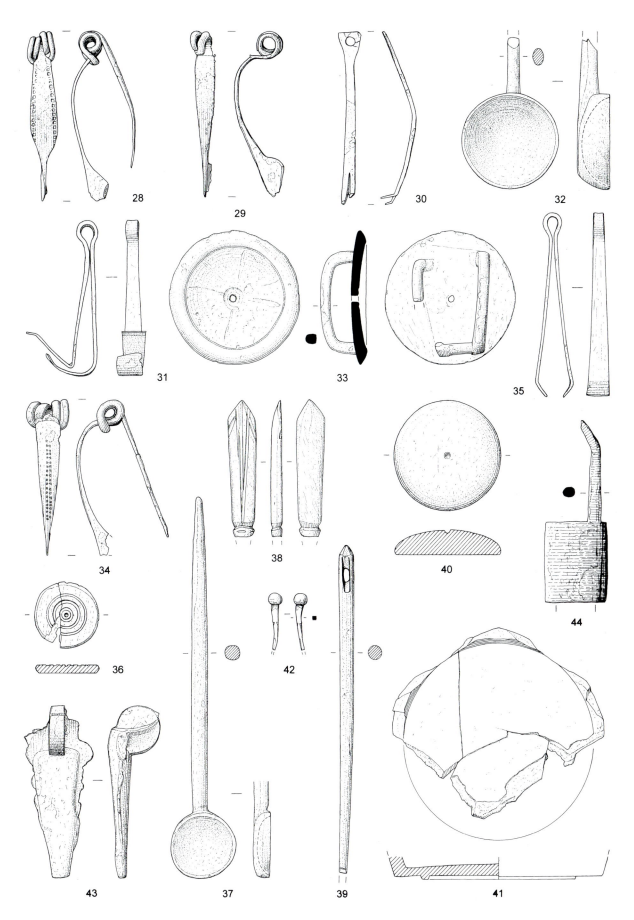

FIG. 57. Small finds: Period 3 south-eastern occupation (Object 701). Scale 1:1. (*Drawn by Brian Williams*)

Type 1 hairpin, a Nauheim derivative brooch (FIG. 57, No. 34, SF 3216) and tweezers (FIG. 57, No. 35, SF 3308). In addition the silts produced a pottery counter, two bone counters, one plain and one decorated with concentric circles (FIG. 57, No. 36, SF 3357), and a probable bar iron offcut, waste debris from blacksmithing.

The assemblage from the possible building MRTB 3, cutting into the silts, is quite unusual. Five of the nine items recovered are of bone, and three of the five are round-bowled spoons. One is complete (FIG. 57, No. 37, SF 3262) and two are damaged. The remaining two bone objects are a fragment of a shaft that may be part of the handle of one of the damaged spoons and a short, pointed terminal (FIG. 57, No. 38, SF 3266) of uncertain identification but bearing some resemblance to bone spatulae (Mikler 1997, Taf. 27, 1–8). The metal objects include a copper-alloy needle.

Part of a round-bowled spoon also came from the clay accumulation overlying the lower silts, with other items from this group including a bone hinge unit, part of a shale armlet, and two needles, one of bone (FIG. 57, No. 39, SF 2391) and one of copper alloy. The upper silts above the clay contained only a fragment of a tanged blade and a plano-convex bone counter (FIG. 57, No. 40, SF 3405) of late Roman form (Crummy 1983, 91, Type 3). The recovery of this example from the silts points to a late second-century appearance for the type, which is not common and is generally found in fourth-century contexts.

As might be expected, the numerous objects from the rubble make-up overlying the upper silts are generally small pieces of scrap, most probably residual and derived from midden waste. Other than a Type 1 hairpin and a small fragment of a round-bowled spoon (both early Roman), none of the items in this assemblage can be dated. They include a small shale dish (FIG. 57, No. 41, SF 2881). Two items are unusual. One is a small gold stud, the square-section shank of which suggests that it was used to ornament a wooden object, perhaps a box or piece of furniture (FIG. 57, No. 42, SF 2245); with evidence for gold-working on Insula IX, the possibility that the stud was locally made cannot be ruled out. The other object is an unfinished casting of one element of a copper-alloy strap-hinge; a fragment of casting debris also came from the rubble. On the hinge the flashings along the line where the two halves of the mould joined together are unfiled, and the lug for attachment to the second element of the hinge is unpierced (FIG. 57, No. 43, SF 2362). This piece is firm evidence for the manufacture of wooden artefacts at Silchester as well as of the metal fittings needed to complete them. Hinges of this type were used on mid-first-century folding game boards (as P. Crummy *et al.* 2007, fig. 111, CF47.20b–c) and on box lids (Riha 2001, Abb. 19, 21 and 23, Tafn 12–23). A closely similar example has been found at the Roman temple at Farley Heath, Surrey (Bird 2007, 56, fig. 24, 98).

The final group of contexts in Object 701 are defined as late second-century occupation, but, like those from the rubble make-up, they produced mostly small pieces of undated scrap, including a small quantity of copper-alloy casting debris. They include an unusual form of iron goad prick, with the point extending from a ferrule made from a rolled strip (FIG. 57, No. 44, SF 2886). A wire armlet with damaged slip-knot join is a form more usually found in late Roman burials and probably represents the latest item in Object 701.

PERIOD 4 MASONRY BUILDING 3 (Object 50046) (Appendix 2, Table 30)

Unlike Object 50019, which contained many complete or near-complete artefacts, Object 50046 produced mainly fragmented pieces, with most complete items being small and/or of durable materials such as pottery or glass. Many are certainly, and others probably, first-century in date and residual in their contexts. These contrast with some items from the dark earth and the robbing of the stone walls, which date to the late third century.

Early items include a Colchester BB derivative brooch, dated *c.* A.D. 65–85 (FIG. 58, No. 45, SF 1077), and two Nauheim derivative brooches, dated *c.* A.D. 43–80/5 (FIG. 58, Nos 47–8, SF 1232 and SF 1286), from the floor levels, and a Rearhook brooch, dated *c.* A.D. 40–60/5, from the construction clays (FIG. 58, No. 48, SF 4044). More unusual are a peltate vessel foot (FIG. 58, No. 49, SF 2013) and a strainer-plate from a strainer bowl. Very little metal survived from the latter, which was very thin and had been crumpled or folded, but was clearly visible as a stain in the soil.

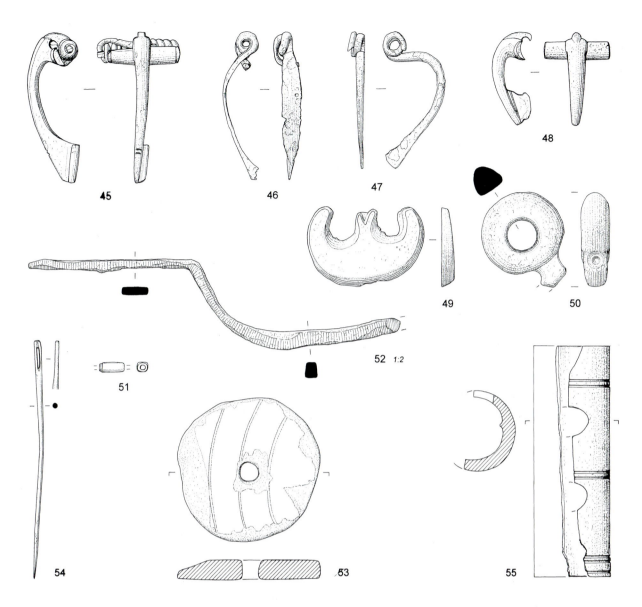

FIG. 58.   Small finds: Period 4 Masonry Building 3 (Object 50046). Scale 1:1 except No. 52 (1:2). (*Drawn by Brian Williams*)

Although found separately, both these objects may originally have been part of the same vessel. The distinctive thin sheet-metal strainer-plates, bearing patterns of small punched holes, were fitted by soldering their edges to the wall, base and spill-plates of strainer bowls. They served to sieve out solids such as herbs and spices used to flavour warmed or brewed drinks before the liquid was served. Such plates can be seen on the strainer bowl from the richly-furnished Welwyn Garden City burial of *c.* 10 B.C. (Stead 1967, fig. 12), and on the mid-first-century bowl from the Doctor's burial at Stanway, Essex (P. Crummy *et al.* 2007, 223, 324–5, fig. 113, f). The Silchester vessel foot is also close to those found on the Stanway bowl; although smaller and lacking the central grooving of the Stanway feet, it is similarly stouter and less elongated than those found on continental metal vessels. The Stanway strainer bowl was of the carinated form that was made in both metal and pottery in the eastern region, where most examples have been found. Exceptions come from Blain, Loire-Atlantique, Alchester in Oxfordshire, Chettle in Dorset, and Kingston Deverill in Wiltshire (ibid.; Worrell 2006, 460–2), a spread westwards that was almost certainly driven by the political upheavals of the Conquest and its aftermath. In the light of these western finds it is possible to see the Silchester foot and strainer-plate as deriving from a strainer bowl of this mid-first-century type.

All the above items are clearly residual in a Period 4 context, and indeed there is little reason to believe that any of the objects in the contexts associated with the construction of the building are of early third-century date. In the construction clays a fragment of an early Roman melon bead and a nail-cleaner from a late first- or early second-century châtelaine brooch are certainly earlier, and many of the other items consist only of small pieces of scrap, including part of an iron stylus and the iron prick from a goad. The latter would have been used in an urban context to drive animals to market or to slaughter, as well as to and from grazing grounds; the goad pricks from this assemblage can be matched to the evidence for the keeping of animals within Insula IX. A plain copper-alloy terret from the harness of a driven animal (FIG. 58, No. 50, SF 3002) is a more unusual find from an urban site. Lacking the lipped mouldings that characterise many Late Iron Age terrets, this plain example is probably Roman, but cannot be more closely dated. One object that may belong to the third century is a small blue glass cylinder bead of rectangular section, a form typical of the small beads found in late Roman burials (FIG. 58, No. 51, SF 2136).

Where the objects in the floor levels can be dated, they are similarly earlier than their contexts, such as the brooches and vessel fragments described above. An exception here may be an iron latchlifter, which is complete apart from the end of the hook (FIG. 58, No. 52, SF 1121). A single link from a loop-in-loop chain found in hearth 1544 derives from a necklace or brooch chain and is unlikely to be contemporary with its context. A spindlewhorl from a post-hole was well used when buried, being worn around the spindle hole and chipped on the edge and on both faces; made of *terra nigra*, it must predate the Flavian period (FIG. 58, No. 53, SF 1805).

The objects associated with the verandah include a pottery counter rough-out made from the base of an orange-ware vessel, probably a flagon, with the edge clipped to form a regular roundel but not worked to a smooth finish. It has none of the features associated with wear as a counter, such as abrasion or spalling on either face. A copper-alloy needle from the same context (FIG. 58, No. 54, SF 3025) is of a form that dates to the third century or later (Crummy 1983, 67, Type 3). Both objects are likely to be contemporary with their contexts, although other items from the verandah are probably residual, such as a large fragment of a bone hinge unit with incised grooving and two dowel-holes (FIG. 58, No. 55, SF 3165).

Although the small finds from Object 50046 cover nearly the entire Roman period, none need be as late as the early fifth century. The latest items are probably two examples of the simple cog-wheel armlet with close-set crenellations, Lankhills Type D1d, which dates to the late fourth century and does not seem to continue in use into the fifth century like the variant with toothing between more widely spaced crenellations (G. Clarke 1979, 305, fig. 37, 437; Crummy 2006a, 129). Both are from the dark earth which developed subsequent to the demolition of MB 3 after A.D. 287 (Fulford *et al.* 2006, 18–19). A fragment of clay tobacco pipe from context 1788 (SF 1143) points to some contamination of the gravel floors by the Victorian explorations in Insula IX.

PERIOD 4 SOUTH-EASTERN PITS AND WELLS (Object 500017) (Appendix 2, Table 31)

Well 1750 (Object 500020)

Well 1750 produced only an intrusive modern iron fitting, found on the surface, and a scrap of leather.

Pit 2601 (Object 500032)

In contrast to the debris found in most of the pits and wells in Object 500017, the secondary fill of pit 2601 contained a complete iron folding-knife or razor with an ivory handle in the form of two coupling dogs (FIG. 59, No. 56, SF 1734; cf. FIG. 43). Traces of leather noted during conservation suggest that it was buried in a leather pouch. As the pit also contained two dog skeletons, the bones of a raven and two doubly-pierced pot sherds, this object can be seen as a deliberate formal deposit, part of the ritual activity focusing on dogs and holed pottery that took

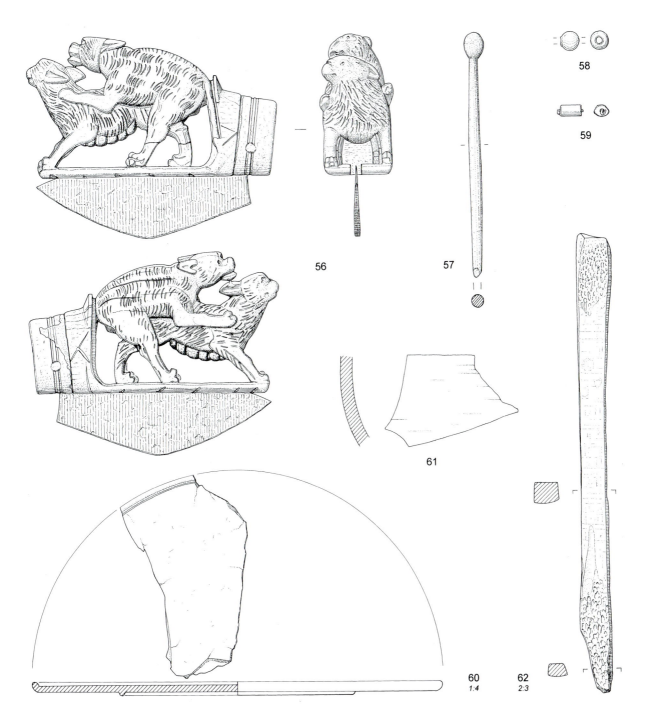

FIG. 59.   Small finds: Period 4 south-eastern pits (1) (Object 500017). Scale 1:1 except No. 60 (1:4) and No. 62 (2:3). (*Drawn by Brian Williams*)

place in Insula IX (Fulford 2001, 201–2; Eckardt and Crummy 2002). The pit dates to the early third century, a date that agrees with the general second- to early/mid-third-century date for many knives of this form.

The lively scene on the handle shows the animals in a typical mating pose, with the dog's back humped as he clasps the bitch's sides, while she braces all four legs firmly on the ground; both animals have their ears laid back. Comparison with mating felines confirms the identification of these animals as dogs — female felines lie on the ground during mating — and the possibility that this is a variation of the hound and hare hunting scene found on copper-alloy folding-knife handles can also be dismissed in the light of the typical humped pose of the male and the swollen teats of the bitch that show her to be already lactating. Their pelts are shown by incised straight and wavy lines and they stand on a small platform with a central slot to allow the blade to pass through when folded. They were intended to be viewed facing right, as from the other side their faces are obscured. As is often the case with figures carved to be seen in profile, when seen full-face they appear asymmetrical.

Behind the dogs the ivory is solid and elliptical in section, with an incised cross at the base on the front side and a single diagonal line at the rear. There is a distinctive concave extension rising behind and attached to the rump of the dog, providing some strength to the carving. The handle is rebated close to the blade and has two grooves around the circumference. This area was originally covered by a band of copper-alloy sheet, which has now almost completely disappeared. The blade is pivoted on a copper-alloy pin set through the lower side of this area. Handles with similar extensions come from Florence, Cologne and Hüttwil in Switzerland (von Mercklin 1940, Taf. 35, 2, 7; Degen 1984, Abb. 5). The iron blade is short and wide, with the straight cutting edge set into the gap in the platform. The back rises slightly before curving down to the tip.

Boon has suggested that blades of this form were probably used for trimming the nails, but they are more widely accepted as razors (Boon 1991, 22–3; Riha 1986, 28–32). The short, wide blade with rounded or angled back compares closely to the form of razors of the Anglo-Saxon period, and the apotropaic imagery used on the handles makes a strong case for their identification as razors. The figure types used on handles from Gaul, Germany and Italy are those associated with fecundity, death and resurrection, prophylactic images that could be invoked to avert the danger inherent in shaving — the misuse of a cut-throat razor could prove fatal. The animals shown on knives where sufficient of the blade remains to identify it as belonging to this group are dogs, monkeys, an owl (on a very small knife, possibly a model), and a long-muzzled animal that has been interpreted as an anteater (aardvark), a species today confined to southern Africa but seemingly among the fauna of Sub-Saharan Africa during the Roman period (von Mercklin 1940, Taf. 35, 5–7; Degen 1984, Abb. 3, 4; Grapin and Sivignon 1994, esp. figs 1–2, 4, 6, 8; Bertrand 1999, fig. 56; Rodet-Berlarbi and Dieudonné-Glad 2008, 152–3, fig. 18). Anthropomorphic images consist of a lyre-player (Apollo or Orpheus), a shepherd carrying a lamb across his shoulders, gladiators and lovers (von Mercklin 1940, Taf. 39, 2, Taf. 41, 1–2; Degen 1984, esp. Abb. 2, 6; Jackson and Friendship-Taylor 2003). An elaborate handle in the British Museum, said to be from Ravenna, shows two tigers attacking a goat (*BMQ* 37 (1973), 128–9, fig. 61), and large felines, chiefly panthers, occur on the handles of a number of razors that are probably also from Italy, along with single examples of a ram and a bull (Venturi 1926, pls 58–61). The association of dogs with chthonic deities and the passage to the underworld is well documented (e.g. Jenkins 1957, 64–5; Merrifield 1987, 46–7, 67; Green 1997, 176–8; Alexander and Pullinger 1999, 45–7, 53–4). Lions denote the all-devouring jaws of death over life, while in the North-West provinces the depiction of African beasts evokes the fecundity of that continent as a symbol of the underworld, teeming with strange and threatening creatures (Henig 1984). Rams and bulls, as well as being sacrificial animals, are also images of fecundity, as are the human lovers, while the lyre-player, the good shepherd, the panthers of Dionysus-Bacchus and the lions through their association with Cybele are images of resurrection (Degen 1984; Henig 1977, 356; Henig and Wickenden 1988, 107). The Silchester handle unites the three themes in a single image, the dog as guide and guardian of the soul on the journey to the underworld, and the coupling pair demonstrating not only fecundity but also rebirth through the cycle of new life evidenced by the female's swollen teats.

The deposition of this razor is laden with meaning not only by reason of its context but also from the associations of the scene shown on the handle; moreover, as a continental-made and uniquely beautiful object, expensive in both material as well as execution, its deliberate burial would not have been lightly undertaken. What remains obscure is whether or not its deposition was directly related to the two dogs in the primary fill of the feature. If genuinely associated, it may be seen as either a grave gift accompanying the burial of a pair of valued dogs or as a votive offering connected with the ritual life of the inhabitants of Insula IX. Even if not associated, it is undoubtedly a deliberate deposit. The possibility that it might have been used in the skinning of dogs, for which there is some evidence in this part of the site, is a potentially new use for this type of object that could impact on the interpretation of the related British and continental material.

Pit 3406 (Object 500033)

The early to mid-third-century pit 3406 contained a large and varied number of objects, with dress accessories, hobnails from footwear and household items predominating. Datable items include early Roman hairpins and one with a globular head (FIG. 59, No. 57, SF 2918), a form that first appears in the mid-second century and was still in use in the fourth century (Crummy 1983, 21–2, Type 3; 1992, 144). Groups of hobnails, in one case consisting of at least 32 examples, were scattered throughout the fill. These clusters are unlikely to derive from a single pair of nailed shoes, sandals or boots but point to the disposal of old footwear over a period of time. The pit may have remained open for waste disposal or was dug for the immediate burial of midden waste. A degree of economic wealth in Insula IX at this period, matched only by the razor deposited in pit 2601, is attested by a silver-in-glass bead (FIG. 59, No. 58, SF 3178) and a short length of gold wire threaded through a bead of beryl (FIG. 59, No. 59, SF 2203). A similar fragment from a beryl and gold wire necklace has been found at Colchester (Crummy 1983, fig. 36, 1422–3); such necklaces were no doubt continental-made items imported for sale by merchants trading in jewellery in the major towns of Roman Britain. Household items from the pit include a long iron rod with knobbed head that may be from a piece of furniture, a large fragment from a low-walled shale platter, with a diameter of about 280 mm (FIG. 59, No. 60, SF 2900), and a sherd from a smaller concave shale vessel, probably a bowl (FIG. 59, No. 61, SF 3148). The platter is similar in size to platters from Silchester and London (Lawson 1976, 262, 80; Marsden 1967, 53, fig. 54).

Two unusual bone implements from pit 3406, both made from long bones, are probably craft tools. One is a long point with a worn tip, the sides of its square-section shaft polished from use (FIG. 59, No. 62, SF 2914). The other has two prongs at one end and has been hollowed out, probably to take a handle in a different material. It also has a perforation cut into one side of the shaft; the sides of the hole are worn but it is not absolutely circular (FIG. 60, No. 63, SF 3097). The prongs also show signs of wear. Shorter double-pronged tools of the medieval period are sometimes described as lucets, used in braid-making, or as thread-twisters, although this identification, or any association with textile manufacture, has not been proven (Walton Rogers 1997, 1790; MacGregor *et al.* 1999, 1994–5). Walton Rogers gives lack of wear on the medieval pronged tools from York as one reason for discounting them as lucets. The wear on the prongs of the Silchester tool may go some way to supporting its identification as such a tool, but its size and sturdiness militate against its use in delicate work and make it more suitable for use in a craft where a greater degree of force would be necessary. Both tools would be suitable for use as awls in leather-working.

Pit 3102 (Object 500034)

The fill of pit 3102 has also been dated to the third century. As with pit 3406, this feature contained scattered groups of hobnails and appears to have been open for some time. Like pit 5693 above and cess-pit 4835 in Object 500029 (the northern pits, see above), it also contained three joiner's dogs that probably come from timbers lining or bracing the sides of the pit, or from a wooden lid, both possible if the pit was in use for a prolonged period. Many of the other objects found in the pit consist of small pieces of scrap, but they include a rake prong — an object type chiefly used in horticulture or for clearing up animal bedding or dung, although this example came from the gravel capping of the pit and may have been used and lost during the course of this work.

Well 5735 (Object 500037)

Among the iron fragments from well 5735 was part of a bucket handle and a joiner's dog, the former perhaps lost during use, the latter perhaps from a wooden superstructure or cover (see above). Organic items, rare in the dry soils of Silchester, consisted of a few scraps of leather and a wooden writing-tablet. Some of the leather may derive from footwear, as groups of hobnails were also found, but two pieces are offcuts, pointing to leather-working in the area. FIG. 60, No. 64, SF 4386 is a maplewood single-leaf writing-tablet (FIG. 36; Watson, below, pp. 116-17), the surface countersunk and scored to hold wax, with the remains of a handle at the top that has broken across a small hole for suspension.

Another remarkable item from the well is the handle from a *Fusshenkelkrug* or foot-handle jug (FIGS 37 and 60, No. 65, SF 4399). These are elegant composite vessels with a cast handle soldered to the body, its terminal in the form of a human foot. Either the right foot or the left, or sometimes both, may be shown; they may be naked or sandalled, with the sandal usually formed of applied white-metal strips. The toenails on SF 4399 are marked, as is usual, but the foot is otherwise quite plain, with no scarring from any appliqués. On some handles the joints of the toes are shown, and the detailing may extend to a realistically modelled leg with defined calf muscles. There is often a small curled leaf above the foot, which on the Silchester handle appears as a knob-like projection. On SF 4399 the top of the handle is marked by a cross between marginal lines. The thumb-rest is usually, although not invariably, in the form of a curled leaf, as here, and the side terminals are often shown as the heads of water birds. The shape of a bird's head with its long beak is clear on the surviving terminal of the Silchester handle (compare with Tassinari 1975, pl. 34, 174 and 179), but the incised decoration is vegetal, obscuring the image. This supports Szabó's suggestion that the detailing on these jugs was done by professional engravers who had not been involved in the manufacture of the mould (1983, 93).

Jugs of this type have a wide distribution from Thrace across to Britain, although they are not particularly numerous. Most examples come from Pannonia, Germany and Gallia Belgica, where they lie along the trade routes of the Danube and Rhine, with a further trail along the Rhône and Saône in Gaul (Reinach 1894, 333, no. 340; *Germ. Rom.* 1924, A2 V, Taf. 7, 4; Radnóti 1938, 167–8; den Boesterd 1956, 81–2, nos 288–90; Tassinari 1973; Szabó 1981; 1983; Vanvinckenroye 1984, 215; Sedlmayer 1999, Karte 3; Pirling 1993; Nenova-Merdjanova 1998). Tassinari has divided them into two groups, an eastern form with ovoid body and a western form with taller and more slender baluster-shaped body, but there is some overlap; an example of the eastern form has even been found in Britain (Crummy 2006c). Szabó suggested that the western form was the earlier, probably being produced in a Gaulish workshop in the late first century A.D., with production then spreading to the Danube region in the second century. Sedlmayer has argued that the more scattered distribution of the eastern form is evidence for a workshop in the Rhine-Danube area aiming principally for an export market. Mould fragments have also been found in both Spain and Syria, demonstrating that, as with distribution, the true pattern of production is more complex than these studies suggest.

Many examples of the eastern form come from graves, while the western examples have often been found in association with rivers, wells and springs in or near sanctuary sites, suggesting that they were purpose-made ritual, rather than domestic, vessels. In a combination of both contexts, a western-type jug was found with pottery vessels in a hoard in a cemetery at Tongeren, Belgium (Vanvinckenroye 1984, 215). The recovery of the Silchester handle from a well makes this a clear example of the association of the vessels from the western provinces with watery contexts, and we can assume that it was a votive offering. Had it simply parted from the vessel when it was lowered down the well to be filled, the body would also have been recovered.

The Silchester handle represents the fourth such jug known from Britain, the others being complete. A slender example of the western type is one of three jugs found at Hauxton Mill, Cambs. (Hurrell 1904, 496, pl. 23, b; Liversidge 1958, 11; Eggers 1966, Abb. 39, c). Its terminal shows a pair of naked feet peeping out from beneath rudimentary drapery, a feature that derives from an earlier Graeco-Roman tradition. The circumstances of the find are unfortunately obscure; the jugs may be from a hoard or grave deposit, or, like the Tongeren find, a combination of both. One of the other jugs has a trefoil mouth, a first-century form that supports the late first-century A.D. date for the appearance of foot-handle jugs proposed by Szabó, but there is unfortunately no guarantee that all three vessels were directly associated when buried. Hauxton lies on the river

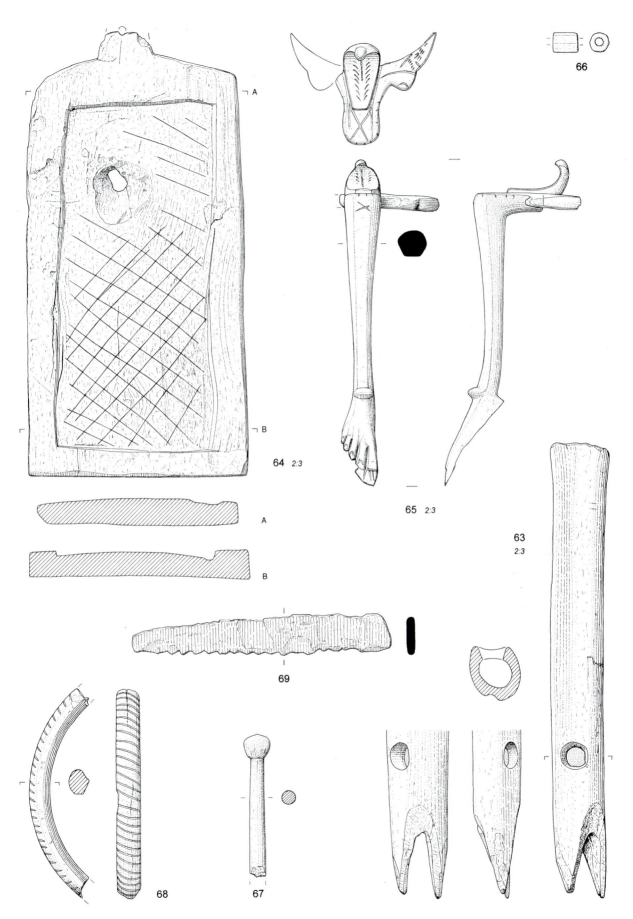

FIG. 60. Small finds: Period 4 south-eastern pits (2) (Object 500017). Scale 1:1 except Nos 63–5 (2:3). (*Drawn by Brian Williams*)

Granta, a location that enhances the possibility that this jug matches the watery associations noted in many of the other western finds. A second western-type jug, also showing a pair of feet, was found at Corbridge in a probable dark earth layer within the eastern military compound just south of the Stanegate (Site 43; Forster and Knowles 1913, 7). Three temples lay on the other side of the compound wall, and a bone plaque carved with the image of a Mother Goddess bearing a mound or basket of fruit in her lap was found near the jug (ibid., 234, 275–6, fig. 22). The compound wall appears to deny any association between the jug and plaque and one or other of the three temples, but their proximity is tantalising; perhaps the objects were tossed over the wall during a clearance or demolition project? The third complete jug is of the ovoid-bodied eastern form. It was found at Heybridge, Essex, in a small pit on a plot of land fronting the approach road to the site's temple precinct (Crummy 2006c, 6), so, as with the Corbridge jug, its association with a temple is close but not direct. The terminal on the Heybridge jug consists of only a right foot, the leaf at the top of the handle has been transformed into a lotus bud, with the calyx incorporating the angular terminals that are here at a considerable remove from the original bird's heads (ibid., fig. 2).

The wooden writing-tablet
By Jacqui Watson

A wooden writing-tablet (SF 4386) (FIGS 36 and 60, No. 64) was found in the basal fill (6436) of well 5735 (for the full conservation report, see Watson 2008). The context in which the tablet was found has been dated to *c.* A.D. 200 (above, pp. 43–4), which puts this example rather later than the more commonly recorded writing-tablets from the first and second centuries. The writing-tablet is made of maple (*Acer* sp.), not the expected silver fir, larch or cedar (see below), and the object seems to be roughly made from a single piece of wood, with little attempt made to produce a neat and symmetrical piece. On closer examination it was possible to see that fine lines have been cut into the surface which would have held the wax. Another piece of wood was attached to the front of the writing-tablet and was identified as being a piece of oak (*Quercus* sp.) and therefore not part of the broken handle as hoped.

Analysis

Attempts were made to see if any traces of wax might remain by examining the object under UV light and using Fourier Transform Infra-Red spectroscopy (FTIR). Unfortunately both techniques proved inconclusive. No traces of wax showed under UV light, but some waxes such as beeswax do not fluoresce. It was possible to produce a FTIR spectrum, but no definite match was found, so samples have been retained for further analysis when more comparative spectra are available.

Wax writing-tablets

Wax writing-tablets have been found on a number of sites in Britain, but most have come from Roman forts along Hadrian's Wall and are associated with the military occupation, and date to the first and second centuries. The woods used for these objects form a small group including silver fir, larch, and cedar, with a few examples of maple or sweet chestnut (see Table 12). Silver fir and larch are native to upland areas of southern Europe, while cedar was more common in the eastern Mediterranean territories of the Roman Empire (Hather 2000, 38–43; Gale and Cutler 2000, 375). Sweet chestnut is not a native tree to the British Isles, and is presumed to have been introduced by the Romans. Out of the five wood species recorded for wax writing-tablets only the examples made from maple could have come from local supplies of timber. Field maple has already been identified among the charcoal residues from Silchester (Smith 2002, 28), and would have been available in the local woodland.

The shape of this writing-tablet is also unusual and more detail was revealed when the object was completely dry and it was possible to remove the soil and concretions from the wood surface. The hole at one end was in fact a knot-hole where the knot in the original piece of timber had

TABLE 12. WOODS USED FOR WRITING-TABLETS FROM VARIOUS SITES IN ROMAN BRITAIN.

	Alder	Birch	Willow	Maple	Silver fir	Larch	Cedar	Sweet chestnut
Vindolanda, Hadrian's Wall[1]	▲	▲	▲			●		
Carlisle, Annetwell St.[2]	▲				●		●	
Carlisle, Millenium excs.[3]							●	
Corbridge. Hadrian's Wall[4]				■	●			●
London, St Thomas' St.[5]					●			
London, St Magnus House[6]					●		●	
Groundwell Ridge, Wilts[7]						●		
Silchester, Hants				■				

▲ ink writing-tablets made from native wood species
■ wax writing-tablets made from native wood species
● wax writing-tablets made from non-native wood

[1] Bowman and Thomas 1983; [2] Jones 1991; [3] Watson pers. comm.; [4] Watson 1987; [5] Keepax 1975; [6] Gale and Cutler 2000; [7] Fell *et al.* 2008

fallen out at some point, probably before burial. It also became clear that all the recessed area had been cut with fine cross-hatched lines, possibly to help key in the thin wax surface; they were not vestiges of writing or graffiti.

This object has probably been whittled out of a piece of wood with a knife, which has resulted in the block having uneven edges and an undulating surface. On the reverse one can see the shallow and slightly discoloured depressions as a result of trying to obtain a flat surface with a short bladed knife rather than using a much larger bladed draw-knife where it would have been possible to produce an even surface by removing one or two shavings of wood.

The handle is broken at the point where a hole has been made for suspension, leaving a dark coloured depression (FIG. 60, No. 64). However, no evidence remains to suggest how the writing-tablet was suspended in use.

Most of the wax writing-tablets that have been found on British sites conform not only to a small specific group of wood species but also to a fairly uniform size and shape; this example is different in many ways, appearing to be roughly made with materials and tools to hand. The majority also come from a different period of the Roman occupation in Britain, most having been dated to the first and second centuries, whereas this tablet comes from an early third-century context.

Unfortunately analytical work to identify traces of residual wax proved inconclusive, but samples of the silt have been retained to re-run at a later date if required.

Pit 2434 (Object 500031)

The latest of the south-east pits was backfilled in the late third century, a date supported by an unworn coin of Carausius (A.D. 287–293) (SF 01612) and the presence of three items typical of the later Roman period: a green glass hexagonal cylinder bead, a bone hairpin with globular head, and a shale armlet with incised grooves imitating cabling (FIG. 60, Nos 66–8, SFs 1826, 1755 and

1754). Hexagonal green glass beads, a cheap substitute for beryl, occur throughout the Roman period but occur more frequently in Britain in late Roman contexts, no doubt largely because the change in burial rite from cremation to inhumation allowed complete necklaces to survive (Guido 1979; Crummy 1983, 34; Riha 1990, type 11.23; Guido and Mills 1993; Bertrand 2003, 69–70). The hairpin is of the long-lived globular-headed Type 3, while the simply-achieved cable decoration on the armlet suits a date in the later third or early fourth century. The pit also contained a badly decayed sole, or pair of soles, from nailed leather footwear, preserved as 'casts' in a hard chalky deposit patchily stained yellow-green, almost certainly from cess. These features fragmented on lifting, but some of the hobnails survive intact and the pieces of leather that made up the composite sole are visible as distinct mineral-replaced layers in section. Also from pit 2434 is the blade of a small saw, one of the few craft tools in the 'City in Transition' assemblage (FIG. 60, No. 69, SF 1542). The thickened handle plate at the upper end would have been fitted with a composite organic handle. The small size of the blade is in contrast to the coarseness of the teeth, which at three teeth/cm mark this saw out as a woodworker's tool rather than a surgeon's (compare with the fourteen teeth/cm of the Stanway healer's saw (Jackson 2007, 250, fig. 121, CF47.28)).

PERIOD 4 SOUTH-EASTERN OCCUPATION (Object 700) (Appendix 2, Table 34)

As with Object 701, the material from the various levels comprising Object 700 is described in chronological sequence.

A curved pick from the path (FIG. 61, No. 70, SF 1939) is a comparatively rare object. There are other examples from London, Verulamium and Colchester (Wheeler 1930, pl. 38, 10; Waugh and Goodburn 1972, fig. 35, 76; Crummy 1983, fig. 66, 1939). They may have been used as toilet instruments, perhaps as toothpicks, as suggested by a superficial similarity to the larger types of nail-cleaner, but there is no firm evidence to support this identification.

From the make-ups for the northernmost building MRTB 5 in this area came a variety of metal fragments, among them part of a knife blade, two stylus fragments and a ring-headed pin, together with a complete iron needle with a long oval eye (FIG. 61, No. 71, SF 1997) and an acorn-shaped weight of lead with copper-alloy sheet cladding the surface (FIG. 61, No. 72, SF 1905). Traces of iron on the weight come from the suspension loop. Among the material from the northern building MRTB 5 was a split-spike loop and a damaged key, while the southern building MRTB 4 produced a well-worn hone (FIG. 61, No. 73, SF 2538), an early Roman hairpin, an iron ferrule, a fragmentary copper-alloy wire armlet and two roughly-shaped pottery counters.

The ?occupation contexts contained another wire armlet or anklet, in this case made of iron, and a variety of other personalia, such as a small ear-scoop (FIG. 61, No. 74, SF 2356), a copper-alloy hairpin of Group 3A (Cool 1990, 154), bone hairpins of Types 1 and 2 (Crummy 1983, 20–1) and a Type 2 variant (FIG. 61, No. 75, SF 2497), a fragment of a simple iron one-piece brooch (FIG. 61, No. 76, SF 2532), and an enamelled umbonate brooch of copper alloy (FIG. 61, No. 77, SF 2521). While the ?armlet may be contemporary with its context, the remaining dress accessories date to the first to second century, with the iron brooch fragment perhaps as early as the first century B.C. The undated objects from this group of contexts include a small fragment from a shale vessel and a wide variety of iron fittings: a joiner's dog, a clamp or piece of binding, a ring or collar, a rove, and part of a strap-hinge. Also present was a complete linch-pin of an unusual form, with a rectangular, rather than crescentic or spatulate, head (FIG. 61, No. 78, SF 2288; see Manning 1985, 72–4, for the commoner forms).

The make-up for the late Roman buildings in this part of the site produced a large collection of objects, many of iron and nearly all fragmentary, such as two hipposandal wings, two keys with missing teeth, parts of two knife blades, some hobnails, and a number of strips and pieces of sheet that probably derived from structural fittings and furniture; a complete stylus with twisted stem is an exception (FIG. 61, No. 79, SF 2058; Manning 1985, 85, Type 4). Non-ferrous pieces include part of an early Roman bone hairpin with lattice-decorated head (FIG. 61, No. 80, SF 1592), a complete nail-cleaner with long plain shaft (FIG. 61, No. 81, SF 1775), a decorative

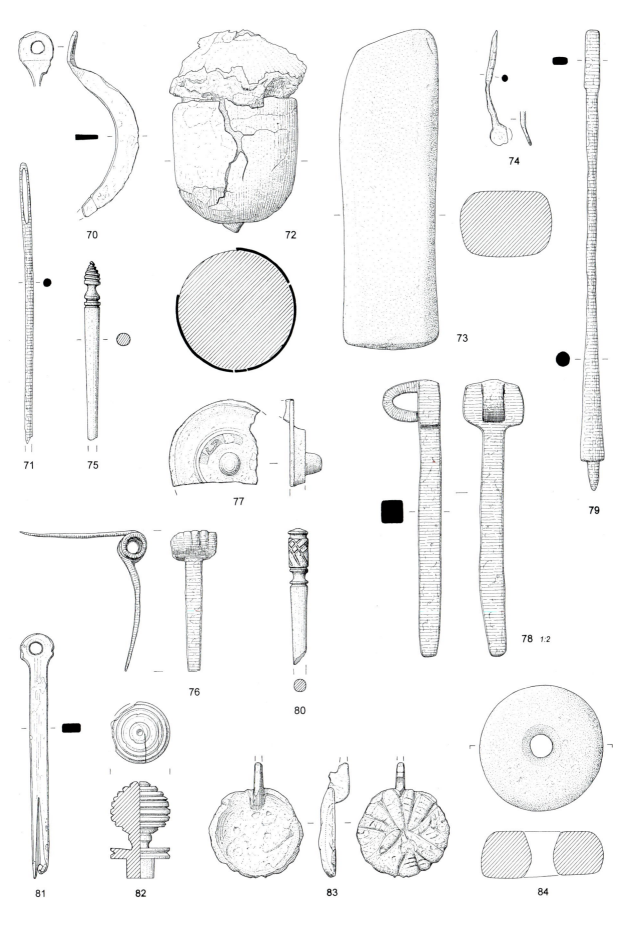

FIG. 61. Small finds: Period 4 south-eastern occupation (Object 700). Scale 1:1 except No. 78 (1:2).
(*Drawn by Brian Williams*)

ivory peg that may have come from the lid of a *pyxis* (FIG. 61, No. 82, SF 2010), a spoon bowl with decorative mouldings on the underside (FIG. 61, No. 83, SF 2224), and two spindlewhorls, one made from a reused pottery sherd, the other stone (FIG. 61, No. 84, SF 2810). Two small fragments of bar iron from the make-up derive from blacksmithing, but in this secondary context such a low number of pieces can be presumed to have travelled some distance from their initial point of disposal, as is the case with the majority of the material from the Period 4 occupation, and with that from so many of the other contexts in this assemblage.

DISCUSSION

Table 13 summarises the functional categories present in the Objects associated with Periods 3 and 4. The northern and southern buildings (MRTB 4 and 5) in Object 700 and the possible building (MRTB 3) in Object 701 have been listed separately in order to highlight their contents. The categories are those defined in Crummy 1983: Category 1, dress accessories; 2, toilet instruments; 3, textile manufacture and working; 4, household equipment; 5, recreation; 6, weighing and measuring; 7, literacy; 8, transport; 10, tools; 11, general fittings and fasteners; 12, horticulture/agriculture/animal husbandry; 13, military equipment; 15, metal-working; 16, bone-working (and here also leather-working); and 18, miscellaneous. No objects were present from Categories 9 (buildings and services, dealt with elsewhere in this volume), 17 (objects associated with the manufacture of pottery and other ceramic objects) and 14 (religion), although religious/ritual activity is evidenced by the contextual use and condition of some artefacts and will be summarised below. Items only doubtfully attributed to a category are not distinguished in Table 13 from items that are positively identified. Iron nails and slags do not form part of this chapter (Tootell, below, Ch. 11), but an unfinished copper-alloy casting, some possible copper-alloy casting waste and some offcuts from blacksmith's bar iron are included here. We should also note that querns and whetstones (household equipment) are catalogued and discussed by Hayward (below, Ch. 9).

As with the late Roman assemblage from Insula IX, the categories best represented are 1 (dress accessories), 11 (fittings) and 18 (miscellaneous), and this is a pattern that occurs on most Roman sites. The remaining categories vary from being represented by only one artefact to a substantial number of artefacts, and it can be from these groups that the character of a site emerges, such as when a high proportion of tools, craft waste, military equipment, or religious regalia points to a specific activity. On an urban site such as Insula IX an individual character only rarely emerges, blurred by earlier residual material, truncation or disturbance of surfaces, the importation of dump and make-up soils, and above all the general wide range of activities that would have taken place in and around the insula over the course of many decades or centuries. Nevertheless, individual finds or small groups of finds within a category may offer glimpses of the economic and intellectual status of the inhabitants, particularly as regards Romanization, ritual practices, literacy and access to imported goods.

The many items in Category 18 consist not only of unidentified or general pieces (such as multi-purpose rings and pieces of wire), but also of small fragments of scrap metal and bone shafts from pins, needles, or spoons. This is probably indicative of material derived from soil that has been turned over or moved, such as midden waste or make-up. The concentration of miscellaneous items outside the Period 3–4 buildings, and particularly in the south-eastern part of the site in Objects 500017, 700 and 701, which include rubbish disposal pits and layers of levelling material, make-up and dump, confirms this interpretation (FIG. 62; Table 13). This distribution pattern is repeated for many of the other functional categories, stressing the secondary nature of the contexts from which much of this assemblage derives. The fittings of Category 11 show a fairly even spread in Period 3, shifting in Period 4 to a bias to the south-eastern area, but in both periods a number of items are associated with the buildings (FIG. 63). As fittings range from copper-alloy studs and nails to iron objects such as keys or hinges, the category is perhaps too broad to allow for close interpretation, and many of the objects are in secondary contexts such as make-up or other imported material, but in some instances a direct connection with a building or its contents may be reasonably assumed, such as the iron latchlifter from MB 3 (Object 50046).

TABLE 13. SUMMARY OF FUNCTIONAL CATEGORIES REPRESENTED IN EACH OBJECT
(For categories, see p. 120)

Object	Category														
	1	2	3	4	5	6	7	8	10	11	12	13	15	16	18
50037	9	5	1	3	3	-	1	1	2	11	-	-	-	-	25
50018	9	-	1	-	2	-	-	-	2	5	-	-	2	-	12
50019	6	3	1	-	1	-	-	-	1	3	-	-	-	-	6
50046	19	2	2	6	5	-	2	1	1	12	1	-	-	-	23
500017/pit 3406	15	-	-	3	-	-	-	1	4	3	-	-	-	-	16
500017/pit 3102	11	-	-	-	1	-	-	-	-	4	1	-	-	-	15
500017/pit 5693	-	1	-	-	-	-	-	-	-	2	-	-	-	-	3
500017/well 5735	4	-	-	2	-	-	1	-	-	1	-	-	-	1	4
500017/well 1750	1	-	-	-	-	-	-	-	-	-	-	-	-	-	-
500017/pit 2434	4	-	-	-	-	-	-	-	1	1	-	-	-	-	4
500017/pit 2601	-	1	-	-	-	-	-	-	-	-	-	-	-	-	-
500017/pit 5039	-	-	-	-	-	-	-	-	-	-	-	-	-	1	2
500017/pit 6290	3	-	1	-	1	-	-	-	-	-	-	-	-	-	3
50029/pit 4835	-	-	-	1	-	-	-	-	-	2	-	-	-	-	2
50029/well 2234	-	-	-	1	2	-	1	1	-	-	-	-	-	-	-
701, general	20	7	2	10	7	-	2	1	4	16	2	1	7	-	64
701, ?building	-	-	1	3	-	-	-	-	-	1	-	-	-	-	4
700, general	18	3	3	4	1	1	5	3	3	23	-	-	3	-	44
700, northern building	1	-	-	-	-	-	-	-	-	3	-	-	-	-	4
700, southern building	2	-	-	-	2	-	-	-	1	3	-	-	1	-	2
Totals	122	22	12	33	25	1	12	8	19	90	4	1	13	2	233

The dress accessories of Category 1 largely conform to this bias to the south-eastern part of the site, although hobnails are concentrated in Period 4 and in only a limited number of contexts, and there is a markedly different concentration of hairpins in a different area in the same period (FIG. 64; Table 13). This might be taken as indicative of different methods of disposal for different items, but is more likely to be the result of different context types deposited at different times. Brooches are more generally scattered across the site, including in the footprints of the Period 3–4 buildings, but most are again likely to be secondary in these contexts as many predate Period 3 (FIG. 64). For example, a second-century enamelled umbonate brooch (FIG. 61, No. 77, SF 2521) was found in Object 700 in association with other early dress accessories and like them was residual (Table 34, Appendix 2).

The brooch assemblage is dominated by copper-alloy Nauheim derivatives of the type that arrived in Britain at the Conquest and continued in use until c. A.D. 80/5 (pace Corney 2000, 337). Nauheim derivatives are present in Objects 50037, 50018, 50019, 50046 and 701, but are noticeably absent from the pit groups, Objects 500017 and 500029, and from Object 700. Other first-century brooch types also occur in many of these Objects, some pre-Conquest (Colchester,

Period 3: Miscellaneous finds

Period 4: Miscellaneous finds

FIG. 62.   Distributions of miscellaneous small finds in Periods 3 (upper) and 4 (lower) (Category 18).

FIG. 63. Distributions of fittings in Periods 3 (upper) and 4 (lower) (Category 11).

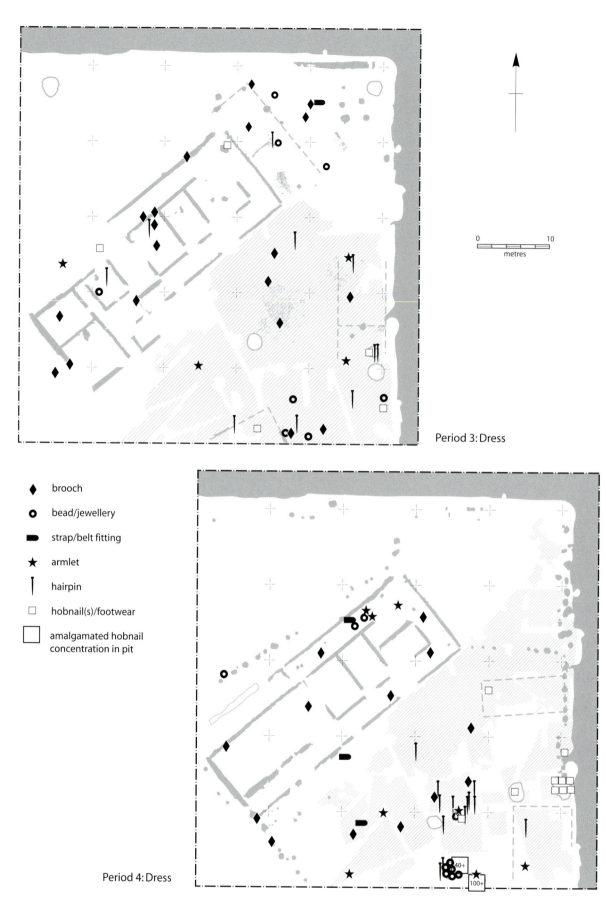

FIG. 64.   Distributions of dress accessories in Periods 3 (upper) and 4 (lower) (Category 1).

Langton Down) and some post-Conquest (Hod Hill, Colchester B and BB derivatives). The dating of these forms in Britain is sufficiently well-established to define them as certainly residual in mid to late second- and third-century contexts. The presence of these early brooches in the features and layers associated with the Period 3–4 buildings can therefore be presumed to be the result of the movement of soil about the area in the course of building works or the manuring of cultivated areas with well-rotted midden waste. In some cases, particularly in the deposits pre-dating MB 1 (Object 50018), first-century brooches might have been used as foundation deposits, or perhaps termination deposits for earlier buildings. Another possible explanation for the presence of some early brooches in later contexts is that they are debris cleared from a nearby temple or shrine, as may also be the case with other items (see below).

The absence of early brooch types from the pit groups points to their no longer being available for disposal in the second and third centuries, and in the case of Object 700 it seems that the soils being utilised no longer contained first-century material. This observation impacts not only upon the date of the other small finds in these various Objects, but most particularly upon the period of manufacture of the forms of early Roman bone hairpins in the pits and in Object 700. Simple tapering-shafted conical-headed Type 1 and 2 hairpins date from the mid-first century into the second century, but it has not been firmly established how long into the second century they were used, and how much they overlapped with the later swollen-shafted globular-headed Type 3, which appeared at the earliest c. A.D. 150 and continued to be used into the late fourth century (Crummy 1983, 20–3; 1992, 144). Only two Type 3 hairpins have been found in the 'City in Transition' assemblage (FIG. 59, No. 57, SF 2918 and FIG. 60, No. 67, SF 1755), respectively in pit 3406, backfilled in the early to mid-third century, and in pit 2434, backfilled in the late third century. Pit 3406 also contained a Type 1 hairpin, suggesting that the early forms continued in use until at least c. A.D. 200/225, giving a broad 50/75-year period for the straight-sided forms to fall into disuse and the swollen-shafted forms to be established as the norm. In practice the change is likely to have been swifter and perhaps centred upon c. A.D. 200.

Unlike the small finds associated with the masonry buildings, the assemblage from the timber building (MRTB 1/ERTB 1 = Object 50037) contains several objects that are likely to be closely associated with its occupation. They include three brooches dating to the late first to second century: two T-shaped brooches, one with Polden Hill spring mechanism, (FIG. 54, Nos 1–2, SFs 2985 and 3256) and a penannular brooch (FIG. 54, No. 6, SF 2877). All three, together with a hairpin of Cool's Group 6 (FIG. 54, No. 5, SF 2860), would suit a late Flavian/Trajanic/Hadrianic date, and to them can be added a crude lead candelabrum that dates at the earliest to the Antonine period. While acknowledging the presence of residual first-century material in Object 50037, this particular combination of artefacts could therefore be defined as late Hadrianic/early Antonine, a date that agrees with that of the early occupation of the building.

Rites of foundation seem to have been behind the deposition of two complete toilet sets in MB 2 (=Object 50019), one from a floor and the other from a wall, and this enhances the presumption that the brooches mentioned above, and also a complete toilet set from MRTB 1/ERTB 1 (=Object 50037), were also used in this way. In early Roman London complete toilet sets show a marked concentration on the Middle Walbrook valley, where, along with a mass of other metalwork, they were used as votive deposits associated with the Walbrook stream (Crummy with Pohl 2008, 18–19). The various Object tables (Appendix 2) and FIG. 65 show that all three of the complete toilet sets on Insula IX are associated with buildings, while most of the individual instruments and other grooming equipment, such as mirrors, stirring rods, and long-handled toilet spoons, are more widely scattered. This is not to say that single toilet instruments were not also used as votives, and some of the tweezers and nail-cleaners from other parts of the site may have been used in this way, particularly if there had been a shrine or temple close to Insula IX, as has been suggested above. Some sanctuary sites, such as Woodeaton in Oxfordshire, Harlow in Essex and the shrine of Apollo at Nettleton, Wiltshire, have produced high proportions of individual toilet instruments, especially nail-cleaners, which have been shown to be a peculiarly Romano-British survival from the La Tène period. The influence of Roman grooming practices seems to have driven nail-cleaners out of use in Gaul and Germany during the Augustan period, whereas the conquest of Britain produced an upsurge in production and a wider percolation

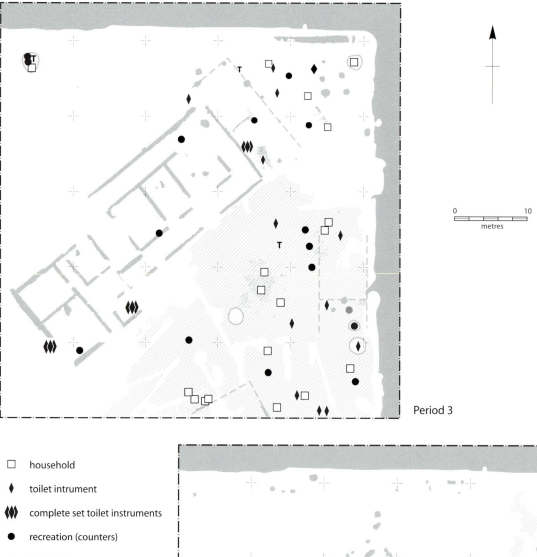

Period 3

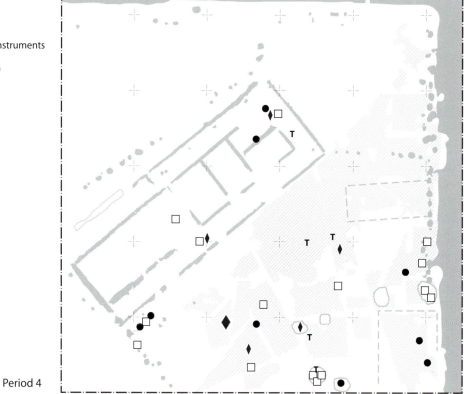

☐ household

◆ toilet intrument

◀◀◀ complete set toilet instruments

● recreation (counters)

T transport

Period 4

FIG. 65. Distributions of toilet instruments, household items, and items relating to recreation and transport in Periods 3 (upper) and 4 (lower) (Categories 2, 4, 5 and 8).

of their use throughout a wider section of society, particularly in southern and central Britain. The proportion of nail-cleaners is higher from small settlements and rural sites than from major towns, and their use as votives, whether individually or as part of a set, was probably driven by their close association with the person and their wider availability for both use and ritual deposition, although they may also have held a deeper resonance for an early Romano-Briton than these considerations imply (Eckardt and Crummy 2008, 69–72, 96–7, 103–4).

In general the contexts associated with the timber building produced objects from a broad range of functional categories, and those associated with the masonry buildings are similar in character (Table 13). Even though a high proportion of items in these Object assemblages are residual, they represent a typical cross-section of the material likely to be found in an average Romano-British urban setting. As well as the dress accessories in Category 1, other small personalia from Categories 2 and 5 are present, together with domestic items from Category 4 and fittings from Category 11 (FIG. 65). Household equipment in the assemblage is largely represented by bone spoons and shale vessels; notable exceptions are a fragment of a bucket handle and the handle from a jug, both from well 5735, although the latter probably had a religious function. The jug handle is discussed in detail above, and, as well as perhaps being from a vessel used in ritual activity, its final use may well have been as an *ex voto*. The bone spoons from Insula IX can be equated to some extent with the early Roman hairpins. They were early imports to the province, no doubt arriving as personal equipment with soldiers and immigrant civilians and rapidly being adopted by the wider Romano-British population. There is evidence for their manufacture and for that of Type 1 and 2 hairpins at Winchester and at Woodcuts Common on Cranborne Chase, Dorset (Crummy 2001, 97–9; Rees *et al.* 2008, 182–94). How long they remained in use is not clear. Although present in second-century assemblages, they are certainly absent from those of the fourth century (ibid.). Whether or not they were used in at least the early years of the third century is uncertain. Seven are listed in the 'City in Transition' catalogue: one from MRTB 1/ ERTB 1 (=Object 50037), the Period 3 timber buildings, and six from Object 701. Of the latter, three came from general contexts within this Object, and a remarkable three from the possible building MRTB 3 in this area. The idiosyncratic nature of the collection of items from the possible building MRTB 3 — principally made from bone and with a high proportion of spoons — provides the structure with a degree of 'authenticity', albeit somewhat diluted by the presence of the other three spoons from scattered contexts in the same Object. As this possible building cut the late second-century silts, it is likely that these spoons were being used up to *c*. A.D. 200 or into the first decade of so of the third century.

Evidence for recreation (Category 5) is present in some quantity, chiefly outside the footprints of the buildings but in some instances inside them (FIG. 65). All these items are counters of bone, glass, recycled pot sherds, and in one instance a piece of tile. Some of the ceramic pieces may have been used for other purposes, particularly the larger ones, but most of these counters would have been used for Roman-style board games such as *ludus latrunculorum* and *duodecim scripta* or for an early version of the Celtic game known in the British medieval sources as *fidhcheall* in Ireland and *gwyddbwyll* in Wales (Schädler 2007, 369–74). Items associated with transport (Category 8) are comparatively low in number and all relate to vehicles and driven animals: fragments of hipposandals, a terret and a linch pin (FIG. 65). None are necessarily related directly to the inhabitants of Insula IX, but they provide a glimpse of how important the movement of goods and people was to urban life.

Apart from a few items associated with spinning and sewing, which are arguably domestic crafts (Category 3), and also some possible bronze-working fragments (Category 15) from the floors of MB 1 (Object 50018), craft- and occupation-specific equipment is markedly absent from the buildings (Table 13; FIGS 66–67). As has already been shown by the dislocation between the dates of some objects and the period of use of the timber and masonry buildings, some of these items are in secondary contexts and need not relate directly to the occupations and the lives of the inhabitants of the insula, but not all rubbish will travel far from its point of origin and so others must.

A noticeable dearth of weighing and measuring equipment (Category 6), with only one large weight having been found in Period 4 (Object 700), suggests that little or no commercial activity

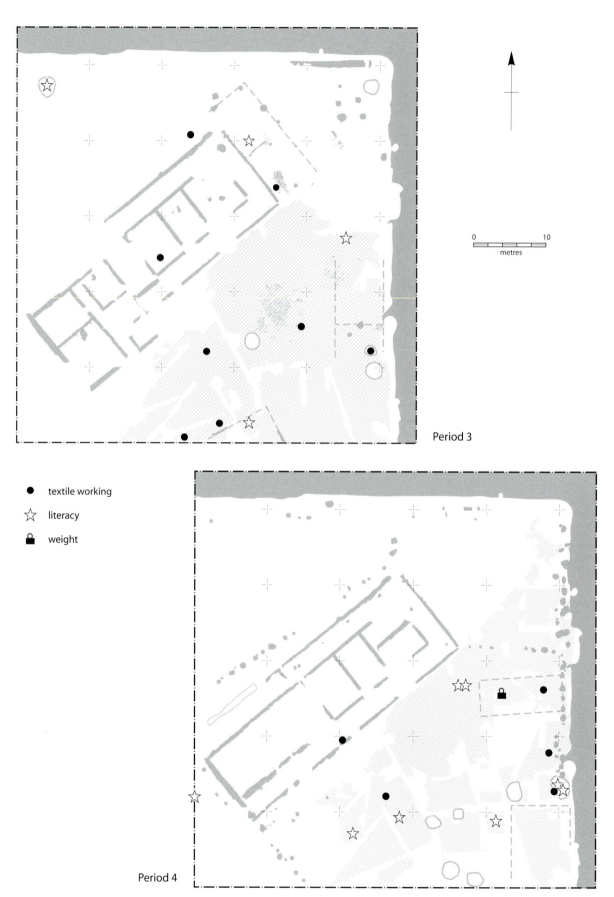

FIG. 66.   Distributions of items relating to textile working, weighing and literacy in Periods 3 (upper) and 4 (lower) (Categories 3, 6 and 7).

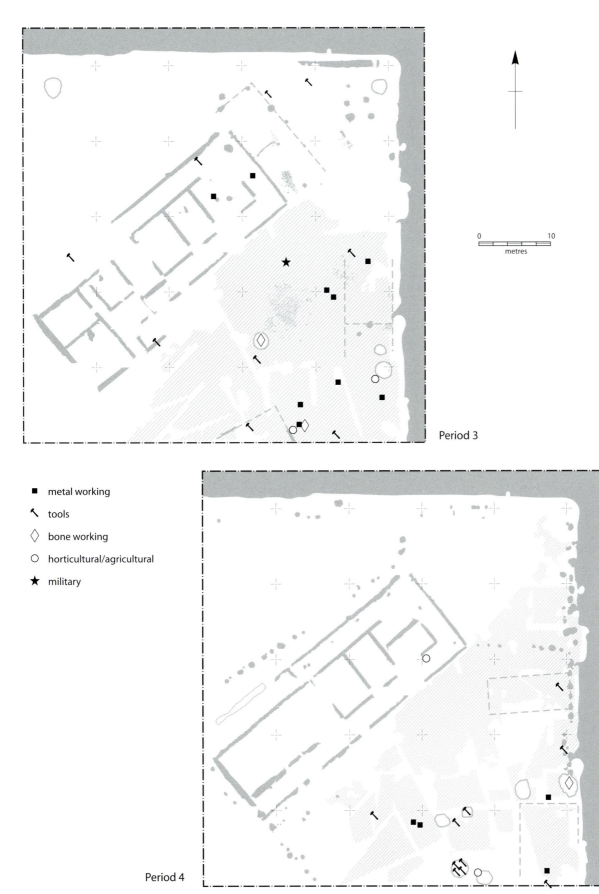

FIG. 67. Distributions of tools, horticultural/agricultural equipment and military equipment, and items relating to metal and bone-working in Periods 3 (upper) and 4 (lower) (Categories 10, 12, 13, 15 and 16).

took place on Insula IX (an observation that might correlate with the paucity of coins from Periods 3 and 4); it is also interesting to note that, while there are a few styli from the buildings (Category 7), the only substantial number also comes from Period 4 (Object 700), two of them from the same make-up context as the weight, and therefore secondary in that context and possibly derived from the same source beyond the insula itself (FIG. 66). There is also a writing-tablet from well 5735. In general the number of styli from Insula IX is fairly high. While this can in part be attributed to the generally good state of preservation of ironwork from the site, it also implies a considerably degree of literacy among the inhabitants of *Calleva*. The presence of styli but absence of seal-boxes from this part of the Insula IX assemblage is matched in the suburbs of Roman Winchester, and may relate both to the type of documents on which seal-boxes were used and the social context of their use (Rees *et al.* 2008, 138–9).

Only four items are associated with horticulture and animal husbandry (Category 12), two goad pricks and two rake prongs. One prick and one prong come from Object 700, the second prick from the construction clays for MB 3 Object 50046 and the second prong from the gravel capping of pit 3102 in Object 500034; only the latter may be in a primary context, although even this is doubtful (FIG. 67). While this provides very little indication that gardening and the keeping of animals took place on Insula IX, it can be linked to the broader picture presented by the objects associated with transport, the animal bone assemblage and the evidence for diet, particularly herbs and spices, demonstrated by the environmental assemblage. Goad pricks may alternatively relate to the possibility that there was a temple or shrine close to Insula IX, as five were found at the shrine of Apollo at Nettleton and one from the shrine of Nodens at Lydney, where they can be associated with driving animals to sacrifice (Wedlake 1982, 49; Wheeler and Wheeler 1932, 189).

Only one piece of military equipment was found, a first-century phalera that is clearly residual in its context (Category 13). That it was recovered from Object 701 is no doubt simply a reflection of the greater number of items from that Object than from any other (FIG. 67). It should be seen in the context of a small quantity of other pieces of early militaria recovered from contexts pre-dating Period 3, together with brooches with military associations, such as Aucissas, Hod Hills and also to some extent Nauheim derivatives, and also the similar material from earlier excavations (e.g. Corney 2000; Boon 2000).

Although there are no finds from Periods 3 and 4 on Insula IX that are specific to Category 14, which covers material with an overtly religious use, the beliefs of its inhabitants have nevertheless been touched on above with regard to rite of deposition. Probable ritual deposits from Period 3 include a mason's trowel in MB 2 (=Object 50019), two brooches and a knife in MB 1 (=Object 50018), a hairpin from MB 2 (=Object 50019), and the complete toilet sets from MB 2 (=Objects 50019) and MRTB 1/ERTB 1 (=50037). Another possible votive is the jug handle from the Period 4 well 5735. The clearest example of formal placement is undoubtedly the razor or knife with zoomorphic ivory handle from the Period 4 pit 2601. The handle clearly resonates with the importance of the dog in the religious life of Silchester (Fulford 2001, 201–2), and the animal's association with a wide range of deities, often those credited with healing or chthonic powers, provides deeper levels of complexity to the deposition of this object in its context. It also implies access to Continental markets in these high-quality items. High-status, continental-made objects do not figure large in the Insula IX Period 3 and Period 4 assemblage, being limited to this handle, a silver-in-glass bead and a fragment of a necklace of beryl and gold found in pit 3406, a decorative ivory peg that is probably all that remains of a *pyxis* from Object 700, and the jug handle from well 5735, all of Period 4. To these can be added a gold stud from Period 3 Object 701 which may be of British or continental origin. That these items existed in isolation is unlikely, especially given the presence of imported pottery on the site, and we can perhaps infer from them a greater degree of economic wealth within Insula IX in particular and mid-Roman Silchester in general than their number seems to imply.

It has been stated above, in the contexts of various groups of finds, that there may have been a temple or shrine adjacent to Insula IX. In an urban context the teasing out of votive from domestic is not necessarily straightforward, witness the literature regarding the Middle Walbrook assemblage (e.g. Merrifield 1965, 93; 1987, 26–7; 1995; Wilmott 1991; Maloney 1991), and

Insula IX is no exception. This is a gradually emerging picture that will be more fully explored at a later date, but it is informed by the presence of such artefact types as goad pricks, a high number of toilet instruments and other personalia, including deliberately bent, broken or rolled dress accessories. A number of items that directly reference health and good fortune are also present in the wider assemblage.

Metal-working (Category 15) is comparatively well-represented here, although not in any great quantity and scattered across the site and across the periods (FIG. 67). It is more fully dealt with elsewhere in this volume (Cook, above, Ch. 3; J.R.L. Allen and Tootell, below, Ch. 11). Again, the high number from Period 3 Object 701 reflects the greater quantity of material in general from that context group. Some of the items recovered are offcuts of bar iron from blacksmithing, while copper alloy working is represented both by casting waste and by an unfinished hinge, the latter also providing evidence for the manufacture of high-quality wooden objects at Silchester, although not necessarily on Insula IX. Category 10 covers general tools, which are similarly scarce (FIG. 67) and none are craft-specific, although the possibility that the zoomorphic razor or knife handle was used in the skinning of dogs raises new questions regarding this class of artefact (pp. 110–13). Two crude bone tools from Period 4 pit 3406 are likely to have been made locally. Although their precise functions are unclear, they are evidence for craft activity in Insula IX, possibly leather-working, which is supported by the recovery of two leather offcuts from Period 4 well 5735. Bone-working is represented by a single fragment, probably an unfinished hairpin, from Period 3 pit 5039 (Category 16). Evidence for bone-working as an intensive craft activity should consist of mixed dumps of discarded offcuts and unfinished or blundered items at various stages of manufacture, sometimes together with the processed but unused raw material, and this is not present here (Crummy 2001, 100; Rees *et al.* 2008, 182–94). This single piece points rather to *ad hoc* manufacture, which is already attested by the two crude tools from pit 3406. Home production of bone and antler objects seems to have taken place occasionally throughout the Roman period, perhaps because the standard products of specialist bone-workers were not always available (Crummy 2001, 102).

As far as the material from the northern and south-eastern pits and wells is concerned, these features contain material from a wide range of functional categories but this is clearly not because a greater number of artefacts was recovered from these contexts, as is the case in Objects 700 and 701. Some of the material may well have been scraped up from surrounding topsoil when the features were backfilled, but in general the artefacts seem to represent a true sample of contemporary detritus. An intriguing characteristic from some of the features is the recovery of joiner's dogs in several pits or wells, suggesting that they derive from superstructures or coverings that were broken up and buried as each open hole was backfilled (FIG. 63). Little organic material was recovered and most of the leather scraps that were found probably come from shoes or sandals, also represented by considerable quantities of hobnails (FIG. 64). The writing-tablet from Period 4 well 5735 is unusual both in form and in manufacture from maplewood rather than an imported softwood; it is probably a local product (above, pp. 116–17).

In terms of date, it had been hoped that Periods 3 and 4 at Silchester might present a clear difference between them as far as artefact type was concerned or at least allow the definition of a mid-Roman assemblage that was characterised by the presence of certain types of artefact rather than the absence of earlier and later material. That little progress in either respect has been made is no doubt partly due to the broad date ranges attributed to many artefact types as well as to the high level of residuality. Many objects are residual first-century pieces in second–century contexts, and there is some likelihood that many pieces in third-century contexts are similarly residual from the second century. The items that can be dated to the third century (or later) with reasonable certainty are few in number and come from Period 4 Objects 50046 and 700 and pits 3406 and 3102 in Object 500017. There are also a couple of 'late' finds in Period 3 Object 701. More broadly 'late' material is also present, in some cases later than the date range for Period 4 might easily accommodate. A copper-alloy needle in Object 50046 is the only distinctively late third-century and later object from the Period 4 masonry building. Two fourth-century armlet fragments also came from Object 50046, but from contexts post-dating the abandonment and demolition of the building rather than its occupation. Period 4 pit 3406 contained a bone peg, a jet bead and a silver-in-glass bead, all late Roman artefact-types (although in the case of the silver-in-glass bead not confined to that period), and other bone pegs came from Period 4 pit 3102 and Object 700. These tapering straight-sided pegs may be hairpins, but they appear at a time when other hairpins have swollen shanks and so almost certainly have an alternative function (Crummy 1983, 162–3). Period 4 pit 2434 contained a bead, a Type 3 hairpin and an armlet that are typical of third to fourth-century assemblages, although in the case of the bead and armlet an earlier date cannot be ruled out. Finally, fragments of wire armlets/anklets that are also typical of the third and fourth centuries came from both Objects 700 and 701, and a plano-convex bone counter from Object 701 is a late Roman form.

In summary, the 'City in Transition' small finds are, in terms of function, typical of most Romano-British urban assemblages, with little to point to either a high-status population or craft activity, although there is evidence for literacy, leisure and of some contact with continental markets. Few items can be closely dated, and those that can are often residual in secondary contexts. Exceptions are often formal deposits of objects associated with rites of foundation or termination. Poised at the transition between early and late, the Insula IX small finds assemblage in Periods 3–4 prefigures the late settlement and also retains the long shadow of the early Roman town, even of the oppidum and a post-Conquest military presence. There can be no doubt that the population retained contact with the wider material culture of post-Conquest Roman Britain, as shown by the presence of western T-shaped brooches and nail-cleaners, while embracing a fully Romanised style of living.

CHAPTER 7

THE GLASS

By Denise Allen

The glass assemblage is catalogued by Period and Object in Appendix 3 and a selection is illustrated (FIG. 68 (Period 3) and FIG. 69 (Period 4)). The numbering of the illustrated glass follows that of the catalogue in Appendix 3.

The distribution of the glass vessels is plotted for each period, both by numbers of fragments (FIG. 70) and, more schematically, by the proportion of the various vessel types (FIG. 71). The distribution of window glass for each period is plotted on FIG. 72. Comparatively little material of any vessel type is associated with the masonry buildings, though there is proportionally more in Period 4 (MB 3). However, very large numbers of fragments, particularly of bottles, are associated with the timber buildings (MRTB 1/ERTB 1) in Period 3, where the density of finds is also significantly greater than among the more extensive occupation spreads to the south (Object 701). Overall, the glass finds from Period 4 amount to less than one third of the quantities from Period 3.

PERIOD 3

The vessel glass from Period 3 includes many types which are traditionally dated to the later first and early second centuries A.D. (FIG. 68).

COLOURED 'CAST AND GROUND' BOWLS

These bowls (made by slumping a flat disc of glass over a former, then rotary-polishing all smooth surfaces) are believed to have been made until the early Flavian period, although many seem to have survived beyond that date. Some are polychrome, in which case the flat disc was a composite of pieces of glass of a variety of colours and patterns, some monochrome. Some have a ribbed outer surface, traditionally known as 'pillar moulded bowls', and now believed to have been made by pinching the ribs from the glass when it was still in disc form. Some have horizontal wheel-cut lines either around the inner surface or the outer. Several variants are represented here:

No. 1 is a simple monochrome bowl with an internal cut line, which would probably have had a moulded foot-ring. The general type is discussed by Price and Cottam (1998, 53–9, fig. 12a–b or fig. 13c–d) and most coloured examples date to the late first century A.D., although colourless vessels were made well into the second century.

No. 11 is a small chip of polychrome glass; the shape is not determinable, but the pattern of yellow spirals in a green ground is not uncommon during the first century A.D.

Nos 27, 28 and 32 (FIG. 68) are all monochrome pillar moulded bowls, apparently one of the commonest glass finds of the first century A.D., but this may be because even very small fragments are easy to recognise. Price and Cottam list many examples from Britain (1998, 44–6, fig. 7); most dated examples belong to the late first century, although there was quite a lot of survival into the early second century.

There is additionally a marbled polychrome and another blue-green pillar moulded bowl (Nos 58 and 59 respectively) amongst the Period 4 glass, but this may be due to redeposition of the fragments rather than survival of the vessels.

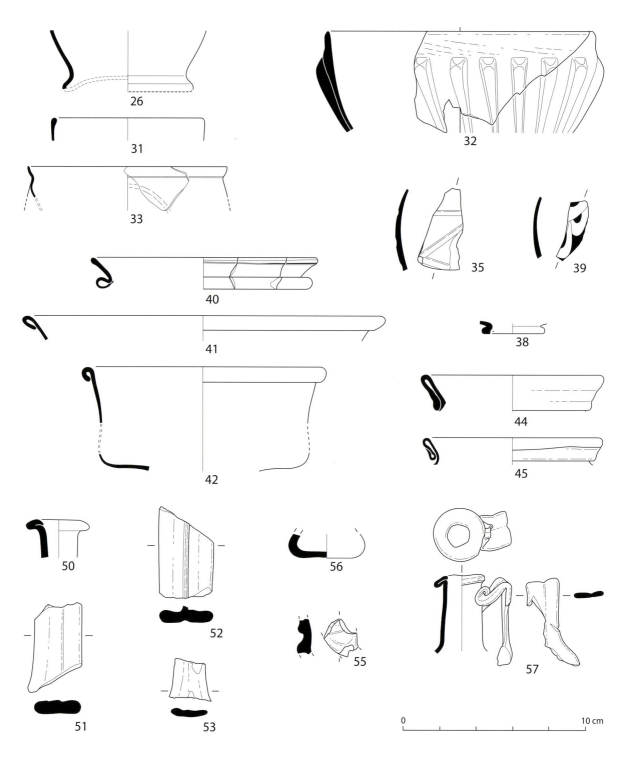

FIG. 68.   Illustrated glass from Period 3. Scale 1:2. (*Drawn by Frances Taylor*)

BLOWN GLASS

Cups and bowls

These are again represented by a number of forms which were common during the late first and early second centuries, as well as some typical of the mid to late second century. They include some finely decorated pieces which must once have been from good quality vessels.

Silchester has produced some very fine cut glass over the years, and this has continued with a small piece of glass with a regular facet-cut design (No. 2) from a probably conical beaker of a

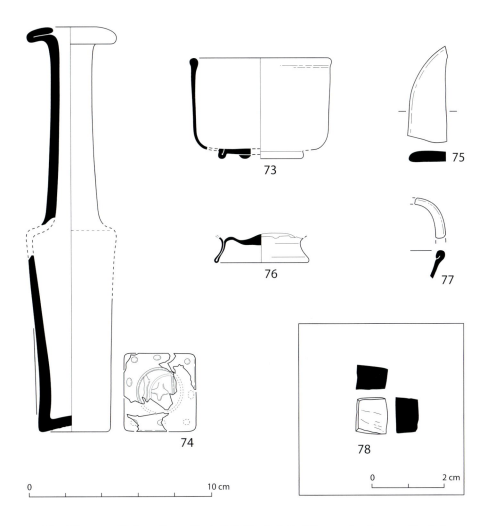

FIG. 69.   Illustrated glass from Period 4. Scale 1:2. (*Drawn by Frances Taylor*)

type which belongs to the Flavian and Trajanic periods (Price and Cottam 1998, 80–3, fig. 26).

No. 35 (FIG. 68) has a more irregular design of broad lines cut at angles to each other. It is difficult to ascertain from a piece of this size exactly what type of vessel is represented, but the curvature of the side suggests that it comes from a curved or hemispherical form. It may belong to the group of geometric-cut hemispherical or deep convex bowls of the second to fourth centuries (Price and Cottam 1998, 115–17, fig. 47), or it may even be from a globular flask of some kind.

The other two decorated vessels from this assemblage have polychrome marvered trails; one of these cannot be assigned with any certainty to a specific vessel type (No. 39, FIG. 68), the other is the rim of a bowl with folded ridge beneath the rim (No. 3). Polychrome marvered trails are most often seen on vessels of the first century A.D., such as the *zarte rippenschalen* or trailed ribbed cup (Price and Cottam 1998, 67–8, fig. 18) or the cantharus (ibid., 68–70, fig. 19), which has a stepped rim, but not usually a complete fold beneath, like No. 40. Bowls with a complete horizontal fold beneath the rim were usually made in monochrome glass from the late second to the fourth centuries (Price and Cottam 1998, 109–10, fig. 43), and a particularly fine complete blue-green example has previously been found at Silchester (Boon 1974, 232, fig. 36 no. 7). No. 61 from a Period 4 context is another example of this type, this time of monochrome yellow-green glass.

There are a good number of cylindrical bowls with tubular rims represented in the Period 3 glass; these are typical of the period from the later first to the later second centuries (Price and Cottam 1998, 78–80, fig. 25). They were made in strong colours as well as blue-green glass, and some had vertical optic-blown ribs. Nos 7, 14, 15, 16, 17, 41 (FIG. 68), 42 (FIG. 68), 43 are all from bowls of this type, and No. 63 from Period 4 is another example.

Larger plate rims of a similar type, but with more flaring rims, are represented by Nos 12 and 13 and also Nos 62 and 63 from Period 4. These occur in both blue-green and colourless glass, as here, and have a fairly long date range throughout the second to fourth centuries (Price and Cottam 1998, 110–11, fig. 44).

Drinking cups and beakers are quite well represented, albeit in many cases only by small fragments about which it can only be said that they are most likely to come from this general vessel type. Two well-cut pieces have been discussed above (Nos 2 and 35) and there are also colourless fragments with horizontal wheel-cut lines or grooves (Nos 25, 36), colourless base-rings (Nos 37, 38 (FIG. 68)), and blue-green body fragments (No. 34). Similar fragments have come from Period 4 contexts (see below). Pieces which can be assigned to specific forms with more certainty include a colourless indented beaker (No. 33, FIG. 68), of a type which usually dates between c. A.D. 65 and the early second century (Price and Cottam 1998, 85–8, figs 28–9), and a probable example (No. 31, FIG. 68) of the cylindrical cup type frequently referred to as Isings 85b, which was perhaps the most popular drinking vessel of the period from the third quarter of the second century to the mid-third century (Price and Cottam 1998, 99–101, fig. 37). There is a more substantial example from Period 4 below (No. 73, FIG. 69).

Jars

There is a form of jar, which was presumably much used for storage in the later first and earlier second centuries (A.D. 65–130), as the folded rims from the type are one of the standard finds of this period. The bodies are globular, the mouths have vertical or slightly sloping tubular collars, they sometimes have vertical optic blown ribs, and they have open base-rings (Price and Cottam 1998, 137–8, fig. 58). Body and base fragments are easily confused with those of the closely related long-necked jugs discussed below. Nos 44 (FIG. 68), 45 (FIG. 68), 46, and 47 are rims of this type, and Nos 3, 4, 26 (FIG. 68), 30, 48, and 49 are body and base fragments which may be from jars or jugs as described below.

Jugs

The long-necked jugs common during the later first and earlier second centuries, and closely related to the jars above, are quite well represented amongst the Period 3 glass. Nos 21, 22 and 50 (FIG. 68) are fragments which include rim and neck pieces which certainly identify them as jugs; Nos 9, 51 (FIG. 68), 52 (FIG. 68) and 55 (FIG. 68) are handles; and Nos 4, 5, 26 (FIG. 68), 30, 48 and 49 are body fragments already listed above which may come from jugs or jars. They represent the range of strong colours, such as brown, amber, dark blue, yellow-green and blue-green, which were popular for these forms. No. 55 (FIG. 68) is likely to be from the extended tail below the handle which was often given pinched decoration. These fragments may represent anything between five and thirteen different vessels.

There are several more fragments which clearly come from various forms of jug, flask or bottle, but which cannot be identified as any specific form: handle fragments Nos 53 (FIG. 68) and 54, rim fragments Nos 8, 18 and 20 (the latter being a spouted rim), and neck fragment No. 29.

Unguent bottles

There are three fragments of unguent bottles of forms which were quite common during the first and early second centuries. Rim No. 5 has the simple fire-rounded finish typical of first-century forms and Nos 10, 19 and 56 (FIG. 68) all have rounded conical reservoirs for the precious liquids once contained in them, representing a type in use during the last quarter of the first and first quarter of the second centuries (Price and Cottam 1998, 172–4, fig. 77).

Bottles

The most numerous vessel type was, as usual, the blue-green bottle. Fragments in Table 14 below

FIG. 70. The distribution of glass finds according to context in Periods 3 (upper) and 4 (lower).

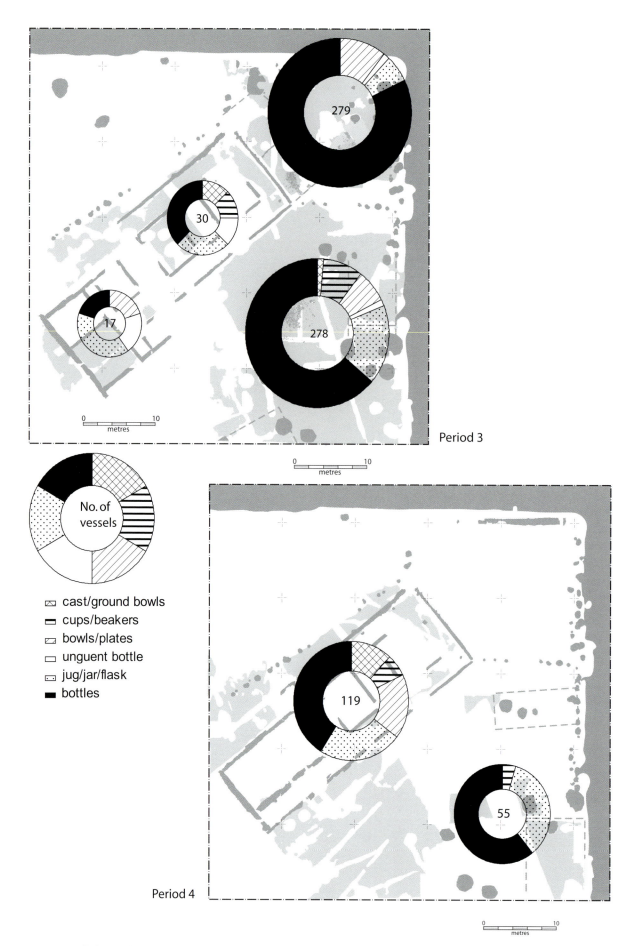

FIG. 71. Schematic representation of the distribution of vessel glass by type in Periods 3 (upper) and 4 (lower). The small quantity of glass from the pits of Period 3 is not included, but that from the Period 4 pits is incorporated into the material from Object 700.

which clearly came from the same vessel have been counted as 1, so a maximum vessel count is 109 bottles from Period 3 contexts, and 32 from Period 4. Some of the other fragments may be from the same vessels, so the actual count may be lower, although there is no way of being certain of this. 'Prismatic bottles' include fragments whose vessel shape was not cylindrical, but may be square, rectangular, octagonal or hexagonal, whereas those in the square category include corners which identify them as such. Indeterminate fragments include neck, shoulder, rim, handle fragments, and others which cannot be assigned to any bottle shape, but whose thickness and colour strongly suggest they belong to this broad group.

Many examples of this vessel category have been listed by Price and Cottam (1998 191–202, figs 88–91). Cylindrical bottles went out of use earlier in the second century than other shapes, and are marginally more numerous in Period 3, but this may not be statistically significant in the light of the amount of glass found in both periods.

A few bottle fragments are catalogued separately: Nos 23 and 24 are substantial square bottle fragments, and No. 57 (FIG. 68) is a rather badly-made square bottle which might be compared to three from a pit at Harlow, Felmongers, Essex, dated A.D. 160–170 (Price 1987, 206, nos 33–4, fig. 4) — possibly later, even locally made, variants of the type.

TABLE 14. BOTTLE FRAGMENTS

Object	Total	Cylindrical	Square	Prismatic	Indeterminate
Period 3					
50018	3	2		1	
50019	1			1	
50037	55	4	7	12	32
500035	1		1		
500036	6	1	4		1
44008	0				
41016	0				
500028	0				
701	43	5	14	1	23
Total	*109*	*12*	*26*	*15*	*56*
Period 4					
50046	18	4	1	6	7
500033	3		2		1
500034	0				
500037	0				
500020	0				
500031	1	1			
500032	3	1	1		1
700	7		3	1	3
Total	*32*	*6*	*7*	*7*	*12*
TOTAL	**141**	**18**	**33**	**22**	**68**

WINDOW GLASS

Only twelve fragments of window glass have been found in Period 3 contexts, all of the 'cast' matt-glossy variety whose method of manufacture has been much discussed with regard to experiments by Mark Taylor and David Hill (Allen 2002, 102–8). Several of the fragments are edge pieces, which have the marks of metal tools impressed in their upper surfaces. One fragment from Period 4, catalogued below as No. 75 (FIG. 69), is interesting in that it may be from a curved pane, which is discussed below.

FIG. 72. The distribution of window glass in Periods 3 (upper) and 4 (lower).

TABLE 15. WINDOW GLASS

Object	Total
Period 3	
50018	0
50019	0
50037	1
500035	2
500036	1
44008	0
41016	0
500028	0
701	8
Total	*12*
Period 4	
50046	9
500033	0
500034	1
500037	0
500020	0
500031	1
500032	0
700	4
Total	*15*
TOTAL	**27**

BEADS AND OTHER OBJECTS

There is just one small fragmentary annular bead of blue-green glass, catalogued as No. 6, which is a long-lived Roman type and cannot be closely dated.

PERIOD 4

Much of the glass from Period 4 contexts represents further examples of the types already discussed above with reference to Period 3. There is generally less glass; the only significant find of a relatively uncommon flask type which is not represented in Period 3 is the 'Mercury flask' discussed below.

COLOURED 'CAST AND GROUND' BOWLS

Nos 58 and 59 are both pillar moulded bowl fragments of first-century type, as discussed above.

BLOWN GLASS

Cups and bowls

There are two colourless glass cups represented here: No. 60 could be from any of a variety of such vessels which were in common use from the Flavian period to the early third century; No. 73 (FIG. 69) is a good example of the common cylindrical cup type often referred to as an Isings 85b, as discussed above with reference to No. 31, dating *c.* A.D. 160–230. The fragment of a high-folded footring, catalogued as No. 76 (FIG. 69), may be from another drinking vessel, perhaps Price and Cottam 1998, 108–9, fig. 42, in use during the third century — but other vessel types had bases like this and the identification is not certain.

No. 61 is a good example of a bowl with a horizontal fold in its body, as discussed above with reference to Period 3 No. 3, in use from the second to the fourth centuries. Nos 62 and 63 are further examples of the bowls and plates with out-flared tubular rims discussed above with reference to Nos 12 and 13, with a similar fairly long date range.

Jugs and flasks

There are fragments from at least six jugs of various types; Nos 64 and 67 may be from the later first-/ earlier second-century group of long-necked jugs discussed above with reference to Nos 21, 22 and 50, but pinched trails occur beneath the handles of other forms too, and there is not enough of No. 67 to identify it with certainty.

Handle fragments Nos 65, 66 and 68 are not sufficiently diagnostic to identify the specific vessel form, nor is the rim elongated towards a spout catalogued as No. 77 (FIG. 69), but they serve to illustrate the variety of vessels in use.

There are fragmentary bodies of three more globular flasks or jugs — Nos 69, 70 and 71 — which again could have come from a variety of specific forms.

More readily identifiable are the substantial remains of a thick-walled, colourless square-bodied flask, No. 74 (FIG. 69). Such vessels are often referred to as 'Mercury flasks' because some examples have been found with a representation of this god on the base (Price and Cottam 1998, 179–81, fig. 81). Dated finds seem to span the second and earlier third centuries, and this example is from pit 2434 filled in the late third century. The design on the base is unfortunately very difficult to make out, as the vessel appears to have moved slightly in the mould as it was inflated, so that the image is blurred — parts of two raised circles which are not concentric may be further evidence for this. Whether the upright within the circle could be identified as a standing figure (i.e. Mercury) is highly debatable, and it might be that this is a simple geometric pattern on the base, with the 'smudging' of the image making it appear more complex. These vessels were described in some detail by Cool and Price with reference to finds from Colchester (1995, 152–3). They are not very common in Britain, and this is the first example from Silchester.

Bottles

See Table 14 above for the numbers from Period 4 contexts. It is notable that there are six finds of cylindrical bottles, which mostly disappeared from use fairly early in the second century.

WINDOW GLASS

Table 15 above shows the nine fragments of matt/glossy window glass from Period 4 contexts, the most interesting of which is the apparently curved fragment (No. 75, FIG. 69), which may just be from a very irregular square pane, or from a circular pane, as discussed with reference to finds from Caerwent (Allen 2002, 106–8, figs 8.7, 8.8). Since the line of the edge is neither entirely straight nor a regular circle, it is difficult to be sure.

OBJECTS

The fragment of twisted glass rod (No. 72) may be from a hairpin, a cosmetic rod or a stirring rod — only a very small piece survives. The small tessera of blue glass (No. 78, FIG. 69) may be from a floor or wall mosaic, or it may be that glass intended for re-use was stored in this form — odd tesserae do turn up in places apparently unconnected with mosaics, so this could be an alternative interpretation.

CHAPTER 8

THE POTTERY

By Jane Timby

With contributions on the samian by Paul Tyers, Joanna Bird and Brenda Dickinson

INTRODUCTION AND METHODOLOGY

The pottery recovered from features and deposits within Insula IX allocated to Period 3 (*c.* A.D. 125/50–200) and Period 4 (*c.* A.D. 200–250) has, as with previous work (cf. Timby 2006), been subjected to different levels of analysis reflecting the importance and integrity of the respective contexts. The approach adopted has been used to maximise the amount of information that can be recovered from an assemblage of this size given certain time and financial constraints. All the pottery identified by the excavator as relevant was initially rapidly spot-dated and the samian extracted for separate study. No quantification was undertaken at this stage.

The assemblage has been split into four groups: the south-east pits (Object 500017), the northern pits (Object 500029), contexts associated with 'House 1', and the south-east layers considered to be contemporary with the house and pits (Objects 701 (Period 3) and 700 (Period 4)). The data from 'House 1' formed the basis of a separately published internet article (Timby 2007). This information will not be repeated in detail here but will be referred to in this report and included in the tables for comparative purposes. The 'House 1' assemblage was recorded by sherd count and weight only. The pottery from the pits and wells, Objects 500017 and 500029, has been fully analysed and quantified by sherd count, weight and estimated vessel (rim) equivalence (EVE). In total this amounts to some 3,867 sherds, 79kg, 7465 EVEs from Object 500017, and 693 sherds, 15kg, 739 EVEs from Object 500029. The final group reported on here is that from the layers in the southern part of the site. This comprised a very large assemblage of material. In the first instance this was subjected to a rapid spot-dating scan which led to some refinement of the group, some contexts being phased as earlier. As it was impractical to attempt to analyse the complete assemblage, a sub-sample was selected, based on the spot-date and focusing on those contexts with larger assemblages containing good samian and datable coarseware falling within the defined chronological periods. In total some 12,669 sherds from Object 701 (Period 3) and 6,828 sherds from Object 700 (Period 4) have been analysed. In addition, a few other special finds from non-analysed contexts have been included. The data have been entered onto an MS Excel spreadsheet, a copy of which is deposited with the site archive. The samian has been studied separately and fully quantified by Paul Tyers. Only the samian (plain and decorated) from the selected contexts for analysis has been fully reported here. The stamps and decorated wares extracted from the complete assemblage have been listed and reported on separately by Brenda Dickinson and Joanna Bird respectively.

In the following report the fabrics and associated forms for all the material studied for Periods 3 and 4 are described first. The report is then split into a detailed description of the material from the Period 3 pits, wells and layers followed by a comparison of the groups from 'House 1', pits and layers. A similar section follows this for Period 4. The report concludes with some general observations. The tables are presented in Appendix 4.

DESCRIPTION OF FABRICS AND ASSOCIATED FORMS

All known named and traded wares are described using the codes set out in the National Roman Fabric Reference Collection (NRFRC) (Tomber and Dore 1998 = T & D 1998). As these have been fully discussed in this publication, these fabrics are not described further. Regional and local wares not in the NRFRC are described in full below using a generic alpha-numeric coding based on firing colour, surface finish or distinctive inclusions. Thus all reduced sandy wares are prefixed GREY, oxidised wares OXID, white wares with WHITE, and white-slipped wares as WSLIP. Wares containing a distinctive temper are coded according to the principal inclusions, for example GROG, FLINT etc. Where relevant all the fabrics are cross-referenced to the codes used in earlier Silchester reports, shown in square brackets after the new code (cf. Timby 1989; 2000b). There is a very wide range of material present but quite a few fabrics are entirely redeposited, brought up from earlier deposits. At the other end of the chronological spectrum some of the later wares and forms post-date Period 4. These relate to contexts on the footprint of 'House 1', but post-dating its demolition.

CONTINENTAL IMPORTS

Fine wares

Samian. Table 35 (Appendix 4) provides a quantified summary of the overall samian assemblage by fabric. The samian from these features comprises some 20.1kg (59 eves, 2,383 sherds). The material is generally rather broken and incomplete with only 20 instances where both the rim and base of the same vessel have been identified. The sherd breaks and surfaces can be rather abraded, although some of the earlier South Gaulish material from even the latest levels in Period 4 seems quite fresh, perhaps suggesting relatively rapid re-deposition from earlier contexts in some cases.

The largest group is from the south-east layers (Objects 701, 700) with over 11.5kg, followed by 'House 1' (6.6kg, 1,029 sherds). Only a very small assemblage was recovered from the pits and wells (0.5kg, 183 sherds).

As can be seen from Table 35, the assemblage is dominated by Central Gaulish (Lezoux) products at 78 per cent by weight (73 per cent by eve) principally of the Hadrianic-Antonine period, with the bulk of the remainder from South Gaulish (La Graufesenque) factories (17 per cent weight, 23 per cent eve). East Gaulish wares are uncommon (*c.* 1.5 per cent by weight, including both Rheinzabern and Trier sherds) and are not represented among either the decorated or stamped vessels.

The remainder of the sherds are small in number, and in many cases residual, but include the following sherds from a Drag. 18 in Pulborough samian (2434 and 3674), of early second-century date (see regional fine wares below); an enigmatic, abraded sherd of a Drag. 33 in an unusual fabric (either Colchester or the Argonne) from a late second- or early third-century context (3412) (see regional fine wares below for fabric description); Montans ware, including a Drag. 15/17 and the base of another platter of the first century and a Drag. 33 of the second century; a sherd of a Drag. 15/17 in early ('micaceous') Lezoux ware (1934) and a base of a cup in an Italian or early Gaulish fabric of the early to mid-first century A.D. (3532).

Argonne colour-coated ware (ARG CC) (T & D 1998, 47). In total some 167 sherds of ARG CC have been recorded, 107 from Period 3 and 60 from Period 4. All the sherds are from beakers, largely bag-shaped with short everted or cornice rims and decorated with mainly rough-casting and less commonly rouletting (FIGS 76.32; 81.104; 83.167).

Central Gaulish black-slipped ware (CNG BS) (T & D 1998, 50). This group comprised some 113 sherds almost exclusively from beakers, including funnel mouthed and everted rim necked forms (FIG. 83.171–2), either plain or with rouletted or barbotine decoration. Some sherds from pit 3406 are decorated with barbotine floral motifs on the exterior but have not been slipped on the interior. Only five sherds came from Period 3, the rest being from Period 4.

Central Gaulish colour-coated ware (CNG CC/ CNG CC2) (T & D 1998, 52) [Silch E53]. This group comprised some 124 sherds, 70 from Period 3 contexts, the rest from Period 4. Most of the sherds are from beakers, although a single tripod leg from a first-century colour-coated bowl, possibly from Lezoux, came from layer 3472. The colour-coated ware beakers, many with cornice or short everted rims, generally have a chestnut-brown or orange-brown colour-coat on a cream fabric and are decorated with barbotine tear drops or hairpin designs or roughcasting.

Central Gaulish white-slipped ware [Silch E19]. Nine residual first-century flagon sherds.

Central Gaulish glazed ware (CNG GL1) (T & D 1998, 52) [Silch E32]. Two residual sherds, one identifiably from a small flask.

Central Gaulish mica-slipped ware (CNG MS). A single residual sherd.

Central Gaulish micaceous Terra Nigra [Silch E20]. A single residual platter *Camulodunum* (*Cam.*) type 2 from Period 4.

Cologne colour-coated ware (KOL CC) (T & D 1998, 58). A good range of beakers are present, evenly distributed across Periods 3 and 4 (FIGS 78.79, 83; 83.148, 164). The group includes some earlier products dating from the Flavian period alongside the later wares. Production continued until the mid-third century.

Eggshell ware (EGG SH). Thin-walled black or white eggshell ware. The latter is probably imported from Gallia Belgica and includes at least two carinated vessels as *Cam.* type 120. The white wares may be imports or British in origin. Probably all residual.

Gallo-Belgic Terra Nigra (GAB TN1) (T & D 1998, 15) [Silch E6]. 47 residual sherds. Forms include *Cam.* platters 2, 8, 12, 12/13, 14 and 16 and cup sherds.

Gallo-Belgic Terra Rubra (GAB TR1A, TR1C, TR2, TR3) (T & D 1998, 17–20) [Silch E7–12]. Residual. Forms include pedestal beaker and platters, in particular *Cam.* type 5, and butt beaker (*Cam.* type 112).

Lyon ware (LYO CC) (T & D 1998, 59) [Silch E26]. A small group of 24 residual sherds, mainly from beakers with roughcast or barbotine scale decoration.

Moselkeramik black-slipped ware (MOS BS) (T & D 1998, 61) [Silch E30]. A small group of 23 beaker sherds, all from Period 4.

South Gaulish colour-coated ware (SOG CC) (T & D 1998, 65). Four pale buff sherds with an orange colour-coat, one from a cup; the others from cornice rim beakers.

White wares

Italian white ware (ITA WH) (T & D 1998, 74). A single cream flagon sherd from Object 50046 (1796) with a black sand fabric. A sherd of oxidised black sand ware also came from layer 4300, probably from the same source.

Central Gaulish (Rhône Valley) mortaria (GLG OX) (T & D 1998, 69). Eight sherds, all from Object 50046 (3313, 3374). A buff fabric with distinctive red iron inclusions.

North Gaulish white ware (NOG WH) (T & D 1998, 22) [Silch E13]. A large number of flagon and butt beaker (*Cam.* type 113) sherds. Probably mainly residual.

North Gaulish white ware mortaria (NOG WH). A moderately large group of 75 sherds. Many are quite worn. One flange from Object 500046 (4454) is stamped by the potter Q. Valerius Veranius, only the latter part of the name being extant, dating to the period A.D. 65/70–100. One example (FIG. 77.49) is similar in form to Exeter type C31 dated *c*. A.D. 80–150 (Hartley 1991, 201).

Rhineland white ware mortaria (RHL WH) (T & D 1998, 79). Four sherds from Period 3 and 4 layers.

Soller mortaria (SOL WH) (T & D 1998, 79). A single rim sherd from 'House 1' Object 50037 (4151).

Coarse wares

Pompeian redware (CAM PR1) (T & D 1998, 42). Four residual sherds recovered from the Period 3 and Period 4 layers.

Amphorae

Amalgro 50 (Peacock and Williams 1986, class 22) (FIG. 81.100). The origin of this amphora form is uncertain but it is generally assumed to be from the Algarve, Portugal (Keay and Williams 2005), although Baetica and Lusitania have also been cited (Bonnet *et al.* 2003). It has been suggested that they contained fish products. Although mainly documented from fourth- to fifth-century contexts, the amphora first appears in France on sites dating to the first half of the third century (Bonnet *et al.* 2003, 165); its earliest appearance is an example from the Capo Ognina wreck dated by associated coins to A.D. 210/215 (ibid.). The sherd, which is in quite a worn state, was recovered from south-east pit/well 3406 (3821) allocated to Period 4; thus, if contemporary, it is amongst the earlier of these amphora types to be recorded.

Asia Minor amphora (British Biv) (ASM AM) (T & D 1998, 83). A single bodysherd was recovered from the Period 3 layer 3849.

Baetican amphorae (BAT AM) (T & D 1998, 84–5). In total some 556 sherds weighing just over 47kg have been recorded in Baetican fabrics. Most of the sherds allocated here are from Dressel 20 amphorae (e.g. FIG. 77.51) but there are also a number of rims (e.g. FIG. 83.155, 165) and handles and undoubtedly bodysherds from the Haltern 70 type (Peacock and Williams 1986, class 15). A Dressel 20 handle from context 4041 (FIG. 86.1) has a poorly impressed stamp, L...T (retro). This may be L▲I▲T (Callender 1965, fig. 9.15–17), although the triangular stops are not visible. Several examples are documented from Britain, including another example from Silchester (May 1916, 280, nos 21–2). It is thought to date to the second half of the second century.

There are several instances of later reuse of sherds. One vessel from Period 4 Object 700 (2420) (FIG. 85.G8) has been reused, with the broken neck ground smooth and an 'X' scratched into the exterior surface. Other ground-down neck sherds came from Period 4 MB 3 Object 50037 (3533, 4152). A handle from Period 3 Object 701 (3424) has been turned into a pestle with a cross marked on the end. One bodysherd from Period 3 Object 701 (4303) has been fashioned into a roundel, 160mm across, whilst one sherd from Period 4 pit 3406 (3821) has had two holes drilled through it.

Cadiz amphorae (CAD AM) (T & D 1998, 87). A modest group of 41 bodysherds and one handle, probably all from *Cam.* 186 amphorae, generally considered to transport *garum.*

Dressel 2-4 amphorae (Peacock and Williams 1986, class 10). A small group of 48 sherds, recognised from handle or rim sherds and largely in Campanian fabrics. Other unfeatured sherds from other sources may exist in the unassigned group.

?Dressel 14 (Peacock and Williams 1986, class 20). An oxidised sherd with a 'gritty' fabric, possibly from a south Spanish or Portuguese Dressel 14 amphora, thought to transport fish products and generally dated from the first to third centuries A.D. A single sherd from Period 3 layer 4063.

Gaulish amphorae (GALAM) (T & D 1998, 93–5). A moderately well represented group of 156 sherds, but with few featured pieces. A complete base came from Period 3 MB 1 (3751).

Palestinian amphorae (PAL AM) (T & D 1998, 103). Eight residual sherds.

Unclassified amphorae (AMP). Mainly unfeatured bodysherds. An unclassified rim is illustrated in FIG. 82.129.

Amphorae lids (AMPLID). A small number of lids were recorded, mainly in fine fabrics.

REGIONAL WARES

Fine wares

Abingdon oxidised ware butt beaker (ABN OX) [Silch S16] (Timby *et al.* 1997). A small group of 30 sherds; residual.

Colchester colour-coated ware (COL CC2) (T & D 1998, 132). A small group of 52 sherds has been identified, with possibly further examples in the miscellaneous group. Mainly cornice rim beakers with roughcast or barbotine decoration (FIG. 83.160).

Colchester samian (COL SA) (T & D 1998, 133). Fabric description: orange (Munsell 5YR 6/8), fine granular texture with finely irregular fracture; darker orange-red slip remains in small patches on inner and outer surfaces, and in light groove on outer face. Under the binocular microscope, moderately abundant fine inclusions of sub-rounded glassy and white sand (up to 0.5mm), flecks of white mica (up to 0.2mm), particularly visible in the surfaces, sparse fine black (Fe rich?) inclusions and occasional sub-angular voids. A single cup Drag. 33 from Period 4 (FIG. 83.175).

Pulborough samian (PUL SA) (T & D 1998, 186). Two sherds only from a Drag. 18 form.

London ware (LON BWF). Fine black ware (see miscellaneous fine black wares).

Lower Nene Valley colour-coated ware (LNV CC) (T & D 1998, 118) [Silch E48]. A small group of 34 sherds from the pit and layer groups. Vessels include examples of barbotine decorated 'hunt' beakers (FIG. 84.181), small bag-shaped beakers (FIG. 82.115), box fragments and a complete intact lid from Period 4 pit 3406 (4041) (FIG. 81.97). Sherds occur in both Periods 3 and 4, but mainly the latter.

New Forest colour-coated wares (NFO CC; NFO RS) (T & D 1998, 141) [Silch E39, 40/41]. A small group of 18 sherds, including examples of beaker (Fulford 1975) types F33 and F44. Probably contamination from later levels.

New Forest parchment ware (NFO PA) (T & D 1998, 141). Two sherds.

Oxfordshire white ware (OXF WH) (T & D 1998, 173) [Silch S43/S47]. A moderately large group of 648 sherds with forms spanning the second to third centuries. A variety of flagons are present: Young (1977) types W2 (FIG. 78.84), W3 (FIG. 82.127), W5, W6, W8, W9 (FIG. 77.52, 59), W11 (FIG. 78.78); W15 (FIGS 82.116; 83.168, 173), and W18. Other forms include small jars, larger jars (type W33), bowls (type W46, W54), and a wall-sided example (FIG. 78.92) and a lid (type W72). Flagon types W9, W11 and W15, of which several examples are present, were originally dated A.D. 240–400 by Young but their frequency here might suggest a slightly earlier date of manufacture.

Oxfordshire red-slipped ware (OXF RS) (T & D 1998, 176) [Silch E27]. A small group of 26 sherds including some fourth-century forms such as Young (1977) types C49, C68 and C69 which must be intrusive here.

Oxfordshire white-slipped ware (OXF WS). Four sherds only.

Verulamium Region white ware (VER WH) (T & D 1998, 154) [Silch S33]. Well represented in the assemblage with a variety of second-century forms, particularly flagons, including a large double-handled type (FIG. 75.19), two semi-complete examples — one without a rim but with a post-firing slot in the body (FIG. 75.20); the other with a pinch-mouth (FIG. 75.21). Several ring-necked and pulley wheel forms also feature (FIG. 83.159). Other vessels include dolia-type jars (FIG. 77.35), a wall-sided bowl (FIG. 78.68) and various bowls, jars and lids (FIG. 75.14).

Mortaria

Caerleon mortaria (CAR RS) (T & D 1998, 205). Four sherds, one a worn rim sherd with no surviving grits from Period 3 layer 3826; the others, a rim and two bodysherds from Period 4 layers 2786 and 4303. Probably second century.

?Colchester white ware mortarium (T & D 1998, 133). A single, stamped mortarium was recovered from Period 4 layer 2467 (FIGS 83.152; 86.4). The incomplete stamp is impressed diagonally across the flange.

Oxfordshire white ware mortaria (OXF WH) (T & D 1998, 173) [Silch M2]. A moderately diverse collection of Oxfordshire mortaria, including examples of Young (1997) types M3, M5, M6, M10 (FIG. 84.180), M13 (FIG. 83.156, 174), M14 (FIG. 83.149, with a distinctive coiled spout), M15, M17, and a single intrusive M22.

One of the M13 examples (FIGS 83.174; 86.5) has a complete stamp. Mrs K.F. Hartley notes that the trademark stamp, impressed vertically down the wall-side rim, is from the same die as another stamp from Silchester (May 1916, pl. lxxxiii, no. 29) and one from Wanborough, Wilts. (Anderson *et al.* 2001, fig. 79, no. 210). These mortaria are products of the Oxford kilns and although the stamp is not represented at Cowley, the stamp has so much in common with Atkinson 1941, fig. 5, no. 54, that one may reasonably believe that both dies were in use there; wall-side mortaria were also being made there. The two Silchester stamps are both on wall-side mortaria, which suggests an optimum date of A.D. 150–180.

Oxfordshire white-slipped ware (OXF WS). Four sherds only from two contexts, probably all intrusive.

Verulamium region white ware mortaria (VER WH) (T & D 1998, 154) [Silch M12]. Several Verulamium mortaria are present including one large, almost complete, example stamped by the potter Matugenus (FIGS 77.36; 86.3). Matugenus is one of the better-known potters working at Brockley Hill, Verulamium, normally thought to have been operating between *c.* A.D. 90 and 120/5. He had a number of dies and this one perhaps most resembles *Verulamium III* fig. 118.84 (Hartley 1984, 286), the clay dies of which were found at the workshop. A similar vessel to the Silchester example, probably stamped using the same die, is published from London (Davies *et al.* 1994, fig. 39.209).

One flange fragment from Period 4 MB 3 (3049) is stamped with the word 'FECIT' and probably dates to the period A.D. 70–100 (cf. Timby 2007). Another much worn double-line stamp is just visible on a flange fragment from 2303 (FIG. 76.25). The edges of seven further stamps were recorded: six from 'House 1', Periods 3 and 4 (Objects 50037, 50018 and 50046) and one from Period 3 well 2234 (2303). One of the examples from Period 4 MB 3 (Object 50046) has the letter 'R' extant.

Coarsewares

Dorset black-burnished ware (DOR BB1) (T & D 1998, 127) [Silch S18]. Dorset black-burnished ware makes a significant contribution to the assemblage with some 1,457 sherds fairly evenly split between Periods 3 and 4. Of the measured sample, jars dominate accounting for 44 per cent by eve (FIGS 77.56; 78.76; 81.96, 109 and 113; 82.119; 83.153, 158; 84.182–4). Flat-rim bowls and dishes account for a further 29 per cent (FIGS 77.39; 78. 82; 83.157; 84.185), grooved-rim bowls for 4.5 per cent (FIGS 77.40; 78.77, 90; 81.105; 82.120; 84.186), plain-rimmed dishes for 21 per cent (FIGS 77.41; 78.81; 83.154), and conical-flanged bowls for less than 1 per cent. These latter vessels must be regarded as intrusive or from mixed later deposits. The only other form present is a handled mug. Flagons, lids and fish-dishes are absent.

Several jars showed traces of use with sooting and internal limescale deposits, whereas bowls were often sooted. At least four sherds had some sort of post-firing graffiti (FIG. 85.G4–7).

Hampshire grog-tempered ware (HAM GT) (T & D 1998, 139). A small group of 68 sherds, including jars, a plain-rimmed dish and a flanged bowl, the latter probably intrusive. Also present is a particularly thin walled, deep bowl (FIG. 77.42).

Savernake ware (SAV GT) (T & D 1998, 191). A single, beaded-rim jar from Period 3 layer 3431 and a possible storage jar (FIG. 82.123).

Shelly ware (SHELL). A generally red-brown ware containing a sparse to moderate frequency of shell. A rare ware here with a small group of mainly unfeatured sherds and just a single jar rim sherd. Possibly originates from Oxfordshire (cf. Evans 2001, 367, fabric C13) where it predates the late Roman Harrold shelly ware.

South-West black-burnished ware (SOW BB1) (T & D 1998, 129). Poorly represented with just a few sherds, including a jar, a handled mug (FIG. 82.114) and a conical-flanged bowl, the latter presumably intrusive.

South-West white-slipped ware (SOW WS) (T & D 1998, 192). Eight sherds, including one base from Period 3 MB 1 (4152) which has been deliberately holed.

LOCAL AND UNPROVENANCED

Fine wares

Miscellaneous colour-coated wares (CC). A diverse group of sherds, mainly from beakers (e.g. FIG. 81.94) which may be local, regional or imported.

Fine black ware (BWF). A fine black ware with no visible inclusions. The core is either grey or dark red-brown. A variant is distinguished with frequent white mica (BWFMIC). The group may include London ware (cf. Seeley and Drummond-Murray 2005, 128ff.). A moderately small group of 78 sherds of BWF is present with a further 36 sherds of the more micaceous variant. Vessels include carinated beakers (as *Cam.* type 120), cornice-rim beakers, copies of samian bowls Drag. 30 (FIG. 75.10), plain-rimmed shallow dishes, and carinated bowls (FIG. 77.50). Various forms of decoration occur including barbotine dots, barbotine stripes, compass-style incised designs, dot-in-circles, rouletting, vertical combing and incised lattice.

Fine grey wares (GYF). A moderately large group of 2,298 sherds in a diverse range of forms and probably represented by more than one source. Several vessels may be products of the early Oxfordshire industry (Young 1977). A significant proportion of the vessels are beakers — globular, poppyhead and cornice-rim forms, some with barbotine dot, rouletted or fine roughcast decoration (FIGS 76.24; 78.63, 85; 82.145; 83.161, 163). Other forms include copies of samian bowls Drag. 30 (FIG. 77.54), ring-necked and disc-necked flagons (FIG. 77.57), flasks (FIG. 82.136), dishes (FIGS 76.23; 77.60), lids (FIG. 77.61), and other bowls (FIGS 75.13; 83.162). One jar or beaker has traces of a post-firing graffito (FIG. 85.G3).

Mica-slipped wares. A diverse group of mainly oxidised wares all with a mica-slipped finish. A significant number of the sherds are burnt, a reflection of the use of these vessels. Forms include indented and bobble beakers, a small lid-seated jar (FIG. 75.12), lids, a flanged hemispherical cup, curved wall dishes, and a tripod bowl. Also within this group is a mica-slipped oxidised fabric, a variant of OXID3 (see below) which includes a bowl (FIG. 82.118).

Fine oxidised ware (OXIDF). A moderately large group sharing a very fine, sandy fabric. Vessels include flat rim bowls and dishes, plain-rimmed dishes, various beakers (e.g. FIG. 78.80), some with barbotine dot decoration and flagons (FIG. 77.55).

Fine white-slipped oxidised ware (WSOXIDF). Limited to flagon (e.g. FIG. 77.46).

Southern glazed ware (SOB GL) (T & D 1998, 213). Two sherds have been noted, one with a greenish glaze and a white barbotine cross from Period 4 MB 3 (1410); the other a base from Period 4 layer 3468 with an orange-brown glaze (FIG. 83.144).

Coarsewares

Silchester flint-tempered ware (SIL FL) [Silch F1]. A moderately hard, smooth, clean matrix tempered with a moderate to common density of white, calcined, angular flint fragments. These vary in size, the larger pieces reaching 4mm across. Sparse quartz and red iron grains are also present. The colour of the paste varies from shades of brown to red, dark grey or black, sometimes on one vessel, the typical result of bonfire firing. Vessels are handmade and the repertoire extremely limited. The commonest forms are jars, which broadly fall into two types: bead rim and everted rim. The only other forms found in this assemblage are lids. The ware is quantitatively well represented in the assemblage accounting for 6 per cent overall (by count), although most, if not all of this must be residual material dating from the first century B.C. to first century A.D. Two vessels have survived in a semi-complete state: a beaded-rim jar from Period 3 MB 2 Object 50019 (SF 2039) (FIG. 76.30) and an exceptionally large jar from Period 3 MB 1 (3259, SF 2377) (FIG. 76.27; cf. FIGS 11–13) possibly used as a *clibanus*.

Finer flint-tempered ware (FL2). The substantial part of an everted, thickened rim jar from Period 4 MB 3 (3313) is the only example of this ware.

Grog-tempered wares [SIL G1, G4, GF1]. As with the flint-tempered wares, many of the grog-tempered sherds are redeposited first-century B.C. to first-century A.D. finds. The three fabrics most commonly found are Basilica fabrics G1, G4 and GF1, all residual here. There is a higher incidence of such redeposited material associated with the 'House 1' contexts.

Grog-tempered ware (miscellaneous) (GROG). Various other grog-tempered wares: handmade and wheelmade jars, bowls and lids. Most of these are probably largely residual, although one exception may be a handmade dish (FIG. 78.75) with a burnished finish.

Grog-tempered storage jars (GRSJ). Large handmade grog-tempered storage jars (FIG. 78.73–4) in fabrics typical of those found in the Oxford region in the second to third centuries are quite common with some 2,065 sherds weighing *c*. 86kg. Interestingly these were not common in the pits; sherds were mainly from contexts associated with 'House 1' and the south-east layers.

Alice Holt reduced wares (ALH RE) (T & D 1998, 138; Lyne and Jefferies 1979). As one of the main suppliers of coarsewares to Silchester, it is not surprising that a large range of vessel types is represented. It is possible that sherds from other non-distinctive local grey ware industries have been subsumed into this group. The ware accounts for between 46.1 and 59.3 per cent by count of the Period 3 pottery (see Table 36) and between 48 and 63 per cent of the Period 4 assemblage (Table 43). Of the groups (pits and layers) measured for eves, jars dominate the assemblage accounting for 75 per cent. A variety of types is present, with flat rim forms and everted or cavetto rimmed types (Lyne and Jefferies 1979, later industry forms class 3A and 3B) being particularly common (e.g. FIGS 77.53; 78.66; 82.124, 128; 83.169). Also quite well represented are earlier types such as the everted rim with an internal bevel, beaded rim, and everted rim cordoned forms (FIGS 75.1–3, 9; 76.22, 28–9, 31; 81.108). One complete, beaded-rim jar has been deliberately holed in the side after firing (FIG. 76.28). Other less common types include a dolium-type jar from Period 3 Object 701 (4308), a miniature jar from Period 3 Object 701 (3849), and a small number of lid-seated forms (FIG. 75.6). A few storage jars were present, including two with cabled rims (Lyne and Jefferies 1979, class 10), which appear at the end of the second century (FIG. 82.122), but generally such vessels are not common. At least one example of a storage jar (ibid.) form 1A (FIG. 84.187), probably of third-century or later date, came from Period 4 layer 3836. Various other jar forms are shown in FIGS 78.64–5, 91; 81.93, 95, 102, 107; 82.117. The diameters of the various jars range from 70mm through to 300mm, with the highest incidence of vessels (47 per cent) in the 130–160mm range. One jar base from Period 3 well 2234 has a post-firing X scratched onto the underside (FIG. 85.G1).

Bowls and dishes contribute a further 16 per cent (eve) of the Alice Holt assemblage. The commonest form being flat and triangular-rimmed bowls and dishes (Lyne and Jefferies 1979, forms 5A and 6B) (FIG. 82.131–4). Various other bowls and dishes are also present, in particular plain-walled dishes, reeded and grooved-rim dishes and bowls, and flat-rim carinated bowls (FIGS 77.43, 58; 78.89; 81.111; 82.130, 141–2). One vessel from Period 3 Object 701 (3424) had two cut marks on the rim (FIG. 78.70). A small sherd from Period 3 Object 50037 had part of a barbotine stem on the upper rim in imitation of a samian dish Drag. 36. At least one scarred base and a detached leg indicate the presence of tripod bowls in the assemblage. Earlier residual forms are also present, notably Atrebatic-type bowls (FIG. 75.7) and shallow dishes with internal mouldings (FIG. 75.4–5) (ibid., class 5 and 6.2).

Lids are also well documented in the Alice Holt assemblage accounting for 6.3 per cent (eve), mainly types falling into Lyne and Jefferies 1979, later industry class 7 (FIGS 77.45, 62; 78.67;

81.110; 83.176–7). In addition, there are several knobs, some perforated to allow steam to escape (FIG. 82.140). The lid diameters peak around 160–180mm which account for 48 per cent of the measured examples. The smallest examples start at around 140mm with the largest at 320mm. It is likely therefore that some lids were designed to go with bowls or dishes as well as jars.

All other forms are present in minor amounts collectively contributing just 2.7 per cent eve. These include beakers (FIG. 77.48), flasks (FIG. 82.135), jugs, a single, ring-necked flagon and an earlier handled flagon (Lyne and Jefferies 1979, class 8) (FIG. 82.138).

Overwey white ware (OVW WH) (T & D 1998, 146) [Silch S31]. Four intrusive sherds including three triangular-shaped jar rims.

Mixed grit. A minor group mainly comprising redeposited finds from the first century. Fabrics include various combinations of flint, grog and quartz sand (SF/GF) and are undoubtedly locally made at Silchester.

SOURCES UNKNOWN

Other miscellaneous wares

Pale wares (PALE/ BUFF/ CREAM). Various fine to medium sandy buff or cream wares probably from various sources. Vessels include flat rim and reeded-rim bowls, small hemispherical bowls (FIG. 83.166), plain-rim dishes, thickened rim jars, beakers, lids and flagons. The basal knob of an amphora is included here which may be a British product (FIG. 75.8).

Grey sandy wares. Local grey wares, medium sandy fabrics, sources uncertain (GREY). Forms include beaded rim (FIG. 82.137), and everted rim jars, beakers (FIG. 81.101), a plain-rim dish (FIG. 81.98), lids, and a flask typologically similar to Young (1977) form W15.

BB1 copies (BB1 COPY). Wheelmade BB1 copies, probably a subdivision within the Alice Holt industry.

Black sandy ware with visible mica (BWMIC). A small group of distinct but unfeatured sherds; possibly continental imports.

Local oxidised wares (OXID; OXID1–6):
OXID. A large miscellaneous group of fine to medium sandy, oxidised wares either in insufficient quantities to classify separately or with non-diagnostic fabrics. It is possible that several are products of the early Oxfordshire industry, in particular some globular beakers with short everted rims (FIG. 78.87), some with cream, barbotine-dot decoration. Forms featuring in this group include a colander, at least two unguent flasks (FIG. 81.106), flat rim and reeded-rim bowls and dishes, ring-necked flagon, lids, beaded rim jars, and a shouldered jar with a decorative cordon (FIG. 82.126).

OXID1. A hard medium-grained, dense sandy ware, oxidised orange with a grey blume. A small group of just five sherds.

OXID2. Medium-fine, orange sandy ware with a slightly rough texture. The core is pale grey and the surfaces, particularly the interior, frequently show grey banding. The paste contains a dense frequency of very fine inclusions, including a sparse scatter of small white grains, and dark brown iron specks. Also present is a light scatter of larger rounded, dark brown, iron inclusions up to 2mm. A small group mainly comprising flat-rim bowls and lids.

OXID3. Orange, medium-fine sandy ware with a slightly powdery texture. The exterior is sometimes slightly blackened. At x20 magnification the matrix shows a moderate scatter of well-sorted, fine (less than 0.5mm), sub-rounded quartz sand, some grains iron-stained, accompanied by a rare scatter of rounded, red iron grains. It appears in quantity in the Trajanic-Hadrianic period and is particularly common as bowls (FIGS 78.86; 83.143), dishes (FIG. 77.38), flagons (FIGS 81.99; 83.146; 84.179), beakers (FIGS 78.88; 83.147), jars, and lids, including several knobs

(FIG. 77.37). Many of the rims of the bowls and lids are deliberately blackened, presumably in firing rather than from use.

OXID4. Hard, well-fired, fine, oxidised ware with a dark orange exterior and core margin, a blue-grey core and a brown, slightly streaky interior. The exterior shows red iron-streaking. At x20 the only visible grains are a sparse scatter of rounded brown and red ferruginous pellets. The main form in this ware is an open lamp (FIG. 77.44).

OXID5. Red-brown exterior with a grey core and brown interior. The smoothed exterior surface shows red iron-streaking. Hard, sandy fabric with a moderate frequency of well-sorted, fine quartz. The matrix appears quite coarse at x20 with black streaks and occasional iron grains. Probably a first-century ware used to make British copies of butt beakers.

OXID6. Bright orange ware with a darker orange core. Sandy texture with visible white mica. The paste contains rare, fine, angular, white inclusions and a sparse scatter of very fine quartz less than 0.5mm in size. Vessels include curved-wall dishes (FIG. 78.72), lids and flagon. One base-sherd from an open form has incised lines, probably cut marks (FIG. 78.71). A fine variant of probably the same fabric has been distinguished (OXIDF6).

Black-slipped wares (OXIDBS; GYFBS):
OXIDBS. Probably a variant of OXID3 but with a black slip. Restricted to a single example of a Hofheim-type flagon (FIG. 75.18). This may originally have been a white-slipped vessel which has post-depositionally changed in a water-logged deposit.

GYBS. Hard, fine grey sandy ware with a black, polished surface slip. Also occurs in a finer variant as indented beakers, cornice rim beakers, a bowl with an unusual rim (FIG. 83.178) and a single, squat jar.

White-slipped wares (OXIDFWS; WSOXID; WSOXID1–4):
WSOXID1. Orange sandy ware, similar in texture to Verulamium ware with a thin white slip.

WSOXID2. A hard, fine- to medium-grained sandy ware with a distinctive streaky grey and orange interior; cream exterior slip.

WSOXID3. A variant of OXID3 with a white slip.

WSOXID4. A variant of OXID4 with a white slip.

WSOXID6. A variant of OXID6 with a white slip.

Most of the white-slipped wares featured as flagons of various types including ring-necked, expanded rim, collared, bifid and disk-necked (FIGS 77.34, 47; 81.112). Also present in this group is a jar or bowl (FIG. 75.15) and fragments of unguent jars, some ribbed.

White wares (WW1–3):
WW1. A creamy-white ware with occasional red streaks. The core is light grey with pale orange-brown margins. At x20 magnification only occasional fine quartz grains are visible in the fine sandy matrix with rare grains larger than 0.5mm and rare grains of large dark grey argillaceous inclusions less than 1mm in size and rounded white calcareous inclusions.

WW2. White to slightly pinkish in colour with a smooth silky fabric. The core is a darker pink with paler margins. At x20 magnification the matrix contains fine, sparse quartz sand and a scatter of ill-sorted, mid-orange ferruginous pellets 0.5mm and finer in size.

WW3. A hard white sandy ware with a pinkish core. Fairly similar texture to a finer Verulamium white ware. At x20 the matrix shows a moderate to sparse scatter of well-sorted, sub-rounded, clear and white quartz sand, rare red iron and rare white rounded argillaceous pellets.

The white wares mainly feature as flagons (FIGS 75.17; 83.150) and beakers (FIG. 76.33).

PERIOD 3

INTRODUCTION

The features and deposits considered to date to Period 3 comprise one pit, 5039, and one well, 5693, in the south-east of the trench (Objects 440088 and 500035), and one well, 2434 (Object 41016) and one pit, 4835, in the group of northern pits (Object 500028). Collectively these features yielded some 1,796 sherds of pottery weighing 38.6kg. The Period 3 assemblage from 'House 1' comprises material from MB 1 (Object 50018); MB 2 (Object 50019) and MRTB 1/ERTB 1 (= 'ERTB 4') (Object 50037), collectively yielding a total of 13,145 sherds weighing 171.8kg. The south-east layers (Object 701) add a further 12,680 sherds weighing 184kg. Table 36 (Appendix 4) summarises the pottery assemblage as a whole from Period 3.

PERIOD 3 SAMIAN

Decorated ware
By Joanna Bird

Summary

The decorated samian from the Period 3 and 4 contexts reported here consists mainly of small sherds, suggesting that it formed part of the general rubbish on the site. It ranged in date from the Tiberian period until the end of the second century, but most of it was of Hadrianic to Antonine date. Surprisingly, in view of the dates assigned to Periods 3 and 4, there was no decorated East Gaulish ware, although the collection of samian from Silchester as a whole, now housed in Reading Museum, contains a relatively high proportion of East Gaulish wares (J. Bird, computerised report for Reading Museum, 1997).

The decorated samian from Object 701 came from a variety of features. There was one small sherd, of Antonine date and possibly by Cinnamus, from the neonate grave (D39; 4465), and a piece of an early to mid-Flavian Drag. 29 bowl from the CBM dump (D23; 4265). The occupation along the north–south road contained a sherd of a Drag. 37 bowl in an unusual style, probably by a potter of the Quintilianus-Laxtucissa group (D11; 3184), of which two further sherds were recovered from Object 700 (3911, 4063), and a small sherd in the style of the X-9/X-10 group at Les Martres-de-Veyre, of early second-century date (D20). The remainder of the Object 701 decorated samian came from dumps, silts and make-up layers; it comprised less than ten sherds and ranged in date from the Neronian period to the Antonine. It included two mould-stamped vessels, a black-slipped beaker by Libertus ii (D41; 517) and a bowl of Cinnamus ii (D4; 59), a black-slipped jar with an applied female head (D40) and a jar with incised decoration (D19).

Only one of the Period 3 cut features in the northern area had any decorated samian: pit 4835 (Object 500028) contained a single sherd in the style of the X-13/Attianus group, of Hadrianic date (D1). There was little more recovered from the south-eastern cut features with a small sherd of Hadrianic-Antonine date (D2) from well 5693 (Object 500035).

Catalogue of Period 3 decorated samian (FIGS 73–74)

Pits and wells

D1.   Drag. 37, Central Gaul; two sherds. The ovolo is Rogers 1974, B7, used by X-13, X-14 and Attianus. Hadrianic. Pit 4835 (4849 and 5835).

D2.   Drag. 37, Central Gaul. Figure in narrow beaded panel. Hadrianic–Antonine. Well 5693 (5747).

Layers: Object 701

D3.   Drag. 37, South Gaul. Panel design, including a lion eating a captive (Hermet 1934, pl. 25, 33/Oswald 1936–7, type 1493), a large satyr (Hermet pl. 19, 83/Oswald 630) and a spray of five corded rods. Below is a wreath of small trifid leaves. There are links with bowls by the Flavian Sabinus, Mees (1995) Sabinus II: a bowl in this style has the lion and captive and similar rods, but corded in the opposite direction (Ricken 1934, Taf. 14, 13). *c.* A.D. 85–110. (5698) (FIG. 73).

D4. Drag. 37, Central Gaul, with mould-stamp of Cinnamus ii (see stamp catalogue S9); six small sherds. The ovolo is on Stanfield and Simpson 1958, pl. 156, 23; the panel design includes a small medallion or festoon, probably containing a bird (pl. 157, 2 and 6), and a figure, possibly the Actaeon on pl. 161, 51. *c.* A.D. 150–180. (2619) SF 1767 (FIG. 73).

D5. Drag. 37, Central Gaul; two sherds. Probably by Divixtus: the Venus is on Stanfield and Simpson 1958, pl. 115, 2, the border, ring terminal and medallion on pl. 115, 7. The motif in the medallion is probably part of an animal. *c.* A.D. 140–170. (2644).

D6. Drag. 37, Central Gaul; two sherds. Panel design in the style of Cinnamus: the ovolo, border, medallion and leopard are on Stanfield and Simpson 1958, pl. 162, 60, the astragalus motif on pl. 160, 41. *c.* A.D. 150–180. (3103).

D7. Drag. 37, Central Gaul. Broken ovolo, probably Rogers 1974, B143, used by the Cinnamus group. Early to mid-Antonine. (3103).

D8. Drag. 37, Central Gaul. Small dolphin in a festoon. Hadrianic–Antonine. (3103).

D9. Drag. 37, Central Gaul. Part of an animal, probably the leopard used regularly by Casurius (Stanfield and Simpson 1958, pl. 134, 22). Mid- to late Antonine. (3103).

D10. Drag. 30, Central Gaul. Panels, with an astragalus at the base. Antonine. (3103).

D11. Drag. 37, Central Gaul, in the style of Quintilianus or his later associate Laxtucissa. The ovolo and wavy line border were used by both, as were the acanthus and the astragalus impressed across a border (Stanfield and Simpson 1958, pl. 68, 2 and 8, pl. 71, 25, and pl. 98, 8 and 10). The horse, lion and column are on Quintilianus bowls, and the bird in the festoon may be one he used (pl. 68, 7, pl. 69, 13, and pl. 73, 46 and 50). The figure may be a cupid used by Laxtucissa, who also used the astragalus border, the rosette and plume motif and the plain festoon (pl. 97, 5 and 7, and pl. 99, 16). The second bird does not seem to have been used by either, while the leaf in the festoon has no parallel in Rogers 1974. The double line at the base was a regular feature on Quintilianus bowls (pl. 71, 32); the other motifs are too fragmentary to identify. A date in the range *c.* A.D. 135–165 is likely. (3184), two sherds, (3911) and (4063) five sherds (FIG. 73).

D12. Drag. 37, South Gaul. Panels, including a hound and hare at the base and a saltire of leaves; probably by M Crestio, who used the hound and what may be the same hare (Mees 1995, Taf. 45, 1), and the large leaf in the saltire (Taf. 38, 1). *c.* A.D. 75–95. (3424 and 3826).

D13. Drag. 37, Central Gaul, in the style of the Sacer-Attianus group. The deer is probably the one on Stanfield and Simpson 1958, pl. 82, 6, by Sacer, and the double-ended trifid motif and the acanthus tip were used by Attianus (pl. 85, 1 and 9). *c.* A.D. 125–150. (3424).

D14. Drag. 37, Central Gaul. The ovolo, Rogers 1974, B47, was used by Criciro. *c.* A.D. 135–165. (3424) SF 2413.

D15. Drag. 37, Central Gaul, in the style of Cinnamus. Narrow panels, including Vulcan and the dolphin and basket motif (Stanfield and Simpson 1958, pl. 158, 22); the element in the left-hand panel is a partial impression of Rogers 1974, L11 (pl. 160, 41). *c.* A.D. 145–175. (3424).

D16. Drag. 37, Central Gaul, in the style of Cinnamus. Panels, including a large medallion with a horse (probably a partial impression of the horse on Stanfield and Simpson 1958, pl. 163, 72) above a stag (pl. 159, 25), and a herm (pl. 160, 35); the borders and lozenge ornament are on pl. 160, 46. *c.* A.D. 145–175. (3424) (FIG. 74).

D17. Drag. 37, Central Gaul, in the style of Casurius. The ovolo and border are on Stanfield and Simpson 1958, pl. 133, 17, the pigeon on pl. 134, 24. *c.* A.D. 165–200. (3424).

D18. Drag. 37, Central Gaul. Scrollery at base. Hadrianic–Antonine. (3424).

D19. Déch. 72, Central Gaul. Decorated with incised facets, arranged as a double-ended spray of leaves bound at the centre, with other facets at the sides. Mid- to later Antonine. (3424) (FIG. 74).

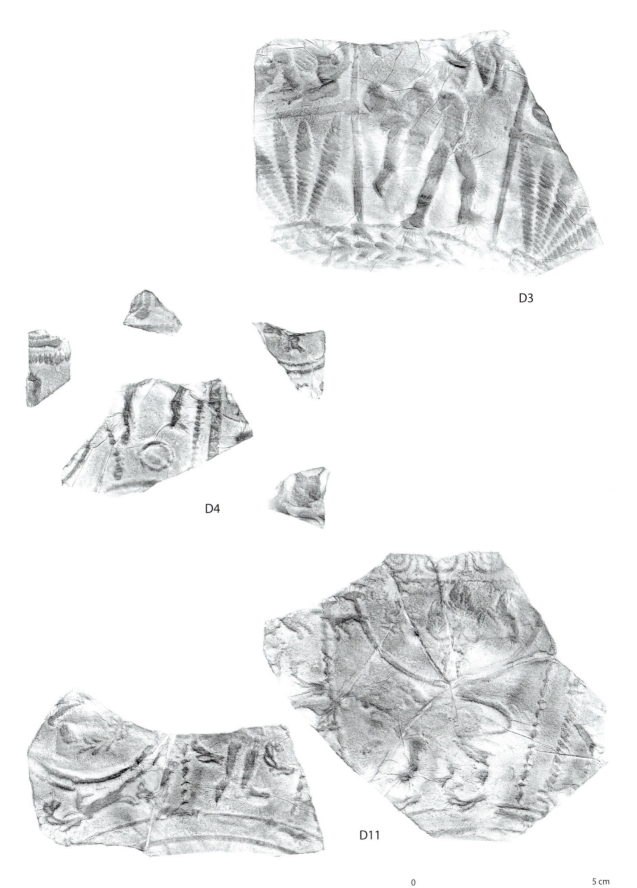

FIG. 73. Decorated samian from Period 3 Object 701. Scale 1:1.

D16

D36

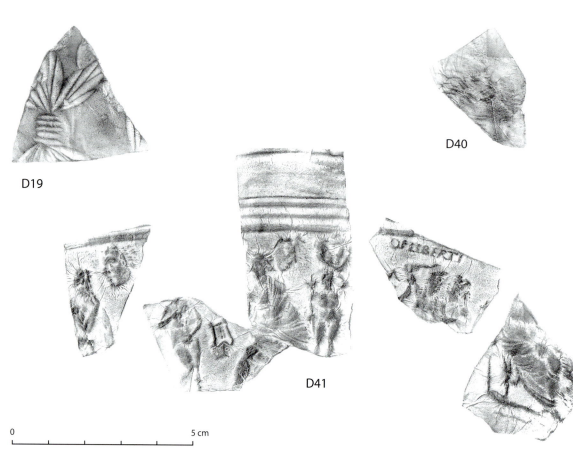

D19

D40

D41

FIG. 74.   Decorated samian from Period 3 Object 701. Scale 1:1.

D20.   Drag. 37, Central Gaul. Ovolo Rogers 1974, B38, used by X-9 and X-10; the border below is rather more untidy than their usual borders. *c.* A.D. 110–130. (3431).

D21.   Drag. 30, South Gaul, in the style of Masclus. The ovolo and rosette are on Mees 1995, Taf. 112, 2, with similar tendrils. *c.* A.D. 50–65. (3435).

D22.   Drag. 37, South Gaul. Spurred leaf. Early to mid-Flavian. (3471).

D23.   Drag. 29, South Gaul; two sherds. The lower zone contains a band of S-shaped volutes above a basal wreath of chevrons. The general style is close to much of the Pompeii Hoard material, where the volutes occur on a signed Memor bowl and similar chevrons on a signed and stamped bowl of Mommo (Atkinson 1914, nos 15 and 74; Dzwiza 2004, nos A15 and A74). *c.* A.D. 70–85. (4265).

D24.   Drag. 37, Central Gaul, probably by Attianus. The leaf is probably that on Stanfield and Simpson 1958, pl. 87, 21; the bird is on pl. 87, 20. *c*. A.D. 125–150. (3826).

D25.   Drag. 37, Central Gaul. Large medallion; the motifs inside are too fragmentary to identify. Antonine. (3826).

D26.   Drag. 37, Central Gaul. The beaded border, ring terminal and caryatid were shared by Divixtus and Cinnamus (Stanfield and Simpson 1958, pl. 115, 1 and 7, pl. 117, 4 and 10, and pl. 158, 19 and 22); the male figure, probably Apollo (Oswald 1936–7, type 93), is not apparently recorded for either potter. *c*. A.D. 145–175. (3849).

D27.   Drag. 37, Central Gaul. Panels with corded borders, ending in a seven- or eight-petalled rosette; they include a small medallion and probably a ring motif. Hadrianic–Antonine. (3849).

D28.   Drag. 37, Central Gaul. Hare in large medallion. Early to mid-Antonine. (4293).

D29.   Drag. 37, Central Gaul. This ovolo is impressed over a plain line on bowls of Pugnus and Secundus I; a bowl attributed to Pugnus has a similar untidy vertical border, taken up into the ovolo (Rogers 1999, pl. 90, 21). *c*. A.D. 145–175. (4063).

D30.   Drag. 37, Central Gaul; three sherds. In the style of Cinnamus: the bear is on Stanfield and Simpson 1958, pl. 163, 66, the scroll with astragalus binding and the medallion on pl. 162, 60. *c*. A.D. 145–175. (3912).

D31.   Drag. 37, Central Gaul, in the style of Drusus II. The Silenus is on Stanfield and Simpson 1958, pl. 89, 16, the rosette and a similar small panel at the base on pl. 88, 1. The other motifs are too fragmentary to identify. *c*. A.D. 125–150. (4308).

D32.   Drag. 37, Central Gaul, in the style of Casurius. The ovolo and beads are on Stanfield and Simpson 1958, pl. 135, 32. *c*. A.D. 165–200. (4063).

D33.   Drag. 30, Central Gaul. Panels, including a large medallion, probably containing an animal, and part of an unidentified figure. Antonine. (4063).

D34.   Drag. 37, Central Gaul. The ovolo is too badly smudged to identify; below, panels, including a large medallion, perhaps containing a leaf, and a ring at the corner. Antonine. (4063).

D35.   Drag. 29, South Gaul. Upper zone scroll with small bifid binding, similar to one used by Modestus (Mees 1995, Taf. 141, 2). *c*. A.D. 50–65. (4067).

D36.   Drag. 30, South Gaul, in the style of Germanus. The ovolo is on Mees 1995, Taf. 72, 1; below is a leaf scroll winding over an area divided horizontally into two zones. The leaf in the scroll and the corded tendril are on Taf. 87, 1 and 4. For the leaf tips in the upper zone, cf. Taf. 83, 1; the motif in the lower zone is too fragmentary to identify. *c*. A.D. 70–90. (4270) one sherd; four sherds from (3836), Object 700, below (FIG. 74).

D37.   Drag. 37, South Gaul. Ovolo with four-pronged tongue, probably one used by the M Crestio group (cf. Mees 1995, Taf. 49, 2). *c*. A.D. 75–95. (4270).

D38.   Drag. 37, Central Gaul; five small sherds. In the style of X-9. The ovolo, border and rosette are on Stanfield and Simpson 1958, pl. 29, 344; the figures include Diana (pl. 29, 353) and probably the sea-horse to left (pl. 32, 376). *c*. A.D. 110–130. (4270).

D39.   Drag. 37, Central Gaul. Panel design, including Vulcan: cf. Stanfield and Simpson 1958, pl. 161, 49, by Cinnamus. Antonine. (4465).

D40.   Black-slipped jar, Déch. 72 or 74, Central Gaul. The applied mask is a female head, not illustrated by Déchelette (1904, II.2) or by Simpson (1957; 1973). Mid- to later Antonine. (5124) (FIG. 74).

D41.   Black-slipped beaker, Déch. 64, with a mould stamp of Libertus ii of Lezoux (S17); as often happens with this form, the slip has only partially fired black. The figure-types are all previously recorded for Libertus: they are a seated man, Venus, a seated woman, Neptune supporting a mask, Bacchus supported by two Bacchantes, and Demeter and Kore, with two further masks and a lyre in the field. Bémont 1977, 73–8, fig. 17, has all the motifs except the Bacchic group, which is on Stanfield and Simpson 1958, pl. 51, 602; for generally similar beakers, cf. pls 52, 608–612, and 53, 622. *c*. A.D. 115–130. (4508) SFs 3278, 3318, 3324, 3325, seven sherds; also sherd from (5698) SF 3961 (FIGS 26, 74).

Stamped samian

By Brenda Dickinson

The stamps from 'House 1': MB 1, MB 2 and 'ERTB 4' are published in Clarke *et al.* 2007.

Pits and wells

S1.   Drag. 18. South Gaulish, La Graufesenque. OF.IVC[VN] Iucundus iii Die 5a. A.D. 75–85. Well 2234 (2254).

S2.   Drag. 31. Central Gaulish, Lezoux. SACER[Sacero Die 1a. A.D. 150–180. Pit 4835 (4832).

Layers: Object 701

South Gaulish

S3.   Drag. 15/17 or 18. La Graufesenque. CARANTI Carantus i, Die 7a. A.D. 75–90. (4253) SF 3051.

S4.   Drag. 18. La Graufesenque. GER[Germanus i, Die incomplete 2. A.D. 65–90. (4270) SF 3070.

S5.   Drag. 27. South Gaulish. INII. Probably illiterate. Flavian–Trajanic. (4475) SF 3328.

Central Gaulish

S6.   Drag. 33. Lezoux. AVITA.MA Avitus iv, Die 1b. A.D. 120–150. (3424) SF 2364.

S7.   Drag. 33. Lezoux. CELSIANIF Celsianus, Die 8a. A.D. 160–190. (3103) SF 2272.

S8.   Drag. 33. Lezoux. CE[? unidentified stamp. A.D. 140–200. (3424) SF 2414.

S9.   Drag. 37. Lezoux. [CIN]NAMIM Cinnamus ii, Die 4b. Stamped in the mould (D4). A.D. 150–180. (2619) SF 1767.

S10. Drag. 38 or 44. Lezoux. CRISPI[NIM] Crispinus ii, Die 1a. A.D. 160–200. (3424) SF 2400.

S11. Drag. 18/31. Lezoux. [DAGO]MARVSF Dagomarus. The die was also used at Les Martres-de-Veyre. *c.* A.D. 100–120. (4475) SF 3337.

S12. Drag. 18/31R. Lezoux. D[unidentified stamp. A.D. 120–160. (4270) SF 3078.

S13. Drag. 31R. Central Gaulish. MA[unidentified stamp. A.D. 160–200. (2435) SF 4571.

S14. Drag. 27. Les Martres-de-Veyre. [NA]TONVS Natonus, Die 1a. *c.* A.D. 115–140. (4475) SF 3322.

S15. Drag. 33. Les Martres-de-Veyre. N[ICEPHORF] Nicephor i, Die 1a. *c.* A.D. 100–120. (4477) SF 3868.

S16. Drag. 46. Lezoux. PINNAFE Pinna, Die 2a. A.D. 135–165. (4303) SF 3176.

S17. Déch. 64. Lezoux. OFLIBERTI Libertus ii, Die 6a. *c.* A.D. 115–130. (5698) SF 3961, with sherds from (4508). Stamped in the mould (D41).

S18. Drag. 27. Les Martres-de-Veyre. SACE[R] Sacer i, Die 14a. A.D. 120–140. (4308) SF 3197.

S19. Drag. 27. Lezoux. [SILVI].OF Silvius ii, Die 2a. A.D. 120–145. (4308) SF 4573.

S20. Drag. 18/31. Lezoux. SILVI[.OF] Silvius ii, Die 2b. A.D. 125–145. (3471) SF 2517.

S21. Drag. 33. Lezoux. SOLIIMNI Sollemnis i, Die 5a. A.D. 130–150. (4303) SF 3171.

S22. Drag. 33. Lezoux. VEGI...M? unidentified stamp. A.D. 140–200. (3424) SF 2411.

S23. Drag. 31. Lezoux. [VE]LOX.F Velox, Die 2b. A.D. 140–170. (3471) SF 2544.

S24. Curle 15 with rosette stamp. Probably Central Gaulish, but in a pale fabric; the slip is rather orange and uneven, perhaps under-fired. Hadrianic–Antonine. (3849).

S25. Drag. 18/31. Les Martres-de-Veyre. VITA[LIS.M.S.F.] Vitalis iii, Die 2a. *c.* A.D. 100–120. (4349) SF 3358.

S26. Drag. 33. Stamped]I or I[, an unidentified Central Gaulish stamp. Hadrianic–Antonine. (4063).

S27. Drag. 33. Les Martres-de-Veyre.]LISF unidentified. Trajanic–Hadrianic. (4070) SF 3348.

DESCRIPTION OF PERIOD 3 GROUPS

Pits and wells (FIGS 75–76 and 80)

Four pits and wells have been placed into Period 3; Objects 500035, 44008, 41016 and 500028. Tables 37–40 (Appendix 4) provide separate quantified summaries for each of these four features. A range of the Period 3 pottery is illustrated in FIGS 75–76 arranged in feature groups. The slumps into 6290 (Object 500036) are considered below under Layers: Object 701.

South-east pits: well 5693 (Object 500035) (Table 37; FIG. 75.1–8)

Well 5693 yielded an assemblage of 375 sherds of pottery weighing 11.1kg. With an average sherd weight of 29.6g, the pottery is particularly well preserved with a number of large sherds. Sherd joins were observed between layers 6285 and 6300. The assemblage comprises a mixture of continental imports, traded regional wares and local wares. Eleven sherds of samian are present, seven South Gaulish and four Central Gaulish. A *terminus post quem* is provided by a decorated Drag. 37 from 5747 dated to the Hadrianic-Antonine period (catalogue no. D2). Samian forms present include Drag. 18/31 and 18 dishes and Drag. 27 cups. Other fineware imports are restricted to a single sherd of ARG CC beaker, three sherds from a closed form in fine black micaceous ware and eight sherds of imported white ware, along with sherds of Dressel 20 olive oil and Gallic wine amphorae and North Gaulish mortaria. Collectively the imports account for just 10.7 per cent by count of the group. Regional imports account for a further 4.3 per cent, with small quantities from the Dorset, Oxfordshire and Verulamium industries. The DOR BB1 vessels are limited to plain-walled dishes and a flat-rim bowl, whilst the Oxfordshire ware includes a ring-necked white ware flagon and Verulamium region wares flagon and mortaria, the latter quite worn from use.

Amongst the local wares, products of the Alice Holt industry contribute 57.3 per cent by count of the assemblage. These include a number of beaded rim jars (FIG. 75.1–3), necked jars (FIG. 75.6), storage jars, small dishes (FIG. 75.4–5), and 'Surrey' bowls (FIG. 75.7). Several jars had sooted exteriors.

Many of the other known local wares in grog- and flint-tempered fabrics are redeposited finds, and this is highlighted by 4.8 per cent of the total assemblage comprising Silchester ware (fabric SIL F1) which had ceased production by this time. Probably more contemporary with the deposit is the presence of several sherds of large grog-tempered storage jar, which accounts for 6.4 per cent by count and 13 per cent by weight.

The remaining fabrics recorded are of unknown source mainly comprising fine grey wares, various oxidised wares and white-slipped ware. A basal knob in a buff ware, probably from a small amphora (FIG. 75.8) could be imported or British. One lid in oxidised ware had a blackened lip as did a flat rim bowl.

In terms of the overall vessel profile for the well, jars dominate accounting for 45.3 per cent (eve) (see Table 50), followed by flagons at 20.9 per cent, dishes at 13 per cent and lids at 6.4 per cent.

South-east pits: pit 5039 (Object 44008) (Table 38; FIG. 75.9–16)

Pit 5039 produced 577 sherds of pottery weighing 10.6kg. Compared to the previous feature the sherds are more fragmented with an average sherd weight of 18.5g. Sherd links were observed between layers 6228 and 6233; 4549 and 6228; 5001 and 4549; and 5005 and 5009. Continental imports make up 10.3 per cent with broadly the same range of material. Samian includes both South and Central Gaulish pieces, including three sherds of Les Martres-de-Veyre/early Lezoux with a *terminus post quem* in the Hadrianic period. Several colour-coated beakers with roughcast decoration are present in Argonne, Central Gaulish and Cologne fabrics. A residual *Cam.* 8 platter in GAB TN came from context 5001. Sherds of Gallic amphora are quite prolific making up 5.6 per cent by count and 17.1 per cent by weight.

Regional wares are very sparse and, unlike well 5693, products of the Dorset and Oxfordshire industries appear to be absent with just seven sherds of Verulamium region ware (e.g. FIG. 75.11 and 14) and a London ware bowl (FIG. 75.10). Amongst the local wares Alice Holt vessels account for 49.2 per cent with some residual flint- and grog-tempered ware. Sherds of grog-tempered storage jars are not quite as prolific as in the former group.

The same spectrum of grey wares, oxidised wares and white-slipped wares is present. Oxidised fabric 3 makes up 7 per cent of the assemblage, again with several lids along with reeded rim bowls. Quite a diverse range of fine grey wares is present, 7.8 per cent, with examples of poppyhead beakers, jars, bowls (FIG. 75.13) and dishes. Amongst the fine oxidised wares is a sherd with white barbotine dots. Some of these may be products of the Oxfordshire industry.

The breakdown of vessels is quite similar to well 5693 with jars dominating followed by bowls, flagons and lids (cf. Appendix 4, Table 56).

Northern pits: well 2234 (Object 41016) (Table 39; FIGS 75.17–21; 76.22–25; 85.G1)

Well 2234 produced a more modest assemblage of 443 sherds of pottery weighing 9715g. A large number of layers were excavated and there is clearly a chronological difference between the lower and upper horizons. Continental imports contribute just 6.2 per cent by sherd count, some 28 sherds, of which 17 are probably pre-Flavian including South Gaulish samian (stamp S1), Gallo-Belgic wares (GAB TN, TR1C), and Central Gaulish white-slip flagon. The latest samian, dating to the early second century, comes from layers 2293 and 2254 in the upper zones of the well.

Regional wares are quite well represented with products from the Dorset, Verulamium region, Nene Valley and Oxfordshire industries. Overall the regional imports account for 19 per cent of the assemblage and 17.7 per cent of these are products of the Verulamium industries, 37.3 per cent by weight. Of particular note are two semi-complete Verulamium region flagons (FIGS 27; 75.20–1), both from layer 2722, a gravel layer. A further double-handled, large flagon came from lower level 3341 (FIG. 75.19). Two mortaria are also present, one rim fragment from 2303 showing the very edge of a stamp. The small fragments of Lower Nene Valley and Oxfordshire colour-coated wares, probably of fourth-century date came from the uppermost layer 2311 and layer 2254. Similarly the DOR BB1 came from the uppermost levels.

Alice Holt products and allied grey wares account for 39.7 per cent by count but only 20 per cent by weight. Jars dominate but two flanged bowls of later third- to fourth-century type came from horizons 2304 and 2311. A jar base from 2330 has a post-firing graffiti (FIG. 85.G1). Two sherds of Overwey white ware, again from the upper levels, reinforce the late Roman accumulation in the upper zone. The grog-tempered storage jar includes a sherd reshaped as a counter (SF 2137).

Of note amongst the other wares present is a flagon in a black-slipped oxidised ware from 3341 (FIG. 75.18). A handle in a similar fabric from 2967 may be from the same vessel. Bodysherds from a very large flagon in a white-slipped, oxidised ware were recovered from layers 2254 and 2311. A further flagon in white ware (FIG. 75.17) came from 3341.

The vessel profile for the well deviates from the usual pattern in that flagons dominate at 47.2 per cent (eve) followed by jars at 27.6 per cent and fineware platters at 10.8 per cent (Table 50). If the handles and concentrations of bodysherds are counted alongside the rims, there is probably a minimum of ten flagons associated with the deposits from layer 2747 and below.

The lowest horizon in well 2234 to produce pottery was 3362, which produced just eight sherds amongst which were two buff flagon handles from two different vessels. The succeeding layer, 3359, produced just five bodysherds, with layer 3341 above this, a concentration of three flagons (FIG. 75.17–19). Both nos 17 and 18 are forms typologically datable to the pre-Flavian period, the latter perhaps continuing up to the later first century. The black-slipped fabric is unique to this vessel, although it is just possible that this is a post-depositional change. The Verulamium region double-handled example (FIG. 75.19) can be paralleled by an example from London sometimes referred to as an amphora (Davies *et al.* 1994, fig. 36.169). It is not one of the commoner forms found and is not closely dated other than later first to early second century. The base of a grog-tempered large jar was also found with the flagons along with five coarsewares

(ALH RE and Silchester ware). Layer 3339 above this also produced a small assemblage of six bodysherds, which included a sherd of South Gaulish samian Drag. 27 cup. A further similar sherd came from 2967 along with three further flagon handles, one in a black-slipped oxidised ware, which may belong with the rim from 3341, and two in a fine oxidised white-slipped ware. The grog-tempered counter also came from this deposit. Above this layer 2722 produced two semi-complete flagons (FIG. 75.20–1), one a pinch-mouthed type in Verulamium region ware; the other missing its rim but with a deliberate body piercing. Pinch-mouthed flagons are again not common in the Verulamium region potters' repertoire and the examples from London lack detailed dating, although typologically the form appears in the Claudian period continuing into the second century. It is possible that this vessel comes from the recently discovered kilns at Northgate House, London, which were also producing Verulamium-type white wares including pinch-mouthed flagons in the first half of the second century (Seeley and Drummond-Murray 2005, 85). Also with this group is a sherd of South Gaulish Drag. 18 dish, a sherd of Central Gaulish white-slipped flagon, an amphora lid and eight coarsewares.

Another small group of 23 sherds came from 2320 which included a jar base with an incised cross (FIG. 85.G1), a large sherd of Baetican amphora, a rim from a grog-tempered storage jar, one sherd of South Gaulish samian, eight of fine micaceous black ware and nine sherds of ALH RE. Layer 2336 produced a large rim sherd of Verulamium mortarium typologically dated to A.D. 100–120 and a lid knob of oxidised ware OXID3 that seems to be an early second-century industry. Further lid sherds are present in 2302 above with a few coarseware sherds. Further coarsewares, predominantly Alice Holt, came from 2275 and 2333, which could again be later first or early second century in date. From horizon 2304 upwards the deposits appear far more variable with a mixture of redeposited first-century material, alongside sherds from vessels potentially of later third- to fourth-century currency, suggesting a later phase of levelling off. In total, 235 sherds (3kg) of material, just over half the total assemblage, came from these later deposits with an average sherd weight of 12.9g indicating the more fragmented nature of these deposits.

Northern pits: pit 4835 (Object 500028) (Table 40; FIG. 76.26)

The only pit from the northern area dated to Period 3 produced a modest assemblage of 246 sherds, 5.9kg. This appears to be quite a mixed assemblage chronologically in that there is quite a high proportion of first-century fine and coarseware present. The *terminus post quem* for the pit is provided by 15 sherds of Central Gaulish samian and 11 sherds of DOR BB1.

Continental imports contribute 15.6 per cent by count, with slightly more samian sherds than seen in the features already discussed above. There are four vessels of Hadrianic or Hadrianic-Antonine date from layers 4849, 4861, 4832 and 5835. One Central Gaulish Drag. 31 dish has a rivet-repair hole. There are sherd links between layers 4849 and 5835. Residual finds include sherds from a *Cam.* 16 platter in GAB TN, a platter in GAB TR2 with the edge of a potter's stamp, and a white ware butt-beaker (*Cam.* 113 (fabric NOG WH)). Regional imports are not prolific, with just DOR BB1 and VER WH; the former includes a jar decorated with diagonal burnished lines and a beaded-rim bowl.

Compared to the previous features the proportions of Alice Holt grey ware and Silchester ware differ with proportionately less of the former, which accounts for 36.4 per cent by count, and more of the latter at 27.2 per cent. There are also several sherds of first-century grog-tempered ware (fabrics G1 and G4) alongside second-century grog-tempered storage jar. The familiar presence of fine grey ware, including barbotine-dot decorated beaker, oxidised ware and white-slipped oxidised ware reflects early second-century types. One sherd of Hadrianic decorated samian was recovered (catalogue no. D1) and one stamp dated A.D. 150–180 (no. S2). An almost complete (*c.* 90 per cent) grey ware burnished dish (FIG. 74.26) came from context 5835.

Curiously the assemblage from this feature deviates from the expected norm in terms of the vessel repertoire in that coarseware bowls dominate the EVEs at 42.7 per cent, followed by jars at 30 per cent and then fineware dishes at 7 per cent (Table 53). Lids also make quite a significant contribution at 5.7 per cent.

Catalogue of illustrated sherds from Period 3 pits and wells (FIGS 75–76)

South-east pits: well 5693 (Object 500035) (Table 37)

1. Large beaded rim jar decorated with a single burnished wavy line. Burnished on the shoulder. Fabric: ALH RE. (6300).
2–3. Two beaded rim jars with sooted exteriors. Handmade, wheel-finished. Fabric: ALH RE. (6300).
4–5. Shallow dishes with external offset. Fabric: ALH RE. (6300).
6. Everted rim jar with internal lid seating. Fabric: ALH RE. (6325).
7. Surrey bowl in a black sandy ware. Fabric: ALH RE. (6326).
8. Amphora base. Buff sandy ware with a dark orange-brown core possibly once with a white slip. At x20 the paste contains a common frequency of well-sorted quartz sand less than 0.5mm and rare red iron. Possibly a Verulamium region product. Fabric: BUFF. (6326).

South-east pits: pit 5039 (Object 44008) (Table 38)

9. Necked, cordoned jar with a carinated shoulder. Slightly sooted exterior. Fabric: ALH RE. (6228/6233).
10. Small bowl imitating a Drag. 30. Rouletted decoration in the upper zone. Fine black 'London ware'. Fabric: LON BWF. (6228).
11. Verulamium ware mortarium. Fabric: VER WH. (6228).
12. Small lid-seated jar. Brownish orange, fine sandy ware with traces of a mica slip. Possibly slightly burnt. Fabric: MICOX. (5009).
13. Deep carinated bowl in fine grey ware. Fabric: GYF. (5001).
14. Verulamium ware lid with a blackened lip. Fabric: VER WH. (4549).
15. Everted rim jar/bowl in a white-slipped oxidised ware. The vessel is slipped on both the exterior and interior surfaces. The narrow cordon at the neck has been cleaned of slip and shows through as orange. Fabric: WSOXID3. (4549).
16. Jar/large beaker with slightly everted rim. Decorated with tooled line vertically bisected diamonds. Fabric: GREY1. (4549).

Northern pits: well 2234 (Object 41016) (Table 39)

17. Pulley-wheel rim, single-handled flagon. Fabric: WW2. (3341).
18. Hofheim-rim flagon. Fine oxidised ware with a black slip. Fabric: OXIDBS. (3341).
19. Large double-handled flagon with a slightly cupped rim. Fabric: VER WH. (3341).
20. Almost complete single-handled flagon missing the rim and handle. The belly of the vessel has a deliberate post-firing vertical slot. Fabric: VER WH. (2722), SF 1737 (cf. FIG. 27).
21. Almost complete pinched-mouth flagon, *c.* 80 per cent present. Some blackening on one side of the body. Fabric: VER WH. (2722), SF 1763 (cf. FIG. 27).
22. Necked, cordoned jar with a carinated shoulder. Fabric: ALH RE. (2275).
23. Shallow dish with a footring. Fabric: GYF. (2254).
24. Globular beaker in fine grey ware. Fabric: GYF. (2254).
25. Mortarium flange with traces of a very worn/poorly impressed potter's stamp. Probably a double line but individual letters difficult to decipher. Fabric: VER WH. (2303) (FIG. 86.2).

Northern pits: pit 4835 (Object 500028) (Table 40)

26. Grey ware dish, probably wheelmade. The interior has an irregular, burnished finish whilst the exterior base is well burnished and slightly sooted. Fabric: GREY. (5835), SF 3756.

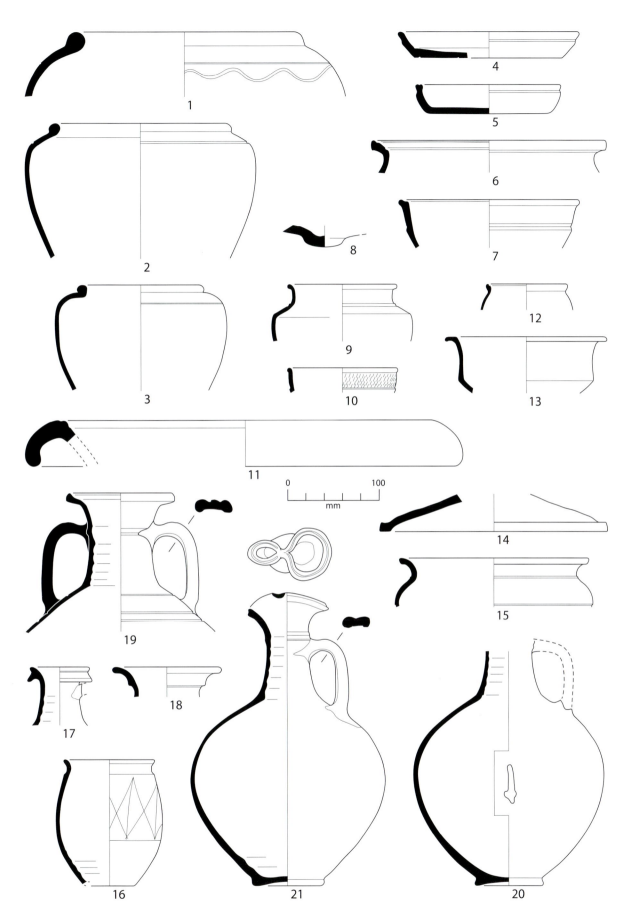

FIG. 75. Pottery from Period 3 pits and wells. Scale 1:4. (*Drawn by Frances Taylor/Jane Timby*)

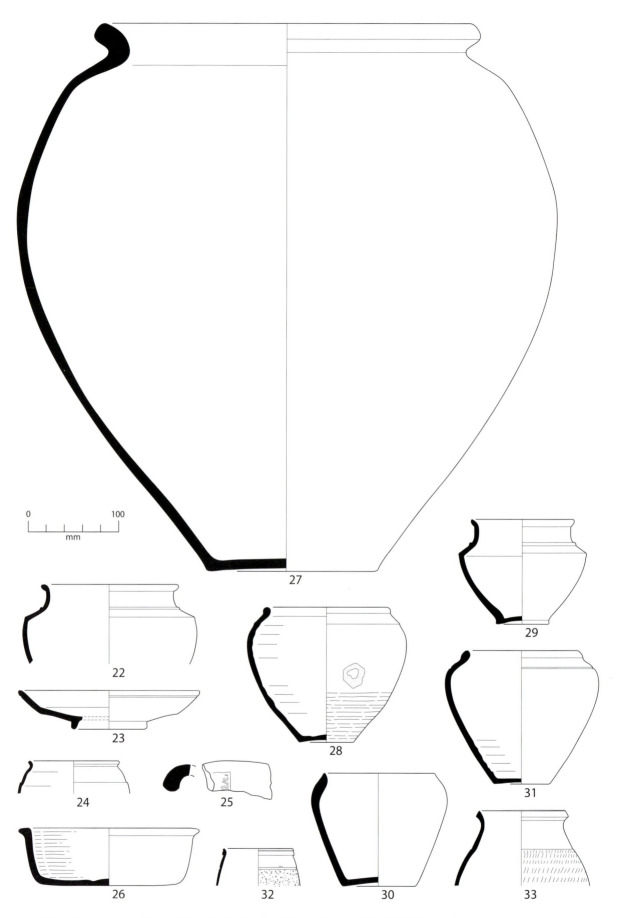

FIG. 76. Pottery from Period 3 well 2234, pit 4835, MB 1 and 2, MRTB 1 and south-east occupation Object 701 (Nos 32–3). Scale 1:4. (*Drawn by Frances Taylor/Jane Timby*)

'House 1' (Table 36)

Summary

The Period 3 contexts associated with 'House 1' (Objects 50018, 50019 and 50037) produced a large assemblage of some 11,756 sherds weighing *c.* 147.50kg (see Table 36 for summary and Timby 2007 for full report). Although the overall average sherd weight is quite low at 12.5g, at least five complete vessels were recovered, one in fragments and not illustrated and several substantial sherds and multiple fragments of others (FIG. 76.27–31). A noticeably high level of redeposited first-century material would also account for the overall lower average sherd weight. An enormous flint-tempered jar, partially reconstructed (FIG. 76.27), is excluded in the quantification. This vessel found placed on its side in Masonry Building 1 was substantially burnt on the lower half strongly suggesting that it may have served as a *clibanus* for baking bread, keeping dishes hot or some other similar function (FIGS 12–13).

MB 1 (Object 50018) produced about 20 per cent of the assemblage by sherd count. The samian is dominated by South Gaulish wares, but the few Central Gaulish wares suggest a Hadrianic date for the group overall. Also present is a small sherd of Moselle black-slip beaker which might suggest a date in the later second century and two small Oxfordshire white ware flagons (Young 1977, type W18), conventionally dated to the second half of the third century. Other regional wares include Colchester colour-coated beakers, Dorset black-burnished ware, and Verulamium white ware.

MB 2 (Object 50019) produced a slightly smaller assemblage of some 1,062 sherds, *c.* 14.9kg. The latest samian dates to the Hadrianic–early Antonine period. As with Object 500018, there is a high proportion of residual material, including a small Silchester flint-tempered ware jar (SF 2039) probably complete when deposited (FIG. 76.30). A complete Alice Holt ware beaded-rim jar (FIGS 15; 76.31) was also recovered. Grog-tempered ware storage jar is also quite prominent with several sherds from a single vessel from context 4123. Despite the mid-second-century date provided by the samian, Dorset black-burnished ware is noticeably absent, suggesting that it perhaps was not being traded much to Silchester at this time.

MRTB 1/ERTB 1 ('ERTB 4') (Object 50037) produced the largest of the Period 3 assemblages from this area with some 9,844 sherds weighing *c.* 124kg. Again the average sherd size is quite low at 12.5g and although there are two complete pots (FIG. 76.28–9), there are few other obviously semi-complete or once-complete vessels. Central Gaulish samian is well represented including five stamped Lezoux pieces, four of which broadly date to the period A.D. 160–190. Regional and continental imports are quite diverse but of moderately low frequency. As with most of the other groups, Alice Holt and allied grey wares dominate, in this case contributing around 56 per cent of the assemblage by count.

Catalogue of illustrated sherds (FIG. 76)

27. Very large handmade jar, semi-complete. Fabric: F1. Internally and externally blackened on one side possibly suggesting it functioned as a *clibanus*. (3259), SF 2377 (cf. FIGS 11–13).
28. Complete beaded-rim jar. Deliberately and slightly clumsily holed post-firing. Fabric: ALH RE. Object 50037. (3930), SF 3095 (cf. FIG. 18).
29. Complete small, necked, cordoned jar with a carinated shoulder. Fabric: ALH RE. Object 50037. (3930), SF 3096 (cf. FIG. 18).
30. Broken but probably once complete Silchester ware jar. Fabric: SIL F1. Object 50019, SF 2039.
31. Complete beaded-rim jar. Fabric: ALH RE. Object 50019. (3933), SF 2549 (cf. FIG. 15).

Layers (Object 701) (Table 41; FIGS 76.32–33; 77.34–62; 78.63–92; 85.G2)

In total the sample of pottery analysed in detail from the Period 3 layers amounts to some 12,680 sherds weighing 184kg, 146.3 EVEs (Appendix 4, Table 41). Looking at the assemblage overall samian accounts for 5.6 per cent by count, other imported fine wares for 1.6 per cent, amphorae for 2.7 per cent, regional wares for 6.4 per cent, and local or unassigned wares for 83.7 per cent. The samian is dominated by Central Gaulish ware but includes sherds of Les Martres-de-Veyre ware, two small sherds of East Gaulish ware and some South Gaulish material (Table 42). The group includes a number of vessels stamped by Antonine Lezoux potters alongside some residual material.

The lowermost layers in the sequence are those slumped into 6290 from which some 1,062 sherds, *c*. 21.5kg, of pottery were analysed, 8 per cent of that from Object 701 numerically. Most of these contexts produced quite modest assemblages with 74 per cent of the analysed sherds coming from context 5698 towards the bottom of the sequence. The assemblage from 5698 comprised some 42 per cent vessels of Alice Holt and allied grey ware including a range of jars, bowls, dishes and lids (FIG. 77.45). Also present were seven sherds of DOR BB1 including examples of flat rim bowls, plain, slightly curved-wall dish and two, possibly intrusive, grooved-rim bowls (FIG. 77.39–41) which imply a date at the end of the second century. Only a single sherd of Central Gaulish samian came from this deposit along with a figured sherd from black-slipped Central Gaulish ware with a mould stamp of Libertus of Lezoux (catalogue no. D41; S17; FIGS 26; 74) dated A.D. 120–140. Sherds from the same vessel came from context 4508 (Object 701). Other contemporary fine wares are sparse. Of particular note is a flat-topped jar or dolium in VER WH (FIG. 77.35) and an almost complete, but worn, VER WH mortarium stamped by the potter Matugenus (FIG. 77.36) dated A.D. 90–120/5. In addition there is a handmade bowl in a Hampshire grog-tempered ware (FIG. 77.42) and a large fragment of an open lamp (FIG. 77.44). White-slipped oxidised flagons came from this and other horizons (e.g. FIG. 77.34, 46–7). Layer 5727 produced sherds of mid to late Antonine Central Gaulish samian. Layer 5183 had an Oxfordshire white ware mortarium (Young 1977, type M5) dated A.D. 100–170, and 5122 two examples of flagons (ibid., type W6) dated A.D. 150–240.

The dump of CBM produced a small assemblage of 159 sherds. Again few fine wares are present with just ten sherds of samian, only two of which are Central Gaulish, the rest South Gaulish (cf. catalogue no. D23). The group includes a fine, black carinated bowl (FIG. 77.50), a North Gaulish mortarium (FIG. 77.49), and an Alice Holt-type grey ware (FIG. 77.48).

A further substantial collection of pottery came from the gravels and dumps with some 2,543 sherds weighing 42kg. This group contained some 63 sherds of Central Gaulish samian with a number of mid-second-century stamps (catalogue nos D31, D36–8; S3, S4, S12, S17–19); Alice Holt grey ware is still prominent accounting for 42 per cent by count with grog-tempered storage jar accounting for a further 10.7 per cent. A small number of DOR BB1 sherds are present, including early jars with acute latticing and flat-rim bowls. The group contains a fairly high residual component reflected in the finewares and coarsewares. Amongst the latest sherds present is an OXF WH walled-sided flagon (FIG. 77.52) (Young 1977, type W9) with a production period A.D. 240–300.

The possible building MRTB 3 produced quite a large, well fragmented assemblage from 3490 with some 632 sherds. The average sherd weight at 9.4g is lower than the previously discussed groups which generally average around 13–16g. The group is very much dominated by two fabrics, ALH RE and oxidised sandy wares accounting for 45.4 per cent and 20.7 per cent respectively. The form profile is slightly unusual in that whilst jars dominate at 42.5 per cent eve, lids are more prominent than normal at 29 per cent. The remainder comprises bowls/dishes at 16.4 per cent and beakers at 10.7 per cent. Most of the lids are in the oxidised fabric along with the majority of the flat-rimmed bowls, possibly forming a complementary set.

The lower, second-century silt horizons collectively yielded 1,148 sherds, 15.2kg. The sherds showed an average weight of 13g. The group showed a similar profile to others in this assemblage in that ALH RE dominates at 55 per cent (count). Of particular note are three decorated sherds of 'black samian' (FIG. 74.D40) dating to the mid-to-late Antonine period. The Central Gaulish samian includes decorated sherds and a stamp, the latest date of which is A.D. 145–175 (catalogue nos D5, D11, D28–30, D32–5; S5, S11, S14–15, S26–7). A sherd link was observed in a decorated vessel between context 4063 in these silts and two sherds from the occupation along the north–south road. The DOR BB1 is confined to mainly flat rim bowls/dishes and jars with a few plain-rimmed dishes. Amongst the Oxfordshire white ware are mortaria (Young 1977) types M10 and M14 (A.D. 180–240) and a further example of a wall-sided flagon type W9 (A.D. 240–300) (FIG. 77.59).

The accumulation layers and upper clays contained slightly less material (557 sherds) in a more fragmented condition (average sherd weight 9.9g). Alice Holt grey ware accounts for 58 per cent, with oxidised wares, fine grey wares and Oxfordshire white ware quite well represented; the latter includes a lid (Young 1977, type W72). One ALH RE vessel has a post-firing inscribed 'X' (FIG. 85.G2). The latest Central Gaulish samian falls into the Hadrianic–Antonine period (stamps S20, S23) with other residual material (e.g. catalogue no. D22).

The upper silts contained a small assemblage of 253 sherds with an average sherd weight of just 8.8g. The range of fabrics and forms very much mirrors the other deposits with no particularly closely datable pieces.

The neonate grave produced a modest assemblage which included 11 sherds of samian which give an Antonine *terminus post quem* (catalogue no. D39). More material was recovered from the rubble make-up layers with some 689 sherds analysed. The material continues to be quite fragmented (average weight 8.9g) and dominated by Alice Holt grey ware which makes up 64.7 per cent. DOR BB1 sherds, although only contributing 4 per cent, include two later jars, one with a right-angle burnished lattice dating to the later second century; the other with an oblique lattice which should belong to the later third century onwards. The samian includes five decorated pieces (catalogue nos D12, D21, D24–5, D39) and one stamp (S24). A link was observed between layers 3826 and 3424 in the rubble make-up layers on the cusp of 700/701.

A group of contexts from the rubble make-up on the cusp of objects 700 and 701 produced some 3,247 sherds, 26 per cent of the total Object 701 assemblage, 48kg. Alice Holt ware accounted for 62 per cent (FIG. 78.64–7, 69–70) with other significant groups of fine grey ware, grog-tempered storage jar, DOR BB1, OXF WH, oxidised ware (FIG. 78.71–2) and Central Gaulish samian. The last accounts for 6.6 per cent, a moderately high figure and has a high incidence of dishes Drag. 31 and cups Drag. 33. A number of stamped and decorated pieces were also recorded (catalogue nos D4, D6–10, D12, D14–20, S6–10, S13, S22); the former date up to *c.* A.D. 200. The DOR BB1 includes a diverse range of forms including a beaded-rim jar and an intrusive conical-flanged bowl. The OXF WH includes four examples of mortaria (Young 1977) type M14 (A.D. 180–240) and two type M3 (A.D. 140–200) along with a small jar and bowl, W54 and W56 (A.D. 300–400). Also of note is a sherd from a LNV CC box, several sherds of Cologne colour-coated beaker, and a Verulamium bowl or small mortarium (FIG. 78.68).

The late second-century occupation along the north–south road also yielded a moderately large assemblage of 2,247 sherds weighing 35kg. Alice Holt grey ware (FIG. 78.89, 91) accounts for 59 per cent by count with the usual accompanying range of fine grey wares (FIG. 78.85), grog-tempered storage jar (FIG. 78.73–4), Oxfordshire white wares, oxidised wares (FIG. 78.72, 80, 86–8), and samian. In total 141 sherds of Central Gaulish samian were documented, including some with stamps dating to the period A.D. 135–165/145–175 (catalogue nos S16, S21, D11, D26–7). The OXF WH included forms (Young 1977) M6, W2, W5, W8 and W11 (FIG. 78.78, 84, 92). The last is dated to the period A.D. 240–400 with most of the other forms extending into the third century but current earlier. The DOR BB1 accounts for just under 5 per cent of the group with examples of flat-rim bowls and grooved-rim dishes (FIG. 78.76–7, 81–2, 90). Again a few sherds with right-angle and obtuse lattice are present, generally indicating some disturbance of these upper levels. Of particular note is a single sherd of East Mediterranean amphora from context 3849, a handmade grog-tempered dish (FIG. 78.75) and some Cologne ware beakers (FIG. 78.79, 83).

Catalogue of illustrated sherds (FIGS 76–78)

32. Colour-coated beaker with roughcast decoration. Fabric: ARG CC. (5698).
33. White ware devolved butt-beaker with rouletted decoration. Possibly a North Gaulish import. Fabric: WW2. (5698).

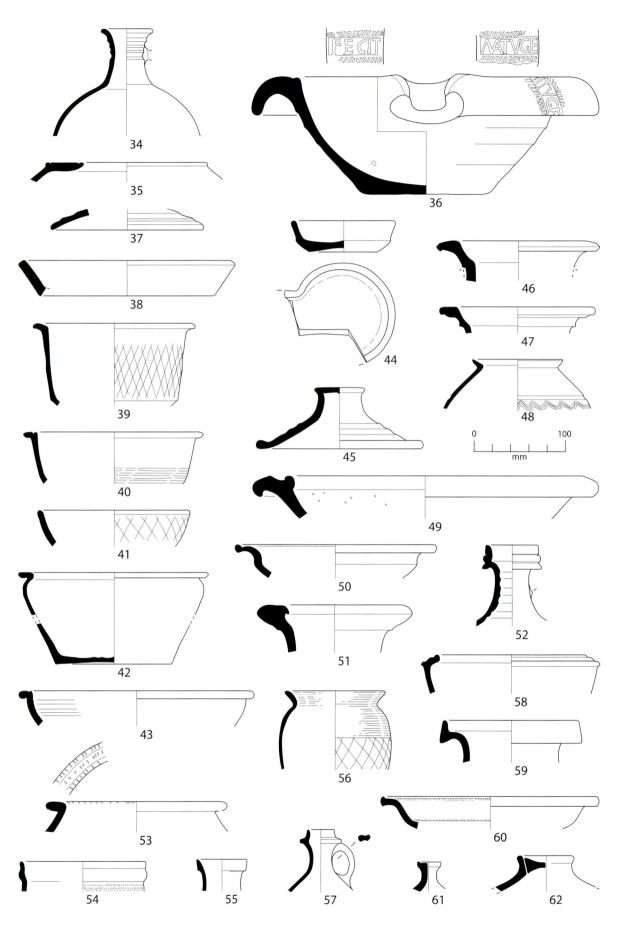

FIG. 77.　Pottery from Period 3 south-east occupation Object 701. Scale 1:4. (*Drawn by Frances Taylor/ Jane Timby*)

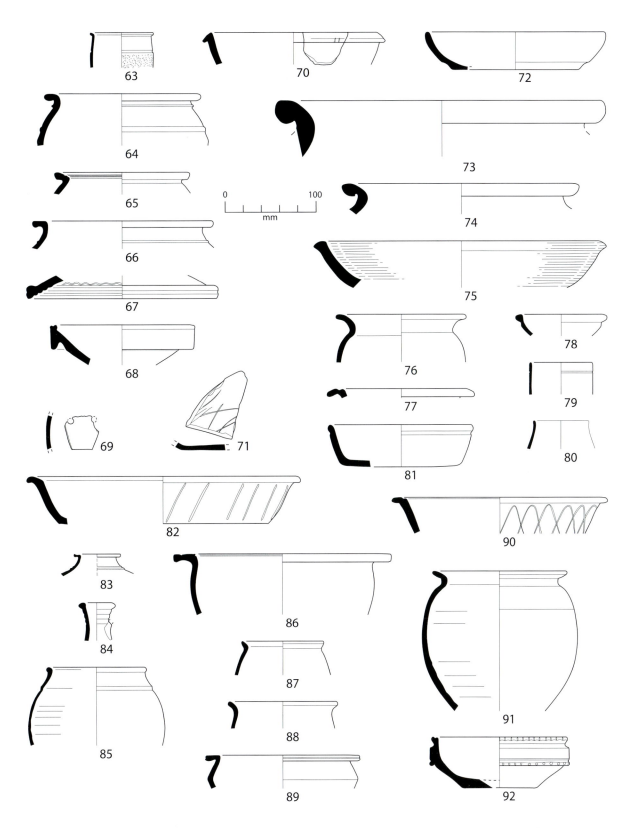

FIG. 78. Pottery from Period 3 south-east occupation Object 701. Scale 1:4. (*Drawn by Frances Taylor/ Jane Timby*)

34. Ring-necked flagon. Fabric: WSOXID3. (5698).
35. Dolium-type jar. Fabric: White ware, possibly VER WH. (5698).
36. Complete but broken mortarium with a worn interior. Stamped either side of spout by Matugenus: MATVGE on one side and with a counterstamp on the opposite side of

FECIT. Both stamps are set within a herringbone border. Fabric: VER WH. (5698), SF 3865 (FIG. 86.3).

37.   Lid with a blackened lip. Fabric: OXID3. (5698).

38.   Shallow dish with a straight, angled wall and squared rim. Fabric: OXID3. (5698).

39.   Deeply chamfered bowl with a slightly angled flat rim and decorated with a burnished lattice. Exeter type 38 (Holbrook and Bidwell 1991, 108). Fabric: DOR BB1. (5698).

40.   Grooved-rim bowl, with a slightly curved wall and burnished on the lower zone only. Fabric: DOR BB1. (5698).

41.   Curved-wall dish decorated with a burnished line lattice. Similar to Exeter type 36 (Holbrook and Bidwell 1991, 108). Fabric: DOR BB1. (5698).

42.   Deep handmade bowl with a flat rim. Thin-walled, grog-tempered ware. Fabric: ?HAM GT. (5698).

43.   Grooved rim, curved-wall dish. Fabric: ALH RE. (5698).

44.   Open lamp. The handle has become detached and the spout broken. Traces of burning around the spout area. Fabric: OXID4. (5698), SF 3867.

45.   Complete profile of a lid. Fabric: ALH RE. (5720).

46.   Large collared, double-handled flagon. Fabric: WSOXIDE. (5129).

47.   Moulded rim, collared flagon. Fabric: WSOXID6 (micaceous). (5121).

48.   Large, short-everted rim globular beaker decorated with combed, wavy line. Fabric: ALH RE-type. (4265).

49.   Mortarium. Fabric: NOG WH. (4265).

50.   Carinated bowl. Fabric: BWF. (4265).

51.   Dressel 20 amphora. Fabric: BAT AM. (4265).

52.   Wall-sided, grooved rim flagon (Young 1977, type W9). Fabric: OXF WH. (4270).

53.   Flat-rimmed jar decorated on the upper rim surface. Fabric: ALH RE. (4270).

54.   Bowl imitating a samian Drag. 30 with rouletted decoration (as Young 1977, type R64). Fabric: GYF. (4270).

55.   Flagon. Fabric: OXIDE. (4270).

56.   Jar decorated with an acute lattice. Fabric: DOR BB1. (4270).

57.   Single-handled, disc-necked flask. Fabric: GYF. (4270).

58.   Bowl with an inturned, reeded rim. Fabric: ALH RE. (5135).

59.   Wall-sided flagon (Young 1977, form W9). Fabric: OXF WH. (4067).

60.   Dish with rouletting or chattering on interior. Fabric: GYF. (4067).

61.   Lid knob with a single perforation. Fabric: GYF. (4067).

62.   Lid knob perforated with eight peripheral and one central steam holes. Fabric: ALH RE. (4067).

63.   Small beaker with very fine sand roughcasting. Fabric: GYF. (4067).

64.   Everted-rim jar with a cordon below the rim and on the barrel-shaped body. Fabric ALH RE. (3103).

65.   Everted-rim, neckless jar. Fabric: ALH RE. (3103).

66.   Flat-rimmed, cordoned jar. (Lyne and Jefferies 1979, Class 3A). Fabric: ALH RE. (3103).

67.   Bifid-rim lid decorated with a tooled, wavy line on the interior. Fabric: ALH RE. (3103).

68.   Wall-sided bowl or small mortarium with no grits. Fabric: VER WH. (3103).

69.   Bodysherd from a jar with two post-firing wall perforations. Fabric: ALH RE. (3103), SF 2373.

70.   Triangular-rimmed bowl (Lyne and Jefferies 1979, type 5A). Two short post-firing incisions on the outer rim edge. Fabric: ALH RE. (3424).

71.   Base of an open form with incised lines, probably cut marks. Fabric: OXID6. (3424).

72.   Curved-wall dish. Fabric: OXID6. (2618).

73.   Handmade storage jar. Fabric: GRSJ. (3849).

74.   Handmade everted, rolled-rim jar. Fabric: GRSJ. (3849).

75.   Handmade dish. Burnished on the interior and exterior surfaces. Fabric: GROG. (3849).

76.   Everted-rim jar. Fabric: DOR BB1. (3849).
77.   Grooved-rim bowl. Fabric: DOR BB1. (3849).
78.   Cup-mouthed, beaded-rim flagon (Young 1977, W11). Fabric: OXF WH. (3849).
79.   Cylindrical beaker. Fabric: KOL CC. (3849).
80.   Flared-rim beaker. Fabric: OXIDF; pale orange, slightly sandy, fabric. (3849).
81.   Beaded-rim, plain-walled dish. Fabric: DOR BB1. (3849).
82.   Flat-rimmed dish decorated with diagonal burnished lines. Fabric: DOR BB1. (3849).
83.   Necked, cordoned flask/beaker. Black colour-coated ware similar to a Cologne colour-coat. Fabric: ?KOL CC. (3849).
84.   Ring-necked flagon (Young 1977, type W2). Fabric: OXF WH. (3849).
85.   Globular-bodied, necked beaker. Fabric: GYF. (3849).
86.   Flat-rimmed bowl. Fabric: OXID3. (3911).
87.   Beaker with a short, everted rim. Fabric: OXID. Hard, orange, slightly granular, sandy fabric. (3911).
88.   Everted-rim jar/beaker. Fabric: OXID3. (3911).
89.   Flat rim, carinated bowl. Fabric: ALH RE. (3911).
90.   Grooved-rim bowl. Fabric: DOR BB1. (3911).
91.   Short, everted-rim jar. Fabric: ALH RE. (3431).
92.   Wall-sided, bifid rim decorated bowl. Fabric: OXF WH. (3432).

Catalogue of sherds with graffiti (FIG. 85)

G1.   Base from a closed vessel with a post-firing graffito cross on the underside. Fabric: ALH RE. Well 2434 (2320), Object 41016.
G2.   Bodysherd from a closed form with an X scratched into the upper body. Fabric: ALH RE. (3225), Object 701.

PERIOD 4

INTRODUCTION

In total some 15,536 sherds of pottery weighing 218kg have been analysed from Period 4. Appendix 4 Table 43 summarises the pottery assemblage as a whole from Period 4. The cut features comprise four pits (Objects 500033, 500034, 500031 and 500032) and two wells (Objects 500037 and 500020) all in the south-east area. Collectively these features yielded some 2,438 sherds of pottery weighing 44.5kg and with 43.32 EVEs. Appendix 4, Tables 44–49 provide separate quantified summaries for each of the five features. MB 3 (Object 50046), part of the 'House 1' sequence contributed a further 6,093 sherds weighing 71kg. The selected sample of pottery from the south-east layers (Object 700) has added a further 7,005 sherds, 102kg, 123.00 EVEs.

PERIOD 4 SAMIAN

Decorated samian
By Joanna Bird

The decorated samian from Object 700 is all residual and comes from a variety of features, mainly from the make-up levels for buildings in the north and south of the site. It ranges in date from the mid-to-later Flavian period to the mid-to-late Antonine, but the greater part is Antonine, with a maximum of six bowls by Cinnamus represented. The latest potter identified is Casurius, with a bowl (D59) from the northern building MRTB 5 (2626). Apart from mould-decorated ware, there is a sherd from a black-slipped jar with an applied head of a faun (D77; 3467) and a sherd from a jar with incised decoration (D72; 3467).

The samian from the Period 4 cut features in the south-east area (Object 500017) all consists of small sherds and is likely to have been deposited with general rubbish. The single sherd from pit 2434 (Object 500031), of Hadrianic to Antonine date, has some sort of concretion on the surface (D42), while the two sherds from a bowl in the style of (Car)atillus (D43) from pit 2601 (Object 500032) and one of the two sherds from pit 3406 (Object 500033), in the style of Cinnamus (D45), are burnt. The samian from these pits and from pit 3102 (Object 500034) represents only seven bowls and ranges in date from the Hadrianic–Antonine period to the mid-to-late Antonine. Well 5735 (Object 500037) contained small sherds of four bowls, two South Gaulish Drag. 29 (one Tiberian, the other Neronian; D51, D52), a probable bowl of Docilis of Hadrianic to early Antonine date (D49), and a mid-to-late Antonine bowl of Paternus II (D50).

Catalogue of Period 4 decorated samian (FIG. 79)

Pits and wells

D42. Drag. 37, Central Gaul. Panels, including a beaded saltire apparently held at the centre by a ring. In the two surviving spaces are a vase (cf. Rogers 1974, T16, T18 and T20), the dolphins and basket ornament (Q58) and an astragalus. The next panel also has the vase. There is a double cordon below the decoration. Hadrianic–early Antonine; surface damaged by concretions. Pit 2434 (2605) (Object 500031) (FIG. 79).

D43. Drag. 37, Central Gaul; two sherds, probably one bowl. The ovolo, here slightly overlapped, is Rogers 1974, B148; this is recorded for a potter identified as Caratillus, but in fact his only mould-stamp is one of Atillus v (Brenda Dickinson, pers. comm.). Beaded borders and saltire; the other motifs are not identifiable. *c.* A.D. 160–200; both sherds are burnt. Pit 2601 (2762, 2785) (Object 500032).

D44. Drag. 37, Central Gaul. Beaded panels, including a robed figure (possibly Minerva) with leaves or rosettes on tendrils, and a double medallion. Row of rings at the base. Hadrianic–early Antonine. Pit 3406 (3829) (Object 500033).

D45. Drag. 37, Central Gaul, in the style of Cinnamus. The ovolo is Rogers 1974, B145, here above panels and festoons (cf. Stanfield and Simpson 1958, pl. 158, 16). *c.* A.D. 145–170; burnt. Pit 3406 (4041) (Object 500033).

D46. Drag. 37, Central Gaul, in the style of Paternus II. The ovolo is Rogers 1974, B139, here above a scroll or large medallion. *c.* A.D. 160–195. Pit 3102 (3827) (Object 500034).

D47. Drag. 37, Central Gaul. The ovolo is too blurred to identify certainly, but cf. Rogers 1974, B7. The motif beneath may be part of an animal. Hadrianic–early Antonine. Pit 3102 (3897) (Object 500034).

D48. Drag. 37, Central Gaul. Panel of slightly rhomboid beads containing a figure, probably Venus (Oswald 1936–7, type 302). Antonine. Pit 3102 (4026) (Object 500034).

D49. Drag. 37, Central Gaul, probably in the style of Docilis; the modelling is rather flat and imprecise, perhaps from use of a worn mould. The ovolo is probably that on Stanfield and Simpson 1958, pl. 91, 3, the lozenge motif is on pl. 92, 12; the other motif may be the large bear on pl. 92, 16. *c.* A.D. 130–155. Well 5735 (6304) (Object 500037).

D50. Drag. 37, Central Gaul, in the style of Paternus II. The ovolo (Rogers 1974, B114) and smaller cupid are on Bird 1986, no. 2.31, the other cupid on Rogers 1999, pl. 78, 29. Paternus regularly used two borders together: for wavy lines and beads, cf. Rogers pl. 78, 28. *c.* A.D. 160–195. Well 5735 (6306) (Object 500037) (FIG. 79).

D51. Drag. 29, South Gaul, with shallow rim and rouletted central cordon. The upper zone has a straight wreath of paired leaves, the upper pair having a smaller third leaf at the base. Closely similar leaves, either slightly narrower or of the same size but reversed, were used on stamped bowls of Firmo i and Salvetus from the Fosse Cirratus at La Graufesenque (Dannell *et al.* 2003: Firmo i E9 and G9, Salvetus A4 and B2, the last from Vechten). *c.* A.D. 30–50. Well 5735 (6407) (Object 500037).

D52. Drag. 29, South Gaul. Upper zone scroll with small rosettes, lower zone gadroons. *c.* A.D. 50–75. Well 5735 (6430) (Object 500037).

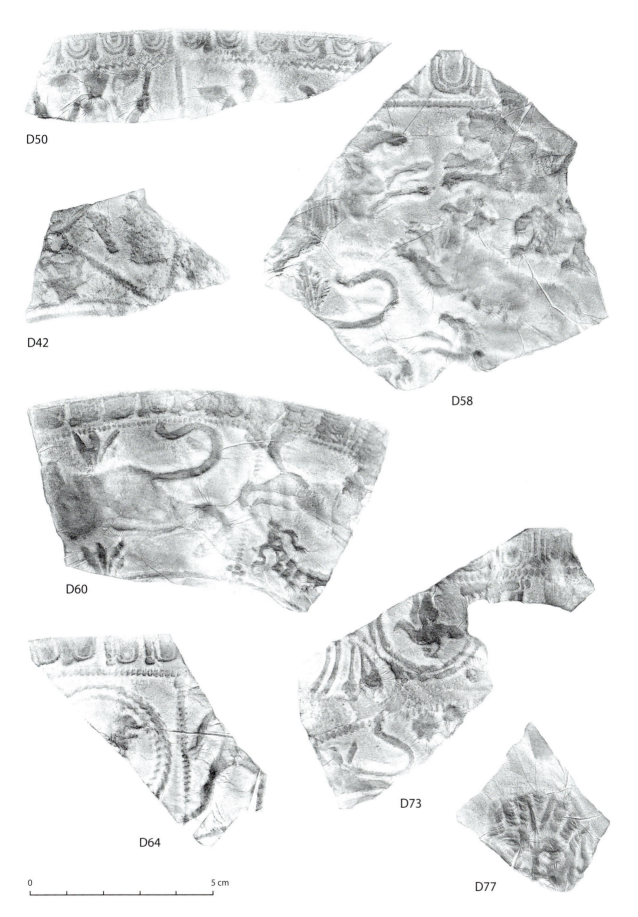

D50

D42

D58

D60

D64

D73

D77

0   5 cm

FIG. 79.   Decorated samian from Period 4 pit 2434, well 5735 and the south-east occupation Object 700. Scale 1:1.

D53. Drag. 37, South Gaul (two sherds). Trident-tongued ovolo above frieze with berries. *c.* A.D. 75–100. Northern pit (5416) (Object 500038). A.2004.30

Layers: Object 700

D54. Drag. 37, South Gaul. Panels, including diagonal wavy lines over a small animal. Mid- to late Flavian. (2420).

D55. Drag. 37, Central Gaul. Broken ovolo, not certainly identifiable; below is a probable panel design. Hadrianic–Antonine. (2420).

D56. Drag. 37, South Gaul, in the style of Germanus. The lion and similar 'rocks' are on Mees 1995, Taf. 70, 1; the straight element is probably part of a spear or javelin (cf. Taf. 75, 4). *c.* A.D. 70–90. (2499).

D57. Drag. 37, South Gaul. The ovolo and border have been badly smeared during the finishing process. The leaf was used by M Crestio (Mees 1995, Taf. 40, 2). *c.* A.D. 75–95. (2613).

D58. Drag. 37, Central Gaul, in the style of Cinnamus. The ovolo, border and lioness are on Stanfield and Simpson 1958, pl. 163, 65, the lioness, leaf and horse on pl. 163, 70, the lion on pl. 163, 73, and the small lion on pl. 159, 23. The leopard, Oswald 1936–7, type 1562, is recorded for Cinnamus. *c.* A.D. 150–180. (2613) SF 1783 (FIG. 79).

D59. Drag. 30, Central Gaul; two sherds. In the style of Casurius. He is recorded for the ovolo (Rogers 1974, B176), here with a wavy-line border (Stanfield and Simpson 1958, pl. 132, 1–2). *c.* A.D. 165–200. (2626).

D60. Drag. 37, Central Gaul, in the style of X-13 ('Donnaucus'). The ovolo, border, lion and grass motif are on Stanfield and Simpson 1958, pl. 47, 558, the rosette terminal and basal line on pl. 49, 578, and the snake and rocks on pl. 49, 584. The smaller animal, probably a second lion, is not certainly identifiable. *c.* A.D. 100–125. (2786) (FIG. 79).

D61. Drag. 37, Central Gaul, in the style of Cinnamus. The large ovolo is on Stanfield and Simpson 1958, pl. 158, 22. *c.* A.D. 150–180. (2925).

D62. Drag. 37, Central Gaul. Panel design, including Venus leaning on a column; the Venus, border and ring would suggest a bowl of Cinnamus (Stanfield and Simpson 1958, pl. 157, 5) but the large rosette terminal has no apparent parallel in his work. Antonine. (3149).

D63. Drag. 37, Central Gaul. The leaf is probably the one shown with a similar scroll and astragalus binding on Stanfield and Simpson 1958, pl. 161, 53, by Cinnamus. *c.* A.D. 145–175. (3412).

D64. Drag. 37, Central Gaul, in the style of Cinnamus. He is recorded as using the ovolo, Rogers 1974, B12; the wreath medallion, here with a cockerel inside, is on Rogers 1999, pl. 33, 58, the cupid on pl. 32, 47, with similar borders and terminals. *c.* A.D. 145–175. (3467) (FIG. 79).

D65. Drag. 37, Central Gaul, probably in the style of Cinnamus. The medallion, border, terminal and ring are on Stanfield and Simpson 1958, pl. 158, 22, the astragalus on pl. 160, 45. *c.* A.D. 145–175. (3467).

D66. Drag. 37, Central Gaul; two sherds. Ovolo Rogers 1974, B206, with wavy-line border. Hadrianic–Antonine. (3467).

D67. Drag. 37, Central Gaul; two sherds. Ovolo Rogers 1974, B106, used by Albucius and Paternus II. Antonine. (3467).

D68. Drag. 37, Central Gaul. Panels, including the feet of a small animal and a ring at the base; the corded border has an astragalus terminal. Hadrianic–Antonine. (3467).

D69. Drag. 37, Central Gaul. Panels, including a medallion with a ring in the corner, and an unidentified figure. The beaded border has a ten-petalled rosette as terminal. Antonine. (3467).

D70. Drag. 37, Central Gaul. Long narrow corded sticks at the base. Antonine. (3467).

D71. Drag. 37, Central Gaul. Fragment of decoration only. Antonine. (3467).

D72. Déch. 72, Central Gaul. Decorated with incised facets, arranged as a lozenge between tall palm leaves. Mid- to later Antonine. (3467).

D73. Drag. 37, Central Gaul; three sherds. In the style of Sacer. The ovolo is on Rogers 1999, pl. 101, 2; the upper zone festoons, trifid pendant and bird are on Stanfield and Simpson 1958, pl. 82, 7, and a similar frieze of animals with the grass motif is on pl. 82, 6. The lioness is on a mould-stamped Sacer bowl from Lyon (Musée de la Civilisation Gallo-Romaine), and was used by his associate Attianus (pl. 86, 15). *c.* A.D. 125–150. (3468) (FIG. 79).

D74. Drag. 37, Central Gaul; two sherds. Probably by Paternus II: the ovolo and border are on Stanfield and Simpson 1958, pl. 105, 12, the small ring and the arrangement of the tendril on pl. 104, 10. The vine leaf is too incomplete to identify certainly. *c.* A.D. 160–195. (3468).

D75. Drag. 37, Central Gaul. Ovolo Rogers 1974, B103, shared by several potters; here with a fine beaded border and a small bird. Antonine. (3468).

D76. Drag. 30, South Gaul, in the style of Germanus. (3836) four sherds; see D36 (Object 701) above.

D77. Black-slipped jar, Déch. 72 or 74, Central Gaul. Decorated with an applied head of Pan. There are several closely similar but larger heads (Déchelette 1904, II.2, types 108 and 109; Simpson 1957, pl. 14, 20, 28 and 29; Simpson 1973, pl. 9, 2 and pl. 11, 25), but another appliqué from Silchester is the same size and may come from the same mould (May 1916, pl. 35, 2; Simpson 1957, pl. 14, 21). May describes the earlier find as 'brown clay … glossy black glaze' (1916, 96); this sherd is in a buff fabric, with the applied head in a paler cream fabric, while the slip is black on the exterior and brownish black on the interior. Mid- to later Antonine date. (3467) (FIG. 79).

Stamped samian
By Brenda Dickinson

Pits and wells

S28. Drag. 33. Central Gaulish Lezoux. MA[retr. Marcus v, Die 5a. A.D. 160–200. Pit 3406 (4041) (Object 500033).

Layers: Object 700

South Gaulish

S29. Drag. 18/31R. South Gaulish. C....? Unidentified. A.D. 70–120. (2439) SF 4574.
S31. Cup. La Graufesenque. EQVRE, Nequres, Die 1a'''. A.D. 55–70. (2420) SF 1744.

Central Gaulish

S32. Drag. 33. Lezoux. ALBVCIM. Albucius ii, Die 4a. A.D. 150–180. (2613) SF 1684.
S33. Drag. 33. Lezoux. CAPELLIVSF, Capellius, Die 1a. A.D. 150–200. (3412) SF 2435.
S34. Drag. 33. Les Martres-de-Veyre. [CA]RATIM, Caratus, Die 2a. A.D. 105–125. (3467) SF 2527.
S35. Drag. 33a. Les Martres-de-Veyre. [DAGOMA]RVSF, Dagomarus, Die 3b. A.D. 100–120. (3468) SF 2505.
S36. Drag. 33. Les Martres-de-Veyre. DIOCIINCIS retr., Diogenes, Die 1a. A.D. 100–120. (3472) SF 2514.
S37. Drag. 33. Lezoux. MALLIACI.E, Malliacus, Die 2a. A.D. 140–170. (3836) SF 2804.
S38. Drag. 33. Lezoux. MICCIONI.M, Miccio iii, Die 2a. A.D. 145–175. (3412) SF 2318.
S39. Drag. 33. Lezoux. PA.VLIM, Paullus iv, Die 5a. A.D. 135–170. (3468) SF 2528.
S40. Drag. 31. Lezoux. TITVR[ONIS], Tituro, Die 5b. A.D. 160–190. (3836) SF 2863.
S41. Drag. 18/31R. Lezoux. TITVS.FE[CIT]. Titus iii, Die 10a. A.D. 150–175. (3468) SF 2534.
S42. Drag. 33. Lezoux.]CVL[? unidentified. A.D. 140–160. (3467) SF 2526.
S43. Drag. 33. Lezoux.]F , unidentified. A.D. 120–160. (3467) SF 2581.

DESCRIPTION OF PERIOD 4 GROUPS

Pits and wells (FIGS 80; 81.93–113; 82.114–123)

South-east pits: pit/well 3406 (Object 500033) (Table 44; FIG. 81.93–102)

Pit 3406 yielded a good assemblage of 593 sherds of pottery weighing 19.4kg. The sherds are in good condition with an overall average sherd weight of 32.7g. A sherd link was observed between 3874 and 3829. Compared to the Period 3 assemblages the group generally contains more regional imports at 26.5 per cent. Continental wares contribute 6.7 per cent, mainly Central Gaulish samian and Baetican amphorae. Of the latter, one handle was stamped and one bodysherd was drilled through with two post-firing holes. Of particular interest is a sherd from an Almagro 50 amphora rim (FIG. 81.100) from layer 3821 towards the top of the feature. Although conventionally seen as late Roman in date, there are now third-century examples recorded from France (cf. Keay and Williams 2005; Bonnet *et al.* 2003).

The regional imports include a significant quantity of DOR BB1, mainly jars (FIG. 81.96) and plain-sided dishes but also including a grooved-rim dish of later second- to third-century type and a flanged conical bowl of later third- to fourth-century type. One dish (SF 3125) (FIG. 85.G4) has a post-firing graffito. Five sherds of Nene Valley colour-coated ware are present, including a complete box lid (SF 3123) (FIG. 81.97). The angularity of the form suggests it is typologically one of the earlier examples of the form, perhaps dating from the later second century to early third century (Perrin 1999, 100). The Oxfordshire wares include white ware flask (Young 1977, type W15) dated A.D. 240–300 and at least one mortarium (ibid., type M14) dated A.D. 180–240.

Amongst the local wares Alice Holt accounts for 39.3 per cent by sherd count. Most of the vessels are everted-rim jars. Several pieces from a single vessel came from layer 4041 (FIG. 81.95). In addition there are also several copies of BB1 jars (FIG. 81.93, 102), most or all of which are likely to be Alice Holt products. Various other grey wares of unknown source are also represented, including dishes (FIG. 81.98) and beakers (FIG. 81.101). Also amongst the wares of unknown provenance is a small partially slipped beaker (FIG. 81.94).

In terms of the vessel forms from this feature jars are dominant at 39 per cent by eve (Table 50) but coarseware dishes/bowls are quite prominent at 20.6 per cent. Lids and mortaria each contribute 8 per cent and flasks 7 per cent.

The lowest fill of the pit/well, context 4316, produced a small assemblage of just nine sherds, including a rim from a copy of a BB1 jar and a tiny scrap of Central Gaulish samian. No pottery came from the slump context 4311 and only four sherds from layer 4306 above this. Layer 4290 above these produced just five sherds and eleven crumbs with none from 4044. From this point the quantity of pottery present increases, perhaps indicative of deliberate backfilling. Horizon 4041 produced an assemblage of 412 sherds weighing 9984g. The sherds are of a moderately good size at 24g, that is to say the pottery does not appear to include much residual material. Ten sherds of samian were recovered, all but one sherd of Central Gaulish origin and including a decorated piece dated to the early Antonine period (catalogue no. D45) and a stamp dated A.D. 160–200 (S28). Also present is a complete Nene Valley colour-coated box-lid, most of a DOR BB1 jar, and substantial parts of several other jars. Curiously there are proportionately more rims of DOR BB1 than bodysherds. There are rim sherds from at least five plain-rimmed dishes, eight jars and one flat-rimmed bowl. The illustrated jar is decorated with an oblique lattice, which would suggest that the deposit is later than suggested by the samian and should be seen as third-century. Further support for such a date is provided by an Oxfordshire white ware mortarium (Young 1977, type M14) with a production date of *c.* A.D. 180–240 and a white ware flask (ibid., type W15) dated to *c.* A.D. 240–300. The small beaker (FIG. 81.94) could be a New Forest product related to Fulford (1975) type 44. Few types of this form have come from reliably dated contexts. Although the Portchester evidence suggested *c.* A.D. 300–350, it could well date back into the third century. One fine grey ware bodysherd shows the very edge of what would have been a graffito and there is a stamped Dressel 20 amphora handle. No pottery was

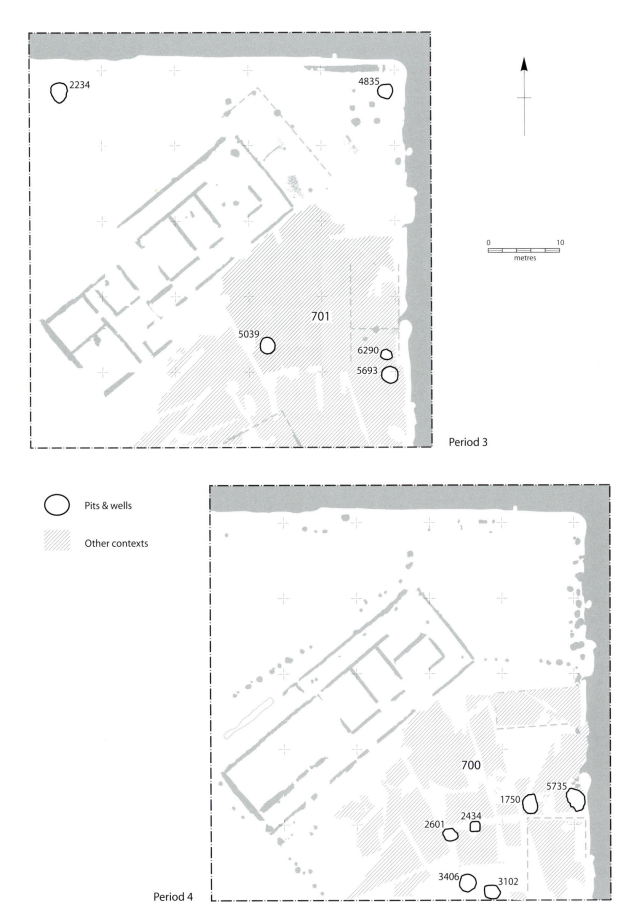

FIG. 80. Location of pits and wells in Periods 3 (upper) and 4 (lower).

recovered from 3875 but a small group of 38 sherds of more fragmented material came from 3874. Of note amongst this are four sherds of Hampshire grog-tempered ware and a DOR BB1 flanged conical bowl typical of the later third to fourth century. Further small groups of pottery were recovered from upper horizons 3829, 3821, 3917 and 3175. A sherd of mid-to-late Antonine decorated samian came from context 3821 (catalogue no. D44). Further examples of DOR BB1 with oblique lattice decoration occur and another Oxfordshire mortarium (type M14). The Almagro amphora rim also came from 3821.

South-east pits: pit 3102 (Object 500034) (Table 45; FIG. 81.103–6)

Pit 3102 produced a similar quantity of pottery to pit/well 3406, with 603 sherds but considerably more fragmented, with a total weight of 9055g and an average sherd weight of just 15g compared to the 24g of the latter. The upper levels of this feature were reported on in an earlier report (Timby 2006). Continental imports account for 10 per cent by sherd count, mainly sherds of Central Gaulish samian. One Drag. 31 dish has a cut for a swallowtail rivet. Other fine wares include sherds of Cologne and Argonne beaker (FIG. 81.104). The regional imports are dominated by DOR BB1 which account for 14.6 per cent of the total assemblage. Several different vessels are present including flat rim, grooved rim (FIG. 81.105) and conical-flanged bowl and jars. Both Oxfordshire and Verulamium region mortaria are present, the former including an example of Young (1977) form M10. The local wares are dominated by Alice Holt and allied grey wares, accounting for just under 59 per cent. These mainly feature as jars and there are no apparent BB1 jar copies as seen in pit 3406. There are also a few grog-tempered storage jar sherds. Of note amongst the other wares is a large white ware flagon (FIG. 81.103) and a small unguent flask with a hole drilled through the side (FIG. 81.106).

The form profile is not that dissimilar to pit 3406 with 37 per cent jars, and 30.4 per cent bowls/dishes. Flagons and samian cups are better represented at 13.4 per cent and 5.3 per cent respectively (cf. Table 50).

In terms of chronology the first horizon to produce pottery was 4030 with 38 sherds amongst which was an Oxfordshire mortarium type M10 dated A.D. 180–240. The samian includes pieces of Antonine date and there are two sherds from a Cologne beaker with rouletted and barbotine decoration. Horizon 4026 produced just six sherds, three from an Antonine decorated Drag. 37 (catalogue no. D48). Horizon 3897 above this also produced just three sherds, but 3827 above this had some 385 sherds, 64 per cent of the whole assemblage from the pit. Amongst the fine wares were several pieces of Antonine samian, the latest dated mid-to-late Antonine (catalogue nos D45–7), and Argonne colour-coated ware. Alice Holt grey ware dominates the coarsewares at 62 per cent (count) and DOR BB1 represents 13.5 per cent of the assemblage from this context. The latest form of the latter is a grooved-rim bowl probably of late second- to early third-century date. Further material of broadly similar date was recovered from layers 3820, 3182, 3154 and 3144. The gravel capping, 3127, yielded several sherds of Antonine samian, further DOR BB1 and two sherds of New Forest colour-coated ware intimating a date at the earliest in the later third century, possibly later. Further New Forest ware came from layers 3115 and 3109 and a sherd of ALH RE with mortar attached came from the former. Conical-flanged bowls in DOR BB1 and SOW BB1 came from layers 3115 and 3108, the latter very abraded again suggesting fourth-century accumulations in the uppermost fills.

South-east pits: well 5735 (Object 500037) (Table 46; FIG. 81.107–12)

Well 5735 again produced an assemblage not dissimilar in size from the other features with 602 sherds, 9335g in weight, and with a similar level of fragmentation to well 3102 at 15.5g. Sherd links were observed between layers 6294, 6304 and 6306. Continental imports are moderately well represented at 17.7 per cent and, whilst this feature contains some later wares, there is evidently quite a high level of redeposition with 15 sherds of South Gaulish samian, one GAB TN platter (Cam. 12/13), and six NOG WH butt-beaker. Beakers in Moselle black-slipped ware and Central Gaulish colour-coated ware are well represented with examples of both folded and bag-shaped beakers. The amphorae include Gallic and Spanish sherds (Dressel 20 and Haltern 70) along with a lid.

Regional imports similarly contain a few residual first-century sherds alongside DOR BB1, which accounts for 23.3 per cent, various colour-coated wares from the New Forest and Nene Valley industries, and Oxfordshire and Verulamium white ware. The DOR BB1 includes plain-rimmed dishes, flat rim bowls and several jars, some with oblique burnished line decoration. One DOR BB1 jar rim has incised line graffiti on the shoulder (FIG. 85.G5). Alice Holt and allied wares account for 39.9 per cent. Silchester ware which should be out of use by this time accounts for 4.8 per cent by count. Fine grey wares are also well represented at 6 per cent, but the arrays of oxidised wares that seem to dominate the Trajanic–early Hadrianic levels are almost absent. The vessel profile also deviates from the expected norm in that whilst jars dominate at 47.4 per cent, coarseware bowls/dishes only contribute 7.6 per cent, with beakers and flagons making up 15.9 and 8.9 per cent respectively and samian cups 6.1 per cent (Table 50). The assemblage as a whole, therefore, appears to have a higher than average incidence of drinking vessels.

The basal fill of the well, 6960, yielded a small group comprising a mixture of first-century sherds, including GAB TN and Silchester ware along with a single small scrap of Central Gaulish samian, not closely datable. The following horizon produced two sherds of mid-to-late Antonine date alongside a DOR BB1 jar decorated with oblique lattice, which is probably early third-century. The small group of 26 sherds from layer 6430 includes a mixture of first-, second- and possibly third-century sherds. Horizon 6234 produced Hadrianic–Antonine samian and several sherds from Central Gaul, black-slipped beakers, both bag-shaped and folded, which could date anywhere between A.D. 180 and 220. Further sherds of black-slipped beaker and Hadrianic–Antonine samian came from 6407. Fineware beaker also features in 6306, with examples of Argonne and Moselle and fine grey ware decorated with barbotine lines. A DOR BB1 jar is decorated with a lattice which is just within the oblique range, again suggestive of a date around the later second and early third century. Sherd links between this and the following two layers, 6304 and 6294, suggest possible contemporaneity. Layer 6294, however, had DOR BB1 with more firmly oblique lattice and a possible sherd of New Forest ware, perhaps placing it more firmly in the third century. The top fill of the well, 5697, contained a moderately large assemblage of 243 sherds, 3775g, which was particularly dominated by sherds of ALH RE and DOR BB1 — 66 per cent of the total by count (cf. FIG. 81.107–11). Seven sherds from a Central Gaulish black-slipped beaker with floral barbotine decoration were present; unusually this vessel had not been internally slipped. A disk-necked flagon in a white-slipped oxidised ware (FIG. 81.112) was also present. Again the deposit would appear to have a third century *terminus post quem*. (Decorated samian nos D49–52.)

South-east pits: well 1750 (Object 500020/500070) (Table 47)

Well 1750, previously excavated in the late nineteenth century, only produced a very small assemblage of some 35 sherds from undisturbed context 2766, with an additional 15 sherds from the well cut. The only fine wares present are four small sherds of Moselle black-slipped ware generally dated to the later second to third century. There is little else in the group to confirm this date, with a mixture of first- and second-century sherds, but there is certainly nothing noticeably later.

South-east pits: pit 2434 (Object 500031) (Table 48; FIGS 81.113, 82.114–15)

Pit 2434 produced a slightly smaller assemblage than seen in some of the other pits with 305 sherds weighing 4610g, but with a similar fragmentation, the average sherd weight being 15g. The overall pattern of wares is very similar to that already documented above; continental imports account for 9.5 per cent and regional imports for 27.2 per cent by sherd count. Of note amongst the regional imports is a sherd from a dish Drag. 18 of Pulborough samian from context 2434, which has a sherd link with context 3674 in MB 3 (Object 50046). Dorset black-burnished ware accounts for 15.4 per cent, with jars decorated with burnished line lattice just turning to an oblique lattice, two conical-flanged bowls and one bowl transitional between a grooved rim and a beaded-flanged rim. A handled mug in SOW BB1 (FIG. 82.114) is also present. Other regional imports include New Forest and Nene Valley colour-coated ware (FIG. 82.115), and Oxfordshire white ware including two mortaria (Young 1977) types M6 and M17 dated A.D. 100–170 and 240–300 respectively.

As with all the other assemblages Alice Holt wares dominate, accounting for 40.9 per cent of the group. A single sherd of Overwey white ware is included in the local wares. The vessel profile for the pit is similar to that from well 5735 (Object 500037), with jars accounting for 46.5 per cent followed by beakers at 16.9 per cent and bowls/dishes at 14.6 per cent, which increases to 19.4 per cent if the fineware examples are added in. There is thus a higher than average presence of drinking vessels — cups, mugs and beakers collectively accounting for 25.6 per cent by eve (Table 50).

The lowest fill to produce pottery, 2776, produced 38 sherds, including a profile sherd of a small colour-coated beaker, probably LNV CC, a handled mug and an almost complete DOR BB1 jar decorated with oblique lattice (FIG. 81.113). Also present is a sherd of LNV CC indented beaker and a Central Gaulish samian sherd (Drag. 40). The DOR BB1 jar, which falls into Dorchester type 3 (Seager Smith and Davies 1993, 231), would suggest a date from at least the mid to late third century.

Horizon 2774 produced a further 74 sherds which include a sherd of Cologne beaker decorated with vertical lines of barbotine leaves, a cornice-rim Argonne beaker and a DOR BB1 jar with a lattice just becoming oblique. This group is also likely to date to the third century. The dark fill of the feature, layer 2605, contained further sherds of imported beaker (CNG BS, MOS BS and KOL CC) and samian, including a decorated bowl dated to the Hadrianic–early Antonine period (catalogue no. D42). The latest sherd, however, is a large piece of DOR BB1 conical-flanged bowl, which places the group in the later third to fourth century. Layer 2602 above this, representing a dump of building material dumped into the feature, contained a further example of a flanged bowl along with a sherd of New Forest colour-coated ware. Small groups of material were recovered from cut 2434 and deposit 2433, eleven and four sherds respectively. The former includes the sherd of Pulborough samian linking with Object 50046. The only Overwey sherd in the group, probably of fourth-century date, came from 2433.

South-east pits: pit 2601 (Object 500032) (Table 49; FIG. 82.116–123)

Pit 2601 produced a similar sized assemblage to pit 2434 with some 366 sherds, 5699g, and a similar level of fragmentation. Again there are a number of redeposited sherds dating from the first century on, reflected in some of the fine wares (a GAB TN dish Cam. 8) and the flint-tempered Silchester ware. Sherd links have been observed between 2785 and 2762, between 2785 and 2623, and between 2762 and 2723. Continental imports contribute just 6 per cent and regional imports 16.7 per cent. The former mainly comprise Central Gaulish samian, the latter mainly DOR BB1 with a few Oxfordshire white wares. Alice Holt and allied grey wares contribute 56.8 per cent. Apart from grog-tempered storage jar at 5.7 per cent, all other wares are present in minor amounts.

The form profile is again dominated by jars at 37.6 per cent followed by flasks at 22.9 per cent. This is somewhat skewed by a complete small flask top. Bowls/dishes account for 14.9 per cent and samian cups 12.2 per cent. Beakers are not as dominant as in the previous two features (pit 2434 and well 5735) (Table 50).

No pottery was recovered from the lower pit fills, the first recorded pottery coming from layer 2785, representing either capping or backfill. The 37 sherds include the complete top of a small Oxfordshire flask (FIG. 82.116) of Young (1977) type W15 dating to the mid-third century on. A decorated samian bowl is dated to the mid-to-late Antonine period (catalogue no. D43). Also present is a DOR BB1 jar decorated with oblique lattice. Layer 2781 produced just three coarsewares but a much larger assemblage of 171 sherds came from 2762, and a further 51 sherds from 2623 and 92 sherds from 2622. There are at least three sherd links between these layers, with other links between 2762 and 2785, and 2723 and 2785, perhaps suggesting a similar source of material and a contemporaneous act of back-filling for these horizons. The

DOR BB1 jars from these layers all have oblique lattice and a grooved-rim DOR BB1 dish came from 2622. One sherd of ALH RE grey ware with wall perforations from 2623 joins a sherd from 2785. A large shallow dish had a reconstructible profile from sherds in 2623 and 2762 (FIG. 82.118). Other wares of note include a cable-rim storage jar (FIG. 82.122) and a grog-tempered storage jar, which appears to be of Savernake type (FIG. 82.123). Just two sherds came from the uppermost gravel fill, one a sherd of Antonine samian.

Catalogue of illustrated sherds (FIGS 81–82)

South-east pits: pit/well 3406 (Object 500033)

93. Small wheelmade jar with burnished line decoration imitating a DOR BB1 form. Fabric: BB1 COPY/ ALH RE. (4041).
94. Small bag-shaped colour-coated beaker with a partial slip. Slipped, matt black interior and upper exterior. Lower zone is a matt red-brown with some drip marks of slip. Hard, fine, pale grey fabric with a scatter of black iron. Fabric: MISC CC. (4041).
95. Large medium-mouthed handmade jar with vertical, burnished-line decoration. The interior of the rim is smoothed and the underside of the base has two-directional scraping marks. Some external sooting. Fabric: ALH RE. (4041).
96. Jar with oblique, burnished-line decoration. Traces of carbonate deposit on the interior surface. Fabric: DOR BB1. (4041).
97. Complete box-lid with rouletted decoration. Orange-brown colour-coat. Fabric: LNV CC. (4041), SF 3123.
98. Dish imitating a DOR BB1 form including a squiggly burnished line on the underside of the base. Brushed on dark blue-grey slip on the interior applied whilst being turned on a wheel. Light grey, hard, dense sandy fabric; possibly from the Colne Valley. Fabric: GREY. (4041), SF 3125.
99. Double-handled flagon with a wall-sided reeded rim. Fabric: OXID3. (3829 and 3874).
100. Rim sherd from an Almagro 50 amphora. (3821).
101. Fine grey ware beaker. Fabric: GREY1. (3821).
102. Wheelmade copy of a DOR BB1 jar. Fabric: BB1COPY/ALH RE. (3821).

South-east pits: pit 3102 (Object 500034)

103. Double-handled flagon. Fabric: WW. (3827).
104. Cornice-rim beaker with rouletted decoration. Fabric: ARG CC. (3827).
105. Grooved-rim bowl. Slightly sooted, plain exterior. Fabric: DOR BB1. (3827).
106. Small unguent flask with a broken, smoothed but uneven rim. The lower body is pierced with a post-firing hole. Fabric: OXID. (4030), SF 2814.

South-east pits: well 5735 (Object 500037)

107. Wide-mouthed jar decorated with girth grooves and a single wavy line. Fabric: ALH RE. (5697).
108. Narrow-necked cordoned jar. Fabric: ALH RE. (5697).
109. Everted-rim jar decorated with burnished, oblique-line lattice. Fabric: DOR BB1. (5697).
110. Lid. Fabric: ALH RE. (5697).
111. Beaded-rim dish (Lyne and Jefferies 1979, type 5A). Fabric: ALH RE. (5697).
112. Disk-necked flagon. Micaceous fine oxidised ware with a white slip. Fabric: WSOXID6. (5697).

South-east pits: pit 2434 (Object 500031)

113. Almost complete jar decorated with a narrow zone of oblique, burnished-line lattice. The base is missing. Fabric: DOR BB1. (2776).

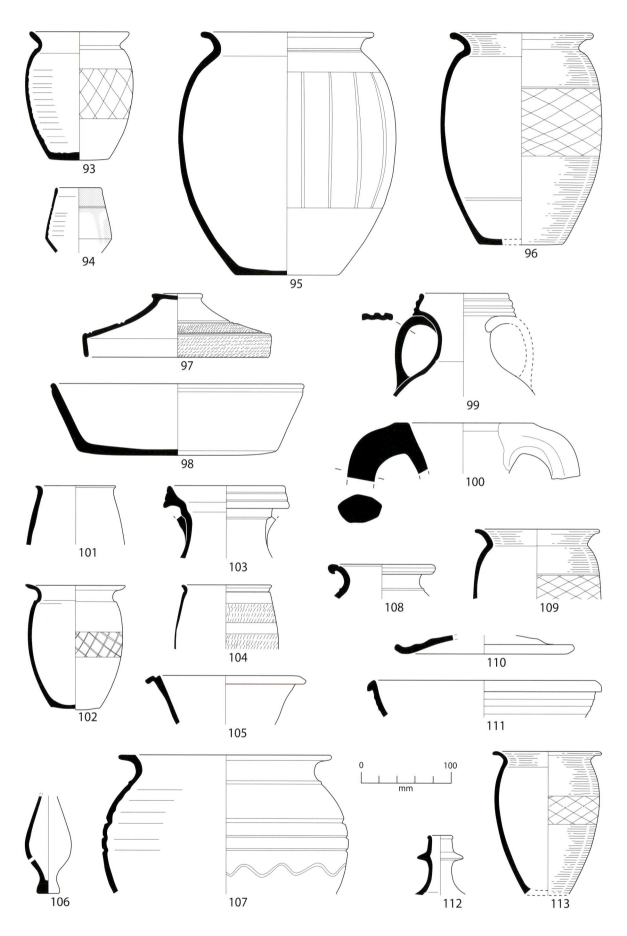

FIG. 81. Pottery from Period 4 pits and wells. Scale 1:4. (*Drawn by Frances Taylor/Jane Timby*)

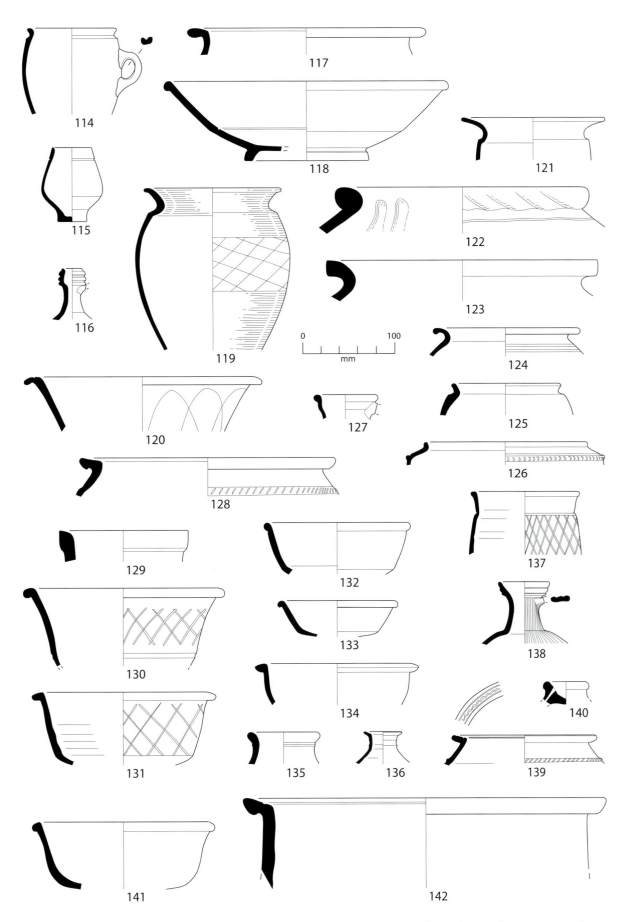

FIG. 82. Pottery from Period 4 pits 2434 and 2601 (Nos 114–23) and from the south-east occupation Object 700 (Nos 124–42). Scale 1:4. (*Drawn by Frances Taylor/Jane Timby*)

114.   Handled mug. Fabric: SOW BB1. (2776).
115.   Small bag-shaped beaker with a black colour-coat which becomes orange-brown where thinner on the rim and base. Fabric: ?LNV CC. (2776).

South-east pits: pit 2601 (Object 500032)

116.   White-ware flask (Young 1975, type W15). Fabric: OXF WH. (2785).
117.   Wide-mouthed jar. Fabric: ALH RE. (2785).
118.   Shallow bowl with footstand. Thin, patchy mica slip visible on the interior surface. Fabric: OXMIC3. (2762/2763).
119.   Everted-rim jar decorated with an oblique-line lattice. Fabric: DOR BB1. (2762).
120.   Grooved-rim bowl. Fabric: DOR BB1. (2622).
121.   Wheelmade, flared everted-rim jar. Fabric: ALH RE. (2622).
122.   Cable-rim storage jar. Fabric: ALH RE. (2622).
123.   Grog-tempered storage jar. Fabric: possibly SAV GT. (2600).

'House 1' (Table 43)

Summary

The pottery from MB 3 (Object 50046) comprises some 6,093 sherds weighing 71kg (Timby 2007). Continental imports account for 10.3 per cent of the group by count of which samian forms the largest component numerically with some 357 sherds, of which nearly half are South Gaulish and thus residual. The Central Gaulish wares include stamped vessels from three Lezoux potters, with the latest material dating to the mid-to-late Antonine period. Much of the accompanying imported fine ware and mortaria is also residual, featuring alongside later colour-coated beakers from Central Gaul, Argonne, Cologne and the Moselle. Regional wares account for just 5 per cent of the assemblage but are quite diverse in nature. Most common is DOR BB1 with forms spanning the second to later third to fourth century, the latter marked by some conical-flanged bowls. Later regional colour-coated wares also feature from the Oxfordshire and New Forest industries some, or most, of which appear to be intrusive, a problem emphasised by the presence of two post-medieval sherds. Many contexts allocated to this period produced exclusively first-century material emphasising the problems of redeposition.

Layers: Object 700 (Tables 51–52; FIGS 82.124–42; 83.143–78; 84.179–93)

In total some 7,005 sherds, weighing 102.4kg, 123.0 EVEs, were analysed from contexts associated with Object 700 (Appendix 4, Table 52). Looking at the assemblage as a whole, samian numerically accounts for 6.5 per cent, with some 455 sherds weighing 5668g. This is dominated by Central Gaulish wares accompanied by sherds from Les Martres-de-Veyre, East Gaul (including Argonne and Rheinzabern) and South Gaul (Table 51). There is one sherd from a Drag. 33 from (3412) in an unusual orange micaceous fabric that may be Argonne, or possibly a Colchester product. Amongst the other imported fine wares are several sherds of Cologne beaker and a single Moselle sherd accompanied by several residual wares. The amphorae are dominated by Baetican sherds accompanied by smaller quantities from South Gaul, Cadiz and Palestine. Two sherds of Rhenish mortaria are also present. Regional wares contribute 10.7 per cent, with DOR BB1 alone accounting for 6.4 per cent. Other contemporary wares include products from the Oxfordshire, Nene Valley, Surrey and New Forest industries along with other wares probably redeposited. Alice Holt and allied grey wares account for 62.1 per cent by count but only 49 per cent by weight. Fine grey wares are quite prominent at 6.2 per cent but all other wares, including the oxidised, white-slipped and white wares fabrics are present in minor quantities.

At the bottom of the sequence are the make-up levels for the northern building MRTB 5, which yielded some 663 sherds, 8.5kg. The sherds were quite fragmented with an average sherd size of 13g. Alice Holt wares account for 61.4 per cent following the overall profile for Object 700 (cf. FIG. 82.124–5, 128). In total 55 sherds of Central Gaulish samian were recorded with a sherd link between adjacent layers 2780 and 2786. The latest material is mid-to-late Antonine (catalogue nos D60, S36). Few sherds of DOR BB1 are present but the Oxfordshire wares include three sherds from a white-slipped mortarium normally dated to after A.D. 240, and examples of a white ware mortarium (Young 1977) type M10 (A.D. 180–240) and a flagon, type W3 (FIG. 82.127) (A.D. 100–240). Amongst the oxidised wares is a shouldered jar with decorated cordon (FIG. 82.126).

The northern building, MRTB 5, produced a much smaller, more broken-up assemblage of some 347 sherds, weight 3.5kg, with an average sherd weight of 10g. Alice Holt products still predominate at 60 per cent. Eight sherds of Central Gaulish samian are present, including a decorated Drag. 30 bowl (catalogue no. D59) dated A.D. 165–200 and a late Drag. 27 cup in a micaceous fabric. The DOR BB1 accounts for 11.8 per cent by count and comprises exclusively jar and plain-rim dish sherds. Some jar sherds have internal limescale deposits. A few fourth-century sherds are also present, including an OXF RS bowl, type C68, an OXF WH mortarium, type M22, and two New Forest beaker sherds, from layers 2626 and 2765.

The southern building, MRTB 4, produced a much bigger assemblage of some 1,033 sherds, 16.7kg, with an average sherd weight of 16g. The ALH RE wares still dominate at 59.4 per cent but DOR BB1 is slightly more prominent at 7.5 per cent, with a similar proportion of samian. The latest samian again appears to be mid-to-late Antonine (catalogue nos D62, D64–72, D77, S34, S42–3). The ALH RE contains a significant number of bowls (Lyne and Jefferies 1979, type 5A) (FIG. 82.130–4) along with two flasks (ibid., type 1A) dated A.D. 270–400 (FIG. 82.135), a single-handled flagon (ibid., class 8) (FIG. 82.138), and a number of jars. The DOR BB1 also shows a high incidence of bowls and dishes, nearly all flat rim or plain rim types with a single grooved rim. Other wares of note include a fine grey ware flask (FIG. 82.136) and OXF WH mortaria (Young 1977, types M10, M14 and M15?), dated A.D. 180–240. The overall vessel profile for the group based on EVEs shows it to comprise 39.5 per cent jars, 27 per cent coarseware bowls and dishes, with an additional 7.5 per cent example in fineware, the remaining 26 per cent split between cups, beakers, flasks, flagons, mortaria and lids.

The small pits and post-holes produced a scrappy collection of 115 sherds, 0.87kg, with an average sherd weight of 7.5g. The assemblage contained much residual material but also a third-century type DOR BB1 jar, part of a barbotine animal decorated LNV CC beaker, an OXF WH bowl type W54 (A.D. 100–300), and a sherd of OXF RS (A.D. 240+).

The path similarly produced a small assemblage of 66 sherds, 449g, which are well broken (average sherd weight 6.8g). The group includes a sherd of decorated samian (catalogue no. D61) dated A.D. 150–180.

The main occupation layer to produce a large assemblage of pottery was 3468 with some 1,663 sherds of pottery, 211kg. The sherds are slightly larger compared to the pits/post-holes and path deposits. The Alice Holt assemblage contains a wide range of forms (FIG. 82.139–42) with several copies of DOR BB1 forms including flanged bowls and plain rim dishes. The ware accounts for 68.5 per cent of the assemblage by count. Samian is well represented with 118 sherds (7 per cent by count) amongst which are four East Gaulish sherds. Several decorated sherds (catalogue nos D73–5) and stamps (S35, S39, S41) indicate a *terminus post quem* in the last quarter of the second century. The DOR BB1 sherds only account for 3 per cent of the assemblage and mainly comprise flat-rim dishes and bowls, plain-rimmed dishes and jars. There are no grooved-rim dishes present. One bowl has a post-firing graffito (FIG. 85.G6). A few oxidised wares are present including a large bowl and a pulley-wheel flagon (FIG. 83.143, 146). A second flagon occurs in the white wares (FIG. 83.150). Fine grey wares contribute another 7 per cent by count and include a flared-rim beaker (FIG. 83.145). Other wares of note include a Cologne beaker (FIG. 83.148), the base of a British glazed vessel (FIG. 83.144), a stamped Oxfordshire reduced-ware dish (FIG. 83.151), and an OXF WH mortarium, type M14, with distinctive curled terminals at the spout (FIG. 83.149). Also present in the group is an indented, New Forest colour-coated beaker decorated with vertical strips of barbotine scales, an Overwey jar with a triangular rim, and an OXF RS dish type C49.

The vessel profile is quite distinct in that small drinking vessels (cups and beakers) are quite prominent, accounting for 24 per cent of the group by eve. Jars make up 32.4 per cent, bowls and dishes (both coarse and fineware) 31.2 per cent. The remaining 12.4 per cent are split between a platter, flasks, flagons, mortaria and lids.

The uppermost levels belonging to Period 4 produced a very large assemblage of some 3,135 sherds, weighing 51.3kg, with an average sherd weight of 16.4g. Alice Holt wares account for 59 per cent and include grooved-rim bowls, flasks, storage jar (Lyne and Jefferies 1979, type 1A, dated A.D. 180–270), large bowls and the usual range of jars, bowls and lids, some copies of DOR BB1 forms. DOR BB1 proper accounts for 8.5 per cent of the assemblage with a mixture of forms including a beaded-rim Flavian-type jar (FIG. 83.158) alongside early third-century types, such as jars with oblique latticing and at least four grooved-rim bowls. Several of the jar sherds have limescale deposits. One sherd has a post-firing graffito (FIG. 85.G7). Samian still features quite strongly, accounting for 2.8 per cent of the total assemblage, mainly Central Gaulish with four East Gaulish and a few residual South Gaulish sherds. There are a number of stamped and decorated sherds present, largely dated to the second half of the second century (catalogue nos D54–8, D63, D76, S29–33, S37, S38, S40). Sherds of the same decorated vessel came from upper layer 3836 and from 4270 associated with the layers and dumps in Object 701. One vessel had a lead rivet-repair. Also present is a Drag. 33 cup in a particularly coarse fabric (FIG. 83.175) of uncertain provenance, either Colchester or Argonne. The group of samian from context 3836 is highlighted as particularly distinct (see discussion below).

A variety of fineware beakers is present, both imported and British (FIG. 83.160–1, 163–4, 167, 170–2 and 181). Amongst the amphorae is a modified Dressel 20, ground off at the neck and with an inscribed 'X' (FIG. 85.G8). Other amphorae include two Haltern 70 rims (FIG. 83.155, 165), a Palestinian *Cam.* 189 sherd, and some sherds of *Cam.* 186 from Cadiz. Oxfordshire white ware continues to feature quite prominently in the assemblage accounting for 3 per cent. Forms include several types current in the period A.D. 180–240, for example, (Young 1977) mortaria types M10, M12, M13 along with bowls W54 and flagons W15 (FIGS 83.156, 168, 173–4; 84.180). One of the M13 mortaria is stamped (FIG. 83.174).

Two sherds of worn Rhenish mortarium came from 2420. No Oxfordshire colour-coated ware is present but a single sherd from a New Forest beaker (Fulford 1975, type 33) came from layer 3836.

Comments on layer 3836

As noted above, the material from context 3836 at the top of the Object 700 sequence contained a distinct samian assemblage. It is the only substantial assemblage in the current study to include a significant number of East Gaulish vessels (Table 51). These are listed below, and illustrated on FIG. 84.188–93. The Central Gaulish ware includes two vessels stamped by mid-to-late Antonine potters (S37, S40), but no decorated wares.

The coarsewares in the deposit are dominated by ALH RE (45.5 per cent by count) and DOR BB1 (21.5 per cent). The overall average sherd weight is moderately high at 20g and the level of residual material is quite low. The DOR BB1 is a particularly good group with large sherds. Amongst the vessels are plain-rimmed dishes, flat-rim bowls/dishes and jars, but of particular note are a grooved-rim bowl (FIG. 84.186) and at least two jars decorated with an oblique lattice demarcated at the top of the decoration by a scored line (FIG. 84.182, 184). This feature of DOR BB1 seems to have appeared before A.D. 250 and is dated in the New Fresh Wharf deposit, London to *c*. A.D. 235–245 (Richardson 1986, 124–5). Further supporting evidence for the date at which this feature appears on BB1 jars comes from Vindolanda (Bidwell 1985, 172), where it is suggested that the evidence points to the obtuse-angled decoration appearing before *c*. A.D. 223–225 at the latest and that the scored line appears rather earlier than the later part of the third century. Bidwell (ibid.) also cites a jar with this feature containing a coin hoard, the latest issues of which are dated A.D. 236–238, from Darfield (South Yorks.) as further evidence for the introduction of this feature. It would seem, therefore, that the DOR BB1 wares are providing a *terminus post quem* for this deposit in the second quarter of the third century. In addition the group contains the rim of a New Forest indented colour-coated beaker (Fulford 1975, type 33) and an unusual black-slipped grey ware bowl (FIG. 83.178).

Given the associations with coarsewares of early third-century date, the samian from this context has been examined by Richard Delage,[1] who comments that while much of the Central Gaulish material is residual at such a date, there are several vessels which could be contemporary. One is the Drag. 36 with a distinct bead on the lower lip (FIG. 84.191), which should post-date the conventional variety of the form that lacks this feature. The thick heavy base of the Drag. 30 (FIG. 84.193) has a section that can be compared with the chronological development of Drag. 30 and 37 bases proposed by Delage (2003, 189, fig. 4) and would be placed in the later second or early third century. A somewhat similar foot-section features on a Drag. 37 bowl from New Fresh Wharf (Bird 1986, 157, 2.54) that is now considered to be the work of the Marcus group, and datable to the early third century.[2]

Although it is clear that the large-scale importation and distribution of Central Gaulish *sigillata* is essentially a phenomenon of the second century, there is evidence that a small number of later vessels did find their way across the Channel. Delage's distribution map of decorated bowls assignable to the Marcus group extends across northern and western Gaul, and into Britain (Delage 2003, fig. 3) and a small number of other Central Gaulish bowls of this period have been identified in southern England.[3]

Catalogue of samian from layer (3836)

1. Drag. 31R/Lud Sb, East Gaulish (probably Rheinzabern) (FIG. 84.188).
2. Drag. 31/Lud Sa, East Gaulish (perhaps Rheinzabern) (FIG. 84.189).
3. Drag. 32, East Gaulish (probably Rheinzabern) (FIG. 84.190).
4. Mortarium, East Gaulish, pale orange slip, worn internally.
5. Drag. 36, Central Gaulish. The curved rim, decorated *en barbotine*, terminates in a distinct rounded bead, and there is a slight offset where the rim joins the outer wall of the body (FIG. 84.191).
6. Drag. 45, Central Gaulish, very worn internally with no grits remaining[4] (FIG. 84.192).
7. Drag. 30, Central Gaulish, very thick heavy base, burnt (FIG. 84.193).
8. Drag. 33, Central Gaulish, stamped by Tituro of Lezoux, A.D. 160–190 (S40).
9. Drag. 31, Central Gaulish, stamped by Malliacus of Lezoux, A.D. 140–190 (S37).
10. Central Gaulish, additional material, not illustrated and mostly fragmentary includes Drag. 27 (3), 31 or 31R (10), 33 (4), 36, 38 (sherd of thick angular flange), 45 (a sherd with incised decoration from near the lion's-head spout), Curle 11 (2), Walters 79.
11. South Gaulish, four sherds from a Drag. 30, A.D. 70–90 (see D36 above, in fresh condition).

TABLE 16. SUMMARY STATISTICS FOR SIGILLATA FROM CONTEXT 3836

Fabric	Sherds	Eve	Weight (g)
Central Gaulish	34	1.43	667
East Gaulish	4	0.28	176
South Gaulish	4	0.08	63

Catalogue of illustrated sherds Object 700 (FIGS 82–84)

124. Everted-rim jar. Fabric: ALH RE with a thin white slip on the exterior and inner rim face. (2786).

[1] Institut national de recherches archéologiques preventatives, Rennes.

[2] Identification by Richard Delage (information from Joanna Bird). For dating and discussion of Marcus see Delage 2003, 188 (as part of a wider discussion of the identification and chronology of third-century Lezoux products); also Bet and Delage 2000, 451–3.

[3] Information from Joanna Bird.

[4] Richard Delage comments further that this vessel may be from a source in the Allier valley rather than Lezoux.

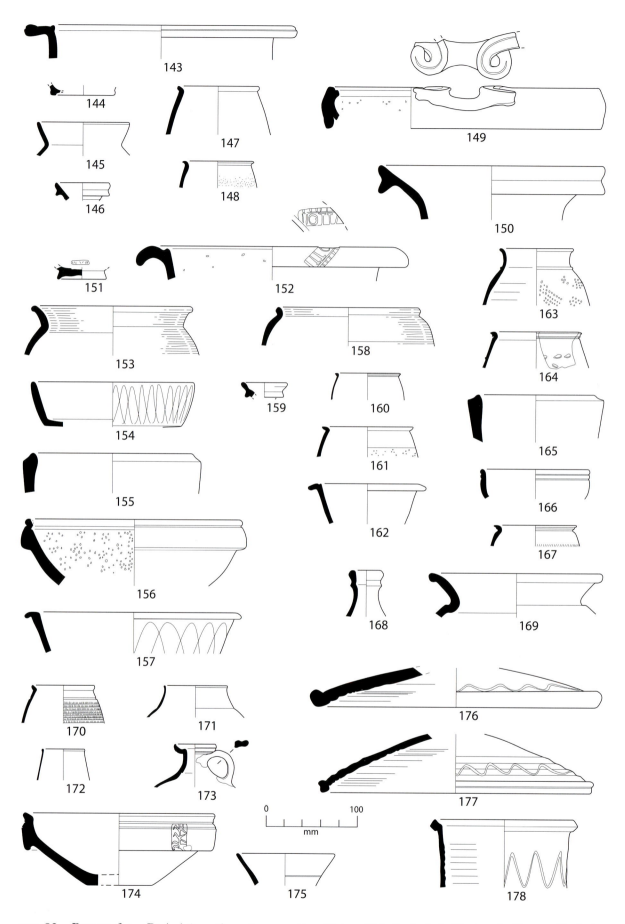

FIG. 83.　Pottery from Period 4 south-east occupation Object 700. Scale 1:4. (*Drawn by Frances Taylor/ Jane Timby*)

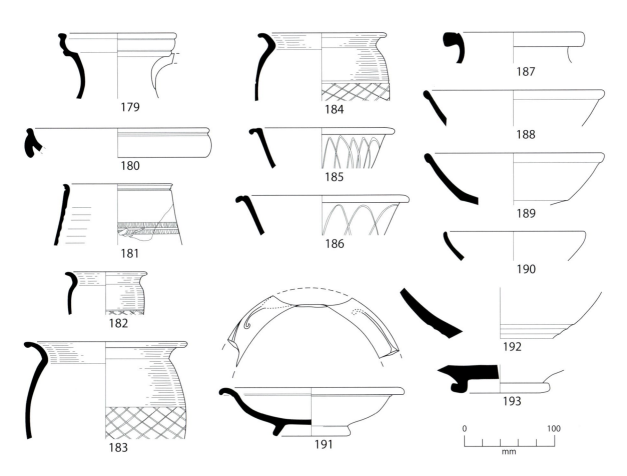

FIG. 84.   Pottery from Period 4 south-east occupation Object 700. Scale 1:4. (*Drawn by Frances Taylor/ Jane Timby*)

125.   Short-rimmed jar. Fabric: ALH RE. (2786).

126.   Shouldered jar marked with a knicked cordon on the shoulder carination. Oxidised sandy fabric with a grey inner core. Fabric: OXID. (2786).

127.   Flagon (Young 1977, W3). Fabric: OXF WH. (2786).

128.   Flat-rim, cordoned jar (Lyne and Jefferies 1979, 3A). Fabric: ALH RE. (2786).

129.   Amphora. Whitish surface with a pinkish orange dense sandy fabric. Possibly North African? (3472).

130.   Deep bowl with rolled rim and straight walls (Lyne and Jefferies 1979, type 5A.2). Fabric: ALH RE. (3467).

131.   Deep bowl with thick flat rim and chamfered base (ibid., type 5A2). Fabric: ALH RE. (3467).

132.   Deep bowl with beaded rim (ibid., type 5A.4). Fabric: ALH RE. (3467).

133.   Shallow bowl with beaded rim (ibid., type 5A.4). Fabric: ALH RE. (3467).

134.   Bowl with curved walls (ibid., type 5A.1). Fabric: ALH RE. (3467).

135.   Flask (ibid., type 1B). Fabric: ALH RE. (3467).

136.   Flask. Fabric: GYF. (3467).

137.   Jar with upright slightly beaded rim. Decorated with a lightly tooled lattice. Fabric: GREY. (3467).

138.   Single-handled flagon. Vertically burnished exterior. (Lyne and Jefferies 1979, class 8). Fabric: ALH RE. (3467).

139.   Flat-rimmed jar decorated with a wavy line and a slashed cordon (Lyne and Jefferies 1979, class 3A). Fabric: ALH RE. (3468).

140.   Knob from a lid, pierced with four holes. Fabric: ALH RE. (3468).

141.   Triangular-rimmed bowl (Lyne and Jefferies 1979, class 5A). Fabric: ALH RE. (3468).

142.   Very large bowl in a light grey sandy ware with a mottled exterior. Fabric: ALH RE? (3468).

143.   Large bowl with a flat bifid-rim beaded on the interior edge. Slightly blackened rim. Fabric: OXID3. (3468).

144.   Base from a small ?closed vessel. Orange sandy fabric with an orange-brown glaze. Fabric: SOB GL. (3468).

145.   Flared-rim beaker. Fabric: GYF. (3468).

146.   Pulley-wheel flagon. Fabric: OXID3. (3468).

147.   Barrel-shaped beaker with a small, everted rim. Fabric: as OXID3 with a matt brown colour-coat. (3468).

148.   Beaker with fine roughcast decoration. Fabric: KOL CC. (3468).

149.   Mortarium with a spout marked by curled terminals. Young 1977, form M14. Fabric: OXF WH. (3468).

150.   Large pulley-wheel flagon. Creamy white with a pink inner core. Hard, granular sandy fabric. Fabric: WW3. (3468).

151.   Base from a small bowl with an illegible, worn potter's stamp. Fabric: OXF RE. (3417), SF 2341 (FIG. 86.6).

152.   Mortarium with a stamp impressed diagonally across the flange. Cream, sandy fabric with very sparse angular flint and quartz trituration grits. Fabric: COL WH? The visible letters read IOTT/ , bordered on one side. (2467), SF 1715 (FIG. 86.4).

153.   Everted-rim jar. Fabric: DOR BB1. (2613).

154.   Plain-sided dish. Fabric: DOR BB1. (2613).

155.   Haltern 70 amphora. Fabric: BAT AM. (2613).

156.   Wall-sided, beaded-rim mortarium. Young 1977, type M13. Fabric: OXF WH. (2613).

157.   Flat-rimmed bowl with arcaded, burnished-line decoration. Fabric: DOR BB1. (2613).

158.   Handmade barrel-shaped, beaded-rim jar (cf. Holbrook and Bidwell 1991, type 3, dated to Flavian period). Fabric: DOR BB1. (2420).

159.   Pulley-wheel flagon. Fabric: ?VER WH. (2420).

160.   Cornice-rim beaker. Fabric: COL CC. (2420).

161.   Short-rim, globular beaker with roughcast decoration. Fabric: GYF. (2420).

162.   Grooved-rim bowl with a sooted exterior. Fabric: GYF. (2420).

163.   Poppyhead beaker with panels of barbotine dots. Fabric: GYF. (2420).

164.   Cornice-rim beaker with barbotine decoration. Fabric: KOL CC. (2420).

165.   Haltern 70 amphora. Fabric: BAT AM. (2420).

166.   Small hemispherical bowl. Fabric: BUFF. (2420).

167.   Cornice-rim beaker with rouletted decoration. Fabric: ARG CC. (2439).

168.   Flagon (Young 1977, type W15.4). Fabric: OXF WH. (2439).

169.   Flared, everted-rim jar imitating a BB1 form. Fabric: ALH RE. (2439).

170.   Barrel-shaped beaker with a short, everted rim. Rouletted decoration. Fabric: GYF. (3412).

171.   Short-necked beaker. Fabric: CNG BS. (3412).

172.   Funnel-necked beaker. Fabric: CNG BS. (3412).

173.   Flagon (Young 1977, W15). Fabric: OXF WH. (3412).

174.   Wall-sided, stamped mortarium (Young 1977, type M13). Partially blackened on the interior and exterior. Heavily worn with no surviving internal grits. Fabric: OXF WH. (3412), SF 2365 (FIG. 86.5).

175.   Drag. 33 cup. Fabric Colchester or Argonne. (3412).

176–7. Lids decorated with tooled wavy lines. Fabric: ALH RE. (3412).

178.   Bowl with a shaped cuboid rim. A grey sandy ware with a black external slip. Decorated with a burnished wavy line. Fabric: GYBSLIP. (3836).

179.   Flagon with a curved, wall-sided rim. One extant handle. Fabric: OXID3. (3836).

180. White ware mortarium (Young 1977, type M10). Fabric: OXF WH. (3836).
181. Cornice-rim beaker with barbotine decoration, probably a hunt scene. Fabric: LNV CC. (3836).
182. Small jar decorated with an obtuse lattice delineated by an upper scored horizontal line. Fabric: DOR BB1. (3836).
183. Larger jar decorated with an obtuse burnished lattice. Fabric: DOR BB1. (3836).
184. Jar decorated with a burnished obtuse lattice delineated by an upper scored horizontal line. Fabric: DOR BB1. (3836).
185. Flat-rim bowl with arcaded decoration. Fabric: DOR B1. (3836).
186. Grooved-rim bowl with arcaded decoration. Fabric: DOR BB1. (3836).
187. Storage jar (Lyne and Jefferies 1979, type 1A). Fabric: ALH RE. (3836).
188. Drag. 31 dish. East Gaulish. (3836).
189. Drag. 31 dish. East Gaulish. (3836).
190. Drag. 32 dish. East Gaulish. (3836).
191. Drag. 36 dish with a slight bead. Central Gaulish. (3836).
192. Drag. 45 mortarium with a worn surface and no surviving grits. Central Gaulish. (3836).
193. Drag. 30 base sherd. Central Gaulish. (3836).

Catalogue of sherds with graffiti (FIG. 85)

G3. Bodysherd from a jar or beaker decorated with a lightly tooled lattice. Two vertical parallel lines scratched after firing. Fabric: GYF. Pit 3406, (4041). Object 500033.
G4. Plain-sided dish. Burnished-line decoration on walls and on underside of base. Incised post-firing graffito in the form of a cross. Fabric: DOR BB1. Pit 3406, (4290), SF 3166. Object 500033.
G5. Everted-rim jar with an incised cross on the shoulder. Fabric: DOR BB1. Well 5735, (5697). Object 500037.
G6. Small flat-rim bowl with a post-firing X on the body. Fabric: DOR BB1. (3468). Object 700.
G7. Bodysherd from a jar with a post-firing X. Fabric: DOR BB1. (3412). Object 700.
G8. Dressel 20 amphora neck, broken but ground smooth for re-use. An X has been incised onto the exterior. Fabric: BAT AM. (2420). Object 700.

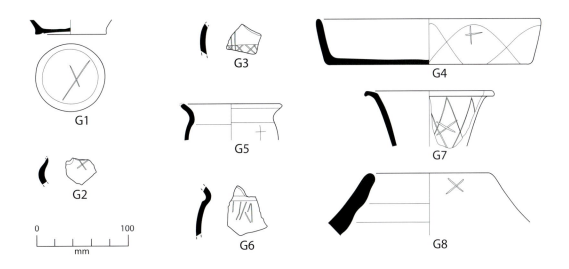

FIG. 85.   Sherds with graffiti from Periods 3 and 4. Scale 1:4. (*Drawn by Frances Taylor/Jane Timby*)

Stamps on amphora, mortaria and coarseware from Periods 3 and 4 (FIG. 86)

Amphora stamp

1. Dressel 20 amphora handle with an impressed stamp reading L...T (retr). Poorly impressed, clogged stamp. Fabric: BAT AM. (4041).

Mortaria stamps

2. Poorly impressed ?double line. Fabric: VER WH. Period 3 (2303) (FIG. 76.25).
3. MATVGE/FECIT. Matugenus. Fabric: VER WH. A.D. 90–120/5. Period 3 (5698), SF 3865 (FIG. 77.36).
4. Diagonally impressed across the flange. Incomplete: IOTT/ bordered on one side. Fabric: ?COL WH. Period 4 (2467), SF 1715 (FIG. 83.152).
5. Vertically impressed stamp down wall-sided rim. Fabric: OXF WH. A.D. 150–180. Period 4 (3836), SF 2365 (FIG. 83.174).

Coarseware stamp

6. Small bowl with an illegible, worn potter's stamp. Fabric: OXF RE. Period 4 (3417) (FIG. 83.151).

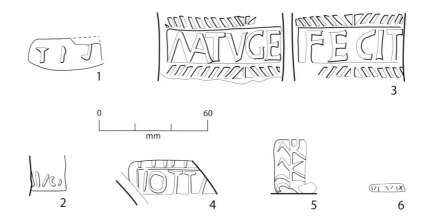

FIG. 86.   Stamps from amphora (No. 1), mortaria (Nos 2–5) and coarseware (No. 6). Scale 1:2. (*Drawn by Frances Taylor/Jane Timby*)

DISCUSSION

In total some 27,260 sherds weighing 394.5kg have been analysed relating to Period 3 contexts and a further 15,536 sherds weighing 218kg for Period 4. If the levels of fragmentation are compared between the three defined groups ('House 1', pits and wells, and layers), it is quite clear that the much smaller assemblages from the pits are considerably better preserved with an overall average sherd weight of 21.5g for Period 3 and 18.3g for Period 4. This compares with 12.3g and 11.7g for Periods 3 and 4 of the 'House 1' material and 14.5g and 14.6g for the layers.

Comparisons were made to see if there were any detectable differences in terms of the fabric and form composition, first between the three spatially-defined groups within the same period, and secondly between the same groups for the different periods. For purposes of comparison the assemblages were broken down into 13 ware groups reflecting both significant individual fabrics and amalgamated groups of fabrics:

> Central Gaulish and East Gaulish samian
> Contemporary imported fine wares (ARG CC, KOLCC, MOSBS, CNG BS)
> Residual imported fine wares (Gallo-Belgic wares, South Gaulish samian, LYO CC, NOG WH, Eggshell wares etc.)

Imported mortaria
Imported amphorae
Dorset black-burnished ware (DOR BB1)
Other regional wares (mainly Oxfordshire wares, but also Verulamium and other products)
Alice Holt and related grey wares
Grog-tempered storage jar
Local residual coarsewares (Silchester ware, first-century grog-tempered wares)
Oxidised wares (unprovenanced)
Fine grey wares (mixed unprovenanced)
Other wares source unknown

FIG. 87 compares the 13 defined ware groups for the pits and wells, layers and 'House 1' Period 3 assemblages. Some differences are apparent between the three groups. The graph demonstrates the higher level of residuality present in the pits/wells and 'House 1' assemblages compared to the layers. This is reflected both in the fineware imports and in the first-century coarsewares. This might argue for the soil disturbed by digging these features to have been partly or wholly reincorporated into their fills. Looking at the other wares there is slightly more Central Gaulish samian featuring in the layers with least from the pits, but the proportions of contemporary fine wares from each are quite similar. Imported mortaria are only present in negligible quantities throughout and amphorae, although again not prolific, show a slightly higher relative presence

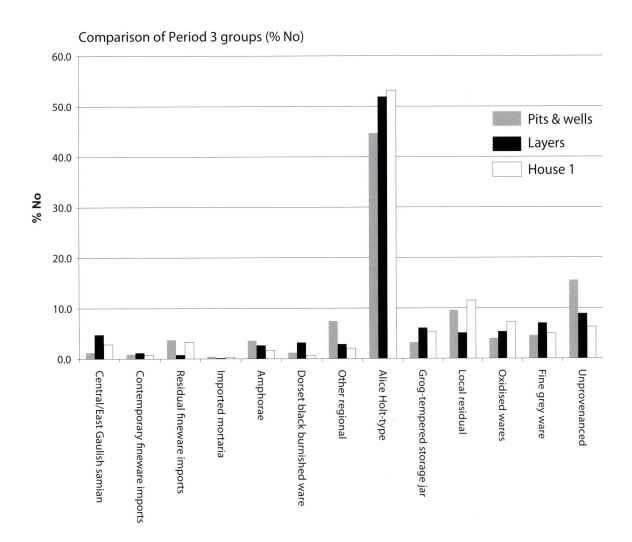

FIG. 87. Comparison of the representation of the principal ware groups from the Period 3 pits and wells, south-east layers and 'House 1'.

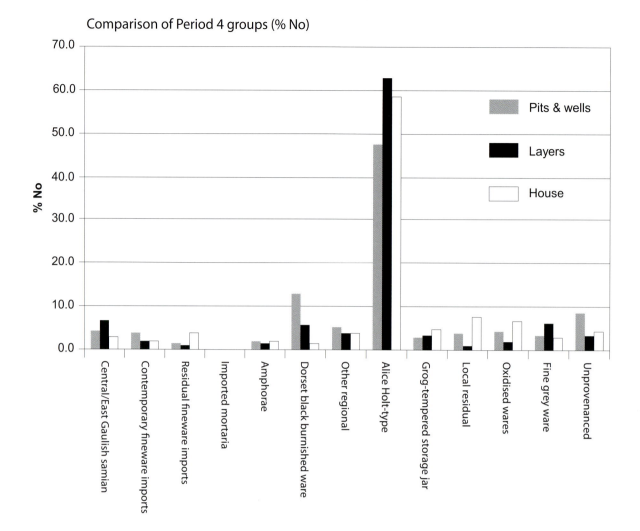

FIG. 88. Comparison of the representation of the principal ware groups from Period 4 pits and wells, south-east layers and 'House 1' (= MB 3).

in the pits. Dorset black-burnished ware is slightly more common in the layers but other regional imports show a higher relative incidence in the pits by quite a margin. Alice Holt wares dominate all three assemblages, but by contrast are slightly lower in the pits but quite close in the layers and 'House 1' deposits. Grog-tempered storage jars also feature less in the pits as do oxidised wares, the latter being most pronounced in 'House 1'. Unprovenanced other wares are most marked in the pits and lowest in 'House 1'.

Appendix 4, Table 53 compares the forms (% EVE) for the Object 701 and the three pits with sufficient measurable eves.[5] Jars dominate both assemblages but with proportionally fewer from the layers, with 27.7 per cent (jars and storage jars) compared to 42.1 per cent from the pits. Fineware bowls/dishes were the second commonest category in the layers assemblage at 15.3 per cent, with a further 12.9 per cent for the coarseware examples. If these two categories of fine and coarse are combined it brings the incidence of bowls very close to that of jars. This compares with just 1.3 per cent from the pits for the fineware and 19.3 per cent for the coarsewares. Other differences are also apparent, fineware cups account for 24.7 per cent of the Object 701 layers but only 1.6 per cent from the pits, with beakers adding a further 7.7 per cent from the layers compared to 2.9 per cent from the pits. By contrast flagons and flasks account for 22 per cent of the pits group but only 4.4 per cent of the layers. It is difficult to know how this can be explained.

---

5 'House 1' eves were not measured.

It is, of course, possible that the amount of material from the pits is too small to be compared realistically with the much larger layer assemblage. Alternatively it may be highlighting different patterns of consumption, different sources for the rubbish material, or distinct activities resulting in different patterns of disposal. There seems to be a predisposition for closed forms, flagons and jars, to be associated with the pits/wells, possibly connected with procuring water, or carrying out activities requiring a nearby water source, and for pits also to be associated with the disposal of kitchen or other waste. Perhaps the containers got thrown in with the waste. Tablewares, including serving, mixing and drinking vessels, show a much higher association with the layers, perhaps reflecting normal household waste deposited into middens prior to its incorporation into the layers, or general domestic rubbish accumulation in peripheral areas. The problem is, however, that this is an accumulation of material which is probably the result of multiple events in the domestic, ritual (celebratory), and commercial spheres.

FIG. 88 compares the main fabric groups for the Period 4 assemblages. Again the pits and MB 3 groups show a higher level of residuality, particularly reflected in the coarsewares and particularly high in the MB 3 assemblage. Alice Holt wares continue to dominate with a slightly lower incidence in the pits. Samian levels are quite close with a slightly higher relative proportion from the layers. Contemporary fine wares, amphorae and regional imports are fairly evenly represented but BB1 is more evident from the pits and wells. As in Period 3 the oxidised wares are quite well represented in MB 3 and fine grey wares in the layers.

Appendix 4, Table 54 compares the forms (% EVE) from the Period 4 layers and pits. In

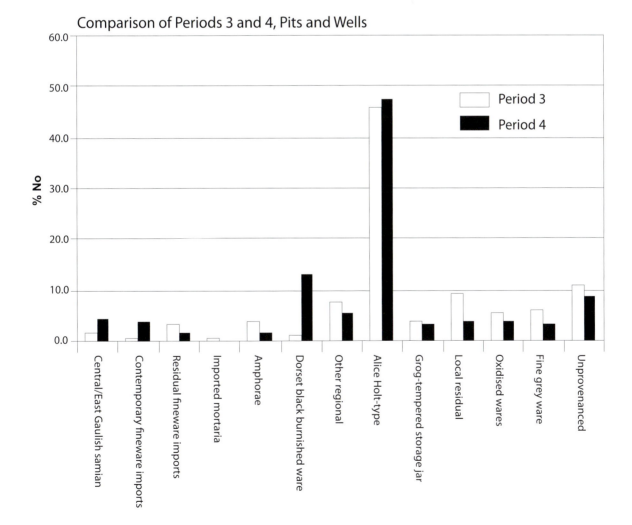

FIG. 89. Comparison of the representation of the principal ware groups from the pits and wells of Periods 3 and 4.

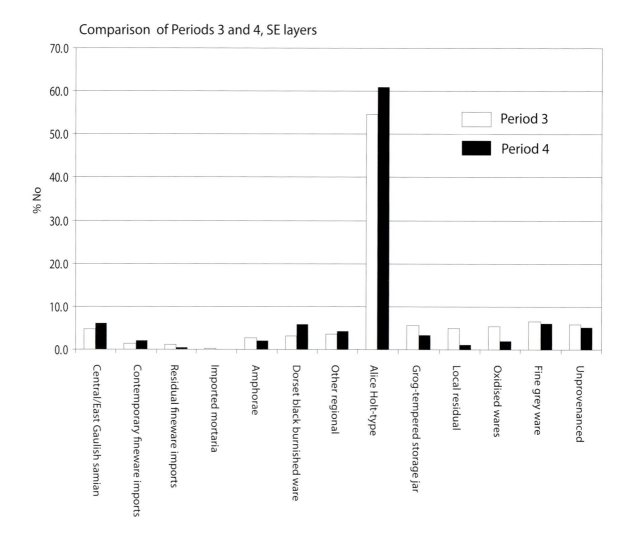

FIG. 90. Comparison of the representation of the principal ware groups from the south-east layers of Periods 3 (Object 701) and 4 (Object 700).

contrast to the Period 3 material there is much greater concordance in the proportions of forms. In both cases jars dominate, accounting for 43.5 and 43.4 per cent respectively followed by bowls/dishes at 17.1 per cent from the pits and slightly higher at 21.9 per cent from the layers. Flagons and flasks are still marginally better represented in the pits at 11.6 per cent compared to 10 per cent from the layers. Cups are quite similar but beakers/mugs more marked in the pits at 10 per cent compared to 4.3 per cent from the layers. The fine wares, largely samian, are less prominent in the overall assemblage reflecting their decline in the market place.

FIG. 89 compares the Period 3 and 4 assemblages from the pits and wells to see if obvious trends or differences are apparent. The proportion of Alice Holt remains fairly consistent but most of the other categories differ. As might be expected the proportion of residual first-century wares declines with time, with proportionately less in Period 4 compared to Period 3. There are higher proportions of samian, contemporary fine wares and Dorset BB1 in Period 4, but slightly more other regional wares, grog-tempered storage jar, oxidised wares, fine grey ware and unprovenanced ware in Period 3. A similar plot for the layers (FIG. 90) shows the same general trends, although the proportion of Alice Holt ware is higher so that the corresponding proportions of other categories are commensurately lower. The differences between Periods 3 and 4 are not as pronounced in the layers as with the pit groups. For the 'House 1' assemblage (FIG. 91) the level of residuality is high throughout Periods 3 and 4 and the incidence of Central Gaulish samian is fairly even. As with the other groups there is slightly more BB1 and other regional wares in Period 4 and more of the other defined groups in Period 3.

Comparison of Periods 3 and 4 and House 1

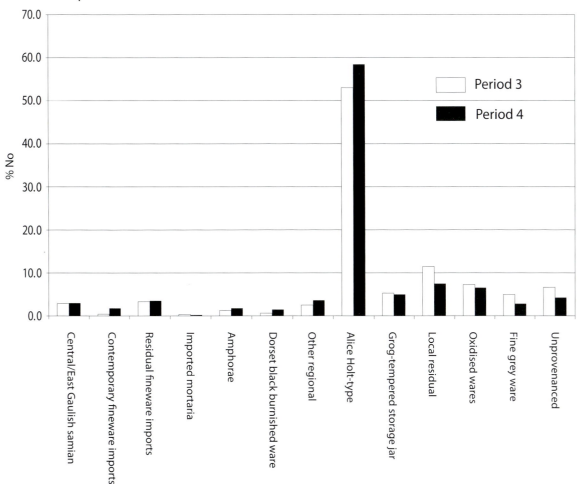

FIG. 91. Comparison of the representation of the principal ware groups from 'House 1' in Periods 3 and 4.

Looking at the form trend, despite the differences between the layers assemblage and pit groups, there is a definite increase in the quantity of jars present in Period 4. The proportion of coarseware bowls/dishes remains fairly constant with a slight increase in the layers but broadly constant for the pits. Cups, which showed such a high incidence in the layers in Period 3, appear at a much lower level in Period 4.

In conclusion, therefore, the following points can be made with regard to the Period 3 and 4 assemblages. First, there is a very marked level of residuality present throughout in all groups in both periods and this is most marked in the 'House 1' assemblage. The markers used to observe this have been the fine wares and the first-century coarsewares. This, therefore, does not take into account the other wares, particularly the Alice Holt wares, which probably also contain a significant residual component. There is a smattering of later material present which must be regarded as intrusive. The occurrence of wares broadly follows the expected trend in market availability, with perhaps the material from the layers being most representative, both in terms of the size of the assemblage analysed and the lower levels of residuality. This is demonstrated in the samian where the layer assemblage is dominated by Central Gaulish wares, principally of Antonine date (89 per cent eve). The proportion from 'House 1' is lower at 49 per cent eve and South Gaulish wares are more common (52 per cent eve). The amount recovered from the pits and wells is probably too small to place much confidence in the proportions of sources represented.

The layer assemblages, therefore, can perhaps be seen as the most reliable in terms of fabrics and forms for defining trends in terms of supply and use for the second and early third centuries

(FIG. 93). In Period 3 (A.D. 125/50–200) continental fine wares are dominated by Central Gaulish samian, accounting for 5 per cent overall of the total assemblage. Other imported fine wares are moderately low in the overall scheme, no individual fabric accounting for more than 0.7 per cent. Vessels from Argonne and Cologne are the most frequent, accompanied by Central Gaulish colour-coated wares. Imported mortaria are rare with largely North Gaulish sherds and two Rhenish sherds from the layers and a single Soller sherd from 'House 1'. Amphorae are also not exceptionally prolific, with Baetican types accounting for 1.4 per cent by count, 8.3 per cent by weight, followed by Gallic wine amphorae at 0.2 per cent. Of note are a single East Mediterranean sherd and one possible Dressel 14 form. The main regional suppliers to Silchester at this time are the Poole Harbour BB1 kilns and the Oxfordshire potters, the latter supplying, in particular, white wares and probably most of the fine grey ware. Also quite marked are white wares from the Verulamium region, both mortaria and other vessels, and Hampshire grog-tempered wares. The BB1 assemblage comprises an almost equal number of jars and flat-rim bowl/dishes, each accounting for 37 per cent by eves. The remainder comprises 17.6 per cent plain-rimmed dishes, 3.3 per cent plain-walled dishes with a slight bead, 4.5 per cent grooved-rim bowls, and 0.5 per cent conical-flanged bowls. The Oxfordshire white wares contain several mortaria, the commonest of which is Young (1977) type M14, dated A.D. 180–240. Most of the vessels in the white wares have a production date which would fall comfortably into the second century (e.g. W2, W5, W6, W8, W33, W46, W54 and W72). However, amongst the flagons are two forms, W9 and W11, both with wall-sided rims, which Young dates to A.D. 240–300. It is possible that these should be associated with a slightly earlier production period. Given the quantity of OXF WH present, it is more than likely that a substantial proportion of the fine grey wares and some of the unattributed, fine oxidised wares also come from the Oxfordshire region. The former contribute 6.6 per cent of the total Period 3 Object 701 assemblage. Other regional imports are rare but include four sherds of Caerleon red-slipped mortaria, and odd sherds of Colchester and Nene Valley colour-coated ware, and South-West white-slipped ware. As noted above, ALH RE (including other related grey sandy wares) is a major supplier to Silchester, effectively accounting for 54.4 per cent by count, 37.6 per cent by weight of the layer assemblage. Other wares of note include grog-tempered storage jar, also possibly originating from the Oxfordshire region and accounting for 5.7 per cent by count. Collectively the pale wares, oxidised wares, white-slipped wares and unattributed white wares account for 9.2 per cent of the assemblage, but individually comprise a range of different fabrics, or wares from the same source with different finishes.

The overall breakdown of forms from Period 3 (layers) shows bowl/dishes to marginally dominate at 28.2 per cent, if both fineware (samian) and coarseware examples are counted, followed by jars at 27.7 per cent. Cups are uncharacteristically high at 24.7 per cent from the layers, although not typically so for the other groups. Beakers account for 7.7 per cent of which 20 per cent are poppyhead beakers and c. 40 per cent cornice-rim or short, everted-rim forms. Mortaria are markedly low at less than 1 per cent which might suggest some of the activities requiring these vessels in terms of food processing and mixing were carried on elsewhere away from Insula IX.

If the Period 3 assemblage from Silchester is compared with other similarly dated assemblages, similarities and differences appear. At Alchester, Oxon., the extramural settlement for Period 5 (c. A.D. 140–190) had a much lower incidence of imports compared to Silchester, the only continental fineware import being samian (Evans 2001, appendix 4, period 5). Central Gaulish samian accounts for 0.6 per cent. Amphorae are limited to Dressel 20 (1.1 per cent) and mortaria to North Gaulish sherds (less than 1 per cent). Where the assemblage shows greater similarity to Silchester is in the dominance of grey wares which account for 70.6 per cent (count). Oxfordshire white wares account for only 1.1 per cent, curious in view of the kilns proximity, and DOR BB1 for 1.3 per cent. This does raise the question as to how much the rise of the Oxfordshire industry, with its more specialist products, was tied into supplying a large town such as Silchester in its early years, perhaps to the exclusion of more local, smaller markets. At Alchester BB1 does not appear before the mid-to-late second century and the Period 5 sample is too small to compare forms (cf. ibid., table 7.27).

At Chelmsford ceramic phases 3 and 4 date to the period A.D. 125–200 (Going 1987, table 9).

These groups have small amounts of Argonne, Cologne and Central Gaulish colour-coat or black-slipped ware. Small quantities of North Gaulish mortaria and amphorae are also present. Grey sandy wares again dominate with very small amounts of DOR BB1 and Oxfordshire white ware. Verulamium white wares are more prominent as might be expected. The range of wares (form and generic category) is broadly the same as Silchester but reflected in products from different sources; the presence of small amounts of recognised regional imports is seen as reflective of the development of a wider provincial trade from around the mid-second century (Going 1987, 110). In the last quarter of the second century (ibid., ceramic phase 4) the provincial colour-coated industries are more important than the continental ones at Chelmsford, which is not the case at Silchester.

Further comparisons can be made with pottery from Borough High Street, Southwark, period 6 (early to mid-second century) (Rayner and Seeley 2002) and London Roman ceramic phases (RCP) 4 and 5 (Hadrianic–early Antonine, c. A.D. 120–160) (Davies et al. 1994, 205ff.). At Southwark, as at Silchester, there is a high residual component reflected in a figure of 5.8 per cent (sherd count) South Gaulish samian and 5.7 per cent Central Gaulish samian in the period 6 deposits. East Gaulish wares also start to appear in minor amounts. Putting the residual problem aside, this still suggests that greater quantities of samian were circulating in Southwark at this time compared to Silchester and indeed other parts of London (see below). The proportions of other fineware imports, such as Central Gaulish and Cologne colour-coats, are minor but comparable from both sites. Southwark also has a significantly greater amount of amphorae present; 11.2 per cent by count overall for period 6, compared with 2.7 per cent from the Silchester Period 3 layers and 1.9 per cent from the Period 4 layers. In both cases Baetican sherds dominate.

In London RCP 4 (A.D. 120–140) all samian accounts for 2 per cent (wt), 8 per cent (eve) compared to 3.35 per cent (wt), 9.7 per cent (eve) at Silchester (Period 3 layers). By London RCP 5 (c. A.D. 140–160) samian accounts for 3 per cent (wt) and 6 per cent (eve). These figures appear closer to the Silchester proportions compared with Southwark. The amphorae from RCP 4 account for 43 per cent weight decreasing to 25 per cent in RCP 5. This compares with 11.4 per cent for Period 3 (layers) at Silchester. The London figure is slightly inflated by the presence of two complete vessels (Davies et al. 1994, 208). Again Baetican types are the most popular.

What is clear from the Southwark and London assemblages and that at Silchester is that the early to mid-second century marks the development of wider regional trading patterns with the appearance of products from the Dorset black-burnished industry, the Nene Valley, Colchester, Alice Holt, Oxfordshire and Verulamium region industries. New imports from the Continent include Rhenish mortaria, North African (London) and East Mediterranean (Silchester) amphorae.

All three sets of data share in common the dominance of reduced wares, although from different suppliers, mainly Alice Holt at Silchester and Highgate Wood and North Kent for London supplemented by Alice Holt products.

Moving further afield, the period 2 assemblage at Wroxeter dating c. A.D. 120–200 comprised some 16 per cent samian (count), of which only 4.86 per cent were Central Gaulish, the rest, presumably largely residual, South Gaulish sherds, and just four East Gaulish sherds (Faiers 2000, 264). This is close to the Central Gaulish totals for Period 3 at Silchester. Other fine wares were present in minor amounts, but include Central Gaulish colour-coats and Cologne ware (ibid., table 4.20). Amphorae account for 6 per cent and continental mortaria included examples from North Gaul, the Rhône Valley, the Rhineland and Aosta. At Wroxeter Dorset black-burnished wares made up 11 per cent; Oxfordshire ware was not present and only minor amounts of Verulamium ware reached the site. Of the BB1 assemblage, jars accounted for 60.8 per cent eve compared to 15.4 per cent bowls, 13.6 per cent dishes and 9.8 per cent lids. Flagons and beakers were also present in minor amounts. Jars were clearly reaching the site in greater quantities compared to the other forms and there are several lids present. In the Silchester assemblage the BB1 is more evenly split between jars (44 per cent eve) and bowls/dishes (55.2 per cent eve), with 0.4 per cent mug hinting at a different marketing pattern for the areas east/north-east of Poole Harbour. Lids and flagons are absent. BB1 also forms a smaller proportion of the overall assemblage (Periods 3 and 4) at just 3.3 per cent by count.

On the limited amount of data available it seems that Silchester is not that dissimilar to other major towns such as London, Wroxeter, Cirencester, Dorchester and Gloucester in terms of the range and quantity of imported wares reaching these sites in the second century. The amounts of samian and other continental imports are markedly higher than the amount reaching the smaller towns such as Alchester and probably Chelmsford. Available figures for London and Southwark might suggest slightly more samian and amphorae at the latter, but in general terms the assemblages seem quite similar. In all cases the assemblages are dominated by the local grey ware industries providing the basic utilitarian wares for domestic use. Other specialist wares are supplied by regional industries but, even on the small amount of data available, there appear to be differences in the types and quantities of vessels supplied.

In the Period 4 (c. A.D. 200–250) layers at Silchester Central Gaulish samian remains high at 6 per cent, accompanied by slightly more East Gaulish pieces. In terms of imported fine ware the levels of Argonne ware remain consistent, joined by increased amounts of Central Gaulish black-slipped ware, Cologne ware and Moselle black-slipped ware. Collectively these account for 2.2 per cent (count) of the Object 700 assemblage. Imported mortaria have declined with just two sherds of Rhenish type alongside probable residual pieces. The proportion of Baetican amphorae remains fairly consistent but other types have declined. Of particular note is the single Almagro rim from the pits. In the regional wares BB1 accounts for 6.1 per cent, almost double that of Period 3, but the Oxfordshire white wares have declined to 3.6 per cent. All other regional wares are present in small amounts, with some probably intrusive pieces from the later Roman colour-coated industries. The vessel profile of the BB1 has changed with jars more prominent at 44.4 per cent eve, but most of the other types remain relatively consistent: flat-rim bowls/dishes at 34.3 per cent, plain-rimmed dishes 17.1 per cent, beaded-rim dishes 1.2 per cent and grooved-rim bowls 3 per cent. The main difference in the OXF WH repertoire is the appearance of at least five small flasks, Young (1977) type W15, which are conventionally dated from A.D. 240. There is a slight increase in the quantity of Alice Holt and allied grey ware to 62.4 per cent with a decrease in grog-tempered storage jar. Many of the other wares remain fairly similar including fine grey ware (6.3 per cent). In terms of the form profile, jars are now more common than bowls/dishes, although they occur at a similar proportion at 41.8 per cent compared to 39.8 per cent in Period 3. All bowls/dishes account for 30.9 per cent. The number of flagons and smaller flasks has increased (11 per cent) but cups have declined to 5.2 per cent and beakers to 4.3 per cent. Lids, storage jar and amphorae are about the same. On balance it would seem there are no significant changes in the assemblages in terms of what is present, but there are more subtle changes in the quantities and vessel types being supplied from the different sources.

This is in contrast to Chelmsford where Going (1987, 113) notes that his ceramic phase 5 (c. A.D. 200/10–250/60) is one of considerable change. Imports are considerably diminished as are colour-coated and buff wares from the Colchester kilns. By the mid-third century the vacuum is filled by products from other industries such as Nene Valley and Oxfordshire. At Alchester period 6 (A.D. 180/90–250) Central Gaulish samian is slightly higher than it was in the preceding period at 2.2 per cent (count) and some East Gaulish ware is also present (Evans 2001, appendix 4). The Oxfordshire white ware industry remains fairly poorly represented at 3 per cent. The level of BB1 has increased from 1.3 to 3.5 per cent and the Oxfordshire oxidised wares have increased from 8.6 to 13.7 per cent. Grey wares remain high at 67.8 per cent.

The proportion of different vessels in the BB1 category from Alchester differs from that at Silchester, with dishes being most common at 45.9 per cent of rim count followed by jars at 32.2 per cent and bowls at 13.5 per cent. The sample is still very small with only 37 rims but this trend continues with dishes and bowls eventually reaching 90 per cent by period 9 (mid-to-late fourth century; Evans 2001, 364). Evans also makes the observation that in northern Britain it is normally the pattern for jars and bowls/dishes to occur at similar levels and attributes the deviance from this trend at Alchester to the availability of similar forms in other fabrics. Similarly sites to the east have few if any BB1 jars. At Silchester the demand for many of the BB1 forms would have been augmented by the Alice Holt industry which produced close copies of all the forms.

It is around this time that the deposit at New Fresh Wharf (NFW), London was formed (Richardson 1986), Silchester Period 4 corresponding to NFW phases 4–6, dated dendrochronologically to A.D. 200/25–245/50. Although not directly comparable in terms of the type of deposit, the diverse range of wares present from these quay deposits demonstrates the sources supplying London at this time. In fact the correspondence with Silchester in terms of similar products is quite low. Apart from obvious, more universal imports (e.g. Dr 20, samian, KOL CC, MOS BS, CNB BS), the only other ware found on both sites is Eastern Mediterranean Biv amphorae, a small group of which came from the quay. Silchester was apparently not receiving the much more diverse range of fineware, mortaria and amphorae imports from North Gaul, the Eifel and the wider Mediterranean world seen in London at this time, which was presumably largely destined for London consumption.

Finally FIG. 92 (Appendix 4, Table 55) compares Periods 3 and 4 at Silchester with the later (fourth- to fifth-century) Roman deposits from Insula IX (Timby 2006). Again, the moderately high level of residuality in these later deposits is highlighted by the incidence of first-century coarsewares and the fact that samian still contributes significantly (4.4 per cent by count) to the late pits despite the fact it is no longer being imported. Other imported fine wares are also quite prominent in the late pits, in fact more so than in Period 4, but essentially consist of the same wares. In the regional wares Dorset BB1 continues the trend seen in Periods 3 and 4, with significantly higher levels in the late deposits where it accounts for 11.1 per cent by count. In terms of vessels, jars accounted for 45 per cent of the late pit assemblage, flat-rim bowls/dishes for 7.8 per cent, plain-rimmed dishes for 35 per cent, grooved-rim bowls for 2.5 per cent, and conical-flanged bowls for 9.9 per cent. The last were not present in the earlier levels. There is

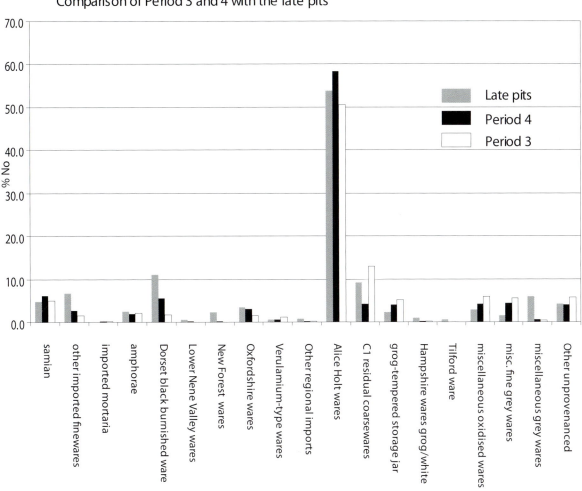

FIG. 92. Comparison of the representation of the principal ware groups from the pits and wells of Periods 3 and 4 and the late Roman pits published in Fulford *et al.* 2006.

Period 3

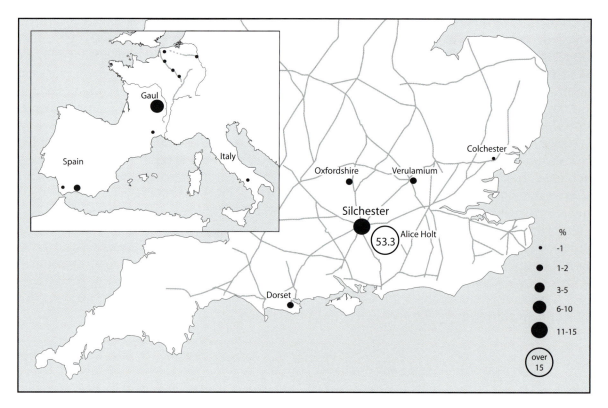

Period 4

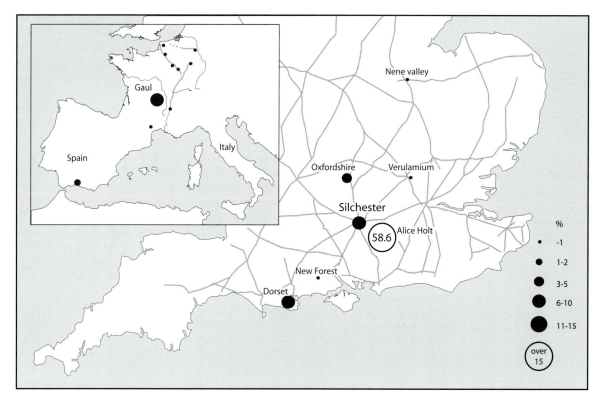

FIG. 93. The representation (by %EVE) of the principal sources of the pottery from Periods 3 (upper) and 4 (lower).

thus a slightly higher incidence of bowls/dishes to jars, but not as marked as that at Alchester where in the later Roman period dishes/bowls account for 90 per cent (rim count) of the BB1 (Evans 2001, 364). The new regional colour-coated industries first appear in quantity in the later pits, for example, New Forest wares, Oxfordshire colour-coated ware and slightly more Nene Valley wares are present. Also Overwey white ware jars are more prominent. The level of fine grey ware, grog-tempered storage jar and oxidised ware is less in the later pits, highlighting that these are essentially second to ?early third century in date. There is a noticeable increase in attributed grey wares in the late pits, perhaps hinting at other small late Roman industries supplying the town in the later Roman period. In terms of overall vessel type nearly half the late Roman assemblage comprised jars (49.6 per cent eve) compared to 27.7 per cent (layers) in Period 3 and 43.4 per cent in Period 4, demonstrating an increasing trend for these forms in the later period. Coarseware bowls/dishes account for 17.9 per cent in the late pits compared to 12.9 per cent and 21.9 per cent (Periods 3 and 4). Most other vessels in the late groups occur at similar levels to Period 4 with jugs and mortaria featuring more in the later groups.

CHAPTER 9

THE WORKED STONE

By Kevin M. Hayward

With contributions on the tesserae and calcite by John R. L. Allen

INTRODUCTION

This chapter assesses the geological character, source and function of the retained 'bulk' and 'small find' stone assemblages from the Period 3 and 4 occupation. It complements an earlier study of the Period 2 to 4 sequence of town-houses and other structures on the 'House 1' footprint (Hayward 2007). The character and source of the stone tesserae assemblage is assessed by John Allen.

The discussion then synthesises both sets of data in order to provide an overview of stone use during Periods 3 and 4. Its purpose is to address two important aspects of stone use in Insula IX, namely, its geological source, including the different scales of quarrying and supply in operation in the Silchester region, and its distribution across the excavation. This will relate the material to the principal structures and features associated with the Periods 3 and 4 occupation: Masonry Buildings 1–3, the south-east pits and the occupation spreads. The study will draw on earlier work from the Insula IX project (Hayward 2007; Shaffrey 2006a) as well as other recent studies of stone used in Silchester, particularly those by Wooders (2000) of the assemblage from the forum-basilica and by Sellwood (1984) of the town wall.

QUANTITY AND CONDITION

Retained 'bulk' stone from Period 3 and 4 features and structures amounted to 422 examples from 111 contexts (total weight 107kg), excluding the flint rubble recorded from the foundations of MB 1–3 of Periods 3 and 4. Nevertheless, it is a sizeable assemblage and, unlike Shaffrey's (2006a) study, which did not consider the residual 'bulk' stone assemblage, and the earlier study of the succession of buildings on the 'House 1' footprint (Hayward 2007), this report takes account of all material from Periods 3 and 4 from the excavation. The condition of the material is mixed, consisting of broken and reused worked stone and walling rubble spread throughout the site, but with discrete zones of deposition in the Period 3 and 4 spreads and pits.

To the above total 1,587 examples (3.2kg) of stone tesserae (including the waste raw material) can be added. Their distribution is comparable to that of the 'bulk' stone assemblage with isolated pockets of waste derived from their manufacture, as well as complete tesserae, deposited in certain Period 3 and 4 pits.

PETROLOGY: METHODOLOGY AND RESULTS

UNWORKED AND WORKED STONE

All retained worked and unworked stone was subject to hand lens inspection in order to identify the type of rock in use. Comparison was then made with the author's reference collection of geological samples so that an outcrop source might be determined. Finally, referral to existing studies of Silchester lithologies (Allen and Fulford 2004; Hayward 2007; Sellwood 1984; Shaffrey 2006a; Wooders 2000) provided further comparative and contextual information.

Including the stone types used solely for tesserae production (FIGS 95–96), 30 different material types could be identified from the retained assemblage, the majority of which could be assigned a geological source. The varieties of material types are comparable with those described previously at Silchester (e.g. Wooders 2000), though the stone types used in architectural and decorative elements are significantly less well represented in Insula IX than in the forum-basilica. Table 17 below lists the main types, their geological source, function and distance from source, whilst FIG. 97 illustrates the position of the sources relative to Silchester.

TABLE 17. PERIODS 3 AND 4 STONE ASSEMBLAGE:
ROCK TYPES, FUNCTION, GEOLOGICAL SOURCE AND DISTANCE FROM OUTCROP

Rock Type	Function	Geological Source (Hayward unless stated otherwise)	Distance to Source
1. *sarsen* – pale grey cryptocrystalline quartz sandstone	walling	Tertiary (Silchester Gravels) Local (Sellwood 1984, pl. 26 no. 1)	0–10km
2. *ironstone* – chocolate-brown coarse-grained iron sandstone	walling whetstone quernstone	Tertiary (Silchester Gravels) Local (Sellwood 1984, pl. 26 no. 2)	0–10km
3. *chalk* – fine white powdery limestone	walling	Upper Chalk (Upper Cretaceous) Nearest outcrop Mapledurwell (Sellwood 1984, 224)	12–30km
4. *flint* – micro-crystalline silica either nodular (walling) or tabular (tesserae) form	walling tesserae	Upper Chalk (Upper Cretaceous) Nearest outcrop Mapledurwell (Sellwood 1984, 224) Lithotype Fa of Allen & Fulford (2004)	12–30km
5. *crystalline calcite*	raw material for plaster	Upper Chalk (Upper Cretaceous) Nearest outcrop Mapledurwell (Sellwood 1984, 224)	12–30km
6. *hard chalk (clunch)* – low density pale yellow rock	walling	Upper Cretaceous – Melbourn Rock Nearest suitable outcrop Berkshire Downs (Blake 1903, 8)	20–30km
7. *calcareous greensand* – fine hard olive-green glauconitic sandstone	walling	Lower or Upper Greensand (Lower Cretaceous) Hampshire/West Surrey Nearest outcrop Kingsclere (Sellwood 1984, 225, pl. 26 no. 6)	25km +
8. fine banded micaceous greensand	walling whetstone	Lower or Upper Greensand (Lower Cretaceous) Hampshire/West Surrey Nearest outcrop Kingsclere (Sellwood 1984)	25km+
9. *pink shelly greensand* – medium-grained glauconitic sandstone with or without black and pink inclusions	walling	Lower or Upper Greensand (Lower Cretaceous) SE England most probably Oxfordshire (Sellwood 1984, pl. 26 no. 5)	25–50km
10. red-brown chert	blades	Mesozoic SE England unknown source	25–100km
11. *ferruginous sandstone* – hard red/black–black ironstone	tesserae	either Tertiary of Hampshire Basin or Early Cretaceous southern English Midlands Lithotype Sb of Allen & Fulford (2004)	25–100km
12. *Lodsworth greensand* – pale-green medium-grained glauconitic sandstone	quernstone	Lower Greensand Pulborough/Lodsworth area of West Sussex (Peacock 1987; Shaffrey 2003, 150)	50km

Rock Type	Function	Geological Source (Hayward unless stated otherwise)	Distance to Source
13. *Culham greensand* – medium-grained glauconitic sandstone with hard black nodular chert	quernstone	Upper Greensand (Lower Cretaceous) Oxfordshire	50km
14. *indurated chalk* – hard chalk	tesserae	Upper Chalk, Upper Cretaceous, Chalk Downlands – Portsdown area of Hampshire or SE Dorset (Wilkinson *et al.* 2008) Lithotype Lb of Allen & Fulford (2004)	50–120km
15. *Stonesfield slate* – oyster-rich mudstone	roofing	Middle Jurassic (Bathonian) North Oxfordshire	60km
16. *coral limestone* – hard fossiliferous ragstone	walling	Corallian (Upper Jurassic), Swindon, Wiltshire (Morley & Wilson forthcoming)	60km
17. *friable sandstone* – light grey sandstone	tesserae	Upper Jurassic (Portlandian), Swindon, Wiltshire Lithotype Sa of Allen & Fulford (2004)	60km
18. *Pusey Flags* (2 varieties) (1) fissile calcareous sandstone – trace fossils (2) fissile calcareous sandstone – shelly	roofing/ paving	Corallian (Upper Jurassic) South Oxfordshire (Arkell 1933) (Morley & Wilson forthcoming)	60km
19. *Combe Down oolite/Box Groundstone* – banded shelly oolitic limestone	architectural funerary	Middle Jurassic (Bathonian) Bath/Box Region (Hayward 2007; 2009)	90km
20. *Pennant Sandstone* – hard grey/green fine micaceous sandstone	paving whetstone	Upper Carboniferous Bristol Region (Kellaway & Welch 1993, 67; Wooders 2000, 87)	110km
21. *Purbeck marble* – hard grey fine shelly limestone with small freshwater snails *Paludina carinifera*	inlay mortar	Upper Jurassic (Portlandian) Isle of Purbeck, Dorset (Arkell 1947, 134; Williams 2002, 126; Wooders 2000, 87)	110km
22. *dolomite cementstone* – dark grey fine mudstone	tesserae	Upper Jurassic (Kimmeridgian) – Dorset Lithotype La of Allen & Fulford (2004)	110–120km
23. *red burnt mudstone*	tesserae	Upper Jurassic (Kimmeridgian) – Dorset Lithotype Mc of Allen & Fulford (2004) (Allen *et al.* 2007)	110–120km
24. *yellow burnt mudstone*	tesserae	Upper Jurassic (Kimmeridgian) – Dorset Lithotype Ma of Allen & Fulford (2004) and Allen (2009)	110–120km
25. *orange burnt mudstone*	tesserae	Upper Jurassic (Kimmeridgian) – Dorset Lithotype Mb of Allen & Fulford (2004)	110–120km
26. *quartz conglomerate* – fractured quartz pebbles, red lithic sandstone inclusions in a fine grey/ brown quartz matrix	quernstone	Quartz Conglomerate Formation, Basal Upper Devonian, Bristol and Forest of Dean (Welch & Trotter 1961, 49; Shaffrey 2003, 147–50)	110–130km
27. *Brownstones* – hard maroon fine sandstone	paving whetstone	Highest division of Lower Old Red Sandstone (Lower Devonian), Forest of Dean (Welch & Trotter 1961, 33)	130km
28. *Millstone Grit* – medium-grained quartz rich sandstone	quernstone	Upper Carboniferous (Namurian), South Wales (Neville-George 1970, 75) or Derbyshire/South Yorkshire	150–300km

Rock Type	Function	Geological Source (Hayward unless stated otherwise)	Distance to Source
29. *basaltic lavastone* (Niedermendig lava) – hard, coarse, dark grey vesicular lava rock with white (leucite) inclusions	quernstone	Tertiary – Andernach Region, NW Germany (Shaffrey 2003, 154)	800km
30. *Cipollino Mandalato* – brecciated grey-green marble	inlay	Tertiary – Pyrenees	2000km

FUNCTION

BUILDING RUBBLE

The retained and recorded building rubble derives principally from two different parts of the excavation: first, from Period 3 MB 1–2 (and Period 4 MB 3) which produced large quantities of *in-situ* flint and Lodsworth Greensand from their foundations; second, from the spreads and pits to the south of these structures.

Excluding the reuse in the internal walls of Period 3 MB 1 and 2 of Lodsworth Greensand, which is more appropriately discussed under quernstones, the material choice for these buildings is almost exclusively nodular flint.

The choice of using many tonnes of flint as the principal building material in the construction of the earliest (Period 3) masonry houses is governed by three factors: Silchester's topographic position, the local geology, and the consequent practicalities and economic cost of transporting bulk stone over distance.

Silchester lies in an area of upland topography characterised by geologically young Pleistocene fluvial gravels which (apart from some sarsen and ironstone blocks) are not hard enough to be used for construction. The nearest suitable outcrop material is the hard flint from the Upper Chalk, seen within 12km of Silchester (Sellwood 1984) and further afield in the Berkshire Downs. A further advantage of using this material is that it can be used along with other stone from this formation, namely white and grey, low density chalk 'clunch' both of which are present in Periods 3 and 4. The choice of flint as the preferred material is therefore determined, as in its use in the late third-century town wall (Sellwood 1984), by the proximity of the outcrops.

Less easy to explain is the purpose and function of *c.* 25kg of building rubble dumped in the later, Period 4 Pits (Object 50033) and spreads (Object 700). This varied assemblage consists not only of local materials (ironstone, sarsen, clunch, chalk) but older Upper Jurassic and Lower Cretaceous sediments, including shelly greensands, grey sandstones and corallian limestone from much further afield (25–100km) than the flint. Some of these materials have been identified from the late third-century town wall (Sellwood 1984), so the possibility of them belonging to a consignment associated with this construction should not be discounted.

ROOFING

Quantities of stone roofing-tile were considerably less (5.5kg) than the recorded assemblage of ceramic *tegulae* and *imbrices* (Warry, below, Ch. 10). Fragments of stone tile were identified only from Period 4 spreads and surfaces in the south-east of the excavation trench (Object 700: 2488, 2610, 3459, 3468) and from the contemporary MB 3 (Object 50046) (FIG. 94).

These thin-bedded (fissile) rocks come in two forms. The calcareous sandstone from Object 700 is from the Pusey Flags (Corallian) of South Oxfordshire (Arkell 1933) (FIG. 98, No. 7). The rock has also been identified in roofing slate from the Groundwell Ridge villa, near Swindon, Wilts. (NGR SU 1408 8935) (Morley and Wilson forthcoming). The second type, an oyster-rich calcareous limestone, comparable with the Middle Jurassic Stonesfield Slate of west Oxfordshire and Gloucestershire, for which quarries have been identified at Brimpsfield, Glos. (Rawes and

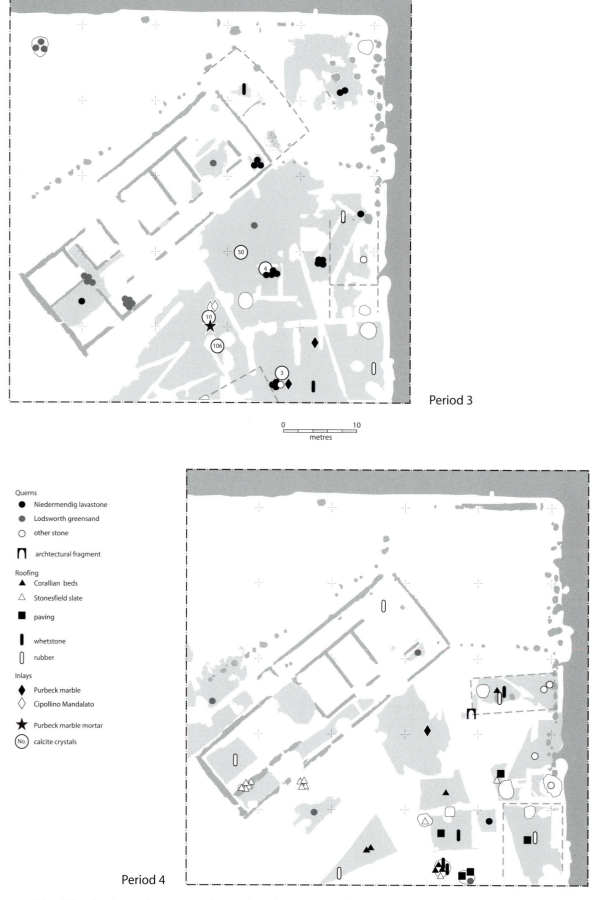

FIG. 94.   Distributions of stone artefacts other than tesserae from Periods 3 (upper) and 4 (lower).

Gander 1978), is only present in MB 3 (Object 50046). The discrete occurrence of Corallian flagstone rock-types away from the main Period 4 building would suggest that these roofing materials were derived from a separate building project elsewhere in Insula IX, or from an adjacent insula.

PAVING

Broken-up paving slabs of Palaeozoic Brownstones from the Forest of Dean (Welch and Trotter 1961) and Pennant Sandstone from the Bristol region (Kellaway and Welch 1993) occurred in Period 4 spreads (Object 700) and may have derived from the flooring of an adjacent building of Insula IX or nearby (FIG. 94). Both of these West Country materials have, like the Pusey Flag roofing, been identified at Groundwell Ridge Villa near Swindon (Morley and Wilson forthcoming).

QUERNSTONE

A sizeable quantity (26kg) and variety (seven) of rotary quernstone materials were recovered from the Period 3 and 4 assemblages (FIG. 94). Many of the fragments, however, had either degraded or been reused as whetstones or building material, making it difficult to determine their original typology. The variety and proportional representation of the different quern materials, which are listed below (Table 18), are comparable with those from the late Roman occupation phases at Silchester noted by Shaffrey (2006a), who also describes their petrology (Shaffrey 2003).

TABLE 18. QUANTIFICATION OF QUERNSTONE (INCLUDING REUSED MATERIAL)

Stone type	No.	No. %	Weight (g)	Wt %
Lodsworth greensand	18	45	17400	67.2
German lavastone	16	40	1523	5.9
Quartz conglomerate	2	5	2538	9.8
Millstone Grit	1	2.5	383	1.5
Culham greensand	1	2.5	478	1.8
Sarsen	1	2.5	2905	11.2
Ironstone conglomerate	1	2.5	700	2.7

A significant proportion (10kg, 38 per cent) of this assemblage consisted of large (1–5kg) chunks of Lodsworth greensand reused as building material in the internal walls (1161, 1163) of Period 3 MB 2 (Object 50019). Lodsworth greensand, a chert-rich, glauconitic sandstone from West Sussex, was used for querns in many Iron Age and Roman settlements in South-Central England and it is well represented at Silchester in the late Iron Age/earliest Roman phases of the occupation on the site of the later forum-basilica (Peacock 1987; Shaffrey 2003; Wooders 2000). The existence of discarded quernstone from the earliest occupation at Silchester through the first century A.D. would have provided a ready source of building stone for incorporation into the earliest masonry buildings of the insula. The absence of greensand from the external walls of the buildings may well be deliberate as the green mineral glauconite is vulnerable to physical and chemical weathering.

  For the majority of the assemblage of quernstone, however, the spread is diffuse, with material deposited either in wells (Object 41016) or in Period 3 and 4 spreads (Objects 700 and 701). Examples of quern fragments in Lodsworth greensand, Millstone Grit, quartz conglomerate and Niedermendig lava are illustrated in FIG. 98, Nos 1–6.

WHETSTONE

Hard, fine-grained sandstones quarried from three geological sources: Brownstones (Lower Devonian, Forest of Dean) (Welch and Trotter 1961), Pennant Sandstone (Upper Carboniferous, Bristol) (Kellaway and Welch 1993), and ironstone (Tertiary, local) were used in the small assemblage (1.5kg) of whetstone in Periods 3 and 4 (FIG. 94).

MORTAR

A large piece of a Purbeck marble mortar (SF 3131) was recovered from Period 3 occupation (Object 701 (3396)) (FIG. 99, No. 9).

DECORATIVE AND ARCHITECTURAL STONE

A handful of decorative stone inlay fragments (total weight 1.1kg) made from hard, polished native limestone (Purbeck marble) and continental, polychrome marble (Cipollino Mandalato) were all identified in the Period 3 and 4 dumps and spreads (Objects 700 and 701). Their presence attests to the demolition or renovation of a major building of some pretension, and of early Roman, probably first-century, date (cf. Fulford 2008).

Pyrenean Cipollino Mandalato, represented by a fragment from the Period 3 dump (3396) (FIG. 99, No. 10), has only previously been identified at Silchester in a stratified context from the Hadrianic-Antonine construction phase (Period 6) of the nearby, masonry forum-basilica (Wooders 2000, 89). Rather than being destined for the forum-basilica, it has been suggested that fragmentary, decorative and architectural material incorporated in its construction (or earlier) contexts probably originated from an earlier building or buildings situated just to the west of the forum-basilica (Fulford 2008). The probability is that the Insula IX Pyrenean fragment, along with the shelly Purbeck marble, was also originally used to adorn the walling or flooring of the same, first-century building or buildings, located to the west of the forum-basilica, but south of the northern part of Insula IX.

Finally, one fragment of worked Combe Down oolite, a Middle Jurassic freestone from the Bath/Box region, was also uncovered from the Period 4 dump (Object 700 (2792)) (FIG. 99, No. 8). As this material is identical in character to over 80kg of architectural stone broken up and reused in one room of Period 2 ERTB 2 (Hayward 2007; 2009) the most likely explanation is that it, too, also originally derived from the same first-century building(s).

CALCITE
By John R.L. Allen

A sizeable assemblage (169 examples, 1kg) of lumps of colourless, coarsely fibrous crystals of calcite without inclusions was concentrated in the Period 3 dumps and accumulation layers from the southern part of the excavation trench (Object 701, particularly 4307, 4469) (FIG. 94). The use of calcite crystals is very probably to be associated with the production of Roman wall-plaster and similar material was recovered from the forum-basilica from Period 5 (Flavian–early second century) (Morgan 2000, 114–15; Wooders 2000, 87, 100). Whether the Insula IX material is waste from the construction of the Period 3 town-houses, or, as has been suggested above for the associated decorative and architectural stone material, derives from nearby first-century building(s) cannot easily be determined.

The many fragments from Insula IX that show the crystals growing at a steep angle from surfaces of chalk assign the material to a provenance in the Upper Cretaceous Chalk Group, but to establish the particular horizon calls for micropalaeontological analysis. The coarsely fibrous crystals, which are a few to several centimetres long, are very similar to the bedding parallel layers of displaced, fibrous calcite known as 'beef' that grow vertically during the early lithification especially of organic-rich shales subject to over-pressure (e.g. Marshall 1982). Arkell (1947), however, does not mention any such masses in the Chalk Group of the Isle of Purbeck, and they are not known in the Group outcropping to the south of Silchester (Osborne White 1909).

TESSERAE
By John R.L. Allen

Periods 3 and 4 afford many examples of the geomaterials known to have been used for floorings and mosaic designs in the earlier Roman period in southern Britain (Allen and Fulford 2004; Allen *et al.* 2007; Wilkinson *et al.* 2008). They take two forms. Stone border tesserae are 2–3cm square and were laid around the margins of a mosaic design. The design tesserae are much smaller, typically 10–15mm square, and are restricted to the pattern itself. The petrology of the border and design tesserae is summarised below, on the basis of new evidence and the types previously described in detail (Allen and Fulford 2004; Allen 2009).

Border tesserae

Although chiefly of ceramic material, this variety includes examples of two kinds of stone. Type Sa is a feebly glauconitic, shelly, pelloidal quartz sandstone that is indistinguishable microscopically from Portlandian (Upper Jurassic) beds once quarried extensively from the restricted outcrop that underlies (Old) Swindon in east Wiltshire (Arkell 1933). The distinctive tesserae assigned to type Sb are of a tough, reddish-black to black sandstone composed of well-rounded quartz grains cemented by iron compounds. They were made from a thin, wind-polished slab (or slabs) of rock probably collected from a Pleistocene gravel deposited periglacially. The ultimate geological source could be in either early Cretaceous beds of the south Midlands or the Tertiary of the London or Hampshire basins.

Design tesserae

These represent a greater range of rock types and include very few made from ceramics. On mineralogical and palaeontological grounds (Allen and Fulford 2004; Allen *et al.* 2007; Allen 2009), a distinctive group comes from sources in the Kimmeridge Clay Formation (Upper Jurassic) of the south-east Dorset coast. Type La is a dark grey, finely granular dolomite cementstone marked by tiny, subparallel shreds of carbonaceous material (kerogen). Type Mc is an originally dark grey, finely laminated, fossiliferous mudrock burnt to a dark red colour. Closely related to it, but pinkish orange in colour, is type Mb. Another burnt mudrock, type Ma, is bright yellow, very fine grained, and only sparsely fossiliferous. As the colour is unchanged by refiring fragments to 750°C in an oxidising atmosphere, the parent mudrock was probably calcareous rather than organic-rich like that of Mc and Mb. A molluscan fauna consistent with a Kimmeridgian age, including a form specific to the stage, has been identified by Dr Jon Todd (Natural History Museum, London) among raw material and *opus sectile* from the Roman Palace at Fishbourne, thus proving earlier speculation concerning the source of this distinctive but poorly fossiliferous lithology (Allen 2009).

Tesserae of hard chalk (type Lb) are common. The microfossils they contain assign them to the uppermost parts of the Upper Cretaceous Chalk Group (White Chalk Subgroup) of southernmost Britain (Wilkinson *et al.* 2008), possibly in the Weymouth-Swanage area from which it is clear that Kimmeridgian tesserae were sourced.

Tesserae of other kinds of rock are very rare. They include a very-fine-grained quartz sandstone (type Sc), a siltstone–very-fine-grained sandstone (type Sd), a yellowish-green, richly fossiliferous limestone (type Lc), a light grey, microcrystalline limestone (type Ld), and flint (types Fa, Fb).

Quantification of the large, loose, stone tessera assemblage from Periods 3 and 4 involved the weighing, measuring and counting of all the individual cubes. This was carried out not only to identify the size and shape of the different materials but the relative importance of each rock-type.

There is not an even distribution of tesserae across the excavation in Periods 3 and 4. With the exception of the concentration of waste from the manufacture of tesserae in Period 4, the bulk of material is to be found within 20m of the southern edge of the excavation (FIGS 95–96). In Period 3 there is a very small number associated with MB 1 and 2 and immediately to the north-east in the area generally assigned as ERTB 4, but in insufficient quantities overall to suggest

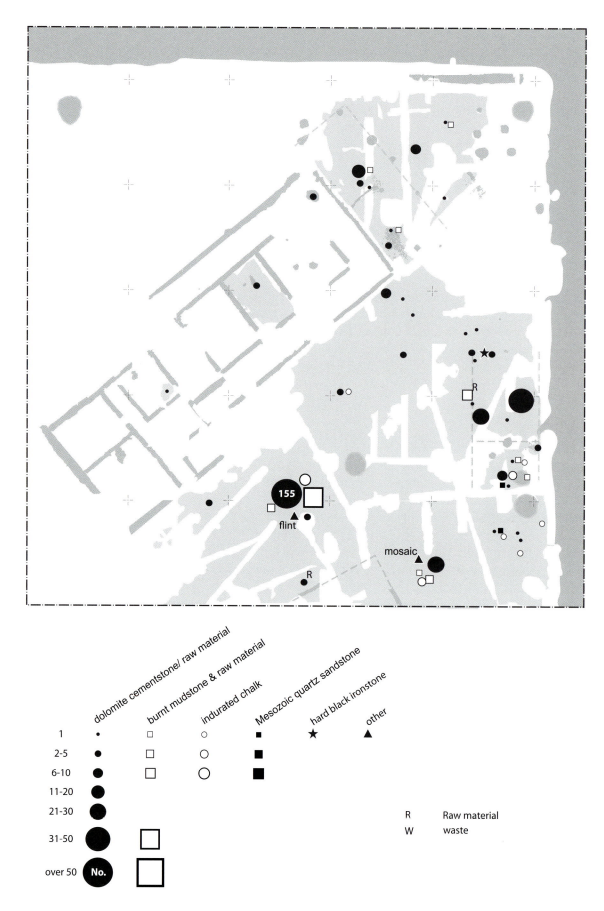

FIG. 95.   Distribution of stone tesserae of Period 3.

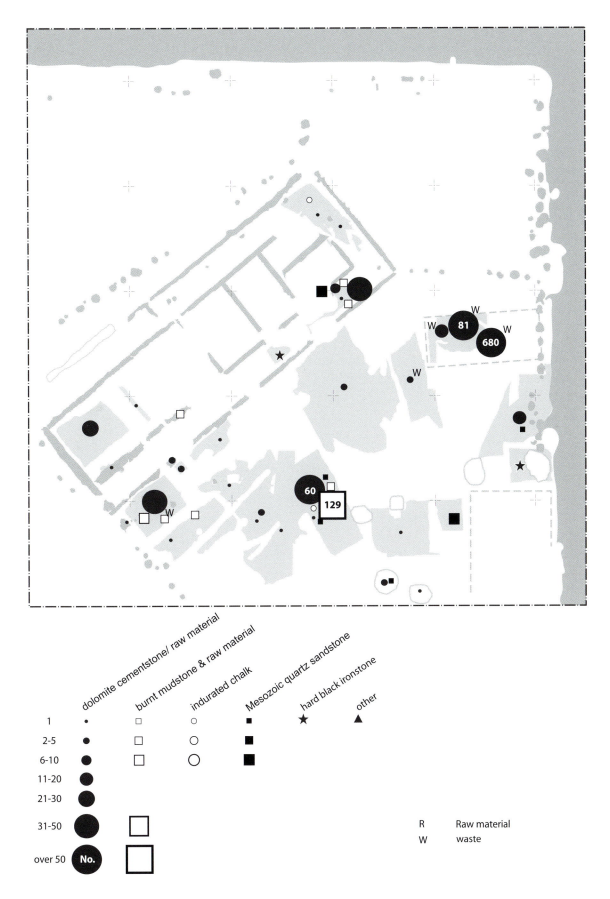

FIG. 96. Distribution of stone tesserae of Period 4.

that they derived from floors of either building. The vast majority of tesserae of this period were found to the south and east of the two houses, with a particularly large cluster to the south of MB 2 (FIG. 95). The same holds for Period 4, with the greatest concentration overlying that from Period 3 (FIG. 96). However, larger numbers were also associated with MB 3 with clusters at each end of the building. The predominant material was dolomite cementstone which was also represented by significant quantities of waste material (*c.* 800 fragments), mostly buried in pits immediately to the east of the house (FIG. 96). This indicates that this material at least continued to be imported from the Isle of Purbeck into Silchester during the late second/early third century, with the probability that it was used in the flooring of MB 3. This use is a little later than the general range proposed by Allen and Fulford (2004, 30–4). Otherwise there is a strong possibility that the tesserae derived from a building or buildings which pre-dated the early second century.

Carbonate tesserae

Kimmeridge cementstone (lithology La) — by far the most common rock-type (1,325 examples: 83 per cent) to be worked into small (*c.* 10mm) cuboidal tesserae from the Period 3 and 4 occupation. These totals also include large quantities of waste derived from on-site tessera manufacture, chiefly in the Period 4 spreads to the east of MB 3 (Object 700) (2609, 2610, 2763).

Indurated chalk (lithology Lb) — small quantities (25 examples: 1 per cent) of these small (*c.* 10mm) cuboidal tesserae are present throughout the excavation trench, apart from Period 3 MB 1 and 2.

Burnt mudrock tesserae

Red burnt mudstone (lithology Mc) — the second most common rock-type from the Period 3 and 4 occupation (199 examples: 13 per cent) has been worked into very small (5–7mm) cuboidal tesserae as well as a range of other shapes (Allen and Fulford 2004, 15). The totals also include the secondary (post-burning) raw material (4070) identified in the Period 3 spreads (Object 701).

Yellow burnt mudstone (lithology Ma) — rare (10 examples: 0.6 per cent), occurring in the Periods 3 and 4 levels as small, 5–7mm cubes.

Orange burnt mudstone (lithology Mb) — very rare (3 examples: 0.2 per cent), occurring only in the Period 4 MB 3 (Object 50046) as small, 5–7mm cubes.

Sandstone tesserae

Medium-grained quartz sandstone (lithology Sa) — small quantities (21 examples: 1.3 per cent) of large (25–35mm), cuboidal, border tesserae, nearly all occurring from the Period 4 spreads (Object 700) and MB 3 (Object 50046).

Iron-cemented sandstone (lithology Sb) — both examples (0.1 per cent) are large (25–35mm), roughly cuboidal, border tesserae, one from the Period 3 spreads (Object 701) (3826), the other from Period 4 MB 3 (2233).

Other stone tesserae

Flint (lithology Fa) — a solitary, sub-cuboidal example (3396) from the Period 4 spreads (Object 700).

Ceramic tesserae

Tesserae representing a range of ceramic materials are not quantified here. They include large, border tesserae made either from roof tiles or specially divided tiles, and tesserae from mosaic patterns produced by clipping pottery sherds (oxidised wares) (see also Warry, below, Ch. 10).

DISCUSSION

GEOLOGICAL SOURCE

A review of the worked stone and tessera assemblage from the Period 3 and 4 occupation has been successful in identifying 30 different geological materials, most of which have been assigned an outcrop source (FIG. 97). One explanation for this diversity, apparent from other studies of the lithologies employed at Silchester (Allen and Fulford 2004; Sellwood 1984; Wooders 2000; Shaffrey 2006a; Hayward 2007; 2009), may be linked to Silchester's central, geographical position in southern Britain.

The region is characterised by a considerable variety of rock types (Jurassic, Cretaceous and Tertiary limestones, sandstones and mudstones), many of which have properties suitable for portable, structural and decorative stonework. Although we cannot so far identify which means of transport were used, possibilities for moving these materials from outcrop are provided both by the road network which radiates from Silchester and the river system of the Thames catchment, which includes the River Kennet. However, it is possible to examine the relationship of the type of stone and the purpose for which it was used at Silchester with its distance from outcrop. Three zones of extraction can be identified:

Local (10–30km)

It has been shown from the assessment of the retained and analysed building-stone assemblage from Periods 3 and 4 (Table 17; FIG. 97) that nearly all of this material was coming from either the Silchester Plateau or within a 10–30km radius of it. The selection of flint and chalk, in particular, both here and in the late third-century town wall (Sellwood 1984) was probably

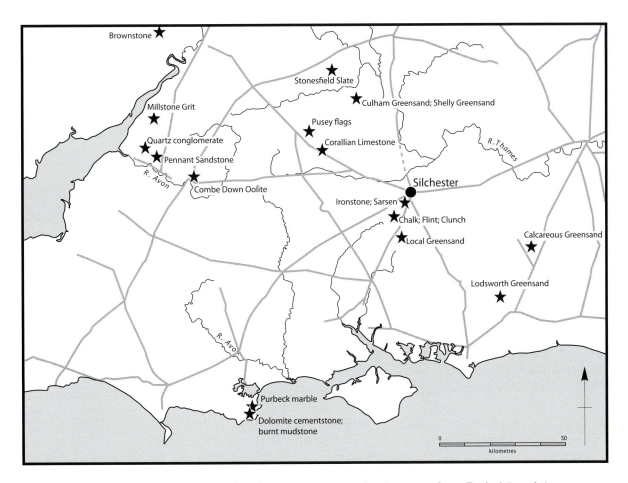

FIG. 97. Map showing the location of rock outcrop sources for the stone from Period 3 and 4 contexts.

made for reasons of economic practicality rather than for its quality as stone. The exception to this is the reuse of Lodsworth greensand quernstone as building rubble in the Period 3 Masonry Building 2.

Regional (30–200km)

A total of 16 stone types from Insula IX could be sourced to outcrops well-away from the local hinterland of Silchester (50–200km) (Table 17; FIG. 97). These materials also had particular attributes that set them apart from the local, poorer quality building-stone, and for this reason it would appear that they were in demand for use throughout the southern half of the province. This is particularly the case with the high-quality freestone from the Bath region and Gloucestershire which was required for architectural and monumental purposes and was widely selected for public and private building in southern Britain. Otherwise, this group of materials embraces Purbeck marble, which is well attested elsewhere in Britain for inscriptions, mortars, statuary, inlays and tombstones as far west as Exeter and north as Chester (Allen *et al.* 2007, fig. 8). Other examples include the use of different coloured, burnt mudstones and carbonates (e.g. white indurated chalk from East Dorset, dark grey dolomitic cementstones, as well as red and yellow burnt mudstones from Kimmeridge Bay) in the tessellated pavements at Silchester and elsewhere (Allen and Fulford 2004; Allen *et al.* 2007, fig. 7). The waste from the production of tesserae in Period 4 indicates that the Isle of Purbeck dolomite cementstone was still being exploited and imported to *Calleva* at the turn of the second and third centuries. Finally, the widespread use of hard, angular, coarse sandstones from the Devonian and Carboniferous of western England and South Wales for paving, roofing and querns (Shaffrey 2006b), as well as the chert-rich greensands for quernstones from West Sussex should also be noted (Peacock 1987). Comparison of the stone assemblage from Insula IX and that from the Groundwell Ridge villa near Swindon, Wilts. (Morley and Wilson forthcoming) illustrates well the widespread use of some of these materials. At both sites Pusey Flagstones for roofing and Brownstones and Pennant Sandstone for paving can be identified.

Overseas

Finally, the presence of continental materials from Insula IX, such as Mayen (Germany) lavastone querns and an example of a Cipollino Mandalato marble inlay, provide further instances of particular types of stone used for specialised purposes.

DISTRIBUTION WITHIN INSULA IX

Differences in the character and function of the stone from the Period 3 and 4 occupation require this section to be divided between the material recovered from the two periods of town-house (MB 1–3) and that from the southern spreads and the south-eastern pits.

Period 3 Masonry Buildings 1 and 2

The construction of two masonry town-houses (MB 1 and 2) during the second quarter of the second century is the first time that only stone is used in the walling of a structure from the excavation trench in Insula IX. The external walling consists almost entirely of flint, a material that would have been readily available at this time as it was used in vast quantities during the construction of the Hadrianic-early Antonine forum-basilica (Wooders 2000, 84). Only the reuse of Lodsworth greensand quern fragments in the internal walling of MB 2 represents a significant departure in the choice of building materials. This may have been on the grounds of cost, or, simply, an opportunistic recycling of locally available material.

The complete absence of either freshly quarried or reworked Bathstone architectural fragments from these town-houses deserves note, particularly given that this material was present in the underlying Period 2 Room 6 of ERTB 2 (Hayward 2007). Two possibilities need to be considered:

either the plundered 'supply' of freestone from an earlier monumental building had all been used up or, more probably, the supply of such stone was now being redirected to meet the demands of a major, contemporary masonry construction, such as the Hadrianic-early Antonine forum-basilica where stone of this variety has been identified (Hayward 2007).

With few exceptions, the tesserae from this period have all been sourced to the Kimmeridge Bay area of Dorset (*c.* 120km) (Allen and Fulford 2004). The very small quantities of dolomite cementstone and the red burnt mudstone from contexts associated with MB 1 and 2 are not such as to suggest that they were necessarily used in flooring, rather than occurring residually.

Period 4 Masonry Building 3

Flint continued to be used in the construction of MB 3, as it was in very large quantities for the construction of the later third-century town wall at Silchester (Sellwood 1984, 224). The use of shelly greensand and ironstone in the town wall (Sellwood 1984) corresponds with a shift towards the use of these materials rather than reused quernstone fragments in the walling of MB 3. Examples of Stonesfield roofing-slate are also associated with MB 3. Larger numbers of tesserae, particularly of dolomite cementstone, from either end of MB 3 suggest that they may have been employed in the flooring of the house. The occurrence nearby of large quantities of waste dolomite cementstone adds weight to this idea.

Southern spreads and layers

Compared to the building-stone used in MB 1–3, there is not only a greater variety of materials (17 alone in Object 700), but also a greater variety of uses to which stone was put in the southern part of the excavation trench. These spreads and dumped layers (Objects 700 and 701), which accumulated over a period of more than a century, not only contain broken up decorative inlays of Purbeck marble and Cipollino Mandalato, but also a wide variety of quernstone materials, as well as a quantity of raw material and waste associated with the production of tesserae and plaster. A wide variety of origins must account for this assemblage, not all of them necessarily associated with activity in Insula IX.

Period 3

One key feature of the earlier dumps and levelling deposits (Object 701) is the presence of a large quantity of calcite crystal, over 1kg, especially in the contexts around the vicinity of context 3396. This material was used in the preparation of wall-plaster. Whether or not plaster production took place within Insula IX is not clear, but the demand for plaster for contemporary private and public building at Silchester would certainly have been considerable. Similar levelling and dump deposits (4070) also contain prepared (red burnt Kimmeridge mudstone) raw material for tesserae and several complete tesserae, including a fragment of a mosaic (3858), as well as Purbeck marble and Cipollino Mandalato inlays (3396). There are also large quantities of other tesserae, particularly of dolomite cementstone, towards the southern edge of the excavation.

What all these materials have in common is their association with decoration and embellishment, presumably of an important, but earlier, public or private building(s). What the archaeological evidence has shown, however, is that such a structure cannot have existed in the north of Insula IX. One possibility is a first-century palatial building immediately to the south of Insula IX and to the west of the forum-basilica (Fulford 2008).

Period 4

The character and function of the spreads from Period 4, the third century, are essentially the same as in Period 3, but with the addition of a small quantity of stone roofing-tile and some types of stone (e.g. Brownstone paving), also associated with the later third- and fourth-century occupation of Insula IX (Shaffrey 2006a). It has been commented that stone roofing in southern Britain is essentially a third- and fourth-century phenomenon (Boon 1974) and the presence of

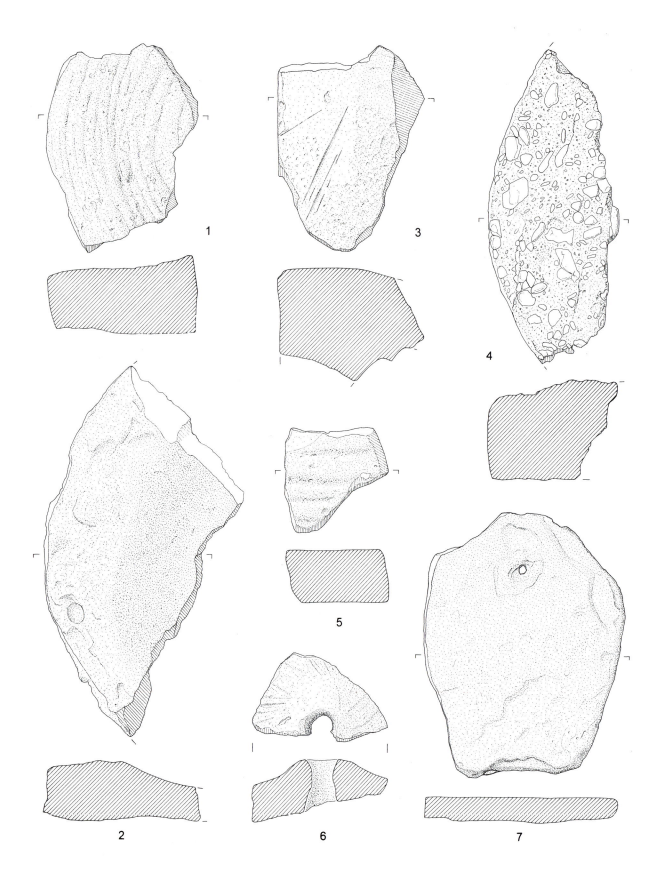

FIG. 98. Fragments of quernstones (Nos 1–6) and a roofing slate (No. 7). Scale 1:3. (*Drawn by Brian Williams*)

such tiles in both the Period 4 town-house (MB 3) and the associated spreads merely supports this. The petrological character and source (Pusey Flags – South Oxfordshire) of the tiles from Object 700 are different to those from MB 3 and they were clearly used to cover another third-century building in Insula IX or its vicinity. Finally, the tesserae are represented by a larger number of calcareous sandstone cubes from the Portlandian (Upper Jurassic) of Swindon (Lithology Sa) (Allen and Fulford 2004) and by the large quantity of waste from the manufacture of dolomite cementstone tesserae from contexts immediately to the east of MB 3.

ILLUSTRATED FINDS

FIG. 98

1.   Quern fragment: Lodsworth greensand (SF 1545): Period 3 well 2234.
2.   Saddle-quern fragment: Lodsworth greensand (SF 2112): Period 3 well 2234.
3.   Quern fragment reused as whetstone: Lodsworth greensand (2613): Period 4 (Object 700).
4.   Quern fragment: quartz conglomerate (SF 1990): Period 4 (Object 700).
5.   Quern fragment: Millstone Grit (3424): Period 3 (Object 701).
6.   Quern fragment: Niedermendig lava (SF 2385): Period 3 (Object 701).
7.   Roofing slate: probably Corallian (Swindon beds) (2610): Period 4 (Object 700).

FIG. 99

8.   Architectural fragment: Combe Down oolite/Box Groundstone (2792): Period 4 (Object 700).
9.   Mortar: Purbeck marble (SF 3131): Period 3 (Object 701).
10.   Marble inlay: Cipollino Mandalato (SF 3297): Period 3 (Object 701).

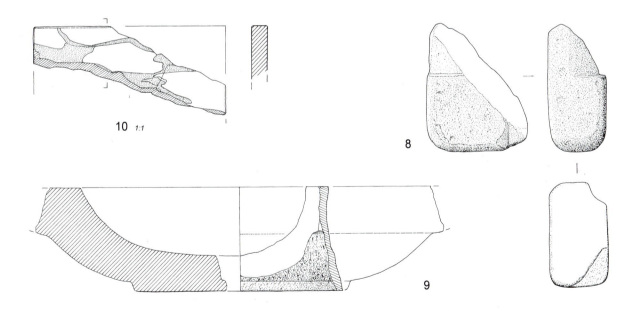

FIG. 99.   Architectural fragment, mortar and fragment of marble inlay. Scale 1:3 except No. 10 (1:1). (*Drawn by Brian Williams*)

CHAPTER 10

THE CERAMIC BUILDING MATERIAL

By Peter Warry

With a contribution on the ventilators/finials by J. R. Timby

QUANTITATIVE ANALYSIS

Overall 2.8 tonnes of ceramic building material have been recovered from Period 3 and 4 contexts. Ignoring material that was too fragmented to be categorised, Table 19 shows that this comprised 65 per cent *tegulae*, 19 per cent *imbrices*, and 16 per cent flat brick. Less than 1 per cent of the assemblage was flue tile. However just over one tonne of material came from the tile dump (Context 4265) which was composed of 80 per cent *tegulae* and therefore very different in character to the rest of the site. If this context is excluded then the figures become *tegulae* 57 per cent, *imbrices* 22 per cent, and flat brick 21 per cent. Some of the pieces recorded as flat brick will inevitably have been fragments of *tegulae* and *imbrices* (*imbrices* are not normally semi-cylindrical but typically have a rounded 'V' profile), so the proportion of roof tile in the overall assemblage is probably somewhat higher than stated.

TABLE 19. QUANTITATIVE ANALYSIS OF CERAMIC BUILDING MATERIAL

	% *tegula*	% *imbrex*	% brick	% flue	Total Tonne
Insula IX Periods 3 and 4	65	19	16	0	2.8
Tile dump (context 4265)	80	14	6	0	1.1
Insula IX excl. tile dump	57	22	21	0	1.7
Later Roman pits	55	24	20	1	0.6
Forum-basilica	21	10	68	1	2.7
Caerwent forum-basilica (Warry, forthcoming)	42	15	42	1	19.0

The proportions of *tegulae*, *imbrices* and brick are virtually identical to those from the later Roman pits in Insula IX and suggest that both the material and its process of distribution around the insula were similar in both the mid and later Roman periods. This is in contrast to the Silchester forum-basilica where the 2.7 tonnes of identifiable material recovered comprised 21 per cent *tegulae*, 10 per cent *imbrices* and 68 per cent flat brick (Timby 2000a, 121). The excess of flat brick in the forum-basilica compared to Insula IX is because most of this material will have been used for tile bonding courses on the basilica which were required for both structural and aesthetic reasons on its taller walls. Nevertheless when compared with the Caerwent forum-basilica there appear to be rather less *tegulae* and *imbrices* than one might expect from the Silchester basilica, which could be consistent with the roof being only partly covered with ceramic tiles. It has been suggested that in the later Roman period the roof was covered in a combination of stone slates, ceramic tiles and, perhaps, flimsier materials such as shingles or thatching (Fulford 2000, 576–9).

Within Insula IX much of the 21 per cent of the assemblage that was flat brick seems to have been derived from hearths and it therefore seems likely that most, and perhaps all, of the buildings would have been single storey. Indeed it is possible that the relative absence of bonding brick could imply that even the buildings with masonry foundations were timber structures built on dwarf masonry walls, but this is taking the evidence too far. Manifestly the virtual absence of flue tile (and *pilae*) demonstrates that none of the buildings had hypocausts.

It has already been noted that the overall ratio of material types was very similar between the mid-Roman Insula IX and the later Roman pits. FIG. 100 looks at the distribution of material types within mid-Roman pits and wells. It can be seen that in nine out of these twelve contexts the proportion of *tegulae* was around 50 per cent which is consistent with the insula average and further evidence that a fairly homogeneous blend of ceramic material had been generated, implying considerable churning.

The proportion of *tegulae* to *imbrices* is also interesting. A *tegula* weighs roughly 2.4 times as much as an *imbrex* (Brodribb 1987, 11) which is closely matched by the ratio 57:22 per cent of *tegulae* to *imbrices* recovered from Insula IX (excluding the context 4265 tile dump). It suggests that, with the exception of the tile dump, most of the roof tile in Insula IX is likely to have come from the collapse or demolition of roofs within the insula. The forum-basilica and later Roman pits have ratios of *tegulae* to *imbrices* close enough to suggest that most of that material was also roof collapse or demolition. It is still, of course, possible that a complete roof was dismantled in another area and imported into Insula IX but in this case one might anticipate that there would have been some deliberate or natural selection of the material that was transported.

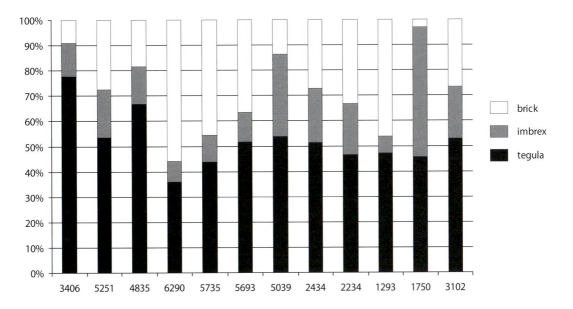

FIG. 100. Make-up of ceramic building material from contexts with >20kg of material from pits and wells of Periods 3 and 4.

DISTRIBUTION OF *TEGULAE*

FIG. 101 shows the distribution of *tegulae* recovered from contexts dated to Periods 3–4 relative to the outline of the structures present during those periods. There is no convincing correlation between the *tegulae* and the structures in any period, the strongest being with MRTB 1/ERTB 1 in Period 3. There is, however, an alignment of *tegulae* in Period 3 along the northern wall of the earlier, Period 2 buildings in the south-east sector; this could imply that these *tegulae* represent the collapse of the roof of this building or that the northern wall (or at least the property boundary) persisted into Period 3 preventing the dispersal of *tegulae* being churned up through building activity on the rest of the site.

An alternative approach to this *tegula* distribution analysis is based on the observation that lower cutaways went through four distinct phases of development (identified as Groups A–D; Warry 2006, ch. 3). The lower cutaways determined the way in which overlapping tiles meshed

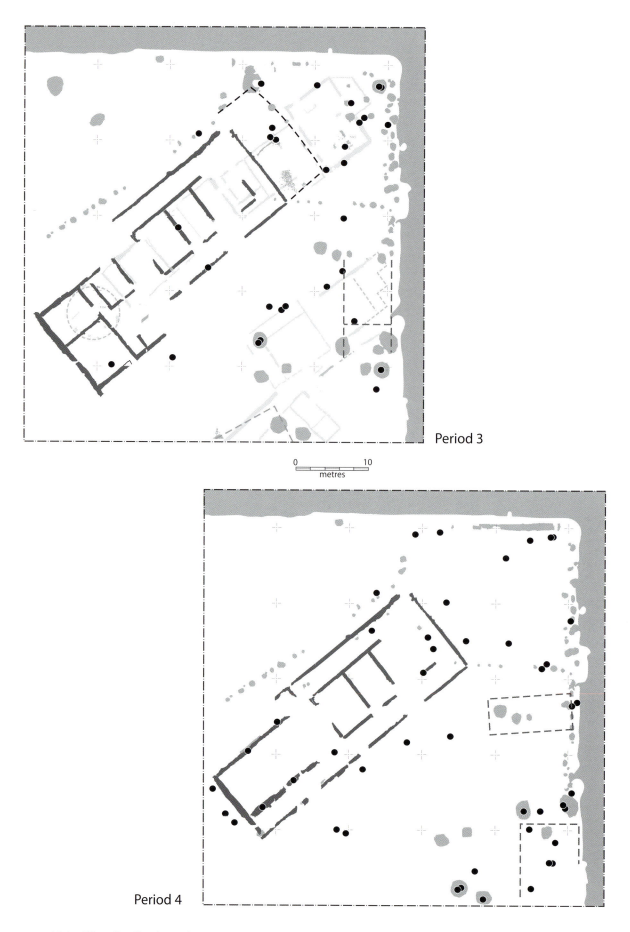

Period 3

Period 4

0   10
metres

FIG. 101. The distribution of *tegulae* in Periods 3 (upper) and 4 (lower).

and as a result any individual roof is only likely to have used *tegulae* from a single, lower cutaway group. Thus the distribution of a particular cutaway group may potentially indicate where the tiles from a roof or small group of roofs ended up, albeit they may have been deposited at different times given the extensive churning activity that the insula appears to have undergone.

The cutaway groups appear sequentially with Group A being the earliest and Group D the latest. No Group D *tegulae* appear in contexts before Period 4 which would imply that these date after A.D. 200. Group C *tegulae* appear in Period 2 as well as Period 3 contexts which could mean that these all originate from Period 2, but the more likely explanation is that production of this group (which is easily the most plentiful variety at Silchester) started in Period 2 and continued through Period 3 and possibly into Period 4. Groups A and B must therefore have originated in the first century in Periods 1 or 2. With the exception of the Group C *tegulae* which appear to start significantly earlier at Silchester, this dating is consistent with that found elsewhere in the province (Warry 2006, ch. 4).

The distributions of these *tegulae* are plotted in FIGS 102–103. Many of the contexts contained examples of more than one cutaway group and in these instances the context has been assigned to the cutaway that appears latest in the sequence. As with the distribution by periods, the distribution by cutaway group shows no meaningful association with any of the buildings, although the alignment of *tegulae* along the northern wall of the Period 2 buildings in the south-east sector is present with the Group C *tegulae* as was also shown with the Period 3 contexts.

Group C *tegulae* were used in four separate contexts (1140, 1141, 1151 and 3595) that formed part of the construction of the Period 4 Masonry Building 3. Two of these contexts also contained Group B *tegulae* which suggests that this was residual material from earlier periods that was being reutilised. Indeed the absence of any meaningful correlation between the buildings and the distribution of *tegulae* when viewed either by cutaway group or context period reinforces the proposition that there has been considerable churning of the ceramic material across the site.

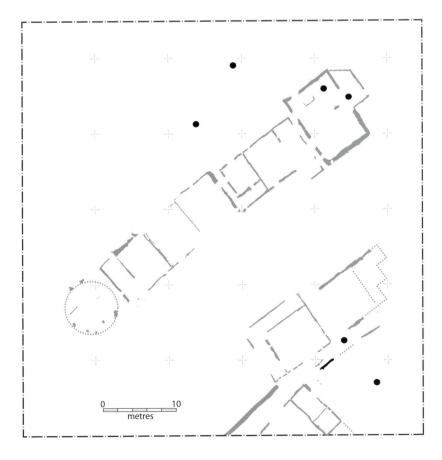

FIG. 102. The distribution of Group A and B *tegulae*.

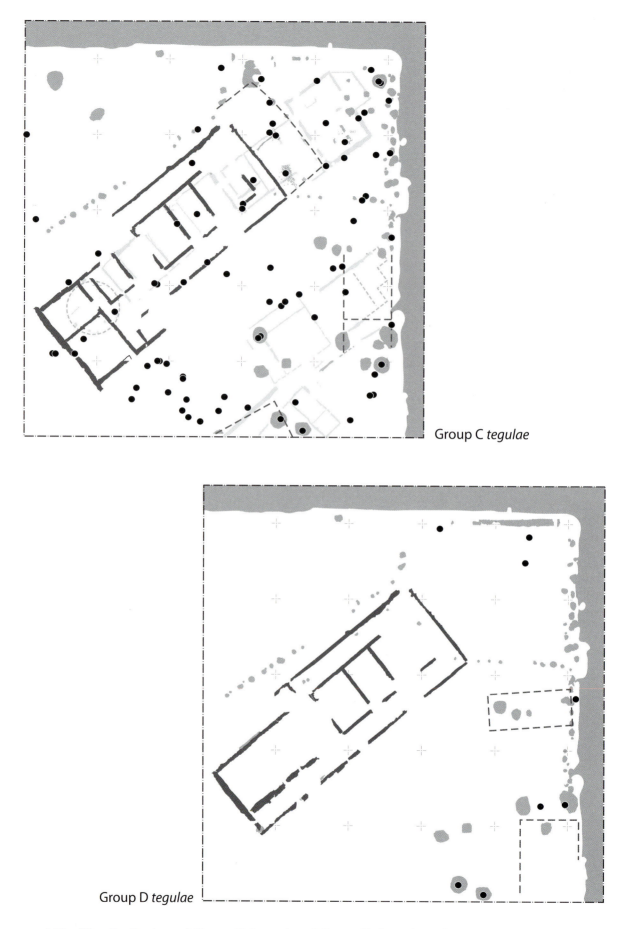

Group C *tegulae*

Group D *tegulae*

FIG. 103. The distributions of Group C (upper) and Group D (lower) *tegulae*.

PITS AND TILE DUMP

Just over a tonne of tile was recovered from context 4265 which, unlike the average for the rest of the site, split 80 per cent *tegulae*, 14 per cent *imbrices* and 6 per cent flat brick. The assemblage included 55 *tegula* lower cutaways which divided into twelve Group A, one Group B, and the remainder Group C. It was not possible to distinguish any particular pattern to the deposition of these tiles as both Group A and C *tegulae* were recovered in each of the two seasons when this context was being excavated. The absence of Group D *tegulae* is in agreement with the stratigraphic sequence which places this deposit prior to A.D. 200. It seems clear both from the very low percentage of *imbrices* and the mix of lower cutaway types that this was not the direct result of a roof demolition. These tiles are therefore likely to have been removed from buildings some considerable time previously and have either been stored or gathered from the general churning on the site before being redeposited.

The weight of *tegulae* equates to some 130 complete tiles which would represent about a fifth of the *tegulae* that would have originally been on one of the roofs of the adjacent buildings of the previous Period 2. This number of *tegulae* should generate 260 lower cutaways compared to the 55 that were recorded. Some of the cutaways will have been broken to the extent that they were either unrecognisable or not worth recording, but the disparity between the actual and expected numbers of cutaways hints at either some selective processing or incomplete recording.

Second-hand roof tiles were a valuable commodity: *inter alia* on Romano-British sites, *tegulae* have been used for drainage channels, flooring and wall construction and *imbrices* used to form *pilae*, flue tiles and pipes. One possibility is, therefore, that the dump represents part of the stock of a used-tile dealer. On stripping a roof, the dealer would have separated the *imbrices* from the *tegulae* for their separate uses. The *tegulae* may have been further processed, for example by knocking off the flanges to generate a flat tile, and it is this processed tile that has directly or indirectly resulted in the dump.

Table 20 lists the diagnostic *tegulae* recovered from the mid-Roman pits, wells and layers and a full listing of all the contexts that provided diagnostic *tegulae* is given in Appendix 5. It is notable that despite the proliferation of Group C lower cutaway *tegulae* there are only 17 contexts containing more than one Group C cutaway which is matched by the number of contexts containing cutaways from two or more different groups: again this suggests that a high proportion of the material had been churned rather than representing primary deposits.

TABLE 20. *TEGULAE* RECOVERED FROM THE PITS, WELLS AND LAYERS OF PERIODS 3–4 AND COMPARATIVE MATERIAL FROM PERIOD 2

Object	Pit/Well	Context	Period	*Tegulae*
701	layer	4528	3	3C
44007	5251	5912	2	C
44008	5039	6228	2	3C
50050	layer	5547	2	3C
500020	1750	1750	4	A
500028	4835	5867	3	2C
500033	3406	3821	4	C, D
500034	3102	3827	4	C
500035	5693	5723	3	C
500037	5735	6436	4	C

TEGULA DIMENSIONS

Only three *tegulae* with complete lengths and breadths have been recovered in the Insula IX excavations, two of these were Group C, which measured 492 by 364mm and 472 by 361mm, and the third was a Group D, measuring 408 by 351mm (breadths being recorded at the upper end). In addition there were a further thirteen *tegulae* where a full length could be measured but not the breadth. Table 21 provides data on all the complete *tegulae* and compares the Silchester measurements with the national average (Warry 2006, 136, fig. 9.1). It is notable that the average for the Group C length is greater than for the Group A which ought to be the larger consistent with the national picture of *tegula* sizes reducing through time. The much larger collection of Group C *tegulae* retained from the Victorian excavations at Silchester in the Reading Museum divides into two distinct lengths, one of which is consistent with the national average and one which is considerably longer. Almost all of these longer Group C *tegulae* are longitudinally convex and were most likely intended to cover a vaulted roof such as on a bathhouse (Warry 2006, 107–8; 116–17 for a fuller discussion of these tiles). The Group C average length in Insula IX is a combination of the standard and longer *tegulae* noted in the Reading collection.

TABLE 21. *TEGULA* DIMENSIONS

| Group | No. | Length (mm) | | | | Breadth (mm) | |
		Average	Longest	Shortest	National	Average	National
A	2	460	465	455	488	n/a	374
B	0	n/a	n/a	n/a	449	n/a	341
C	11	463	492	430	416	363	317
D	3	408	430	386	407	351	315

Only two complete *imbrices* were recovered with lengths of 403 and 405mm respectively.

FLUE TILE

Under 1 per cent of the ceramic building material assemblage was flue tile. Most of this was fragmentary and most appeared to be of standard form with typical scored or combed surfaces. However there were a number of fragments of relief-patterned tile (discussed below) and one fragment (unstratified) of *parietalis* (context 3100, FIG. 104, No. 1).

One of the box-flue tiles (unstratified) had a distinctive vent hole (context 4021, FIG. 104, No. 2). Vents were made in the sides of box-flue tiles to allow the hot air to circulate sideways as well as upwards and they normally take the form of rectangular or circular openings in the walls of these tiles. This fragment of box-flue would have had a vent comprised of two opposed triangles making an opening like an hourglass. Examples of this type of opening have been noted at Liss (Annelay 2008), Chilgrove 1 (Down 1979, 176, fig. 64.2) and Upmarden (Down 1979, 177, fig. 65.6); all of these lie along the Silchester to Chichester road which would suggest either a common production source or some stylistic linkage between multiple producers along the road. However the vent has also been recorded at Bignor (Brodribb 1987, fig. 33d) on the Chichester to London road. At Chilgrove the tile was used as a voussoir in a fourth-century arch so the dating is likely to be fourth century if the tile was new when fixed in position or late third century if it was reused from the original bathhouse.

Two fragments of relief-patterned tile of Die 39 were recovered from contexts 3468 (Period 4) and 3833 (Period 3) (FIG. 104, No. 3). The fabric was very grey, typical of many *parietalis* tiles and similar to the *parietalis* fragment from context 3100, but no lug holes remained to confirm this identification and the thickness at 24mm was less than the 33mm of context 3100 but not inconsistent with Brodribb's national average of 28mm (Brodribb 1987, 143). The distribution of Die 39 is Gloucestershire, Wiltshire, Berkshire and Hampshire with a suggested date range of A.D. 80–150 (Betts *et al.* 1997, 109). If the fragment comes from a *parietalis* then the date should be towards the start of this range.

A further three fragments of relief-patterned tile of Die 27 came from context 2420 (Period 4) in a red fabric, most probably from a box-flue (FIG. 104, No. 4). Die 27 has a distribution ranging from Dover to Lincoln but is found primarily in the London area. It has not been recovered from any well-dated context (Betts *et al.* 1997, 98–9).

No relief-patterned tile has previously been found in the very extensive Fulford excavations

FIG. 104. No. 1. Fragment of a *parietalis* (context 3100); No. 2. Flue-tile with hour-glass-shaped vent-hole (context 4021); No. 3. Flue-tile with relief-patterned stamped decoration: Die 39 (context 3468); No. 4. Flue-tile with relief-patterned stamped decoration: Die 27 (context 2420); No. 5. Fragment of *tegula* or flue-tile deeply scored with a rectilinear pattern in preparation for production of tesserae (context 3424). Scale 1:3. (*Drawn by Brian Williams*)

around Silchester although both these dies are reported by Lowther as occurring at Silchester (Betts *et al.* 1997, 98, 109).[1] Indeed in all of its excavations, Silchester has yielded only four different dies of relief-patterned tile which is very surprising for a *civitas* capital located relatively

---

[1] The authors attribute some Die 27 fragments to the Fulford forum-basilica excavation but this is incorrect as Timby 2000, 119 states that no relief-patterned tile was found.

close to the centre of this tile production in the south-east of the province. By way of comparison, Table 22 gives the number of different dies recorded from other major towns (ibid., 26–8). It seems unlikely that Silchester was particularly impoverished, so does this simply reflect an absence of construction of buildings with hypocausts at Silchester when relief-patterned dies were in fashion?

TABLE 22. NUMBER OF RELIEF-PATTERNED DIES FOUND IN TOWNS

Town	Different dies
London	68
Canterbury	22
St Albans	22
Chichester	11
Colchester	9
Chelmsford	8
Cirencester	6
Leicester	5
Wall	5
Winchester	5
Silchester	4
Lincoln	2

OTHER CERAMIC MATERIAL

Insula IX has yielded the normal range of ceramic building material including fragments of floor, wall and *pilae* tiles. Fragments of ventilators or finials (Timby, below, pp. 229–31) and a probable fragment of water pipe were also observed. The dimensions of complete examples are given in Table 23.

TABLE 23. DIMENSIONS OF COMPLETE CERAMIC PIECES

		Silchester (mm)			National average (mm) (Brodribb 1987, 142)		
	Context	length	breadth	depth	length	breadth	depth
Opus spicatum	2774	148	82	50	114	62	26
Bessalis	2602	200	200	28	198	198	43
Lydion		440	310		403	280	41

An object of interest was a deeply scored *tegula* (or possibly flue tile) with a rectilinear pattern which was recovered from context 3424 (Period 3/4) (FIG. 104, No. 5). It has been speculated that this was a fragment of a gaming-board but in fact it is clearly a tile prepared for tessera production. The scoring generated squares 25mm wide which, with a tile thickness of 19mm, would have produced tesserae absolutely typical of those found on the site. Tesserae have already been removed from three sides of the piece. The scoring is on the underside of the tile and was made before firing, after the tile had dried to a leather-hard state as is evidenced by the 'polish' on the scoring. The flanges of the *tegula* had been broken off (which would not have been possible until the tile was leather-hard) to produce a flat tile and then presumably flipped over such that the scoring could more easily extend over the whole tile including the area where the flanges had been. A similar example of tessera production on a tile of typical *tegula* thickness has been observed by this author at Colchester but that fragment did not extend as far as the flanges.

It is worth speculating on the circumstances that might have led to the use of *tegulae* rather than flat tiles for tessera production. *Tegulae* were much more expensive and time-consuming to produce than flat tiles so one must assume that an urgent order had gone out to the tile manufacturer to convert some of his existing production to tesserae. As the order was urgent the tilemaker could not do the sensible thing and produce some flat blanks which would have then had to stand for several days before becoming sufficiently leather-hard to be scored out for tesserae. As a result he had to take *tegulae* which had already reached the leather-hard stage, knock off the flanges and then score these out. *Tegulae* were chosen because this was the only product at the leather-hard stage that was of a suitable thickness for tesserae. If more time had been available then the moulds used for *imbrex* production, which were flat (prior to the blank being turned out and placed over a shaped former) and of suitable thickness, could have been used. After firing these tesserae slabs were sent to Silchester where the individual tesserae were broken off with pliers. A more efficient approach would have been to break the slabs into individual tesserae in a workshop where a bench, perhaps with a clamp or vice, was available to allow the tesserae to be broken off more easily and effectively. However an alternative hypothesis is that the *tegula* used for this tessera production was a green waster: a tile that had been trodden on or been spoiled in some other way during the drying process. If this were the case then, far from this being an example of inefficiency, it would be a demonstration of efficiency where even wasters were recycled for economic use.

Whether these tesserae were required for an urgent order or an opportunist recycling of wasters one cannot know, but it does suggest that the practice was to source such ceramic tesserae locally rather than a master pavement maker arriving on site with supplies made in his own workshop.

THE VENTILATORS OR FINIALS (FIG. 105)
By J.R. Timby

INTRODUCTION

To date the archaeological excavations in Insula IX have produced 18 fragments of ceramic ventilator or roof finial weighing 3,321g. Some fragments join; others may belong to the same object but do not link. Most of the pieces have come from Period 3 layer 4265 (Object 701), but to these can be added one piece from Period 3 MRTB 1/ERTB 1 (Object 50037), five fragments from the Victorian backfill pit 1057 and trench 1204, one complete collar from late Roman pit 1463, and one piece from cleaning (Object 500061).

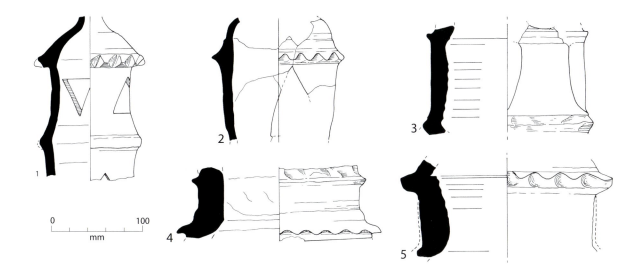

FIG. 105.   Fragments of ceramic ventilators or finials. Scale 1:4. (*Drawn by Jane Timby/Frances Taylor*)

DESCRIPTION

All the pieces are in a red-orange, quite smooth, sandy clay resembling a fine tile clay. At x20 magnification the paste shows a sparse frequency of very fine quartz sand, some grains facetted, and a rare scatter of rounded red-orange iron, mainly less then 0.5mm. The individual segments of the ventilator are wheel-thrown, the sections being luted together, probably with a coil of clay and the joins masked by a frilled or plain band. Apertures have been cut through the walls prior to firing and appear to be either triangular or with rounded edges. The two illustrated examples (FIG. 105, Nos 1–2) from the upper part of two ventilators show slightly different styles: one conical, the other more domed. Further fragments come from the wall or lower part of the ventilator (FIG. 105, Nos 3–5), two surviving as complete or joining collars. None of the pieces shows any evidence of sooting or burning to support their function as chimney pots to convey smoke from a building.

Where from datable contexts, most of the Silchester fragments come from second-century levels. The pieces from later contexts are probably residual.

Catalogue (FIG. 105)

1. Three joining fragments from the conical top of a ventilator. Triangular-cut apertures alternating in orientation. Additional non-joining fragment (not illus.). A1997.25, pit 1057 (1046). SF 355. Victorian backfill.
2. Three joining fragments from the top of a ventilator with a domed profile. Triangular-cut aperture. A2006.50, layer 4265. Object 701, Period 3.
3. Body fragment from a ventilator with three apertures with curved cut edges. A2006.50, layer 4265. SF 4567. Object 701, Period 3.
4. Two joining pieces forming the lower collar from a ventilator with a frilled lower edge and a coil break marking another frill above. Four further non-joining pieces probably from the same object (not illus.). A2004.30, 4265. SF 4566. Object 701, Period 3.
5. Lower collar from a ventilator with a degraded outer surface. Orientation uncertain. Slightly oval in plan, 120mm by 130mm (internal). A1998.12, late Roman pit 1463, (1347). SF 862.
6. Not illus. Bodysherd from near the top. External diameter 220mm. A1997.25. Victorian trench 1204, (1005).
7. Not illus. Small bodysherd. Object 50037, (3905), Period 3.
8. Not illus. Top fragment. Diameter 200mm. A2004.30, (4331), Object 500061, cleaning. SF 4568.

DISCUSSION

These forms of roof accessory have been documented on a number of sites in Britain (Lowther 1976; Brodribb *et al.* 1977; Brodribb 1987, 31; Timby 1991). Their precise purpose(s) still remain slightly enigmatic and various interpretations have been put forward, the most favoured being some sort of roof ventilator (cf. Lowther 1976). As with the examples here, few, if any, show traces of sooting to indicate the passing of hot gases. Some examples have an aperture at the base whilst others are sealed, the latter perhaps serving as finials. Whether these were reserved for a specific type of building, or, if acting as a ventilator, some specific function within a building, can only be speculated. An earlier find from Silchester (Reading Museum) cited by Lowther (1976, 39, pls IIIa, b; IVa and fig. 4, 2–3) shows the lower part of a chimney still attached to a ridge tile but without any opening, proving conclusively a more likely function as an ornamental roof finial, but, again, whether this denoted a specific type of building is unknown. Other examples, such as a complete one from Norton, East Yorks., have an integral ridge tile with an opening indicating direct communication with the roof space (ibid., 38).

The domed top of one of the Silchester examples most closely resembles the complete example from the Roman house at Ashtead, Surrey (cf. Wheeler and Wheeler 1936, pl. LVIII) and a fragment from Verulamium (Goodburn and Grew 1984, fig. 48.17). A complete example from the triangular temple at Verulamium (Wheeler 1936, pl. LVIII and fig. 32.43) has a wider, flat, open top and comprises six tiers divided by obliquely scored bands with a round-headed opening; it was recovered from early second-century levels. An example from Chalk, Kent, possibly from a villa, similarly has a wider top (Lowther 1972, fig. 20). Here it is suggested from melted lead on some of the *tegulae* that the ventilator stood on the slope of the roof (Johnston 1972, 117). The reconstructable example from the pottery production site in Gloucester also has an open top, four tiers and a sloped base, suggesting it too was designed for fixing to a sloped roof rather than the apex. The Gloucester example is also likely to date to the late Flavian-Trajanic period.

Chimney fragments seem to be associated with two sorts of site: occupation sites, both military and civilian, particularly town sites (e.g. Caerleon, Verulamium, London, Silchester, Chester, Cirencester, York), less commonly villa sites (e.g. Chalk), and with pottery or tile production sites, e.g. Ashtead (Lowther 1934); Heighington (Brodribb *et al.* 1977, 315); Gloucester (Timby 1991). The few examples that have been found in datable contexts seem to indicate a second- or third-century date (Lowther 1976, 37).

CHAPTER 11

THE METALWORKING

By John R. L. Allen and Klare Tootell

This chapter reports the evidence for non-ferrous metalworking from crucibles and for the making and working (forging) of iron. Further evidence for non-ferrous metalworking in Periods 3 and 4 can be found in Cook's report on the geochemistry (Ch. 3) and Crummy's report on the 'small finds' (Ch. 6). The latter also reports pieces of bar iron from Period 4 as evidence of blacksmithing.

NON-FERROUS METALWORKING: THE CRUCIBLES
By John R.L. Allen

Four fragments were available and examined by hand-lens, in two cases also in thin-section. Three different crucibles are represented, two of which were found in third-century, Period 4 contexts (Object 700) (FIG. 106). The third was unstratified.

1. SF 1191 (1996) and SF 4962 (2610) (Object 700)

These are joining fragments from the lower parts of a flat-based crucible the size of probably a cup. The fabric, observed in hand-specimen and thin-section, is pale grey, hard, and slightly vitrified with very abundant quartz silt and scattered inclusions of fine- to medium-grained quartz sand and occasional grains of flint and feldspar, chiefly microcline and some plagioclase. Adhering to the outside of the joined fragments — the underside of the crucible — is a thick, uneven mass of greenish-black, highly vesicular, glassy material with scattered fine- to medium-grained quartz sand showing microfractures under the microscope. This mass reveals the moulds of several fragments of charcoal on which it rested. On the inner surface of one of the joined fragments (2610) is a small, blister-like body ranging in colour between off-white and pale green, probably corroded dross. X-ray fluorescence analysis by Dr Stuart Black using portable equipment revealed the presence in this dross of copper, zinc, lead and arsenic.

2. SF 2888 (Unstratified)

This doubly-curved fragment is 12mm thick and in a different, mid-grey, hard, slightly vitreous fabric with very abundant fine- to medium-grained quartz sand. The outer surface is pale grey but on the inner surface are a number of fused, smooth, glassy-looking, blister-like protuberances of off-white to pale green colour, probably corroded dross. This was also found by X-ray fluorescence analysis by Dr Black to contain copper, zinc, lead and arsenic. This fragment was found in a late Roman context.

3. SF 2297 (3412) (Object 700)

This context yielded three tiny fragments clearly different from those above. The fabric is pale grey and semi-vitreous, with abundant fine- to medium-grained quartz sand and many tiny vesicles.

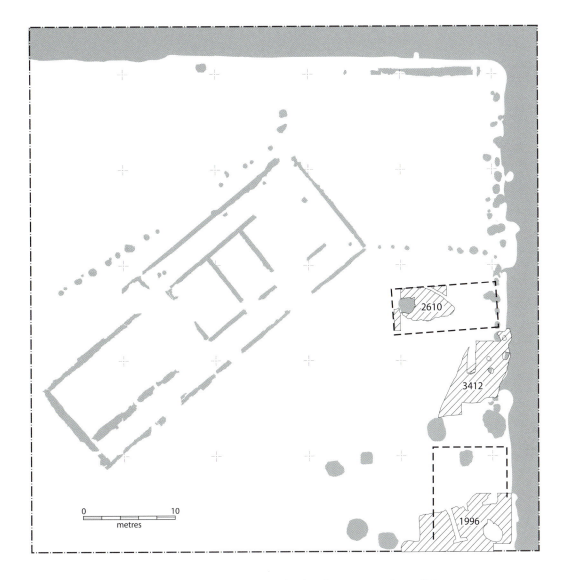

FIG. 106. Location of Period 4 contexts producing fragments of crucible.

OVERALL INTERPRETATION

The vitreous but quartz-rich character of the fabrics, and the association in the case of No. 1 with a highly vesicular outer layer, perhaps added as an additional protection, points to a ceramic designed to withstand, and be operated at, high temperatures. The composition of the two joining fragments is consistent with manufacture from the local Tertiary sediments. There is evidence for charcoal as a fuel. The green-coloured, blister-like bodies found on the inner surfaces (SFs 2888 and 4962), probably corrosion products formed from dross, strongly suggest that the crucibles were last used for melting copper alloys, probably a brass for casting.

Very many crucible fragments have been described in considerable detail from the forum-basilica at Silchester, the great majority from first-century A.D. (pre-Flavian) contexts (Fulford and Timby 2000, 395–405). Bronze residues and corrosion products were recognised in two of these. In terms of fabric, the fragments described above most resemble the Roman-style, Form 4 crucible from the forum-basilica.

The remains of the two crucibles from Object 700 were found close together in contexts beneath late Roman Building 5. The sherd representing the third crucible is unstratified.

IRONMAKING AND IRONWORKING: CONTEXT AND DISTRIBUTION
By Klare Tootell

A total of 8.88kg of slags derived from ironmaking and ironworking was recovered from Period 3 and Period 4 contexts. The great majority were found through hand-excavation, but hammerscale and other spheroidal spatter, the microscopic residues of ironworking, as characterised by Allen (1987) and Allen and Fulford (1987, 273), were also recovered as a product of flotation and the sorting of the associated residues. This sampling technique was applied selectively, primarily to contexts from pits and wells with the principal aim of recovering charred plant remains, but also to other layers which hand-excavation revealed to have significant charcoal or other charred remains. Wherever possible, samples up to 20 litres in volume were taken. There was no attempt to recover hammerscale and other microscopic residues of ironmaking through a systematic programme of wet-sieving across the excavation area. Nevertheless both the absolute quantities of microscopic slag in any sampled context and the proportion of sampled contexts yielding slag are indicators of the intensity of ironworking. Of the slag from Periods 3 and 4, 61 per cent was associated with the south-east layers, 38 per cent with MB 1–3 and MRTB 1/ERTB 1 (=ERTB 4), while 1 per cent derived from the pits and wells.

PERIOD 3 (FIG. 107)

Masonry Buildings 1 and 2 and MRTB 1/ERTB 1 (=ERTB 4)

The incidence of slags associated with these buildings was very low. A total of 1.04kg of slag was excavated from 5 of 436 (1.1 per cent) contexts associated with the Period 3 buildings. Of the 26 contexts sampled by flotation, 8 (30 per cent) produced microscopic slags.

MB 1

Microscopic slags only were recovered from contexts associated with this building. Hammerscale flakes (24) and a single globule were identified from hearth context 3707. Very small quantities were found in samples from clay floor 3202 (3 flakes) and gravel wall foundation 3248 (1 globule).

MB 2

A small quantity of smithing slag was associated with clay layer 3396 (95g), while a charcoal rich context (3367) in a corner of the north-east Room 4 produced 70g including fuel-ash and smithing slags. Very small quantities of hammerscale were recovered from floor layer 5506 (5) and occupation layer 4449 (2).

MRTB 1/ERTB 1

A total of 0.88kg of slag was recovered from three contexts associated with this building, of which 56 per cent was associated with context 3732. This included a slag basin (340g). Fragments of smelting and processing slag (245g) were also found in context 3533, the remaining bulk slag (140g) occurring in context 3847. Only one context, 3532, produced a quantity of hammerscale flakes (56) and globules (8). Very small quantities of microscopic slag were produced from two other contexts.

Pits and wells

Northern pits: no slag was recovered from well 2234 and only a single, microscopic globule from cess-pit 4835.

South-eastern pits: no bulk slags were recovered from any of the south-eastern group of pits and wells. However, a significant quantity of microscopic slag was identified from pit 5039 with

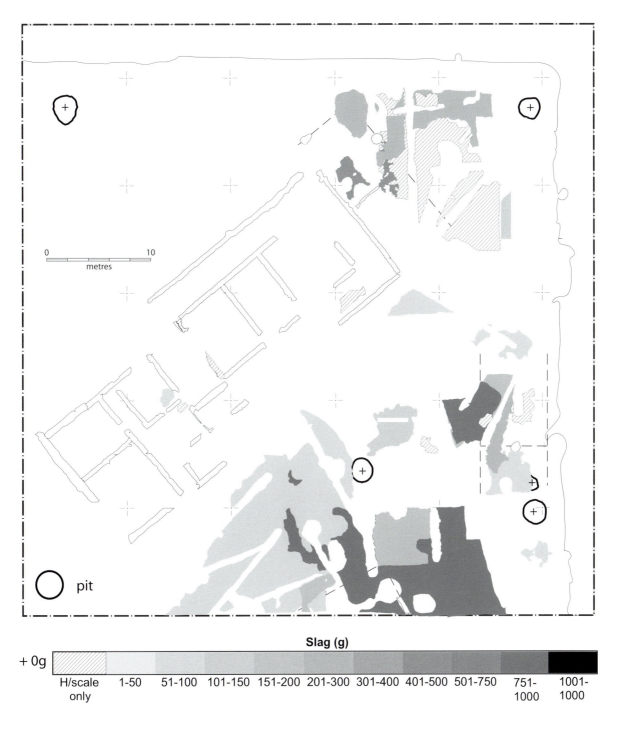

Slag (g)

| + 0g | H/scale only | 1-50 | 51-100 | 101-150 | 151-200 | 201-300 | 301-400 | 401-500 | 501-750 | 751-1000 | 1001-1000 |

FIG. 107. The distribution of slags associated with ferrous metalworking in Period 3.

over 200 hammerscale flakes and 4 globules from contexts 6213 and 6228. A lesser quantity of hammerscale flakes (25) and globules (2) was associated with the slumps into 6290 and context 6284 in well 5693.

South-east layers

In contrast to the south-east pits, a total of 2.15kg of slag was associated with the occupation spreads to the south and south-east of the Period 3 buildings. Out of the 156 contexts associated with this Object, only 12 (7.6 per cent) contained bulk slag. Of the 20 contexts sampled for charred plant remains, only 5 (25 per cent) produced microscopic slag.

Almost half of the slag derived from only two contexts, one of which (3833) produced a single slag basin (285g). The latter was the only certain evidence of ironmaking, the remaining slags from the south-east layers representing residues of ironworking. None of the sampled contexts produced significant quantities of microscopic slag. The largest amount (15 flakes and one globule) was associated with context 4273, while 11 flakes and 2 globules were associated with context 3833 and the larger slags described above.

PERIOD 4 (FIG. 108)

Masonry Building 3

A total of 2.33kg of slag was recovered from the contexts associated with MB 3. The great majority of this derived from only ten (4 per cent) of the excavated contexts, with microscopic slags associated with three (42 per cent) of the small number of only seven contexts sampled for charred plant remains. Just over half (54.5 per cent) derived from a single context, 1788, a make-up layer for Room 4, among which were two slag basins. Further possible evidence of iron smelting, in the form of dense pieces of slag, was identified from contexts 1397, 1410, 1796 and 3313, while the remaining iron-forging slags included fragments of furnace lining and fuel-ash slag. Small quantities of hammerscale, ranging from thirteen to four flakes and two globules, were recovered from three contexts, 1544, 3268 and 3276.

South-east pits and wells

Only two (1.4 per cent) of the 135 contexts associated with all the south-eastern pits and wells of Periods 3 and 4 produced bulk ironworking slags. A small quantity was recorded from the adjacent pits or wells 3102 and 3406 of Period 4. The larger amount (105g) derived from 3102 and included fuel-ash and microscopic slags (<10 flakes and globules in total) from contexts 3144, 3182 and 3827. Pit or well 3406 produced only 4 flakes of hammerscale from context 4041.

South-east layers

A total of 3.26kg of slag was recovered from the Period 4 layers to the south and south-east of MB 3. Of the 114 contexts associated with this Object only 14 (12 per cent) contained slag, while half of the small sample of 18 contexts processed for charred plant remains produced microscopic slags from their residues.

Southern building (MRTB 4) and associated make-ups

A slag basin (210g) was recovered from clay surface 3911 associated with the putative building itself, while microscopic slag (19 hammerscale flakes; 3 globules) was recorded from 3467 and 3912, also in association with the building. Other processing slag, including 11 hammerscale flakes and 3 globules, was found in association with, respectively, dump deposit 4067 and make-up or possible occupation layer 3444.

Make-ups and occupation layers

A third (34 per cent) of the slag from Object 700 came from this group of contexts. It included a slag basin (250g) and a larger slag mass (575g) derived from smelting from make-up or possible occupation layer 3468.

Make-ups for Late Roman Buildings 1 and 5

Over half of the slag, accounting for 53 per cent of the total from the south-east layers of Period 4, came from the late third-century make-ups for Late Roman Building 1, in particular from deposit 2419 and levelling layer 3424. Slag basins, weighing respectively 420g and 300g, were found in these layers and in the gravel spread 2488 (190g). Two further probable slag basins (190g; 180g) were also recovered from 3424. A make-up layer (3412) for Late Roman Building

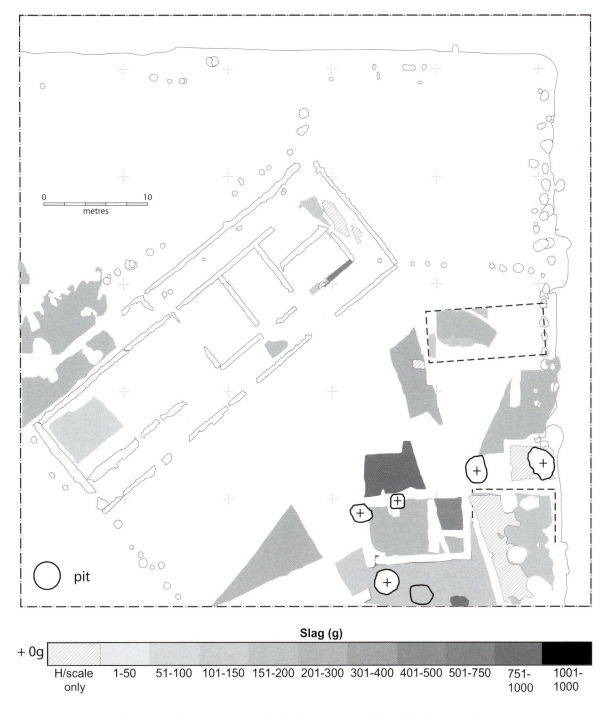

FIG. 108. The distribution of slags associated with ferrous metalworking in Period 4.

5 produced one piece of possible smelting slag and microscopic slags (22 flakes of hammerscale and 7 globules). Three further contexts produced microscopic slags but with a collective total of eleven hammerscale flakes and globules.

DISCUSSION

The total quantity of slags, including microscopic material, from Periods 3 and 4 is small, a little over half the total amount recovered from the late Roman occupation (16.43kg) (Tootell 2006); two thirds (64 per cent) of the total derived from the third-century Period 4 contexts. With the exception of Period 3 pit 5039, which contained the largest quantities of microscopic slag (hammerscale) (>200 flakes) from any Period 3 or 4 context, the pits and wells of both periods produced almost no slag. The south-east layers of both periods were the most productive, together accounting for almost two thirds (62 per cent) of the total recovered from Periods 3 and 4. As with the total amount, the distribution between periods was also approximately one third:two thirds in favour of Period 4 (60 per cent). In both periods the greatest quantities were found towards the southern edge of the excavation trench, particularly in contexts pre-dating the construction of Late Roman Building 1. Among the buildings the greatest quantity was associated with Period 4 Masonry Building 3 and the distribution was again one third:two thirds in favour of Period 4 and MB 3 (62 per cent).

The quantities and character of slag recovered do not indicate any sustained ironmaking or ironworking and there is the possibility that all was imported from elsewhere in the town to Insula IX, for example in the context of preparing the ground for building work. Certainly the majority of the slag, including the slag basins indicative of smelting activity, is concentrated in the area later occupied by Late Roman Building 1. The same might also be true of the microscopic slag, a key indicator of iron-forging, that it was imported from elsewhere in *Calleva* in association with other materials. Indeed some flakes and globules may have been introduced casually, for example, on the soles of muddy hob-nail boots. However, there are concentrations, notably from Period 3 pit 5039 (>200 flakes) and MRTB 1/ERTB 1 (3532) (>50 flakes), which suggest some smithing activity nearby or within the latter building. Further concentrations (>20 flakes) were associated with two contexts in Period 3 (MB 1, 3707 and the slumps into well complex 6290). A third deposit of this size coincides with the concentration of bulk slags associated with the make-ups for Late Roman Building 1 and may indicate that, despite the absence of evidence from the adjacent pits and wells, some ironmaking and ironworking were taking place in association with the predecessor of Late Roman Building 1. In the case of Period 4 MB 3, where there is a small amount of evidence for both smelting and forging from the bulk slags, the significant contexts in question were not further sampled for microscopic slags.

Further interpretation of the microscopic residues is hindered by the lack of comparative, quantitative data and different approaches to the determination of the content of such residues in the soil. While there is clearly a higher incidence associated with the late Roman occupation, very few individual contexts produced quantities in excess of 100 flakes (Tootell 2006). By comparison a very large quantity was recovered from pre-Boudican Building 3 and also from the post-Boudican Period Structure 2, Borough High Street, Southwark (Drummond-Murray and Thompson 2002, 28; 612). With a total of over 60kg of microscopic slags recovered from these Borough High Street excavations, almost all of which derived from the above two structures, the interpretation of them as smithies seems unassailable (Keys 2002, 241). Elsewhere in Southwark a different approach was taken by Starley who used magnetic susceptibility to gauge the density of hammerscale (2003, 132–3). Sim's experimental work concentrated on the spatial distribution and morphology of microscopic residues in relation to a series of blacksmithing experiments (1998, 97–145). Although there is no directly comparable quantitative data, the experiments do reveal how concentrated the distribution of hammerscale and other spatter is around the anvil, and how steep the fall-off is away from it (Sim 1998, 97–145). Bearing in mind the sampling strategy which produced the Insula IX data, the larger quantities of microscopic residues (>20 flakes and spheroids) would not be inconsistent with smithing events (as opposed to the existence of a smithy) within the insula in Periods 3 and 4.

In conclusion, the total amount of slag is small and some may have been introduced from outside or elsewhere in the insula. In the case of Period 3 the evidence is such that it may only indicate limited and episodic ironworking, particularly in association with MRTB 1/ERTB 1 and pit 5039. A very small quantity of smelting slag is also associated with MRTB 1/ERTB 1. For Period 4 the concentration of bulk and microscopic slag in the area occupied by the predecessor to Late Roman Building 1 indicates a small amount of both ironmaking and ironworking, activities which continue in this location into the fourth century. In the absence of positive evidence of microscopic slags, we can be less certain of a similar interpretation for the slags from MB 3.

One important taphonomic observation arises from the study of the Period 3 and 4 slags. Microscopic slags were recovered as a product of a sampling strategy primarily designed to recover charcoal and charred plant remains. The largest quantity of microscopic slag was found in contexts within a pit which otherwise produced no bulk slag. The second largest quantity, from MRTB 1/ERTB 1, derived from contexts which did not themselves otherwise produce bulk slags, although the latter were found in adjacent, associated contexts. Given the aim of the environmental sampling strategy, we cannot extrapolate from its findings more generally about ironworking activity across the excavation trench in the second and third centuries, except in the case of the pits and wells which were subjected to intensive sampling for charred plant remains, etc. This suggests that a parallel sampling strategy, including magnetic susceptibility, ought to be developed for occupation layers with the principal purpose of recovering microscopic slags (as well as, of course, other surviving microscopic evidence).

IRONMAKING: ANALYSIS OF SLAG BASINS
By John R.L. Allen

Each of the eight masses of slag interpreted as furnace bottoms (see below), was cleaned and sliced vertically along the longitudinal axis. The cut faces and other surfaces were subjected to hand-lens examination. In selected cases, the distribution, form and orientation of vesicles exposed on the cut faces was emphasised by rubbing these moistened surfaces with a bar of white, cold-cream soap, a simple process which infills these cavities with a material of contrasting colour.

PERIOD 3

Two contexts each yielded a single furnace bottom. That from MRTB 1/ERTB 1 (context 3732) weighs 340g and is roughly oval in plan and weakly concavo-convex in profile. Many small scraps of charcoal are trapped on the underside and a little is captured on the uneven top. The almost black slag is dense and uniform, with evidence of crystallinity, and marked by frequent vesicles, the smaller spheroidal, the larger more irregular. There is no sign of internal stratification and the vesicles are fairly evenly distributed, but without any conspicuous radial orientation. The furnace bottom from the south-eastern layers (context 3833) weighs 285g and is roughly triangular in plan and deeply plano-convex. The underside, incorporating a few chips of charcoal, is irregular on a scale suggesting that the slag chilled against granular soil. One extensive face on this surface is flat and could be the mould of the tip of a spade with a V-shaped blade where it had dug into a substrate. The upper surface is very uneven. The slag is black, dense, uniform, partly crystalline, and with radially arranged vesicles near the lower and upper surfaces. Evidence of internal stratification is lacking.

PERIOD 4

There are six furnace bottoms, two from MB 3 and four from the south-eastern layers. The slags from MB 3 come from a single context (1788). Two contexts represent the south-eastern layers.

One furnace bottom (410g) from MB 3 is oval in plan, deeply convex, and with a slightly concave top. The underside shows small-scale irregularities compatible with the slag having chilled against granular soil. Ochreous material occludes the top. The slag is black, uniform and partly crystalline, with small- to medium-sized spheroidal vesicles dispersed throughout. Signs of internal stratification are lacking.

The second mass of slag (335g) solidified at a level above that of the furnace bottom proper and is very irregular in plan and sliced section. The slag extends inward from a doubly-curved fragment of furnace lining which displays a short baking-sequence of dark red through grey to almost black glassy and vesicular sandy clay with scattered flint pebbles (<12mm). Beneath, the surface of the slag is uneven, with the moulds of fragments of charcoal. On the upper surface is a smooth, concave central area surrounded by an irregular zone. The slag is black, dense, uniform and partly crystalline, with numerous vesicles of very variable shape and size. Locally, these show a strong radial orientation. There is no internal stratification.

Context 3424 from the south-eastern layers gave three furnace bottoms. The smallest (175g) is oval with a shallow plano-convex profile, a few fragments of charcoal and chips of flint appearing on the base. Dispersed in the black, dense, uniform, partly crystalline slag are occasional spheroidal to elongated vesicles, those near the base having a strong radial orientation. The next largest furnace bottom (190g) is oval and plano-convex. The base and top are uneven, the former revealing entrapped charcoal, and the latter charcoal fragments and flint pebbles (<15mm). The slag is black, dense, uniform, partly crystalline and with very few vesicles. Signs of internal stratification are lacking. The third furnace bottom from this context (300g) has a shallow, concavo-convex profile. On the underside is a relatively smooth, flat face which could be the mould of a surface cut by some kind of digging tool. The almost black slag is dense, uniform and partly crystalline, with abundant, evenly dispersed, radially arranged spheroidal to elongated vesicles of small to medium size. Stratification is lacking. The furnace bottom (210g) from the only other context (3911) affording slag is oval and shallowly plano-convex. A few fragments of charcoal are trapped on the uneven base; just below the top occur a little quartz sand and a few chips of flint. The slag is black, dense, uniform and partly crystalline. A strong radial arrangement typifies the frequent small- to medium-sized vesicles. The sand and flint just below the top are the only indications of internal stratification.

OVERALL INTERPRETATION

The main question is whether the described slags represent iron smelting (furnace bottoms) or iron smithing (hearth bottoms). Although bodies of slag of similar form result from the two processes, those from Insula IX can be assigned with some confidence to smelting, referring to Schrüfer-Kolb's (2004) and Allen's (2008) recent reviews. The main reasons are the high density, uniformity, absence of significant internal inclusions and lack of internal stratification displayed by the slags. The relatively small size and generally spheroidal form of their vesicles, and their frequent radial arrangement relative to the undersides of the slag bodies, together with the slag density, indicates that each mass represents a single cooling event from a silicate melt of comparatively low viscosity because of its high temperature. These are not the conditions associated with smithing, where the episodic operation of the hearth at a lesser temperature results in a layered mass replete with irregular vesicles and many different inclusions. As furnace bottoms go, however, those from Silchester are on the small side, suggesting small-scale operations of low efficiency. The form of the fragment of furnace lining to which one of the slags from MB 3 (Period 4) is attached, is consistent with the use of a non-tappable bowl furnace dug into the ground surface (Tylecote 1986). As no tap slags have so far been recovered from any part of the excavations, this simple technology seems likely to have been in more extensive use as, for example, reported in the context of the late Roman occupation of Insula IX (Allen 2006).

CHAPTER 12

THE HUMAN REMAINS

By Mary Lewis

With the exception of fragments of skull from one adult, all the human remains from Periods 3 and 4 derived from infants. The surviving remains may represent as many as six individuals of which only one was represented by more than a single bone and was retrieved from a single burial cut. In terms of the possible number of individuals, these are equally divided between Periods 3 and 4, but all remains, irrespective of period, are clustered in the south-eastern area of the trench (Objects 700, 701) (FIG. 109).

PERIOD 3 (Object 701)

Skull fragments (5641)

The two small finds, 3546 and 3549, comprise, respectively, left and right parietal bones of the skull. SF 3546 also includes a piece of non-human bone, possibly from a skull. All of the breaks along the skull margins are post-mortem.

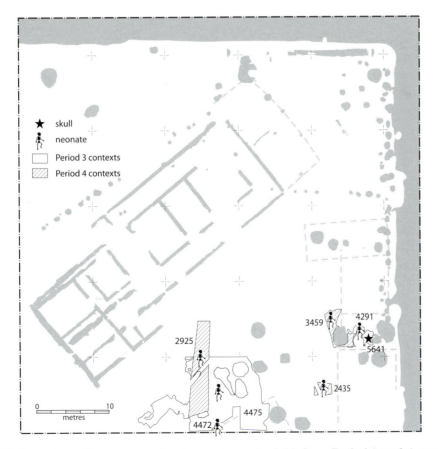

FIG. 109. Location of human remains (neonates and adult) from Period 3 and 4 contexts.

The human parietal bones can be fitted together at the sagittal suture along the centre of the skull, and therefore represent one individual. It is impossible to assess the sex of an individual from the cranial vault alone, and age at death cannot be determined, other than that this skull belongs to an adult. There is evidence of pitting on the parietals that is often interpreted as representing iron deficiency anaemia (i.e. porotic hyperostosis). However, this is a very slight change and may also be indicative of a mild scalp infection.

Infant burial (4472)

Two small finds were excavated from this context. SF 3115 comprises four left rib fragments and one shaft fragment of a right rib from a neonate. SF 3331 also contains rib fragments, one of which can be matched with a fragment from 3115. Therefore, these remains are considered to belong to one individual. Skull fragments, the left and right clavicle, and a shaft fragment of an unidentified long bone were also recovered. A tentative age assessment can be made from the intact left clavicle. The maximum length (42.93mm) indicates that the child was between 38 and 42 weeks (Scheuer and Black 2000, 250). Birth is traditionally estimated to be between the ages of 38 and 40 weeks, suggesting that the child was full-term. Such neonatal deaths are generally the result of internal (endogenous) factors caused by maternal illness, low birth weight or birth trauma, rather than being caused by the external environment into which they were born (Scott and Duncan 1999).

Context 4475

SF 3364 comprises an intact left humerus. The maximum length of the humerus (57.49mm) suggests this child was 35 weeks old (range 33–37 weeks, Scheuer and Black 2000). It is likely that this child was either born prematurely, before its lungs were developed enough for the child to breathe unaided, or was stillborn.

Context 4291

This context contained the proximal end of a right tibia. Although a precise age could not be assigned, a comparison of the bone with the tibia from 2435 (below) suggests the child was older and therefore full-term.

PERIOD 4 (Object 700)

Context 2435

This context included a complete left tibia and fibula (lower leg). The maximum length of the tibia (64.56mm) indicates that the child was between 36 and 40 weeks, with a mean age of 38.6 weeks (Scheuer and Black 2000, 415). This child was full-term at the time of death.

Context 2925

This context comprised the distal end of a left femur. It was not possible to assign a precise age to this neonate.

Context 3459

The remains comprise three fragments representing one right femur and a distal left femur. It is possible that these remains are a pair. The fragmentary nature of the bones means that a precise age could not be assigned to them. However, the size of the distal femur suggests that the neonate was slightly younger than that from 2925.

CONCLUSION

Of the four infants who could be aged, three were full-term or probably full-term and one was about 35 weeks. Although the phasing suggests an equal division of the remains between the second and third centuries, all those from Period 3 came from later contexts in the sequence, suggesting that the majority belong to the third century. The skull fragments, however, may be reworked from late Iron Age levels from which adult inhumations have been recovered (Firth 2000).

CHAPTER 13

THE ANIMAL BONE

By Claire Ingrem

The focus of this report is the animal bone recovered from Period 3 (*c.* A.D. 125–150—*c.* A.D. 200) and Period 4 (*c.* A.D. 200—*c.* A.D. 250/300) deposits, the majority of which came from layers in the south-east area of the excavation and is associated with occupation along the north–south street frontage. A small amount of material also came from miscellaneous pits and wells. Ceramic evidence suggests that some material may be residual (Timby, Ch. 8*)*.

An assemblage of animal bone was also recovered from the Period 2–4 'House 1' sequence, including MBs 1–3, and this has already been published (Ingrem 2007). However, basic data from the 'House 1' sequence included in the tables and the results of that analysis are also included here to allow the entire Period 3 and 4 material from Insula IX to be viewed as a whole.

METHODOLOGY

Anatomical elements were identified to species where possible with the exception of ribs and vertebrae which were assigned to animal-size categories. Mandibles and limb bones were recorded using the zonal method developed by Serjeantson (1996) to allow the calculation of the minimum number of elements (MNE) and individuals (MNI); this is based on the most numerous zone of a single element taking into account size. Percentage survival of selected elements is based on the minimum number of elements (MNE) calculated as a percentage of the maximum number possible according to MNI. In addition, all bone fragments over 10mm in the hand-recorded material and over 2mm in the sieved samples were recorded to species or size category to produce a basic fragment count of the Number of Identified Specimens (NISP). Fragments categorised as large mammal are likely to belong to horse or cattle, those in the medium mammal category to sheep/goat or pig.

The presence of gnawing, butchery and burning, together with the agent responsible, was recorded. Measurements were taken according to the conventions of von den Driesch (1976) and Payne and Bull (1982) for mammals, and Cohen and Serjeantson (1996) for birds. The wear stages of the lower cheek teeth of cattle, caprines and pig were recorded using the method proposed by Grant (1982) and age attributed according to the method devised by Payne (1973), Legge (1981) and O'Connor (1988). The fusion stage of post-cranial bones was recorded and age ranges estimated according to Getty (1975). Measurements of the crown height of horse teeth were recorded and age estimated according to the method of Levine (1982).

A selected suite of elements was used to differentiate between sheep and goat (Boessneck 1969; Payne 1985): the distal humerus, proximal radius, distal tibia, distal metapodials, astragalus, calcaneus and deciduous fourth premolar. No elements were positively identified to goat, but for the purposes of this report the caprine remains are referred to as sheep/goat. It is likely that the birds identified as 'galliformes' are all domestic fowl. None of the characteristic features of pheasant were present on tarsometatarsi or femurs (Cohen and Serjeantson 1996). Duck have been assigned to species on the basis of size in comparison to reference specimens and using the criteria of Woelfle (1967).

The dog assemblage is the subject of a separate report (Clark, Ch. 14) although basic quantification data are included in Appendix 6, Table 57.

DATA

A total of 26,990 fragments of animal bone were recovered from Period 3 and Period 4 deposits (including the 'House 1' sequence) by hand collection, of these 57 per cent are identifiable to species, taxa, or size category (Appendix 6, Table 57a). Overall, cattle and specimens assigned to the large mammal category dominate the material, with caprines only slightly more numerous than pig. A number of other mammals are represented including horse, dog, badger (*Meles meles*), roe deer (*Capreolus capreolus*), red deer (*Cervus elaphus*), hare (*Lepus europaeus*), and rat (*Rattus rattus*). Several species of bird are present including domestic goose (*Anser anser*), duck (*Anas/Aythya spp.*), galliform (probably domestic fowl), woodcock (*Scolopax rusticola*), pigeon/dove (*Columbus spp.*), raven (*Corvus corax*), rook/crow (*Corvus frugilegus/corone*), and thrush (*Turdidae spp.*). Fish are represented by salmonid and flatfish.

In addition, a further 5,317 fragments came from sieved samples of which 7 per cent are identifiable to species, taxa, or size category (Appendix 6, Table 57b). The remains of pig dominate this assemblage, although specimens assigned to the large mammal category are also numerous. The only mammal not present in the hand-collected material is wood mouse (*Apodemus sylvaticus*). A greater range of fish is present with cyprinid, common eel (*Anguilla anguilla*), sea bream (*Sparidae spp.*), and flatfish present; in addition single bones tentatively identified to scad (*Trachurus trachurus*) and mullet (*Muglidae spp.*) were recovered. A few amphibian bones are present including two ilia belonging to frog (*Rana temporaria*).

In general taxa representation is very similar in the assemblages recovered from both the south-east layers and the 'House 1' sequence, although caprines and pig are more numerous in the Period 4 'House 1' sequence (=MB 3), at the expense of cattle.

PERIOD 3 (*c.* A.D. 125–150–*c.* A.D. 200)

TAXA REPRESENTATION

South-east layers (Object 701)

Deposits dated to Period 3 (*c.* A.D. 125–150–*c.* A.D. 200) produced 5,191 identifiable specimens (Appendix 6, Table 57). The major domestic animals — cattle, sheep/goat and pig — dominate the assemblage with cattle most numerous and pig more frequent than caprines. Specimens assigned to the large mammal category are more numerous than those belonging to medium mammal. Horse and dog are present in small numbers. Several species of wild mammal are represented including roe deer, red deer and hare but all comprise less than one per cent of the identifiable assemblage. Galliformes dominate the bird assemblage, although greylag goose, duck, woodcock, pigeon/dove and corvid are all represented by a few specimens. The small fish assemblage contains bones belonging to salmonid, cyprinid, eel, flatfish, and probably also scad and mullet.

Excluding the dog remains (see Clark, Ch. 14), few articulated or paired bones were recovered. Two horse bones — a distal metapodial and 1st phalanx — belong to the same animal, as do a cattle radius and ulna, matching pairs of sheep metacarpals and metatarsals, and a pair of pig mandibles (Appendix 6, Table 58a).

In contrast to the NISP figures, the calculation of the minimum number of elements shows a fairly equal representation of cattle, sheep/goat and pig and the minimum number of individuals suggests there were fewer cattle (Appendix 6, Table 59a). Roe deer are represented by three individuals and red deer by one.

The majority of the material came from miscellaneous layers with a small proportion derived from pits and wells. There is some variation in the proportion of the major food animals according to feature type with cattle less well represented in the pits and layers than in the well which is dominated by cattle bones (FIG. 110a).

'House 1' sequence (=MB 1 & 2, 'ERTB 4' = MRTB 1, ERTB 1)

The majority of the assemblage from the 'House 1' sequence also derives from miscellaneous

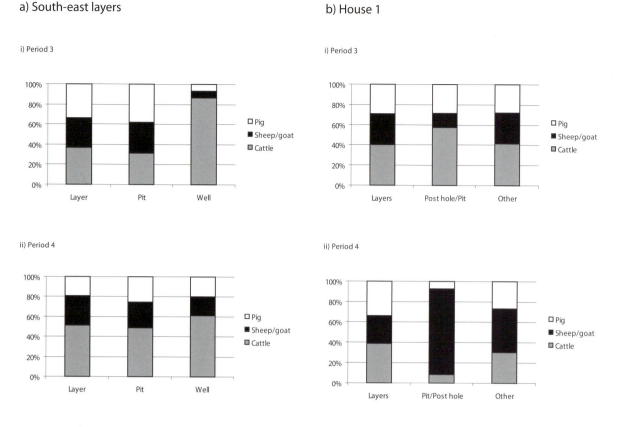

a) South-east layers

b) House 1

i) Period 3

i) Period 3

ii) Period 4

ii) Period 4

FIG. 110.   Proportion of major domestic animals according to feature type (%).

layers and is very similar in terms of representation of cattle, sheep/goat and pig (Appendix 6, Table 57). Although cattle appear to be more numerous in the pits and post-holes (FIG. 110b), this is likely to reflect the small sample size (n=7) rather than depositional practices.

BODY PART REPRESENTATION

South-east layers (Object 701)

Anatomical representation according to NISP is shown in Appendix 6, Table 60a. Few horse bones were recovered and most are either loose teeth or foot bones. Cattle and sheep/goat are represented by elements from all parts of the body — head, major limbs and feet — with vertebra and rib fragments belonging to large and medium-sized mammals also present. Most parts of the pig skeleton are also present. The high frequency of metapodials is likely to reflect their naturally occurring frequency in the pig skeleton and the grouping of metacarpals and metatarsals during recording has also created a bias in their favour. As a result, pig metapodials are not directly comparable with cattle and caprines so have been omitted from the calculation of MNE and MNI (Appendix 6, Tables 59a–b).

Most of the roe and red deer bones are from the head and feet, although the presence of roe deer scapulae and red deer pelves suggests that some good quality venison was available. As would be expected for an animal usually cooked whole, the small hare assemblage includes bones from the head, major limbs and feet.

The galliform assemblage similarly includes elements from the trunk and the limbs. Other bird taxa are represented mainly by limb bones (Appendix 6, Table 61a). Apart from a few unidentifiable ribs, all of the fish bones are vertebrae.

Percentage survival has been calculated using, and is compared with, the method of Brain

(1969) in which the elements are listed according to their expected survival in a goat assemblage that has been subjected to density mediated taphonomic processes such as gnawing (FIG. 111a). In respect of the cattle assemblage, most major limb bones, tarsals and foot bones are over-represented with only the mandible, atlas, and axis notably under-represented. A similar pattern is visible for caprines although the mandible is better represented. The most notable characteristic of the pig assemblage is the scarcity of mandibles and over-representation of hind limbs.

'House 1' sequence (=MB 1 & 2, 'ERTB 4' = MRTB 1, ERTB 1)

In most respects the 'House 1' sequence is generally similar to that from the south-east layers although some forelimb bones belonging to horse and roe deer are present (Appendix 6, Table 60a, FIG. 111b).

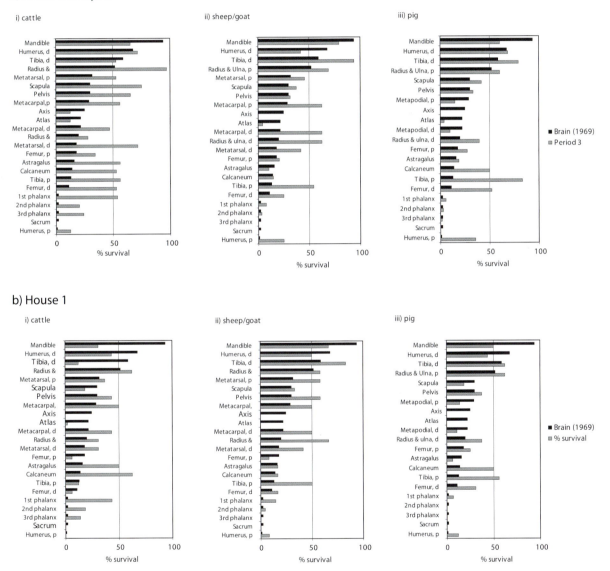

FIG. 111.   Period 3: percentage survival (elements arranged according to Brain 1969).

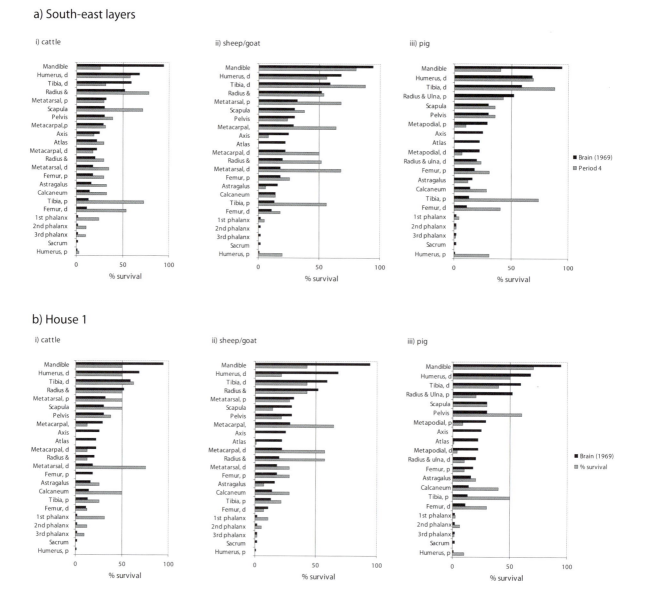

FIG. 112.   Period 4: percentage survival (elements arranged according to Brain 1969).

MORTALITY AND SEX

Tooth eruption and wear data are given in Appendix 6, Tables 69–70 and bone epiphyseal fusion data can be found in Appendix 6, Tables 71–72.

South-east layers (Object 701)

All of the horse teeth derive from adults and no bones with unfused epiphyses indicative of immature animals are present.

Cattle teeth derive from animals ranging in age from very young to very old; however two clear peaks occur between 26 and 36 months and between 6 and 8 years, each representing approximately a third of the population (FIG. 113a, i). Bone epiphyseal fusion data broadly support this pattern but might suggest that the first peak in slaughter occurred later, between 3 and 4 years of age (FIG. 114a, i).

According to the dental data most sheep and goats were slaughtered between the ages of 1 and 4 years (FIG. 113a, ii). Epiphyseal fusion data similarly suggest that most (80 per cent) caprines

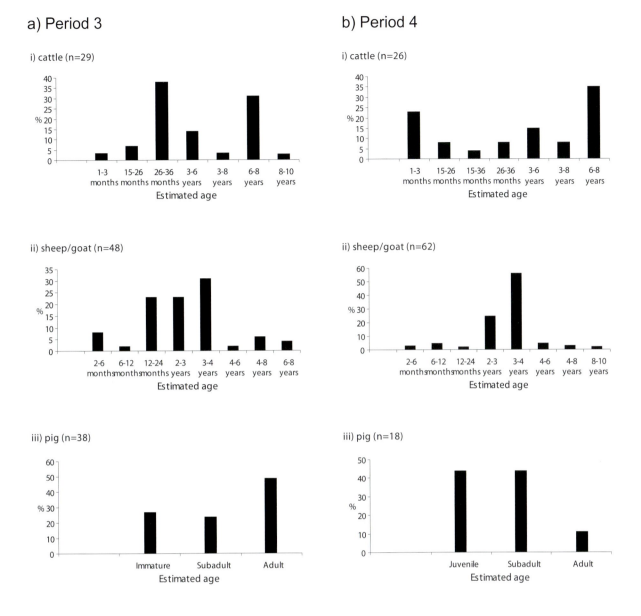

FIG. 113.   South-east layers: estimated age of domestic animals according to tooth eruption and wear.

died before fully adult (FIG. 114a, ii). A few bones belonging to foetal/neonatal animals attest to the presence of very young lambs/kids.

Tooth eruption and wear data provide evidence that approximately half of the pig remains derive from animals that were immature or sub-adult, and the other half from adults (FIG. 113a, iii). The epiphyseal fusion data contradict this suggesting a steady rate of slaughter up until three years of age with few animals surviving into adulthood (FIG. 114a, iii). A few bones belonging to foetal/neonatal piglets are also present. Out of 26 pig canines that can provide an indication of sex, 18 belong to males.

The presence of a few immature galliform bones (10 per cent) is evidence that a small proportion of domestic fowl were slaughtered before reaching maturity. Three out of 22 metatarsal bones possess a spur or spur scar and so probably belong to male chickens (Sadler 1991).

'House 1' (= MB 1 & 2, 'ERTB 4' = MRTB 1, ERTB 1)

The evidence for age and sex of the remains from the 'House' 1 sequence broadly matches that

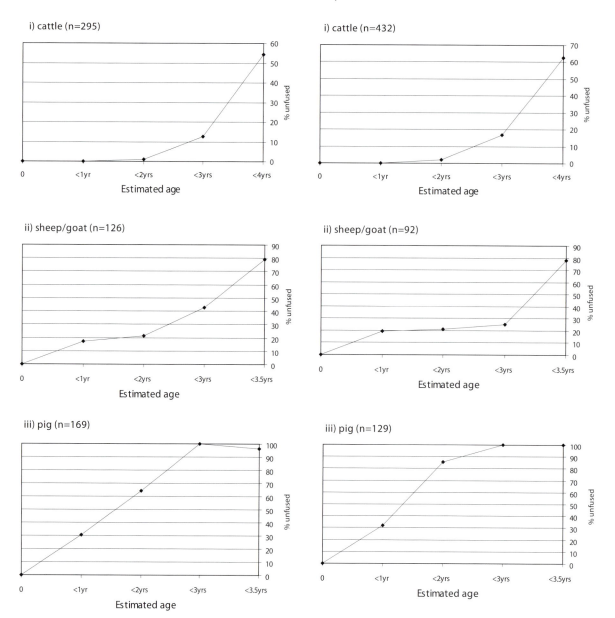

FIG. 114. South-east layers: estimated age of death according to bone epiphyseal fusion.

from the contemporary layers although male and female pigs are equally represented, by three canines each. A single galliform tarsometatarsal is without a spur.

TAPHONOMY

South-east layers (Object 701)

As discussed above, survival of the different parts of the skeleton indicates that bone density is not the only factor influencing the survival of bone and therefore it is likely that cultural factors have influenced the composition of the assemblage.

A small proportion (2 per cent) of the identifiable assemblage shows evidence for gnawing, probably by canids, and one bone displays marks associated with rodent gnawing (Appendix 6,

Table 62a). A higher incidence is visible on the bones of cattle (4 per cent) and pig (6 per cent) than on those of caprines (2 per cent).

Butchery evidence is clearly visible on 5 per cent of the identifiable assemblage (Appendix 6, Table 63). Cattle display the highest incidence (12 per cent) with chops more numerous than cut marks and a cattle metatarsal has been sawn transversely through the distal shaft. A smaller proportion of caprines (4 per cent) and pig (3 per cent) display blade marks, although cut and chop marks are more equally represented. In addition, a number of specimens possess shave marks where their surfaces have been sliced with a blade; most occur on the bones of cattle and large mammal, although a few are visible on caprine and pig specimens.

Some butchery marks occur repeatedly. In particular, numerous cattle scapulae display evidence of breakage that is suggestive of a hook being pushed into the blade and many possess chop marks where the distal part of the spine (acromion) was removed (FIG. 115). Transverse cut marks on the posterior face of cattle first phalanges indicative of skinning are also common (FIG. 116).

FIG. 115. Butchered cattle scapula showing removal of acromion.

During recording it became evident that a considerable number of bones preserve evidence suggestive of their having been broken open for marrow extraction and/or have split epiphyses likely to result from butchery even though they do not preserve blade marks. These marks can result from natural breakage but in order to gain an idea of their frequency they were recorded for Object 701 where 4 per cent of the assemblage is affected (Appendix 6, Table 64).

The incidence of burning is low (<1 per cent) with just a few fragments calcined and/or charred (Appendix 6, Table 65a).

'House 1' (= MB 1 & 2, MRTB 1, ERTB 1)

Evidence for gnawing is similarly scarce in the 'House 1' sequence (Appendix 6, Table 62b). A small proportion of the identifiable assemblage exhibits clear evidence for butchery in the form of cut and chop marks, with cuts more numerous and again mostly occurring around joint articulations (Appendix 6, Table 63b). Very few fragments are burnt (Appendix 6, Table 65b)

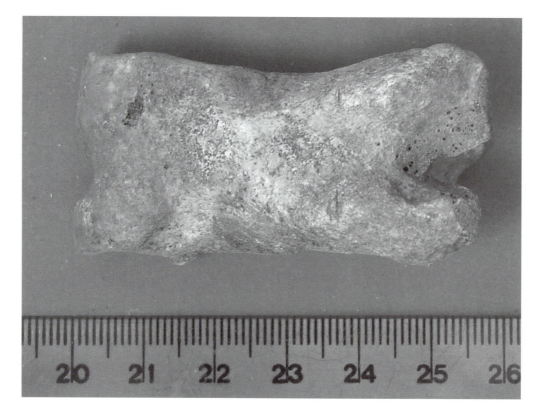

FIG. 116.   Cut marks on cattle 1st phalanx.

PATHOLOGY
(comments by Kate Clark)

Several specimens display evidence of pathology including a cattle pelvis, navicular cuboid (FIG. 117) and 1st phalanx that display evidence of degenerative osteoarthritis. Another cattle 1st phalanx displays exostosis at the site of tendon insertion which is often associated with draught or traction (FIG. 118). A third cattle 1st phalanx has evidence of an early arthropathy with articular extension and early periarticular exostosis which is also age or draught related. A cattle

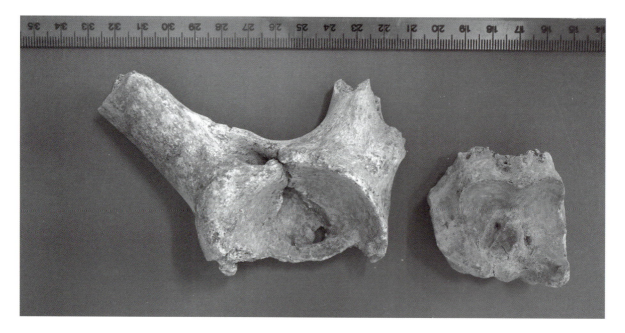

FIG. 117.   Cattle pelvis and navicular cuboid with evidence of degenerative osteoarthritis.

FIG. 118.   Cattle 1st phalanx with exostosis at the site of the tendon insertion.

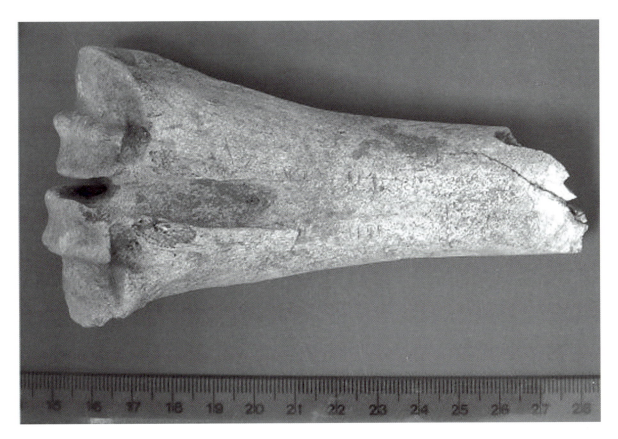

FIG. 119.   Abnormally splayed cattle metatarsal with shave marks from Period 3 deposits.

metatarsal (FIG. 119) possesses abnormally splayed distal condyles that is also probably draught related (Bartosiewicz *et al.* 1993).

In addition, a galliform scapula displays swelling probably as the result of a healed fracture.

METRICAL DATA

South-east layers (Object 701)

Metrical data are given in Appendix 6, Tables 73–74. Where possible measurements have been compared with those held on ABMAP (http://ads.ahds.ac.uk/catalogue/resources.html?abmap) and in general they fall within the range recorded at other Roman sites. There are a few exceptions but most of these are less than 1mm outside of the range, although more notable in the cattle assemblage are the distal breadth of a humerus that is 1.5mm smaller, a metacarpal whose distal breadth is 2.4mm smaller, and a metatarsal whose proximal breadth is 3.1mm larger, than the ABMAP specimens.

The only caprine bones able to provide an estimate of size are two metacarpals that belong to a sheep with an estimated withers height of 566mm and 610mm (Appendix 6, Table 66) according to the factor of Teichert (in Boessneck and von den Driesch 1974). Several cattle metapodia are also complete; however the factors used to calculate withers height from these bones are sex dependent. The samples of metrical data are not large enough to separate males from females with certainty. However, proximal breadth and depth measurements have been plotted on scatter-graphs (FIG. 120) and whilst distinct clusters are not visible, females are likely

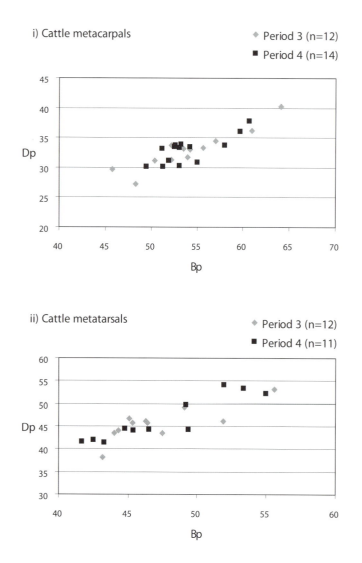

FIG. 120. South-east layers: proximal breadth and depth of cattle metapodials.

to be represented at the lower end of the scale and males at the upper. This has allowed the few metapodials that have a known greatest length to be assigned a sex and to be used to obtain an estimate of withers height using the factors of Teichert and Matolsci 1970 (in von den Driesch and Boessneck 1974). This suggests that cows were between 1.07m and 1.10m high at the withers which compares well with estimates of the average size of cattle obtained from early Roman deposits at Dorchester (Greyhound Yard) and from Roman Exeter. However, the one element assigned to the male category produced a slightly higher estimate of 1.23m (Appendix 6, Table 66) giving an overall average of 1.12m, suggesting that cattle at Silchester may have been slightly larger than those from contemporary sites in the South-West.

Metrical data for birds are given in Appendix 6, Table 75. Where possible measurements taken on bones belonging to duck (*Anas/Aythya* spp.) have been compared with modern comparative material and the data of Woelfle (1967) and all fall within the range for mallard duck.

SPATIAL ANALYSIS

South-east layers (Object 701)

The majority (86 per cent) of the Period 3 animal bone came from miscellaneous layers in the south-east quarter of the excavated area that is associated with the north–south street frontage. Taxa representation according to Object is shown in FIG. 121 and, although animal size categories are omitted, it is worth noting that large mammal comprises a considerable proportion of the samples (Appendix 6, Table 67a). Cattle (32 per cent) and pig (29 per cent) are the most frequent taxa in the layers (Object 701) although caprines are also numerous (25 per cent), with the remaining 15 per cent comprised of other taxa (FIG. 121 and Appendix 6, Table 67a).

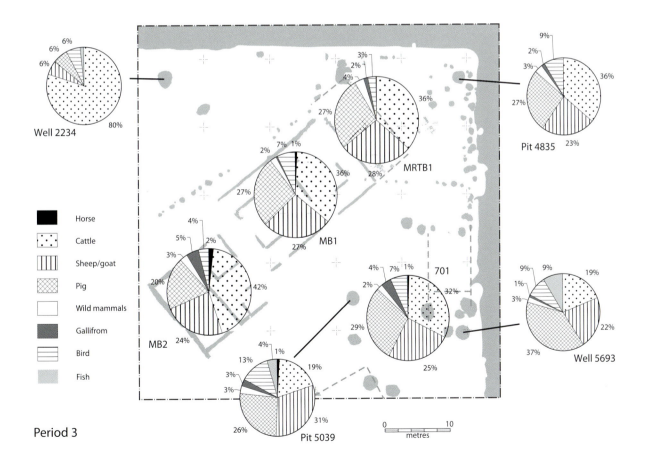

FIG. 121.   Period 3: 'House 1', pits, wells and south-east layers: taxa representation according to Object.

Unsurprisingly given the large sample size, most of the horse, dog and the trace taxa came from the layers including partial fore and hind feet belonging to red deer from context 4067. Roe deer, hare, galliform, goose, duck, pigeon/dove, woodcock, rook/crow, thrush, salmon and eel are all represented (Appendix 6, Table 67a).

The pits and wells produced relatively small samples. Cattle are the least frequent of the major domestic animals in south-east pit 5039 (Object 44008) where caprines (31 per cent) are slightly more numerous than pig (FIG. 121). Other taxa comprise almost a quarter of the sample and include a few dog bones, a roe deer metacarpal, and a hare radius. Galliform, woodcock and cyprinid are also represented (Appendix 6, Table 67a).

Cattle show a similar representation in the other south-east pit, 5693 (Object 500035), in which pig is the most numerous taxa (FIG. 121). Wild animals are represented by a roe deer mandible and scapula and a hare pelvis. Goose, galliform and woodcock are amongst the bird remains and fish are represented by a few bones belonging to cyprinid and eel. The remains of two dogs, including a tibia with skinning marks, also came from this pit (Appendix 6, Table 67a).

In contrast, well 2234 in the northern area (Object 41016) contained mainly cattle bones (80 per cent) with the remaining 13 specimens belonging to sheep/goat, pig and other taxa that include two woodcock bones and a fragment of fish (FIG. 121; Appendix 6, Table 67a).

Cattle (36 per cent) are also the most numerous taxa in the northern pit 4835 (Object 500028), where pigs are slightly more numerous than caprines (FIG. 121). Wild species and other animals are scarce with only a roe deer mandible, two wood mouse, a few dog and two galliform bones identified (Appendix 6, Table 67a).

'House 1' sequence (= MB 1 & 2, 'ERTB 4' = MRTB 1, ERTB 1)

MB 2 (Object 50019) produced a rather high proportion of cattle fragments and fewer caprines than either MB 1 (Object 50018) or ERTB 4 (=MRTB 1, ERTB 1) (Object 50037) (FIG. 121).

PERIOD 4 (*c.* A.D. 200–*c.* A.D. 250)

TAXA REPRESENTATION

South-east layers (Object 700)

The assemblage recovered from Period 4 deposits is larger than the Period 3 sample comprising a total of 7,515 identifiable specimens (Appendix 6, Table 57). In addition to the taxa present in the earlier period, badger, rat, raven, eel, sea bream, flatfish and frog are all represented. Wood mouse, rook/crow, thrush and cyprinid were absent.

According to the NISP figures, cattle are slightly more numerous in this phase (Appendix 6, Table 57) comprising approximately 50 per cent of the material from layers and pits (FIG. 110b). Cattle bones also dominate the well deposits, although not to the extent seen in Period 3. A similar range of wild mammal is present including roe deer, red deer and hare, but again all represent less than one per cent of the identifiable assemblage. Galliform is the most numerous bird taxon, although greylag goose, mallard duck, woodcock, pigeon/dove and raven are all represented by a few bones (Appendix 6, Table 57). The small fish assemblage includes eel, sea bream and flatfish.

A few bones were recovered as matching pairs or articulations and 34 are from partial skeletons (Appendix 6, Table 58), including a partial piglet that came from context 3836 and a partial badger recovered from pit 2434 (context 2602).

Calculation of the minimum number of elements and individuals also indicates that cattle are considerably more numerous than caprines (Appendix 6, Table 59a).

'House 1' sequence (= MB 3)

The Period 4 assemblage from the 'House 1' sequence is smaller than the sample from the preceding period (Appendix 6, Table 57). The NISP and MNI figures are slightly contradictory (Appendix 6, Tables 57 and 59b, ii), although caprines are more numerous whichever method is employed. The range of wild animals is narrower than was observed for the Period 3 'House 1' sequence with only roe deer, duck and woodcock represented.

BODY PART REPRESENTATION

South-east layers (Object 700)

Anatomical representation according to NISP and MNE is shown in Appendix 6, Tables 59a, ii and 60b. Despite the small size of the horse assemblage, elements from the head, major limbs and feet are all present. As with Period 3, cattle, caprines and pig are represented by elements from all parts of the body with major limb bones well represented. Vertebrae and rib fragments belonging to large and medium-sized mammals are also present. Of particular note is the large number of limb-bone fragments assigned to the large mammal category.

Roe deer are represented by a fragment of antler, mandibles, scapulae and metapodials belonging to a minimum of one individual. Several pieces of red deer antler, two tibiae, a scapula, pelvis, metatarsal and a 2nd phalanx representing at least two individuals are also present. In addition, hare major limb and foot bones are present (Appendix 6, Table 60b).

As in Period 3, the galliform sample contains elements from both major limbs and trunk with the tarsometatarsal most numerous (Appendix 6, Table 61b). Raven is represented by trunk and limb bones, whilst the rest of the bird assemblage is dominated by limb bones.

Salmon, eel and sea bream are represented solely by caudal vertebrae and flatfish by an anal pterygoid.

Percentage survival is shown in FIG. 112a alongside the model proposed by Brain (1969). As in Period 3, it appears that bone density is not the only factor affecting assemblage composition, with the general over-representation of limb bones and under-representation of some of the densest bones suggesting that cultural practices have also played a part.

'House 1' sequence (= MB 3)

The assemblage recovered from the 'House 1' sequence is very similar with the major domestic animals represented by elements from all parts of the body (Appendix 6, Table 60b). Density is clearly not the only factor affecting the assemblage as indicated by the comparison with Brain's ethnographic data (FIG. 112b).

MORTALITY AND SEX

Tooth eruption and wear data are given in Appendix 6, Tables 69–70 and bone epiphyseal fusion data in Appendix 6, Tables 71–72.

South-east layers (Object 700)

Ageing evidence for horse is again scarce. Only one bone has an unfused epiphysis, a distal tibia which provides evidence that one horse died before reaching two years of age.

The sample of cattle mandibles and loose teeth able to provide tooth eruption and wear data, although relatively small, displays two peaks in slaughter between one and three months and between six and eight years of age (FIG. 113b, i). A tibia belonging to a neonatal/foetal calf is the only evidence for the death of very young animals, with epiphyseal fusion suggesting that most animals died after reaching three years of age (FIG. 114b, i).

A larger sample of dental data is available for caprines and shows that the majority (81 per cent) were slaughtered between the ages of two and four years (FIG. 113b, ii). Epiphyseal fusion data suggest that most were culled between three and three and a half years of age (FIG. 114b, ii). The presence of very young caprines is evidenced by a few foetal/neonatal specimens.

With regard to pig, tooth eruption and wear data indicate that most pigs (89 per cent) were slaughtered before reaching adulthood (FIG. 113b, iii). Similarly, there is no evidence from bone epiphyseal fusion data to suggest that any pigs survived past three years (FIG. 114b, iii).

A few bones belonging to foetal/neonatal piglets were also recovered. Fourteen pig canines provide an indication of sex; seven belong to males and seven to females.

Only two immature galliform bones (2 per cent) were recovered from Period 4 deposits. Six out of nineteen tarsometatarsal bones possess a spur or spur scar and probably belong to cocks. Medullary bone is present in two out of seven galliform femora.

'House 1' sequence (= MB 3)

There is no evidence for very young calves although dental data provide evidence for the culling of both immature and adult cattle (Appendix 6, Table 70). Most of the caprine mandibles and loose teeth belong to animals that died after reaching three years of age, although bone data suggest that a considerable proportion were culled in their first and second years. There is evidence for adult pigs, although bone fusion data again show that most pigs were less than three years old when slaughtered. Five pig canines provide an indication of the sex of the pigs: three belong to males and two to females. Of three galliform tarsometatarsals, one has a spur.

TAPHONOMY

South-east layers (Object 700)

As with the Period 3 assemblage, percentage survival (FIG. 112) indicates that most major limb bones are present in greater numbers than would be expected in an assemblage that has been subjected to density mediated taphonomic processes alone. Cultural practices such as differential butchery and disposal have clearly played a significant role in affecting assemblage composition.

There is some evidence that dogs had access to the bones with 3 per cent of the identifiable component displaying gnaw marks (Appendix 6, Table 62a). Pig (8 per cent) possesses a higher incidence than cattle (5 per cent) and sheep/goat (5 per cent).

The incidence of butchery marks is similar in this phase with 6 per cent of the identifiable assemblage affected (Appendix 6, Table 63b). Cattle display the highest frequency (12 per cent) with cut and chop marks occurring in almost equal numbers. A smaller proportion of caprines (2 per cent) and pig (5 per cent) have blade marks, although again cut and chops occur in similar numbers. In addition, shave marks occur on a considerable proportion of the cattle and large mammal assemblages but are absent on sheep/goat and pig bones. Saw marks are visible on two pieces of red deer antler.

As in Period 3, cattle scapulae and 1st phalanges display classic evidence for butchery associated with meat processing and skinning respectively.

The incidence of burning is low (<1 per cent) with just a few fragments calcined and/or charred (Appendix 6, Table 65b).

'House 1' sequence (= MB 3)

A slightly smaller proportion of the assemblage displays gnaw marks (Appendix 6, Table 62b). Cattle and pig bones are less affected by butchery with cut marks more numerous than chops and, as in the earlier period, most are associated with disarticulation.

PATHOLOGY
(comments by Kate Clark)

South-east layers (Object 700)

Several specimens in the Period 4 assemblage display evidence of pathology. These include a cattle 2nd phalanx that exhibits early signs of stress on the tendon attachment. A caprine metacarpal has ossification at the site of tendon attachment that is probably age-related (FIG. 122). A pig humerus displays evidence for osteomyelitis which seems to have partly resolved and part of a draining sinus is visible (FIG. 123). In addition, the shortened and deformed diaphysis of a galliform tibiotarsus is probably the result of a fracture.

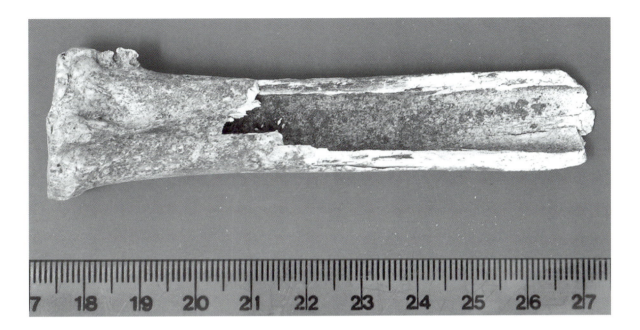

FIG. 122. Sheep/goat metacarpal from Period 4 deposits with ossification at the site of the tendon attachment.

FIG. 123. Butchered and pathological pig humerus from Period 4 deposits.

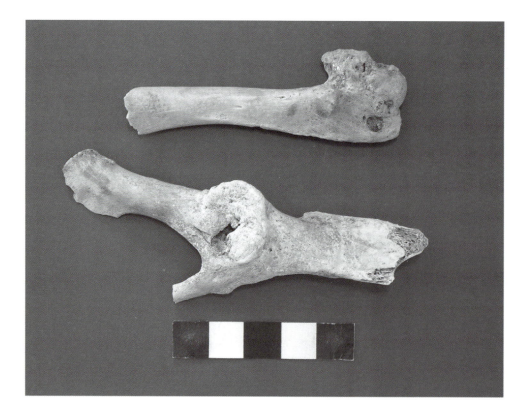

FIG. 124. Evidence for hip dysplasia on a badger pelvis and femur from Period 4 deposits.

An articulating pelvis and femur (FIG. 124) belonging to an immature badger display significant bony proliferation below the femoral caput and the acetabulum is filled indicating that the animal suffered from hip dysplasia. It is clearly a long standing lesion and so the dislocation must have occurred at a very young age.

A hare ulna displays pronounced ossification of the tendon attachment which flexes the elbow joint and suggests that the animal was aged.

METRICAL DATA

South-east layers (Object 700)

Metrical data are given in Appendix 6, Table 73 and where possible have been compared with those held on ABMAP (http://ads.ahds.ac.uk/catalogue/resources.html?abmap). Most specimens fall within the range recorded for elements from contemporary sites and the majority of those which fall outside only do so by a very small amount (less than 1mm). The exceptions are: a pig humerus that has a shaft diameter 1.6mm larger, a cattle radius that has a breadth of the proximal facies 1.2mm smaller, and a pig radius with a proximal breadth 1.2mm smaller. More notable is the presence of several relatively large cattle metatarsals, one with a proximal breadth 2.5mm larger, and three with proximal depths 2.9mm, 4mm and 4.8mm larger than those held on ABMAP, and, therefore, probably representative of large bulls.

Three metacarpals and four metatarsals provide an estimate of size (Appendix 6, Table 66a) and suggest that sheep stood between 577mm and 657mm at the withers with an average of 624mm, according to the factor of Teichert (in Boessneck & von den Driesch 1974). The sample is small but does suggest that sheep may have been larger in Period 4.

Metrical data for birds are given in Appendix 6, Table 75. Where possible measurements taken on bones belonging to duck (Anas/Aythya spp.) have been compared with modern comparative material and the data of Woelfle (1967); most fall within the range for mallard duck, although one tarsometatarsal is slightly smaller. The greatest length of a duck humerus indicates that it belongs either to teal *(Anas crecca)* or garganey *(Anas querquedula)*.

SPATIAL ANALYSIS

South-east layers, pits and wells

More than three-quarters (76 per cent) of the animal bone from Period 4 deposits in this area of Insula IX came from miscellaneous layers associated with occupation that took place along the north–south street frontage (Object 700). The remaining small quantity derives from the south-eastern pits and wells (Appendix 6, Table 67b). Taxa representation is shown graphically in FIG. 125 which indicates that there is some variation in the representation of cattle, sheep/goat and pig according to feature, with cattle generally having a higher representation in the layers than in the pits and wells.

In the layers (Object 700), cattle are more numerous (47 per cent) than they were in Period 3 and caprines outnumber pig. Other taxa are scarce with galliform, goose, duck, pigeon/dove, woodcock and raven comprising a total of 6 per cent of the assemblage (FIG. 125). Specimens belonging to wild animals make up just one per cent, although roe deer, red deer, hare, salmon and eel are all represented (Appendix 6, Table 67b). A proportion of this assemblage derives from contexts associated with two ephemeral buildings, MRTB 4 and 5, and a comparison of these samples with the material recovered from the more general layers indicates that the northern

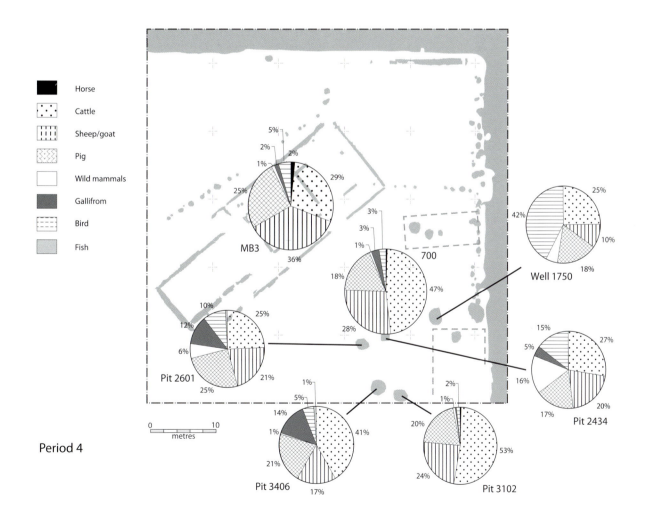

FIG. 125.   Period 4: 'House 1', pits, wells and south-east layers: taxa representation according to Object.

building produced a relatively high proportion of sheep/goat at the expense of pig (Appendix 6, Table 68). A minimum of four dogs came from these deposits (Clark, Ch. 14).

The sample from well 1750 (Object 500020), although small, is dominated (43 per cent) by bird remains (FIG. 125). Of particular interest are twelve raven bones — including pairs of humerii, ulnae and tibiotarsii — that probably belong to the same skeleton, and which came from a timber structure that forms the basis of the well shaft (context 2767). A few bones belonging to domestic and wild animals, including several dog bones (Clark, Ch. 14), a red deer tibia, a pathological hare ulna and a woodcock bone, also came from the well.

Cattle are the most numerous taxa in pit 2434 (Object 500031). Other animals make up a sizeable proportion of the sample with wild animals and birds other than galliform comprising 15 and 14 per cent respectively (FIG. 125). The remains of at least three dogs (Clark, Ch. 14), three pieces of red deer antler, two partial badger skeletons, a pair of cattle horn cores, and galliform scapulae are amongst the remains. Woodcock, goose and galliform are also represented.

Pit 2601 (Object 500032) produced fairly equal quantities (25 per cent) of the major domestic animals (FIG. 125). Galliform, red deer, hare and rat are all present. Five raven bones (probably from the same individual) came from context 2762 and two pig metapodials that probably belong to the same foot also came from this pit. In addition, a minimum of two dogs are represented, at least one of which was male (Clark, Ch. 14).

Cattle remains that include a partial skull, dominate the material from pit 3406 (Object 500033) (FIG. 125). A matching pair of foetal/neonatal pig humerii also came from this pit. Galliform is present in significant numbers (14 per cent) and a few bones belonging to goose, woodcock and corvid are present (Appendix 6, Table 67b). Dog is represented by at least two individuals and also a neonate (Clark, Ch. 14).

Similarly, cattle remains dominate pit 3102 (Object 500034) but, although it produced a larger sample than any of the other pits or wells, only odd bones belonging to red deer, galliform, woodcock and dog are present (FIG. 125; Appendix 6, Table 67b).

Cattle comprise half of the sample from well 5735 (Object 500037). Dog, red deer, hare, rodent and goose are all represented. Nineteen amphibian bones came from this deposit of which two pelves belong to frog (FIG. 125; Appendix 6, Table 67b).

'House 1' sequence (= MB 3)

A single structure, MB 3 (Object 50046), occupied the site during Period 4. As in the earlier phase, most of the assemblage derives from miscellaneous layers, spreads and deposits within this structure. The largest concentrations of animal bone came from two clay levelling deposits outside and to the south of the house (contexts 3396, 4454) which produced 165 and 88 identifiable specimens respectively; pig is the most numerous species in both (FIG. 125).

Several deposits are worthy of note. These include the partial skeleton of an immature sheep, aged between 12 and 24 months, recovered from a shallow pit (context 2006). Several cattle foot bones that probably represent the disposal of feet came from an occupation deposit (context 2471) and a robber trench (context 3636). In addition, another levelling deposit (context 4454) produced a scapula and metacarpal belonging to a foetal/neonatal caprine.

INTERPRETATION AND DISCUSSION

ANIMAL EXPLOITATION

The assemblages from the south-east layers and the 'House 1' sequence are clearly dominated by the three major domesticates — cattle, caprines and pig — during both Period 3 and Period 4. Variation in the relative frequencies of these animals is generally believed to reflect the type of settlement and its degree of 'romanisation'. Highly romanised sites such as *coloniae* and those associated with the military tend to produce high values for cattle and pig, while native, rural settlements are more often associated with a high proportion of caprines (King 1991). More recently, changes in taxa frequency have been seen as part of the general intensification of agriculture that was taking place at the time rather than simply indicating dietary preference (Hamshaw-Thomas 2000). The increased frequency of cattle that occurs in the Period 4 layers from the south-east area of Insula IX conforms to the pattern expected for an urban settlement and suggests that Insula IX became increasingly 'romanised' with time. An increasing emphasis on cattle at Silchester is also attested by the recovery of a cattle-dominated assemblage from fourth-century deposits in Insula IX (Ingrem 2006) and many other areas of the site (Maltby 1984; Barker 1983; Hamilton-Dyer 1997).

There is some variation in taxa representation, chronologically, spatially and according to the method of quantification. For instance, in contrast to the fragment counts, calculation of the minimum number of individuals for the Period 3 assemblages recovered from both the south-east layers and the 'House 1' sequence suggests that caprines and pig outnumbered cattle. This may have been the case; however the larger body size of cattle almost certainly suggests that beef was the meat most commonly eaten even in the early period and the increasing romanisation of the diet is also evidenced by the contribution made by pork. No such discrepancy occurs in the material from the Period 4 south-east layers; cattle remains are clearly dominant regardless of the method of quantification leaving little doubt that in general more beef was eaten, at the expense of pork, by the third century.

The higher frequency of caprines and pig in the Period 3 pits located in the south-eastern area compared with those in the northern part of the excavation trench is probably related to their having been used for the disposal of household food waste. During Period 4, evidence from the 'House 1' sequence and MRTB 5 suggests that mutton made a greater contribution to the diet of certain inhabitants. This has led to the suggestion (Ingrem 2007) that a pattern midway between those generally associated with native and highly romanized sites might reflect an early stage in the process of economic intensification. However, in light of the evidence now available from the south-eastern area of the excavated area, the relatively high frequency of sheep/goat appears unusual and seems more likely to suggest that some occupants, including those of 'House 1', had ready access to their preferred meat — mutton — and perhaps were slow to adopt a more Roman diet.

Spatial variation in taxa representation has been shown to exist in other areas of Silchester and at other Roman towns; it is often associated with human activities that result in differential disposal such as butchery and industrial processes. For instance, previously excavated early Roman deposits suggest that primary butchery of cattle took place on the outskirts of Silchester, with waste discarded in ditches away from the main settlement areas (Maltby 1984). Such practices would explain the relatively low number of cattle bones in central areas and would account for the under-representation of cattle jaws. At Exeter Maltby (1979) also showed that taxa frequency varied according to location within the Roman town, again as the probable result of differential butchery and disposal practices (Maltby 1985a).

A high incidence of pig, similar to that seen in the Period 3 assemblage from the south-east layers and throughout the 'House 1' sequence, also occurred in early Roman deposits at the forum-basilica prompting Grant (2000) to suggest that pigs were bred to supply the towns. More recently, this high frequency was interpreted (Grant 2002) as 'confirmation of the importance and comparative wealth of the settlement'. An abundance of pig at sites such as Skeleton Green, Herts. (Ashdown and Evans 1981), and Fishbourne, West Sussex (Grant 1971), has also been associated with high status and wealth during both the Iron Age and Roman periods. Evidence for a high frequency of pig in very early (Period 2) Roman deposits from Room 2 of ERTB 1 (Object 50030) suggests that a tradition of feasting may have been in place for some time in Insula IX and that some inhabitants may have held considerable status (Ingrem 2007).

In terms of taxa representation, the Period 3 assemblage from Insula IX appears to have much in common with that recovered from contemporary deposits (Period 6) at the forum-basilica (Grant 2000, 426). Interestingly, this similarity extends to comparisons between the Period 4 MB 3 sequence and the Period 7 (c. A.D. 250–400) assemblage from the basilica area in respect of the unusually high proportion of caprines, even if the chronology of the basilica assemblage is slightly later. As in MB 3, the high incidence of sheep/goat is at odds with evidence from contemporary sites and other areas of the town which led Grant (2000, 474) to suggest that it might be explained either by an unusual food supply and local economy or by particular activities that took place in the forum-basilica, rather than representing the general pattern of food consumption in the town. In the case of MB 3, however, we should allow for residuality.

CONSUMPTION AND DISPOSAL PRACTICES

The assemblage recovered from Period 3 deposits contains bones from all parts of the cattle, sheep/goat and pig skeletons, providing a clear indication that at least some, probably most animals arrived at Silchester on the hoof in both periods. According to percentage survival cattle and pig mandibles are quite scarce, particularly in the 'House 1' sequence, suggesting that joints of beef and pork were imported. Good quality meat bones are abundant and clearly good quality cuts of meat were available to the people living in Insula IX. However, the presence of some mandibles and lower limb bones is an indication that poorer cuts of meat were also consumed and it is likely that, as was suggested for Exeter (Maltby 1979), all parts of the carcass were distributed to the town's inhabitants. It may be that the servants ate the less desirable parts of the carcass such as cattle brains (Serjeantson, pers. comm.). This pattern continues into Period 4 when the greater scarcity of cattle and pig mandibles suggests that joints of meat were increasingly imported. At the same time, a reduced incidence of mandibles in MB 3 suggests that some caprines were also arriving in a decapitated form during the third century.

Other anomalies in terms of body part representation indicate that bone survival is not solely density-dependent; human activities, including butchery, disposal and industrial processing, are likely to have had a role in determining which bones survive. As discussed above, there is evidence to suggest that in the early Roman period the preliminary butchery of cattle was carried out on the outskirts of Silchester (Maltby 1984). In the past, horn cores and foot bones were commonly left attached to the hides and taken to the tanner's/horner's workshop where they would be disposed of (Serjeantson 1989, 136) and practices of this nature would account for the scarcity of horns and feet. At Dorchester Greyhound Yard, discreet concentrations of cattle bones reflecting the dumping of waste derived from large-scale specialist activities were found in pits and other features with material dated to Period 6 (late first/early second century A.D.). The bones comprised predominantly upper limbs and scapulae. This led to the suggestion (Maltby 1993, 334) that the creation of large quantities of waste by butchers and slaughterers operating inside the town created major problems for waste disposal and resulted in the use of open spaces and available pits for this purpose. A similar problem may have existed at Silchester and would account for the mixed nature of the material recovered from many of the layers and features in Insula IX.

In addition, small foot bones — carpals, tarsals and phalanges — belonging to medium and small animals may have been missed during excavation or destroyed by dogs. There is clear evidence that dogs were present at Silchester (Clark, Ch. 14), although the generally low incidence of gnaw marks suggests that bone refuse was not readily available to dogs and that households did not generally feed dogs at the table but cleared away their rubbish.

The large number of large mammal limb-bone fragments amongst the assemblage from the south-east layers is noteworthy, particularly in Period 4, and may account for the more patchy survival of major limb bones in general in this period if fragmentation had rendered them unidentifiable. A similar pattern has been noted in the fourth-century assemblage from Insula IX (Ingrem 2006) and at contemporary sites such as *Augusta Raurica* (Augst), Switzerland (Schmidt 1968; 1972, 48) where they are believed to result from glue boiling. This activity is discussed alongside the evidence for butchery in more detail below.

ANIMAL HUSBANDRY PRACTICES

During the early Roman period, the majority of cattle were slaughtered in their third year — an age when they would have been in their prime for beef production — or as adults (6–8 years) suggesting that secondary products (milk, blood, manure and traction) were also important. More cattle were kept into adulthood during Period 4 when there is also evidence for the slaughter of young calves (1–3 months) — a pattern often associated with dairying whereby young calves are killed off to prevent competition for milk. It is impossible to be certain whether or not the cattle remains recovered from Insula IX represent a true cross-section of the cattle exploited. However, a predominance of adult cattle is not restricted to Insula IX, the Period 5 and 6 assemblages from the forum-basilica similarly consisted mainly of adults (Grant 2000) and this pattern is commonly seen throughout the Roman period. For instance, at Greyhound Yard, Dorchester, the majority of cattle mandibles belonged to adults and there is also evidence for the slaughter of calves (Maltby 1993). An increase in elderly and immature cattle in third-century deposits from Lincoln similarly suggested that 'the production of beef, veal and dairy produce became more organised than it had been in the early Roman period (Dobney *et al.* 1999, 22). Consequently, the increasing emphasis on older cattle during Period 4 in Insula IX may, as Maltby (1981, 182) suggested for contemporary sites, reflect the chronological development of organised cattle marketing in response to urban demands.

The presence of very young animals is evidence that some cattle were raised in the environs of Silchester, indicating a degree of self-sufficiency. Pollen samples suggest that the surrounding land was suitable for cattle pasture (Keith-Lucas 1984) and some previously excavated buildings at Silchester are believed to have functioned as barns, cattle stalls and pig sties (Boon 1974). According to Maltby (1994, 85), it is likely that much of the land around urban settlements was farmed by their inhabitants and cattle would have been important animals for traction. Evidence from York and Lincoln led Dobney *et al.* (1999, 22) to suggest that cattle were multi-purpose animals bred primarily for traction and only utilised for beef once their working lives were over. The range of joint disorders seen on cattle bones also provides an indication of the importance of cattle as beasts of burden (ibid.) and there is documentary evidence for their importance for traction in ancient Italy (White 1970, 276–7).

An increasing emphasis on secondary products is also seen in respect of sheep/goat. Most were culled before reaching four years of age suggesting that although prime quality meat was important during Period 3, secondary products were a consideration, with much of the mutton derived from animals which had produced several clips of wool. The decrease in the number of young (less than two years) caprines slaughtered during Period 4 suggests, as with cattle, that there was an increasing emphasis on secondary products. This pattern is not dissimilar to that seen in the area of the basilica where, according to Grant (2000, 467), most of the sheep consumed were mature. At rural sites such as Winnall Down (Maltby 1985b) and Balksbury (Maltby 1995) Roman deposits produced a higher proportion of older caprines than their Iron Age counterparts and according to Maltby (1993, 336) the slaughter of animals for meat when they were approaching full size is a feature of many Roman assemblages. At Greyhound Yard, Dorchester a similar increase in the number of mandibles belonging to sheep aged between two and four years in later Roman deposits led Maltby (1993, 336) to suggest that this might be indirect evidence for the increasing importance of wool in the regional economy.

At rural sites such as Odell and Abingdon, the wider spread of ages displayed by the caprine population is believed by Grant (2000) to reflect a close involvement with sheep rearing. A wide range in the age of slaughter was also seen in the Period 2 deposits from the 'House 1' sequence (Ingrem 2007) and similarly suggests an involvement in caprine farming which may have decreased over time. However, the recovery of a few very young lamb/kid bones suggests that some breeding continued to take place locally and it is likely that some inhabitants were still engaged in sheep rearing outside the town. At the same time, the majority of sheep/goat may have been supplied by local farming communities. A side-effect of the increased age of cattle and caprines would have been an increase in livestock density and, according to King (1991, 17), farming communities must have been generally richer with animal husbandry playing a more visible part in the agricultural economy.

According to the dental evidence pork came from immature and adult pigs during the early Roman period and a similar pattern was seen at Fishbourne, Sussex (Grant 1971), where it was suggested that pigs were kept locally. Evidence from early Roman deposits in the basilica suggests that most pigs had been killed before, or just after, reaching dental maturity — a pattern more typical of a consumer site whereby surplus males are supplied for consumption in the towns (Grant 2000). The probability that joints of pork were imported to Insula IX was discussed above and may account for the discrepancy that exists between the dental and bone data. The presence of a few foetal/neonatal remains is evidence that some pig husbandry took place locally throughout the Roman period, although Silchester was clearly developing its role as a consumer from the early Roman period onwards. This is supported by the predominance of male canine teeth in Period 3 deposits both in Insula IX and in the basilica where pork came from surplus males. At Greyhound Yard, Dorchester Maltby (1993, 337) suggested that boars were deliberately selected because they may have reached a greater carcass weight than sows and because they were surplus to breeding requirements. During Period 4 the majority of pork came from juvenile and immature pigs, perhaps indicating that Silchester had become more dependent on outside supplies. Boars and sows are more equally represented by canine teeth but the scarcity of mandibles suggests that the sample may not represent a true cross-section.

One of the minor changes noted by King (1991, 17) is the increasing consumption of domestic fowl in the early Roman period compared to the late Iron Age. Poultry, including chicken, duck, goose and pigeon, would have provided a welcome addition to the diet with secondary products — eggs and feathers — also valued. Evidence for young domestic fowl is scarce as are metatarsal bones with spurs, suggesting that most of the chickens represented in Insula IX were adult females, some of which were in lay. Egg production was considered a factor in the exploitation of chickens at Dorchester (Maltby 1993, 336) and it is quite possible that individuals living in towns kept hens primarily to produce eggs. This contrasts with the high proportion of males and immature birds seen in the basilica which is explained by the suggestion that eggs and young birds were brought into the town from nearby villages to be sold (Serjeantson 2000, 499). The possibility that the high proportion of young cocks might reflect sacrificial activities or cockfighting was also considered likely given the commercial nature of this area (ibid.).

BUTCHERY AND BONE PROCESSING

Throughout the Period 3 and 4 sequences there is evidence to suggest that animal carcasses were commonly disarticulated by cutting through the soft tissue surrounding joint articulations, a pattern similar to that seen on Iron Age sites. However, at the same time major limb-bone shafts and epiphyses were routinely chopped through in a manner suggestive of intensive processing in much the same way as was noted for the late Roman assemblage (Ingrem 2006). The increased ratio of cut to chop marks in Period 4 in MB 3 suggested a move away from the Iron Age tradition towards more romanised practices involving the use of metal chopping tools. However, evidence from Insula IX as a whole indicates that the use of metal tools was already well established in Period 3.

The presence of cuts on phalanges (FIG. 116) and large mammal limb articulation suggests that knives may have been the preferred tool of skilled butchers familiar with animal anatomy for carrying out certain activities such as skinning and disarticulation. However, chopping tools were also used for disarticulation and to further sub-divide the carcass into manageable-size joints. The repeated position of many cut and chop marks suggests that butchery practices were standardised. Particularly noticeable is the removal of the spine on numerous cattle shoulder blades that also have their articular surfaces chopped through and appear to have been punctured, probably by a metal hook (FIG. 115). Similar damage has been seen at other Roman sites including Greyhound Yard, Dorchester (Maltby 1993) and Augusta Raurica in Switzerland where it was suggested that the Romans smoked shoulders of beef by hanging them in the chimney (Schmidt 1972, 42). Evidence from Tongeren also attests to the preparation of meat, in this case smoked ham, which appears to have taken place on a far greater scale than domestic needs demanded (Vanderhoeven and Ervynck 2005).

Another type of damage commonly seen on the bones from the south-east layers, particularly on cattle bones, are shave/slice marks, caused by a heavy blade during filleting and resulting in small pieces of bone being removed with the meat. Marks of this nature are generally only found on urban or military sites such as Greyhound Yard, Dorchester and, according to Maltby (1993), bones processed in this way are sometimes found in large dumps suggesting that the method was employed by specialist butchers. In this respect the assemblage from the 'House 1' sequence differs from that recovered from the south-east layers, perhaps unsurprisingly given that waste from large-scale butchery is less likely to be incorporated into waste from domestic households (Maltby 1993).

Animal bone would have been a valuable resource from which a wide range of products were derived, such as marrow, marrow oil, fat, bone grease and glue. At Tongeren, the production of secondary products appears to have become important with the general intensification of cattle husbandry and was soon organised on a large scale within the town (Vanderhoeven and Ervynck 2005). A similar situation may have arisen at Silchester as there is clearly evidence for the intensive processing of bone in the Roman assemblages from Insula IX. Other sites that have produced similar evidence include Zwammerdam, Netherlands (Mensch 1974), Augusta Raurica (Augst), Switzerland (Schmid 1972), and Greyhound Yard, Dorchester (Maltby 1993). Experimental work has shown that fragmentation of the shaft of limb bones is sufficient to achieve marrow extraction, especially if aided by heating the diaphysis to liquefy the fat content of the marrow, so that it only has to be poured out (Vanderhoeven and Ervynck 2005). The resulting oil would be of a high quality suitable for use in cosmetics, soap, medicine and lamps (Dobney 2001). This type of activity would clearly account for the numbers of deliberately broken limb bones in Insula IX.

Another characteristic of the Insula IX assemblage is the large number of cattle and large mammal limb-bone fragments, particularly in Period 4. The recovery of heavily fragmented limb bones from contexts at other Roman sites including Augusta Raurica (Schmid 1972, 48) has led several researchers to investigate the processes involved in grease and glue extraction. It has been suggested (Vanderhoeven and Ervynck 2005) that, following marrow extraction, bones were broken into smaller pieces in order to increase their surface area and then boiled to release the superficial fat and that contained within the bone itself. The resulting grease would be skimmed off after cooling, the liquid reheated and the bone fragments removed before the liquid was reduced further to produce glue composed of bone collagen. According to Stokes (2000), the end product was a crystallised glue that could easily be liquefied simply by adding tepid water before use.

HORSES

A general scarcity of horse remains is normal in towns and is often explained by the increased emphasis on the acquisition of beef by the urban population (Maltby 1985b). King notes the absence of butchery marks on horse bone and considers this as evidence that horsemeat was no longer eaten, whilst noting the possibility that different methods of food preparation may be responsible. Differences between military and native beliefs and disposal practices may also explain this pattern, as evidence from the Netherlands suggests. Here, horses were buried inside native settlements (Lauwerier 1999) but not on military sites; this is explained by Lauwerier as reflecting the existence of a taboo against eating horsemeat in the Roman military world but not among the native population. There is no evidence of butchery on the horse bones from either the south-east layers or the 'House 1' sequence, although the occasional consumption of horsemeat in the town, perhaps by a servant, is attested by a cut-marked humerus from the forum-basilica (Grant 2000, 467). If the European evidence applies to Britain then the low proportion of horse remains seen at Silchester may reflect the romanization of the town, where a taboo against horsemeat was already in existence.

Horse remains have been associated with foundation deposits during the Roman period (Luff 1982, 190) and are commonly found in Iron Age deposits where the skulls in particular are believed to have a symbolic association (Grant *et al.* 1991). A number of horse bones came from Period 4 occupation deposits, walls and gullies associated with the 'House 1' sequence and whilst the possibility exists that some of these isolated bones might represent symbolic offerings, without firm evidence for deliberate placement, it is equally plausible that the equid remains represent the mundane disposal of old or sick animals. According to Green (1992, 98), one way of minimizing economic loss was to bury deposits consisting of parts of animals rather than whole carcasses, consequently ritual sacrifices and offerings need not consist of entire carcasses. In graves, individual bones such as a tooth, a toe, or a mandible have been interpreted as the symbolic representation of the animals concerned (ibid., 108). In this light it is interesting that most horse specimens occur in isolation, and it is possible that the 1st phalanx recovered from a Period 3 pit (5039) and the tibia from a Period 4 pit (3102) reflect ideological activities. In contrast, there is little to suggest that the horse bones recovered from the south-east layers represent anything other than the routine disposal of animals that had reached the end of their working lives.

EXPLOITATION OF WILD ANIMALS

The similarities that have been shown to exist between the assemblages recovered from Insula IX and the forum-basilica extend to wild animals, with roe deer, red deer and hare represented at both in small numbers. Clearly, these animals were occasionally hunted and eaten but made only a small contribution to the diet. Antler would have been valued as a raw material during the Roman period and the presence of a shed antler indicates that some was collected. Hunting appears to have taken place for occasional sport rather than as an activity which produced meat, but the fact that game is present at all is suggestive of a romanized household (King 1991).

A similar range of wild fowl — duck and woodcock, typical game birds of the period — was hunted and eaten in Insula IX and the forum-basilica (Serjeantson 2000). Pigeons and thrushes may be incidental but it is quite likely that they were deliberately caught and consumed. In their translation of Apicius, *The Roman Cookery Book*, Flower and Rosenbaum (1958, 145) give recipes for sauces to accompany roast and boiled wood pigeon and other birds including thrushes.

Ravens are known to have had symbolic associations and were unlikely to have been considered suitable as food. The ritual role played by ravens is strongly suggested by the recovery of skeletons from other Roman sites as well as Iron Age sites such as Danebury (Grant 1984). At Jordan Hill, Weymouth the remains of ravens were found set between tiles in a dry well associated with a Romano-Celtic temple (Green 1992, 104). Green (1992, 126) suggests that ravens and crows were seen as 'messengers from the Otherworld because of their black plumage and habit of feeding off dead things'. The primary fill of a Romano-British ritual shaft at Springhead, Kent produced the skeletons of a raven, a goose and domestic fowl (Grimm 2007). The articulated remains of a raven that was recovered from Late Iron Age (Period 3) deposits at the forum-basilica were similarly interpreted by Serjeantson (2000, 485) as a deliberate deposit because many of the bones were found in articulation. The partial raven skeletons that came from context 2762 of Period 4 pit 2601 in Insula IX appear to have symbolic associations given that an overlying context (2622) produced an ivory razor handle depicting two coupling dogs as well as the remains of at least two dogs, one of which is male.

The raven remains from the Period 4 well 1750 in Insula IX were probably also deliberately deposited, although whether these acts simply represent the disposal of natural casualties or have ideological associations is uncertain without supporting contextual evidence. According to Serjeantson (pers. comm.) the bottom of a well and within a pit are the type of contexts that one might expect to find a deliberate raven burial; however the associated material appears to be food remains and therefore fails to confirm the possibly ritual nature of the deposit.

Badgers are likely to have been valued for their distinctive pelts which, in light of the evidence for the systematic skinning of dogs (Clark, Ch. 14), may account for the presence of the two partial badger skeletons in the Period 4 pit 2434, which also produced the remains of at least three dogs. Evidence in the form of cut marks is not necessarily inflicted on the bones as a result of skinning (Serjeantson 1989, 131), although when it does occur it is normally the skull and foot bones that are affected — elements which are absent from the deposit. One of the badgers may have been relatively easy to catch given that it suffered from hip dysplasia (Clark, pers. comm.). There is documentary and archaeological evidence to suggest that the pelts of wild animals were valued by the Celts. According to Diodorus Siculus (in Green 1992, 53) the fur of wild animals was used as bedding and for covering floors. At Hochdorf, Germany there is evidence that the

Halstatt prince was laid on a couch covered by a badger skin (in Green 1992, 42). Closer to home there is evidence that badgers and foxes were trapped for fur at Danebury (ibid.).

Rodent and amphibian bones are scarce and most likely represent natural casualties that became trapped in pits and wells. The black rat arrived in Britain during the Roman period and its remains have been recovered from contemporary deposits at Wroxeter, London and York (Armitage *et al.* 1984).

Fish bones are scarce in both Period 3 and Period 4 deposits but provide evidence that some freshwater and marine fish were eaten in Insula IX during this period. The range of species present in Insula IX is similar to that found in Roman deposits from the forum-basilica area of the town and from contemporary sites such as County Hall, Dorchester (Hamilton-Dyer 1993) and York (O'Connor 1988). According to Locker (2007) the consumption of fresh marine fish such as sea bream and scad would have been associated with high-status inland sites, such as Silchester. These could have been quite easily transported from the coast either by road or by boat via the Thames, possibly kept alive in barrels of water. Freshwater taxa such as eel, carp and salmon were probably caught locally. Eel are commonly found on Roman sites and salmon also occur at many sites. That they are both migratory fish may, according to Locker (2007), have afforded them totemic status in the Celtic world.

STRUCTURED DEPOSITION

The 'House 1' sequence produced a few deposits worthy of mention, including the probable burial of an immature sheep from a pit in Room 1 of Period 2 ERTB 1 and the partial skeleton of another from a Period 4 pit associated with MB 3. Burials of domestic animals are not unusual on sites of Iron Age and Roman date but their interpretation, particularly those from Iron Age sites, has been controversial (Grant 1984; Wilson 1996; Wilson 1992; Hill 1995). Ethnographic studies have since led to much wider acceptance of the possibility that disposal of animal skulls, skeletons and articulated remains was intrinsically linked to ideology (Szynkiewicz 1990; Tambiah 1969; Wilson 1999). In addition, it is now generally accepted that complicated relationships can exist between features and finds and ritual and rubbish and that structured deposition within individual features, and, perhaps, the site as a whole, might result from ideologies that today would be considered irrational (Hill 1995; Fulford 2001).

Evidence from other areas of Silchester (Fulford 2001) and other Roman sites, including Dorchester Greyhound Yard (Woodward and Woodward 2004), indicates that pits and wells often contain deliberately placed deposits associated with foundation rituals. The raven and dog remains from the Period 4 pit discussed above almost certainly have symbolic associations. The possibility exists that some of the other more interesting deposits in Insula IX also have symbolic associations but, in the absence of contextual evidence to suggest otherwise, this must remain speculative as it is equally possible that they simply represent the more mundane disposal of butchery waste and old or sick animals that had died of natural causes.

CONCLUSION

The Period 3 and Period 4 assemblages from Insula IX conform well to the pattern seen at contemporary urban sites; consequently accidental incorporation of residual material does not appear to have masked the overall pattern. The increasing frequency of cattle throughout the early to late Roman periods reflects the development of the urban centre and the increasing romanisation of its inhabitants. The transitionary nature of Periods 3 and 4 is illustrated by characteristics of the animal bone assemblage, such as taxa representation and mortality profiles, that are generally mid-way between those associated with the Late Iron Age and the later Roman period. There is evidence for variation at the household level, with the relatively high incidence of caprines in the Period 4 assemblage from the 'House 1' sequence suggesting that some households continued eating a diet based on mutton. A range of industrial activities was clearly taking place at Silchester and there is clear evidence to suggest that intensive, systematic butchery and waste processing was well underway in Period 3. In addition to the deposition of material resulting from routine activities, there is also evidence to suggest that some of the more unusual deposits may have had symbolic associations.

CHAPTER 14

THE DOG ASSEMBLAGE

By Kate Clark

A total of 503 fragments of dog bone was recovered from:

Period 3

Pits (SE)	Object 500017	19
Pits (N)	Object 500029	7
SE Layers	Object 701	118
MB 1	Object 50018	3
MRTB 1/ERTB 1 [=ERTB 4]	Object 50037	24

Period 4

Pits (SE)	Object 500017	186
SE Layers	Object 700	128
MB 3	Object 50046	18

THE ASSEMBLAGE BY CONTEXT

PERIOD 3 (FIG. 126)

Northern pits (Object 500029)

Dog remains were recovered only from pit 4835. This pit yielded two metacarpals and one metatarsal (5835), a scapula, ulna and skull fragment (5867), and a single neonate humerus (4832). The proximally unfused ulna indicates an animal of less than 32 weeks of age.

South-east pits (Object 500017)

Pit 5039

Only three fragments were recovered, a metatarsal (4549), tibia (4535) and cervical vertebra (4542). The unfused proximal ulna again suggests an animal under the age of 32 weeks; the metatarsal and tibia both exhibit skinning marks.

Pit 5693 (16 fragments)

The remains suggest the presence of two dogs, and are predominantly from context 6300. With the exception of one mandible with early adult dentition, all the remains are of limb bones of which one (tibia) exhibits a skinning mark. Epiphyseal fusion indicates that one animal was less than 40 but older than 24 weeks, and the other less than 32 weeks.

Nos of fragments

·   1

•   2-10

●   11-20

⬤   21-40

⬤   41-60

⬤   61-80

⬤   81-100

Period 3: Density of dog remains

0   10
metres

•   1

●   <10

Period 3: Evidence of skinning

FIG. 126.   Period 3: density of dog remains (upper) and evidence of skinning (lower).

South-east layers (Object 701)

Accumulation deposits (85 fragments)

The majority of the fragments were recovered from context 5698. At least two individuals, with estimated shoulder heights of 37cm and 42cm, are present in these contexts, and all areas of the skeleton with the exception of tibiae are represented. One animal was less than 36 weeks, the other older than 40 weeks. Only one cut mark was visible, on a maxilla fragment (3225).

Building make-up

Only two fragments were recovered, from context 3435; a fifth metatarsal from an animal standing 34cm at the shoulder, and a pelvic fragment.

Dump deposits (10 fragments)

A minimum of two animals are represented in these deposits, one older than 20 weeks and one less than 28 weeks. In addition a foetal metatarsal was recovered (4270). Skinning marks are visible on two humeri (4308) and a mandible (4254).

Occupation deposits

Five fragments were recovered. A femur of an animal of less than 36 weeks exhibited a skinning mark (4469), as did a scapula from context 4277.

Silt (10 fragments)

One animal less than 32 weeks of age (4307), and one older than 40 weeks (4070) are represented in these deposits; a skinning mark is visible on a mandible (4307).

Small pits

Context 6284 contained two 2nd and two 3rd phalanges, and context 6286 a radius of an animal older than 24 weeks.

Floor

Context 3431 produced a single mandibular fragment.

MRTB 1/ERTB 1 [=ERTB 4] (Object 50037) (24 fragments)

Context 4151 yielded eight bones (mandibles, radius, ulnae and tibiae) which may well be from one individual older than 32 weeks. Further limb bone remains from Object 50037 were recovered from floor deposit 4170 (4 fragments), occupation deposit 5335 (2 fragments from an animal older than 40 weeks), layer 3732 (2 fragments indicating an animal over 32 weeks of age), and accumulation deposit 4811 (1 fragment). Mandibular fragments were present in layers 3847 and 3532, the latter context representing two individuals.

Object 50030

The four fragments from these contexts (4153 gravel spread, 4774 post-hole and 5275 occupation/demolition layer) are all of limb bones.

MB 1 (Object 50018)

The floor deposit context 4152 produced forelimb elements (humerus, radius and ulna) which are likely to be from one individual less than 40 weeks of age.

PERIOD 4 (FIG. 127)

South-east pits (Object 500017)

Well 1750 (8 fragments)

Context 2767 produced the femur of an animal older than 24 weeks, the tibia of a dog older than 44 weeks which exhibits a very well-healed fracture of the distal shaft, and three articulating cervical vertebrae. A mandible and ulna were recovered from context 1750.

Pit 2434 (86 fragments)

A minimum of three dogs are represented in this pit, and in addition a neonate scapula (2776) and metacarpal (2774) were recovered. All areas of the skeleton are present. At least one animal is older than 40 weeks (2774) and two are less than 32 weeks (2776). One dog, over 44 weeks, has bowed tibiae (2605).

Pit 2601 (56 fragments)

In this pit context 2622 produced the partial skeleton of a dog whose fusion status indicates an age of between 24 and 36 weeks. Further discussion of this animal is given below (pp. 277–8).

   The other dog remains from context 2622 which are not constituents of the partial skeleton comprise a femur, two radii from separate individuals, one of which was less than 32 weeks of age, and three articulating left metatarsals. A baculum, the only occurrence of this element in the assemblage, is also present but cannot be directly associated with the partial skeleton. Context 2623 contained a right maxillary fragment, and context 2762 produced two vertebrae, the left portion of a pelvis, and a rib fragment.

Pit 3102

The single fragment from this pit (3827) is a 4th metatarsal from an animal standing 36cm at the shoulder.

Pit 3406 (28 fragments)

Remains from a minimum of two animals plus a neonate radius were recovered primarily from context 4290. One dog was older than 40 weeks, another younger than 32 weeks. Skinning marks were visible on a humerus (3826) and tibia (3829).

Well 5735 (6 fragments)

The femur of a dog younger than 32 weeks (5697), together with two metacarpals (6294 and 6430), a tibia (6430) and a scapula (6436) exhibiting a skinning mark were present.

South-east layers (Object 700)

Building make-up (94 fragments)

A minimum of four dogs are represented in these contexts. Two of these were older than 44 weeks (3468 and 3836) and two younger than 32 weeks (3468, 3498), and immature dentition in one mandible indicates the presence of a pup less than 10 weeks (3468). 24 fragments, including that of the pup, exhibited skinning marks. One dog had bowed tibiae (2916).

Dump

A single fragment of humerus was recovered from context 3467.

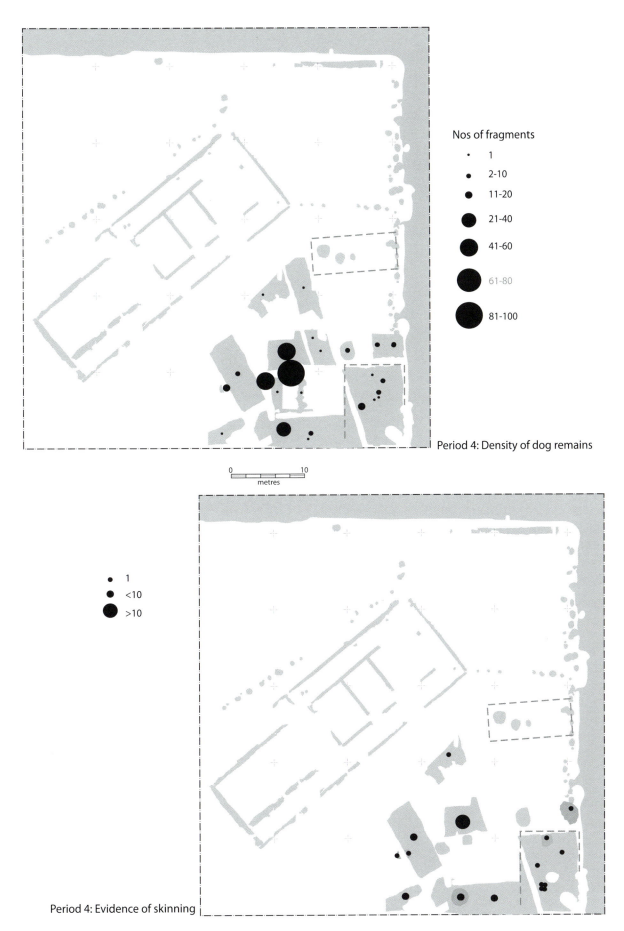

Nos of fragments
·   1
•   2-10
●   11-20
●   21-40
●   41-60
●   61-80
●   81-100

Period 4: Density of dog remains

0   10
metres

1
<10
>10

Period 4: Evidence of skinning

FIG. 127. Period 4: density of dog remains (upper) and evidence of skinning (lower).

Levelling

Context 2467 produced a single maxilla with a skinning mark below the orbit.

Occupation

These contexts (3911 and 3849) produced a pair of mandibles and four fragments of scapula, radius, maxilla and mandible. One of the paired mandibles and the mandibular fragment exhibited skinning marks.

Post-holes

2650: four fragments were recovered — fibula, fibula fragment, ulna and tibia. The tibia exhibited skinning cuts.
2651: the femur of an animal older than 32 weeks, and a rib.
2658: two mandibles (one juvenile, the other neonate), humerus, 2nd metatarsal and 1st phalanx. From the metatarsal a shoulder height of 35cm is calculated, and the humerus exhibits skinning cuts.
2670: 13 fragments and small bones were recovered from this post-hole, including a neonate scapula. A 2nd metacarpal and 4th metatarsal both produce estimated shoulder heights of around 40cm.

MB 3 (Object 50046) (18 fragments)

The majority of the remains (15 fragments) are from the levelling deposit (3396) where at least two dogs are represented in limb bones and pelvis. Further contexts yielding single dog fragments are cut 3636 (sacrum) and occupation deposit 2471 (mandible).

AGE AND SEX

Fusion evidence (Sumner-Smith 1966) for Period 3 layers suggests only one animal of full skeletal maturity (Object 701 context 5698), supported by a single case of moderate mandibular tooth wear from the same context. The remaining dogs from the early layers appear to be between 20 and 36 weeks of age. The age profile for the Period 3 pits (Objects 500029 and 500017) indicates that all the animals were between 20 and 32 weeks. The presence of foetal or neonate animals is restricted solely to two metapodia from the dump context 4270.

In the Period 4 layers (Object 701) there is evidence for one dog of skeletal maturity (humerus from building make-up context 3468), the remainder being between 24 and 36 weeks. Period 4 building make-up also provided the single instance of age-related pathology — a pelvic fragment exhibiting minor periarticular exostosis (context 3498). Neonate/foetal material occurred only in post-holes 2658 (mandible) and 2670 (scapula). In the Period 4 pits mature remains were recovered from pit 3406 (humerus from context 4290) and well 5735 (tibia in context 6430). The remaining animals appear to be between 20 and 32 weeks of age. Neonate or foetal remains again were rare, occurring in pit 2434 (metacarpal context 2774, scapula context 2766), pit 3406 (radius context 4290), and pit 4825 (humerus context 4832).

Tooth wear in the cheekteeth cannot be used to age dogs directly as the degree of wear depends on diet and the proclivity to chew. However youthful animals can be identified by unworn dentition, and Appendix 7, Table 76 shows the level of wear observed in mandibular and maxillary teeth *in situ*. These observations concur with the results from the fusion data, where only one aged animal is visible in each period.

The only baculum recovered was from Period 4 pit 2601, context 2622. While negative evidence cannot be take as conclusive, it would appear likely that the majority of dog remains of both periods are from females. This, together with the fusion data and the paucity of neonate/ foetal material, may tentatively indicate that bitches were despatched as they achieved sexual maturity.

SIZE

Selected measurements of skull, mandible, axial and appendicular remains are shown in Appendix 7, Tables 77–86. Measurable limb bones, including the metapodia, have been used to estimate shoulder height using the factors of Harcourt (1974) and Clark (1996), and the results of these calculations are shown by period and deposit type in Table 87.

The size ranges within each period are similar (Period 3: 32–45cm, n=7; Period 4: 30–49cm, n=15), and are both firmly within the range for Romano-British dogs. By amalgamating the two periods it is possible to compare this assemblage with recorded Romano-British dogs of the mid-second to mid-third century A.D. (Harcourt 1974; Clark 1996; 2000), and this comparison is shown in FIG. 128. By this period the bifurcation of the Romano-British dog population into smaller and larger animals was becoming apparent, but this is not reflected in the Silchester assemblage which shows a higher degree of uniformity.

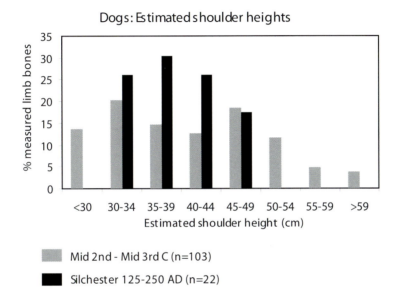

FIG. 128. Estimated shoulder heights of dogs from Silchester and elsewhere in Roman Britain, second to third centuries.

SKINNING (FIGS 126–127)

Cut marks were visible on remains from both Period 3 and Period 4, and these are described in Appendix 7, Tables 88–89 by context, element and location. The cuts are fine and precise, and all are consistent with skinning, rather than disarticulation. With the exception of a cut mark on the lateral face of a scapula from well 5735, they are confined to the limb bones, the metapodia, and the mandible.

However, there is a notable difference between the incidence of cut marks on these elements, both between periods and between deposit type and this is summarised in Appendix 7, Table 90. Skinning marks are most abundant in the Period 4 layers, and are predominantly found in the building make-up contexts.

PIT 2601 CONTEXT 2622

Photographic evidence suggests that the animal in this context was originally deposited as a complete carcass, carefully placed on the right side in a tightly curled-up position with the muzzle typically tucked against the tarsal joints. As the body has decomposed and compressed from above the pelvis has disarticulated and the left femur has been depressed into the skull.

The right forelimb has been recovered in the humerus, radius and ulna, and the left hindlimb in the femur, tibial fragment and the metatarsals. The axial elements comprise one cervical, three thoracic and five lumbar vertebrae together with the sacrum, complete pelvis and both scapulae. The skull is fragmented but largely complete, as are both mandibles.

The dog is aged between 24 and 36 weeks, and there is no wear on the teeth. The shoulder height, calculated from measurements of the radius and metatarsals, is estimated at around 48cm.

Sufficient measurements were available in the skull and mandibles to enable comparison with modern specimens, and there is a notable concordance with the dimensions of a modern crossbred Staffordshire terrier (Appendix 7, Table 91), the only significant divergence being that the pit 2601 animal has a slightly more robust development of the mandibular articulation.

DISCUSSION

Although there is a marked constraint in age and size within this group of dogs, and possibly of sex, the notable characteristic is the incidence and consistency of the skinning evidence in Period 4. Skinning of dogs in the Late Iron Age/early Romano-British period is occasionally reported, as at first-century Owslebury (Maltby 1987a), Brighton Hill South (Maltby 1987b), and Coombe Down and Chisenbury Warren (Powell *et al.* 2006), and from later Romano-British sites as at the second/third-century deposits at Rope Lake Hole (Coy 1987) and the later contexts at Chisenbury Warren (Powell *et al.* 2006). Definitive evidence of an actual dog skin was present in the third/fourth-century child's grave from Asthall (Booth *et al.* 1996). However, with the exception of the Asthall material, observations of skinning cuts are intermittent and are invariably accompanied by disarticulation evidence within the same assemblage, suggesting that some dogs were eaten and the skins were removed as a by-product or to facilitate cooking. This does not seem to be the case at Silchester in the early third century. Here, skins appear to be systematically removed from young adult or sub-adult animals and, by invoking negative evidence, those animals may have been predominantly female.

CHAPTER 15

THE OYSTER SHELL

By Sandie Williams and Elizabeth Somerville

A small quantity of oyster (*Ostrea edulis*) was recovered from the south-east pits and wells and from the south-east layers (6.004kg) (Table 24). No oyster was found in association with any of the buildings of Period 3 and 4 or the northern pits. The majority of the oysters were in fragmentary condition and were quantified by weight.

TABLE 24. QUANTIFICATION OF THE OYSTER SHELL IN THE PITS IN THE SOUTH-EAST OF THE TRENCH

Pit/Well	Weight (g)
3406 (P4)	25.08
3102 (P4)	87.11
5693 (P3)	8.55
5735 (P4)	205.01
1750 (P4)	2.66
2434 (P4)	1.66
2601 (P4)	26.79
6290 (P3)	1070.10
5039 (P3)	362.90

PERIOD 3

Oysters were present in all three of the south-east pits and wells, but the only significant quantity (1.070kg) was found in a single context in the layers slumping into 6290 and dating to the early to mid-second century. From the south-east layers as a whole 3.329kg were recovered from 34 contexts. The largest quantity from any context amounted to only <700g, while the majority of those contexts with oysters produced <100g from each.

PERIOD 4

Oysters were present in very small quantities in each of the Period 4 pits and wells with the largest quantity only 205g from well 5735. Mussels were present in two pits. A small quantity of oyster was recorded from the south-east layers (885g) from nine contexts. The largest quantity from a single context was <650g, with the majority of layers with oysters only producing <100g from each

AGEING AND INFESTATION
By Elizabeth Somerville

From the very small available sample of complete umbos and valves, infestation by *P. ciliata* was identified from 15 umbos and one valve (Table 25). *C. celata* was identified on two valves and a single incidence of infestation by *P. hoplura* was noted on one fragment. Despite the virtual absence of evidence of the latter infestation, the pattern of infestation compares with that identified among the later second-century assemblage at the North Gate (Silchester) and at Fishbourne and suggests an origin for the oysters from the south coast (Somerville 1997; 2006). In terms of age the material is also similar to that of the North Gate and Fishbourne assemblages with a modal age of five years (Table 25). There were only two umbos with an age of more than ten years.

TABLE 25. OYSTERS: SUMMARY OF INFESTATION AND AGE

umbos showing infestation:

	pc	ph	cc	none	n/a
u/s	5	0	0	6	13
left	8	0	0	3	0
right	2	0	0	6	4
total	15	0	0	15	17

valves showing infestation

	pc	ph	cc	none
left	1	0	1	0
right	0	0	1	0
total	1	0	2	0

Ages

yrs	no umbos	no valves
3	3	
4	4	
5	6	
6	4	
7		1
8	1	
9		
10+	2	
not aged	28	3

DISCUSSION

Although the total quantity of oysters was significantly greater than from the fourth century (1.308kg) (Williams 2006), oysters made a very marginal contribution to diet in the second and third century in the north-east of Insula IX. It is likely that the very small quantities recorded from the pit and well contexts as well as from certain of the south-east layers were residual and redeposited. The largest single assemblage (>1kg) from the Period 3, early second-century slumps into 6290 might be contemporary with the date of the deposit and may have derived from a single meal. This may also be the case with the only two other contexts, one from Period 3 and one from Period 4, which produced notable, but still small quantities (<700g) of oyster. The distribution between Periods 3 and 4 was approximately 3:2. In terms of the pattern of infestation and age the small assemblage compares both with that from the Silchester North Gate and from Fishbourne. The oysters probably originated from the south coast.

CHAPTER 16

THE MACROSCOPIC PLANT AND INVERTEBRATE REMAINS

By Mark Robinson

INTRODUCTION

The programme of sampling which was implemented for the late Roman archaeological contexts of Insula IX was continued with the excavation of mid-Roman deposits. These again included non-waterlogged deposits containing carbonised plant remains, waterlogged sediments in well-bottoms containing waterlogged macroscopic plant remains, and latrine deposits with calcium phosphate replaced (mineralised) plant and arthropod remains. In addition, conditions of waterlogged preservation in some well-bottom sediments were sufficiently good that insect remains also survived and some of the latrine deposits contained rather poorly-preserved waterlogged seeds. The results for waterlogged plant remains from the latrines are presented along with the results for mineralised remains from those deposits. As with the study of the pollen (Dark, below, Ch. 17), pit 5251, assigned by spot-dating to Period 2 and therefore not reported in Ch. 2 , has also been included in this report; it was filled by *c.* A.D. 125, the start of our Period 3. The sources of the samples are shown by period on FIG. 129.

The remains were analysed and interpreted in a similar way to those from the late Roman contexts (Robinson 2006). Only limited description of these techniques will be repeated here. The tables are presented in Appendix 8.

WATERLOGGED MACROSCOPIC PLANT AND INSECT REMAINS

METHODS AND RESULTS

Waterlogged sediments were discovered during the excavation of Period 4 well 5735 (Object 500037). The preservation of organic remains in context 6960, the lowest deposit, and context 6436, the layer above, was relatively good but the concentration of remains was extremely low, perhaps because the sediments accumulated rapidly. Whereas it is usually possible to obtain sufficient waterlogged seeds from a sample of between 0.25kg and 1.0kg, it was decided to wash bulk samples of up to 20 litres onto a 0.25mm mesh in order to extract the organic material. The heavy residues were sieved to 2mm to recover any larger items which had not been washed over. The flots were sorted in water using a binocular microscope for potentially identifiable macroscopic plant and insect remains which were stored in ethanol. Identifiable macroscopic plant remains which had been preserved by waterlogging were also found in the dried flots of Sample 386 from context 2778, from the Period 4 well 1750 (Object 500020). The remains were identified with reference to the collections of the Oxford University Museum of Natural History. The results for seeds from Sample 1715 context 6960, Sample 1646 context 6436, Sample 1581 context 6436, all from well 5735, and Sample 386 context 2778, from well 1750, are quantified in Appendix 8, Table 93 and the results for other macroscopic plant remains are given in Appendix 8, Table 94. Nomenclature follows Stace (1997). Useful numbers of insects were only found in Samples 1715 and 1646. The results for Coleoptera (beetles) are given in

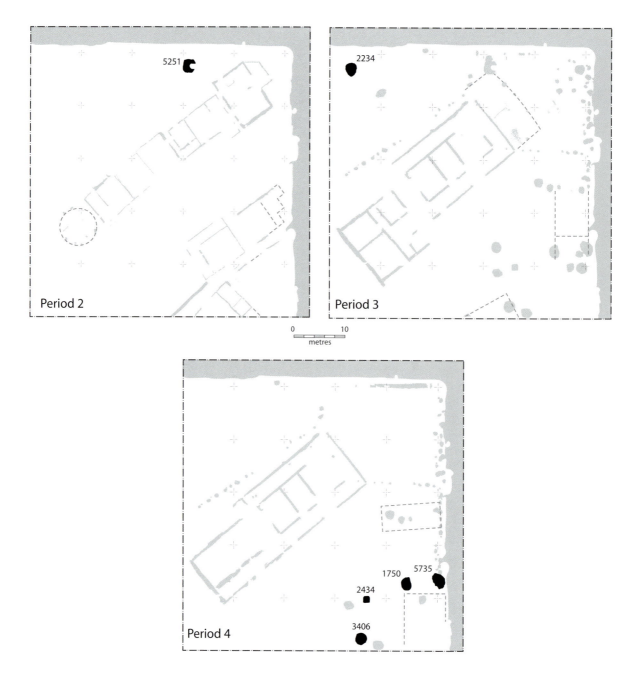

FIG. 129.   Location by period of pits and wells producing macroscopic plant and invertebrate remains.

Appendix 8, Table 95, the nomenclature following Kloet and Hincks (1977), and the results for other insects are given in Appendix 8, Table 96. The Coleoptera have been divided into species groups after Robinson (1991, 278–81) and the results displayed in FIG. 130.

Although the concentration of remains was low, there was no evidence that these waterlogged deposits had experienced any disturbance or contamination since they were laid down in the third century. The samples contained remains from a very diverse range of plant and beetle species.

The most numerous seeds were from plants of disturbed-ground habitats. Annual weeds of nutrient-rich disturbed ground predominated in Samples 1715 and 386; *Urtica urens* (annual nettle) and *Stellaria media* gp. (chickweed) were the most numerous in Sample 1715, whereas *Chenopodium album* (fat hen) was abundant in Sample 386. Perennials of neglected nutrient-rich habitats predominated in Sample 1581, especially *Urtica dioica* (stinging nettle) and *Sambucus nigra* (elder). There was a more even distribution of seed numbers in Sample 1646, although seeds of *Rumex* (docks), including *R. obtusifolius*, were well represented.

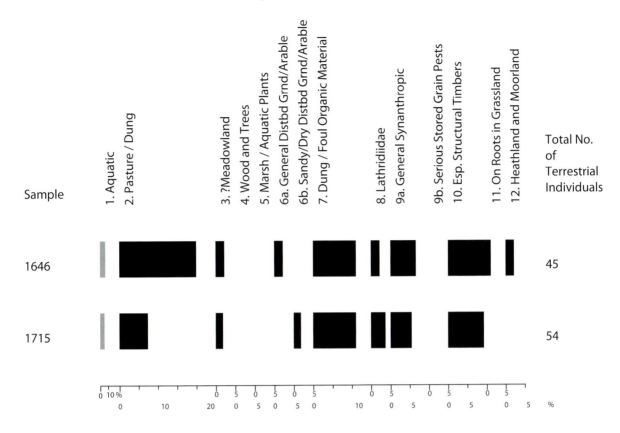

FIG. 130. Percentage of terrestrial Coleoptera: species groups expressed as a percentage of the total terrestrial Coleoptera (i.e. aquatics excluded). Not all the terrestrial Coleoptera have been classified into groups.

Seeds of plants of marsh and wet-ground habitats were present in all the samples but they comprised around 20 per cent of the seeds in Samples 1645 and 1581. In Sample 1645 they were mostly *Eleocharis palustris* or *uniglumis* (spike rush) and *Carex* spp. (sedge). *Juncus* spp. (rushes) were the most numerous in Sample 1581.

The samples also all contained seeds of grassland plants. They were not nearly as abundant as the seeds from plants of disturbed and waste-ground habitats but a diverse range of species was found. They included *Ranunculus* cf. *acris* (meadow buttercup), *R.* cf. *repens* (creeping buttercup), *Potentilla* cf. *erecta* (tormentil), *Prunella vulgaris* (selfheal), and *Hypochoeris* sp. (cat's ear). *Trifolium* sp. (clover) was represented by some floral parts in Samples 1715 and 1646. There were also some pod fragments of *Vicia* or *Lathyrus* sp. (vetch or tare) in these two samples.

Heathland or open woodland on acid soil was represented by frond fragments of *Pteridium aquilinum* (bracken) in Sample 1646. Remains from trees or shrubs included some bud scales, seeds of *Rubus fruticosus* agg. (blackberry), and, as noted above, seeds of *Sambucus nigra* (elder).

There was a slight presence of remains of cultivated plants in all the waterlogged samples. They were best represented in Sample 1646 which contained seeds of *Ficus carica* (fig), *Brassica nigra* (black mustard), *Vitis vinifera* (grape), *Anethum graveolens* (dill), *Coriandrum sativum* (coriander), *Apium graveolens* (celery), as well as a nut-shell fragment of *Juglans regia* (walnut), stones of *Prunus domestica* ssp. *domestica* (plum) and *P. domestica* ssp. *insititia* (bullace), an endocarp (core) fragment of *Malus* sp. (apple), and glumes of *Triticum spelta* (spelt wheat). Fragments of *Corylus avellana* (hazel) nut-shells were present in a couple of the samples. While Sample 1715 did not have the range of remains of edible plants, there were leaf fragments of *Ilex aquifolium* (holly) and *Buxus sempervirens* (box).

The most numerous insects in Samples 1715 and 1646 were Coleoptera (beetles) of terrestrial habitats from grassland to rather sparsely vegetated disturbed ground. They included various Carabidae (ground beetles), such as *Trechus obtusus* or *quadristriatus* and *Pterostichus melanarius*, and Staphylinidae (rove beetles), such as *Stenus* spp. and *Tachinus* sp. Phytophagous species included *Brachypterus urticae*, which feeds on *Urtica dioica* (stinging nettle), and *Apion* spp. which feeds on various Fabaceae including *Trifolium* sp. (clover) and *Lathyrus* spp. (vetchling). Scarabaeoid dung beetles which feed on the droppings of domestic animals on pasture (Species Group 2), such as *Aphodius contaminatus* and *A. granarius*, comprised 7 per cent of the terrestrial Coleoptera in Sample 1715 and 20 per cent of the terrestrial Coleoptera in Sample 1646. Beetles occurring in a wider range of categories of foul organic material including dung (Species Group 7), for example *Cercyon* spp. and *Megasternum obscurum*, comprised 1 per cent of the terrestrial Coleoptera in both samples. Beetles which commonly attack structural timbers (Species Group 10) were well represented, at 9 per cent of the terrestrial Coleoptera in Sample 1715 and 11 per cent of the terrestrial Coleoptera in Sample 1646. *Anobium punctatum* (woodworm beetle) in both samples was joined by *Lyctus linearis* (powder post beetle) in Sample 1646. Other beetles of indoor habitats included *Tipnus unicolor* and *Ptinus fur* of Species Group 9a, general synanthropic beetles, comprising 6–7 per cent of the terrestrial Coleoptera. Water beetles (Species Group 1) averaged 6 per cent when expressed as a percentage of the terrestrial Coleoptera in both samples. Beetles which feed on marsh and aquatic plants were, however, absent. There were no beetles associated with trees and shrubs.

Most of the remains of other orders of insects were unidentified puparia of Diptera (flies). However two heads of workers of *Apis mellifera* (honey bee) were found in Sample 1646.

INTERPRETATION

The waterlogged macroscopic plant and insect remains from the samples had been derived from many different sources but have a good potential for facilitating the reconstruction of the site environment and activities. Few, if any, of the insects lived in the wells. The few water beetles need only have been attracted by the reflection from the surface of the water. The absence of a full aquatic fauna and the very low concentration of organic materials suggests that the wells supplied high-quality clean water. Some of the plants and insects were from habitats in the vicinity of the wells, while others had been transported to the site, in some instances from very great distances.

Working outwards from the wells, the beetle *Lesteva longoelytrata* probably lived in gaps between the well timbers. The annual herbaceous plant *Polygonum aviculare* agg. (knotgrass) perhaps grew sparsely on trampled ground around the top of the wells. This vegetation probably graded into a Chenopodietalia community of *Urtica urens* (small nettle), *Stellaria media* (chickweed) and *Chenopodium album* (fat hen), annual herbs of nutrient-rich soil, where there was less trampling and some input of decayed refuse and dung. Where disturbance was only sporadic this community is likely to have given way to a waste-ground tall-herb vegetation of *Urtica dioica* (stinging nettle), *Rumex obtusifolius* (broad-leaved dock), *Ballota nigra* (black horehound), and some grasses. *Rubus fruticosus* agg. (blackberry) and *Sambucus nigra* (elder) appear to have become established in the most neglected corners of the site. Various of the carabid beetles, such as *Nebria brevicollis*, *Pterostichus melanarius* and *Agonum dorsale*, could have lived on the ground amongst one or more of these categories of disturbed/neglected-ground vegetation. The various phytophagous beetles feeding on the vegetation included *Brachypterus urticae* on *Urtica dioica* (stinging nettle), *Chaetocnema concinna* on *Rumex* spp. (docks) or other members of the Polygonaceae, and *Ceuthorhynchidius horridus* on *Cirsium* and *Carduus* spp. (thistles).

It is uncertain to what degree the seeds of grassland plants represented the vegetation of Insula IX or were brought to the site either by domestic animals which deposited them as droppings or as hay. However, there is no reason why there should not have been small grassy areas with plants such as *Ranunculus* cf. *repens* (buttercup), *Prunella vulgaris* (selfheal) and *Hypochoeris* (cat's ear) growing on them. There would have been an insufficient area of Insula IX available for pasture to sustain any domestic herbivores without the import of fodder. However, the high proportion of scarabaeoid dung beetles such as *Aphodius* spp. in Sample 1646 suggests that domestic animals were concentrated nearby. These beetles are not characteristic of manure heaps or middens. The glumes of spelt wheat, arable weed seeds such as *Agrostemma githago* (corn cockle), and the remains of plants characteristic of hay-meadow vegetation, including *Thalictrum flavum* (meadow-rue), *Filipendula ulmaria* (meadowsweet), *Centaurea nigra* (knapweed) and *Vicia* or *Lathyrus* sp. (vetch, vetchling etc.), were perhaps from dry fodder given to the animals. The remains of Cyperaceae, such as *Eleocharis palustris* or *uniglumis* (spike rush) and *Carex* spp. (sedges), along with other wet-ground plants such as *Mentha* cf. *aquatica* (water mint), could either have been introduced in cut vegetation or in the droppings of animals which had been grazed on marshy pasture. The bracken is likely to have been brought to the site as animal bedding. It is a plant of acid sites as are some of the grassland plants which were represented by seeds, for example *Potentilla* cf. *erecta* (tormentil). Suitable soils for these plants occur around Silchester.

Both *Ilex aquifolium* (holly) and *Buxus sempervirens* (box) are native to the British Isles, the former being a reasonably common shrub of scrub and woodland, the latter a very rare shrub of calcareous escarpments. Both could easily have been grown on the site. Holly and box make good ornamental shrubs which can readily be clipped to shape. Pliny the Elder (*Naturalis Historia* 26.28) describes the use of box as a garden plant and it is possible that the leaves were hedge-cuttings from a small garden area attached to one of the buildings on Insula IX. There could also have been a religious significance given to the evergreen nature of these shrubs, perhaps sprigs of them were used to dress shrines. The occurrence of bud scales suggests that there could have been a few deciduous trees or bushes on the insula. Some of the fruit (see below) could have been grown within the town.

The buildings of Insula IX provided habitats for at least two communities of insects. Some of their timbers were presumably infested with woodworm beetles, particularly *Anobium punctatum*. These beetles are rare away from man-made structures because their requirement of old dry wood is uncommon in nature. There was also a significant presence of the synanthropic beetles *Tipnus unicolor* and *Ptinus fur*. They feed on a wide range of rather dry, starchy or protein-rich material. These beetles can live independently of human influence, for example feeding on debris in birds' nests; however, they are now most often found inside buildings, eating food waste in neglected areas of kitchens and amongst old hay or straw in barns or stables. Although they often occur in very old grain residues, they are not primarily pests of stored grain.

The beetles of general decaying organic material were no more abundant than might be expected given that domestic animals were apparently kept on the site and that cut vegetation was being imported. The insects do not suggest the proximity of any large midden. Some decayed organic material does, however, appear to have been incorporated into the soil of the site increasing its fertility. It has already been noted that the flora of the site included plants of nutrient-rich soils and seeds of *Hyoscyamus niger* (henbane), a plant which was formerly particularly characteristic of dung-enriched soil around settlements, were present in three of the samples.

The occurrence of honey bee remains raises the possibility that there was bee-keeping at Silchester. During the winter honey bees need water to dilute their honey stocks as they feed on it and the workers of a colony will tend to use a single source nearby. It is possible that the well was providing water for a hive within the town and some of the bees drowned.

As was suggested for the late Roman, fourth- to fifth-century, waterlogged material (Robinson 2006, 208), the various remains of food plants probably represent a background scatter of domestic refuse on the site. The possible origins and uses of most of the food flavourings and fruit are discussed below for the mineralised residues. There is little doubt that the majority of them were cultivated locally or imported for consumption. However, it should be noted that *Brassica nigra* (black mustard) would readily have grown as a weed on the insula as well as being cultivated as a condiment. Both *Juglans regia* (walnut) and *Corylus avellana* (hazel) would have given higher yields of nuts in the Roman period than now because grey squirrel was absent. The production of hazel nuts could have been combined with the coppicing of hazel for poles and fuel.

The waterlogged macroscopic plant remains from the third-century (Period 4) contexts were better preserved than those from the late Roman, fourth- to fifth-century contexts, but many similarities can be seen when preservational factors are taken into account (Robinson 2006, 207–9). Both give evidence of vegetation of disturbed to neglected ground. Likewise, both include remains of various food plants which were introduced by the Romans, some of which were probably grown locally and others imported from the Mediterranean region. Probably the greatest difference is that the late Roman deposits contained a higher proportion of seeds from wet-ground vegetation, although the samples from both periods included plant material which, it was argued, had either been brought to Insula IX as animal fodder or deposited by domestic animals which had grazed outside the town. Almost all the plant remains found in the mid-Roman waterlogged deposits were of species recorded from Silchester by Reid in his study a hundred years ago, including fig and box (Reid 1901–1909).

Insect remains were not preserved in the late Roman deposits but they were studied from the late nineteenth- to early twentieth-century excavations (Amsden and Boon 1975). A very similar range of species was found, including many Carabidae, Staphylinidae and Scarabaeidae. *Anobium punctatum* (woodworm beetle) was present in most of the samples. Serious pests of stored grain were absent from both groups of samples.

CARBONISED PLANT REMAINS

METHODS AND RESULTS

Bulk samples averaging 12 litres were floated onto a 0.25mm mesh and the residues which did not float were sieved to 2mm. 138 samples totalling 1,583 litres were analysed from 118 contexts. The seed and chaff remains recovered were identified and the results incorporated into the site database. The full list of taxa identified from the mid-Roman contexts is included in Appendix 8, Table 92. The detailed results from the only samples to contain twenty or more items are given in Appendix 8, Table 97. Summary results are also given in FIG. 131 and the location of the contexts with relevant samples is given in FIG. 129.

The concentration of remains from the Periods 3 and 4 contexts of Insula IX was very low, averaging only 0.20 items per litre. Remains were found in 41 samples from 36 contexts,

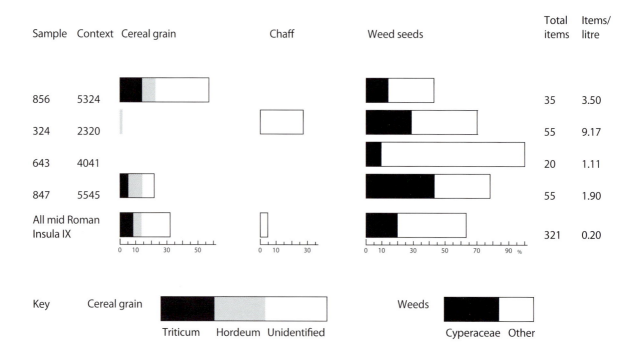

FIG. 131.   Summary of the incidence of carbonised plant remains.

although in the majority of samples with remains the charred items were both sparse and poorly preserved. Only seven samples contained more than 1.00 items per litre (with two containing more than 2.00 items per litre: Sample 856, context 5324 and Sample 324, context 2320). The most consistently represented items were cereal grains and weed seeds but a limited quantity of cereal chaff was also present.

The majority of the identifiable cereal grains were of *Triticum* sp. (wheat) but *Hordeum* sp. (barley) was also quite well represented. The only wheat which could be identified to species was *Triticum spelta* (spelt wheat), which was represented by both grain and chaff. Some wheat grain and glumes could only be taken to *T. dicoccum* or *spelta* (emmer or spelt) but all the hulled wheat could have been spelt wheat. Three of the *Triticum* sp. grains were very short, a characteristic that usually leads to an attribution to a free-threshing wheat (rivet or bread-type wheat). However, the angularity of these grains suggested that they could instead be of a hulled wheat, probably a variety of *T. spelta*. The only other cultivated cereal to be identified with certainty was hulled *Hordeum vulgare* (six-row hulled barley), represented by a few lateral grains. The majority of the barley grain could only be identified to the level of hulled *Hordeum* sp. but there was no reason to believe any two-row barley was present. There were a very few grains of *Avena* sp. (oats) but it was not possible to determine whether they were from a wild or cultivated species. They have both been included in the weed seeds in the tables of results (Appendix 8, Table 97). No other charred crop remains were found and there were no remains of gathered wild food plants.

Weed seeds outnumbered cereal grains by about two to one. The largest group amongst them were members of the Cyperaceae, perennial herbaceous plants of damp to marshy habitats. Most common amongst these were *Eleocharis palustris* or *uniglumis* (spike rush) and *Carex* spp. (sedges). Grassland plants including *Ranunculus* Sect. *Ranunculus* sp. (buttercups), cf. *Trifolium* sp. (clovers) and *Plantago lanceolata* (ribwort plantain) as well as seeds of grasses themselves comprised a distinctive group. There were few seeds of annual weeds which commonly occur as weeds of cultivation, for example members of the Chenopodiaceae were absent and there were only single examples of *Bromus* cf. *secalinus* (chess) and *Galium aparine* (goosegrass). Seeds of *Rumex* spp. (docks) were rather more numerous; these plants are herbaceous perennials which are able to tolerate cultivation but can live in a variety of other habitats including grassland.

INTERPRETATION

The charred plant remains appear to have been from at least two, possibly three, habitat types: arable fields, marsh and grassland, although it is possible that the grassland from which some of the seeds originated had marshy areas within it. Assemblages of cereal-processing remains have been found which include seeds of plants of wet ground and grassland. Indeed, *Eleocharis* cf. *palustris* is of quite frequent occurrence amongst Iron Age and Roman crop-processing waste. The interpretation often given for such material is that cereal cultivation had extended up to the edge of marshy ground and that the arable fields included recently ploughed-up grassland (e.g. Jones 1978). However, at second- to third-century Silchester the low proportion and low concentration of cereal remains suggest that the seeds of marsh and grassland plants had a separate origin. They were not cereal-processing waste.

The richest sample for cereal grain, Sample 856, only contained 20 grains while the richest sample for cereal chaff, Sample 324, only contained 15 chaff fragments. It is clear there was no major activity generating carbonised crop-processing remains occurring on the site during the second and third centuries. It is thought likely that the rather poorly-preserved cereal grains occurring in very low concentrations in most cases represented reworked material either derived from earlier contexts of Insula IX or scattered from the de-husking of grain elsewhere in the town. It is also possible that some of the charred spelt wheat and barley grains, for example those in Sample 856, resulted from cooking accidents to cleaned grain.

It is likely that the cereal remains in Sample 324, however, had a different origin. Chaff predominated, with both glumes of *Triticum spelta* and cereal culm nodes (straw 'joints') present. Such material probably represented burnt thatch or animal bedding or fodder for domestic animals. This sample also contained seeds of grassland plants appropriate to cut fodder.

Triticum spelta (spelt wheat) and hulled *Hordeum vulgare* (six-row hulled barley) were the main cereals cultivated in Britain so their use at mid-Roman Silchester was as might be expected. A short-grained variety of *T. spelta* could have been grown as a crop in its own right but it is thought more likely that the local landrace of spelt in the second to third centuries had a tendency to produce occasional short-grained mutants.

The mixed nature of the weed seed assemblages means that little can be said about the crop ecology. However, the occurrence of *Rumex* S. *Acetosella* sp. (sheep's sorrel), which could have grown either as an arable weed or in grassland, was appropriate to the light acid soils of the Silchester area.

It is thought that the seeds of marsh and grassland plants had been brought to the site amongst vegetation cut as fodder for domestic animals. While such seeds could also have been present in the droppings of animals grazing in such habitats, the flots did not contain the characteristic charred fragments which result from the burning of dung. *Eleocharis palustris* or *uniglumis* (spike rush) is not a typical hay-meadow plant but it would readily grow along with *Carex* spp. (sedges) in rough marshy pasture that was grazed some years and cut others. The seeds of grassland plants included some from plants characteristic of managed hay-meadows, such as *Centaurea* cf. *nigra* (knapweed) and *Leucanthemum vulgare* (ox-eye daisy).

The second- to third-century results from Silchester Insula IX are similar to those from the fourth- to fifth-century contexts of the insula in that neither gave any evidence for large-scale crop-processing and concentrations of remains were low. Likewise it was not possible to detect areas where particular processing activities were occurring. However, there were also differences. Spelt wheat predominated amongst the fourth- to fifth-century cereal remains and most of the weed seeds were from annual weeds, with seeds of *Bromus* cf. *secalinus* (chess) being the most numerous. In contrast, barley was also well represented in the second- to third-century samples and there were few seeds of annual weeds, with only a single seed of *B.* cf. *secalinus*. Instead there were seeds of marsh and grassland plants. It would be wrong to interpret these results as implying a major difference between the agricultural economy of mid- and late Roman Silchester. All that would have been needed, given the generally low concentration of charred remains, to have created these differences was for some old hay to have been burnt on the site in the mid-Roman period and for some spelt wheat with arable weed seeds to have been burnt on the site in the late Roman period.

MINERALISED AND WATERLOGGED MACROSCOPIC PLANT AND ARTHROPOD REMAINS FROM LATRINE DEPOSITS

METHODS AND RESULTS

The bulk flotation onto a 0.25mm sieve and the heavy-residue sieving down to 2mm that were undertaken to extract charred plant remains also resulted in the recovery of calcium phosphate mineralised plant and invertebrate remains. They were found in eight samples from eight contexts. One large deep pit, Period 2 pit 5251, was identified as a latrine during excavation and a sewage deposit, context 5276, extended over the bottom (FIG. 129). It had a 'crust' of calcium phosphate beneath which was sediment rich in calcium phosphate replaced organic remains. Some parts of context 5276 also contained rather poorly-preserved waterlogged macroscopic plant remains. At the southern half of the pit, Sample 857 was taken from the lower waterlogged part of context 5276, Sample 855 from the middle part including the crust, and Sample 852 from the upper part. Sample 792 comprised a series of 1-litre sub-samples distributed over the northern half of context 5276. All the samples from context 5276 were washed over onto a 0.25mm sieve to extract any waterlogged organic remains. The residues were sieved to 0.5mm and dried. Flots and residues were sorted under a binocular microscope, identified and the results incorporated into the site database. Full lists of all the taxa identified from the Period 2 contexts are given in Appendix 8, Table 92 for the plant remains. The detailed results for Sample 804, context 5303, pit 5251 (one of the samples floated for charred plant remains), and the samples from context 5276, the sewage deposit in pit 5251, are given in Appendix 8, Tables 98–99 for mineralised remains and Table 100 for waterlogged remains. The results for the sub-samples of Sample 792 have been combined. Nomenclature for the plant remains follows Stace (1997).

The comments made on the means of preservation of remains and the difficulties experienced with their identification for the late Roman mineralised remains (Robinson 2006, 212) are equally applicable to the mid-Roman material. For example the *Prunus* stones were represented by internal casts which filled the void enclosed by the woody exterior to the stones once the embryo had decayed. There were only a few examples where some of the woody part of the stone had become mineralised.

As was the case for the late Roman period, the range of archaeological features which contained mineralised material was very restricted. All but one of the samples were from contexts related to Period 2 pit 5251 (Object 44007), the large latrine pit at the north of the site. The remaining sample was Sample 350 from context 2605, the fill of Period 4 pit 2434 (Object 500031), one of the south-east corner pits (FIG. 129). This too could have been a cess-pit but only four mineralised items were found in a 25-litre sample.

The majority of the mineralised seeds were of edible species, with fruits, flavourings, cereals and pulses all being well represented. Seeds of *Prunus* sp. were particularly conspicuous in most of the samples. The internal casts of their stones have the superficial appearance of seeds of *Malus* sp., and in the absence of the woody part of the stone were difficult to identify to species. They mostly had a size and shape appropriate to a small variety of plum such as *P. domestica* ssp. *insititia* (bullace) and indeed waterlogged stones of this type of plum were found in context 5276. One, however, resembled *Prunus avium* (cherry). The most numerous mineralised seeds in the samples from context 5276 were of *Ficus carica* (fig). Other mineralised seeds included *Rubus fruticosus* agg. (blackberry) in all the samples from context 5276, *Morus nigra* (black mulberry) in Sample 792, and *Vitis vinifera* (grape) in Samples 857 and 792. Possible seeds of *Pyrus* sp. (pear) or *Malus* sp. (apple) were found in Samples 852.3 and 792.

Seeds either used as culinary herbs and spices or from plants with leaves used as flavourings were found in all the samples from context 5276. *Anethum graveolens* (dill) was probably the most numerous, although their preservation was not good and they were only identified with certainty from Samples 857 and 792. Most of the 104 indeterminate Apiaceae seeds from Sample 857 and 42 from 792 had a shape and vittae impressions suggestive of *An. graveolens*. Seeds of two other Apiaceae commonly used as flavourings, *Coriandrum sativum* (coriander) and *Apium graveolens* (celery), were found in several samples from context 5276. Additional seeds of flavourings from this context were *Satureja hortensis* (summer savory) and *Mentha* sp. (mint) from Sample 792, *Brassica* or *Sinapis* sp. (mustard etc.) from Sample 857, and *Papaver somniferum* (opium poppy) from Samples 855.3 and 792. A seed of *P. somniferum* was also found in Sample 804 from context 5303.

Mineralised cereal remains were present in all four samples from context 7276 but they were only abundant in Sample 857. They were mostly in the form of hulled grains with some mineralised fragments of husk adhering to them but few could be identified. They included both *Triticum spelta* (spelt wheat) and *Hordeum vulgare* (hulled six-row barley). The less-closely identified grain showing some resemblance to *Triticum* sp. was considerably greater in quantity than that which resembled *Hordeum* sp. Cereal bran was observed in some of the amorphous fragments of calcium phosphate from Samples 857, 855.3 and 792.

Sample 857 from context 5276 contained many mineralised legume seeds most of which resembled *Pisum sativum* (pea). The seed coat and broad oval hilum survived on a few, enabling this identification to be confirmed. *Lens culinaris* (lentil) was also present in this sample. The only other sample to contain edible legume seeds was Sample 792 from context 5276, in which a single example of *Vicia faba* (field or Celtic bean) joined company with a lentil and a few peas.

One further cultivated plant with edible seeds which was represented amongst the mineralised seeds was *Linum usitatissimum* (flax) from Sample 855.3, context 5276. There were many mineralised seeds and parts of seeds in the samples which could not be identified. The majority of them were of a size and shape appropriate to larger fruit seeds and peas.

Edible species also predominated amongst the waterlogged seeds from context 5276 in the large latrine pit 5251 (Object 44007). About 97 per cent of the seeds were of *Rubus fruticosus* agg. (blackberry) and a further 2 per cent of the seeds were of various species of *Prunus* (plum etc.). There was inevitably much variability amongst the 1880 seeds of *Rubus* spp. in the samples but only two, from Sample 857, fell outside the range shown by reference material of *R. fruticosus* agg. They were smaller, more elongate and had a finer network of ridges on the surface. They most closely resembled seeds of *R. idaeus* (raspberry). The *Prunus* stones were very poorly preserved and less than half could be identified beyond generic level, although none fell within the morphological range of *P. persica* (peach), *P. dulcis* (almond) or *P. armenaica* (apricot). Preservation was best in Sample 857, in which the majority of identifiable stones resembled *P. domestica* ssp. *insititia* (bullace, damson etc.) but there was at least one larger stone resembling that of *P. domestica* ssp. *domestica* (plum) and there was a single stone of *Prunus spinosa* (sloe).

Mineralised weed seeds were greatly outnumbered by seeds of edible plants in the samples from context 5276. Some were from annual weeds which readily grow as weeds of cultivation, such as *Agrostemma githago* (corn cockle), *Lithospermum arvense* (corn gromwell), *Gallium aparine* (goosegrass), and *Carduus* or *Cirsium* sp. (thistle). Others were from grassland habitats such as *Prunella vulgaris* (selfheal) and marsh habitats such as *Carex* sp. (sedge). A few, such as *Urtica dioica* (stinging nettle) and *Conium maculatum* (hemlock), were from waste-ground plants. In contrast, weed seeds predominated in Sample 804 from context 5303. By far the most numerous seeds in this sample were of *U. dioica*.

Many mineralised vegetative plant fragments, most of which could not be identified, were present in Samples 857, 855.3 and 792 from context 5276. They included straw-like material and wood. A couple of frond fragments of *Pteridium aquilinum* (bracken) were recognised in Samples 857 and 792.

Mineralised arthropod remains were present in all the samples in which mineralised plant remains were abundant. They were mostly Diptera (fly) pupae and puparia belonging to *Psychoda alternata* (trickling filter fly), Sphaeroceridae indet. (sewage fly) and *Fannia* sp. (latrine fly). There were also some sclerites (skeletal plates) of Diplopoda (millipedes) and Isopoda (woodlice).

INTERPRETATION

The occurrence of a latrine-fauna of insects, the range of seeds of edible plants and the calcium phosphate replacement of biological remains all suggest that the pits which contained the mineralised material were latrine pits and that the contexts with remains were derived from sewage deposits. The process of mineralisation is described in detail in the report on the late Roman mineralised remains from Silchester (Robinson 2006, 214–15).

The plant and invertebrate remains from the latrine deposit of context 5276 (pit 5251) can be divided into three categories: various flies whose larvae lived on the sewage in the pit, items, especially seeds, which entered the pit having passed through the human digestive tract, and remains that either fell or were thrown into the pit. The occurrence of pupae of the fly *Psychoda* cf. *alternata* (trickling filter fly) and puparia of the fly *Fannia* cf. *scalaris* suggest that the pit held liquid or semi-liquid contents. Such conditions seem to be necessary for the process of phosphatic mineralisation but in the late Roman cess-pits they must have been intermittent because remains preserved by waterlogging were absent. However, the survival of seeds preserved by waterlogging in context 5276 suggests that the pit permanently held liquid sewage, probably because it extended below the water table.

The majority of seeds in context 5276 were from edible species for which it is plausible that some seeds would have been consumed and that they would have passed through the gut intact. The strong contrast between the seeds preserved by mineralisation and those preserved by waterlogging shows that preservation was highly selective. The waterlogged preservation was poor: only the most woody seeds were preserved by this means. However, by far the most abundant seeds preserved by waterlogging were of *Rubus fruticosus* agg. (blackberry). They were not particularly abundantly or even well preserved by mineralisation. It is thought possible that the reason *Rubus* seeds did not also dominate the mineralised assemblages is that their robust nature enables them to remain alive for much longer than the seeds of many other taxa in the deposits and thus resist the diffusion of the ions into them which leads to mineralisation. The contrast in preservation serves as a reminder that while the results provided much useful evidence on the plant components of the early second-century diet at Silchester, it is not a complete or balanced picture.

What the results do suggest is a mixed diet showing a strong Roman influence, although the majority of the food plants could have been grown locally. The staples included spelt wheat, hulled barley and peas. Depending on the scale of consumption of peas, they could either have been grown as field crops along with the cereals or in horticultural plots along with lentils and beans. It was argued for the late Roman period that cereal grains would have been de-husked then milled into flour or crushed before cooking and consumption: those hulled grains which were preserved by mineralisation were the few which escaped the seed cleaning and grinding (Robinson 2006, 265). The same appears to have been true for the mid-Roman period. However, less preparation would have been needed for peas, which could have been consumed after soaking and boiling. The peas which became mineralised were perhaps ones which had not been fully rehydrated and so remained hard when consumed.

The various seeds of plants used as flavourings are mostly well known from Roman Britain and the quantity of Apiaceae seeds resembling *Anethum graveolens* (dill) suggests that they were used profusely. *Mentha* sp. (mint) is the only one for which there is much doubt about its use because there are no other records from Roman latrines to confirm its usage and plants of *Mentha aquatica* (water mint) could readily have been amongst the marsh plants which it has been argued were brought to the site as fodder. Some of the herbs and spices, for example dill and coriander, are Roman introductions probably of south-west Asian or Mediterranean origin but all could have been grown in horticultural plots at Silchester. They could have been used to flavour bread, porridge, boiled peas and stews. *Linum usitatissimum* (flax, linseed) seeds, although not imparting any strong flavour, were, perhaps, eaten for their high nutritious oil content.

There was no certain evidence for the consumption of any root or leaf vegetables. *Apium graveolens* (celery) could also have been cultivated for its edible leaf-petioles or roots (celeriac) and species of *Brassica* grown for their edible leaves (e.g. cabbage) or roots (e.g. turnip) but their vegetative tissues would have been much less likely to have been preserved in an identifiable state than their seeds.

Prunus domestica (plum, bullace etc.) seems to have been a Roman introduction to Britain (Moffett *et al.* 1989) which was readily adopted for local cultivation. It is very plausible that there were plum orchards around Silchester. However, *P. domestica* ssp. *insititia* (bullace) spreads rapidly by suckering and can compete effectively with native hedgerow shrubs so it is also possible that it had been planted along field boundaries. *Morus nigra* (black mulberry) was also a Roman introduction to Britain, indeed the first archaeological record was from Silchester (Reid in Hope 1907, 449). Unlike plum it has only been found on a few sites, all high-status, even though mulberry can easily be grown in Britain and it has a long season of cropping in the summer. The disadvantages of mulberry are that it takes about twenty years for a tree to begin large-scale cropping, it gives a light crop in comparison to, for example, plum, and the fruit have a very short life. Perhaps there was a mulberry tree between the buildings of Insula IX.

Vitis vinifera (grape) could either have been grown locally or imported dried from the Mediterranean region (Robinson 2006, 215). *Ficus carica* (fig) was also likely to have been a Mediterranean import (Robinson 2006, 208–9, 215). Neither of these fruits is likely to have made a major contribution to the diet.

The numerous seeds of *Rubus fruticosus* agg. (blackberry) were presumably from wild fruit collected in the vicinity of the town. Neglected hedgerows and pasture experiencing thorn-scrub colonisation are likely to have been productive sources. The blackberry bushes which it has been argued grew on neglected corners of the site are not thought to have provided a major supply of fruit. The stone of *Prunus spinosa* (sloe) hinted that wild fruit could have been collected to supplement the plum crop.

The mineralised arable weed seeds were probably contaminants of cereal products which had escaped any crop cleaning and the effects of food preparation. They were not abundant and it is possible that the separation of weed seeds from grain was generally efficient.

Not all the seeds in these samples had passed through the human digestive tract. Seeds of plants of nutrient-rich neglected ground such as *Urtica dioica* (stinging nettle) were probably from vegetation growing in the vicinity of the latrines. Material likely to have been imported as fodder for domestic animals or animal-bedding also seems to have been discarded into context 5276 (pit 5251). The seeds of grassland and marsh plants were perhaps from hay, while dry *Pteridium aquilinum* (bracken) makes good bedding which is reputed to be vermin-repellent.

The results for the mineralised remains from early second-century context 5276 showed many similarities to the mineralised remains from the fourth-century latrine pit 3235 (Robinson 2006). Both latrines had faunas of fly larvae feeding on their liquid contents and gave evidence of diets rich in cereals, legumes, fruits and flavourings. They showed a romanised diet which included various species introduced to Britain by the Romans. In both cases the fruit remains suggest the consumption of some imported exotics as well as the use of local produce. The most striking difference between them is that the mineralised assemblages from the early second-century (Period 2) samples were dominated by stones of *Prunus* spp. (plum, bullace etc.) whereas the fourth-century samples were dominated by seeds and skin fragments of *Malus* sp. (apple). There were only a couple of possible *Malus* seeds from the mid-Roman samples. It seems implausible that this was the result of a simple change in food preference. The main plum season is late summer, whereas apples are mostly autumn- to winter-ripening fruit but it is not believed that the latrines had such short lives that the difference was due to seasonality. It was noted that it has recently been discovered that cultivated apple (*Malus domestica*) was derived from a Central Asian species and is not a hybrid descended from *M. sylvestris* (crab apple) (Robinson 2006, 217). It was also suggested that *M. domestica* could have been a Roman introduction to Britain but that details are uncertain. It is possible that *M. domestica* was not widely established as an orchard crop in Britain until the late Roman period.

DISCUSSION

The second- and third-century deposits of Insula IX were very unusual in having organic remains preserved by waterlogging, charring and mineralisation. Although such lines of evidence were also available from the fourth- to fifth-century contexts, the preservation was not as good and was largely restricted to seeds. Insect remains preserved by waterlogging were absent. The second- and third-century deposits were also unusual in that there were some with both mineralised and waterlogged preservation of remains. It had already been appreciated that there were biases as to what tended to be preserved by the different means (Robinson 2006, 216), these results showed unexpectedly that some robust seeds which were readily preserved by waterlogging seemed rather resistant to preservation by mineralisation.

The environment of Insula IX in the second and third centuries seems to have been very similar to that of the fourth to fifth centuries. There were again areas of waste-ground vegetation, such as stinging nettles, alongside some of the buildings but domestic animals dropping dung were also enclosed in the insula. Cut vegetation was imported for their fodder and bedding. The structural timbers of the buildings were infested with woodworm and synanthropic beetles scavenged in food-waste and old animal bedding inside the buildings. Sewage flies bred in the latrine but otherwise there do not seem to have been large accumulations of foul organic material. There was possibly an ornamental garden area with clipped box and holly bushes and it is likely that there was a honey bee colony nearby. Box has been recorded from many sites in Roman Britain, both rural and urban, for example Farmoor, Oxon. (Lambrick and Robinson 1979, 101), Claydon Pike, Glos. (Robinson 2007, 361), and York (Hall *et al.* 1980), as well as elsewhere in Silchester (Reid in Hope 1909, 485). Holly leaves have been found in a Roman well at Hunt's Hill Farm, Havering, London (Trickett 1999, 27) and at Silchester (Reid in Hope 1906, 164). Honey bee remains have been found on several rural Roman sites in Britain, for example at Claydon Pike, Glos. (Robinson 2007, 362), and were found in sufficient quantity at a site on the edge of Godmanchester, Cambs., to suggest beekeeping (Robinson, unpublished). The Romans, at least in Italy, had quite sophisticated hives which could be opened so that some comb could be harvested without the destruction of the colony (Varro, *Re Rustica* 3.16).

Just as in the fourth to fifth centuries, spelt-wheat and six-row hulled barley appear to have been the main cereals used in the insula, but the grain was being processed elsewhere. It is likely that there was large-scale storage of dehusked grain in Silchester. Evidence of grain storage has been provided by discoveries of a range of beetles such as *Oryzaephilus surinamensis* and *Sitophilus granarius*, which are serious granary pests, in other towns in Roman Britain, for example Alcester (Osborne 1971a). However, grain beetles were absent from the mid-Roman, Periods 2 to 4, samples suggesting no more than a small-scale presence of stored grain in the buildings of Insula IX. Some cereal chaff was being brought to Insula IX, perhaps for use as fodder.

The results for the mineralised remains from both the second and third and the fourth to fifth centuries drew attention to the consumption of legumes, particularly peas in the case of the former period and lentils in the latter. This aspect of the diet is likely to be under-represented in the archaeological record because their seeds are not readily preserved by waterlogging and, although they are preserved well by charring, they are less likely to come into contact with fire than grains of hulled cereals. Legumes are generally recognised as a component of the Romano-British diet but it is possible they were a more important part than previously appreciated.

The early second-century (Period 2) latrine deposits and to a lesser extent the third-century (Period 4) waterlogged well samples gave evidence for a rich range of flavourings and fruit in the diet. Such a diet was probably typical of that enjoyed by the wealthier occupants of the larger towns of Roman Britain (Veen *et al.* 2008, 25). By the mid-Roman period the diet even on low-status settlements was becoming very romanised, with non-native plants introduced by the Romans, such as coriander and plum, being cultivated and used. In addition, there was a luxury element to the diet at Silchester with the consumption of exotic fruit which, although capable of being grown in Britain, do not seem to have been widely planted, such as mulberry, and the importation of fruit unlikely to have been grown in Britain, such as fig. This luxury aspect of the diet continued until the end of Silchester as a Roman town.

The evidence from the macroscopic plant and invertebrate remains suggests that Silchester had developed a mature urban character by the second to third century. While some domestic animals were being kept in the town, a full range of agricultural activities was not occurring in Insula IX. While the majority of food was presumably being obtained from the hinterland, there were sufficient resources for a diet more varied than all but the highest-status rural settlements and there was at least a little long-distance importation of foodstuffs.

CHAPTER 17

THE POLLEN AND TRICHURID OVA FROM PIT 5251

By Petra Dark

INTRODUCTION

Pollen analysis was undertaken on waterlogged deposits in the southern half of Period 2 pit 5251, identified as a cess-pit which was filled by *c.* A.D. 125 (see Preface, p. xix). The pit lay immediately next to the east–west street and was beside, and contemporary with, ERTB 1 (FIG. 132). The samples were from the lower cess (Sample 800.6), middle calcium phosphate 'crust' (Sample 800.5) and upper cess (Sample 800.4) from the sewage layer (5276). In addition to abundant pollen grains, the samples were found to contain small numbers of whipworm eggs, which were measured to allow specific identification. The same layers were sampled by Robinson (above, Ch. 16) for macroscopic plant remains from the southern half of the pit, providing the opportunity to compare the different types of botanical evidence.

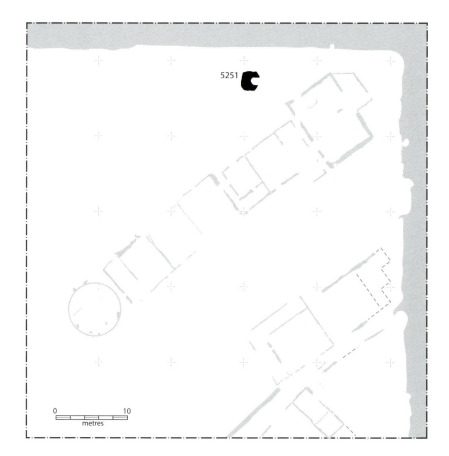

FIG. 132. Location of pit 5251 (Period 2).

METHODS

POLLEN ANALYSIS

Samples were collected during hand excavation of the pit, and sub-samples $1cm^3$ in volume were prepared for pollen analysis following standard procedures (Berglund and Ralska-Jasiewiczowa 1986). Pollen was counted using a Leica DMLB microscope at a magnification of 400x, with a magnification of 1000x for critical determinations. A minimum of 300 identifiable pollen grains and Pteridophyte (fern) spores was counted for all samples. Pollen and spores were identified using the key of Moore *et al.* (1991) and by comparison with the reference collection in the Department of Archaeology, University of Reading. Vascular plant nomenclature follows Stace (1991) and pollen and spore nomenclature follows Bennett *et al.* (1994). The criteria of Andersen (1979) were used in identification of cereal pollen. Unidentifiable deteriorated pollen grains and spores were classified according to the categories of Cushing (1967).

Pollen percentage calculations are based on a sum including all identifiable pollen grains and Pteridophyte spores (no pollen of obligate aquatics was present). Calculations for the different categories of unidentifiable pollen grains are based on the main sum plus the sum of unidentifiable grains.

TRICHURID OVA

Eggs of the genus *Trichuris* were counted from the same samples used for pollen analysis. Their numbers are expressed in relation to the main pollen sum plus sum of *Trichuris* eggs. The length and width of all eggs were determined as whipworms of different hosts are distinguishable by their size.

RESULTS

POLLEN ANALYSIS

Pollen percentages for all taxa are shown in FIG. 133. The samples contained abundant pollen, but preservation was variable and a high proportion of corroded and/or crumpled grains occurred in all samples. Most pollen grains remained identifiable, however, with total indeterminable pollen never exceeding 10 per cent, so there is no reason to believe that the assemblages have been significantly biased by poor preservation. It is likely that the pollen deterioration reflects fluctuations in the degree of waterlogging in the pit.

The composition of the pollen assemblages from all three samples is very similar. Tree pollen is sparse, reaching a maximum value of just 6 per cent of the pollen sum in the upper cess, and all samples are dominated by pollen of the Brassicaceae (cabbage) family (peaking at 52 per cent in the lower cess). This family includes many familiar native plants of cultivated and other open ground, such as garlic mustard (*Alliaria petiolata*) and shepherd's purse (*Capsella bursa-pastoris*), but also crops such as cabbage (*Brassica oleracea*) and mustard (*Sinapis alba*). The pollen grains of most members of the family are too similar to allow separate identification, so unfortunately it is uncertain whether any of the pollen represents crops. Robinson (Ch. 16) identified two seeds of *Brassica* or *Sinapis* sp. in the same deposit.

The other main taxa present are Apiaceae (carrot family) (maximum 16 per cent) and Poaceae (grasses) (maximum 18 per cent). Again, most members of these large families have pollen grains too similar to allow identification to genus or species level (although fortunately cereal pollen is an exception). The Apiaceae includes a wide range of both wild (e.g. cow parsley, *Anthriscus sylvestris*, and hogweed, *Heracleum sphondylium*) and cultivated plants occupying a variety of habitats. It includes several culinary herbs, such as coriander (*Coriandrum sativum*), dill (*Anethum graveolens*) and celery (*Apium graveolens*), all of which were represented by seeds in the same deposit (Robinson, Ch. 16). The assemblages of macroscopic plant remains were dominated by seeds classed as Apiaceae undiff., most of which resembled *Anethum graveolens*.

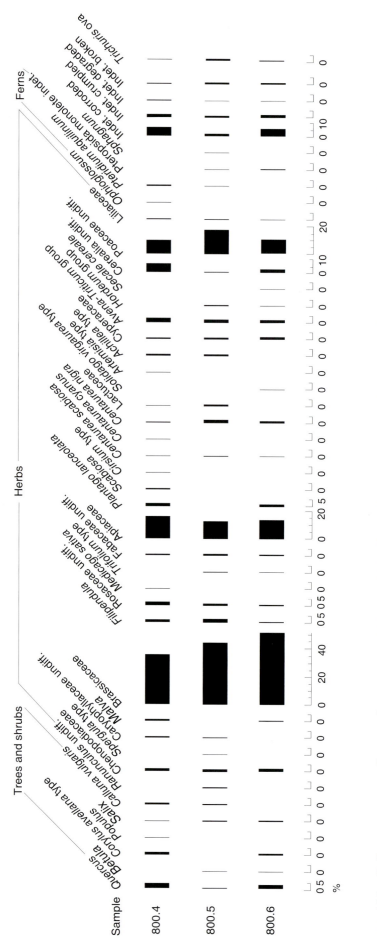

FIG. 133.   Pollen percentage diagram from context 5276, pit 5251. For pollen sums see text. Presence of Trichurid ova is also indicated.

The undifferentiated Poaceae pollen could derive from plants of a wide range of mainly open habitats, but there is also a substantial presence of cereal pollen in the deposits (peaking at almost 10 per cent of the pollen sum in the upper cess). Pollen of *Avena-Triticum* group (which includes *Avena* (oat) species and *Triticum* (wheat) species apart from *T. monococcum*) is most abundant, but *Hordeum* group (which includes *Hordeum vulgare* (barley), *T. monococcum* and a few native grasses) is also present, as well as a single pollen grain of *Secale cereale* (rye) in the lower cess. Mineralised cereal remains werc abundant in the lower part of the sewage deposit, including both spelt wheat (*Triticum spelta*) and hulled six-row barley (*Hordeum vulgare*) (Robinson, Ch. 16). Robinson reports that remains of *Triticum* were more abundant than those of *Hordeum*, and this applies to the pollen also.

Pollen of several characteristic arable weeds is present, some of which are thought to have been introduced in the late Iron Age but are seldom recorded before the Roman period (e.g. cornflower (*Centaurea cyanus*)). Common knapweed (*Centaurea nigra*) is characteristic of hay meadows, although it also occurs in other grassy places and on rough ground, where other plants represented in the pollen assemblages, including *Malva* (mallow), *Medicago sativa* (medick), *Scabiosa* (scabious) and *Centaurea scabiosa* (greater knapweed), may also be found.

TRICHURID OVA

Trichuris eggs were present in small numbers in all three samples (reaching a maximum of 1.4 per cent of the pollen sum in the middle cess) (FIG. 133). Preservation was generally good, but all eggs lacked their polar plugs (FIG. 134). The eggs range from 41–49 μm in length and 24–31 μm in width.

Given the context of the eggs, attribution to the human whipworm, *T. trichiura*, seems a virtual certainty, but there are several species of whipworm that infect other mammals, and it is possible

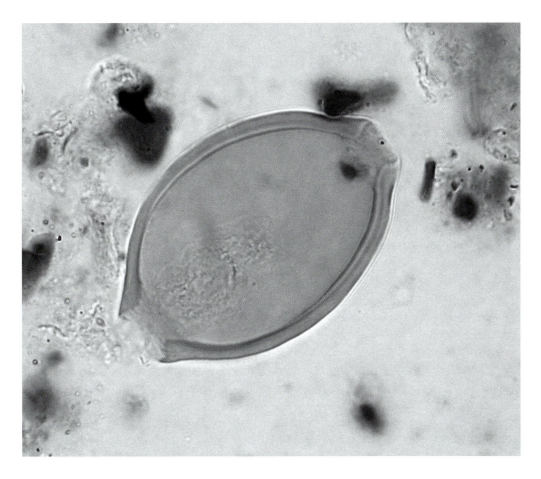

FIG. 134.   Egg of human whipworm (*Trichuris trichiura*) from context 5276.

that dung of domestic animals may have been deposited in the pit as well as human waste. These include dogs (infected by *T. vulpis*), cattle (*T. ovis* and *T. globulosa*), sheep (*T. ovis*), and pigs (*T. suis*). Eggs of the different species of *Trichuris* are morphologically similar but differ to varying degrees in size. Beer (1976) provides detailed measurements for modern eggs of *T. trichiura* and *T. suis*. *T. trichiura* eggs have a mean length without polar plugs of 49.8 μm (range 45.3–56.0 μm), and width of 25.5 μm (range 23.1–28.7 μm), while *T. suis* eggs have a mean length of 51.5 μm (range 35.1–62.8 μm) and width of 30.1 μm (range 26.8–34.5 μm). Thus *T. trichiura* eggs are, on average, slightly smaller than those of *T. suis*, but the size ranges overlap. The eggs of *Trichuris* species of other domesticated and wild mammals are generally larger than those of *T. trichiura* and *T. suis*. For example, Thienpoint *et al.* (1979) give size ranges of 70–80 μm length (with polar plugs) and 30–42 μm width for *T. ovis*, and 70–90 μm length and 32–41 μm width for *T. vulpis*.

Consideration of the size of the eggs from Silchester must take account of the fact that they were from samples subjected to the chemical treatments used for pollen preparation, and mounted in glycerine jelly. These procedures are known to cause some shrinkage of *Trichuris* eggs. Working on samples from Viking Age York, Hall *et al.* (1983) found that *T. trichiura* eggs untreated and mounted in water had a mean length without polar plugs of 55.3 μm (range 48.1–61.6 μm) and width of 26.6 μm (range 23.1–30.8 μm), while those subjected to chemical pollen preparation procedures and mounted in glycerine jelly had a mean length of 41.2 μm (range 34.7–47.0 μm) and width of 22.1 μm (range 17.7–30.0 μm). The Silchester eggs are thus similar in size to the treated *T. trichiura* eggs and, even allowing for shrinkage, would seem to be too small to derive from whipworms of dogs or ruminants. Given their size, the eggs are almost certainly all from whipworm of humans.

INTERPRETATION

The key factor in interpreting the pollen assemblages is consideration of the sources of pollen to the deposits. The main possibilities are:

1. Pollen that has passed through the digestive tract after ingestion with food. Greig (1994) notes that significant amounts of pollen may persist in many plant materials after the flowers have disappeared, including various fruits, legumes and dried herbs.
2. Pollen from plants brought to the town for various purposes, e.g. cereals and other plant foods, hay for animal fodder or bedding, straw for thatch, and deposited in the pit through various routes.
3. Pollen from plants growing on disturbed ground or garden/horticultural plots within the town.
4. Pollen from plants growing at varying distances outside the town.

Previous pollen assemblages from latrine fills (most examples of which have been medieval or later in date) have often been found to be dominated by cereal pollen, accompanied by macroscopic remains of cereals, suggesting that much of their pollen content may be from food (Greig 1994). Food is the most likely source of much of the pollen in the Silchester pit also, although cereal pollen was not the most abundant pollen type here. Other possible sources for the cereal pollen include pollen dispersed by threshing (Robinson and Hubbard 1977), pollen present in straw or animal dung which might have been dumped in the latrine, or even pollen derived from run-off from thatch on adjacent buildings. With regard to the first of these possibilities, Robinson (Ch. 16) suggests, on the basis of the macroscopic plant remains, that cereal grain was being processed elsewhere. The use of hay and straw in the town might account for the pollen of hay meadow plants and arable weeds.

As noted above, the abundant Apiaceae pollen is mirrored by the dominance of the assemblages of macroscopic plant remains by seeds closely resembling those of dill, suggesting that this was a popular culinary herb. The Brassicaceae pollen can probably also be attributed to culinary use of plants of this family, such as cabbage and mustard. Other pollen types that may derive largely from food are Rosaceae undiff. and Fabaceae undiff. The former may relate to the large number of blackberry (*Rubus fruticosus* agg.) seeds and plum (*Prunus* spp.) stones in the deposits, and the latter to the peas (*Pisum sativum*). While pollen of all of these potential food plants is perhaps most likely to have reached the pit in sewage, another possibility is that kitchen waste from food preparation was deposited in the pit.

The records of pollen of *Malva* (mallow) are interesting, as this plant is rarely represented in off-site pollen sequences. *Malva* pollen was also recorded in sewage deposits from the Roman fort at Bearsden, Scotland (Knights *et al.* 1983), and Dickson and Dickson (2000) suggest that its presence there may reflect a medicinal use.

The very low tree pollen frequencies from the Silchester cess-pit need not be indicative of limited woodland around the town, as the pollen assemblages probably contain very little pollen deposited aerially from outside its walls. Apart from pollen derived from plant foods, most of the herbaceous pollen types in the assemblages, including Chenopodiaceae (goosefoot family) and *Plantago lanceolata* (ribwort plantain), probably represent plants growing on patches of disturbed ground within the town.

Assuming that much of the pollen in the sewage deposit is indeed from food, it is tempting to consider whether the minor differences between samples (such as the apparent decline in abundance of Brassicaceae, and increase of Rosaceae, towards the top of the layer) may represent changes in food consumption over time. However, it is likely that the pit was periodically cleared out (M.G. Fulford, pers. comm.), so the sewage layer analysed may have accumulated over a very short period of time. Furthermore, many factors other than diet might be responsible for variability between samples, such as use of the pit by different households, and variation in the relative abundance of different types of materials (e.g. waste from food processing, floor sweepings etc.) deposited in the pit.

Differences between the pollen assemblages from different parts of context 5276 might be expected due to variation in the nature of the sediment and degree of waterlogging within the layer. Robinson (Ch. 16) found considerable variation in the preservation of macroscopic plant remains, with the best preservation in the basal part of the context, but the pollen preservation is less variable and unlikely to have caused significant differences in assemblage composition.

DISCUSSION AND CONCLUSIONS

The availability of both pollen and macroscopic plant remains from the same contexts at Silchester has provided an interesting (and unusual) opportunity to compare the two types of evidence. They are complementary because of differences in source areas, potential for preservation, and level of identification possible. While pollen grains are, in many cases, less closely identifiable than seeds, where pollen can be identified to species level it has the potential to indicate the presence of plant taxa missing from the macroscopic assemblages. An example of this at Silchester is rye (*Secale cereale*), which is absent from the assemblages of macroscopic plant remains from the pit, but which is represented by a single pollen grain from the lower cess. Similarly, pollen grains, but not seeds, of cornflower (*Centaurea cyanus*) and greater knapweed (*C. scabiosa*) were present.

As much of the pollen from the pit is likely to derive from food, or from the immediate area around the pit, the assemblages shed little light on the broader environment of the town in the mid-Roman period. The basal part of the pollen sequence analysed by Keith-Lucas (1984) from waterlogged deposits below the town rampart may be contemporary with the deposits analysed here. There the assemblages were dominated by grass pollen, indicating substantially open conditions, but pollen of oak (*Quercus*), hazel (*Corylus avellana*) and alder (*Alnus glutinosa*) together comprised over 25 per cent of the pollen sum in one sample, suggesting the presence of some local woodland (Keith-Lucas 1984). Interestingly, the pollen type dominant in the cess-pit samples, Brassicaceae, was absent from the basal part of the rampart sequence, and pollen of Apiaceae did not exceed 2 per cent of the pollen sum. This supports the suggestion that much of the pollen of these groups in the sewage deposit is derived from food.

The abundant pollen of Brassicaceae and Apiaceae suggests that both plant groups made a significant contribution to the diet at Silchester, and in the case of the Apiaceae the evidence from the macroscopic plant remains makes it possible to suggest that much of the pollen may derive from dill. Macroscopic remains of dill have been found quite frequently on Roman-period sites in Britain, including Colchester (Murphy 1984), York (Hall and Kenward 1990), and Bearsden (Dickson and Dickson 2000), and it was evidently a popular and widely used culinary herb. The plant could have been grown locally at Silchester, perhaps even within the town.

The origin of the Brassicaceae pollen is less certain, as few seeds of this family were present. Mustard and cabbage are both possible, providing flavouring and leafy vegetables respectively, and could also have been grown locally. The great abundance of Brassicaceae pollen may indicate that shoots either close to or actually flowering were consumed. Flowering shoots of several native members of the family are edible, including watercress (*Rorippa nasturtium-aquaticum*) and charlock (*Sinapis arvensis*), but it is also possible that a vegetable similar to broccoli was available (Robinson, pers. comm.).

The presence of whipworm eggs in the deposits at Silchester adds strength to the interpretation of the pit as a cess-pit, although this was hardly in doubt in view of the character of the deposit and presence of calcium phosphate mineralised plant remains. Whipworm infection was probably commonplace in the human population of the Roman period. The eggs have been quite widely recorded in prehistoric and later sites where coprolites and/or cess deposits are preserved: other examples from Roman Britain include the forts at Bearsden (Knights *et al*. 1983) and Carlisle (Jones and Hutchinson 1991) and the *colonia* at York (Hall and Kenward 1990).

CHAPTER 18

THE MID-ROMAN PITS IN CONTEXT

By Hella Eckardt

The late Roman occupation of Insula IX was characterised by large groups of pits and wells located in the backyards of properties, and in many cases attributable to specific houses. This offered an opportunity to examine the spatial distribution of 'special' deposits such as dogs and infants, but also to compare the proportions of artefact categories such as building materials, animal bones and pottery across the insula, and within selected pits and wells (Eckardt 2006). The results showed some striking differences between the northern and southern half of the insula in particular, with proportionally much more animal bone deposited in the pits to the south of the main fence-line. Analysis also highlighted the potential of exploring pit assemblages in detail, by not just identifying features that contained unusual deposits, but also studying individual layers within those pits. Such an approach makes use of the meticulously recorded stratigraphic and finds information, and adds a more detailed and temporal dimension to our understanding of pit use. It also, however, highlights the difficulty of defining 'ritual' deposits in wells and pits by examining associated material, which, for example, demonstrated that complete dog carcasses were deposited with other animal waste, or infants in fills that also contained what appears to be rubbish. The study of the late Roman pits thus illustrated both the potential and the difficulty of mapping and understanding structured deposition in the Roman period, a theme that will be developed below.

This chapter broadly follows the structure used for the comparative section in the late Roman report, but there are fewer pits, and it is much harder to attribute them to specific properties. Much of the discussion will focus on Period 4, as most of the cut features are attributed to that phase.

CHARACTER AND USE OF PITS

The discussion of excavated features has already covered cut features in some detail (above, Ch. 2), and only a brief summary is given here. In Period 3, we have identified three pits and two wells. Presumably associated with MRTB 1/ERTB 1 (former ERTB 4) is cess-pit 4835, located near the intersection of the streets in the north-east corner of the insula. Probably associated with MB 1 and/or MB 2, and located in the south-eastern area of the excavation, are pit 5039, the slumps into pit 6290, and well 5693. Finally, there is an earlier well used as a pit in Period 3 (2234); this feature is located to the north-west of the main buildings, and probably belongs to a separate property located outside of the excavated area.

In Period 4, all the major cut features are located to the south-east of MB 3, and are associated with that building, and/or with the more ephemeral MRTBs 4 and 5. There are two certain wells (5735 and 1750), with well 1750 already partially excavated by the Victorians. Pits 3102 and 3406 may have functioned initially as wells, while 2601 and 2434 are certainly pits, with the latter used as a cess-pit.

Table 26 records the depths, number of fills, and any special deposits found within these pits and wells. The table suggests use as a cess-pit where mineralised deposits were recorded, using a '?' to indicate field observations not supported by the plant remains. It is clearly difficult to define 'special deposits' within archaeological contexts, but, as for the late Roman material, it is possible to map the distribution of infants, complete pottery vessels and dogs. The articulated remains of wild animals have been added as a new category for this period.

Complete, and almost complete, pottery vessels were found in five of the eleven cut features examined here (FIG. 135). Fulford and Timby (2001) have suggested ritual deposition for complete pierced vessels which may represent the symbolic 'killing' of a vessel while at the same time allowing for the gradual release of fluid offerings. In this assemblage, complete vessels such as the worn mortarium from the slumps into pit 6290 and the Nene Valley colour-coated box-lid from pit/well 3406 may represent offerings, or discarded household utensils. Fills within pits and wells may have been subject to considerable disturbance and compression, and that may explain 'almost complete' pottery vessels such as the dish from pit 4835, the three flagons from well 2234 and the BB1 jar from pit/well 3406. It is also possible that partial vessels (such as the base fragment from pit 4835 and the flagon necks from pit 5039) represent *pars pro toto* offerings. Alternatively, of course, damaged vessels may simply have been discarded as rubbish.

Jane Timby (above, Ch. 8) has explored other aspects of the pottery assemblage, such as the relative proportions of imports and functional categories. An interesting pattern to pick up here is the emphasis on drinking vessels amongst the pottery contained in well 5735; this may represent the disposal of pottery relating to fluid storage and consumption in a watery feature. Such an association of specific pottery forms is perhaps mirrored in the three almost complete flagons from well 2234, but the sample is too small for certain conclusions, and flagon necks were also recorded from a pit (5039). Complete and almost complete pottery vessels were recorded from four Period 3 and one Period 4 features, but the sample is too small to suggest a trend; there is no apparent spatial patterning.

In contrast to the late Roman period, none of the infants recorded from mid-Roman features were found in pits or wells (FIG. 109). Parts of the skull, clavicle and ribs of an infant aged 38–42 weeks were found in context 4472, the fill of a small grave cut (4516). This burial is located

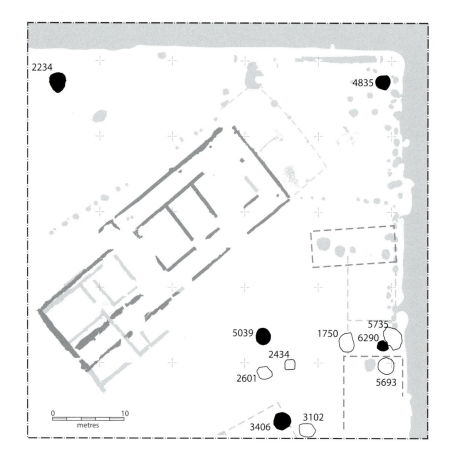

FIG. 135. Pits with complete or near complete pots (Periods 3 and 4).

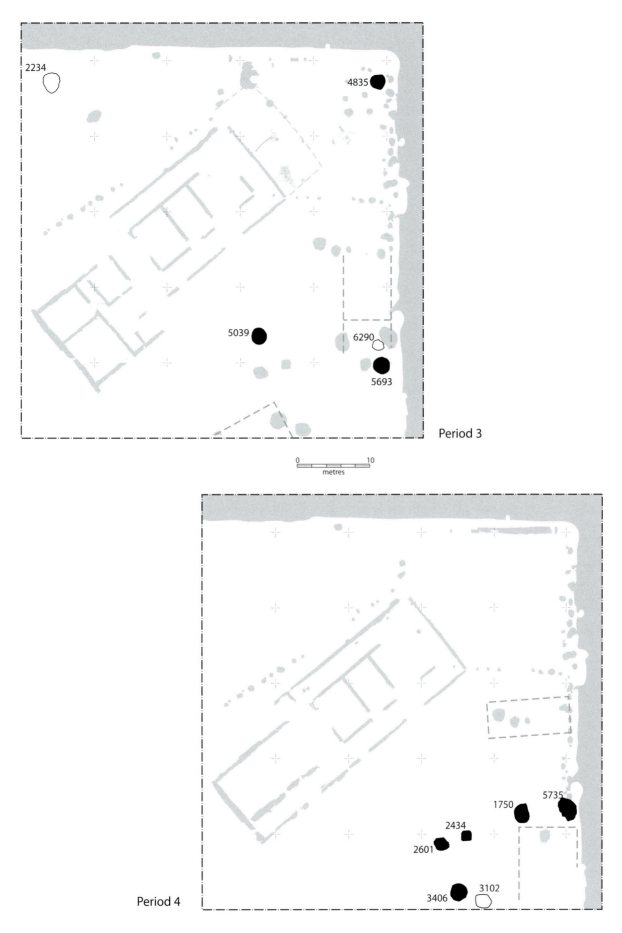

FIG. 136. Pits with dog remains (Periods 3 and 4).

adjacent to a beam slot, possibly indicating a timber building (MRTB 2), in the occupation deposits close to the southern edge of the excavation trench (Object 701). The left humerus of a premature infant was found in the nearby deposit 4475.

Dog remains were recovered from pits, wells and occupation layers (Clark, above, Ch. 14) (FIG. 136). These usually consist of fragmentary bones, and while two or more individuals are represented in five pits and wells, only the neighbouring pits 2434 and 2601 contained more than 50 fragments, representing at least three dogs. Articulated skeletons have been interpreted as ritual deposits (cf. Eckardt 2006, 227–8, with further references) and Black (2008, 1–8) has recently argued that the deposition of dogs and vessels in pits, wells or shafts may have been associated with the god Sucellos. He interprets the dog as representing the devouring and transforming nature of this god, rather than any healing properties. However, with the exception of the curled up carcass in pit 2601 and the skull in pit 4835, there are no other articulated skeletons, or complete skulls, from the mid-Roman features. This can be contrasted with the late Roman pits, where three pits contained the articulated remains of multiple dogs. These three pits were all located in the southern half of the site, and possibly associated with Building 1 (3235 and 3251) and Building 5 (1707). These pits also yielded infant remains and, in two cases, complete pots; closer analysis did, however, demonstrate that these deposits did not necessarily occur within the same layers.

The detailed stratigraphy of selected pits containing dogs will be examined below, but it should be noted here that there appears to be no temporal or spatial patterning, or association with specific buildings, in the deposition of dog remains in the mid-Roman phases. They also occur in both pits and wells, including cess-pits. While there are fewer mid-Roman pits, this discussion includes all substantial features, and the relative rarity of articulated remains may thus reflect a change in depositional practice rather than an accident of survival and recording. It may also relate to the changing management and exploitation of the canine population. Clark (2006, 189–95) noted that while some of the animals had been mistreated and killed, indications of butchery in the late Roman assemblage were few. By contrast, there is considerable evidence for the skinning of dogs in the mid-Roman assemblage (Clark, above, Ch. 14), perhaps suggesting that dog remains were much more intensively processed in the mid-Roman period, and perhaps not perceived to have the same ritual importance as in the late Roman period. It is striking that the only pit to yield an almost complete carcass (2601) also contained the unusual folding-knife depicting two mating dogs (see below for further discussion and Crummy, Ch. 6).

The apparent use of dog furs may also provide an explanation for the presence of badger remains in mid-Roman pits and features, in particular the deposition of two carcasses in pit 2434. While it is possible that badgers were killed as pests, it seems more likely that they were trapped for fur. That badger fur was valued in the Iron Age is demonstrated by its use to cover the elaborate bronze couch of the Hochdorf burial (Green 1992, 53; Biel 1985, 117–18). Badger remains occur at Danebury, where the deposition of a young fox and badger in the same fill within a pit was interpreted as a special deposit (Grant 1984, 526; Grant 1991, 478; cf. Cunliffe 1986, 126–35). Other wild animals are relatively rare in the Silchester pits (FIG. 137), but Ingrem (Ch. 13) also highlights the deposition of raven remains in mid-Roman features.

Ravens are striking birds, and their presence at Silchester, especially in pit 2601 and well 1750, may not simply signify the disposal of food waste or vermin, but again relate to ritual practices. Ravens may have been eaten, or hunted because they threatened crops (Green 1992, 52), or even attacked young lambs (Luff 1982, 63). Ravens are omnivorous birds, well suited to scavenging amongst urban debris, and their 'slow, low take-off flight means ravens are especially vulnerable to target practice' (Parker 1988, 218). Ravens can be kept well in captivity if taken young, and may have been valued for their ability to mimic human speech. Toynbee (1973, 273–5) discusses a number of literary sources recording Roman fascination with their ability to talk, most famously the story about a raven trained to greet the emperor Augustus after his victory at Actium (Macrobius, *Satires* 2.4.29, 30).

However, ritual significance has been suggested for both the Iron Age and the Roman period, with subtly changing symbolic meaning attached to these birds. Beliefs about the supernatural association of ravens may reach as far back as the Bronze Age (Needham and Bowman 2005,

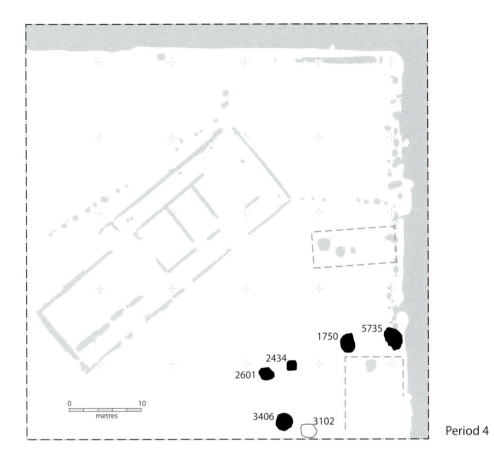

FIG. 137. Pits with the remains of wild animals (Period 4).

119–22). For Celtic Europe, Green (1992, 87–9, 177–81, fig. 4.17) discusses the association of ravens, who scavenge on dead flesh, with death and war, citing examples such as the third/second-century B.C. helmet from Ciumeşti in Romania crowned by a raven with flapping wings. The association with death is also reflected in later Irish vernacular tales, where ravens are often perceived to predict the future, acting as birds of omen and harbingers of doom (cf. Ross 1967, 242–70).

Archaeologically, ravens are strongly represented in Iron Age pits within, for example, the Hampshire hillforts of Danebury and Winklebury. At Danebury, it has been suggested that ravens may have nested on the site, 'frequenting the rubbish dumps and picking at carcasses' (Coy 1984, 530), and their deposition in pits may relate to other ritual deposits of animals in pits on that site (Grant 1984, 533–43; Serjeantson 1991, 479–81; cf. Cunliffe 1986, 158–9; Hill 1995, 29, 63–4). Even more strikingly, a raven was found with spread wings at the bottom of a pit at Winklebury, which also contained the complete carcass of a pig (Wait 1985, 138; Hill 1995, fig. 2.1).

Ravens continued to be deposited in striking ways in the Romano-British period (cf. Parker 1988, 206–9). A dry well associated with the Romano-Celtic temple at Jordan Hill in Dorset contained, amongst other structured deposits, pairs of tiles, between each of which were a coin and a bird skeleton, with raven, crow, buzzard and starling represented (Ross 1968, 266–7). On several sites, unusual deposits of raven are also associated with dog remains, as in our mid-Roman pits. At Portchester the fourth-century pit 236 contained a complete Great Northern Diver as well as two ravens, numerous other birds and domesticated animals, with a noticeable concentration of complete or almost complete skulls of cattle, sheep, pig and dog (Cunliffe 1975, 172–6). Eastham (1975, 412–14) suggests that the Great Northern Diver may represent an accidental catch while the ravens may have been kept as pets, but does not comment on the fact that they are all associated in the same pit. At Sheepen pit 120, dated to A.D. 49–61, produced a 'curious assortment of bones', including two nearly complete raven skeletons, the remains of two white tailed eagles, a complete dog skeleton and a puppy (Luff 1982, 63). At Dunstable two human skeletons had been buried amongst the subsiding top fills of a 9m-deep shaft, interpreted in the report as a well re-used as a cess-pit, and dated to the first half of the second century A.D. (Mathews *et al.* 1981, 63–73). Amongst the fills was the skeleton of a sea eagle, found in a layer with parts of a raven, several small rodents, a frog and a water vole. The excavators interpret this assemblage as 'the remains of food given to a captured eagle, or they may have been in the bird's stomach' (Mathews *et al.* 1981, 67). The ritual associations of this feature are, however, strengthened by the presence of an infant burial and several complete dog and puppy skeletons in other layers within this shaft.

Raven remains were recorded from the forum-basilica excavation at Silchester (Serjeantson 2000, 485–6), with a raven skeleton from an Iron Age feature interpreted as possibly ritual in nature. Ravens were also deposited in late Roman pits in Insula IX, but occur only in the pit group associated with Building 1 (Late Roman Object 116); in particular raven and jackdaw remains are concentrated in pit 3251 (cf. Ingrem 2006, 174, tables 32a–c). This is a pit that also contained infant, cat and articulated dog remains, and a complete pottery vessel (Eckardt 2006, 242–4).

These finds from Romano-British contexts suggest that ravens continued to have ritual significance, with the deposition in pits and wells indicating a chthonic motif, perhaps harking back to the association with death and the underworld apparent in Celtic beliefs (Green 1992, 211). In the Roman world ravens are also credited with prophetic powers, acting as oracles and associated with a variety of deities (Toynbee 1973, 273–5). The raven was sacred to Apollo and Helios, and also appears on Mithras reliefs (ibid., 275).

Black (2008, 5–8) also discusses the finds of ravens from Roman Britain, and notes that ravens are the bird of the Gaulish Romano-Celtic Nantosuelta, the consort of Sucellos (cf. Ross 1967, 244–6, figs 151–2). Ravens are also found with the god Lugos (ibid., 249–56, fig. 154), and other healing and underworld deities (Green 1989, 61–9, fig. 25). Given the association of ravens with dogs in structured pit deposits, a relief from Moux, Burgundy, is of particular interest. This depicts a bearded god standing with a dog at his feet and a raven on each shoulder (Green 1992, 212, fig. 7.10; Deyts 1976, no. 160).

While ravens are clearly significant in Roman Britain and beyond, we again come up against the difficulty of conclusively proving ritual deposition, as opposed to the structured deposition of unusual material (see below). Possible links between ravens and dogs will be explored below through the detailed examination of selected pits.

CHRONOLOGY OF PITS

For the late Roman pit assemblages, it was possible to map the distribution of not only coins, but also dated pottery (Eckardt 2006, 228–33, figs 98–103). For the mid-Roman phases, there are far fewer coins, and almost none contemporary with the occupation come from pits. The only exception is an unworn coin of Carausius (A.D. 287–93) that came from the uppermost fill (2602) of pit 2434, which also contained quantities of building material dumped prior to the construction of Late Roman Building 1, whose foundations overlay the pit. This coin not only provides a *terminus post quem* for the construction of that late Roman building (cf. Fulford *et al.* 2006, 18–19), but also a *terminus ante quem* for the abandonment of well 1750, which lies underneath the building. Radiocarbon dating suggests that the construction of well 1750 should be in the period of 202–240 cal AD (Galimberti *et al.* 2004, 920–1, see above, pp. 44–6). A combination of pottery dating and stratigraphic relationships in Period 4 then allows us to suggest a chronological sequence, with well 5735 the earliest, followed by 1750 (of which only the earliest contexts were undisturbed by Victorian excavations), then 2601, 3102, 3406 and finally 2434 (see pp. 41–51 above).

A recurring feature of both the layers and pits is the amount of residual material, noted both for pottery and small finds (see Chs 6 & 8 above), a characteristic that prevents further spatial analysis.

PIT ASSEMBLAGE COMPOSITION

For the late Roman report, the quantities of tile, pottery, bone, slag and nails were compared for each group of pits (Eckardt 2006, figs 105–109). As pit size and depth clearly have an impact on the amounts of material contained within a feature, pit volumes were calculated (Eckardt 2006, 236). For this purpose, pits are described as truncated cones, and volumes calculated using three basic parameters: the top diameter, the bottom diameter, and the depth (see Table 26). Finds can then be shown as estimated densities, and for the late Roman pit groups there were some interesting trends. As expected, tile was by far the most common material by weight, and was spread relatively evenly across the site; it was often dumped in upper fills, presumably to seal pits and wells prior to further building activity. By contrast, nails and slag occurred in much smaller quantities, with some spatial patterning. Perhaps the most striking result for the late Roman features was the differential deposition of domestic waste, namely pottery and animal bone. Analysis demonstrated that proportionally much more animal bone was deposited in the features associated with the buildings in the southern half of the excavated area (Eckardt 2006, figs 107 and 109).

For the mid-Roman assemblage, the dataset is much smaller, and there are no clear-cut spatial groupings of pits and wells. It is, however, possible to compare Period 3 features with those from Period 4, and to contrast the use of wells with that of pits. In the graphs that follow, pits (P) and wells (W) are distinguished, and features are shown in the same order as in Table 26 below. Pits/wells 4835, 5039, 6290, 5693 and 2234 belong to Period 3, the remainder to Period 4.

Ceramic building material is so dominant by weight, that it should be examined separately from domestic waste. While dominating assemblages in most features, tile is especially strongly represented in two features, pits 4835 and 2434 (FIG. 138a). Pit 4835 is located at the street intersection in the north-eastern corner, making it potentially an easily accessible site for the dumping of tile from anywhere in Silchester. On the other hand, and especially if the street frontage was fenced, the tile may be derived from earlier tiled structures within the insula. The tile is largely derived from two middle fills (5873 and 5867), with smaller quantities in the top fills (5821 and 4862); this may represent opportunistic disposal of unwanted building material rather than a sealing deposit.

Pit 2434 is located to the south-east of MB 3, and to the west of the potential building MRTB 4 in the south-eastern corner of the excavated area. There is no indication from where the ceramic building material is derived. The ceramic building material is largely from the uppermost fill (2602), where it appears to have been dumped prior to the construction of Late Roman Building 1 whose foundations overlay the pit. This context also included an unworn coin of Carausius (see above).

FIG. 138a also illustrates the deposition of stone; this is presumably derived from nearby demolished buildings and thus similar to the ceramic building material discussed so far. Stone occurs more commonly in Period 4 features, in particular in the neighbouring pits 2601 and 2434 to the south-east of MB 3. The especially strong showing of stone and tile in pit 2434 reflects the deliberate dumping of building material.

It is interesting that not that much tile was recovered from the mid-Roman wells, in contrast to the late Roman pattern (cf. Eckardt 2006, 234).

Other than tile, the bulk of the fills is made up of domestic waste, in particular broken pottery vessels and animal bone. FIG. 138b illustrates that pottery is generally more strongly represented than animal bone, with only pit/well 3102 and well 1750 containing noticeably more animal bone than pottery. Both are located in the south-eastern part of the insula, but not immediately next to each other. It is interesting to note that the two pits with very large amounts of tile (4835 and 2434, see above) are not dominated by pottery, but contain relatively similar quantities of pottery and animal bone. Does this indicate that bulky and 'harder' material was specifically selected to fill and seal these features? There are no clear-cut differences between Period 3 and Period 4, apart from a slight increase in the quantities of animal bone deposited.

The deposition of nails (FIG. 138c) may relate to casual loss, or the dismantling and disposal of timber structures, with wood deposited in wells and pits without the prior removal of structural

TABLE 26. 'SPECIAL' DEPOSITS IN PITS AND WELLS IN PERIODS 3 AND 4

Pit/Well	No. of fills	Depth	Cess	Special deposits: Objects	Special deposits: Dogs	Special deposits incl. wild animals
Pit 4835	14	1.75m	Yes	1 almost complete dish, 1 jar base	Remains of, including skull fragment. 7 fragments altogether including neonate humerus	
Pit 5039	15	1.65m	Yes?	Part of jar, flagon necks	Remains of ?1 dog; 3 fragments, 2 with skinning marks	
Pit 6290 (excavation not complete)	8	2.5m		Complete mortarium		Oyster dump
Well 5693	13	2.2m		Mirror fragment	Remains of 2 dogs concentrated in context 6300; 16 fragments, one with skinning marks	
Well 2234	32	3m		3 almost complete flagons		
Well 5735	9	2.2m		Writing-tablet, bucket handle, foot jug handle	Remains of 1 dog, 6 fragments, skinning marks	red deer, hare, rodent and goose bones, but no complete carcasses
Well 1750 (partial Victorian excavation)	4 un-disturbed lower fills	1.5m			Remains of 2 dogs, including articulated vertebrae and well-healed tibia fracture. 8 fragments	Faunal assemblage dominated by birds, including raven; some red deer bone
Pit/well 3102	14	2.75m	Yes?		1 fragment	
Pit/well 3406	10	2.8m		Complete Nene Valley lid, most of BB1 jar, substantial parts of other jars. Bead and gold wire, shale vessels, bone hairpins, shoes?	Remains from at least 2 dogs, plus neonate radius. 28 fragments, mainly from context 4290. Skinning marks on 2 bones	Partial cattle skull; substantial representation of galliform bone
Pit 2601	7	1.45m	Yes?	Dog folding-knife	Complete carcass of young, curled up dog; remains of 2 further dogs. 56 fragments	Partial raven skeletons
Pit 2434	6	1.8m	Yes	CBM dump; bead, bone hairpin, shale armlet	Remains of 3 dogs, and 2 neonate dog bones. 86 fragments	2 partial badger skeletons; red deer antler pieces

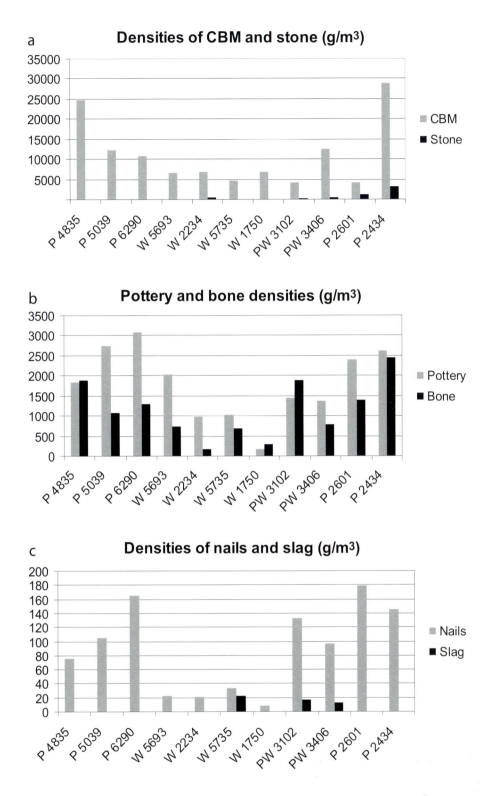

FIG. 138. Densities of (a) cbm and stone, (b) pottery and bone, and (c) nails and slags from pits and wells of Periods 3 and 4.

nails. Slag relates to metalworking, although as with all material deposited in cut features, it is not possible to say whether this occurred in the immediate vicinity of the pit or well. Nails appear to be more common in pits as opposed to wells, perhaps reflecting the disposal of decaying timber.

Slag only occurs in Period 4 cut features, a finding echoing the less frequent occurrence of

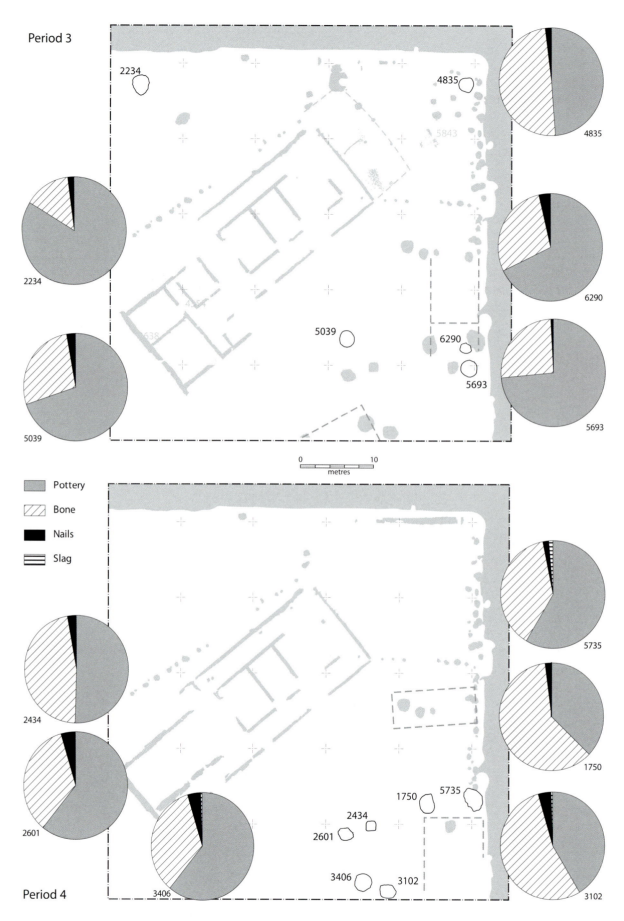

FIG. 139. Proportional representation of principal categories of finds from pits and wells of Periods 3 and 4.

slag in Period 3 layers (Tootell, above, Ch. 11). However, hammerscale and microscopic slag were recovered from pits 5039 and 6290. For Period 4, three cut features contained slag. Well 5735 is located immediately next to the north–south street, and adjacent, too, to the putative building MRTB 4 in the south-eastern corner of the excavation. The neighbouring pits/wells 3102 and 3406 are located just to its west, perhaps suggesting that one of the functions of this elusive structure was as a workshop, perhaps servicing MB 3, the structure with which most of the metalworking evidence was associated (Tootell, above, Ch. 11).

We can map the proportional representation of domestic waste in individual pits and wells (FIG. 139). This reiterates the point that in Period 3 both pit and well assemblages are dominated by pottery vessels, with the exception of pit 4835 in the north-east corner of the insula. In Period 4, animal bone is generally more strongly represented, perhaps indicating a change in disposal practices for butchery and food waste. Well 1750, which was already almost totally excavated by the Victorians, should perhaps be ignored, but it is interesting that the other two Period 4 features with a high proportion of animal bone (2434 and 3102) are located immediately to the west of the possible workshop/service building MRTB 4 in the south-eastern corner of the excavation. The spatial patterning is, however, not as marked as it was for the late Roman period, where pits containing relatively large amounts of animal bone clustered in the southern part of the site, and appeared to be associated with the main masonry buildings (cf. Eckardt 2006, fig. 109). It remains to be seen whether these more subtle variations will be echoed in the early Roman and late Iron Age pits.

SELECTED PITS IN DETAIL

As for the Late Roman report, three pits and wells (2601, 5735 and 2434), distinguished by the presence of what appear to be 'special' deposits, were selected for more detailed analysis (cf. Eckardt 2006, 238–44). The overall assemblage composition for each feature is already illustrated in FIGS 138–9 above, but here, first, the distribution of material across fills and, secondly, the composition of selected fills, in particular those containing 'unusual' finds, will be examined. In the bar charts, fills are illustrated with the topmost fill to the left, running towards the basal fill on the right.

PIT 2601

This probable cess-pit contained an articulated dog skeleton and the ivory folding-knife depicting two mating dogs (FIG. 59, pp. 49–50), and represents perhaps the clearest example amongst the mid-Roman pits of structured deposition. We do not have all the material originally deposited in this pit as its fills were truncated and effectively bisected by the construction of Late Roman Building 1. It is dated to Period 4.

FIGS 140–141 illustrate the deposition of ceramic building material across fills; this is uneven, with most of this bulky material dumped in the middle fills 2623 and 2762. Fill 2762 also contained a relatively large amount of pottery, while most other fills have a more even mixture of pottery and animal bone. Overall, jars predominate in the assemblage and drinking vessels are not significantly represented. Amongst the upper fills several cross-joins between sherds from different contexts were noted, suggesting rapid infill of the pit. Animal bone occurs in most fills, but only context 2758 has more animal bone than pottery. The partial skeleton of a dog, probably originally deposited as a complete carcass, was found in context 2622, which also contained the remains of further dogs. Fills 2623 and 2762 also contained dog remains. Partial raven skeletons were found in fill 2762.

No slag was recovered from pit 2601, and there is a relatively even scattering of nails throughout the fills. Stone is concentrated in fill 2623, which also contained very large amounts of tile, suggesting deliberate dumping.

In terms of small finds, the most outstanding find from this pit, and indeed the site, is a folding-knife or razor with an ivory handle in the form of two coupling dogs (FIGS 43 and 59; above, pp. 110–13; SF 1734). This was found in context 2622, which also contained the articulated dog

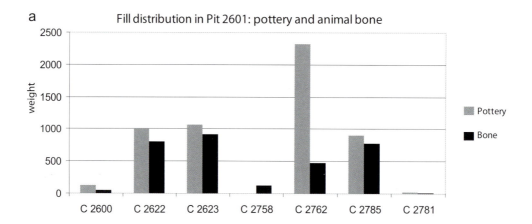

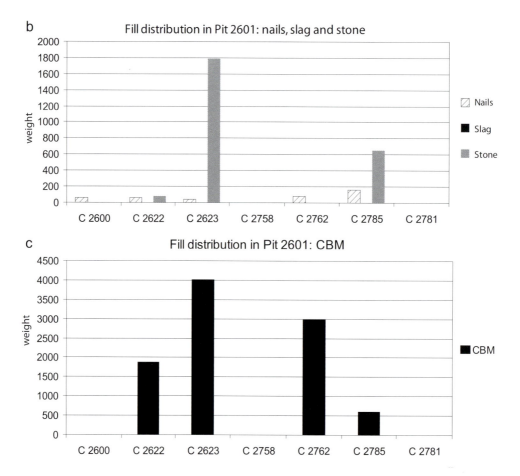

FIG. 140. Weights of (a) pottery and animal bone, (b) nails, slag and stone, and (c) cbm from each context of Period 4 pit 2601.

skeleton. The other small find of note from this pit is a Republican silver coin dated to 55 B.C. (SF 02431) in context 2623.

FIGS 140–141 illustrate that fill 2622, so outstanding in terms of the knife and dog skeleton, is not very different from the fills preceding it in terms of the overall representation of finds. There are of course differences, such as the strong showing of stone in fill 2623, and the varying amounts of pottery, but it would be difficult to argue that 2622 is different in terms of the material deposited with the dog carcass and knife. One interesting pattern to emerge is that 2623 and especially 2762 contain relatively little animal bone other than the dog and raven remains.

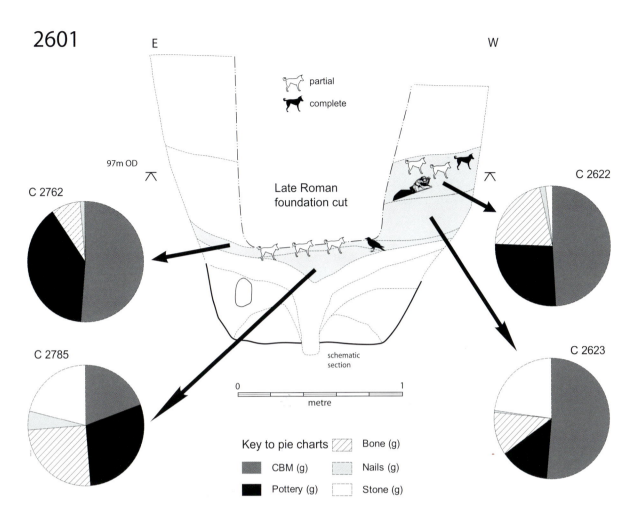

FIG. 141.   Proportional representation of principal categories of finds from each context of Period 4 pit 2601.

WELL 5735

For the earlier of the Period 4 wells, 5735, there is clearly an uneven distribution of artefacts by weights across fills (FIGS 142–143). The top fill (5697) contains the most ceramic building material, with quantities of tile decreasing markedly in the lower fills. This suggests the deliberate dumping of material to consolidate the top of the feature, prior to the construction of the late Roman buildings. Pottery is, by weight, more strongly represented than animal bone in most fills, with the largest quantities again recorded in the top fill 5697. Fulford (see above, p. 44) has already commented on the high proportion, almost one third (31 per cent), of vessels associated with drinking (beakers, cups and flagons) in this well. Relatively large quantities of animal bone are recorded in fills 6294 and 6436.

Nails have only been recorded from the top two fills of this feature; together with the ceramic building material, this perhaps suggests the deliberate dumping of structural remains (that is timbers with nails remaining) to stabilise the feature prior to further building activity. Slag and stone only occur in fill 6424.

We have already noted the presence of a number of 'special' deposits of small finds from this well, and these are concentrated in one fill. The lower fill 6436 had a depth of 0.8m and was waterlogged, preserving fragments of wood and the leaves of box and holly. In this one context were found a writing-tablet of maple (SF 4386), a bucket handle (SF 4413) and the handle of a copper-alloy foot-handle jug (SF 4399, see Crummy, above, pp. 114–16; FIGS 36, 37 and 60). The dog remains may represent one individual, but were scattered over several fills; a scapula

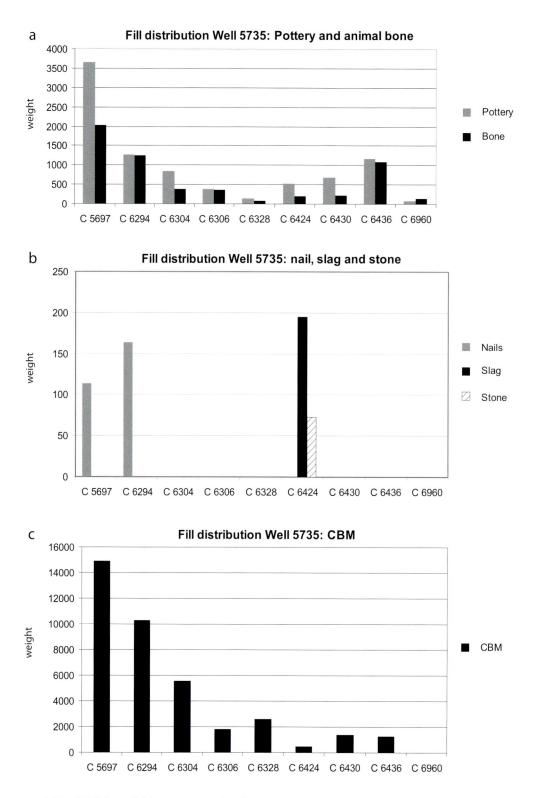

FIG. 142. Weights of (a) pottery and animal bone, (b) nail, slag and stone, and (c) cbm from each context of Period 4 well 5735.

came from fill 6436, which also contained multiple small finds; 6430 contained a tibia and metacarpal and the top fills (6294 and 5697) contained a further metacarpal and femur.

FIGS 142–143 illustrate the proportional representation by weight of the various find categories within individual fills. This once again illustrates the dominance of tile in the top two fills, and to a lesser extent in fill 6430. 6424 stands out for the occurrence of slag and stone. 6436 contains

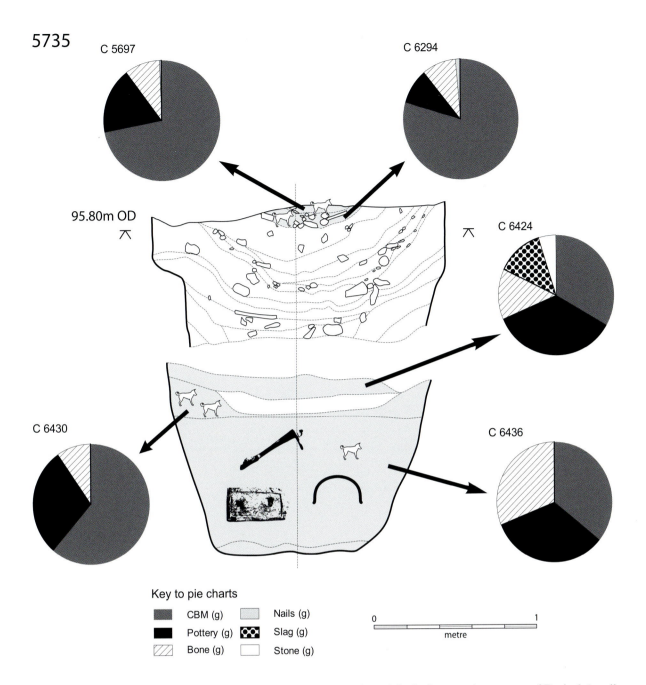

FIG. 143. Proportional representation of principal categories of finds from each context of Period 4 well 5735.

a relatively even mixture of bulk finds. In terms of the dog remains, it is interesting that, with the exception of fill 6436, none of the fills containing dog bones contains large amounts of other animal remains.

PIT 2434

As with well 5735, analysis shows an uneven distribution of material across the fills of cess-pit 2434, also dated to Period 4. The uppermost fill (2602) is dominated by ceramic building material prior to the construction of Late Roman Building 1 whose foundations overlay the pit. This context also included an unworn coin of Carausius (SF 01612). Smaller quantities of tiles occur in fill 2605, but tiles are otherwise relatively rare in the lower fills.

FIGS 144–145 illustrate that while animal bone is strongly represented in the top three fills,

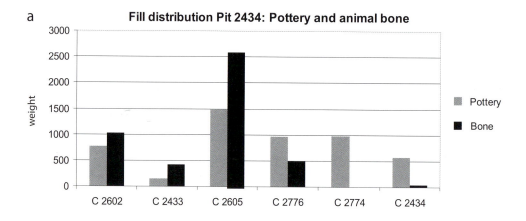

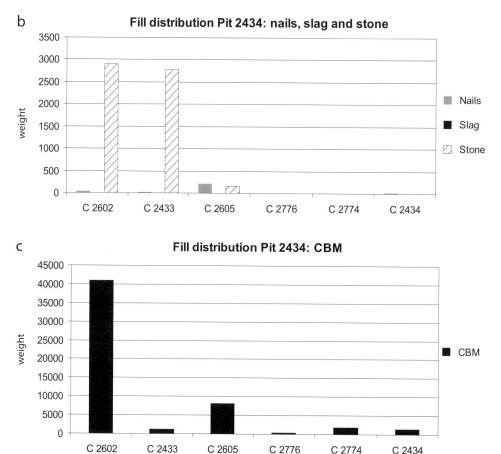

FIG. 144. Weights of (a) pottery and animal bone, (b) nails, slag and stone, and (c) cbm from pit 2434.

pottery is more dominant in the lower fills. This change in the disposal of domestic rubbish may relate to a change in function from cess to rubbish pit.

The small assemblage of pottery contained a high proportion (26 per cent) of drinking vessels (cups, mugs and beakers). The faunal assemblage is dominated by cattle, but there are significant proportions of wild animals, in particular two partial badger skeletons (contexts 2602 and 2605). Overall, context 2605 contains most of the animal bone and pottery, perhaps representing concentrated rubbish disposal prior to the consolidation and subsequent building in the area.

No slag was found in this pit. The relative concentration of stone in the top two fills supports their interpretation as deliberate dumps prior to construction. Nails are most common in fill 2605, but they also occur in the top two and the basal fills.

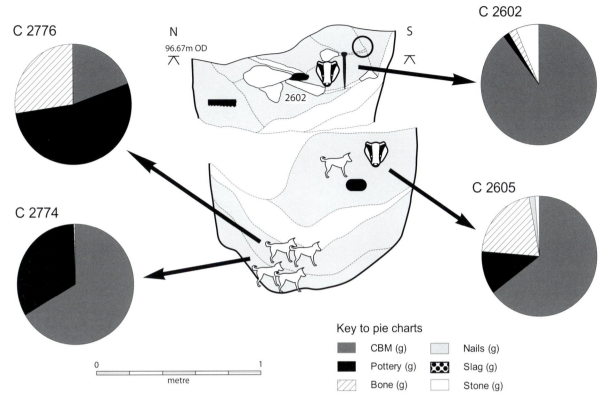

FIG. 145. Proportional representation of principal categories of finds from Period 4 pit 2434.

For pit 2434, the most obviously 'special' deposit is that of the two partial badger skeletons from fills 2602 and 2605. Fill 2605 also contained 25 dog bone fragments. Dog remains also occur in fills 2774, 2776, 2602 and 2433, suggesting the repeated disposal of partial dog remains in this area, perhaps from nearby middens. The combined occurrence of dog and badger in fills 2602 and 2605 may reflect how these animals were treated in death, or simply the fact that these two fills contain large amounts of animal waste generally.

While there are small finds from this pit, many are items of personal adornment, potentially easily lost amongst other household rubbish. A glass bead (SF 1826) comes from fill 2605, while a bone hairpin (SF 1755) and a shale armlet (SF 1754) are both from the top fill 2602. There was also a saw (SF 01542) from context 2433.

DISCUSSION

The preceding analysis has shown differences in the deposition of the main categories of finds across the site, but in contrast to the late Roman period there was no clear-cut spatial patterning in, for example, the deposition of animal bone within pits. There are changes between the two mid-Roman phases, with, for example, slag only occurring in Period 4 features; shown in relation to pottery, animal bone is also more strongly represented in the later period. While infants were only recorded from Period 3 features and complete or almost complete pottery vessels are more common in Period 3, dogs and the articulated remains of wild animals are more common in Period 4. However, given the small sample size, these observations cannot be described as clear trends. Re-uniting bulk find assemblages with their contexts does also allow for the identification of deliberate dumps, often prior to the construction of new buildings in the same area. Future work should include more detailed comparison of finds assemblages from pits with material from layers and spreads.

A number of cut features contained deposits which may be seen as 'special', in particular articulated animal skeletons and complete pottery vessels. How to define and interpret 'special' deposits has been debated for some time in prehistoric archaeology (e.g. Hill 1995, 13–15, 27–9) and the question is beginning to be addressed within Roman contexts (cf. Fulford 2001). Whether animal remains in particular should be seen as 'ritual' as opposed to being interpreted in functional and economic terms as butchery waste can be addressed using criteria such as those suggested by Wait (1985, 138–45), which include the presence of articulated skeletons and skulls. This approach does, however, fail to allow for the possibility that the disposal of waste was almost certainly governed by symbolic attitudes to rubbish, dirt and pollution, expressed through structured deposition in daily, weekly or monthly activities (cf. Hill 1995, 16, 95–101).

It should also not be forgotten that while chthonic associations of cut features persisted into the Roman period, most of the 'ritual' pit deposits on Iron Age sites such as Danebury relate to grain storage pits, and may well be linked to specific beliefs about crop fertility (Cunliffe 1995, 80–8). In Roman Silchester, we are essentially dealing with wells and cess-pits, and while a secure water supply must have been of considerable importance, there appears to be little difference in the material deposited in wells as opposed to pits. We may also have to consider the periodic emptying of cess-pits, a practice effectively leaving only the very last fill of a feature for analysis.

In any case, by comparison with the late Roman period 'special' deposits appear to be rarer in Periods 3 and 4, and no infant remains were found within mid-Roman pits and wells. This may be an accident in sampling, or reflect real changes in the deposition of such remains. The difference is especially striking for dogs, with only one articulated skeleton recovered from mid-Roman pit 2601.

Archaeologists studying prehistoric sites have led the way in the detailed examination of pit fills (Bersu 1940, 48–64; Cunliffe 1995, 80–8; Hill 1995, 37–44). Such analysis can potentially distinguish between erosion and natural infill from rain-wash and wind-blown material and the rapid or slow filling of pits. There may also be trends, such as the deposition of 'special' finds in lower fills (Cunliffe 1995, 84; Hill 1995, 46–8), and patterns of association and exclusion (Hill 1995, 54–5). This chapter has analysed three cut features in detail, to examine whether there are differences across pit fills, and whether fills containing 'special' deposits are also distinguished in other ways.

In the late Roman pits 3235 and 3251 articulated dogs were found in the lower fills, and infants in the top and middle fills respectively. For the mid-Roman period, only pit 2601 contained an articulated dog skeleton within one of its middle fills, and while dog remains occur only in the lower fills of pit 2434, they do occur both in the lower and upper fills of well 5735. Small finds can occur with dog remains (e.g. well 5735) but only in pit 2601 is there a striking combination of a knife decorated with mating dogs and a complete dog carcass. Analysis has demonstrated that quantities and types of material vary between fills, but the multiple variables make it difficult to identify clear patterns. Apart from providing a context for the material, and re-uniting the diverse range of materials studied by archaeological specialists, perhaps the greatest value of such an analysis will lie in the final comparison with the late Iron Age and early Roman pits, when it will be possible to track changes in the disposal of 'rubbish' within a single insula over more than 400 years.

CHAPTER 19

VISUALISING THE BUILDINGS OF INSULA IX AND THEIR CONTEXT

By Margaret Mathews

Pictorial visualisations are a popular way of putting across interpretations of excavated evidence, finding a place even in more academic publications, if only to enliven the front cover. They are also influential in shaping our view of what the past was like. The windswept British villas of Alan Sorrell and the sunlit buildings of Peter Conolly's Pompeii influenced a generation of illustrators who continue to reinforce our concept of 'Roman' life through their work. The term 'reconstruction', which is commonly applied to this type of image, often implies that it is more faithful to the evidence from a particular site than is actually the case and glosses over the contribution of the creative imagination of the artist, which draws to a generally unknown extent on established evidence. For this reason 'pictorial visualisation/interpretation' seems a better term. The term 'reconstruction' is better applied to a more technical type of illustration, often using isometric or axonometric projections, for example, those produced for some of the waterlogged structures from Roman London, where structural timbers have been preserved (Brigham *et al.* 1995). The uncertainty of excavated evidence can also be dealt with by alternative reconstructions, as with the medieval structure from Cowdery's Down drawn by Simon James (Millett with James 1983, figs 70–1).

In this chapter I have set out some of the issues I have addressed myself in relation to producing pictorial images of structures from Insula IX both for this volume and for the cover image of *Life and Labour in Late Roman Silchester* (Fulford *et al.* 2006). My aim has been to show the buildings, including alternative interpretations, at the same time as creating an engaging image that captures our interpretation of life in the round.

As an illustrator, rather than a structural engineer, Roman specialist or expert in vernacular building, I am conscious of the influence on the viewer of my illustrations and aware of the responsibility to be as thoroughly informed as possible and to produce something that I can defend, even when the end result is still inevitably speculative and open to alternative interpretation. The buildings uncovered by the excavations are the core of any attempt to do this and, in producing pictorial reconstructions based on the Silchester excavations, this has meant studying comparative evidence for materials, structural elements and dimensions of Romano-British buildings to make my own interpretations of the evidence, rather than be unduly influenced by the visualisations of others.

The process starts with such excavated evidence as relates to structural elements — foundations, wall coursing, beam slots, post-holes and drip-gullies, along with internal features such as floors and hearths. Walls and wall foundations provide a ground plan from which we can infer the layout of rooms and the horizontal extent of the building. However, the visual appearance of a building is largely that of the superstructure for which, on most excavations, there is scant evidence and for which we have to look elsewhere.

Sites in Britain and in northern Europe provide the nearest parallels for buildings at Silchester, though evidence from the wider Roman world is more plentiful. There are a number of British and northern European rural sites where collapsed walls or gables have been preserved (Keevill 1996; King 1996; Ling 1992; Burnham *et al.* 1994). These give an indication of the possible height, construction and dimensions of masonry buildings, although, as they represent buildings that have failed, not necessarily of their structural soundness. Generally these are later Roman in date, but whether they represent progress or decline in technique from the early or mid-Roman is unclear. In addition, there are examples of early Roman waterlogged timber structures from excavations in London, which provide models for timber buildings (Brigham *et al.* 1995).

Evidence from these sources can be augmented by examples from the wider Roman world, though it should be remembered that Britain was not the centre of the empire nor would Mediterranean buildings have been best suited to the climate. Wall paintings and other contemporary artefacts can also provide clues, particularly if they are British or northern European, for example the stone shrines in the form of winged corridor houses and pottery stands apparently depicting timber-framed structures (Perring 2002, figs 47–8).

The evidence of regional vernacular traditions is also relevant; for example the use of flint and brick is clearly evidenced from the Insula IX excavation and has continued in the region to the present day, indicating a natural preference for easily available building materials. The buildings already depicted for late Roman Silchester (Fulford *et al.* 2006, cover) could be argued to be both geographically and temporally closer to succeeding early medieval buildings than to those of first-century A.D. Rome.

Bringing these strands of evidence together, I have first used isometric projections to test possible interpretations of what the mid-Roman town-houses of Insula IX may have looked like. This method allows the reconstruction to be done to scale and can show whether chosen roof pitches and wall heights, for example, are feasible.

MASONRY BUILDING 1: RAISING THE SUPERSTRUCTURE (FIG. 146a)

The ground plan of this building suggests a central range of three rooms, surrounded by a portico or corridor. The general dimensions of the central block and the corridor are consistent with those from other ground plans at Silchester as recorded on the Antiquaries' plan and form a basis for visualising the superstructure.

The height of a building will depend on whether it is interpreted as single storey or having an upper floor. The presence of upper floors in Romano-British buildings is much debated (Neal 1996; Perring 2002, 111–16). Previously at Silchester upper floors have been inferred where foundations have been particularly substantial (Fulford *et al.* 2006, 21). There has been no clear evidence for stairwells in any of the buildings, though some corridor spaces could have accommodated stairs.

The walls of the central block of MB 1 were well built, though not exceptionally wide (0.5m average) and might be interpreted as supporting an upper storey. In that case, with a surrounding corridor, the ground floor rooms would have no natural lighting. This might be so if they were storage areas, or windows were not considered necessary for lighting the interior. Pre-Roman roundhouses are normally depicted as being without windows and we might argue that a romanised indigenous population may not have radically changed their use of domestic space. However, the assumption here for MB 1 is that some level of daylight would be intended. Furthermore, the presence of burnt patches and hearths in two of the rooms, without evidence of chimney structures, suggests that any smoke or fumes would have to escape through the roof, implying a single-storey structure.

Lack of light could also be a problem in a single-storey building with a surrounding corridor. For the central rooms to be adequately lit, it is suggested that the central block rises above the level of the corridor roof to allow clerestory lighting (FIG. 146a).

There are few examples of windows from Roman Britain to draw on, exceptions being the round-arched windows from Meonstoke and the rectangular, stone window surround from Colliton Park (King 1996; Drew and Selby 1939), though reconstructions generally assume that windows were a common feature. Ground-floor windows raise considerations of security and are likely to have been small or provided with lockable shutters or metal grilles (Perring 2002, 116–18).

For the reconstruction of MB 1 (FIG. 146a), the height of the corridor wall has been set at *c.* 2.0m, implied by evidence from a wall painting at Verulamium, quoted in Perring (2002, 115). The height of the main wall is 5m, 7m to the gable, which is less than that suggested for Carsington, Meonstoke or Redlands villas, all of which may have supported upper storeys. The

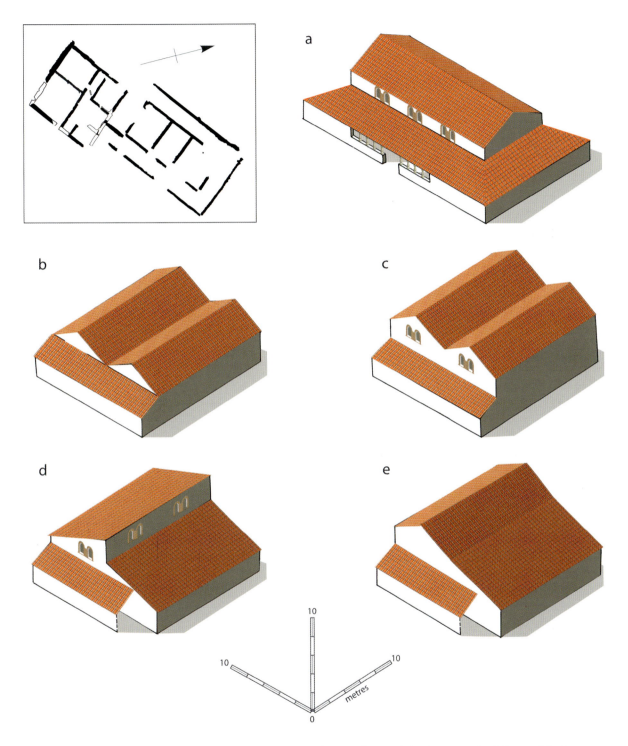

FIG. 146. (a) Isometric interpretation of MB 1 assuming an elevated single-storey building, with clerestory windows to the central rooms and a surrounding corridor on all sides. (b) MB 2 as a single-storey building with a double-pitched roof and schematic representation of the verandah area. (c) The same interpretation but with elevated walls to allow clerestory windows and the possibility of some of the space being divided vertically. The roofs in these last two interpretations could also be argued to run in the opposite orientation. (d) A suggestion for a 'split-level' building divided by the continuous cross-wall and a shorter verandah which is consistent with the arrangement of post-holes. (e) A further interpretation along the same lines. (*By Margaret Mathews*)

roof has been shown as ceramic tile with a pitch of *c*. 30°. The central block has been interpreted as stone-walled and the windows, one for each of the central rooms on the visible façade, are based on those from the Meonstoke gable.

Excavated stone footings may represent full-height stone walls or dwarf walls for a timber superstructure. The outer corridor footings of MB 1 were less substantial and less well laid and could represent a dwarf wall supporting timber framing, rather than one of full height. A closed corridor seems more likely in a northern climate, but a partial or entirely open portico is an alternative possibility. The portico may have had dwarf columns similar to the Silchester Ogham stone (Fulford *et al.* 2000) or wooden posts. Despite lack of direct evidence, a corridor extending around all four sides of the building seems more likely to be part of the original 'architectural concept'. However, it would have brought the south-west end of MB 1 very close to MB 2 and it is possible that the two buildings were joined at a later stage as discussed in Chapter 2.

Both stone and timber walls may have been left exposed, rendered over and/or painted and there is some evidence, commonly, though not solely, from military sites, for the decorative use of red paint to pick out masonry coursing (Bidwell 1996). However, it is also possible that timber framing, being cheap and cost effective to assemble, may have been left unrendered (Ulrich 2007, 98).

MASONRY BUILDING 2: THE PROBLEM WITH ROOFS (FIG. 146b–e)

Excavations rarely provide direct evidence for roof structure but this is important in determining the appearance of buildings. Thatched roofs need to be of a steeper pitch (45–50°) compared to the 20–30° considered to be usual for ceramic tile. Evidence from Carsington (Ling 1992), probably roofed with stone tiles, suggests a roof pitch of 40°, with modern roofs of this type being pitched at 52.5° (Warry, pers. comm.), though vernacular buildings in eastern Europe with stone slab roofs are shallow pitched. Slates or wooden shingles also need a steeper pitch, as suggested for the building at Meonstoke (King 1996, 64–6). Once the pitch angle is chosen for a reconstruction, the vertical height of the roof must increase proportionally with the horizontal distance covered and an isometric reconstruction is helpful here, particularly for testing the feasibility of lean-to roofs over corridors where, for example, upper floor or clerestory windows might be assumed.

The ground plan of MB 2 indicates a building *c*.13m square, the same total width as MB 1 but without an external corridor, though there is evidence for a timber-post verandah to the south-west. The walls were well-laid flint, averaging 0.6m wide, and may have supported an upper storey, though slight traces of hearths in two of the rooms would argue against this, as discussed for MB 1. For the mid-Roman stone town-houses a ceramic tile roof seems more in keeping with the well-laid walls, though there is no conclusive evidence.

Although the roof timbering would not be visible in an exterior visualisation, it is important to think about how a roof would be supported as a tile roof would weigh upwards of 100kg per square metre (Warry, pers. comm.). Though Roman engineering was equal to roofing buildings of a greater size than MB 2 (Adam 1994, 205–12), these were public buildings and involved more complex roof timbering than was likely for what was essentially a vernacular building. It is safer to assume a simple triangulated truss as roof support but, in this case, MB 2 was deemed too wide to support a single span. The largest Byzantine example of this type of roof noted by Adam had a span of less than 10m (Adam 1994, 210, fig. 494). In Britain, the distance spanned by the roof at the fourth-century building at Carsington was *c*. 9m, the walls being 0.5–0.6m in width. The collapsed wall at Batten Hanger, described as an 'end' wall and gable, seems to have roofed a building 11–12m wide, apparently without interior supports, as inferred from the published plan (Burnham *et al.* 1994). At Silchester, a span of *c*. 7m seems a more likely model and MB 2 may, therefore, have had a double pitched roof (FIG. 146b–c). Alternatively, the continuous cross-wall bisecting MB 2 NW/SE could have had a structural function in relation to the roof and allowed, in effect, pent roofs, which could be supported on rafters of not more than 7m (FIG. 146d–e). Other possibilities are similarly based on the building being divided in two with separate roof structures.

MID-ROMAN TIMBER BUILDING 1: ADDING A TIMBER EXTENSION

Buildings at Silchester include both masonry or part-masonry buildings as well as timber-framed structures. Timber framing, *opus craticium*, was a technique used in Roman times and examples have been preserved in urban contexts in Pompeii and Herculaneum (Adam 1994, 119–24). Timber-framed panels, erected on sleeper beams or dwarf walls, may be infilled with wattle and daub, stone, brick or tile, or provide window apertures, and parallels can be drawn with present-day vernacular buildings of a type found widely in Europe (Adam 1994, 124, fig. 286). As commented previously, such walls may have been finished in a variety of ways or left unfinished.

The structural evidence for MRTB 1 is fragmentary and difficult to interpret. On the basis of the excavation evidence it seems most likely that the earlier Period 2 ERTB 1 survived, at least partly, into Period 3 for some time and continued to serve, in dilapidated form, as an animal byre. Succeeding, or even alongside this, MRTB 1 was defined by post-holes and a carefully swept floor. Rather than timber-framed walls, this suggests a structure of earth-fast posts infilled with wattle and daub panels or with planked walls. In visualising this structure, the most striking feature is that it does not seem to form part of the original architectural concept of MB 1, being built hard against its end wall, supporting the suggestion that there was a blank corridor wall here rather than a portico.

MASONRY BUILDING 3: ALTERATIONS AND ADAPTATION (FIG. 147)

The ground plan of MB 3 cannot be determined with certainty, but an attempt has been made to suggest possible reconstructions. On the basis of the phase plans, we have an example of a building which has evolved from earlier structures and appears to incorporate elements of these. It is possible that all the earlier walls were taken down and rebuilt in a single operation. However, it is equally possible that the different parts of the building were developed piecemeal, offering a number of variations for a reconstruction, inevitably tenuous as they are based on the equally hypothetical reconstruction of the earlier building MB 1. What might have happened to the core of MB 1? Was it razed to the foundations and rebuilt, or did it survive in its earlier form, but perhaps cut down to two rooms? Were the walls maintained at the same height, lowered or raised?

The extension over the former MB 2 (Room 4) was raised on foundations that were slighter than in the core of MB 1 and seem too flimsy to support anything other than single-storey timber construction, though an upper storey has been suggested. However, it is also possible that just part of the area could have been boarded out as a loft. If, as seems probable, there was no corridor on the north-west side of this room, lighting a single-storey extension would be no problem, though this could also have been elevated to create a single roof-line if the core of MB 1 survived to a higher level.

One possibility for roofing the building is that the whole area of the building, whether single or two storey, had a single roof. However, if there was no continuous corridor along the north-west-facing side of the building, a single roof would have had to span two parts of different widths, 11m and 13m. This would have necessitated complex roof-timbering to span the distance and a roof structure to accommodate differing roof pitches or ridge lines, if we assume all the outer walls were of the same height. A simpler interpretation would be to preserve the distinction between the central block and the corridors, with the central portion, equivalent in width to the central block of MB 1, extending the length of the building (FIG. 147a).

In either case the roofs may have been either tiled or thatched (FIG. 147b). However, if there were a corridor, the pitch needed for thatching would not leave much room for windows in the upper part of the central block, as previously suggested, without the walls being raised. Alternatively, the central block may have been thatched but the corridor roofs tiled, which would be similar to the suggested reconstruction of the Meonstoke gable (King 1996, 65–6). MB 3 is a slightly smaller building than Meonstoke but the walls are considerably less robust.

The north-east end of MB 1 (Room 1) saw more substantial remodelling than the other two rooms, taking in the former corridor area to make one large workshop. The presence of the industrial hearths argues for an open roof and against an upper storey here, though part of the area might have contained an upper loft level for storage. The foundation for a possible roof support at right angles to the cross walls might suggest that the roof at this end of the building

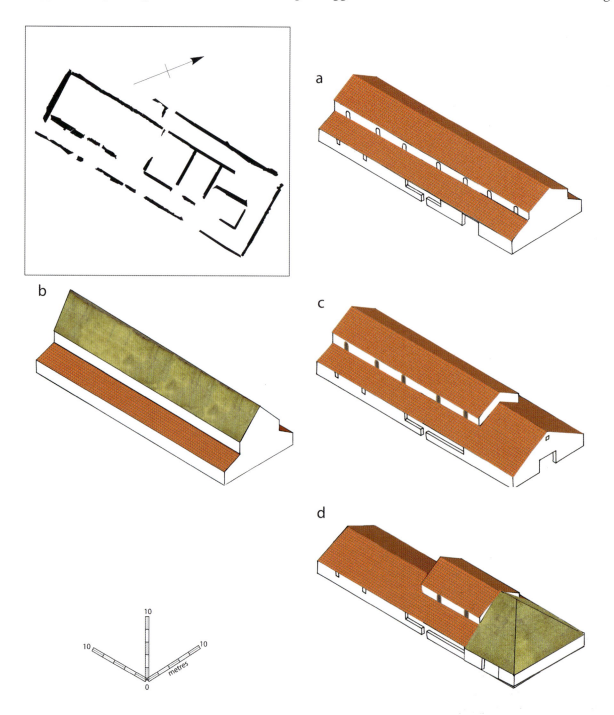

FIG. 147.   Selected interpretations of MB 3 as isometric projections. (a) The building is extended the full length of the ground plan with a central core, tiled roof and corridor throughout. (b) The same arrangement but with the main block of the building thatched. The corridor roofs are tiled since the steeper pitch of a thatched roof would need the suggested wall height to be raised. (c) The building is extended over the area of MB 2 to match the height of the surviving MB 1, but with a single-storey workshop area. The upper roof is shown tiled but could equally well be thatched. (d) A single-storey extension over MB 2 and a thatched roof over Room 1, just reaching the same height as the main block at its apex. This would necessitate some awkward junctions with the tiled corridors but might be consistent with piecemeal development. (*By Margaret Mathews*)

was constructed in a different way, perhaps to address the problem of roofing the 13m span. This is appealing to the illustrator as it offers the opportunity to show alternative approaches and conveys the idea of piecemeal development.

BEYOND THE STRUCTURAL DETAIL: DEPICTING TIME DEPTH AND URBAN LIFE

There are other factors that can play a part in the life of the building and be included in a visualisation. Exterior decoration and paint will deteriorate more quickly in a northern climate and rising damp would have been prevalent, causing the lower parts of rendered surfaces to flake away, attacking the mortar between stones and rotting any timberwork at ground level. Added to that, the buildings of Insula IX were frequently built over earlier, infilled pits and wells and clearly, in some cases, must have been prone to subsidence, as is the case with the south-western wall of MB 2/MB 3. In contrast to a visualisation which resembles an architect's model in its cleanliness and order, Roman Silchester would have been an ever-changing landscape of new building, dilapidation, demolition and repair.

It has not been the purpose of this chapter to discuss in detail how the evidence for the use of the buildings and the life of the inhabitants are incorporated into images. However, to produce a complete visual interpretation, as opposed to a solely architectural one, these elements must be included. Finds and samples have all produced their own narratives for Insula IX, as detailed in preceding chapters and, while we cannot say definitively, for example, that amphora finds represent consumption by the inhabitants of the buildings discussed, it seems reasonable to include this suggestion in a picture. All the elements included in the images reproduced in Chapter 20 should have some justification and this is indicated in the captions.

CHAPTER 20

SYNTHESIS AND CONCLUSIONS

By Michael Fulford

INTRODUCTION

Insula IX occupies a central position within *Calleva*, close to the forum-basilica. The principal north–south street of the town runs along the east side of the block, while the south side fronts on to the principal east–west street. This report on the continuing excavations in Insula IX has focused on the occupation between the early second and the late third century A.D. It begins (Period 3) with the building in stone of two town-houses (MB 1 and 2) on the footprint of, and thus on the same alignment as, a range of timber buildings constructed in the late first century A.D. (Period 2). This alignment is diagonal to, and thus at significant variance with, the Roman street-grid which is aligned on the cardinal points. Associated with the two town-houses is a further, new timber building to the north-east, filling the gap between the first town-house and the decaying remains of the timber building (ERTB 1) retained from the previous period. A spread of occupation to the south includes a well and a single pit as well as possible traces of further timber buildings to the south and south-east of the excavated area. The slight and ambiguous evidence for structures contrasts markedly with that for the buildings which occupied the south-east quarter of the excavated area in the late first and early second centuries (Period 2). An absence of evidence for a boundary to define a southern limit to the property suggests that all the occupation south of the two town-houses within the excavated area was associated with them. Equally, the lack of evidence of any division between the two houses suggests that they both belonged to the same over-arching property. A second well is associated with the backyard of a second property in the north of the excavation area which extended beyond the north-western limits of the trench. This property was separated from the two town-houses by a fence and, within the area of the excavation, produced no evidence of a building.

A striking feature of this period of occupation of Insula IX is its apparent inward-looking character, with evidence of a sturdy fence separating occupation inside the insula from the bustle and movement along the flanking north–south and east–west streets. The only indication of the owners of the main property within the excavated area taking any advantage that access to the main north–south street might have offered is presented by the remains of one, possibly two timber buildings built side-by-side up to and against the street frontage in the south-east corner of the excavation trench. While convincing structural evidence in support of this building(s) is lacking, it is difficult to interpret the defined clay spreads as representing anything other than floor surfaces. Tentatively, we suggest one or two buildings of slight, sleeper-beam construction in this location. This lack of evidence for interaction with the town beyond the limits of the insula is further borne out by the lack of weighing and measuring equipment and of coins. Indeed, all of the coins of the second and third century were found in fourth-century or later and unstratified contexts. Symbolic in a way of this inward-looking character is the location of the one certain latrine pit of Period 3, situated right at the intersection of the north–south and east–west streets, and very close to the position beside the east–west street of the earlier, very large cess-pit 5251 from Period 2. Further to the south, rubbish continued to be dumped into the subsiding fill of an early well or inter-cutting wells (6290). However, whether passers-by would have found the frontages of Insula IX any more noisome than those of other insulae is hard to determine. Indeed the inhabitants of *Calleva*, as of any other contemporary urban community, may not have been sensitive to foul smells at all.

In the 150 years or so covered by this report there is little substantial, structural change within the excavated area. The two houses are merged to become one house (MB 3) from the early third century (Period 4) and a concentration of pits in the south-east of the trench indicates a more substantial occupation beside the north–south street. Nevertheless the details of the associated structures, including the manner of their construction and even their precise extent, remain elusive. There is no significant break between our two periods across the excavated area and, in terms of the occupation spreads to the south of the masonry houses, it is hard to define a clear break-point in the stratigraphic sequence.

Most of the evidence with which to characterise the occupation derives from the occupation spreads to the south of the two town-houses rather than from pits which are very few in number. The general occupation has, perhaps inevitably, produced a proportion of residual material dating back to, and through the first century A.D. This immediately raises the very serious question as to how representative the material associated with Periods 3 and 4 is of the occupation and life of the inhabitants over two or three generations. How much material was disposed of outside the insula? This problem is brought into sharp focus by the difficulties surrounding the interpretation of the timber buildings to the north-east of town-house MB 1. While the micromorphological and geochemical study has helped to define the building (ERTB 4) formerly seen as a single structure into two buildings (ERTB 1 and MRTB 1) and to characterise their occupation, it has also presented us with a paradox. The quality of the finds from the area occupied by MRTB 1 and ERTB 1, which includes a range of copper-alloy items as well as a major assemblage of glass, is at odds with the evidence that this space was used as a byre to accommodate animals, unless it was also used as a midden for the adjacent town-houses, the bulk of whose contents were periodically removed. In this regard it is interesting to note the low average weight per pottery sherd and the large number of highly fragmented glass scraps — as if the larger material had been removed. Material taken from the midden may account for all or some of the finds incorporated in the spreads to the south (Object 701). Nevertheless, the very real possibility that we only have a fraction of the occupational material associated with Period 3 makes the task of reconstructing the life and occupations of the inhabitants more difficult. On the other hand, while soils, such as clays used in foundations and flooring, and building material, both newly made or quarried, or in the form of rubble, were undoubtedly brought in, it seems unlikely, but not provable, that discarded material, in the form of domestic waste from other household middens, was introduced to the insula from elsewhere in the town.

The situation is little different in Period 4 where, again, the inference is that the occupation spreads (Object 700) to the south of MB 3 also largely derived from it. However, in this period there is also a larger number of pits than in the second century and, typically, they are not so 'contaminated' with residual material. However, the fact that they are concentrated in the south-east of the excavation area suggests that they may relate specifically to the occupation of the adjacent timber building rather than to the town-house MB 3.

PERIOD 3

THE TOWN–HOUSES (MB 1 AND 2 WITH MRTB 1/ERTB 1) (FIG. 148)

However, let us begin with what can be inferred from the two town-houses themselves. While both appear to be of modest size, it has to said that we have precious little evidence from Britain of the scale and character of town-houses in the early second century A.D. While Silchester itself boasts the largest number of different house types, without further excavation of a number of examples to elucidate their phases of development, it would be difficult to determine what the state of any one house was in the second century. However, examples of town-houses, admittedly of timber construction (cf. Frere 1983, fig. 7), from early second-century Verulamium are also relatively modest. In Insula XXVIII, for example, a two-room strip building (3B), of *c.* A.D. 105–130, was significantly enlarged, *c.* A.D. 130–150, to an eight-roomed house (3A), which, in its turn, was replaced, *c.* A.D. 150–155, by a new, L-plan, timber-built town-house (3) of some ten rooms and with a fine, polychrome, figured mosaic in the principal reception room. In the course of about half a century the surface area of the successive buildings had increased by 200 per cent from *c.* 48m² to *c.* 136m², to *c.* 206m² (ibid., 231–41). In the adjacent insula, XXVII, sizeable buildings (2A, 2B), comparable to XXVIII.3, and also of timber-frame construction, were built new in the middle of the second century. Of the ten rooms of 2A no less than seven possessed tessellated floors (ibid., 203–9). A perhaps more typical, general trend in south-east Britain in the first half of the second century is for the construction of *de novo* masonry town-houses, replacing timber predecessors, as here in Insula IX, from about *c.* A.D. 125. This can be seen, for example, in the *colonia* at Colchester, with Buildings 112–14 in Insula XXXIV recorded in the Culver Street

A

B

FIG. 148.   Two pictorial interpretations of the Period 3 buildings by Margaret Mathews.
(a) The two town-houses are newly built and reflect the presumed status of the occupiers. MB 2 is shown with a double-pitched roof as in FIG. 146c. The portico area has dwarf columns modelled on the Ogham stone, small barred windows, formed by timber framing, on the corridor and clerestory windows modelled on the Meonstoke gable. ERTB 1 is falling into decay and used to stable cattle or other livestock (see Ch. 4). Beyond, other buildings are visible in Insula XXVI to the north and, on the left, the building on the west side of Insula IX, detected by air photography. The clipped box plants and the vegetable garden reflect the evidence for garden plants and crops (see Ch. 16).
(b) Some time later, the buildings are showing some signs of wear and repairs and improvements are in hand. MRTB 1 has replaced the cattle shed and perhaps serves as a kitchen area. The amphorae reflect pottery finds, indicative of imported oil and wine. The woman sweeping and the figure with a tray of glassware reflect evidence from the excavation (see Chs 4 and 7). A verandah is added to MB 2 and an extension links the corridor of MB 1 to MB 2 (Ch. 2). The tile dump in the foreground suggests a possible trade in used roofing materials.

excavations; these include two substantial row-type houses with corridors (Crummy 1992, 31–3; 76–83). The Middle Brook Street excavations in Winchester also produced a *de novo*, masonry town-house (XXIII.1), a row-type house with corridors around three sides (like our MB 1) of about 350m², dating from about the mid-second century (Scobie *et al.* 1991, 19–21).

The first of our houses is of a three-room type with surrounding corridor on at least three sides, a form which, in general terms, can be well paralleled in town and country in Britain and northern Gaul in the early Roman period and has been classified as a simple, row-type house with corridor (Perring 2002, 64–5; Smith 1997, 46–64). The square plan of the second house has no obvious parallel, either in Silchester or elsewhere. It is interesting to note that the footprint of MB 2 completely encapsulates that of the underlying circular building of Period 2, ERTB 3; its plan, therefore, may, in part at least, be determined by its predecessor (FIG. 148).

In both houses the walls had been robbed down to foundation levels and, more particularly in the case of MB 2, significant lengths of the foundations had been robbed out as well. As a result no trace of plaster attaching to any wall survived and in only one room, the central space of MB 1, did remains of a decorative floor surface survive *in situ*. This consisted of a small area of tile-tessellation in one corner of the room, perhaps representing the remains of the border to a patterned mosaic occupying the centre of the floor. The flint cobbles of Room 3 were clearly designed as a foundation for a surface now lost, but whether the floors of Room 1 and the surrounding corridor were originally finely finished is uncertain. What is apparent, however, is that before the end of Period 3, and, possibly after no more than two generations of use, Room 1 was reduced to a rough, clay and gravelled surface and occupation in the corridor rested on the clay make-up associated with the primary construction of the house. As for MB 2, there is no surviving *in situ* evidence with which to reconstruct the original state of the flooring. The excavation has, however, produced large numbers of loose stone, notably of Purbeck materials, and ceramic tesserae, particularly from the south of the excavation trench. Indeed, a small number of loose stone tesserae were found associated with both houses. However, it is far from certain that this material should be linked with the Period 3 buildings; more likely is that it is residual from the construction or destruction of major, first-century building(s) located to the south of the excavation trench (Fulford 2008). The same is true of the ceramic building and roofing material from the excavation. While it is highly probable that the two town-houses were roofed with ceramic tile, there is no hard, supporting evidence. Notwithstanding the excavation boasting a major deposit of ceramic roofing material to the south of the houses in Period 3, Warry argues persuasively (Ch. 10) that it is highly unlikely to have derived from any Period 2 building within our excavated area. Rather he suggests that it may represent the stock of a dealer in used tiles.

It has been assumed that the two houses had an upper storey, with the flint walling carried up to the eaves. However, Warry (Ch. 10) has argued on the basis of the scarcity of flat tile for use in bonding that this may not have been the case. Indeed he suggests either all-masonry houses of single-storey, or houses with timber-frame construction on dwarf-wall foundations. The lack of flat-tile is not perhaps surprising, given the overall lack of contexts which may be associated with the construction and demolition of both houses, and the likelihood that materials were either recycled into MB 3, or taken off site for re-use elsewhere. The truth is that there can be no certainty, but where we do have structural evidence surviving above foundations, such as in Pompeii and Herculaneum, the norm is for buildings to have upper storeys. In the case of the timber building MRTB 1 which filled the gap between the end of MB 1 and the decaying ERTB 1 there can be little doubt that it was single-storey. Phytoliths of phragmites reed indicate a thatched roof for this and for the decaying ERTB 1. Against a simple extrapolation from two cities from the heart of the Empire in favour of upper storeys, we should recall the evidence for hearths from both houses — Rooms 1, 2 and the northern end of the outer corridor of MB 1, and Rooms 1 and 4 of MB 2. Unless chimneys were in place, an upper storey above these spaces would have prevented smoke from escaping. As the hearths in MB 2 are close to walls, it is possible that they were served by chimneys, but this cannot have been the case in MB 1 where hearths are, for example, in the centre of Room 1. So, despite the robustness of their foundations, we do need to be cautious about assuming the existence of two, rather than one-and-a-half storeys in both of the houses, as reconstructed by Mathews (Ch. 19).

FAMILY MATTERS: THE OCCUPANTS OF MB 1 AND MB 2

The two houses and the associated timber building MRTB 1 to the north-east occupy the footprint of the underlying houses ERTB 2 and 3 (Clarke *et al.* 2007). In recalling that the footprint of MB 2 encapsulates that of the roundhouse, ERTB 3, we might also note that the mosaic-floored, reception room of MB 1 overlies the equivalent room of ERTB 2 which also divides that building between two symmetrically arranged suites of rooms. Not only does the correspondence between aspects of the layout of the two new houses with their predecessors suggest a continuation of occupation by the same kin group, but the construction of separate houses seems to affirm the duality of the accommodation of ERTB 2 (cf. Smith 1997). Two related families now each occupy their own house.

OCCUPATIONS AND LIFESTYLE

The two masonry houses have produced very slight evidence with which to reconstruct the lifestyle and occupations of their inhabitants. Not surprisingly there was little evidence from the buildings themselves, because so few contexts could be linked to the occupation of the buildings as opposed to their construction. However, the corridor of MB 1 produced the remains of a large pottery storage vessel, probably used in cooking or baking (FIGS 11–13, 76), while geochemical analysis of the burnt areas in the corridor towards the north-east end of the building and on the floor surface of the adjacent Room 1 suggest that metalworking, principally of copper alloys, but also of gold and silver, took place within the house. Further evidence of the working of copper alloy in the form of crucible fragments and metal waste, including an unfinished strap-hinge, was found from the Period 3 occupation spreads to the south of the house, as was a small gold stud. There is also some evidence for ironmaking and ironworking in Period 3. In addition to small concentrations of hammerscale from MB 1 and from pit 5039 to the south, and an offcut of bar iron from the southern spreads, there are also a couple of slag basins indicative of iron smelting from MRTB 1/ERTB 1, and from the spreads to the south. While it is possible that the slag basins may have been introduced to the excavation area from elsewhere in the insula or the town, the concentrations of hammerscale are more likely to represent *in-situ* activity. As Crummy argues in respect of the copper-alloy strap-hinge, metalworking in Insula IX was probably not an end in itself. She sees the hinge as proxy evidence for the making of wooden artefacts, such as boxes or folding gaming-boards, themselves a rare category of find in Britain (p. 108). However, tools associated with any craft are notably scarce from Period 3 contexts.

To metalworking we can add animal husbandry as an occupation of the inhabitants of our town-houses. This can be inferred from the study of the soils associated with the decaying ERTB 1 in the north-east corner of the insula, which indicate the presence of herbivores. The presence of the foetal/neonatal remains of caprines and pigs and the bones of very young cattle provide further evidence that animal husbandry formed part of the subsistence strategy of the occupants of the town-houses. On the other hand, clear evidence is lacking for the cultivation of crops, whether cereals or legumes, in the immediate vicinity of the town. However, notwithstanding the scarcity of tools associated with animal husbandry or horticulture, it seems likely, though not proven, that fruit and flavourings, such as blackberry and plum, and coriander and dill, were grown in or close to the town.

For the status and lifestyle of the occupants of our town-houses, we can turn to the proxy evidence from MRTB 1 and the decaying ERTB 1 in the north-east corner. Importantly, finds of styli imply literacy. Otherwise, from the perspective of material culture, the 'small finds' emphasise the importance of personal appearance and grooming, including a range of dress accessories and toilet instruments. The presence of numerous glass bottles and an unguent flask indicate a lifestyle with access to scented unguents or cosmetics and whatever other precious commodities the bottles contained. A similar emphasis on dress and toilet accessories, as well as bottles among the glass assemblage, is to be found in the spreads to the south of the houses (Object 701). The pottery assemblage from the timber buildings in the north-east corner includes a variety of imported tablewares and drinking vessels, some 8 per cent of the assemblage, as well as a large proportion of kitchen wares, characteristics shared by the material from the occupation spreads to the south where imported vessels account for 10 per cent of the assemblage. Altogether, in terms of the range of the finds and their quality, including imports versus local and regional products, the total ceramic finds assemblage from MRTB 1/ERTB 1 and from the occupation spreads to the south appears average for households from the larger urban communities in southern Britain, with the possible exception of London. We should emphasise that this picture is one of consumption which includes a very significant proportion of material manufactured in the first and early second centuries. Of that significant proportion we should allow for material already discarded before Period 3 and simply re-worked through the excavation of foundations, pits and post-holes into Period 3 stratigraphy. Attempting to distinguish between material which remained in use into Period 3 before discard and that which was re-worked rubbish of earlier date is beyond the scope of this report.

For reconstructing diet we are fortunate in having a combination of faunal and botanical evidence that we can associate with the town-houses. The proxy evidence from the 'midden' of MRTB 1/ERTB 1 shows consumption of the three main domesticates, but with a slight preference for sheep/goat, as well as of wild animals — red and roe deer and hare — and bird, particularly domestic fowl. Fish, both freshwater and marine species, is present in small quantities, as is oyster. There is a very small amount of oyster with the largest deposit of about 1kg from a single context in the south-east quarter. However, cattle predominate in the small assemblage from cess-pit 4835 in the angle between the streets and cattle are marginally the most important of the three main domesticates from the occupation spreads to the south. As far as the evidence of plant remains is concerned, we are fortunate in having a well-preserved assemblage, including mineralised, waterlogged and charred seeds, from the latrine pit 5251 which was assigned to Period 2 in Clarke *et al.* 2007. However the latest fills which contained the assemblage in question belong to around the end of Period 2 and the beginning of Period 3, i.e. *c.* A.D. 125, and can very reasonably be seen as indicative of diet in the early second century. Indeed, as Robinson points out, there are close similarities with the range of species represented in the late Roman period. The main staples are spelt wheat, six-row hulled barley and peas, with flavourings such as coriander and dill, and fruit, notably plum and (abundant) blackberry. The pollen from this latrine pit is also helpful in complementing the evidence of the seeds in adding brassicas, probably mustard and cabbage, to the list, as well as emphasising the importance of Apiaceae, probably dill in this context. Imported varieties, including fig, grapes and mulberry, point to the relative prosperity of the inhabitants. Imported amphorae, predominantly Dressel 20 types from Baetica and Gauloise forms from southern Gaul, also attest to the consumption of olive oil and wine. The presence of whipworm eggs in this pit serves as a reminder that the inhabitants of Insula IX were not spared from infestation by this parasite. Though not life-threatening, it causes irritation of the bowel and certainly impinges on the quality of everyday life.

While the two town-houses and MRTB 1/ERTB 1 provide the most convincing evidence of structures within the excavated area, we should not overlook the possible remains of one or two timber buildings from the south and south-east. While the small structure, MRTB 2, appears truncated by the southern edge of the excavation, the trench captures the full extent of the possible building MRTB 3, alongside the north–south street. Associating a particular identity with the inhabitants, and distinguishing material to be associated with one building within the excavated area rather than another is very problematic. However, we can perhaps point to the dump of ceramic building material, mostly of roofing tile, and speculate that a trade in used roofing materials was located here. Crummy also points to the unusual collection of bone objects associated with MRTB 3, the majority of which are round-bowled spoons. Although the spoons are more to be expected in a first-century context, so this could well be a residual collection, the possibility remains that the occupants of MRTB 3 also specialised in a trade in bone artefacts. There is certainly insufficient evidence of waste to suggest that bone-working took place in this part of Insula IX. However, although more a feature of Period 4, evidence for the skinning of dogs is present in pit 5039 and well 5693.

Further evidence for the working of bone for a variety of purposes should also be considered here, though some of it is probably as relevant for the occupants of the houses to the north as it is for those who occupied MRTB 3. Ingrem reports the incidence of cattle scapulae having been pierced, probably for suspension during smoking of the meat. We should also note the incidence of bones from the south-east spreads with evidence of having been broken open for the removal of the marrow, for possible use in cosmetics, soap, medicine and lighting. There is also some evidence for the further working of this bone in Period 3 by boiling up the fragments in order to extract grease and glue. With all of these activities it is difficult to characterise the scale of activity and thus distinguish between those undertaken for household consumption and those also with a commercial aim in mind. Smoked shoulders of beef, for example, were certainly consumed in Insula IX, but were some also prepared for sale?

While well 5693 did not produce an assemblage of plant remains, the sole evidence for diet of the inhabitants of the insula to the south of the town-houses, including those of MRTB 3, derives from the faunal assemblages from it and the south-east pit 5039. Possibly significant, then, is the high proportion of sheep/goat and the low proportion of cattle recovered from 5039 and 5693, compared with the northern pits. Taxa other than the main domesticates, but including, particularly, bird and wild animals, account for up to a quarter of the faunal assemblage from pit 5039. It is difficult to distinguish between economic and cultural factors influencing the composition of these assemblages since the meat of wild animals and birds is generally regarded as indicative of (high) status, while the preference for mutton over beef might be an issue of affordability or an indication of the continuation of preferences from the late Iron Age (cf. King 1991).

POPULATION AND WATER

Any attempt to reconstruct the number of inhabitants living within the excavated area of the insula is fraught with difficulty. Many of the problems, including the vexed question of whether houses had upper storeys, have been rehearsed by Boon (1974, 61–2, 193–4), who took both a maximising and a minimising approach. With the former he calculated a total household size of 20 individuals, including dependants and slaves, on the basis of single-storey houses for each of the large houses. In the case of MB 1 and MB 2 we might assume that households were half the size of those of the larger houses and estimate a total of 20 individuals for both. With the total surface area of the two houses amounting to some 500m², this gives a ratio of one person to about 25m². This ratio would remain the same if we allowed for an upper storey and doubled the occupancy to 40. In the case of our timber buildings further uncertainty attaches to their occupancy, not least because of lack of clarity about the nature of the structures themselves. Of the timber buildings to the north-east of MB 1, it would seem that one (ERTB 1) was occupied at least in part by domestic animals. The cleaner MRTB 1, on the other hand, may have provided the quarters for servants or slaves belonging to one or both of the adjacent town-houses. To the south we have suggested one or two timber buildings with a total floor area of 160m². What we have not been able to establish through the application of micromorphology is whether any of these buildings were also occupied by animals, with correspondingly fewer human inhabitants. If we allowed for twice the density of occupation for the poorer timber buildings, of which MRTB 1 and MRTB 3 together account for about 225m², these would account for a further 18 (single storey) or 36 individuals (two storey). Thus, for the excavated area of Insula IX these give totals of either 38 (single-storey building) or 76 (two-storey building). These calculations take no account of the truncated MRTB 2 or the backyard of the house lying beyond the north-west limits of the trench. Since all of our structures appear to belong to the one property, our estimates also relate to that entity. Boon's minimising approach (ibid., 62), which developed alternative and smaller models of family size, allowed for only 12 in the 15 larger houses and 8 in the 135 smaller houses. This gives figures for the overall population within the walled area of 600–750 inhabitants between the second and fourth centuries which seems to us altogether too small and does not allow for more than one kin group per house.

Another way of evaluating the contribution that the discovery of timber buildings makes to the population is to represent their total surface area as a percentage increase on the total surface area of the masonry buildings. In this case the additional space amounts to a 45 per cent increase. If we extrapolate this figure across the whole of the (later) walled area it increases

Boon's (larger) estimate of the total population of the town by at least 1,800 to 5,800. If we allow for a consistently greater density (x2) of occupation of the timber buildings, the population rises to 7,600. If we allow for two-storey buildings across the town within the (later) walled area, the total rises to 15,200 (8,000 + 7,200).

The estimated population within our excavated area appears to have been served by only one well, located some distance from the two town-houses towards the south-east corner of the excavated area and in a position where well(s) had been located earlier. It is always possible, however, there may have been a further well associated with the property containing MB 1 and 2 beyond the limits of the trench. A second well, in the north-west of the trench, appears to relate to the property located in the north-west corner of the insula, beyond the excavated area. On the face of it one well would seem small provision for the households associated with the larger property identified within the excavated area. However, well water could also be supplemented by water captured in storage jars from the run-off of rainwater from roofs, particularly the tiled roofs of MB 1 and 2, or drawn from sources outside the insula.

RITUAL BEHAVIOUR

Crummy and Timby have drawn attention, respectively, to 'small finds', mostly of metal, and pottery vessels, whose condition and position are hard to explain other than as votive deposits. Ingrem, too, proposes that certain deposits of articulated animal bone may be regarded as votive. The majority of these are associated with the construction contexts of the two town-houses and the timber buildings to their north-east and may be regarded as offerings to ensure the life, safety and security of the buildings in question. Crummy draws attention to the complete sets of toilet instruments from relevant contexts associated with MB 2, while a third complete set is associated with MRTB 1. While individual toilet instruments are widely scattered, these three are the only complete sets from the excavated area. An iron mason's trowel incorporated in the walling of MB 2 may probably be regarded as a further offering. Crummy also suggests that three complete, individual items — two brooches, both of first-century date, and an iron knife — can also be regarded as foundation deposits in MB 1. Timby notes the deposition of a complete pottery vessel in the make-ups at each of two adjacent corners of MB 2. One of these was of Silchester ware and thus, like the brooches noted above, of considerable antiquity at the time of deposition. Was this a deliberate, symbolic choice? Curiously it echoes the deposition of a complete Silchester ware jar in the underlying, Period 2 roundhouse ERTB 3 (Clarke *et al.* 2007). A further two complete Alice Holt vessels, one clearly with deliberate piercing of the belly, were found side-by-side in the clay make-ups associated with the construction of both MB 1 and MRTB 1. Such pierced vessels are frequently found in the lower levels and at the bottom of wells (cf. Fulford and Timby 2001) and we should note the occurrence of three flagons from well 2234, one of which has a deliberate slot cut into the belly. Crummy also notes the occurrence of pairs of iron joiner's dogs from pit 4835 and well 5693, an association which recurs in Period 4 (below, p. 342), but then offers a functional interpretation of their presence. As far as deposits of articulated animal bone are concerned, Ingrem notes the articulated foot of a roe deer from the interface between ERTB 2 and MB 1 and the partial skeleton of a dog from MRTB 1/ERTB 1 (Ingrem 2007). We might also note the occurrence of the bones of wild animals and birds, particularly roe deer, which occurs in the basal fills of all the Period 3 pits and wells, while hare and woodcock occur in all but one.

HUMAN REMAINS

In addition to the partial remains of an adult cranium, there is evidence for three infants from Period 3: one burial of a neonate infant and two further finds of single bones from different infants. While it is possible that the adult bone was re-worked from an earlier context associated with the late Iron Age occupation when human burials are known at Silchester (Firth 2000), infant remains are not unexpected in an urban context. The single bones imply re-working of earlier burials.

DOGS

With the exception of the partial skeleton noted above, no articulated dog remains are recorded from Period 3, although pit 4835 and well 5693 produced significant numbers of bone, 6 and 16 bones, respectively.

LEISURE

Evidence for recreation is provided by finds of bone, glass and ceramic counters associated with a variety of board games. Also a possible musical instrument, a bone tube with a small slit cut through one side, which may have formed part of a syrinx or set of pan pipes, was recovered from the south-east corner of the excavation (FIG. 58).

RELATIONS BEYOND *CALLEVA*

Although the presence of imported foodstuffs, such as figs and grapes, among the mineralised plant remains, or the remains of oysters and rare saltwater fish illustrate both the importation of some exotics from outside Britain and trade from the coastal regions, it is probably the ceramics which give a more reliable picture of *Calleva*'s contacts beyond its immediate hinterland. Although residuality is a major problem with the second-century assemblages, there is a consistent representation of imported tablewares, mostly from Lezoux in Central Gaul, and transport amphorae. Including drinking vessels from Cologne and the Argonne, imported tablewares account for *c.* 7 per cent, while amphorae, principally olive-oil carriers from Baetica and wine containers from Narbonensis, amount to 2 to 3 per cent of the pottery, making a total of *c.* 10 per cent imported from outside Britain. From within Britain there is some representation of regional wares, particularly of Verulamium region wares, produced in workshops up to 55 miles distant by road from Silchester. In well 2234, for example, where complete vessels were present, these amounted to some 17 per cent of the assemblage. However, the total representation of regional wares, which also consistently include pottery from South-East Dorset (BB 1) and Oxfordshire, as well as minor representation, for example, from London, Colchester and the Nene Valley, on the one hand, and from Caerleon, on the other, otherwise amounts to little more than 5 per cent of the pottery assemblage. As Timby points out, this may be an under-estimate, given uncertainty over the source of a number of wares likely to be of a regional, southern British origin. Altogether the representation of pottery, both that imported from the Continent and that from beyond the immediate hinterland of *Calleva*, i.e. beyond about 15 miles, within Britain, generally amounts to *c.* 15 per cent in Period 3, the second century A.D. With its complete or near-complete vessels, well 2234, with a combined representation of imported and regional wares of about 25 per cent, appears exceptional. Local production is well attested at Alice Holt and wares from this source, probably traded via the small town at Neatham, account for about half of the Period 3 pottery assemblage from Insula IX. Dorchester-on-Thames may have played a similar, mediating role in the distribution of Oxfordshire pottery south to *Calleva*.

Residuality is also a major issue with the remaining finds assemblage. Nevertheless there is a small quantity of glass that is considered representative of the second half of the second century and some of this is probably imported. Niedermendig lava from north-west Germany is present among the materials used for querns, but the assemblage is dominated by the West Sussex Lodsworth Greensand, much of which is demonstrably residual through its use in the foundations of the town-houses. Lodsworth Greensand is the material of choice for the manufacture of querns found at *Calleva* from its origins in the late first century B.C. (Wooders 2000). How long that continued to be the case is unclear. There are also small quantities of querns of Quartz Conglomerate from the west, from Bristol and the Forest of Dean, and Millstone Grit from either South Wales or the Pennines. It is interesting to note that among the small amount of 'small finds' likely to be 'in period', two are of probable western British manufacture from the lower Severn region.

A different perspective on relations with the hinterland is provided by the evidence for the exploitation of building materials. Period 3 saw investment in two masonry town-houses and two or three timber structures. While we cannot be precise about the origins of the timber, we can assume a local source, given the pollen evidence for woodland in the vicinity of the town at the turn of the second and third centuries (Keith-Lucas 1984). The phytolith evidence from MRTB 1/ERTB 1 indicates that phragmites reed was probably used for thatching, a material which points to the valleys of the Kennet, Loddon and Thames, within a radius of about 10 miles, as likely sources. In the case of the two houses, MB 1 and MB 2, nodular flint quarried from the chalk is the main material used in the foundations and superstructure and, while a precise origin cannot be identified, suitable outcrops of chalk are located within 10 miles of *Calleva*. Ceramic building materials were also likely to have been produced very locally and some evidence of manufacture has been recovered from near the amphitheatre (Fulford *et al.* 1997, 161) and, possibly, from Little London (cf. Boon 1974, 277–9), a little less than two miles to the south-west of the town. Uncertainty surrounds how much of the other building material reported by Hayward and Allen can be associated with the second-century occupation of Insula IX, rather than be dismissed as residual from the monumental/palatial building of the first century A.D. (Fulford 2008). MB 1 certainly had one tessellated floor which is likely to have contained a mosaic. It is reasonable therefore to surmise that it employed some of the Purbeck (south-east Dorset) mosaic materials identified by John Allen. The Isle of Purbeck and the shores of Poole Harbour were also the source of the Kimmeridge shale, the black-burnished pottery BB 1 (above), and the Purbeck marble used for mortars, as well as for building decoration, from Insula IX.

The evidence from both capital projects, the building of the Period 3 houses and structures, and recurrent activity emphasises the variety and importance of the interactions with the immediate hinterland, extending as far as the Alice Holt potteries, some 15 miles to the south-east of *Calleva*. Beyond the local in this definition we can point to a variety of regional links: to the south-west to the Isle of Purbeck and Poole Harbour in south-east Dorset; to the west to the Forest of Dean and South Wales; to the north towards the Oxfordshire pottery kilns; to the south towards Lodsworth (West Sussex) (if that source of querns continued in the second century); and to the east to London, the likely source of all the imported pottery, etc. in Insula IX. In terms of quantity it is the (ceramic) imports and, therefore, London which dominate the regional relations of *Calleva* in the second century A.D.

PERIOD 4

The notable developments of Period 4 and the third century were the demolition of MB 2 and the expansion of MB 1 to create a single, large town-house, MB 3. Apart from the demolition and robbing of walls at the north-east end of MB 1, which united Room 1 with the surrounding corridor, it is not certain whether this house was otherwise completely demolished. Even if the remains of other structures in the excavated area are difficult to define, a further major development of Period 4 is the intensification of pit digging in the south-east of the excavated area. Some of this activity is probably to be associated with a timber building, MRTB 4, and the hearth 2037. This and a second timber building, MRTB 5, were constructed at right angles to the north–south street.

For reconstructing the life and occupation of the new town-house MB 3 we are almost entirely dependent on the material recovered from the occupation spreads to the south and the assumption that they relate to the inhabitants of the house. There is no evidence for the continuation of the Period 3 timber building in the north-east corner of the insula and this space appears to have become derelict. The concentration of pits and wells in the south-east of the excavated area suggests that their contents should be directly linked with MRTB 4. However, closer examination suggests the possibility of two groups, since two pits, 3102 and 3406, lie a little to the south of the others and may be linked with a building beyond the limit of the excavation to the south. The remaining two pits are also close to the two wells 1750 and 5735, which are the only two functional wells within the entire excavated area in Period 4. Despite their relative distance from the main house, it seems unlikely that they did not serve it, as well as the occupants of MRTB 4 and 5. If the wells were connected with the town-house, it remains possible that their filling and associated finds also reflect the life of the house, rather than the adjacent MRTB 4.

THE TOWN-HOUSE MB 3 (FIG. 149)

With the exception of Room 1 at the north-east end of the building with its associated hearths and traces of metalworking, it is not possible to identify contexts which are certainly associated with the life of the building rather than its construction, or, in a few cases, where fourth-century material has been identified, activity which post-dates the demolition of the building. Although we have been inclined to interpret the house as having an upper storey, there can be no certainty of this. Peter Warry has commented on the scarcity of flat tile, which would normally have been used for bonding courses in the otherwise flint fabric of the building, and it

A

B

FIG. 149.   Two pictorial interpretations of Period 4 by Margaret Mathews.
(a) This, based on FIG. 147c, shows MB 3 as a fairly smart town-house with a timber-framed extension over the former MB 2 and a single-storey workshop area on the right, all roofed in tile. Metalworking is in progress in the workshop and the amphora attests the continuing evidence for imported goods. The fence on the right is suggested by excavated post-holes and the figures in the foreground hold pelts, suggested by the evidence for the skinning of animals at this time.
(b) Here the upper part of the building is shown as a continuous build in timber with a thatched upper roof as in FIG. 147b. The suggestion is of a less prestigious building than its predecessor in Period 3. The presence of livestock is not directly evidenced for this phase, but is assumed. The bee skeps and the herb bed reflect the environmental evidence in Ch. 16.

is true that the foundations of the new walls which extended the wall lines of MB 1 were slight — indeed, in the case of the extended, internal, south-east-facing wall of MB 1, no more than 0.12m in depth. However, it is quite possible that the superstructure of the new building was of timber frame resting on dwarf-wall foundations. We should also take into account the effect of hearths on the configuration of internal space. These are concentrated at the northern end of the house, suggesting that this space, at least, was open to the roof. In the light of the evidence and constraints, several interpretations present themselves: that the original MB 1 was entirely built of masonry and included an upper, full or half storey, but that the extension which replaced MB 2 was only of a single, or one-and-a-half storeys in masonry. Alternatively, the entire building was of timber frame and of one-and-a-half or two storeys, or the new extension was of two-storey, timber-frame construction alongside a retained, one-and-a-half or two-storey MB 1 entirely of masonry (see Mathews, Ch. 19).

In earlier interim reports we interpreted MB 3 as an aisled hall (e.g. Clarke and Fulford 2002, 139–41), placing emphasis on the layout of the new wall-foundations cutting through the remains of MB 2. This assumed that all the room divisions of MB 1 were also taken down to give a continuous internal space, and that the north-west-facing outer wall originally extended the full length of the building. In fact we cannot be certain either that Rooms 2 and 3 did not remain intact, in which case the open areas of the building are confined to each end, or that the north-west-facing outer wall of MB 1 was extended south-west.

Uncertainty about the structure and ground-plan of the new town-house also extends to its interior decoration. There is no surviving trace of wall plaster and, apart from Room 2 of the old MB 1, no indication of the floor surfacing of the new house. However, a number of loose tesserae of dolomite cementstone in Room 4 of the new house may be linked with the waste from the manufacture of tesserae of similar material from shallow, Period 4 pits, immediately to the south of the house, and taken as evidence for the existence of a nearby tessellated floor.

FAMILY MATTERS: THE OCCUPANTS OF MB 3

MB 3, described as House 1 by the Victorian excavators in 1893, was created by extending the footprint of MB 1 over that of the demolished MB 2. We have already argued that those two earlier town-houses belonged to the same property and that they represented the homes of two kin groups, representing a development of the two units identified in the underlying ERTB 2, a pairing which has been observed by John Smith (1978; 1997) in villas. The implication of the merging of the two houses is that it represents significant change, either of family organisation, perhaps through the departure of one kin group, or a reduction in the size of households, such that they could be housed under a single roof, or the occupation of the property by a new or unrelated family group. Perhaps the only pointer for there being continuation of occupation by the same kin group is that, although significant change was introduced at the north-east end of MB 1, its footprint was retained. Indeed those changes to MB 1 could have been undertaken at a different time to the construction of the extension which replaced MB 2. However, the new house, MB 3, contains two 'halls', one at each end of the building, but with one containing more evidence of hearths and possible metalworking than the other, while the mosaic-floored reception room in MB 1 appears to have been downgraded with no evidence for the refurbishment of the floor. The new hall at the south-west end may have become the principal room of the new house, while at the same time, with its counterpart at the opposite end of the building, preserving the duality of the two earlier houses.

The new building is impressive in its size, and one of the larger town-houses of *Calleva Atrebatum*, even if almost nothing survives to determine the degree of internal splendour. Aggrandisement, rather than reconstruction to match the changing needs of the resident kin group, may have been a significant motivating force behind the project. There is undoubtedly a trend, already evident in successive phases of timber building in Verulamium up to the fire of A.D. 155, towards larger houses from the mid-second century onwards (Frere 1983). This can also be seen at Colchester (e.g. Culver Street and Lion Walk) (Crummy 1984; 1992). It is likely, too, that the larger, winged corridor and courtyard-plan houses, such as those across the north–south street in Insula I, at

Silchester originate from the mid-second century onwards. The decision to build MB 3 may have been driven solely by the desire to emulate peers.

MRTB 4 AND 5

The evidence of further buildings within the excavated area is confined to the south-east where there are traces of two structures, one which coincides with the footprint of Late Roman Building 5 and the other whose ground-plan partly coincides with that of Late Roman Building 1. Neither of these structures has much substance in terms of wall outlines, rather than floor surfaces, but we can be more confident in the existence of the southern building, given the association of a hearth and the close configuration of pits. Of the latter (and excluding the two wells) two (2434 and 2601) contain material which suggests they were filled after about the middle of the third century. In the case of the other two (3406 and 3102) the majority of the fills seem to be somewhat earlier in the third century. Whether the fills of these pits give a reliable clue as to the date of construction and the life of the building we cannot be so confident, since both they and MRTB 5 lie at the upper end of the Period 4 (Object 700) stratigraphic sequence. This would point to their belonging more to the second half of the third century.

OCCUPATIONS: MB 3 (FIG. 150)

The only certain evidence of the nature of the occupation associated with MB 3 is that which derives from the house itself. In this case elemental concentrations from hearths and burnt areas in Room 1 suggest continuity of metalworking from Period 3, in particular of both precious metal (gold and silver) and copper alloys. Although waste from both ironmaking and ironworking was recovered from Period 4 contexts, in particular from Room 4, it is not certain whether they can be associated with the occupation of the house, rather than with make-ups imported for its construction phase.

OCCUPATIONS ELSEWHERE

Waste from ironmaking and ironworking was recovered from across the excavated area. Though larger than in Period 3, the total amount is small and, as with the context of the slag associated with MB 3, the presence of relatively large quantities in the make-up layer for Late Roman Buildings 1 and 5 suggests the possibility that it was imported for this purpose from outside the insula. By comparison the quantities of the larger slag masses recovered from the pits and wells are very small and no significant collections of microscopic hammerscale were recovered from contexts which were wet-sieved. If we see the contents of the pits as reflecting more closely the activities carried out in their immediate vicinity, then ironmaking and ironworking were insignificant in the third century in our area of Insula IX, though, by implication, of greater importance elsewhere in the town.

The only other craft activity which can certainly be associated with this area of Insula IX is the preparation of tesserae, evidenced by the waste deposited in pits associated with MRTB 5 immediately to the south of MB 3. However, it is possible that this activity related only to the construction of the house MB 3.

Although we do not have the micromorphological evidence to indicate the presence of herbivores within the excavated area in Period 4, the presence of bone of neonatal/foetal sheep/goat and of pig as well as one of a calf strongly suggests that animal husbandry continued to be an important strand in the life of the inhabitants of Insula IX. Indeed, beetles which feed on the droppings of domestic animals on pasture and on their bedding and fodder, as well as those which occur in other categories of foul organic material including dung, were found in the waterlogged fills of the early third-century well 5735. To animal husbandry we should also add the possibility of bee keeping. The remains of honey bee from well 5735 suggest the presence of a colony close by.

Systematic exploitation of animals is evidenced in two ways. First, there is the incidence of large mammal limb bone with evidence for the removal of the marrow for a variety of possible purposes and subsequently for boiling to produce grease and glue. This practice is more common than in Period 3 (above, p. 332). Second, study of the dog bone has revealed systematic evidence of the knife marks associated with skinning, rather than disarticulation in preparation for cooking (and there is no other evidence for butchery of dogs in this period). These bones are concentrated in the pits and make-ups around MRTB 4 in the south-east corner of the excavated area and suggest that the inhabitants prepared the pelts from young adult or sub-adult, probably female, dogs for the market. Although present in Period 3, this practice is well established in Period 4. The bones of two badgers also show the same evidence for the removal of their pelts.

For the status and lifestyle of the occupants of MB 3 and of the timber buildings to its south, we have a comparable range of evidence as for Period 3, but, given the scarcity of occupational contexts associated with the house, we have to look to the material from the spreads to the south of MB 3 (Object 700), where there is still a considerable element of residuality in the 'small finds' assemblage, which includes bone hairpins, brooches and toilet instruments. There is not a single third-century brooch — indeed, only a wire armlet or anklet may be of third-century date! The majority of items which might be contemporary with the third-century occupation, such as the beads and hairpin from pit 3406 and the bead, hairpin and armlet from pit 2434, are confined to the south-east area.

While the ratio of all types of imported tableware pottery remains high at about 8 per cent in the large assemblage from the Period 4 occupation spreads, it is dominated by residual material. This is particularly true of the closely datable samian, with only one context (3836) at the top of the stratigraphic sequence of Object 700 with probable third-century material. This layer also contains a high proportion (21 per cent) of South-East Dorset BB1, which otherwise doubles its overall representation from Period 3 to Period 4 to 6 per cent, partly at the expense of slightly reduced supply from the other, main regional producer, the Oxfordshire ware industry.

The absence of samian contemporary with its date of deposition in the third century is also evident in the case of the south-east pits and wells, which otherwise have comparable ratios of imported tableware to the southern occupation spreads, but a high representation of regional wares, particularly BB1, comparable to that from the late context 3836 in Object 700. Altogether there is nothing to distinguish the composite character of the ceramic assemblages from the south-east pits and wells from that single, late context in the southern occupation spreads. However, in comparison with Object 700 as a whole, there is a distinctively higher proportion of regional (cooking) wares from the south-east pits and wells.

If we look to the glass from Period 4 for evidence of the replacement of ceramic table and drinking wares with glass, we find almost none. Denise Allen comments that there is less glass altogether from Period 4 and notes that there are no more than five examples (fragments) altogether of third-century glass bowls, cups and plates, some of which may be imported. There is, therefore, almost no evidence for tableware, including drinking vessels, of either ceramics or glass, in Period 4. One possibility to explain these lacunae is that the third century saw the rise of the manufacture of pewter tableware. Notoriously difficult to date, with deposition predominantly associated with the fourth century, it is worth noting that the one stratified example of a pewter mould from the large collection from the nearby forum-basilica is associated with a late third-century coin (Fulford and Timby 2000, 72, 390–1). Another possibility is that, on grounds of economy, perhaps, more wood was being used for vessels in the third century.

Assuming that the high representation of regional wares has some status implications, it is interesting to note that, with one exception, the only high-status and continental-made items from Period 4 were also found in the south-east pits and well 5735. These include the complete knife or razor with its unique, zoomorphic, ivory handle, the handle of the rare 'foot-handled' copper-alloy jug, the silver-in-glass bead, and the fragment of the necklace of beryl and gold. The exception is the decorative peg from an ivory *pyxis* from the occupation spreads of Object 700. The evidence of the glass tells a similar story to that of the 'small finds'. With one possible exception, all the glass of early third-century date, and thus contemporary with Period 4, was found in the south-eastern pits and wells. This includes the (rare in Britain) continental-made 'Mercury flask' from pit 2434. The concentration of the high-status finds from the south-east area of the excavation raises the question whether they might derive from the occupants of MRTB

FIG. 150. A view from the doorway of MB 3 south-eastwards across the gravel yard by Margaret Mathews. The scene incorporates several aspects of the evidence for life in Period 4. There is little evidence for the structural detail of the two buildings aligned at right angles to the street but they are located as found, the far building (MRTB 5) here shown with a stone-tile roof to reflect evidence for stone roofing (Ch. 9). Activity in the vicinity surrounds the skinning and preparation of pelts, including those of dogs, as suggested in Ch. 14. Well 1750 is shown with a wooden cover suggested by the evidence of joiner's dogs in several pits and wells (Ch. 6). The shack on the right is located over cess-pit 2434, although there is no direct evidence of a covering structure. The bee skeps and the herb bed and the presence of animals, evidenced by their dung, are derived from the environmental evidence in Ch. 16. The enjoyment of imported goods is represented by the amphora and the more elegant lady in the background is suggested by the many finds of bone pins and other dress items from this area. Beyond the confines of the potholed yard, the next property is shown as representative of a state of dilapidation that must have always been an element of the townscape. Across the north–south street a more imposing building, facing away from the street, is on the location of the large courtyard house in Insula I excavated by Joyce and the Antiquaries. In the background on the right the Roman forum can be seen above some other smarter houses in the 'town centre'.

4, rather than from MB 3, or from a combination of the latter and a household to the south beyond the edge of the excavated area. With one unique and two very rare (for Britain) objects, this would imply a higher status for MRTB 4 than its insubstantial structural remains would otherwise indicate. This point is developed further in relation to the associated food remains.

   Overall, the problem remains that there are very few finds, except among the regional and local pottery, which clearly belong to the third century. This raises the question as to how much of the 'residual' material was really rubbish churned up from earlier occupation as opposed to long-lived items disposed of for the first time in the third century.

   Importantly, however, the greater incidence of styli than in Period 3 and the wooden writing-tablet from well 5735 point to the continuing literacy of the inhabitants of our area of Insula IX, including from the town-house and MRTB 4. There are also graffiti on pottery attributable to Period 4.

   The evidence of diet derives principally from the animal bone and from the waterlogged seeds and plant remains which were recovered from well 5735 in the south-east of the excavated area. Of the main domesticates cattle is a little more important as a source of meat in Period 4 than earlier, and caprines outnumber pig. Along with domestic fowl, wild animals and birds, a small amount of, mostly freshwater, fish was also eaten. There is a very small amount of oyster both from the south-east pits and wells and from the occupation spreads of Object 700. Unlike in the Period 3 pits in the south-east, cattle predominate in all the Period 4 pits in the south-east (except the Victorian-excavated well 1750). Domestic fowl, wild birds and wild animals are also present in all these pits. The remains recovered from well 5735 point to the consumption of fruits — apple, blackberry, bullace, damson, plum and imported fig and grape — while other cultivated plants such as black mustard, celery, coriander, dill and spelt wheat were also present, as were shell fragments of hazelnuts and walnuts. Together this evidence supports that of the material finds that the inhabitants of the south-east MRTB 4 enjoyed a varied diet including imported fruits. Imports also extended to olive oil (Dressel 20 from Baetica), also found in the occupation spreads, and to imported fish, if that is the correct identification of the contents of the single (and early) find of a southern Portuguese or Spanish Almagro 50 amphora from pit 3406.

POPULATION AND WATER

In terms of the definite, well-defined floor area of buildings associated with Period 4, there is almost no change from Period 3, since the new house MB 3 simply represents the amalgamation of the two earlier masonry houses, amounting to just under 500m². Taking account of the loss of the timber building to the north-east of MB 3, there is a reduction by 42 per cent to 130m² in the surface area of associated timber buildings, in this case MRTB 4 and 5, with their less well defined structural arrangements, compared with Period 3. All of this might suggest that the number of inhabitants within the excavated area was also slightly reduced. Such an interpretation would be supported by the evidence of the wells. Although there are two associated with Period 4 in the south-east of the excavation trench, where there was only one in Period 3, the dating evidence would suggest that one (1750) followed the other (5735). The final filling of the latter appears to precede the felling of the wood for the lining of 1750. We do not know for certain when well 1750 was filled because the Victorian excavation removed the vast majority of the fill. However, there was sufficient recognition of the slumping caused by the consolidation of the fill at the time of the construction of Late Roman Building 1 at the end of the third century for an extra depth of foundation to be provided. This might well indicate a recent infilling, perhaps just prior to the building of the new house in *c.* A.D. 300. While the number of inhabitants of the larger property within the excavated area may have declined a little compared with Period 3, there is less certainty for the northern property where we do not have evidence of a Period 4 well. Given that we probably only have a small proportion of that property within the excavated area, it is possible that a Period 4 well lies just beyond the edge of the trench. Overall, therefore, we suggest that the number of inhabitants within the excavated area, and particularly those associated with the larger property, was slightly less (at 30 (single storey) or 60 (two storey)) than in Period 3.

RITUAL BEHAVIOUR

The nature of possible votive or 'structured' deposits in Period 4 differs considerably from Period 3 (cf. Eckardt, Ch. 18). Whereas, as we have seen, objects of ceramic or metal dominate such deposits belonging to the earlier period and particularly in association with the construction of buildings, in Period 4 there is a greater emphasis on deposits involving articulated animal remains, particularly in association with pits and wells. In relation to buildings, however, we should also note the burial of a partial sheep skeleton in the make-ups associated with MB 3. Perhaps the most striking deposit of Period 4 is that of the articulated skeleton of a 6–8-month-old dog, probably a complete carcass at the time of deposition, associated with the knife or razor with ivory handle depicting mating dogs, from pit 2601, which has been commented on by Crummy, Clark and Eckardt (above, Chs 6, 14 and 18). That there is considerable meaning to the deposited artefacts and animal bone in this pit is given added weight by the presence of the remains of two other dogs and, perhaps more significantly, the associated occurrence of five raven bones, probably from the same bird. Was the young dog a sacrifice? Timby also notes the occurrence of the sherd of a vessel which had been doubly pierced before deposition. Of course the latter may be part of the otherwise apparently insignificant material culture associated with this pit — sherds in the soil with which it was filled, but a find like this does raise the question as to what might or might not have meaning beyond that of household rubbish. In this particular case we are not helped by the massive disturbance of the pit, and consequent 'loss' of finds, by the digging of the foundations for Late Roman Building 1. In trying to gain insight into this deposit, it is interesting to note, and this may well be more than a coincidence, that, as we have seen above, dogs, through the pelts which they provided, made an important contribution to the livelihood of the inhabitants of MRTB 4. But what prompted this deposit, which involved the loss of what has proved to be the most exceptional find from Periods 3 and 4, remains tantalisingly elusive.

Pit 2601 represents the only example of the deposition of a complete carcass of a dog from Period 4, and in circumstances which would appear to have a strong ritual connotation. Elsewhere, with one exception of articulating vertebrae from well 1750, the basal contexts of pits and wells contain disparate bones of dogs from up to four different animals.

This mixed character of the dog bone assemblage is also typical of other animal and bird remains from the lowest contexts of the wells, which also merit comment. In particular we can point to the occurrence of the bones of raven, probably from a single bird, in a primary construction context of well 1750. Possibly just as significant are the bones of further wild animals and bird — hare, red deer and woodcock — from the same context. Red deer, hare and goose are also reported from well 5735 and there is similar representation of wild animals and birds from other pits. Ingrem (above, p. 268) also raises the question whether the deposition of single bones of horse may have a symbolic significance, for example, the single tibia from pit 3102.

Other than the association of dog and dog-handled knife, there is no clear patterning in the material culture deposited in the Period 4 pits and wells. Crummy makes the case for the handle of the very rare, foot-handled jug from the basal fill of well 5735 being a deliberate votive deposit, observing that, had the body of the vessel broken away, it, too, would have been recovered. The exceptionally rare find of a writing-tablet, in this case of maple wood, was also recovered from the bottom of this well. At a more mundane level, and recalling comparable pairs of such finds in Period 3, Crummy notes the occurrence of three iron joiner's dogs from pit 3102. Also from the base of this pit Timby records that a small unguent flask had been deliberately pierced, recalling the sherds from pit 2601, while from the basal fills of pit 3406 came the only other complete vessel from Period 4 — a Nene Valley colour-coated box lid, an item rare in a Silchester context. Associated with the latter was most of a BB1 jar and substantial parts of other jars. Most of a BB1 jar was also recovered from the basal fills of pit 2434, which also produced the partial skeletons of two badgers as well as bones of other wild animal and bird.

Altogether there are items and associations of items which have attracted comment in relation to the possibility of purposive, votive deposition from all the Period 4 pits and wells, including 1750, from which the majority of the contents were removed without description in 1893.

HUMAN REMAINS

The remains of three neonates were recovered from Period 4, from three different contexts among the occupation spreads to the south of MB 3. In two cases the remains were represented by two bones, in the third by a single bone. As with the remains in Period 3, we must suppose that these occurrences resulted from the disturbance of complete burials.

DOG REMAINS

There are more than twice as many dog bones from Period 4 as from Period 3, the great majority deriving from young adult or sub-adult animals. This increased incidence may relate to a concentration of dog-processing activity in this period as evidenced by the knife marks left by the skinning of the animals. There is only one example where a dog was probably deposited as a complete carcass, from pit 2601, discussed above. However, articulating cervical vertebrae were found at the base of well 1750. Bones from up to four different dogs were recovered from individual pits and wells, while up to five times as many individual dog bones were represented in Period 4 pits and wells compared with those from Period 3.

LEISURE

Period 4 includes further examples of counters of bone, glass and recycled pot sherds, some of which would probably have been used in Roman-style board games.

ENVIRONMENT

A frequently asked question by the public during the excavation of the masonry houses was whether we had found evidence for gardens. From the northern property, the backyard of a house situated in the north-west corner of the insula, there is evidence for the cultivation of the soils, but we cannot be more specific about the nature of the horticulture. It is only from well 5735 that we have any particular insight into the possible condition of the larger area occupied by MB 3. The presence of plants such as stinging-nettle indicates an unkempt appearance to the property associated with this town-house, a picture which would be in keeping with the evidence for the presence of domesticated animals and their waste. However, the presence of box and holly, also in the well, suggests that there was an ornamental garden somewhere in the vicinity, either further south in Insula IX, or across the street in Insula I to the east.

RELATIONS BEYOND *CALLEVA*

It is the material culture, particularly the ceramic, glass and stone, which gives insight into the wider connections of Insula IX in the third century. As we have seen there are also clearly imported — and rare — artefacts among the 'small finds', such as the foot-handled jug or the ivory-handled knife, while the water-logged deposits from well 5735 provide a few examples of imported foodstuffs, particularly fig. In that they contain less residual material than the layers, the contents of the pits and wells are particularly helpful in developing a picture of the wider contacts of the inhabitants of the insula, but Timby and Tyers also isolate a particular context among the occupation spreads (Object 700) south of the town-house which contains less obviously residual material than other layers among these deposits. Nevertheless it is still hard to isolate goods which were definitely imported, rather than simply finally deposited, in the third century. Central Gaulish samian, for example, accounts for 6 per cent of the pottery assemblage in the Period 4 layers but, with the exception of layer 3836, it is all residual. This is also true of the material from the south-east pits. In the case of layer 3836, which contains a small quantity of both Central and Eastern Gaulish (Rheinzabern) sigillata, the typology of the South-East Dorset BB1 suggests a *terminus post quem* of c. A.D. 225–250. Conspicuous in this context is the representation of the regional ware, Dorset BB1, at 21.5 per cent by count of the group. The production of this ware is centred around Poole Harbour, more than 65 miles distant from Silchester. While Oxfordshire ware, also classified as a regional ware, is present in this assemblage, its production is centred only some 25 miles north of Silchester and may therefore be considered as more local. Alice Holt production, which accounts for more than half of the pottery assemblage, was located about 15 miles distance from Silchester. If we therefore discount one 'regional' ware as 'local' in this context, nevertheless over one fifth of the assemblage is otherwise non-local, with material imported from Gaul present, too. South-East Dorset BB1 is also well represented among all the south-east pits and wells with percentages by sherd count ranging from 14 to over 23 per cent. Nene Valley wares, produced in workshops about 90 miles distant from Silchester, are also present in these pits. Thus, if we discount the definitely residual material, it is clear that the contribution of extra-provincial trade in pottery is negligible in the third century. This is also true of the glass, where, of the handful of fragments which are 'in period', some were undoubtedly imports. On the other hand, connections are not just reduced to relations with near-neighbours, because of the significant presence of distantly-produced regional wares, among which South-East Dorset BB1 is by far the most conspicuous. In terms of the ceramics, the rise of Dorset BB1 and the decline in representation of pottery from outside Britannia are the most notable features of Period 4 and the third century, representing significant change from Period 3. In terms of functionality the inhabitants of Insula IX acquired almost no new tableware, including drinking vessels, in the third century. As we have seen above, the dominant regional import, Dorset BB 1, whose representation in the Period 4 assemblage is equivalent to or greater than the combined representation of continental imports and other British regional wares, contributed only cooking wares.

Just as in Period 3, construction provides a different perspective on *Calleva*'s relationship with both its immediate and more distant hinterland. MB 3 involved the use of similar, if not the same materials as those used for MB 1 and 2. Indeed there is a strong possibility that the building of MB 3 simply involved the re-cycling of the existing materials for foundations and walls. As Warry points out, it is difficult to re-use ceramic roofing materials unless they conform to one specification of size and cut-out, otherwise they will not fit together. There is also a singular lack of his later, type D *tegulae* from Insula IX. Whether this means that MB 3 was roofed with thatch or with stone slates, which begin to appear at Silchester in Period 4, is unclear. Roofing materials of both Stonesfield slate from west Oxfordshire and Gloucestershire and Pusey Flags from south Oxfordshire are present in Period 4. Some of the Brownstones, typically used for roofing as well as paving, could also have been employed in this way for MB 3. These new elements in the stone used at Silchester in the third century are paralleled by the appearance of other lithologies, either new to Silchester, or exploited in a significant way in the third century. These include shelly greensands, grey sandstones and Corallian limestone, all of which have been identified in quantity (along with flint, significantly in the majority) in the later third-century town wall (Sellwood 1984). Some of these 'new' materials are used in the foundations of MB 3. For decoration of the Period 4 town-house we have pointed to the waste from the manufacture of tesserae of Purbeck (south-east Dorset) dolomite cementstone as evidence of the possible use of this material in the flooring of MB 3. With a date of *c.* A.D. 200 this is the latest example of the use of this material in tessellated flooring outside south-east Dorset. Period 4 also sees the deposition of large numbers of tesserae of Portlandian sandstone from Swindon (Wilts.). Whether or not these were used in MB 3, they add to the Period 4 horizon of new lithologies employed both in Insula IX and Silchester more generally. While the pattern of stone exploitation points to a significantly greater regional presence in Period 4 than in Period 3 (allowing for the recycling of local flint), we should not overlook the continued requirement for resources likely to have been obtained locally, such as timber, thatch, chalk (for lime), gravel and clay for both the masonry and timber buildings.

The use of more regionally located stone sources complements the evidence of the ceramics which points to significantly greater regional interaction in the third century. Here there is greater emphasis on links with the north, west and south-west at the expense of the south and the east. To the north newly-exploited sources of stone complement existing links with the Oxfordshire potteries; to the west the presence of the Portlandian sandstone and the greater volume of material — roofing slates and paving — sourced from the Forest of Dean point to the intensification of this link; to the south-west the strong presence of SE Dorset BB 1 emphasises the importance of the connection with Purbeck and Poole Harbour. New Forest pottery, either supplied from the south via Winchester, or via the Portway, begins to appear in Period 4. While the local link to the south-east and the Alice Holt potteries, probably via the small town of Neatham, remains as strong as ever, the scarcity of imports and the end of the Verulamium-region pottery production indicate a decline in traffic to the east and London. With no convincing evidence to suggest the continuation of production of Lodsworth querns beyond the early second century, there is little or no indication of contacts to the south/south-east.

CONCLUSIONS

The period between the construction of the two small town-houses, MB 1 and 2, and the demolition of their successor, MB 3, was essentially one of continuity. Property boundaries appear to have remained unchanged and, despite the demolition of the earlier houses and their replacement by a single dwelling, it is reasonable to suppose continuity of ownership, but change in family structure. Difficulties surround the nature and extent of ancillary, timber buildings and different levels of confidence can be placed in each of them — the main issue being the difficulty of identifying consistent evidence of structural supports, in the form of either posts or sleeper-beam-type construction. The existence of hearths, as in MRTB 1 and 4, or of pits grouped in close proximity, as with MRTB 4, provides good supporting evidence. While continuity of use into Period 3 is proposed for the Period 2 ERTB 1, a further five structures were newly built between Periods 3 and 4. With the exception of MRTB 1 and 2 whose footprints follow the 'diagonal' alignment, the remaining buildings, the first of which (MRTB 3) was built in Period 3, align with, and potentially open onto the north–south street. The three buildings, MRTB 3–5, which align with the north–south street indicate a gradual acceptance of the potential advantages of proximity to a main thoroughfare and point the way to the radical re-organisation of Insula IX towards the end of the third century. Together, they represent the gradual transition from a defiance towards the realities and consequences of the new-planned *Calleva* of the later first century A.D. to a full engagement by *c.* A.D. 300 (cf. Fulford *et al.* 2006, 249–52). By the third century we can identify at least one specialist trade associated with one of these timber buildings: the furrier, or processor of dog and other pelts, of MRTB 4.

The importance of these timber buildings is not only in their positioning and relationship with each other and the masonry town-houses, but in their very existence, complementing the stone-built structures and providing evidence of the density of building and occupation of the town which was not at all evident when Silchester was first excavated extensively in the later nineteenth and early twentieth centuries. With a manner of construction which is very different from, say, the sleeper-beam and post-in-trench of the pre-Flavian and Flavian buildings on the site of the forum-basilica (Fulford and Timby 2000), it requires open-area excavation well beyond the limits of the masonry buildings to recognise their existence and recover their plans. While in Period 3 the new timber buildings (excluding the partial footprint of MRTB 2) add a further *c.* 178m² (27 per cent) to the built environment, additional to the surface areas of MB 1 and 2, in Period 4 the figure is 134m², 21 per cent more than the footprint of MB 3. Setting aside ERTB 1 with its presumed function as a byre in Period 3, this suggests a population of Insula IX approximately 20–25 per cent greater than that which might be inferred from the masonry buildings alone. In both periods, however, successive wells in a single location remained the sole source of ground water for the larger property, which also embraced all the buildings located within the excavation area. On the whole, therefore, the population derived from our excavated sample of Insula IX seems to have remained relatively stable throughout Periods 3 and 4.

We have been concerned to identify different occupations among the inhabitants of our area of Insula IX. What we cannot do, without experimentation, is to easily assess the scale of the various activities which we have recognised, beyond the fact that they take place in a domestic or domestic-cum-workshop environment. We can, however, trace continuities and discontinuities and, to a degree, the changing intensity of different occupations through time. However, there is also the question of residuality. We have seen that there is a strong residual element in all categories of material culture, which, by implication, must also extend, but in a way impossible to systematically identify, to the faunal remains. Therefore we can attach greater confidence to the presence of occupations among the households within Insula IX when they can be localised by *in-situ* evidence. At a second level of confidence we could include the evidence of the contents of pits and wells and, to a lesser extent, some of the occupation spreads which tend to include a greater proportion of contemporary material than, say, the make-ups of buildings. The latter, with a significantly high proportion of residual material, as we have found to be the case with MB 1 to 3, present the third, or least reliable source of evidence.

In the case of metalworking we could be persuaded by the macroscopic remains of crucibles and slags that this was a very minor concern and that, possibly, all the waste documented within the excavation area was introduced from elsewhere in the town to be used as make-ups, etc. However, the geochemistry localises the working of copper alloy and of precious metals to MB 1 and, in Period 4, MB 3 and the restriction to the same part of the successive buildings implies a continuity of activity through the second and third centuries. Our few crucible fragments and the unfinished copper-alloy casting may well belong to this activity. Our assumption is that production, at a household level of manufacture, was, however, for sale or exchange beyond the household. There is also the evidence of ironmaking as evidenced by the slag basins and the forging residues. This could also be described as at a household level, but, unlike the working of the non-ferrous metals, we can demonstrate a greater volume of activity in Period 4 (and greater still in the fourth century (Tootell 2006)). With the need for iron for fittings and nails for the various buildings, it is quite possible that all of this activity was dedicated to meeting domestic needs within Insula IX. However, the relative increase, period to period, might suggest otherwise. In contrast, there is no evidence for the working of copper alloys or precious metals from the fourth century and later within the excavated area of Insula IX.

The difficulty of distinguishing from this scale of evidence between production for home consumption and for the market is also highlighted by the evidence for agricultural activities, particularly animal husbandry. In addition to the skeletal evidence of neonates of cattle, sheep or goat, and pig, there is also the proxy evidence of the insect remains from the Period 4 well and the micromorphology from the decaying Period 3 ERTB 1 for the presence of herbivores within this excavated area of Insula IX. The absence of the application of micromorphological approaches other than to ERTB 1/MRTB 1 for either Period 3 or 4 means that we cannot use evidence from this methodology to compare between periods. The piercing of scapulae taken to indicate that some of the meat was cured is also difficult to read. It could have been just to meet domestic needs, or for sale or exchange, or for a combination of all of these. In contrast with animal husbandry, there is a marked absence in the botanical record of evidence for the local cultivation and processing of cereals. This is supported not only by the absence of carbonised, botanical evidence, as residues of the drying and processing of the crop, but also by the rarity of querns in Periods 3 and 4, and beyond into the fourth century. The bulk of the assemblage of (fragmentary) handmills, often with evidence of re-use as whetstones, is made up of the Lodsworth variety which seems to have ceased to be manufactured by the late second/early third century (Shaffrey 2003, 161–3). Once that category is taken out, we are left with very small numbers, of which a proportion is probably residual. Although the botanic record indicates the presence of some whole grain, is it possible that cereals were also reaching Insula IX already processed into flour? Might we interpret the negative evidence from Insula IX as further support for the increased use of animal or water-powered mills in Roman Britain?

Pointing more to the meeting of needs beyond the household is the evidence for the extraction of marrow and fats from the long bones, particularly of cattle. Once again the quantities are not great, and experimentation is required to understand better the scale of this activity in terms of the quantities of derived fats, but there does appear to be an increase in this processing activity over time with the greatest incidence in the fourth century (Ingrem 2006). On the other hand the household engaging with the skinning of dogs and badgers for their pelts is confined to Period 4. In all cases the occupational activity attested from our excavation area can be associated with either *in-situ* evidence, or that derived from pits and wells, with further confirmation from occupation spreads.

This thread of occupational activity through Periods 3 and 4 complements the evidence from both the houses themselves and from the associated material and biological evidence that our households are not particularly wealthy. In terms of masonry buildings we have two modest town-houses in Period 3 and, though the Period 4 house is larger, it does not show evidence of having been well decorated. Indeed, while we have lost the majority of the evidence for the internal decoration of the three town-houses, it would appear that either MB 1 was not completed, with, for example, no surface laid over the north-west-facing corridor, or that no attempt was made to make repairs after heavy wear had reduced the surface to the underlying clay and some of the space was thereafter dedicated to cooking. So, too, it is questionable whether a surface was laid in Room 1 before it was turned over to metalworking. After the demolition of MB 2 to make way for the single dwelling MB 3, no attempt appears to have been made to repair or replace any internal surface within the footprint of the predecessor building, MB 1. The extent of the robbing of MB 2 is such that we cannot draw any conclusions about its finished state or that of the south-west end of the successor dwelling, MB 3. While the initial construction of the shells of the three masonry buildings represents two phases of substantial, but short-lived investment, their successive occupants did not enjoy a high standard of physical environment in terms of internal decor. The question of how far the town-houses were decorated internally recalls similar debate about the degree of finish of the flooring and interior decor of the nearby Hadrianic-Antonine forum-basilica (Fulford and Timby 2000, 573–6).

This is in some contrast with the evidence for daily life as seen through their diet which shows considerable variety: domesticated and wild meat and a range of cereals, legumes and fruits. Fish, both freshwater and marine, in comparison with the fourth century (Ingrem 2006), are rare, but, though equally not plentiful, there are exotic imports of figs and grapes as well as of wine and olive oil, the latter carried in ceramic amphorae. Oysters are also not abundant — a situation which pertains through the fourth century (Williams 2006). It is difficult to make judgements about the overall availability of food, and it is reasonable to assume years of plenty and years of shortages, but the consistent variety suggests a good standard of living.

With the material culture the evidence of affluence, identity and status becomes more difficult and paradoxical. All the chapters reporting and discussing the material culture draw attention to the significant amounts of residual material of first or first/early second-century A.D. date. The question is how much of this material is genuinely residual — rubbish recycled through the excavation of earlier deposits for wall foundations, pits and wells — and how long-lived it was, remaining in use well beyond its period of manufacture. We can obtain some insight into the length of the life (and, presumably, the use) of an object when we have indisputable evidence of its continued use as a complete or near-complete item. So, for example, we note the continuing use of the large, Silchester ware jar, latterly probably for cooking, during the life of MB 1, for more than a century after the time when this pre-Flavian ware was being produced. A Silchester ware jar, at least fifty years old at the time of deposition, provided one of two foundation deposits in the make-ups of MB 2. The glass 'Mercury' bottle from the Period 4 pit 2434 may also have been about one hundred years old when it came to be deposited. Less surprising, perhaps, is the likely one hundred years or more age of the handle of the copper-alloy *Fusshenkelkrug* deposited at the base of well 5735, filled in the early third century. If we do not allow for numerous long-lived items in our Period 3 and 4 contexts, we are confronted with a serious dearth of material culture for the second and third centuries. The paradox of our finds is that the more representative collections, in terms of the number of items approximately contemporary with the presumed date of deposition, are associated with the poorer and least robust structures. In Period 3, on the face of the range and number of finds — copper-alloy, glass, ceramic, etc. — associated with it, MRTB 1/ERTB 1 would appear to be relatively rich. While it may be correct to take this evidence at face value and assume that the rigorous cleaning of the two town-houses and their yards has removed all trace of contemporary material and biological culture, we have advanced the suggestion that the area of the decaying ERTB 1 was used as a midden and a byre, with the possibility of continued human occupation not completely discounted. The contrast between the relative affluence, sophistication and 'Romanisation' displayed through the material culture found in and around MRTB 1 and the stalling of animals is striking. But the animals indicate another source of wealth and the implication of nearby pasture for grazing links our occupants of MB 1 and, perhaps, too, of MB 2, to land owned or rented outside the urban centre. We have argued that the continuity of building alignment from Period 2 to Period 3 can be seen as at least the second generation of occupation by the same extended family. Nina Crummy has made a strong case (2007) that the toilet instruments, particularly the nail-cleaners, deposited in the foundations of the houses 'clearly demonstrate that the builders, and presumably therefore also the inhabitants, of MB 1 and 2 were of British origin'. It is hard, therefore, not to identify the occupants of MB 1 and 2 as well established 'old family', if not particularly affluent members of Callevan society, and, perhaps, of the town's *ordo*.

In accounting for the relatively rich collection of material culture, including a unique knife with ivory handle, from the Period 4 pits in the vicinity of MRTB 4, we have argued that it probably does derive from its occupants, rather than those of MB 3. The combination of the particular material find, its association with the dog and other finds within the pit, and, from adjacent contexts, with the skinning of dogs and other animals generates a powerful identity for at least some of the occupants. While some special circumstances may surround these deposits, as they certainly do in the case of pit 2601, we might otherwise regard the total assemblage from these south-east pits as a benchmark of the circumstances of a poorer household in third-century *Calleva*. If we accept this association, however, we are still left with the almost complete absence of finds to be associated with MB 3. Nevertheless, the continuation in use of the same footprint as the masonry buildings of Period 3 suggests the third generation of occupancy by the same family with broadly comparable ranking in Callevan society as in Period 3, but working the income to be derived from rental somewhat harder; with the buildings MRTB 4 and 5 occupying about 25 per cent more of the north–south street frontage than the equivalent building in Period 3. To conclude: if, in general, we infer that a significant proportion of material culture had a life expectancy well beyond its period of manufacture, and that much of the first and first/early second century was indeed used in the second and third centuries, none of the households associated with our two periods of town-house was materially prosperous, an observation which goes against the traditional association of masonry town-houses with relative prosperity, and which contrasts with the dietary evidence. Indeed, craft and occupational activity were more important in Period 4 than in Period 3.

To add to the contradictory or ambiguous messages about relative wealth and status, just as we have noted that Period 4 has more indications of craft activity than earlier, particularly in respect of the processing of animal bone and the making and forging of iron — two trends which further increase in the fourth century — so, too, it has produced more evidence of regional trade (at the expense of overseas traffic), with interactions extending more than 100km from *Calleva*. This derives from two sources in particular, pottery and stone. Both commodities represent goods which were consumed within the town, rather than raw materials to which value was added by further processing. While the ceramic proxy of long-distance, overseas trade is almost completely lacking in Period 4, it is important to note the presence of figs and grapes/raisins, which are not normally associated with those ceramic amphorae which might be contemporary and are usually linked with olive oil and wine. In other words overseas trade continues, but not leaving much in the way of material culture residues. Earlier we commented that the lack of proxies for overseas trade implied a reduction of links between *Calleva* and London in Period 4. However, we note the occurrence of SE Dorset BB 1 in London, which, while relatively high in the third century with representation by weight of 5 to 11 per cent, is considerably lower than comparable figures from Period 4 in Insula IX (Symonds and Tomber 1991, 71–7). This might suggest that it reached London by road, via Silchester, rather than by sea, the proxy operating in the reverse direction than in the periods with relatively rich overseas imports reaching Silchester via London. Alice Holt/Farnham wares might also have reached London by road via Silchester.

The amount of evidence which can be attributed, admittedly with varying levels of confidence, to rituals within the domestic context in Insula IX is considerable, but changes over time. In particular we have noted the association of votive deposits with the construction of the Period 3 houses MB 1 and 2 and MRTB 1. While the burial of complete pots is the most obvious form of dedicatory deposit in these contexts, Crummy has made a strong case for interpreting the placement of complete sets of toilet instruments, as well as other artefacts, in the foundations in the same way. Ingrem has made a similar case in respect of certain articulated animal bone remains. By contrast the construction of MB 3 did not produce comparable evidence of convincing foundation deposits. On the other hand, there is a variety of evidence from the basal contexts of wells of both periods of rites associated with their commissioning or continued use. Again, and most obviously, this includes complete or near-complete ceramic flagons, as from Period 3 well 2234, but also the handles of containers for liquids, as the flagon and bucket handles from Period 4 well 5735. The animal and bird bone, including raven, from the construction contexts of 1750, which was otherwise emptied of its contents in 1893, are also very suggestive of deliberate deposition. Obviously votive deposits are by no means a *sine qua non* of wells. Of the four certain wells of Periods 3 and 4, it is not possible to identify with confidence a votive character to any of the contents of Period 3 well 5693. However, more comparative work needs to be done on the incidence and character of the faunal remains from wells. Pottery vessels deliberately pierced at or about the point of maximum girth are also a regular feature of deposits in wells or pits (Fulford and Timby 2001) and we can identify two such occurrences in Periods 3 and 4 — a flagon from well 2234, and a small unguent flask from the basal layers of pit 3102. However, one of the two, otherwise complete, Alice Holt jars from the clay make-ups for MB 1 and MRTB 1 was also deliberately pierced. Isolated body sherds with evidence of perforations have been noted, e.g. from Period 4 pits 3102 and 2601. While discerning votive intent behind the contents of pits is fraught with difficulties (cf. Eckardt 2006), there can be some confidence in a ritual interpretation of the deposit of the fine, ivory-handled knife associated with the complete carcass of a young dog and the bones of a raven in Period 4 pit 2601. What thinking lies behind these acts of deposition is hard to imagine, but the focus of the evidence on dogs, including the skinning of dogs in the same, associated household, seems hardly a coincidence.

In considering change over time, and looking ahead to the fourth century, there does seem to be a shift away from deposits associated with house construction to special deposits in pits, and it is also true that the latter increase in their frequency from Period 4 onwards. Although special deposits cannot be identified in all wells, however, they do remain a consistent theme through the second and third centuries into the late Roman period. We can have no certainty about meanings, but if offerings associated with the construction of houses are to do with ensuring their success as buildings as well as their continuing existence, just as placed deposits in the bottom of wells may be to ensure a continuing flow of water, it is more difficult to rationalise the possible range of intent behind structured deposition in pits, other than to draw attention to the chthonic associations. Is there a deeper significance behind the increased incidence of the special deposits in pits other than wells in the later Roman period, from the third century onwards? Our consideration has so far been towards deposition where material culture is prominent, with biological remains less obvious. However, we should not overlook interments of complete skeletons of animals or humans, which remain exceptional in Periods 3 and 4. There is one example of a possibly complete infant burial from late in Period 3 and one probably complete dog carcass from Period 4, but the latter certainly associated with material culture. The remaining incidence of animal and human bone is almost exclusively of bones without evidence of articulation. This is not to say that dogs and infants were not originally buried intact, but that their remains have subsequently been disturbed and become widely distributed horizontally and vertically through the stratigraphic sequence. In the case of the remains of the skull of the adult human, we have to be alert to the possibility of residuality from the late Iron Age when there is evidence of adult inhumation within the settlement.

While the larger conclusion to be drawn from Insula IX in the second and third centuries is of stability over time, there is undoubted evidence, difficult though it is to quantify, of some change, particularly in regard to increased reliance on production and processing within the insula, rather than on income raised outside the insula or the town, or on food and materials brought in from the country estates of the town-dwellers. This was sufficient to ensure that quality of life as reflected in the evidence for diet and material wealth remained more or less unchanged over time. Nevertheless, together, and symbolised by the increased use of the frontage of the property along the north–south street, the changes point the way to the very marked dislocation evident at the end of Period 4 with the demolition of the town-house, the re-organisation of property boundaries and rebuilding within the insula. The fourth century then sees further intensification of the evidence for urban production, but in association with more modest architecture. Such evidence as there is for food and diet, however, shows, if anything, increased diversity compared with the situation in the second and third centuries, particularly in the exploitation of marine and freshwater fish.

A major implication for the consideration of the population of *Calleva Atrebatum* (and of Roman towns more generally in Britain and the North-Western provinces) is the potential impact of the addition of timber buildings to the plan of stone-founded structures. In Periods 3 and 4 the estimated increase of the built environment is, respectively, about 45 per cent (Period 3) and 25 per cent (Period 4). As we have seen (above, p. 332–3), if we extrapolate these kinds of increases across the town within the walls, and include provision for upper, or one-and-a-half storeys, the population of the town rises significantly by a factor of almost four from Boon's calculations

(1974, 61–2) — to over 15,000 in the second century, with the more conservative figure being about half, 7,500. With the extent of the built environment within the excavated area of Insula IX in the fourth century less, perhaps by about 30 per cent, than that of the third century, the local picture suggests a continued decline in the town's population after *c.* A.D. 300. When matched against the provision of wells in the second and third centuries, we note a probable reduction from two to one in the latter period, but rising again to three in the fourth century.

APPENDIX 1

THE IRON AGE AND ROMAN COINS FOUND AT SILCHESTER, AS RECORDED AND CATALOGUED BY GEORGE BOON, 1951–54

By Dave Wythe

It was not my good fortune to have known the late George Boon; my acquaintance with him comes entirely through his work. Of that work, perhaps the most significant was the cataloguing and recording of the 13,400 Iron Age and Roman coins found in and around the Silchester area, which, according to notes on the museum accession documentation, Boon accomplished between 1951 and 1954. The majority of the coins originated from two great collections: that of the Duke of Wellington, which was subsequently accessioned to the Reading Museum and Art Gallery, and that held at Stratfield Saye House. The coins comprising the Duke of Wellington's Collection had been obtained either from excavations at the site over the better part of the preceding century, or had been found on or near the site. Those held at Stratfield Saye House had been found by Joyce and his successors prior to 1890 and had been catalogued by Boon in 1952–53. A number of minor collections and gifts to the museum also contributed towards the total.

The coins had been listed before: by Mill-Stephenson in *c.* 1910 in a series of notes which had been left with the museum and then later, in 1928, by Pearce who had published an abbreviated account in the *Numismatic Chronicle* 1929, p. 328ff. Boon refers to these lists as appropriate in the accession notes. Mill-Stephenson certainly would have been unable to provide Roman Imperial Coinage references for the coins, Pearce's account includes no more than total coin quantities next to specific emperors.

Boon's listing, however, was altogether more comprehensive. Evans references, where possible, were noted for the Iron Age material, while Sydenham and Cohen references were used for the Roman Republican coins. *RIC* references were included, again where possible, for all coins up until A.D. 296, while after that, a combination of Cohen and Maurice references were used for the Tetrarchic and Constantinian coinage. The then published *RIC* Vol. IX was used to catalogue the Valentinianic and Theodosian coinage.

No doubt as a result of his knowledge of then current developments in the study of numismatics and in particular the recording of Roman coins, Boon, prior to the publication of *RIC* Vols VI, VII and VIII and the two volumes of *Late Roman Bronze Coinage*, organised the late third- and fourth-century coins on a mint and date of issue basis and then manually transcribed the mintmark details onto the accession cards.

The principal aim of the current work has been to take that information as preserved by Boon and to translate it into the appropriate *RIC* and *LRBC* references. The coins themselves have also been re-organised into Reece's 21 periods. This, it is hoped, will make them both accessible and usable for future studies. It should be noted that the Iron Age and Pre-Flavian coins listed here also appear within George Boon's extended, synthetic catalogues of these types published in Fulford and Timby (2000) ('Schedule B: the British and Gaulish coins from Silchester' (163–70) 'and Schedule C, the Pre-Flavian coins from Silchester' (170–9)). These provide fuller details and a more up-to-date categorisation of the numerous irregular issues of the first century A.D.

Thanks are due to Ian Leins of the British Museum and Dr Kris Lockyear of the Institute of Archaeology for their assistance with the Iron Age and Republican coinage respectively. My chief thanks, however, are to Dr Richard Reece, initially for facilitating, and then acting as a constant support through the entirety of this project; his assistance was invaluable. Finally, thanks are equally due to Edward Besly of the National Museum of Wales for allowing the project to go ahead and to Professor Michael Fulford for agreeing to its publication.

Reference works cited:

BMC   Hobbs, R., 1996, *British Iron Age Coins in the British Museum*, London, The British Museum Press

CK   Carson, R.A.G., and Kent, J.P.C., 1960, *Late Roman Bronze Coinage, Part II*, London, Spink and Co.

Craw   Crawford, M.H., 1974, *Roman Republican Coinage*, Cambridge, Cambridge University Press

HK   Hill, P.V., and Kent, J.P.C., 1960, *Late Roman Bronze Coinage, Part I*, London, Spink and Co.

IRBCH   Robertson, A.S., 2000, *An Inventory of Romano-British Coin Hoards*, London, Royal Numismatic Society Special Publication 20

RIC   Mattingly, H., Sydenham, E.A., Sutherland, C.H.V., and Carson, R.A.G., 1923ff., *Roman Imperial Coinage*, London, Spink

(note: all editions cited are first editions)

IRON AGE

1	Brigantes	*BMC* 208? plated silver
2	Catuvellaunian	*BMC* 1921, bronze illeg.
1	Dobunni	*BMC* 445 plated
4	Durotriges	*BMC* 1290 (2), 35 debased gold, 2790 base silver
1	Trinovantes	*BMC* 2453
1	Lingones	rev.: bear devouring serpent
1	Treveri	rev.: GERMANVS INDVTIL (bull l.)
6	Cunobelinus	*BMC* 1804, 1827 (2), 1956, 1961 (2)
1	Epaticcus	*BMC* 2270 plated
2	Eppillus	*BMC* as 1016, uncertain rev.: EPPI
3	Tasciovanus	*BMC* 1722, 1739, rev.: 'animal'
1	Tincommius	*BMC* 811
7	Uncertain	*BMC* as 498, 1690, ?2450 debased, ?2484 (Kentish), base silver scyphate disc, base silver flan, fragment (Gaulish)

ROMAN REPUBLIC

12   Craw 364/?, 383, 458, 494/23, 517/2, 544 (2), illeg. Denarii (legionary type) (2), illeg. Denarii (3)

COINS STRUCK UNDER AUGUSTUS

2	Augustus	*RIC* 305, illeg. As
2	Tiberius	*RIC* 370, ?370

COINS STRUCK UNDER TIBERIUS

1	Divus Augustus	*RIC* 6
5	Agrippa	*RIC* 32 (5)

COINS STRUCK UNDER CALIGULA

2	Caligula	*RIC* 30 (2)
1	Germanicus	*RIC* 44

COINS STRUCK UNDER CLAUDIUS

77	Claudius	*RIC* 29, 64 (3), 66 (3), 69, illeg.: Asses (3), copy as 65 (grade IV) (2), copy of 66 (grade I) (20), copy of 66 (grade II) (12), copy of 66 (grade III) (16), copy of 67 (grade I), copy of 67 (grade II) (2), copy of 67 (grade?) (2), copy of 68 (grade I), copy of 68 (grade II), copy of 68 (grade III), copy of 68, copy of 69 (grade I), copy of 69 (grade II), illeg. copies: Asses (5)
5	Antonia	*RIC* 82 (5)
1	Drusus	*RIC* 78

NERO

221   *RIC* 52, 58, 304, 306, 315, 319, 321, 329 (5), 319–322, 325–331 (3), 342, 364, 315/317, rev. illeg.: Asses (3)

OTHO

1   *RIC* 3

COINS STRUCK UNDER VESPASIAN

99	Vespasian	*RIC* 10 (3), 15, 37, 42, 52, 59(a) 74, 77–78, 90 (2), 92, 124(a), 287/288, 443, 473(2), 475 (2), 489(2), 497(2), 500 (2), as 500, 502 (2), 528(b) (2), 528/747, as 592, 740 (4), 744 (2), as 744, 746, as 746 (3), 753(b) (5), 754(b) (2), 758 (4), 764(a)(2), 764(b), rev. illeg.: Sestertii (4), Dupondii (10), Asses (17), indet. (11), plated denarii as 22, 71.
8	Titus	*RIC* 185, 219, 668(a), 775(b)(2), 786 (3)
9	Domitian	*RIC* 238, 244, 724 (7)

COINS STRUCK UNDER TITUS

7	Titus	*RIC* 22(a), 24(b), 87, rev. illeg.: Dupondus, Asses (2), indet.
1	Domitian	*RIC* 42

DOMITIAN

63   *RIC* 244, 262, as 301(b), 313, 325, 326, 332, 333 (2), 335 (4), 337(2), 340, 353(a), 354(a) (3), 354 (b) (2), 356 (a) or (b) (2), 356(b), 357, 369?, 435, rev. illeg.: Sestertii (3), Dupondii (10), Asses (17), plated Denarius copy of 88?

NERVA

15   *RIC* 7, 14, 19 (2), 55, 64, 83, 105, rev. illeg.: Denarius, Sestertius, Dupondius, Asses (4)

TRAJAN

97   *RIC* 13, 49 (2), 58, 96, 120, 122, 129, 147, as 184, 198, 331, 384, 385, 392, 393, 395, 416, 417 (3), 418, 432, 434, 486, 489, 490, 496, 497? (2), 503 (2), 512, 515, 515?, 519 (2), 525 (2), 534, 538, 543 (2), 545, 550, 560 (2), 563 (2), 586, 624/625, 639, 663, 664, 665, 672, 674 rev. illeg.: Sestertii (12), Dupondii (20), indet. (7), plated denarius copy of 239

COINS STRUCK UNDER HADRIAN

116   Hadrian   *RIC* 41, 42, 67, 85, 96, 128, 137(b), 161, 163, 206, 299, 300, 541(c), 552/567, 563(b), 577(a) or (b) (2), 577(b), 579(a) (2), 583 (a) and (b) (2), 585(b), 586(b), 600(c), 605, 605 var., 617 (2), 623(a) var., 634 var., 669 (5), 673, 678 (2), 706, 714, 716 (3), 751, 759, 777 (2), 860, 861–863, 967, 967? (2), 969 var., 970 (2), 973 var. (2), 974, rev. illeg.: Denarius, Sestertii (25), Dupondii (14), Asses (3), indet. (14)

8   Sabina   *RIC* 395(a), 1023 (3), 1024, 1029 (2), 1035

COINS STRUCK UNDER ANTONINUS PIUS

99   Antoninus Pius   *RIC* 64, 136, 240, 313, 597, 598, 601, 618, 657, 663 (2), 679, 699(a), 716, 719, 747(a), 770, 772, 774, 777 (2), 779 (3), 784 (2), 861, 885, as 886 (2), 886/906, 904, 907, 928 (2), 932 (2), 933 var., 934 (11), 964, 981, 1006?, 1031 (2), 1220A (2), rev. illeg.: Denarii (3), Sestertii (11), Dupondii (10), Asses (3), indet. (12), copy as 933, copy of Sestertius, copy of Dupondii (2)

10   Marcus Aurelius   *RIC* 1236, 1240(a), 1248, 1309(a), 1317, 1354(a), copy as 1316, rev. illeg.: Denarius, Asses (2)

36   Faustina I   *RIC* 328(a), 358, 363, 1098, 1103(a), 1118, 1127, 1128(a), as 1154, 1156, 1157, 1158, 1161 (2), 1164, 1164A, as 1169, 1187, 1190, 1199, rev. illeg.: Denarius, Sestertii (7), Dupondii (2), Asses (4), indet. (2)

9   Faustina II   *RIC* 506(b), 508(a), 509, 1395 (2), 1405, 1405(a), rev. illeg.: Sestertius, As

COINS STRUCK UNDER MARCUS AURELIUS

59   Marcus Aurelius   *RIC* 163, 207, 231, 254?, 272, 403, 798, 828, 843 (2), 870, 874, 891, 898 (2), 907, 911 (2), 922, 923, 931, 948 (2), 957 (4), 979, 992, 1031, 1033, 1037, 1064, 1077, 1160, 1214, 1218, 1227, rev. illeg.: Sestertii (10), Dupondii (3), As, indet. (7)

7   Lucius Verus   *RIC* 463, 576, 1439, 1461, 1462, rev. illeg.: Denarius, plated Denarius

18   Faustina II   *RIC* 774, 1628, 1630 var., 1638, 1642 (2), 1645/1646, 1651, 1688, 1693, rev. illeg.: Sestertii (4), Dupondius, Asses (2) copy of 686

15   Lucilla   *RIC* 1747, 1755, 1756 (2), 1757, 1763 (2), 1767 (2), 1779, rev. illeg.: Sestertii (3), Dupondius, As

2   Commodus   *RIC* 1599, Sestertius

3   Antoninus Pius   *RIC* 441, 1263, 1273

COINS STRUCK UNDER COMMODUS

27   Commodus   *RIC* 236 (2), 254(a), 292(a), 331, 354, as 419, 440, 462, 463, 497, 499, 513 (4), 545 (2), 582, 585, rev. illeg.: Sestertii (7)

7   Crispina   *RIC* 665, 668, 669, 672(a), rev. illeg.: Dupondii (2), As

3   Marcus Aurelius   *RIC* 660 (2), 662

CLODIUS ALBINUS

1   *RIC* 7

COINS STRUCK UNDER SEPTIMIUS SEVERUS

39   Septimius Severus   *RIC* 49 (2), 53 or 61 or 68, 58, 64, 69, 74, 79, 87, 105, 107, 113, 118, 143(a), 152, 153, 167, 167(a) (2), 216, 236, 265, 289, 364, 369, 424, 424 var., 435, 441(b) var., 499 (2), 671, 700, rev. illeg.: Denarii (2), copy of 160, copy of 308, plated denarii (3)

10   Caracalla   *RIC* 30(b), 64, 68, 108, 130(a), 149, 448, copy of 39(a), copy of 88, plated denarius

| 12 | Julia Domna | *RIC* 476, 556, 560 (2), 572 (3), 574, 577, 637, rev. illeg.: Denarius, copy of 572 |
| 9 | Geta | *RIC* 6, 9(a) (2), 18 (2), 34(b), 51, copy as 161, copy as 308 |

CARACALLA

| 4 | | *RIC* 223, 281(b), 284, 528(a) |

COINS STRUCK UNDER MACRINUS

| 1 | Macrinus | *RIC* 30 |
| 1 | Diadumenianus | *RIC* 116/117 |

COINS STRUCK UNDER ELAGABALUS

13	Elagabalus	*RIC* 46, 56, 77, 87, 88, 95, 107, 123, 160, 161 (2), copy of 150, plated denarius
1	Julia Paula	*RIC* 222
5	Julia Soaemias	*RIC* 238, 241 (3), 243
3	Julia Maesa	*RIC* 271 (3)

COINS STRUCK UNDER SEVERUS ALEXANDER

35	Severus Alexander	*RIC* 5 or 7, 7, 14 (2), 19, 37, 64 (3), 70 (2), 83, 139, 178 (2), 185, 190, 193, 205, 208, 218/219, 254, 298, 302, as 325, 435, 512, 628, 648, rev. illeg.: Denarii (2), AE Medallion, copy of 57, copy of 230, plated denarius
7	Julia Mamaea	*RIC* 331, 343, 360, 366, 668, 669, 676
1	Julia Maesa	*RIC* as 173

MAXIMINUS I

| 6 | | *RIC* 1, 7(a) var., 13, 14, 16, 23 |

1st TO EARLY 3rd CENTURIES

| 75 | | 1st–2nd centuries: Denarii (2), Sestertii (26), As, indet. (34), plated denarius 3rd century: Denarii (5), indet. (4), plated denarii (2) |

GORDIAN III

| 14 | | *RIC* 90, 91, 95, 150, 196?, 277, 294(b), 297(b) (2), 304(a), copy of *RIC* 86, rev. illeg.: Denarius, copy of Sestertius, plated radiate |

COINS STRUCK UNDER PHILIP I

6	Philip I	*RIC* 26(b), 47, 49(b), 168(a), 175(a), copy of 3
1	Philip II	*RIC* 254(a)
1	Otacilia Severa	*RIC* 203

TRAJAN DECIUS

| 3 | | *RIC* 28, 21(b) var., 112(a)/(b) |

TREBONIANUS GALLUS

| 1 | Trebonianus Gallus | *RIC* 34 |
| 4 | Volusian | *RIC* 140, 166, as 193, rev. illeg.: plated radiate |

COINS STRUCK UNDER VALERIAN I AND GALLIENUS (A.D. 253–260)

18	Valerian I	*RIC* 6/89, 7, 12, 12 var., 13, 86, 92, 106, 113, 115, 117 (2), 127 (2), 134, copy as 113, rev. illeg.: radiates (2)
11	Gallienus	*RIC* 42, 44 (3), 45, 132, 143, 155, 181 (2), copy of 119(a)
1	Saloninus	*RIC* 9
3	Valerian II	*RIC* 3, 20 (2)
8	Salonina	*RIC* 6 (2), 7, 29 (2), 59, 63, 66

COINS STRUCK UNDER GALLIENUS (A.D. 260–268)

341	Gallienus	*RIC* 157 (18), 159 (4), 160 (15), 163 (9), 164 (11), 165, 176 (4), 177 (6), 179 (18), 181 (12), 182 (4), 192(a) (5), 193 var., 193/482 (3), 205 var., 206 (4), 207 (4), 208, 210 (3), 214 (dub.), 216, 227 (2), 227/228, 230 (7), 233 (4), 236 (14), 242/245, 245 (3), 245 (dub.), 249 (4), 256 (4), 256 (dub.), 267 (7), 270 (7), 274(a) (2), 278, 280 (6), 280 (dub.) (2), 280? (2), 283 (8), 284 (2), 287 var. (14), 287 var. (dub.), 297 (4), 320 (dub.), 321, 321 var., 459, 465(a), 471, 481, 483, 484, 489, 490, 495 (2), 499 (2), 513, 518, 525, 560, 572 (11), 575 (2), 580, 581, 584, 585, 585? (3), 586; rev. illeg.: radiates (77)
26	Salonina	*RIC* 5 (3), 5(a), 11 var., 12, 13, 16 (2), 24 (3), 25, 31, 32 (2), 58, 62, 65 var., 68, 78, 80, rev. illeg.: radiates (4)

CLAUDIUS II

496	*RIC* 10 (2), 11, 14 (8), 14/15 (2), 15 (6), 18/19, 19, 22 (3), 27, 32 (4), 32 and 33 var. (2), 32/33 (2), 33 (3), 34 (2), 34/35, 36 (18), 38, 40, 41, 45 (5), 45/46 (6), 46, 48 (11), 48/49 (4), 52 var. (3), 54 (6), 54/55 (5), 55 (3), 56 (4), 57 (4), 60, 62 (4), 66 (7), 66/67, 67 (3), 80 (5), 81 var., 91 (5), 94 (2), 98 (3), 98/99 (3), 99, 100, 104 (6), 105 (6), 107 (2), 109 (9), 109/110 (5), 110 (6), 141, 144, 168, 171 (2), 181 (4), 183, 191, 193 var., 259 (2), 261 (80), 265 (2), 266 (88), 270, 274, 279, 283, 289, var. rev. illeg.: (106), copy of 107, copy of 261 (16), copy of Provid Avg

QUINTILLUS

22	*RIC* 6, 7, 9, 18 (5), 25, 26 (2), 28 (2), 31 (2), 33 (3), 36, 45, 52, 62

AURELIAN

18	*RIC* 56, 71, 118, 127, 128 (2), 129 (2), 135, 142, 142 var., 149, 150, 151, 216, 247, 351, rev. Oriens Avg

TACITUS

12	*RIC* 21 (2), 30, 41 (2), 45, 55, 60, 65, 83 (2), 89

FLORIAN

1	*RIC* 29?

PROBUS

20	*RIC* 31, 37/83, 38, 38/84 (4), 53, as 102, 104, 116, 157 (2), 198, 220, 282, 706, 801, rev. illeg. (2)

CARUS

2	*RIC* 75, 82

CARINUS

1   *RIC* 214

DIOCLETIAN

4   *RIC* 28, 117, 206, 244

MAXIMIAN HERC

6   *RIC* 384, 442, 506, 559, rev. Pax Avgg, rev. illeg.

GALERIUS

1   *RIC* 678

POSTUMUS

65   *RIC* 54 (4), 60, 64, 67, 73 (2), 74, 75/315 (7), 77/316 (2), 79, 80/323 (2), 83/325, 87 (3), 89
     (6), 90, 93, 289, 303, 304, 309 (2), 311 (3), 316, 317 (4), 320, 323 (2), 381, rev. Salus, illeg. rev.
     (12), copy of 60

LAELIAN

1   *RIC* 9

MARIUS

1   *RIC* 17

VICTORINUS

253 *RIC* 57 (17), 57/59, 61 (21), 67 (5), 67/122 (18), 71 (30), 75 (2), 78 (33), 109 (3), 111, 113,
     114 (50), 117 (2), 118 (40), rev. Pax, rev. illeg. (25), copy of 54?, copy of 114, copy of 117

TETRICUS I

434 *RIC* 56 (11), 57 (4), 70 (5), 71 (4), 77, 79 (4), 80 (27), 80 var., 86 (2), 87 (3), 88 (37),
     88/90 (12), 90 (14), 100 (47), 100/101, 101 (3), 113, 114, 118, 121/123, 123, 126 (19),
     127 (12), 129 var. (2), 136 (16), 140 (2), 141 (9), 143, 148 (14), reverse types (65),
     rev. illeg. (111), brockage (2)

TETRICUS II

198 *RIC* 224 (4), 244, 248 (9), 254 (4), 254–6 (3), 255 (5), 258 (9), 258/259, 259 (9), 260, 270
     (38), 270/271 (8), 272 (30), 272/274 (13), 280, reverse types (32), rev. illeg. (30)

CARAUSIUS

371 *RIC* 1A, 5, 10, 11, 11 var., as 36, 53, 56, 57–59, as 61, 75, 80, 85, 98 (14), 101 (15), 116 (2),
     141 (3), 143 (4), 149, 150, 155, 209 var., 237 var., 243 var., 248, 255, as 255, 287 (4), 288, 300
     (3), 301 (4), 303 (2), 303 var., 314 (2), 345/351, 348 var., 350, 351, as 353, 456 (2), 457, 458
     (2), 465, 470, 475 (4), 475 var., 476 (5), 478 (36), 484 (3), 498 (3), 527/529, 532, 581, 686?,
     733, 736, 738, 747/750, 783, 787 (5), 855 (2), 869, 871, 878 (2), 880 (7), 881, 883?, 893 (2),
     895 (3), 896, 897, 929, 940, 942, 947, 983 (6), 988, 990, 1013, 1015, 1037, 1061, 1092, reverse
     types (76), rev. illeg. (60), overstruck (6), brockage, irregular/blundered reverses (33)
     Struck for Maximian: *RIC* 34

ALLECTUS

95 *RIC* as 4, 20, 22 (6), 28 (6), 33 (12), 34, 35, 36, 38, 55 (16), 69, 69 var., 77, 79 (4), 82/83 var., 85, 86 (2), 91, 108 (2), 111 (4), 112, 117, 124 (2), 125 (5), 126 (2), 128 (6), 129, 130 (3), var. rev. types (8), rev. illeg., overstruck (on Carausius)

LATE THIRD CENTURY

1621 Regular radiates (553), Barbarous radiates (1068)

COINS STRUCK A.D. 294–317

107	London	*RIC* 6 as 1(a), as 6(b), 7 (2), as 14(a) (3), as 15 (2), as 16 (2), 30, 33, as 33, 58(a), 77(b), as 80, 85 (3), 89(a), 89(b), 103 (3), 104 (2), 110 (3), 118, 153 (3), 165, as 165, 209(b) (6), 209(c), as 214 (3), 227, as 243, 249, as 279, 280 (3), 282 (3), Maximian: MARTI PACIF, corroded; *RIC* 7 3 (4), as 5, as 9, 10 (7), 27 (4), as 32, 43 (2), as 43, as 47 (3), 84, 89 (7), 90 (12), 91, 107, 109, 123, Licinius I: GENIO POP ROM
83	Trier	*RIC* 6 as 146(a), as 154(a), as 170(a) (2), 176(a), 203(a), 264, 305(a), 368(b), 462(b), as 511, 530(a), 574, 582(b) (2), 595(b) (2), 676(b), as 684, 766, 770, 784, 790, 825, 845(a) (3), 845(b), 846(b), as 886 (3), 897 (5), 899 (12), Constantine I: GENIO POP ROM, MARTI PATRI CONSERVATORI, MARTI PATRI PROPVGNATORI, PRINCIPI IVVENTVTIS; *RIC* 7 40 (5), 45, 47, as 48 (4), 50, as 50, 102 (4), 105 (5), 121 (7), as 132
18	Lyon	*RIC* 6 108(a), 136(b), 164(b) (2), as 166(b), as 174(A), 287, 307, 309. Constantius I: GENIO POPVLI ROMANI; *RIC* 7 2 (3), 7, 16 (2), 30, Licinius I: SOLI INVICTO COMITI
3	Ticinum	*RIC* 6 92, 101, 106
2	Rome	*RIC* 6 76(a); *RIC* 7 as 52
5	Arles	*RIC* 7 22, as 72, 80 (2), as 80
1	Ostia	*RIC* 6 84
1	Carthage	*RIC* 6 as 30(b)
32	Uncertain mint	GENIO POPVLI ROMANI (7), GENIO POP ROM (3), SOLI INVICTO COMITI (21), Galerius: SACRA MONET AVGG ET CAESS NN

COINS STRUCK A.D. 317–330

105	London	*RIC* 7 143, as 154 (2), as 156 (3), as 158 (5), as 180, 185 (3), as 185, 190 (4), 191 (3), as 191, 196 (3), 198 (4), as 199, 210, 214, 216 (2), 222 (2), 229, 230 (6), 231 (4), 236 (2), 243 (2), 249, 250, 251, 257 (2), 258 (4), 264, 267 (2), 275, 278, 285 (2), 286, 287 (9), 289 (3), 291, 292 (2), 293 (4), as 293 (3), 295 (5), as 297 (4), House of Constantine: BEATA TRANQVILLITAS, VICTORIAE LAETAE PRINC PERP (2), copy as 291
181	Trier	*RIC* 7 135, 167, 200, as 200, as 208A (8), 209 (9), as 221 (2), 258, 261, 265 (3), 266 (2), 269 (2), 270, 271, 280, 303 (12), as 303 (2), 305 (2), 306, 307 (3), 312 (3), as 312 (3), 321 (2), 341 (13), 342 (6), 347 (5), 353, as 353 (2), 368 (8), 369 (2), 372, 382 (2), 389 (3), 401, 412 (2), 416 (2), 429, as 430, 431, 433 (4), as 433, 435 (7), 440 (4), 441 (7), 449 (3), 451, 454 (2), 458, 463 (3), 475 (2), 479 (2), 480 (4), 484, 489, 504 (5), 505 (3), 506, 508, 509 (2), 514, Constantine II: VOTIS X, House of Constantine: VIRTVS EXERCIT (banner), VICTORIAE LAETAE PRINC PERP (2). Irregular: Crispus CAESARVM NOSTRORVM VOT V; HK as 12 (4), as 21, as 25
30	Lyon	*RIC* 7 as 79 (2), 88, as 98, 107, 109, 121, as 148, 153, 155 (2), 156, 159, 167, 188 (3), 189 (2), 198 (2), 199, as 209 (2), 215, 216 (2), 234, Licinius II: BEATA TRANQVILLITAS, House of Constantine: BEATA TRANQVILLITAS

13	Arles	*RIC* 7 145, as 190, as 222, as 230, 233, 240, as 252 (2), 291, as 291, 314, 322, Licinius II: SARMATIA DEVICTA
6	Aquileia	*RIC* 7 51, 68, as 77 (2), 85, as 94
1	Cyzicus	*RIC* 7 14
2	Heraclea	*RIC* 7 52 (2)
2	Nicomedia	*RIC* 7 44, as 49
11	Siscia	*RIC* 7 47, as 76, 148 (2), as 148, 155, 159, 163, 175, 181, copy of 163
2	Thessalonica	*RIC* 7 128; HK 811
7	Ticinum	*RIC* 7 67, as 82 (2), as 140 (2), 163, 202
9	Rome	*RIC* 7 as 115, 237, as 238, 281, as 281, 285, 286, 290; HK 509
75	Uncertain mint	BEATA TRANQVILLITAS (17), PROVIDENTIAE AVGG/CAESS (7), VICTORIAE LAETAE PRINC PERP (28), VIRTVS EXERCIT (banner), SARMATIA DEVICTA, VOT V, VOT X (4), VOT XX (6), VOTA (9), IOVI CONSERVATORI AVG (eastern mint)

COINS STRUCK A.D. 330–348

1054	Trier	HK 48, as 48 (22), 49 (35), as 49 (10), 50 (2), as 50 (3), 51 (5), as 51 (57), as 51/48, as 51/52, 52 (8), as 52 (94), 53 (19), as 53, 56 (4), 57 (13), as 57, 58 (26), 59 (30), 60 (11), as 60 (3), 63 (18), 64 (9), 65 (18), 66 (28), as 66 (3), 67 (2), 68 (3), 69 (4), 70 (8), 71 (4), 72 (2), 73 (10), 75 (2), 76 (16), 77 (4), 78 (3), as 78, 81 (3), 83 (2), 84, 85 (8), as 85 (5), 86 (9), as 86 (3), as 87 (3), as 88, 90 (2), 92 (4), 93 (20), 94 (19), as 94 (4), 95 (5), as 98, as 99 (6), as 100 (35), as 102 (25), as 104 (11), as 105 (6), 106 (2), 107, 108 (3), as 108 (5), as 109, 112 (19), as 112 (4), 113 (17), as 113 (8), 114 (4), as 114, 117 (2), 119 (5), 120 (5), as 120 (3), 122 (7), as 124, 126 (3), 127, 128 (9), 129 (6), 130, 131, 133 (14), as 133, 137–137(a) (2), as 137 (31), 138 (2), as 138 (108), 139 (2), 140, 141, 142 (8), 145–147 (7), as 145, 148 (38), as 151, 153 (14), 158 (20), as 158 (10), 162 (4); copy as 88 (3), copy as 99 (9), copy as 112/113 (3), copy as 138 (4); *RIC* 8 56, 71, 72 (2), 94, 105
272	Lyon	HK 180, as 180 (17), 181 (9), as 181 (5), 182 (7), as 182 (5), 184 (16), as 184 (28), 184/185, 185 (5), as 185 (29), 186 (4), as 186 (2), 187 (9), 188 (4), 190 (11), as 190, 191 (3), as 191, 192, as 192, 193 (5), 196 (3), 197, as 197, 198 (2), 199 (2), 200 (10), 201 (8), 202, 204, 205 (4), as 211, 222, as 222 (4), 223 (2), 226, as 226 (3), 228 (2), 229, as 230, 232 (3), 237, 239, as 239 (2), 241 (3), 242 (2), as 242 (9), 243, as 243 (5), 245, as 245 (2), 253, 256 (2), as 256 (5), as 257, as 259, 260 (4), 266, 269; copy of 184, copy as 222 (5), copy as 226 (3), copy as 242, copy as 243 (2)
161	Arles	HK 351(a) (4), 352 (2), as 352 (11), 353, as 353, as 354 (2), as 355, 356 (6), as 356 (5), 360, 362 (3), as 363, 367 (9), as 367, 368 (5), 369, 370 (2), 372 (6), 373 (5), 374 (4), 375 (4), 376 (5), 377, 378 (2), 379 (2), as 381 (2), 382 (2), 389, as 389 (2), 390 (3), 399, as 399 (2), 400, 402, as 417 (5), 420, 421 (3), 438 (3), 441 (4), 442 (4), as 444 (5), 445, as 445 (2), 447, 449, 455 (9), 456 (4), 458, 462; *RIC* 7 341 (8), as 341, 343 (4), 344, 408; *RIC* 8 88
19	Rome	HK 532, as 532, as 533 (2), as 536, 540, as 540, 541 (2), as 541, 543, 546, as 556, as 557, 580, as 609, as 639, 640; *RIC* 7 382
12	Aquileia	HK 652, 654 (4), 657 (2), 670, 673, as 675 (2), 686
9	Siscia	HK 745, as 754, 758, 762 (2), 769, as 774, 782, 791
9	Thessalonica	HK as 835 (2), as 836 (4), 846, as 859, 861
3	Heraclea	HK 907, 909, 914
17	Constantinople	HK as 1005, 1010, 1028, 1030, 1046, 1066 (3), 1067 (9)
2	Nicomedia	HK 1117, as 1136
5	Cyzicus	HK as 1218, as 1221, 1227, 1265 (2)
2	Antioch	HK 1357, 1365

1132	Bronze: reverses regular but mint uncertain	GLORIA EXERCITVS (two standards) (133), CONSTANTINOPOLIS (78), URBS ROMA (65), VOT XX MVLT XXX, GLORIA EXERCITVS (one standard) (459), VIRTVS AVGG NN (2), PAX PVBLICA (38), PIETAS ROMANA (41), SECVRITAS REIP (5), quadriga (4), VICTORIAE DD AVGGQ NN (216), rev. illeg. (90)
180	Bronze: Irregular	GLORIA EXERCITVS (two standards) (62), GLORIA EXERCITVS (one standard) (99), quadriga, VICTORIAE DD AVGGQ NN (18)

COINS STRUCK A.D. 348–364

29	Amiens	CK 2 (2), 5 (3), as 5 (7), as 6, 13 (3), 16, 18, 19 (3), 25, copy as 58 (2); *RIC* 8 13 (3), as 13 (2)
121	Trier	CK 28, as 28, 29 (5), as 29 (2), 32 (8), as 32 (8), 33 (14), as 33 (19), 34, as 34, 35 (10), as 35, 40 (2), as 40, as 41 (3), 43, 46, as 47 (2), 48 (2), 49 (2), as 49 (3), as 53 (3), 55 (4), as 56, as 58 (3), 66, 67 (4), as 67 (3), 72 (5), as 77 (2), copy as 40 (2), copy as 58 (3); *RIC* 8 364, as 364
64	Lyon	CK 178, as 185 (2), 196, as 209 (2), 214, as 214 (3), 217, as 217, as 220, as 222, 224 (2), 228, as 238, 244 (2), 245, as 252 (31), as 257, 270, as 270, copy as 58, copies of siliquae: VOT V MVLT X, VOTIS V MVLTIS X; *RIC* 8 90, 180 (2), 210, as 218, as 234, copy as 218, copy as 227
16	Arles	CK 401, 409, as 421, as 450, 455 (4), as 455, 457 (3); *RIC* 8 as 207 (2), as 263 (2)
13	Rome	CK as 593 (3), 603, 604 (3), 606, 607, 670, 677, 684, 687
4	Aquileia	CK 886 (2); *RIC* 8 108, 200
1	Thessalonica	CK as 1637
1	Cyzicus	CK 2490
1	Nicomedia	CK 2314
112	Bronze: reverses regular but mint uncertain	GLORIA ROMANORVM, VICTORIAE DD NN AVG ET CAE, VICTORIAE DD NN AVG ET CAES (15), SALVS DD NN AVG ET CAES (7), FELICITAS REIPVBLICE, SPES REIPVBLICE (9), SALVS AVG NOSTRI (2), VOT X MVLT XX, FTR (phoenix) (12), FTR (phoenix on pyre) (9), FTR (phoenix with globe) (8), FTR (galley) (10), FTR (hut) (4), FTR (fallen horseman) (32)
663	Bronze: Irregular	GLORIA ROMANORVM (3), VICTORIAE DD NN AVG ET CAES (60), SALVS DD NN AVG ET CAES (3), FELICITAS REIPVBLICE (8), SPES REIPVBLICE (3) FTR (phoenix), FTR (fallen horseman) (584), 'Carausius II'

COINS STRUCK A.D. 364–378

21	Trier	CK as 78, 79, 82 (2), as 82 (2), as 86 (2), 87, 102, 106, illeg.; *RIC* 9 siliquae: as 27(c) (2), as 27(e) (3), as 46(a) (2), aes: 47(a) (2)
256	Lyons	CK 273 (2), 275, as 275 (20), 276, as 276 (38), 277, as 279 (18), as 280 (18), 282, as 282, 285 (2), 286, 287, 289 (3), 290, 291, 293 (3), as 293, 294, as 294 (2), as 296 (10), as 297 (35), as 299 (5), 300 (2), as 300, 303 (4), as 303 (3), 304 (2), 305 (2), 307 (3), 308 (2), 311, 313 (6), 315, 316, 318, 319 (5), 321 (3), as 321 (3), 322 (4), 324 (2), as 330, as 332 (3), 333 (2), 335 (2), 338, 339 (4), 340 (8), as 340, 341 (3), as 343, as 345, 348, 350, as 350, 352 (2), 353, as 353 (7), 356, 357; as 368, Valens SECVRITAS REIPVBLICAE
553	Arles	CK as 477 (36), as 478 (47), 479 (9), as 479 (37), 480 (9), as 480 (41), 481 (8), as 481 (9), 483 (12), as 483 (7), 487 (2), 489 (3), 490 (6), as 493, 495, as 498, as 499, 501 (4), as 501 (2), 502 (2), as 503 (128), 506, 508 (3), 510, 511 (6), 513, 514 (2), 516 (5), as 516 (2), 518 (4), 520 (7), 521, 523 (10), 523(a) (11), 525 (4), 526 (2), 527 (12), 528 (2), as 528 (43), 529 (27), 531 (2), as 531 (4), 533 (10), as 533 (19), 536 (2), as 536, 538, as 541 (2), 543

40	Rome	CK as 703, as 704 (3), as 705 (6), as 709, 713 (2), as 713, as 714, 719 (9), 721, 724 (3), as 725 (6), as 726 (5); *RIC* 9 solidus 2 (c)
97	Aquileia	CK as 965 (5), 966 (4), as 966 (7), as 967 (6), 968 (4), as 968 (10), 969 (2), 971 (2), 972 (3), 973, 974 (2), 980, 986, as 986, 990, 991, 996, 997, 999, 1003, 1006, 1011 (3), 1012 (3), as 1012 (3), 1014 (2), as 1014 (5), 1015 (3), 1018 (2), 1020 (4), as 1020 (2), 1021, 1022, 1028 (2), 1029 (2), as 1030, 1031 (2), 1032 (3), 1033, 1036
79	Siscia	CK as 1271 (9), as 1272 (2), as 1273 (14), as 1274 (8), 1277, 1289, as 1301 (2), as 1331, 1334, 1342, as 1348, 1360, 1363, as 1393 (2), as 1395 (8), 1405, 1408 (3), as 1408 (3), 1409, as 1411 (4), as 1412, 1413 (3), 1421, as 1421, 1422 (2), as 1424 (2), 1427, 1428 (2); *RIC* 9 miliarense light as 10(b)
1	Sirmium	CK 1632
1	Nicomedia	*RIC* 9 Solidus: 2(a)/15
1	silver copy	plated Siliqua (halved): Julian or Valentinian I: vota
594	Bronze: reverses regular but mint uncertain	Valentinian I: RESTITVTOR REIP, GLORIA ROMANORVM (37), SECVRITAS REIPVBLICAE (32), illeg., (2); Valens: GLORIA ROMANORVM (24), SECVRITAS REIPVBLICAE (133); Gratian: GLORIA ROMANORVM (13), SECVRITAS REIPVBLICAE (9); Valentinian II: SECVRITAS REIPVBLICAE; House of Valentinian: GLORIA ROMANORVM (143), SECVRITAS REIPVBLICAE (198)
3	Bronze: Irregular	?Gratian: GLORIA NOVI SAECVLI; House of Valentinian: GLORIA ROMANORVM, SECVRITAS REIPVBLICAE

COINS STRUCK A.D. 378–388

5	Trier	CK 155, as 156, as 157; *RIC* 9 siliquae 57(a), 84(b)
7	Lyons	CK 377 (4), as 377, 386, as 387
11	Arles	CK 546, as 546 (4); 552, as 552, 560 (3), as 560
3	Rome	CK 753, 766, as 783
8	Aquileia	Aquileia as 1069, as 1081 (2), 1091, as 1091, 1093, as 1102, 1103
2	Milan	*RIC* 9 siliqua: 12(b) (2)
34	Bronze: reverses regular but mint uncertain	Magnus Maximus: SPES ROMANORVM; Flavius Victor: SPES ROMANORVM; Gratian: VOT XV MVLT XX (7); Valentinian II: REPARATIO REIPVB, VICTORIA AVGGG (15); Theodosius I: VICTORIA AVGGG (two victories) (2), VOT XV MVLT XX; Arcadius: VICTORIA AVGGG (two victories); House of Theodosius: VICTORIA AVGGG (5)
1	Bronze: Irregular	Valentinian II: VICTORIA AVGGG

COINS STRUCK A.D. 388–402

9	Trier	CK as 163 (2), as 164, as 166, as 167 (2), as 171, as 173; *RIC* 9 106(b)
28	Lyons	CK 389 (5), 391 (3), as 391 (12), 392 (5), as 392 (3)
69	Arles	CK 562 (5), 565 (10), as 565 (25), 566 (18), as 566 (6), 570 (3), as 570, Valentinian II: SALVS REIPVBLICAE
29	Rome	CK as 766, 796, as 796, 797 (3), as 797 (9), as 798 (5), 800 (2), as 806 (6), as 809
22	Aquileia	CK 1105 (6), as 1105 (6), 1106 (2), as 1106, 1107 (6), as 1107
4	Milan	*RIC* 9 solidus: 35(b); clipped siliquae: as 32(a) (3)
1	Siscia	CK AE 4: as 1577
2	Nicomedia	CK as 2414, 2417
1	Antioch	CK 2771
1	Thessalonica	*RIC* 9 solidus: 64(e)

| 394 | Bronze: reverses regular but mint uncertain | Eugenius: VICTORIA AVGGG; Valentinian II: SALVS REIPVBLICAE (7); Theodosius I: VICTORIA AVGGG (39), SALVS REIPVBLICAE (11); Arcadius: VICTORIA AVGGG (69), SALVS REIPVBLICAE (15); Honorius: VICTORIA AVGGG (9), SALVS REIPVBLICAE (5); House of Theodosius: VICTORIA AVGGG (156), SALVS REIPVBLICAE (80); SPES ROMANORVM (2) |
| 2 | Bronze: Irregular | House of Theodosius: VICTORIA AVGGG, SALVS REIPVBLICAE |

FOURTH-CENTURY COINS

| 870 | 3rd–4th centuries (210) 4th century (509) House of Constantine illeg. (81), House of Theodosius illeg. (70) |
| 17 | Cast-piece, late Roman (tremiss), leaden copies (3), coins and coin-like discs (12) |

HOARDS

The hoards are numbered as published by Boon (*Numismatic Chronicle* 1960, 247–52). Where his museum accession card numbering differs, this is indicated.

Hoard I (*IRBCH* 362) — found in a pottery flask buried 3–4 ft below turf in side but not in Pit D of Insula XI, July 1894.

9	M. Antony	Craw 544 (6), rev. illeg. (3)
4	Nero	*RIC* 46, 52 (3)
1	Galba	*RIC* 4
4	Vitellius	*RIC* 1/26, 2 (2), 26
39	Vespasian	*RIC* 9, 10 (5), 15 (2), 29, 30 (2), 36, 37 (2), 43, 50 (2), 52, 53, 57, 63, 65 (3), 67, 73, 77, 84, 90 (5), 103 (3), 110, 131(a), 132
3	Titus	*RIC* (Vespasian) 191(b), 218, 366
4	Domitian	*RIC* (Vespasian) 233, 242, 244, 246
6	Titus	*RIC* 6, 21(b), 24(a), 25(a), 27(b)
3	Domitian	*RIC* 140, 155, 175
28	Trajan	*RIC* 11, 37 var., 49, 58, 59, 80, as 88, 98, 100, 108 (2), 118 (3), 119 (2), 122, 128, 147(b), 165, 176, 204, 228, 243, 252, 343, 355, *BMC* Lycia 9–11
47	Hadrian	*RIC* 3(b), 9, 12 (2), 38, 39(b) (3), 42 (3), 44, 67, 77 (2), 88, 101 (2), 127, 137, 137(c), 139, 147 (2), 158, 160, 169, 175, as 181, 202, 222, 241A (2), 256, 260, 267 (2), 268, 276, 282, 290, 325, 326, 338 (2), 361, 363
4	Sabina	*RIC* (Hadrian) 390, 395(a) (2), 399(a)
29	Antoninus Pius	*RIC* 12, 37, 49, 61, 64, 111(b), 127, 136, 154, 155, 156 (2), 178, 200(c), 204, 219, 222 (2), 239, 264, 273, 286, 291(b), 293(a) (2), 294B(a), 305, 313(c), *BMC* 846
16	Faustina I	*RIC* (Antoninus Pius) as 185, 344 (3), 346(b), 347, 351, 360, 362 (3), 368, 373, 384, 393, 400
3	Faustina II	*RIC* (Antoninus Pius) 496, 497, 517(c)
25	Marcus Aurelius	2, as 6, 23, 24, 50, 59 (2), as 64, 170, 171, 212, 252, 330, 348?, 352, 369, 377, 429(a) (4), 443, 466(a), 468, 473,
3	Antoninus Pius	*RIC* (Marcus Aurelius) 431, 436, 441
7	Faustina II	*RIC* (Marcus Aurelius) 674, 676, 686, 702, 712(2), 715
3	Lucius Verus	*RIC* (Marcus Aurelius) 576, 596(a), *BMC* 380–382
3	Lucilla	*RIC* (Marcus Aurelius) 786 (2), rev. illeg.
13	Commodus	*RIC* 32, 146, 150(a), 160, 161, 167, 202(a), 218, 220, 222(a), 239, as 246, *BMC* 368
1	Crispina	*RIC* (Commodus) 282

| 1 | Clodius Albinus | *RIC* 7 |
| 1 | Septimius Severus | *RIC* 22 |

Hoard II (*IRBCH* 843) — found in Room 15 of House 2, Insula XVIII, 1897.

1	Gallienus	*RIC* 325
1	Claudius II	*RIC* copy of 261
1	Victorinus	*RIC* 118
1	Tetricus I	*RIC* 80
18	Carausius	*RIC* 98 (3), 101 (2), 102, 118 (4), 141, 334, 371, 458, 475 (2), 484, rev. illeg.

Hoard III (*IRBCH* 842; listed by Boon as being held at Stratfield Saye House) — found lying on the floor of the room to the west of the hypocaust, south wing, House 1, Insula I, 24 November 1865.

2	Claudius II	Rev. illeg. (2)
2	Victorinus	Rev. illeg. (2)
36	Carausius	Various rev. (24), overstruck (4), rev. illeg. (8)
1	?Helena	PAX PVBLICA
1	Uncertain 3rd–4th century	Rev. illeg.

Hoard IV (*IRBCH* 1182; Boon, Accession cards: VI) — found in a house south of the forum stuck together, 1892.

3	Trier	HK 49, 77(2)
3	Lyon	HK 191 (2), 203
2	Arles	HK 367, 370

Hoard V (*IRBCH* 1268; Boon, Accession cards: III) — found under a broken quern in a passage leading from the south face of Insula I, 1891.

1	Tetricus II	Copy of VIRTVS type
5	London	*RIC* 7 243, 287, 289, 292; 297
7	Trier	*RIC* 7 372, 382, 435, 461, 505, PROVIDENTIAE CAESS; HK 70
1	Lyon	HK 232
2	Arles	*RIC* 7 321, PROVIDENTIAE AVGG
1	Thessalonica	*RIC* 7 153
1	Constans	FEL TEMP REPARATIO (fallen horseman)

Hoard VI (*IRBCH* 1231; Boon, Accession cards: V) — found in Block 7, Insula XXIX, 1908.

43	Trier	HK 93, 95 (2), 113 (2), 116, 126, 128, 129 (2), as 133 (2), as 137, 140, 148 (7), 151, 153 (2), 158 (2), 162 (7), GLORIA EXERCITVS (one standard), VICTORIAE DD AVGGQ NN (8), copy of GLORIA EXERCITVS (one standard)
3	Lyons	HK as 239, as 266, 269
4	Arles	HK 445, 453, 456, GLORIA EXERCITVS (one standard)
1	Aquileia	HK 692(b)
29	Bronze: reverses regular but mint uncertain	GLORIA EXERCITVS (one standard) (6), PIETAS ROMANA, VICTORIAE DD AVGGQ NN (21), rev. illeg.
7	Bronze: Irregular	GLORIA EXERCITVS (two standards) (2), PAX PVBLICA, GLORIA EXERCITVS (one standard) (2), VICTORIAE DD AVGGQ NN (2)

Hoard VII (*IRBCH* 1230; Boon, Accession cards: IV) — found in a broken pot in the south-east corner of Insula III, 1891.

| 1 | Aurelian | ORIENS- type |

1	BR (Tetricus I)	Pietas (implements)
17	Trier	HK 52, 128, 138, as 138 (4), as 145, 148, as 151, 153, as 158, GLORIA EXERCITVS (one standard) (3), VICTORIAE DD AVGGQ NN (2)
2	Lyon	*RIC* 7 271, GLORIA EXERCITVS (one standard)
1	Lyon	CK as 285
1	Rome	HK 547
1	Heraclea	GLORIA EXERCITVS (one standard)
12	Bronze: reverses regular but mint uncertain	PAX PVBLICA, GLORIA EXERCITVS (one standard) (3), VICTORIAE DD AVGGQ NN (8)

APPENDIX 2

THE SMALL FINDS

By Nina Crummy

TABLE 27. PERIOD 3 TIMBER BUILDINGS MRTB 1/ERTB 1, OBJECT 50037, SUMMARY CATALOGUE OF SMALL FINDS
(D: diameter, L: length, T: thickness, W: width; H: height, cu-al: copper-alloy)

Context	Context description	SF No.	Material	Identification	Dimensions (mm)	Notes	Functional Category	Date
3042	latest phase MRTB1/ERTB1	2079	cu-al	toilet set on wire suspension loop: a) tweezers, b) nail-cleaner, c) ear-scoop	a) L 55, b) L 41, c) L 39	ear-scoop and suspension loop damaged	2	–
3533	latest phase MRTB1/ERTB1	2421	lead	candlestick	L 61, W 22	2 legs missing	4	2nd–4th century
3533	latest phase MRTB1/ERTB1	2422	cu-al	tweezers	L 43	–	2	–
3533	latest phase MRTB1/ERTB1	2426	cu-al	stud head?	D 23	–	11	–
3042	latest phase MRTB1/ERTB1	2477	cu-al	needle (?stylus)	L 109	spatulate head, rectangular eye	3	–
3533	latest phase MRTB1/ERTB1	2508	iron	hipposandal wing	L 88	–	8	–
3533	latest phase MRTB1/ERTB1	2535	cu-al	finger-ring, small	D 14	round bezel flanked by mouldings, traces of ?enamel in bezel	1	–
3533	latest phase MRTB1/ERTB1	2548	lead	disc or sealing	D 48	plain	18	–
3533	latest phase MRTB1/ERTB1	2552	iron	?blade fragment	L 89, W 23	–	10	–
3533	latest phase MRTB1/ERTB1	2553	iron	a) split-spike loop fragment; b) 7 nail shank fragments	a) L 58; b) longest 42	–	11	–
3533	latest phase MRTB1/ERTB1	2554	iron	sheet fragment	L 62, W 28	–	18	–
3533	latest phase MRTB1/ERTB1	2563	iron	2 sheet fragments	48 x 23; 40 x 25	–	18	–

Context	Context description	SF No.	Material	Identification	Dimensions (mm)	Notes	Functional Category	Date
3595	latest phase MRTB1/ERTB1	2576	cu-al	toilet spoon	L 100.5	long-handled, round dished scoop with spiral groove above	2	-
3597	latest phase MRTB1/ERTB1	2595	ceramic	counter	D 30, T 6.5	white ware base, wall/base junction trimmed	5	-
3732	latest phase MRTB1/ERTB1	2639	cu-al	Nauheim derivative brooch	L 25	pin and part of spring missing	1	c. A.D. 43–80/5
3597	latest phase MRTB1/ERTB1	2650	iron	ring (?finger-ring)	D 20	-	18	-
3597	latest phase MRTB1/ERTB1	2655	iron	strap-plate	L 86, W 26	one end folded back to hold hinge-bar	1/8	-
3732	latest phase MRTB1/ERTB1	2659	iron	bit from lift-key	W 46, L 25	L-shaped, 3 teeth	11	-
3732	latest phase MRTB1/ERTB1	2660	iron	wall-hook	L 82.5	-	11	-
3533	latest phase MRTB1/ERTB1	2692	iron	strip	L 59, W 14	uncorroded, ?modern	18	-
3595	latest phase MRTB1/ERTB1	2721	lead	sheet fragment	44 x 32	-	18	-
3532	latest phase MRTB1/ERTB1	2767	bone	round-bowled spoon	L 69	part of handle missing	4	mid-1st–2nd century
3751	latest phase MRTB1/ERTB1	2785	iron	?coiled ring	-	delaminated	18	-
3532	latest phase MRTB1/ERTB1	2793	cu-al	nail-cleaner	L 47	plain, one point missing	2	-
3751	latest phase MRTB1/ERTB1	2795	iron	rectangular loop	L 87, W 24	-	18	-
3751	latest phase MRTB1/ERTB1	2796	frit	melon bead	D 20, L 15	complete	1	mid-1st–early 2nd century
3532	latest phase MRTB1/ERTB1	2805	bone	shaft fragment	L 50	-	18	-
3751	latest phase MRTB1/ERTB1	2831	iron	stylus fragment	L 56	point only	7	-
3751	latest phase MRTB1/ERTB1	2832	iron	loop-headed shank	L 108	?part of chain link	11	-
3532	latest phase MRTB1/ERTB1	2859	iron	disc	D 36	thin, ?part of ferrule	11	-
3532	latest phase MRTB1/ERTB1	2860	cu-al	hairpin, Cool Group 6	L 104.5	complete, shaft slightly bent	1	mid-1st–2nd century

2877	3532	latest phase MRTB1/ERTB1	cu-al	penannular brooch, Fowler Type D2	D 30	cast moulded terminals, nicks on upper face of hoop	1	mid-1st–2nd century
2882	3532	latest phase MRTB1/ERTB1	iron	ring	D 53	-	18	-
2957	4151	?wall	iron	ring	D 44	-	18	-
2985	4150	?wall	cu-al	T-shaped brooch, Hull Type 122	L 43	headloop, expanded lozenge on bow, enamelled	1	late 1st to mid-2nd century
2964	3812	occupation	cu-al	fragment	30 x 14	-	18	-
3029	4179	occupation	iron	3 strip fragments	largest L 46.5, W 26	-	18	-
3031	4179	occupation	iron	strip fragment	L 49.5, W 22	-	18	-
3075	4225	occupation	cu-al	furniture nail	L 57	-	11	-
2975	4152	clay floors	cu-al/lead	boss	D 24	filled with tin-lead solder	11	-
3086	4152	clay floors	cu-al	fragment	32 x 25	-	18	-
3112	4152	clay floors	cu-al/lead	boss	D 24	filled with tin-lead solder	11	-
3154	4152	clay floors	iron/cu-al	sheet fragment	46 x 34	with cu-al rivet	18	-
3155	4152	clay floors	cu-al	wire	L 140	-	18	-
3169	4152	clay floors	cu-al	sheet fragment	37 x 20	-	18	-
3173	4152	clay floors	iron	sheet fragment	55 x 30	-	18	-
3496	5307	clay floors	iron	strip/shank fragment	L 45, W 18	-	18	-
3361	4772	clay/gravel floor	iron	knife blade fragment	L 60, W 33	-	10	-
3365	4772	clay/gravel floor	cu-al	stud	L 12	-	11	-
3001	4169	post-hole fill	glass	counter	D 15	black	5	-
3256	4170	later floors	cu-al	Polden Hill/T-shaped brooch	L 64.5	enamelled, Hull Type 110	1	late 1st–mid-2nd century
3260	4170	later floors	ivory	?peg	L 20.5	groove below top; fragmented	18	-
3484	4170	later floors	cu-al	tweezers	L 63	with wire clip	2	-
2999	4170	later floors	cu-al	sheet fragment	27 x 15	folded in two	18	-
3037	4188	later floors	lead	candelabrum	H 20, L 62	open lamp slotted onto tripod candlestick	4	2nd century
3393	4854	later floors	cu-al	strip	L 77, W 13	rivet hole at one end	18	-
3581	5360	tile spread	ceramic	counter	D 30, T 13	oxidised ware base, trimmed wall/base junction	5	-
3482	5825	tile spread?	iron	stud head	D 15.5	shank missing	11	-
3493	5825	tile spread?	frit	melon bead	D 15, L 11	-	1	mid-1st–early 2nd century
2928	3178	soil over building	iron	strip fragment	L 51	-	18	-
2713	3178	soil over building	bone	curved strip	L 6	?part of stud or cap	18	-

TABLE 28. PERIOD 3 MASONRY BUILDING 1, OBJECT 50018, SUMMARY CATALOGUE OF SMALL FINDS
(D: diameter, L: length, T: thickness, W: width; H: height, cu-al: copper-alloy)

Context	Context description	SF No.	Material	Identification	Dimensions (mm)	Notes	Functional Category	Date
3385	deposits preceding stone construction	3381	shale	armlet fragment	L 39, T 9	decorative grooves	1	–
3646	deposits preceding stone construction	3717	iron	knife with integral handle	L 93, W 16	complete, Manning Type 8	10	early Roman
3646	deposits preceding stone construction	3913	cu-al	Nauheim derivative brooch	L 44.5	complete, knurled margins, knife-edge foot	1	c. A.D. 43–80/5
3646	deposits preceding stone construction	3933	cu-al	Colchester B derivative brooch	L 44	complete, incised zigzag on bow	1	c. A.D. 50–70
3646	deposits preceding stone construction	4028	cu-al	sheet fragment	L 17, W 12	–	18	–
3646	deposits preceding stone construction	4031	iron	strap-hinge	L 52, W 18	most of one arm missing, nail hole in complete arm	11	–
3646	deposits preceding stone construction	4036	iron	strip fragment, ?tang	L 40, W 10	–	18	–
3646	deposits preceding stone construction	4057	iron	hobnails	–	–	1	–
3246	walls	2155	cu-al	brooch spring and pin	L 49	–	1	–
3247	walls	2263	cu-al	nail	L 22	possibly from two-piece stud	11	–
3247	walls	2331	cu-al	circular sheet object	–	survived only as corrosion layer	18	–
3247	walls	2437	ceramic	spindlewhorl	D 31, T 6, spindle hole D 9	oxidised ware sherd, edge neatly ground, spindle hole worn	3	–
3247	walls	2486/2501	cu-al	Polden Hill brooch	L 56	with side mouldings and crest on top of bow	1	Flavian
3247	walls	2487	cu-al	hairpin, tip missing	L 58.5	Cool Group 6, with knob head above two reels	1	late 1st–2nd century
3247	walls	2568	iron	strip fragment	L 70, W 10	–	18	–
1174	walls	2614	cu-al	shaft fragment, bent into loop	17 x 12	–	18	–
1533	walls	2617	ceramic	counter	D 42, T 14	base of small grey ware vessel, wall/base junction trimmed	5	–
1476	floors in ?Room 1	805	cu-al/lead	boss with tin-lead infill	D13	damaged, may have had a flange	11	–
3214	floors in ?Room 1	2277	cu-al	sheet fragment	L 32, W 7	–	18	–

floors in ?Room 1	3214	cu-al	fragment	L 13, W 13	?metal-working waste/offcut	15?	–
Room 2 floors?	1912	iron	sheet fragment	L 56, W 33	-	18	–
Room 2 floors?	3288	iron	amorphous fragment	L 58, W 25	-	18	–
floor in Room 3	1905	cu-al	Langton Down brooch fragment	L 27.5	foot only, with longitudinal mouldings; parts of catchplate survive	1	c. A.D. 10–50/5
floors in NE aisle	3281	glass	counter	D 17	dark blue/black	5	–
floors in NE aisle	3281	iron	knife blade fragment	L 73, W 17	-	10	–
floors in NE aisle	3281	iron	strap fragment	L 68, W 32	-	18	–
floors in NE aisle	3707	iron	strip fragment	L 62, W 16	-	18	–
floors in NE aisle	3707	iron	cleat	L 33	-	1	–
floors in NE aisle	3989	cu-al	sheet fragment	L 37.5, W 18	-	18	–
floors in NE aisle	3989	cu-al	stud shank fragment	L 11	-	11	–
floors in NE aisle	3989	bone/cu-al	sheet fragments attached to rib fragment	31 x 9	-	18	–
floors in NE aisle	3989	cu-al	small stud	L 9	-	11	–
floors in NE aisle	3989	cu-al	?casting debris	L 26	-	15?	–

TABLE 29. PERIOD 3 MASONRY BUILDING 2, OBJECT 50019, SUMMARY CATALOGUE OF SMALL FINDS
(D: diameter, L: length, T: thickness, W: width; H: height, cu-al: copper-alloy)

Context	Context description	SF No.	Material	Identification	Dimensions (mm)	Notes	Functional category	Date
3619	walls	2389	cu-al	sheet fragment	L 26	with punched hole	18	–
3619	walls	2786	cu-al	Colchester brooch	L 78	complete	1	c. A.D. 10–50/5
3601	walls	2961	cu-al	toilet set, a) tweezers, b) nail-cleaner, c) ear-scoop; held on penannular loop	a) L 53.5, b) L 46.5, c) L 35.5	tweezers and nail-cleaner notched on edges, ear-scoop damaged	2	1st century
1746	walls	3083	cu-al	strip	L 34, W 6.5	–	18	–
1150	walls	3133	cu-al	Nauheim derivative brooch	L 35	wire bow; pin and part of spring missing	1	A.D. 43–80/5
1160	walls	3140	iron	mason's trowel	L 156	tang damaged	10	–
3619	walls	3485	cu-al	strip fragment	L 44, W 10	–	18	–
3619	walls	3495	cu-al	sheet fragment, ?stud head	D 9	–	18	–
1818	floors	2269	cu-al	Hod Hill brooch	L 41	with small lugs at top of bow, tinned	1	c. A.D. 43–60/5
2023	floors	2560	iron	shank/rod	L 73	–	18	–
3382	floors	2635	frit	melon bead fragment	D 19	–	1	mid-1st–early 2nd century
3382	floors	2642	cu-al	hairpin	L 135	complete but deliberately bent; with mouldings beneath globular head, allied to Cool Group 21	1	2nd–3rd century
2023	floors	2866	cu-al	shaft fragment	L 24.5	–	18	–
3375	floors	2924	glass	counter	D 12	blue/green	5	–
3680	floors	2942	cu-al	toilet set, a) tweezers, b) nail-cleaner, c) ear-scoop; held on penannular loop	a) L 54, b) L 50.5, c) L 41	nail-cleaner has angular top, bellied blade and long points	2	1st century
4354	floors	3082	cu-al	nail	L 14	globular head	11	–
4386	floors	3179	cu-al	nail	L 12	globular head	11	–
4010	burning	2828	cu-al	binding, two pieces	L 107, L 41	–	11	–
4130	'lobby' deposits	3011	cu-al	brooch pin fragment	L 15.5	hinged	1	–
4563	post-hole	3021	iron	needle	L 60	long eye	3	–
4578	post-hole	3098	cu-al	tweezers	L 50	one blade and part of loop only	2	–

TABLE 30. PERIOD 4 MASONRY BUILDING 3, OBJECT 50046, SUMMARY CATALOGUE OF SMALL FINDS
(D: diameter, L: length, T: thickness, W: width; H: height, cu-al: copper-alloy)

Context	Context description	SF No.	Material	Identification	Dimensions (mm)	Notes	Functional category	Date
3213	construction clays	2040	iron	strip fragment	L 80, W 18	from hinge or strap-fitting?	11	-
3048	construction clays	2136	glass	cylinder bead	D 3, L 7	opaque blue, ends pinched	1	-
3213	construction clays	2166	iron	goad prick	D 16, L 29	-	12	-
3049	construction clays	2289	iron/cu-al	strip with cu-al binding	L 23.5, W 11	binding attached by 3 rivets	11	-
3259	construction clays	2304	cu-al	furniture nail	L 29.5, D 7	-	11	-
2074	construction clays	2344	cu-al	stud	L 11, D 14	convex-headed	11	-
2455	construction clays	2355	cu-al	belt-plate	plates 23 x 10, 20 x 9	double plate, with two rivet holes	1	-
3048	construction clays	2447	iron	strip fragment	L 29	-	18	-
3282	construction clays	2589	cu-al	pick from châtelaine brooch	L 54	-	1 (2)	late 1st–early 2nd century
3049	construction clays	2613	cu-al	shaft fragment	L 76	from pin, needle, etc.	18	-
3049	construction clays	2634	iron	shank fragment	L 40	-	18	-
3313	construction clays	2824	cu-al	boss	D 17.5, H 8.5	flanged	11	-
3375	construction clays	2924	glass	counter	D 12	opaque green/blue	5	-
3049	construction clays	2953	cu-al	strip fragment	L 14, W 9.5	-	18	-
4111	construction clays	2965	cu-al	fragment	L 27, W 13	-	18	-
3049	construction clays	2983	lead	sheet fragment	L 114, W 43	?offcut	18	-
4111	construction clays	3002	cu-al	terret	D 21	stump of basal projection	8	-
3313	construction clays	3017	cu-al	sheet fragment	L 31.5, W 10	broken across a perforation	18	-
3313	construction clays	3018	frit	melon bead fragment	D 29, L 23	-	1	mid-1st–early 2nd century
3313	construction clays	3363	cu-al	stylus	L 99	point missing, moulded shaft	7	-
3313	construction clays	3543	iron	wire	L 49	-	18	-
4454	construction clays	4018	cu-al	strip/plaque fragment	L 12, W 8	-	18	-
4454	construction clays	4039	iron	stylus	L 62	shouldered eraser, point missing	7	-
4454	construction clays	4044	cu-al	Rearhook brooch	L 25	spring and pin missing; small/miniature example	1	c. A.D. 40–60
4454	construction clays	4053	iron	pintle?	-	-	11	-
4454	construction clays	4086	iron	tanged tool, ?knife	L 37, W 21	-	10	-
2687	earlier post-hole?	1805	ceramic	spindlewhorl	D 37, T 5, spindle hole D 4 mm	terra nigra, spindle hole worn	3	pre-Flavian

Context	Context description	SF No.	Material	Identification	Dimensions (mm)	Notes	Functional category	Date
2057	clay/gravel floors	1286	cu-al	Nauheim derivative brooch	L 30	wire bow, pin and part of spring missing, catchplate damaged	1	c. A.D. 43–80/5
3221	clay/gravel floors	2958	cu-al	strainer-plate	L 30, W 22	metal perished, tiny fragments only	4	c. A.D. 40–60
1457	gravel floors	774	cu-al	brooch spring fragment	L 6	-	1	-
1580	gravel floors	930	cu-al	strap-end	L 30, W 11.5	split socket with central rivet	1	-
1788	gravel floors	1077	cu-al	Colchester BB derivative brooch	L 39	pin and part of chord missing	1	c. A.D. 65–85
1788	gravel floors	1078	cu-al	curved strip fragment	L 14	?part of flange from large stud	18	-
1788	gravel floors	1143	ceramic	tobacco pipe stem	L 35	with small damaged foot	-	19th century
1757	gravel floors	1121	iron	latchlifter	L 205	end of handle and hook missing	11	-
1792	gravel floors	1180	glass	counter	D 17.5	black	5	-
1934	gravel floors	1232	cu-al	Nauheim derivative brooch	L 38.5	?plain bow, catchplate missing	1	c. A.D. 43–80/5
1796	gravel floors	1247	cu-al	convex-headed stud	D 16, L 17.5	-	11	-
1796	gravel floors	1254	bone	hinge unit fragment	L 30, D >22	with dowel hole	4	-
1796	gravel floors	1257	cu-al	binding fragments	L 61	U-section	11	-
2009	gravel floors	1260	glass	counter	D 12	black	5	-
2009	gravel floors	2013	cu-al	vessel foot	L 32, W 21	pelta-shaped	4	mid-1st century?
3231	gravel floors	2080	iron	strip fragment	L 42, W 22	from strap-fitting?	18	-
1544	hearth	2198	cu-al	chain link fragment	L 8	loop-in-loop type	18	-
3377	robbing of Period 3 stone walls / construction of Period 4 walls	2856	cu-al	penannular brooch pin	L 19	-	1	-
1393	new walls	746	cu-al	strip or plaque fragment	L 22.5, W 11	-	18	-
1151	new walls	2756	cu-al	brooch pin	L 55	from large bow brooch	1	1st century B.C./ A.D.
1151	new walls	3142	iron	strip fragment	L 50, W 22	-	18	-
3346	verandah	2353	cu-al	small fragments	largest L 7.5, W 7	-	18	-
3698	verandah	2579	iron	?key, fragmented	L 102	-	11	-
3999	verandah	2752	cu-al	brooch spring fragment?	D 7	-	1	-
3999	verandah	2776	cu-al	strap-ring fragment	D 28	ribbed section; from box	4	mid-1st–mid-2nd century

Context	Context no.	SF	Material	Object	Dimensions	Description	Phase	Date
verandah	3396	3006	iron	strip fragment	L 55, W 12	-	18	-
verandah	3396	3008	iron	sheet fragments	largest L 115, W 51	-	18	-
verandah	3396	3025	cu-al	needle	L 64	rectangular eye	3	3rd–4th century
verandah	3396	3048	cu-al	buckle fragment?	L 40, D 5.5	bar with grooved ends	1	-
verandah	3396	3077	iron	sheet fragment	L 23.5, W 19	-	18	-
verandah	3396	3085	shale	armlet fragment	D 90	plain	1	-
verandah	3396	3165	bone	hinge unit fragment	D 21.5, L 61.5	incised pairs of grooves, two dowel holes	4	-
verandah	3396	3167	ceramic	counter	D 68, T 4	orange ware base; wall/base junction neatly trimmed	5	-
later robbing of walls	1775	1204	cu-al	shaft fragment	L 45.5	-	18	-
robbing of stone house walls	1397	742	cu-al	crenellated armlet fragment	L 48	-	1	mid–late 4th century
robbing of stone house walls	1397	814	iron	ring fragment (bent nail shank?)	-	-	18	-
robbing of stone house walls	1488	830	glass	stirring rod fragment	L 27, D 6	-	2	-
robbing of stone house walls	1397	856	ceramic	counter	D 17	white ware, worn edge	5	-
dark earth	1461	807	glass	green globular bead	D 15.5, L 13.5	as SF 718	1	-
dark earth	1461	838	cu-al	?armlet fragment	L 47.5	plain curved strip	1	-
dark earth	1656	962	cu-al	curved strip fragment	L 28	?part of flange from large stud	18	-
dark earth	1656	971	cu-al	crenellated armlet fragment	D 52	-	1	mid–late 4th century
dark earth	1656	979	cu-al	boss	D 16, H 8	with flanged rim, pointed on one side	11	-
dark spread	2233	1460	iron	shank fragment with discoid terminal	L 55, D 23	?box or structural fitting	11	-
dark spread	2657	1711	cu-al	nail-cleaner	L 30.5	straight sides, points missing	2	-
dark spread	3252	2211	iron	flesh-hook fragment?	L 70	bar fragment with one bifurcated end	4	-
dark spread	3252	2214	cu-al	strip fragment	L 35, W 3	-	18	-
dark spread	3252	2217	iron	shank fragment?	L 23	-	18	-

TABLE 31. PERIODS 3 AND 4: SOUTH-EASTERN PITS, OBJECT 500017, SUMMARY CATALOGUE OF SMALL FINDS
(D: diameter, L: length, T: thickness, W: width; H: height, cu-al: copper-alloy)

Object	Context	Context description	SF No.	Material	Identification	Dimensions (mm)	Notes	Functional category	Date
500033	3175	upper fill of pit 3406	2151	cu-al	penannular ring	D 7	small, perhaps from earring	18	-
	3175	upper fill of pit 3406	2163	iron	2 fragments	L 52.5, W 29, L 27, W 27	-	18	-
	3175	upper fill of pit 3406	2184	iron/cu-al	blade from folding-knife	L 47, W 22	remains of cu-al fixing on each side	10	-
	3197	fill of pit 3406	2201	iron	fragment	L 10, W 11	-	18	-
	3197	fill of pit 3406	2203	beryl/gold	bead on fine gold wire	L 5	-	1	-
	3821	fill of pit 3406	2633	iron	tongue-ended strap terminal	L 54, W 24	terminal pierced, with nail hole adjacent	11	-
	3821	fill of pit 3406	2637	bone	shaft fragment	L 62	-	18	-
	3829	fill of pit 3406	2720	bone	peg	L 74.5	-	18	later Roman
	3829	fill of pit 3406	2732	bone	shaft fragment	L 55.5	-	18	-
	3874	fill of pit 3406	2711	iron	fragment	L 35, W 17	-	18	-
	4041	fill of pit 3406	2836	iron	spike	L 84	-	18	-
	4041	fill of pit 3406	2838	iron	hobnails	L 14	group, little iron left	1	-
	4041	fill of pit 3406	2840	iron	rod	L 181, D 8	knobbed head; possibly from furniture	4?	-
	4041	fill of pit 3406	2858	iron	hobnails	L 14	group, little iron left	1	-
	4041	fill of pit 3406	2861	iron	finger-ring	D 26	with expanded bezel	1	-
	4041	fill of pit 3406	2879	jet/shale	spacer bead	D 3, L 0.5	-	1	3rd–4th century
	4041	fill of pit 3406	2898	iron	?tang fragments	L 46, 30	fragment of bone attached, ?from handle	10?	-
	4041	fill of pit 3406	2900	shale	platter fragment	D 280 approx.	shallow rim and footring	4	-
	4041	fill of pit 3406	2901	iron	hipposandal wing	L 65	-	8	-
	4041	fill of pit 3406	2902	iron	fragment	L 45, W 40	-	18	-
	4041	fill of pit 3406	2905	bone	shaft fragment	L 60	-	18	-
	4041	fill of pit 3406	2910	bone	shaft fragment	L 70	-	18	-
	4041	fill of pit 3406	2911	iron	strip fragment, ?blade	-	-	18	-

Context	Feature	SF	Material	Object	Dimensions	Notes	Fig	Date
4041	fill of pit 3406	2914	bone	crude pointed tool	L 180, W 15, T 7	made from a long bone; shaft square in section, sides polished from use	10	–
4041	fill of pit 3406	2917	iron	strip/sheet fragment	L 50, W 30	–	18	–
4041	fill of pit 3406	2918	bone	hairpin, Type 3	–	–	1	A.D. 150–400+
4041	fill of pit 3406	3090/3093	bone	hairpin, Type 1	L 95	tip missing	1	c. A.D. 43–150/200
4041	fill of pit 3406	3091	cu-al	stud	L 12	convex head	11	–
4041	fill of pit 3406	3092	glass	shattered cylindrical bead	D 4, L 5	clear glass; as SF 3218	1	–
4041	fill of pit 3406	3097	bone	double-pronged tool	L 182, T 29.5	hollow shaft, side perforation	10	–
4041	fill of pit 3406	3102	iron	hobnail clusters	–	–	1	–
4041	fill of pit 3406	3103	iron	round sheet fragment	D 70	–	18	–
4041	fill of pit 3406	3105	iron	hook	L 34	–	11	–
4041	fill of pit 3406	3120	iron	hobnail cluster	51 x 32	–	1	–
4041	fill of pit 3406	3122	iron	strip fragment	L 35, W 22	bent	18	–
4041	fill of pit 3406	3132	iron	8 hobnails	L 13	–	1	–
4041	fill of pit 3406	3137	iron	32 (approx) hobnails	L 13	–	1	–
4041	fill of pit 3406	3148	shale	bowl fragment	37 x 22, T 3, max D >100	–	4	–
4041	fill of pit 3406	3178	glass	globular bead	D 5, L 5	silver-in-glass	1	–
4041	fill of pit 3406	3217	glass	pellet	D 3.5	setting from jewellery?	1?	–
4041	fill of pit 3406	3218	glass	shattered cylindrical bead,	D 6, L 3	clear glass; as SF 3092	1	–
4290	fill of pit 3406	3152	iron	rod/shank fragments	–	severely decayed	18	–
3108 (500034)	fill of pit 3102	2036	cu-al	sheet fragments	L 7, W 5	–	18	–
3127	gravel capping of pit 3102	2059	cu-al	sheet fragment	L 25, W 14	?vessel fragment	18	–
3127	gravel capping of pit 3102	2070	iron	4 sheet fragments	46 x 37, 28 x 21, 32 x 21, 22 x 19	–	18	–
3127	gravel capping of pit 3102	2071	iron	a) nail shank fragment; b) amorphous fragment	a) L 44; b) 17 x 12	–	18	–
3127	gravel capping of pit 3102	2087	iron	rake prong fragment	L 131	–	12	–
3144	fill of pit 3102	2082	iron	sheet fragment	45 x 23	–	18	–
3182	fill of pit 3102	2181	iron	39 hobnails/hobnail fragments	L 13	–	1	–

Object	Context	Context description	SF No.	Material	Identification	Dimensions (mm)	Notes	Functional category	Date
	3182	fill of pit 3102	2182	bone	shaft fragment	L 47	-	18	
	3182	fill of pit 3102	2216	bone	peg	L 60	tip missing	18	late Roman
	3820	fill of pit 3102	2664	bone	shaft fragment	L 62	-	18	-
	3827	fill of pit 3102	2591	iron	12 (approx) hobnails	L 14	-	1	-
	3827	fill of pit 3102	2592	bone	shaft fragment	L 46	-	18	-
	3827	fill of pit 3102	2593	iron	fragment	40 x 37	-	18	-
	3827	fill of pit 3102	2594	iron	18 (approx) hobnails	L 13	-	1	-
	3827	fill of pit 3102	2603	iron	14 hobnails	L 14	-	1	-
	3827	fill of pit 3102	2619	iron	7 (approx) hobnails	L 12	-	1	-
	3827	fill of pit 3102	2672	iron	fragment	-	-	18	-
	3827	fill of pit 3102	2674	iron	joiner's dog	W 70, L 30	-	11	-
	3827	fill of pit 3102	2676	iron	fragment	L 60	-	18	-
	3827	fill of pit 3102	2684	iron	loop-hinge fragment	L 49, W 25	-	11	-
	3827	fill of pit 3102	2685	iron	joiner's dog	W 70, L 40	-	11	-
	3827	fill of pit 3102	2688	iron	hobnail cluster	51 x 35	-	1	-
	3827	fill of pit 3102	2690	iron	hobnail cluster	47 x 29	-	1	-
	3827	fill of pit 3102	2693	iron	hobnail cluster	35 x 30	-	1	-
	3827	fill of pit 3102	2694	iron	strip fragment	-	-	18	-
	3827	fill of pit 3102	2695	ceramic	counter	D 59, T 4	Alice Holt grey ware	5	-
	3827	fill of pit 3102	2707	iron	rod fragment	L 83	-	18	-
	3827	fill of pit 3102	2708	iron	strip fragment	37 x 34	-	18	-
	3827	fill of pit 3102	2710	iron	4 hobnails	L 14	-	1	-
	3827	fill of pit 3102	2712	iron	joiner's dog	W 35, L 30	-	11	-
	3827	fill of pit 3102	2715	iron	5 hobnails	-	-	1	-
	3827	fill of pit 3102	2718	shale	armlet fragment?	L 32, W 9	-	1	-
500035	5692	fill of pit 5693	3575	iron	2 strip fragments	L 32, W 25; L 39, W 22	-	18	-
	5692	fill of pit 5693	3636	iron	joiner's dog fragment	W >38, L 40	-	11	-
	5692	fill of pit 5693	3681	iron	joiner's dog fragment	W > 45, L 15	-	11	-
	5723	fill of pit 5693	3863	cu-al	2 mirror fragments	20 x 20; 20 x 15	-	2	-
	6300	fill of pit 5693	4269	bone	shaft fragment	L 40	-	18	-

			Material	Object	Dimensions	Description	Count	Date
500037	6343	fill of pit 5693	iron	fragments	-	-	18	-
	5697	upper fill of well 5735	cu-al	finger-ring	D 23, max W 12	hoop worn at back, expanded bezel with remains of green glass setting	1	-
	5697	upper fill of well 5735	iron	shank fragment	L 73	-	18	-
	6304	fill of well 5735	iron	fragment	89 x 28	-	18	-
	6306	fill of well 5735	iron	joiner's dog	W 83, L 62	arm clenched; one arm missing	11	-
	6436	fill of well 5735	leather	fragment	(lost)	-	18	-
	6436	fill of well 5735	wood (maple)	writing-tablet	L 178, W 92, T 6 (before freeze-drying)	single, with pierced handle; surface lattice scored	7	-
	6436	fill of well 5735	leather	two fragments	55 x 38	both oftcuts	16	-
	6436	fill of well 5735	cu-al	jug handle	L 139	foot-handle type	4	2nd century
	6436	fill of well 5735	leather	two fragments	60 x 71; 106 x 92	from shoe uppers	1	-
	6436	fill of well 5735	iron	bucket handle fragment	L 225	-	4	-
	6436	fill of well 5735	leather	small scrap	51 x 28	-	18	-
	6960	basal fill of well 5735	iron	hobnail	L 14	-	1	-
	6960	basal fill of well 5735	iron	hobnail	L 15	-	1	-
	6960	basal fill of well 5735	leather	two small scraps	22 x 12, 31 x 15	-	18	-
500020	1750	well 1750	iron	cast iron fitting	82 x 81	intrusive	-	modern
	2778	fill of well 1750	leather	fragment	45 x 30	?from footwear	1	-
500031	2433	fill of pit 2434	iron	saw blade	L 71, W 10.5	3 teeth/cm	10	-
	2434	pit 2434	silver	wire	L 33, D 1.5	-	18	-
	2602	dumped fill of 2434	shale	armlet fragment	internal D 60 mm, H 6.5, T 6	cable-imitative incised grooves on outer face	1	2nd–3rd/4th
	2602	dumped fill of 2434	bone	hairpin fragment, Type 3	L 36	-	1	A.D. 150–400+
	2605	fill of pit 2434	mineral replaced iron/leather	fragmented 'casts' of nailed soles	-	-	1	-
	2605	fill of pit 2434	glass	cylinder bead	D 3, L 5	green, hexagonal section	1	-

Object	Context	Context description	SF No.	Material	Identification	Dimensions (mm)	Notes	Functional category	Date
	2605	fill of pit 2434	1876	iron	staple	W 72, L 29	-	11	-
	2605	fill of pit 2434	1908	bone	shaft fragment	L 42	-	18	-
	2605	fill of pit 2434	1946	cu-al	strip fragment	L 14, W 11	folded into three	18	-
	2774	fill of pit 2434	1925	cu-al	strip fragments	a) L 19, W 7; b) L 10.5, W 16	rivet holes present	18	-
500032	2622	secondary fill of pit 2601	1734	ivory/iron	folding-knife/razor with zoomorphic handle	L 60, W 40	handle in the form of mating dogs	10/2	2nd century
44008	4542	fill of pit 5039	3801	lead	sheet fragments	80 x 65	partly folded; probably offcuts	18	-
	4549	fill of pit 5039	3841	iron	strip fragments	18 x 16; 19 x 17	-	18	-
	5001	fill of pit 5039	3555	bone	bone-working debris	L 68	probably unfinished hairpin		-
50036	4315	dumps & gravels; slump into 6290	3174	bone	shaft fragment	L 37	-	18	-
	5663	dumps & gravels; slump into 6290	3577	bone	shaft fragment	L 51	-	18	-
	5698	dumps & gravels; slump into 6290	3966	iron	rod/shank fragment	L 90	-	18	-
	5698	dumps & gravels; slump into 6290	3878	iron	hobnail	L 16	-	1	-
	5698	dumps & gravels; slump into 6290	3888	glass	counter	D 17, H 7	dark blue/black	5	-
	5698	dumps & gravels; slump into 6290	3929	cu-al	hairpin fragment	L 121	two grooves below missing head	1	-
	5698	dumps & gravels; slump into 6290	3935	bone	tube (?bobbin)	L 89, D 13	length of hollow bone with slit cut a mid-point	3?	-
	5698	dumps & gravels; slump into 6290	3956	lead	sheet fragment	45 x 34	-	18	-
	5722	dumps & gravels; slump into 6290	3806	bone	hairpin, Type 2	L 49	tip missing	1	mid-1st–2nd century

TABLE 32. PERIOD 3 NORTHERN PITS, OBJECT 50029, SUMMARY CATALOGUE OF SMALL FINDS
(D: diameter, L: length, T: thickness, W: width; H: height, cu-al: copper-alloy)

Object	Context	Context description	SF No.	Material	Identification	Dimensions (mm)	Notes	Functional category	Date
50028	4849	fill of cess-pit 4835	3223	bone	hinge unit	D 21, L 31	-	4	-
	5821	clay cap of cess-pit 4835	3738	iron	strip fragment (?blade)	L 55, W 30	-	18	-
	5867	fill of cess-pit 4835	3808	iron	joiner's dog	W 50, L 5	-	11	-
	5867	fill of cess-pit 4835	3816	iron	joiner's dog fragment	W 25?, L 4	-	11	-
41016	2162	upper fill of well 2234	1416	iron	hipposandal fragment	L 78, W 95	part of base plate and hook only	8	-
	2254	fill of well 2234	1317	iron	stylus fragment	L 7	shouldered eraser, point missing	7	-
	2333	fill of well 2234	1676	cu-al	furniture nail	L 19	-	4	-
	2967	fill of well 2234	2137	ceramic	counter rough-out	D 54, T 10	grey ware wall sherd, roughly trimmed to shape	5	-
	2967	fill of well 2234	2138	tile	counter	D 70, T 24	-	5	-

TABLE 33. PERIOD 3 SOUTH-EASTERN OCCUPATION CONTEXTS, OBJECT 701, SUMMARY CATALOGUE OF SMALL FINDS
(D: diameter, L: length, T: thickness, W: width; H: height, cu-al: copper-alloy)

Context	Context description	SF No.	Material	Identification	Dimensions (mm)	Notes	Functional category	Date
4253	dumps & gravels	2993	cu-al	fragment	20 x 12	-	18	-
4254	dumps & gravels	3108	iron	sheet fragment	46 x 40	-	18	-
4256	dumps & gravels	3009	bone	hairpin fragment, Type 1	L 32	head not quite conical	1	early Roman
4270	dumps & gravels	3065	cu-al	furniture nail	L 17	-	11	-
4270	dumps & gravels	3066	cu-al	nail-cleaner	L 46	plain straight shaft, expanded pierced head	2	-
4270	dumps & gravels	3067	cu-al	tweezers	L 42	plain flared blades	2	-
4270	dumps & gravels	3072	cu-al	Nauheim Derivative brooch	L 45	complete, bow tapers to knife-edge foot, knurled margins	1	c. A.D. 43–80/5
4270	dumps & gravels	3081	iron	knife blade fragment	L 85	straight edge, back straight, angled sharply to tip	10	-
4308	dumps & gravels	3210	bone	shaft fragment	L 43	very thin	18	-
4308	dumps & gravels	3212	iron	shank fragment	L 67	-	18	-
4307	dumps & gravels	3315	bone	hairpin, Type 2	L 56	single groove; shaft broken and repointed for continued use	1	early Roman
4523	dumps & gravels	3450	cu-al	Nauheim Derivative brooch	L 44	pin missing, bow tapers to knife-edge foot	1	c. A.D. 43–80/5
4523	dumps & gravels	3464	iron	bar or shank fragment	L 55	-	18	-
4523	dumps & gravels	3474	cu-al	phalera	D 36	tinned, double loop on underside	13	mid-late 1st century
4523	dumps & gravels	3744	cu-al	shank fragment	L 28	-	18	-
4523	dumps & gravels	3745	cu-al	brooch pin	L 27	with one coil of spring	1	-
4265	CBM dump	3052	bone	round-bowled spoon	L 39, bowl D 26	deep bowl, most of handle missing	4	early Roman
4265	CBM dump	3061	bone	needle shaft fragment	L 70	tip & top of eye missing	3	-
4265	CBM dump	3436	bone	shaft fragment	L 50	-	18	-
4528	CBM dump	3426	bone	hinge unit	L 28, D 21	dowel hole	4	early Roman
3490	?building	3232	bone	round-bowled spoon	L 75	bowl incomplete	4	early Roman
3490	?building	3238	cu-al	needle, spatulate head	L 135	rectangular eye	3	-
3490	?building	3241	bone	round-bowled spoon	L 69	only small part of bowl remains	4	early Roman
3490	?building	3254	bone	shaft fragment	L 36	-	18	-

Context	Find no.	Material	Object	Dimensions	Description		Date
?building	3490	iron	fitting fragment	L 48, W 29	?key	11	–
?building	3490	cu-al	sheet fragment	23 x 12	-	18	–
?building	3490	iron	thin shank fragment	L 34	-	18	–
?building	3490	bone	round-bowled spoon	L 102, bowl D 18	complete, small bowl	4	early Roman
?building	3490	bone	terminal	L 37	incised decoration	18	–
lower silt horizon	3858	iron	?loop-hinge fragment, bent	125 x 75	-	11	–
lower silt horizon	3858	cu-al	shaft fragment	L 17	bent	18	–
lower silt horizon	3858	iron	right-angled fitting	arms 52 x 34	?from box	4?	–
lower silt horizon	3858	cu-al	ring fragment	D 27	-	18	–
lower silt horizon	3858	iron	stylus	L 138	Manning Type 1	7	–
lower silt horizon	3858	stone	counter	D 13.5	small, flat	5	–
lower silt horizon	3858	bone	hairpin fragment, as Type 2	L 60	tip and top of head missing, single groove remains of head	1	early Roman
lower silt horizon	3858	iron	bar fragment	40 x 40	dense metal, probably offcut from smith's blank	15	–
lower silt horizon	3858	iron	finger-ring	D 22	expanded bezel	1	–
lower silt horizon	3858	cu-al	stud	D 9.5	convex head, shank missing	11	–
lower silt horizon	3919	iron	knife blade fragment	L 83, W 27	straight edge, curved back	10	–
lower silt horizon	4063	iron	8 hobnails	L 14	corroded together	1	–
lower silt horizon	4063	iron	tumbler-lock slide key	L 75	teeth missing	11	–
lower silt horizon	4063	cu-al	tiny fragments	-	-	18	–
lower silt horizon	4067	bone	hairpin fragment, Type 1	L 53	-	1	early Roman
lower silt horizon	4067	iron	sheet fragment	51 x 37	?from hipposandal	18	–
lower silt horizon	4067	bone	counter, Type 1	D 19	countersunk centre	5	early Roman
lower silt horizon	4067	bone	shaft fragment	L 35	-	18	–
lower silt horizon	4067	bone	inlay	L 27, W 19–20.5, T 3.5s	slightly tapering	4	–
lower silt horizon	4067	bone	shaft fragment	L 25	-	18	–
lower silt horizon	4070	iron	sheet fragment	L 68, W 31	-	18	–
lower silt horizon	4070	bone	counter, Type 2	D 18	flat	5	–
lower silt horizon	4070	ceramic	counter	D 37, T 6	oxidised ware wall sherd; trimmed and worn, but still slightly rough	5	–
lower silt horizon	4307	cu-al	D-shaped plaque	L 31, W 37	-	18	–
lower silt horizon	4307	cu-al	Nauheim Derivative brooch	L 40	bow tapers to knife-edge foot, central band of knurling	1	c. A.D. 43–80/5
lower silt horizon	4307	cu-al	shank fragment bent into coil	D 21	?votive, or used as a crude finger-ring	18	–

Context	Context description	SF No.	Material	Identification	Dimensions (mm)	Notes	Functional category	Date
4307	lower silt horizon	3246	lead	folded sheet offcut	50 x 37	-	18	-
4307	lower silt horizon	3308	cu-al	tweezers	L 49	plain flared blades	2	-
4329	lower silt horizon	3249	cu-al	stud	D 17, L 7.5	flat head, down-turned rim	11	-
4342	lower silt horizon	3294	iron	right-angled fitting	L arms 48, 36	?pintle fragment	11	-
3396	clay accumulation	3006	iron	strip fragment	55 x 12	-	18	-
3396	clay accumulation	3008	iron	sheet fragment	115 x 51	-	18	-
3396	clay accumulation	3025	cu-al	needle	L 63	oval eye	3	-
3396	clay accumulation	3048	cu-al	bar	L 40	grooved at ends	18	-
3396	clay accumulation	3077	iron	sheet fragment	23 x 19	-	18	-
3396	clay accumulation	3085	shale	armlet fragment	D 90	plain	1	-
3396	clay accumulation	3165	bone	hinge unit	L 61, D 21	two dowel holes	4	-
3396	clay accumulation	3167	ceramic	counter	D 68, T 4	orange ware, neatly trimmed	5	-
3469	clay accumulation	3209	lead	disc fragment	D 23	crushed and scored	18	-
3603	clay accumulation	2391	bone	needle	L 87	rectangular eye, tip missing	3	-
3603	clay accumulation	2454	iron	pin	L 24	narrow round-section shank, tip missing	18	-
3603	clay accumulation	4729	iron	strip	L 19	probably corrosion layer flaked from larger object	18	-
4293	clay accumulation	3138	bone	round-bowled spoon fragment	L 35, D 23	part of bowl and most of handle missing	4	early Roman
4293	clay accumulation	3162	bone	shaft fragment	L 48	-	18	-
4305	clay accumulation	3299	iron	fragments of two joiner's dogs	a) W 85, b) W 76	-	11	-
4320	clay accumulation	3231	iron	strip fragment	L 42, W 23	-	18	-
4320	clay accumulation	3244	iron	hipposandal wing	L 75	-	8	-
4035	upper silts	3405	bone	counter, Type 3	D 29	-	5	later Roman
4257	upper silts	3146	iron	tanged blade fragment	L 82, W 19	straight back and edge	10	-
3424	rubble make-up	2329	cu-al	tiny fragments	-	-	18	-
3424	rubble make-up	2334	iron	sheet fragment	34 x 23	-	18	-
3424	rubble make-up	2358	cu-al	fragment	L 10	-	18	-
3424	rubble make-up	2359	glass	bead fragment	D >3	blue round-section cylinder	1	-
3424	rubble make-up	2363	cu-al	discoid terminal	L 20, D 16	-	18	-
3424	rubble make-up	2388	cu-al	?brooch pin fragment	L 31	-	1	-
3424	rubble make-up	2390	iron	strip fragment	L 33, W 22	-	18	-
3424	rubble make-up	2397	iron	strip fragment	L 52, W 8	expanding towards one end	18	-
3424	rubble make-up	2398	iron	right-angled strip fitting	L arms 58 and 68, W 6	terminals missing; from box	4	-

Context	Context no.	Find no.	Material	Object	Dimensions	Notes	Phase	Date	
rubble make-up	3424	2403	silver	loop-in-loop chain fragments	terminal: L 35; link L 15	possibly from body chain	1		–
rubble make-up	3424	2404	cu-al	shaft fragments	longest L 13	–	18		–
rubble make-up	3424	2409	cu-al	strip fragment	L 26, W 22	–	18		–
rubble make-up	3424	2417	iron	key fragment	L 114	bit missing, looped terminal	11		–
rubble make-up	3424	2419	iron	vessel handle fragment	L 85	loop terminal; probably from bucket	4		–
rubble make-up	3424	2427	cu-al	tiny fragments	–	–	18		–
rubble make-up	3424	2428	cu-al	mirror fragment	44 x 22	high-tin bronze; plain	2		–
rubble make-up	3424	2461	iron	strip fragment	L 52, W 22	one nail hole	18		–
rubble make-up	3439	2354	bone	hairpin fragment, as Type 1	L 64	head almost flat	1	early Roman	–
rubble make-up	3439	2361	cu-al	mirror fragments	Largest 28 x 14	high-tin bronze, plain	2		–
rubble make-up	3439	2362	cu-al	unfinished casting	L 46.5, max W 13	one element of a strap-hinge	15		–
rubble make-up	3446	2394	cu-al	stud	D 28	flat head	11		–
rubble make-up	3446	2401	cu-al	spatula fragment	L 25	shaft made from rolled sheet	2		–
rubble make-up	3826	2706	cu-al	fragment	L 28	–	18		–
rubble make-up	3826	2714	cu-al	shaft fragment	L 13	–	18		–
rubble make-up	3826	2755	iron	strip fragment	L 137, W 14	plano-convex section	18		–
rubble make-up	3826	2757	iron	wire/shank fragment	L 28	–	18		–
rubble make-up	3826	2761	iron	strip fragment	–	–	18		–
rubble make-up	3826	2768	iron	stylus fragment	L 58	point missing	7		–
rubble make-up	3826	2770	iron	strip fragment	L 72, W 13	each end expanded but broken	18		–
rubble make-up	3826	2774	bone	round-bowled spoon	L 27	small part of bowl and short length of handle only	4		–
rubble make-up	3826	2881	shale	dish	D 59, H >6	low footring	4		–
rubble make-up	3826	2884	shale	armlet fragment	D 90	plain	1		–
rubble make-up	3833	2638	lead	puddle	L 52, W 19	–	15		–
rubble make-up	3833	2641	lead	drip	L 36	–	15		–
rubble make-up	3833	2647	cu-al	shaft fragment	L 65	–	18		–
rubble make-up	3833	2652	iron	shank fragments	L 34	–	18		–
rubble make-up	3833	2657	iron	strip fragment	L 38, W 21	–	18		–
rubble make-up	3833	2679	cu-al	brooch fragment	L 27	pin and spring only	1		–
rubble make-up	3833	2737	lead	sheet fragment, ?offcut	56 x 57	–	18		–
rubble make-up	3833	2744	lead	sheet fragment	62 x 25	partly folded, ?offcut	18		–
rubble make-up	2645	1758	cu-al	stud	D 29.5	flat head, shank missing	11		–
rubble make-up	3103	2236	iron	chain fragment	L 74	figure-of-eight-shaped links	18		–
rubble make-up	3103	2238	iron	hobnails	L 12	minimum of 17	1		–
rubble make-up	3103	2245	gold	stud	L 15	globular head	11		–

Context	Context description	SF No.	Material	Identification	Dimensions (mm)	Notes	Functional category	Date
3103	rubble make-up	2248	cu-al	ring or shaft fragment	L 27	-	18	-
3103	rubble make-up	2250	cu-al	wire loop fragment	D 19	?earring fragment	18	-
3103	rubble make-up	2253	cu-al	strip fragment	L 20, W 9	-	18	-
3103	rubble make-up	2256	iron	rake prong fragment	L 135		12	-
3103	rubble make-up	2259	iron	?pipe fragments	L 161, W 70	incomplete U-section strip	18	-
3103	rubble make-up	2270	cu-al	sheet fragments	largest 9 x 8	-	18	-
3103	rubble make-up	2274	iron	?punch	L 82	simple tapering shank	10?	-
3103	rubble make-up	2294	iron	rotary key	L 47, W 20	most of shank missing	11	-
3103	rubble make-up	2299	iron	?bar	L 122, sx 3 x 3	narrow, square-section	18	-
3103	rubble make-up	2308	cu-al	casting debris	L 26		15	-
3103	rubble make-up	2372	iron	joiner's dog	W 75, L 24		11	-
3400		3400	iron	strip fragment	L 53, W 20		18	-
3426		2351	iron	sheet fragment	47 x 33		18	-
3431		2582	iron	tiny fragments	-		18	-
3432		2987	bone	counter, Type 2	D 22	flat	5	-
3849		2671	iron	T-shaped fitting	L 45, W 29	surviving terminals round and pierced	11	-
3849	occupation	2673	iron	wire/shank fragment	L 19	-	18	-
3849	occupation	2687	bone	shaft fragment	L 54	-	18	-
3849	occupation	2705	iron	bar iron fragment	L 23, W 31	dense metal	15	-
3849	occupation	2709	cu-al	finger-ring	D 18	with transverse grooves	1	mid–late Roman
3849	occupation	2722	cu-al	tag	L 34	tubular binding with rivet hole	11	-
3849	occupation	2723	bone	shaft fragment	L 32	-	18	-
3849	occupation	2724	bone	shaft fragment	L 22	-	18	-
3849	occupation	2736	cu-al	casting waste	largest L 16	-	15	-
3849	occupation	2741	bone	shaft fragment	L 40	-	18	-
3849	occupation	2777	iron	penannular ring	D 43	oval	18	-
3849	occupation	2784	iron	?pipe or vessel rim fragment	L 51, D 90	rounded rim	18	-
3911	occupation	2886	iron	goad prick	D 13, L 47	strip ferrule with extended point, rather than coil	12	-
4285	occupation	3118	cu-al	nail-cleaner fragment	L 12	only top of shaft with damaged suspension loop	2	-
4291	occupation	3134	cu-al	armlet	D 98	plain wire with damaged slip-knot join	1	mid–late Roman
4301	occupation	3189	cu-al	stud	D 11	spool-shaped, probably from box	11	-

TABLE 34. PERIOD 4 SOUTH-EASTERN OCCUPATION, OBJECT 700, SUMMARY CATALOGUE OF SMALL FINDS
(D: diameter, L: length, T: thickness, W: width; H: height, cu-al: copper-alloy)

Context	Context description	SF No.	Material	Identification	Dimensions (mm)	Notes	Functional category	Date
2499	path	1935	iron	strip fragment	L 50, W 6	-	18	-
2499	path	1939	cu-al	curved pick	L 50	tip missing	2	-
2684	pit/post-hole	1841	cu-al	stud fragment	D 23	part of head only	11	-
2684	pit/post-hole	1877	shale	armlet fragment	D 70 approx.	plain	1	-
4524	pit/post-hole	3402	cu-al	brooch fragment	L 20	axial bar, spring and part of chord only	1	-
2780	make-ups for northern building	1997	iron	needle	L 77	long oval eye	3	-
2780	make-ups for northern building	2018	iron	knife blade fragment	L 58, W 19	-	10	-
2786	make-ups for northern building	1905	cu-al/lead	weight	L 53, D 34; weight 234 g	acorn-shaped, damaged	6	-
2786	make-ups for northern building	1948	iron	strip fragment	L 56, W 27	-	18	-
2786	make-ups for northern building	1981	iron	fitting	arms L 38	narrow pointed arms, set at obtuse angle	11	-
2786	make-ups for northern building	2075	iron	sheet fragment	49 x 28	-	18	-
3472	make-ups for northern building	2512	iron	a) two S-shaped wire/shank fragments; b) strip fragment	a) L 51, 17 (bent); b) L 19, W 8	-	18	-
3472	make-ups for northern building	2523	iron	sheet fragment	26 x 21	-	18	-
3472	make-ups for northern building	2537	iron	stylus fragment	L 66	point missing, part of eraser only	7	-
3472	make-ups for northern building	2559	iron	stylus fragment	L 73	point missing, part of eraser only	7	-
3472	make-ups for northern building	2602	iron	ring-headed pin fragment	L 99	-	11	-
3472	make-ups for northern building	2625	iron	strap fragment	L 52, W 17	doubled over	18	-
2603	northern building	1615	cu-al	ring fragment	D 18	?finger-ring	18	-
2603	northern building	1624	cu-al	fitting	L 22, W 15	-	11	-
2609	northern building	1768	iron	?cleat	53 x 28	damaged	1?	-
2609	northern building	1871	cu-al	sheet fragment	16 x 9	-	18	-

Context	Context description	SF No.	Material	Identification	Dimensions (mm)	Notes	Functional category	Date
2610	northern building	1806	iron	tumbler-lock slide-key	L 65	teeth missing	11	–
2610	northern building	1809	iron	split-spike loop	L 95	–	11	–
2610	northern building	1840	iron	strip fragment	L 83	bent	18	–
2610	northern building	1875	iron	sheet fragment	21 x 18	–	18	–
3149	southern building	2009	iron	wire/shank fragment	L 34	–	18	–
3149	southern building	2060	lead	offcut strip fragment	L 44, W 11	–	15	–
3149	southern building	2102	cu-al	armlet fragments	D 70 approx	most fragments distorted	1	–
3149	southern building	2104	iron	sheet fragment	32 x 31	–	18	–
3149	southern building	2199	iron	ferrule	L 50	bent	11	–
3444	southern building	2405	cu-al	nail	L 24	very small flat head	11	–
3467	southern building	2507	cu-al	?stud	D 10	head	11	–
3467	southern building	2612	bone	hairpin, Type 1	L 93	–	1	early Roman
3467	southern building	2538	stone	hone	L 84, x 27 x 20	slightly glauconitic, calcareous, fine-grained sandstone, ?Upper Jurassic Portlandian (J.R.L. Allen); square section, one end spalled but worn, one surface very worn in the centre	10	–
3467	southern building	2536	ceramic	counter rough-out	D 31, T 7	oxidised ware base sherd; edge partly rough, partly trimmed and abraded	5	–
3467	southern building	2588	ceramic	counter rough-out	D 5, T 15	colour-coated ware base; wall-base junction partly trimmed and worn	5	–
3417	?occupation	2279	iron	strip fragment	L 37, W 14	–	18	–
3417	?occupation	2288	iron	linch-pin	L 146	rectangular head, with loop	8	–
3417	?occupation	2293	iron	wire loop	L 28	from chain?	18	–
3417	?occupation	2328	cu-al	nail	L 25	–	11	–
3417	?occupation	2350	iron	sheet fragment	40 x 28	high slag content	18	–
3417	?occupation	2356	cu-al	ear-scoop	L 30	flat scoop, shaft not suspensible	2	–
3417	?occupation	2357	iron	spike	L 121, D 7	–	18	–
3417	?occupation	2369	iron	sheet fragment	24 x 11	–	18	–
3417	?occupation	2464	cu-al	stud	L 7	convex head	11	–
3468	?occupation	2493	iron	strap fragment	L 175, W 23	broken across a nail hole	11	–
3468	?occupation	2495	iron	strap fragment	L 84, W 31	bent, two nail holes	11	–

Phase	Context	SF	Material	Object	Dimensions	Notes	Period	Date
?occupation	3468	2496	cu-al	split-spike loop	L 26	-	11	-
?occupation	3468	2497	bone	hairpin, Type 2 variant	L 48	spiral-grooved head above a spool and two grooves	1	early Roman
?occupation	3468	2499	iron	strap-hinge fragment	L 45	with two lugs	11	-
?occupation	3468	2500	bone	hairpin, Type 2	L 110	-	1	early Roman
?occupation	3468	2502	iron	wire ring fragments	D 85	?armlet/anklet	18	-
?occupation	3468	2503	bone	hairpin, Type 2	L 42	-	1	early Roman
?occupation	3468	2504	bone	hairpin fragment	L 40	damaged, ?Type 2	1	early Roman
?occupation	3468	2513	bone	hairpin, ?Type 2	L 54	head missing above grooves	1	early Roman
?occupation	3468	2519	bone	hairpin, Type 1	L 56	-	1	early Roman
?occupation	3468	2521	cu-al	umbonate brooch	D 32	decayed enamel band around central nipple	1	2nd century
?occupation	3468	2522	bone	shaft fragment	L 67	-	18	-
?occupation	3468	2530	iron	wire fragments	L 29, 28	?part of SF 2502	18	-
?occupation	3468	2532	iron	one-piece brooch fragment	L 38	foot and tip of pin missing	1	mid-1st century A.D.
?occupation	3468	2539	cu-al	hairpin, Cool Group 3A	L 107	-	1	1st–2nd century
?occupation	3468	2542	iron	ring/collar	D <30	crushed	18	-
?occupation	3468	2546	iron	strap fragment	L 107, W 30	two nail holes	11	-
?occupation	3468	2551	iron	rove	26 x 28	-	11	-
?occupation	3468	2564	iron	joiner's dog	W 50, L 17	-	11	-
?occupation	3468	2630	cu-al	coil fragment from brooch spring	D 5	-	1	-
?occupation	3468	2636	shale	vessel base	D 57, H 11	small footring	4	-
?occupation	3468	2651	cu-al	ring	D 20	penannular	18	-
?occupation	3468	2665	iron	clamp or binding	W 99, L 155	broad curved head, end of longest arm curves inwards	11	-
?occupation	3468	2683	lead	sheet fragment,	L 32, W 19	?offcut	18	-
make-up for late Roman timber buildings	2419	1719	iron	stylus	L 117 approx.	fragmented	7	-
make-up for late Roman buildings	2420	1592	bone	hairpin fragment	L 36	spool and latticed cylinder on head	1	1st–2nd century
make-up for late Roman buildings	2420	1609	iron	blade fragment	L 82	edge straight, back curved	10	-
make-up for late Roman buildings	2420	1635	iron	hipposandal fragment	L 77, W 38	one wing only	8	-
make-up for late Roman buildings	2420	1654	iron	strip fragment	L 79	bent, crumpled	18	-

Context	Context description	SF No.	Material	Identification	Dimensions (mm)	Notes	Functional category	Date
2443	make-up for late Roman buildings	1751	iron	key	L 72	teeth missing	11	-
2467	make-up for late Roman buildings	1642	iron	hipposandal fragment	L 75, W 31	one wing only	8	-
2488	make-up for late Roman buildings	1775	cu-al	nail-cleaner	L 65	-	2	-
2497	make-up for late Roman buildings	3927	cu-al	strip fragment	L 23, W 15	folded	18	-
2498	make-up for late Roman buildings	1688	bone	hairpin fragment	L 44	top of head missing above single groove	1	early Roman
2613	make-up for late Roman buildings	1687	cu-al	shaft fragment	L 39	-	18	-
2613	make-up for late Roman buildings	1832	iron	delaminated fragments	-	-	18	-
2916	make-up for late Roman buildings	2010	ivory	terminal	L 26, D 17	?from pyxis	4?	-
2916	make-up for late Roman buildings	2017	iron	fragment	54 x 19	-	18	-
2916	make-up for late Roman buildings	2023	iron	sheet fragments	32 x 39, 26 x 38, 16 x 16	-	18	-
2916	make-up for late Roman buildings	2037	iron	bar	L 77, W 10	-	18	-
2916	make-up for late Roman buildings	2046	iron	shaft fragment	L 28	-	18	-
2916	make-up for late Roman buildings	2054	iron	strip fragment	L 18, W 11	-	18	-
2916	make-up for late Roman buildings	2058	iron	stylus	L 125	twisted stem; Manning 1985, Type 4	7	early Roman
2916	make-up for late Roman buildings	2066	iron	rove	20 x 20	-	11	-
2916	make-up for late Roman buildings	2148	iron	strip/bar	L 46, W 10	dense metal, ?offcut from smith's blank	15	-
2916	make-up for late Roman buildings	2448	iron	sheet fragment	28 x 32	dense metal, ?bar iron	15	-
3183	make-up for late Roman buildings	2176	cu-al	shaft fragment	L 56	-	18	-
3183	make-up for late Roman buildings	2187	iron	L-shaped slide-key	L 124	teeth missing	11	-

3183	make-up for late Roman buildings	cu-al	2195	sheet fragment	14 x 6	-	18	-
3412	make-up for late Roman buildings	cu-al	2223	triangular plaque	L 24, W 17	burred punched hole for attachment	18	-
3412	make-up for late Roman buildings	cu-al	2224	spoon	D 26, L 31	underside of bowl has radiating mouldings, most of offset handle missing	4	-
3412	make-up for late Roman buildings	iron	2243	rod/shank fragment	L 92	-	18	-
3412	make-up for late Roman buildings	cu-al	2260	strip fragment	L 23, W 15	possibly part of belt-plate	18	-
3412	make-up for late Roman buildings	iron	2275	clench-bolt	nail L 39, rove 32 x 32	nail and rove separate	11	-
3412	make-up for late Roman buildings	iron	2290	sheet fragments	38 x 27, 35 x 16	-	18	-
3412	make-up for late Roman buildings	iron	2305	sheet fragments	38 x 18, 36 x 16	-	18	-
3412	make-up for late Roman buildings	iron	2309	knife blade fragment	L 113	with long flat tang, back and edge straight; ?Manning Type 1C	10	early Roman
3412	make-up for late Roman buildings	iron	2320	ring	D 29	-	18	-
3412	make-up for late Roman buildings	cu-al	2321	shaft fragment	L 46	plano-convex section; ?handle	18	-
3412	make-up for late Roman buildings	iron	2330	8 hobnails	L 16	-	1	-
3412	make-up for late Roman buildings	iron	2337	ferrule	L 80, W 20	with split socket	11	-
3412	make-up for late Roman buildings	cu-al	2338	fragment	26 x 10	-	18	-
3412	make-up for late Roman buildings	bone	2342	peg	L 93	-	18	-
3412	make-up for late Roman buildings	iron	2349	sheet fragment	26 x 22	-	18	later Roman
3412	make-up for late Roman buildings	iron	2395	strip with pointed terminal	L 38, W 17	?awl	18	-
3412	make-up for late Roman buildings	shale	2430/2436	bowl fragments	D 240 approx.	small fragment only	4	-
3412	make-up for late Roman buildings	iron	-	sheet fragment	32 x 22	-	18	-

Context	Context description	SF No.	Material	Identification	Dimensions (mm)	Notes	Functional category	Date
3412	make-up for late Roman buildings	2255	ceramic	spindlewhorl	D 38, T 11; D of spindle hole 5	grey ware sherd, well worn	3	-
3412	make-up for late Roman buildings	2333	ceramic	counter	D 43, T 9	buff-ware base sherd; wall/base junction trimmed, smoothed and abraded	5	-
3498	make-up for late Roman buildings	2586	cu-al	2 shaft fragments	L 32, 19	-	18	-
3836	make-up for late Roman buildings	2778	iron	strip fragment	34 x 22	-	18	-
3836	make-up for late Roman buildings	2779	iron	a) bar fragment; b) fragments	a) L 29, W 17; b) -	a) dense metal, probably offcut from smith's blank	15	-
3836	make-up for late Roman buildings	2780	iron	fragments	-	possibly from nail shank	18	-
3836	make-up for late Roman buildings	2789	cu-al	stud	D 30	-	11	-
3836	make-up for late Roman buildings	2803	iron	stylus fragment	L 96	eraser missing	7	-
3836	make-up for late Roman buildings	2808	iron	?collar fragment	L 42	centre expanded and pierced	11	-
3836	make-up for late Roman buildings	2810	stone	spindlewhorl	D 34, T 12.5, spindle hole D 5	Pennant Sandstone (J.R.L. Allen)	3	-
3836	make-up for late Roman buildings	2813	iron	split-spike loop fragment	L 44	-	11	-
3836	make-up for late Roman buildings	2852	iron	ferrule	L 67	solid socket	11	-
3836	make-up for late Roman buildings	2867	iron	terminal	L 62	shank fragment with rounded foot at right angles; possibly from furniture	11	-
3836	make-up for late Roman buildings	2872	iron	8 hobnails	L 13	-	1	-
3836	make-up for late Roman buildings	2873	iron	>5 hobnails	L 13	corroded together	1	-
3836	make-up for late Roman buildings	2876	bone	shaft fragment	L 32	-	18	-
3836	make-up for late Roman buildings	3038	iron	hobnail	L 13	with two shank fragments	1	-

APPENDIX 3

CATALOGUE OF THE GLASS

By Denise Allen

Note: selected glass is illustrated in FIGS *68–69. The numbers of the catalogue coincide with the numbers of the illustrated pieces.*

PERIOD 3: A.D. 125/150–200

THE BUILDINGS

MB 1 (Object 50018)

Total 30 vessels: 1 yellow-green cast-and-ground bowl; 1 colourless facet-cut beaker; 1 unguent bottle; 3 bottles (2 cylindrical, 1 prismatic); 1 amber, ribbed jug or jar; 1 yellow-green jug or jar; 21 indeterminate blue-green; 1 indeterminate amber.
   Also 1 bead.

Cast and ground

1. Context 3701
Small rim fragment of a bowl of yellow-green glass: out-flared, and rotary-polished on both surfaces, with horizontal wheel-cut line on exterior below rim. Diam. of rim: *c.* 140mm.

Blown

2. Context 3646 SF 3963
Body fragment, almost certainly from a beaker, of colourless glass. Outer surface very well-cut with diamond-shaped facets arranged in quincunx. Diam. of vessel: *c.* 70mm.

3. Context 1961
10 fragments from the base of a vessel of yellow-green glass. Open base-ring, concave base, probably a jug or a jar. Diam. of base-ring: *c.* 90mm.

4. Context 3989
3 body fragments of amber glass with optic-blown ribs, probably from a globular jug or jar.

5. Context 3646 SF 4017
Rim fragment of an unguent bottle of blue-green glass. Rim out-flared and fire-rounded, cylindrical neck. Diam. of rim: *c.* 35mm (slightly irregular).

Bead

6. Context 3646 SF 4023
Two fragments of a bead of blue-green glass, annular and irregular.

MB 2 (Object 50019)

Total 17 vessels: 1 bowl; 1 flask/jug; 1 jug; 1 prismatic bottle; 1 unguent bottle; 5 indeterminate blue-green; 2 indeterminate blue; 1 indeterminate amber; 2 indeterminate very dark blue, appearing black.

7. Context 3619
Fragment from the rim of a jar or bowl. Part of a tubular-folded rim extant, yellow-green glass. Diam. indeterminable.

8. Context 4725

Rim of a flask, jug or unguent bottle of blue-green glass. Rim folded outward, upward and inward. Diam. of rim: *c.* 30mm.

9. Context 6103

Fragment of a jug handle of dark blue glass, flat-sectioned with raised central rib. Width 21mm.

10. Context 3601

Rounded-conical body fragment of an unguent bottle of blue-green glass. Diam. of body *c.* 40mm.

MRTB 1/ERTB 1 (formerly ERTB 4) (Object 50037)

Total 276 vessels: 7 bowls/plates; 1 unguent bottle; 3 jugs; 1 flask or jug; 55 bottles (of which 7 are certainly square, 4 cylindrical, 12 prismatic and 32 indeterminate); also 139 indeterminate blue-green frags; 2 indeterminate colourless frags; 3 indeterminate blue frags; 42 indeterminate yellow-green frags. (117 of the blue-green and all 42 of the yellow-green indeterminate fragments are very tiny indeed.)

Plus 1 probable fragment of matt/glossy blue-green window glass (context 3521).

Cast and ground

11. Context 4150

1 chip of polychrome cast glass, emerald green with one yellow spiral extant.

Blown

12. Context 4170

1 fragment of a bowl or plate of colourless glass; outer surface rotary-ground to produce a relief-cut ridge. Diam. indeterminable.

13. Context 3533

Three rim fragments of a plate of blue-green glass; rim folded upward and inward, then outward again. Diam. *c.* 260mm.

14. Context 3595

Three joining fragments of the base of a bowl of yellow-green glass; true base-ring, with diagonal tool marks visible. Diam. *c.* 80mm.

15. Context 4170

Two joining base fragments; true base-ring, as above, blue-green glass. Diam. of base-ring *c.* 80mm.

16. Context 4170

Rim fragment of a bowl of amber glass; tubular rim, folded inward and downward, then outward and downward. Diam. *c.* 110mm.

17. Context 4170

Folded rim fragment of a bowl, as above, blue-green glass. Diam. *c.* 140mm.

18. Context 4170

Two very small rim fragments of a flask or jug of blue-green glass; rim folded inward and downward, with part of a pinched trail still adhering.

19. Context 4170

Base fragment of an unguent bottle with rounded conical body, flattened base. Diam. *c.* 30mm.

20. Context 4170

Two joining rim fragments of a jug of blue-green glass. Rim folded inward and downward, and stretched into a spout. Diam. indeterminable.

21. Context 4170

Neck and body fragments of a jug of blue-green glass; vertical optic-blown ribs.

22. Context 4170

Neck and body fragments of a jug of yellow-green glass; spiral optic-blown ribs.

23 Context 4170

Body and base fragments of a square bottle of blue-green glass. Width of sides *c.* 180mm.

24. Context 2170
Body and base fragments of a large, square bottle of blue-green glass; part of two circles extant on the base.

PITS AND WELLS

Well 5693 (Object 500035)

Total 6 vessels: 1 blue-green square bottle (5709); 1 indeterminate blue-green; 1 indeterminate amber; 3 indeterminate colourless (2 with many tiny frags).
   Plus 2 matt/glossy window glass fragments (both from 5723).

'Pit' 6290 (Object 500036)

Total 16 vessels: 6 bottles, including 1 large cylindrical (5698), 4 square (5698, 5774), 1 indeterminate (5698); 8 indeterminate blue-green; 2 indeterminate greenish-colourless.
   Plus 1 matt/glossy window glass fragment (5698).

Pit 5039 (Object 44008)

Total 5 vessels: 1 cup; 1 jar or jug; 1 indeterminate blue-green; 2 indeterminate colourless.
   No window glass.

25. Context 6208
2 indeterminate colourless fragments, horizontal, wheel-cut groove, probably beaker.

26. Context 4535 (FIG. 68)
Base fragment, probably of a jar or jug, blue-green glass. Open base-ring. Diam. *c.* 70mm.

Well 2234 (Object 41016)

Total 8 vessels: 2 pillar-moulded bowls; 1 jug or jar; 1 jug, flask or bottle neck; 4 indeterminate blue-green; 1 indeterminate greenish-amber; 1 indeterminate colourless; 1 indeterminate yellow-green.
   No window glass.

Cast and ground

27. Context 2162
1 rim of a large pillar-moulded bowl, blue-green.

28. Context 2254
Lower body fragment probably from a pillar-moulded bowl of greenish amber glass. Part of two ribs extant. 2 indeterminate blue-green frags.

Blown

29. Context 2292
1 neck fragment of blue-green glass, jug, flask or bottle.

30. Context 2967
1 substantial body fragment of yellow-green glass; large globular body with two-optic blown ribs, probably a long-necked jug, possibly a jar.

Pit 4835 (Object 500028)

Total 2 vessels: 1 cup; 1 indeterminate colourless.
   No window glass.

31. Context 4832 (FIG. 68)
1 colourless cup rim, Isings 85b.

SOUTH-EAST LAYERS (OBJECT 701)

Total 278 vessels: 1 cast and ground bowl; 6 cups; 5 probable bowls; 4 jars; 2 jars or jugs; 6 jugs; 1 unguent bottle; 44 bottles (see list below); 177 indeterminate blue-green; 13 indeterminate colourless; 11 indeterminate amber; 9 indeterminate yellow-green; 3 indeterminate brown.

Plus 8 fragments matt/glossy window glass (3431, 3833, 3912, 4253).

Cast and ground

32. Contexts 4254 SF 5698, 5121 joining (FIG. 68)
2 joining large rim and side fragments of a pillar-moulded bowl of blue-green glass. Diam. of rim *c.* 140mm.

Blown

Cups/beakers

33. Context 4307 (FIG. 68)
1 rim fragment of an indented beaker of colourless glass. Rim out-flared and ground smooth, band of horizontal wheel-abraded lines beneath, part of one indent extant. Diam. of rim 105mm.
10 colourless body fragments, probably from a beaker, possibly same vessel as above.

34. Context 3858
5 fragments from the same vessel, probably a cylindrical, blue-green beaker.

35. Context 4253 (FIG. 68)
1 blue-green fragment with broad horizontal and diagonal, wheel-cut grooves; possibly from the body of a cup, or a flask.

36. Context 3469
1 colourless fragment with horizontal, wheel-cut lines, probably from a cup, but could be a flask.

37. Context 5183
9 fragments probably from the same colourless beaker, including two fragments of pushed-in base-ring.

38. Context 5614 (FIG. 68)
1 folded solid base-ring fragment of colourless glass, probably from a cup. Diam. *c.* 34mm.

Bowls

39. Context 4170 SF 3074 (FIG. 68)
1 fragment of very dark glass, appearing black, with opaque white, marvered trail on outer surface – looped pattern. This is most likely to be from a bowl or possibly a cup.

40. Context 4279 SF 3157 (FIG. 68)
1 rim fragment of a bowl with folded ridge beneath; dark blue glass, with opaque white, marvered trail around edge of rim. Diam. *c.* 120mm.

41. Context 4307 (FIG. 68)
Rim fragment of a bowl of blue-green glass; tubular rim folded outward and downward. Diam. *c.* 190mm.

42. Context 4308 (FIG. 68)
8 fragments, some joining, of a tubular-rimmed cylindrical bowl of pale green glass. Diam. of rim *c.* 130mm.

43. Context 4307
Body of an amber, cylindrical bowl, similar vessel to above.

Jars

44. Context 3491 (FIG. 68)
Rim fragment of a jar of yellow-green glass; tubular rim folded outward and downward into hollow tube. Diam. *c.* 96mm.

45. Context 4279 (FIG. 68)
Rim fragment of a jar of amber glass; tubular rim folded inward and downward, then outward and downward. Diam. *c.* 94mm.

46. Context 4307
1 folded rim fragment, blue-green, of a jar or beaker. Diam. indeterminable.

47. Context 4334
1 folded rim fragment from a jar or bowl with tubular rim, blue-green. Diam. indeterminable.

Jars/jugs

48. Context 4257
2 amber fragments with faint swirling optic blown ribs, almost certainly from a long-necked jug, but possibly from a jar.

49. Context 5121
2 blue-green fragments with optic-blown ribs, probably a globular jar or jug.

Jugs

50. Context 4307 (FIG. 68)
Rim and neck fragment of a jug of amber glass; rim folded outward, upward and inward. Diam. *c.* 34mm.

51. Context 3833 (FIG. 68)
2 joining fragments of a dark brown handle, straight and flat-sectioned with central rib, probably from a long-necked jug; width of handle *c.* 24mm.

52. Context 4334 (FIG. 68)
Blue-green, handle fragment, straight and flat-sectioned with central rib, probably from a long-necked jug; width of handle *c.* 30mm.

53. Context 4251 (FIG. 68)
Blue-green handle fragment, narrow, flat-sectioned with slight central rib; width of handle *c.* 18mm.

54. Context 3912
1 blue-green handle attachment fragment.

55. Context 4307 (FIG. 68)
1 blue-green fragment, probably part of a pinched trail from beneath a jug handle.

Unguent bottle

56. Context 4528 (FIG. 68)
Base fragment of a conical-bodied unguent bottle of blue-green glass. Diam. of body *c.* 40mm.

Bottles

57. Context 4307 (FIG. 68)
6 rim, neck and handle fragments from the same, very badly made, square bottle; blue-green glass with many streaks and impurities, rim irregularly folded, flat-sectioned handle. Diam. of rim *c.* 26mm.

Further bottle fragments:
3431	1 frag. probably bottle, blue-green
3826	1 square bottle, base frag., part of one circle extant
3833	1 lower body and base frag. of a square bottle, blue-green, part of two concentric circles with central dot extant
3919	1 neck frag., thick blue-green glass
3431	1 thick blue-green frag., probably bottle
3490	2 joining fragments of the neck of a very large blue-green bottle
3858	1 prismatic bottle body frag., blue-green
	1 square bottle base frag., blue-green, part of one circle extant
4067	2 blue-green frags, probably bottle

4253   1 neck frag. of a large blue-green bottle
4256   1 frag. square bottle, blue-green
4257   1 body frag., blue-green square bottle
4265   1 large, 1 small frag. of a large cylindrical bottle, blue-green; vertical scratches on outer surface
4270   1 indeterminate square bottle frag. blue-green
        1 cylindrical bottle, body frag. blue-green
4275   1 large bottle rim frag., blue-green
        1 square bottle body frag., blue-green
4293   1 thick blue-green frag., probably a bottle
4303   1 lower body and base frag., cylindrical bottle, blue-green
        1 corner frag., square bottle, pale blue-green
4307   6 rim, neck and handle fragments from the same, very badly made, square bottle; blue-green glass with many streaks and impurities, rim irregularly folded, flat-sectioned handle
        1 square bottle fragment blue-green
4469   1 wide, flat handle frag., blue-green, probably a bottle
4070   4 thick blue-green frags, probably bottles
4265   21 body frags, some joining, of a large cylindrical bottle of blue-green glass; vertical scratches on outer surface around shoulder and body
4305   6 frags from the same blue-green vessel: lower neck, shoulder and upper body of a large square bottle
4523   6 thick blue-green frags, probably bottles
        1 folded rim fragment, blue-green, probably a bottle
4528   9 body and base frags, probably from the same large cylindrical bottle of blue-green glass
5134   1 square bottle frag., blue-green
5614   1 square bottle frag., blue-green
5641   1 square bottle frag., blue-green
5727   3 thick blue-green frags, probably bottles

PERIOD 4: *c.* A.D. 200–250

BUILDING

MB 3 (Object 50046)

Total 119 vessels: 5 bowls/plates; 1 beaker; 8 jugs or flasks; 18 bottles (of which 1 certainly square, 4 cylindrical, 6 prismatic and 7 indeterminate); also 60 indeterminate blue-green fragments; 8 indeterminate colourless fragments; 2 indeterminate blue fragments; 12 indeterminate yellow-green fragments; 5 indeterminate amber fragments.

  Plus 9 matt-glossy window glass fragments; 1 twisted glass stirring rod or pin.

Cast and ground

58. Context 3049
Small fragment of a marbled pillar-moulded bowl: yellow-green ground with horizontal marbling of opaque white, opaque blue, wine and opaque yellow.

59. Context 3231
Fragment of a blue-green pillar-moulded-bowl.

Blown

Cups/beakers

60. Context 3674
Many tiny fragments of a beaker of colourless glass; folded tubular base-ring. Diam. *c.* 50mm.

Bowls/plates

61. Context 2232

Fragment from the side of a bowl of yellow-green glass, with folded-out ridge around side. Another fragment almost certainly from the same vessel came from context 3259.

62. Context 3396
Rim fragment of a plate of colourless glass; tubular rim, folded outward and downward. Diam. *c.* 180mm.

63. Context 1461
Rim fragment of a bowl, as above, blue-green glass, folded outward and downward. Diam. *c.* 150mm.

Jugs/flasks

64. Context 3313
Fragment of a pinched trail from beneath the handle of a vessel, probably a jug, blue-green glass.

65. Context 3674
Handle fragment, blue-green glass; curved, flat-sectioned handle, max. width 20mm.

66. Context 1397
Fragment from beneath the handle, probably of a jug, blue-green glass.

67. Context 1358
6 body fragments probably from a conical jug, blue-green glass, vertical optic-blown ribs.

68. Context 3669 SF 4108
Handle of a jug or flask of blue-green glass; rim still adhering — outflared and folded upwards and inwards. Diam. *c.* 40mm. Narrow, elegant, round-sectioned handle, diam. *c.* 40mm.

69. Context 3049
Base fragment of a conical flask or jug of blue-green glass; concave base, diam. *c.* 100mm.

70. Context 3374
17 small, thin-walled body fragments of a globular vessel, probably a jug or flask, pale blue-green glass.

71. Context 4454
Many small, thin-walled body fragments of a globular vessel, probably a jug or flask, blue-green glass.

Object

72. Context 1488 SF 830
Fragment of a twisted rod of blue-green glass, diam. *c.* 80mm.

PITS AND WELLS

Pit 3406 (Object 500033)

Total 32 vessels: 1 cup; 1 jug/bottle handle; 3 bottles (2 square (3821, 4290)); 1 handle (4041); 12 indeterminate blue-green; 16 indeterminate colourless.
    No window glass.

73. Context 4041 (FIG. 69)
1 large rim fragment of a colourless cup, Isings 85b, and 1 double base-ring fragment, probably from same cup. Diam. of rim *c.* 74mm; diam. of base-ring *c.* 44mm.

Pit 3102 (Object 500034)

Total 4 vessels: 3 indeterminate blue-green; 1 indeterminate colourless.
    1 matt/glossy window glass fragment (3827)

Well 5735 (Object 500037)

Total 7 vessels: 2 indeterminate blue-green; 5 indeterminate colourless.
    No window glass.

Well 1750 (Object 500020)

Total 6 vessels: 4 indeterminate blue-green, including one folded base-ring (1750); 2 indeterminate colourless.

No window glass.

Pit 2434 (Object 500031)

Total 4 vessels: 1 flask; 1 cylindrical bottle (2434); 2 indeterminate blue-green; 1 indeterminate yellow-green.

1 matt/glossy window glass fragment (see No. 75 below).

74. Contexts 2605, 2776 (FIG. 69)
Many fragments from the rim and neck of a colourless flask — from two contexts but almost certainly the same vessel. Rim folded outward, upward and inward and flattened to form lip. Diam. *c.* 48mm. Also many fragments from the body and base; design on base difficult to determine, possibly a cross within a circle, raised boss in each corner, another in centre of each side? Width of sides *c.* 48mm.

75. Context 2602 (FIG. 69)
Edge fragment matt-glossy window glass; it appears to be very rounded corner, which could be part of a very irregular square pane, or a circular pane.

Pit 2601 (Object 500032)

Total 6 vessels: 1 jug, jar or beaker; 1 jug or bottle neck (2623); 3 bottles (1 cylindrical (2622), 1 square (2623), 1 indeterminate (2600)); 1 indeterminate blue-green.

No window glass.

76. Context 2623 (FIG. 69)
Complete base, jug or, possibly, jar, or beaker of blue-green glass; high tubular-folded base ring, diam. 50mm; pontil mark on underside of base.

SOUTH-EAST LAYERS (OBJECT 700)

Total 14 vessels: 2 jugs; 1 jug, bottle or flask neck; 1 body of yellow-green globular jar or jug (3472); 7 bottles (see list below); 10 indeterminate blue-green; 1 indeterminate colourless; 1 indeterminate yellow-green.

Also 4 matt/glossy window glass fragments (3467, 3468), 1 tessera.

77. Context 3468 (FIG. 69)
1 rim fragment of a jug; flaring rim, folded inward and downward, and elongated into spout (not extant).

Bottles:
   3459   1 shoulder frag. of a prismatic bottle, blue-green glass
   3467   1 body frag., square bottle, blue-green
             1 base frag., square bottle, blue-green, two concentric circles extant
             1 thick blue-green frag., probably bottle
             1 bottle rim frag., pale blue-green
   3468   8 rim and neck frags of a bottle of pale blue-green glass; rim folded and flattened
             1 body fragment of a square bottle, blue-green glass

Tessera
78. Context 3219 SF 2829 (FIG. 69)
Tessera of blue opaque glass

APPENDIX 4

THE POTTERY

By Jane Timby

TABLE 35. QUANTIFIED SUMMARY OF SAMIAN FABRICS

Fabric	Description	eve		No.		wt	
?	unknown	0	0%	3	0%	6	0%
apts	Aldgate-Pulborough	0	0%	2	0%	50	0%
cg	Central Gaulish	4348.5	73%	1663	70%	15621	78%
cg?	Central Gaulish?	26	0%	8	0%	20	0%
cg/eg	Central/East Gaulish	8	0%	1	0%	7	0%
cg.mlez	Central Gaulish: micaceous Lezoux	2	0%	1	0%	2	0%
cg.mv	Central Gaulish: Martres de Veyre	114.5	2%	45	2%	410	2%
cg.mv?	Central Gaulish: Martres de Veyre?	4	0%	1	0%	1	0%
cg.mv/elez	Central Gaulish: Martres de Veyre/early Lezoux	14.5	0%	3	0%	54	0%
co/ar	Colchester/Argonne	5.5	0%	1	0%	10	0%
eg	East Gaulish	24	0%	8	0%	248	1%
eg.ar	East Gaulish: Argonne	0	0%	1	0%	13	0%
eg.rz	East Gaulish: Rheinzabern	22	0%	3	0%	40	0%
eg.tr	East Gaulish: Trier	0	0%	1	0%	2	0%
it/earlygaul	Italian/early Gaulish	0	0%	1	0%	11	0%
sg	South Gaulish	1389	23%	627	26%	3501	17%
sg.mo	South Gaulish: Montans	18.5	0%	14	1%	106	1%
		5976.5	100%	2383	100%	20102	100%

TABLE 36. QUANTIFIED SUMMARY OF POTTERY ASSEMBLAGE FROM PERIOD 3

PERIOD 3	Code	Description	PITS AND WELLS				LAYERS (701)				HOUSE			
			No.	No. %	Wt	Wt %	No.	No. %	Wt	Wt %	No.	No. %	Wt	Wt %
IMPORTS	SG SAM	South Gaulish samian	29	1.6	241	0.6	99	0.8	461	0.3	291	2.2	1426	0.8
fine wares	Ital/Gaul	Italian/ early Gaulish samian	0	0.0	0	0.0	0	0.0	0	0.0	1	0.0	11	0.0
	CGSAM	Central Gaulish samian	30	1.7	179	0.5	613	4.8	5535	3.0	381	2.9	2914	1.7
	EGSAM	East Gaulish samian	0	0.0	0	0.0	2	0.0	3	0.0	1	0.0	5	0.0
	ARG CC	Argonne colour-coat	6	0.3	12	0.0	88	0.7	350	0.2	10	0.1	67	0.0
	CNG BS	Central Gaulish black slip	2	1.0	5	1.0	4	0.0	23	0.0	1	0.0	6	0.0
	CNG CC	Central Gaulish colour-coat	1	1.0	2	1.0	18	0.1	78	0.0	51	0.4	131	0.1
	CNG GL1	St Remy green glazed ware	0	0.0	0	0.0	1	0.0	7	0.0	0	0.0	0	0.0
	CNG WS	Central Gaulish white slip	1	0.1	54	0.1	8	0.1	125	0.1	4	0.0	124	0.1
	CNG MS	Central Gaulish mica-slipped	0	0.0	0	0.0	1	0.0	2	0.0	0	0.0	0	0.0
	EGGSH	eggshell ware	1	0.1	1	0.0	1	0.0	1	0.0	5	0.0	5	0.0
	GAB TN	Gallo-Belgic Terra Nigra	10	0.6	93	0.2	2	0.0	22	0.0	23	0.2	393	0.2
	GAB TR1A	Gallo-Belgic Terra Rubra	0	0.0	0	0.0	1	0.0	2	0.0	13	0.1	63	0.0
	GAB TR1C	Gallo-Belgic Terra Rubra	1	0.1	2	0.0	1	0.0	6	0.0	5	0.0	31	0.0
	GAB TR2	Gallo-Belgic Terra Rubra	4	0.2	38	0.1	3	0.0	21	0.0	9	0.1	85	0.0
	GAB TR3	Gallo-Belgic Terra Rubra	0	0.0	0	0.0	1	0.0	2	0.0	5	0.0	24	0.0
	IMP WH	imported whiteware	6	0.3	108	0.3	1	0.0	16	0.0	40	0.3	217	0.1
	ITA WH	Italian whiteware	0	0.0	0	0.0	2	0.0	25	0.0	0	0.0	0	0.0
	KOL CC	Cologne colour-coat	5	0.3	40	0.1	58	0.5	434	0.2	14	0.1	49	0.0
	LYO CC	Lyon colour-coated ware	0	0.0	0	0.0	8	0.1	24	0.0	4	0.0	18	0.0
	MOS BS	Moselle black-slipped ware	0	0.0	0	0.0	0	0.0	0	0.0	0	0.0	0	0.0
	NOG WH	North Gaulish whiteware (Cam. 113)	4	0.2	27	0.1	4	0.0	24	0.0	29	0.2	133	0.1
	SOG CC	South Gaulish colour-coat?	0	0.0	0	0.0	1	0.0	3	0.0	2	0.0	5	0.0
coarseware	CAM PR1	Pompeian redware fabric 1	0	0.0	0	0.0	1	0.0	16	0.0	2	0.0	19	0.0

Group	Code	Description	Count	%	Count	%	Count	%	Count	%	Count	%	Count	%
mortaria	NOG WH(M)	North Gaulish mortaria	5	0.3	431	1.1	16	0.1	636	0.3	40	0.3	2377	1.4
	RHL WH	Rhineland whiteware mortaria	0	0.0	0	0.0	2	0.0	194	0.1	0	0.0	0	0.0
	SOL WH	Soller whiteware	0	0.0	0	0.0	0	0.0	0	0.0	1	0.0	194	0.1
amphorae	ASM AM	E Mediterranean (British Biv)	0	0.0	0	0.0	1	0.0	48	0.0	0	0.0	0	0.0
	BAT AM	Baetican amphora	23	1.3	3832	9.9	175	1.4	14688	8.0	141	1.1	9728	5.7
	BAT AM	Haltern 70	0	0.0	0	0.0	6	0.0	482	0.3	5	0.0	114	0.1
	CAD AM	Cadiz amphora	0	0.0	0	0.0	23	0.2	1569	0.9	7	0.1	236	0.1
	Dressel 2-4	Dressel 2-4 amphora	0	0.0	0	0.0	47	0.4	1793	1.0	1	0.0	77	0.0
	?Dressel 14	S Spanish/Portuguese amphora	0	0.0	0	0.0	1	0.0	20	0.0	0	0.0	0	0.0
	GAL AM	Gallic amphora	40	2.2	2013	5.2	58	0.5	1374.5	0.7	9	0.1	829	0.5
	PAL AM	Palestinian amphora *Cam.* 189	0	0.0	0	0.0	0	0.0	0	0.0	5	0.0	44	0.0
	AMPLID	amphora lid	1	0.1	4	0.0	4	0.0	14	0.0	2	0.0	8	0.0
	AMP	unassigned amphora	7	0.4	174	0.5	20	0.2	829	0.5	44	0.3	1893	1.1
REGIONAL	ABN OX	Abingdon oxid butt beaker	0	0.0	0	0.0	6	0.0	20	0.0	4	0.0	13	0.0
	BWF LW	fine black 'London ware'	6	0.3	21	0.1	0	0.0	0	0.0	0	0.0	0	0.0
	CAR RS	Caerleon mortaria	0	0.0	0	0.0	4	0.0	156	0.1	0	0.0	0	0.0
	COL CC	Colchester colour-coated ware	0	0.0	0	0.0	1	0.0	32	0.0	48	0.4	136	0.1
	COL WH	Colchester whiteware mortaria	0	0.0	0	0.0	1	0.0	92	0.1	0	0.0	0	0.0
	DOR BB1	Dorset black-burnished ware	22	1.2	435	1.1	413	3.3	7301	4.0	82	0.6	1247	0.7
	HAM GT	Hampshire grog-tempered	0	0.0	0	0.0	48	0.4	544	0.3	0	0.0	0	0.0
	LNV CC	Lower Nene Valley colour-coat	1	0.1	2	0.0	4	0.0	37	0.0	0	0.0	0	0.0
	OXF BHW	Oxfordshire burnt whiteware	0	0.0	0	0.0	0	0.0	0	0.0	2	0.0	14	0.0
	OXF WH	Oxfordshire whiteware	8	0.4	65	0.2	257	2.0	2339	1.3	81	0.6	659	0.4
	OXF WHM	Oxfordshire whiteware mortaria	0	0.0	0	0.0	78	0.6	3325	1.8	22	0.2	1081	0.6
	OXF RS	Oxfordshire colour-coated ware	2	0.1	1	0.0	2	0.0	6	0.0	0	0.0	0	0.0

PERIOD 3	Code	Description	PITS AND WELLS				LAYERS (701)				HOUSE			
			No.	No. %	Wt	Wt %	No.	No. %	Wt	Wt %	No.	No. %	Wt	Wt %
	OXFWS	Oxfordshire white-slipped ware	0	0.0	0	0.0	0	0.0	0	0.0	4	0.0	47	0.0
	OVW WH	Overwey whiteware	2	0.1	24	0.1	0	0.0	0	0.0	0	0.0	0	0.0
	SAV GT	?Savernake grog-tempered	0	0.0	0	0.0	1	0.0	55	0.0	0	0.0	0	0.0
	SOW BB1	South-west BB1	0	0.0	0	0.0	0	0.0	0	0.0	3	0.0	53	0.0
	SOW WS	South-west white-slipped	0	0.0	0	0.0	1	0.0	14	0.0	5	0.0	152	0.1
	VER WH	Verulamium white ware	94	5.2	3950	10.2	44	0.3	1017	0.6	121	0.9	1873	1.1
	VERWH M	Verulamium white ware mortaria	5	0.3	735	1.9	14	0.1	5647	3.1	35	0.3	1468	0.9
LOCAL	ALH RE	Alice Holt/ reduced wares	825	45.9	13995	36.2	6924	54.6	69583	37.8	6970	53.0	66092	38.5
	SIL F1	Silchester flint-tempered ware	152	8.5	2904	7.5	558	4.4	13050	7.1	1112	8.5	21731	12.6
	GRSJ	grog-tempered storage jar	64	3.6	2944	7.6	713	5.6	29274	15.9	699	5.3	23246	13.5
	SIL G1	LIA-ERO grog-tempered	5	0.3	46	0.1	4	0.0	74	0.0	49	0.4	448	0.3
	SIL G4	wheelmade C1 grog-tempered	7	0.4	76	0.2	3	0.0	17	0.0	117	0.9	632	0.4
	GROG	Misc. grog-tempered	3	0.2	53	0.1	41	0.3	789	0.4	11	0.1	143	0.1
	SIL SF/GF	mixed grit	9	0.5	118	0.3	25	0.2	251	0.1	219	1.7	1798	1.0
UNKNOWN	BUFF	misc. buff/ cream wares	27	1.5	316	0.8	196	1.5	1640	0.9	133	1.0	7878	4.6
	BWF	fine black ware	6	0.0	21	0.0	8	0.1	120	0.1	29	0.2	145	0.1
	BWFMIC	fine black micaceous ware	15	0.8	57	0.1	11	0.1	77	0.0	1	0.0	1	0.0
	BWMIC	black micaceous ware	1	0.1	9	0.0	0	0.0	0	0.0	0	0.0	0	0.0
	CC	miscellaneous colour-coat	0	0.0	0	0.0	21	0.2	95	0.1	11	0.1	51	0.0
	GYF	fine grey wares	107	6.0	1072	2.8	832	6.6	5795.5	3.2	652	5.0	4025	2.3
	GREY	misc. grey wares	12	0.7	164	0.4	49	0.4	363	0.2	26	0.2	247	0.1
	GYBSLIP	black-slipped grey ware	2	0.1	2	0.0	8	0.1	64	0.0	0	0.0	0	0.0
	GYMIC	grey micaceous ware	0	0.0	0	0.0	5	0.0	57	0.0	0	0.0	0	0.0
	MICAOX	mica-slipped oxidised ware	1	0.1	1	0.0	43	0.3	673	0.4	23	0.2	355	0.2
	MICOXIDF	mica-slipped fine oxidised ware	1	0.1	6	0.0	0	0.0	0	0.0	0	0.0	0	0.0

Code	Description												
MORT	unknown oxidised mortaria	0	0.0	0	0.0	4	0.0	121	0.1	4	0.0	124	0.1
OXIDF	oxidised fine ware	5	0.3	36	0.1	33	0.3	387.5	0.2	89	0.7	772	0.4
OXID	miscellaneous oxidised	12	0.7	135	0.3	433	3.4	4667	2.5	0	0.0	0	0.0
OXID1	oxidised ware	0	0.0	0	0.0	5	0.0	57	0.0	312	2.4	3329	1.9
OXID2	oxidised ware fabric 2	9	0.5	253	0.7	2	0.0	16	0.0	0	0.0	0	0.0
OXID3	oxidised ware fabric 3	55	3.1	1238	3.2	105	0.8	1932	1.1	516	3.9	7620	4.4
OXID4	oxidised ware fabric 4	3	0.2	12	0.0	2	0.0	176	0.1	0	0.0	0	0.0
OXID5	oxidised ware fabric 5	1	0.1	10	0.0	0	0.0	0	0.0	0	0.0	0	0.0
OXID6	micaceous oxidised ware	3	0.2	18	0.0	52	0.4	641	0.3	12	0.1	76	0.0
OXIDBLSL	black-slipped oxidised ware	3	0.2	187	0.5	0	0.0	0	0.0	1	0.0	14	0.0
OXIDMIC3	mica-slipped oxid fabric 3	3	0.2	140	0.4	0	0.0	0	0.0	0	0.0	0	0.0
SHELL	shelly ware	0	0.0	0	0.0	0	0.0	0	0.0	20	0.2	283	0.2
WSGREY	white-slipped grey ware	0	0.0	0	0.0	3	0.0	23	0.0	2	0.0	9	0.0
WSOXIDF	white-slipped fine oxidised ware	4	0.2	112	0.3	50	0.4	528	0.3	230	1.7	2087	1.2
WSOXID	white-slipped oxidised ware	5	0.3	12	0.0	65	0.5	564.5	0.3	241	1.8	2104	1.2
WSOXIDMIC	white slip micaceous oxid ware	2	0.1	31	0.1	7	0.1	122	0.1	0	0.0	0	0.0
WSOXID2	white slip oxidised ware fabric 2	4	0.2	88	0.2	0	0.0	0	0.0	0	0.0	0	0.0
WSOXID3	white slip oxidised ware fabric 3	56	3.1	834	2.2	159	1.3	1805	1.0	0	0.0	0	0.0
WSOXID4	white slip oxidised ware fabric 4	30	1.7	808	2.1	0	0.0	0	0.0	0	0.0	0	0.0
WW	miscellaneous whiteware	5	0.3	9	0.0	29	0.2	292.5	0.2	109	0.8	675	0.4
WW2	whiteware fabric 2	22	1.2	386	1.0	0	0.0	0	0.0	0	0.0	0	0.0
WW3	whiteware fabric 3	1	0.1	14	0.0	8	0.1	107	0.1	0	0.0	0	0.0
WW4	white granular ware	0	0.0	0	0.0	95	0.7	854	0.5	0	0.0	0	0.0
WWF	fine white ware	0	0.0	0	0.0	40	0.3	335.5	0.2	1	0.0	13	0.0
MISC	miscellaneous	0	0.0	0	0.0	0	0.0	0	0.0	1	0.0	10	0.0
CRUMBS	small unidentified crumbs	20	1.1	15	0.0	2	0.0	4	0.0	2	0.0	1	0.0
TOTAL		1796	101.5	38611	101.9	12680	100.0	183968	100.0	13145	100	171878	100

TABLE 37. QUANTIFIED SUMMARY OF POTTERY FROM PERIOD 3 WELL 5693 (OBJECT 500035)

	Code	Object 500035	No.	No. %	Wt	Wt %	Eve	Eve%
IMPORTS	SG SAM	South Gaulish samian	7	1.9	24	0.2	12	1.7
	CG SAM	Central Gaulish samian	3	0.8	18	0.2	0	0.0
	MV SAM	Martres-de-Veyre	1	0.3	2	0.0	3	0.4
	ARG CC	Argonne colour-coated ware	1	0.3	6	0.1	0	0.0
	BWF MIC	fine black micaceous ware	3	0.8	21	0.2	0	0.0
	IMP WH	imported whiteware	6	1.6	108	1.0	0	0.0
	NOG WH	North Gaulish whiteware	2	0.5	2	0.0	0	0.0
	NOG WH(M)	North Gaulish mortaria	3	0.8	301	2.7	7	1.0
	BAT AM	Baetican amphora	9	2.4	1554	14.0	0	0.0
	GAL AM	Gallic amphora	5	1.3	159	1.4	0	0.0
REGIONAL	DOR BB1	Dorset black-burnished ware	5	1.3	124	1.1	0	0.0
	OXF WH	Oxfordshire whiteware	4	1.1	53	0.5	100	14.2
	VER WH	Verulamium whiteware	6	1.6	96	0.9	0	0.0
	VER WH(M)	Verulamium whiteware mortaria	1	0.3	68	0.6	0	0.0
LOCAL	ALH RE	Alice Holt/ reduced wares	215	57.3	5821	52.4	418	59.2
	SIL F1	Silchester flint-tempered ware	18	4.8	453	4.1	12	1.7
	GRSJ	grog-tempered storage jar	24	6.4	1440	13.0	24	3.4
	SIL SF	mixed temper	2	0.5	46	0.4	0	0.0
UNKNOWN	BWFMIC	black micaceous fine ware	3	0.8	15	0.1	0	0.0
	GYF	fine grey wares	25	6.7	255	2.3	0	0.0
	MICSLOX	mica-slipped oxidised ware	3	0.8	18	0.2	0	0.0
	OXID	oxidised wares	1	0.3	4	0.0	0	0.0
	OXID2	oxidised ware fabric 2	9	2.4	253	2.3	70	9.9
	OXID3	oxidised fabric 3	2	0.5	22	0.2	10	1.4
	OXID5	oxidised ware fabric 5	1	0.3	10	0.1	0	0.0
	PALE	misc. buff/ cream wares	8	2.1	129	1.2	50	7.1
	WSOXID	white-slipped oxidised ware	1	0.3	1	0.0	0	0.0
	WSOX2	white-slipped oxidised fabric 2	6	1.6	94	0.8	0	0.0
	WW3	whitewares fabric 3	1	0.3	14	0.1	0	0.0
TOTAL			375	100.0	11111	100.0	706	100.0

TABLE 38. QUANTIFIED SUMMARY OF POTTERY FROM PERIOD 3 PIT 5039 (OBJECT 44008)

	Code	Object 44008	No.	No. %	Wt	Wt %	Eve	Eve%
IMPORTS	SG SAM	South Gaulish samian	4	0.7	36	0.3	0	0.0
	CGSAM	Central Gaulish samian	2	0.3	15	0.1	0	0.0
	MV/ELEZ	Martres-de-Veyre/early Lezoux	3	0.5	54	0.5	24	3.1
	ARG CC	Argonne colour-coated ware	2	0.3	4	0.0	0	0.0
	CNG CC/BS	Central Gaulish colour-coat	2	0.3	5	0.0	0	0.0
	GAB TN	Gallo-Belgic Terra Nigra	2	0.3	11	0.1	7	0.9
	KOL CC	Cologne colour-coat	4	0.7	33	0.3	0	0.0
	NOG WH	imported whiteware	1	0.2	6	0.1	0	0.0
	NOG WH(M)	North Gaulish mortaria	1	0.2	93	0.9	0	0.0
	BAT AM	Baetican amphora	7	1.2	979	9.2	0	0.0
	GAL AM	Gallic amphora	32	5.5	1824	17.1	0	0.0
REGIONAL	BWF	black fine ware (London ware)	6	1.0	21	0.2	7	0.9
	VER WH	Verulamium whiteware	6	1.0	187	1.8	21	2.7
	VER WH(M)	Verulamium whiteware mortaria	1	0.2	362	3.4	10	1.3
LOCAL	ALH RE	Alice Holt/ reduced wares	283	49.0	3505	32.9	345	44.9
	SIL F1	Silchester flint-tempered ware	33	5.7	718	6.7	5	0.7
	GROG	miscellaneous grog-tempered	2	0.3	13	0.1	0	0.0
	GRSJ	grog-tempered storage jar	11	1.9	460	4.3	7	0.9
UNKNOWN	BWMIC	black micaceous ware	1	0.2	9	0.1	0	0.0
	GYF	fine grey wares	45	7.8	425	4.0	125	16.3
	GYBSLIP	black-slipped grey ware	2	0.3	2	0.0	10	1.3
	MICAOX	mica-slipped ware	2	0.3	12	0.1	0	0.0
	MICOX3	mica-slipped oxidised fabric 3	2	0.3	129	1.2	6	0.8
	OXID	oxidised wares	5	0.9	75	0.7	11	1.4
	OXIDF	fine oxidised ware	2	0.3	6	0.1	0	0.0
	OXID3	oxidised ware fabric 3	40	6.9	381	3.6	78	10.2
	PALE	misc. buff/ cream wares	8	1.4	131	1.2	0	0.0
	WSOX3	white-slipped oxidised fabric 3	38	6.6	360	3.4	12	1.6
	WSOX4	white-slipped oxidised fabric 4	30	5.2	808	7.6	100	13.0
TOTAL			577	100.0	10664	100.0	768	100.0

TABLE 39. QUANTIFIED SUMMARY OF POTTERY FROM PERIOD 3 WELL 2234 (OBJECT 41016)

	Code	Object 41016	No.	No. %	Wt	Wt %	Eve	Eve%
IMPORTS	SG SAM	South Gaulish samian (apts)	12	2.7	72	0.7	7	1.2
	CGSAM	Central Gaulish samian	5	1.1	25	0.3	10	1.7
	ARG CC	Argonne colour-coat	1	0.2	1	0.0	3	0.5
	CNG CC	Central Gaulish colour-coat	1	0.2	54	0.6	0	0.0
	CNG WS	Central Gaulish white-slip flagon	1	0.2	54	0.6	0	0.0
	GAB TN	Gallo-Belgic Terra Nigra	3	0.7	59	0.6	18	3.0
	GAB TR1C	Gallo-Belgic Terra Rubra	1	0.2	2	0.0	0	0.0
	BAT AM	Baetican amphora	3	0.7	409	4.2	0	0.0
	AMPLID	amphora lid	1	0.2	4	0.0	16	2.7
REGIONAL	DOR BB1	Dorset black-burnished ware	3	0.7	59	0.6	21	3.5
	LNV CC	Lower Nene Valley colour-coat	1	0.2	2	0.0	0	0.0
	OXF WH	Oxfordshire whiteware	1	0.2	4	0.0	0	0.0
	OXF RS	Oxon colour-coated ware	1	0.2	2	0.0	0	0.0
	VER WH	Verulamium whiteware	76	17.2	3620	37.3	137	22.9
	VERWH(M)	Verulamium whiteware mortaria	2	0.5	222	2.3	11	1.8
LOCAL	ALH RE	Alice Holt/ reduced wares	176	39.7	1955	20.1	137	22.9
	SIL F1	Silchester flint-tempered ware	28	6.3	614	6.3	7	1.2
	GRSJ	grog-tempered storage jar	12	2.7	513	5.3	5	0.8
	GROG	grog-tempered	2	0.5	43	0.4	7	1.2
	SIL G1	C1 handmade grog-tempered	4	0.9	41	0.4	0	0.0
	SIL G4	C1 wheelmade grog-tempered	2	0.5	21	0.2	0	0.0
	OVW WH	Overwey whiteware	2	0.5	24	0.2	7	1.2
	SIL SF	mixed grit	6	1.4	48	0.5	10	1.7
UNKNOWN	BWFMIC	fine black micaceous ware	8	1.8	13	0.1	0	0.0
	GYF	fine grey wares	26	5.9	68	0.7	56	9.3
	OXID	oxidised ware	6	1.4	56	0.6	0	0.0
	OXIDFBS	fine oxidised with black slip	3	0.7	187	1.9	37	6.2
	OXIDFMIC	mica-slipped fine oxidised	1	0.2	6	0.1	0	0.0
	OXIDFWS	oxidised fine ware, white-slipped	2	0.5	83	0.9	0	0.0
	OXID3	oxidised ware fabric 3	5	1.1	612	6.3	0	0.0
	PALE	misc. buff/ cream wares	10	2.3	52	0.5	5	0.8
	WSOXID	white-slipped oxidised ware	2	0.5	5	0.1	0	0.0
	WSOX3	white-slipped oxidised fabric 3	10	2.3	393	4.0	5	0.8
	WW	miscellaneous whiteware	4	0.9	6	0.1	0	0.0
	WW2	whiteware fabric 2	22	5.0	386	4.0	100	16.7
TOTAL			443	100	9715	100.0	599	100.0

TABLE 40. QUANTIFIED SUMMARY OF POTTERY FROM PERIOD 3 PIT 4835 (OBJECT 500028)

	Code	Object 500028	No.	No. %	Wt	Wt %	Eve	Eve%
IMPORTS	SG SAM	South Gaulish samian	7	2.8	111	1.9	12	8.6
	CGSAM	Central Gaulish samian	15	6.1	63	1.1	11	7.9
	ARG CC	Argonne colour-coat	1	0.4	1	0.0	0	0.0
	GAB TN	Gallo-Belgic Terra Nigra	5	2.0	23	0.4	2	1.4
	GAB TR2	Gallo-Belgic Terra Rubra fabric 2	4	1.6	38	0.6	0	0.0
	NOG WH	North Gaulish whiteware	3	1.2	25	0.4	0	0.0
	BAT AM	Baetican amphora	4	1.6	890	15.1	0	0.0
REGIONAL	DOR BB1	Dorset black-burnished ware	11	4.5	236	4.0	5	3.6
	VER WH	Verulamium whiteware	2	0.8	9	0.2	0	0.0
	VERWH (M)	Verulamium whiteware mortaria	1	0.4	83	1.4	0	0.0
LOCAL	ALH RE	Alice Holt/ reduced wares	87	35.4	2594	43.9	49	35.0
	SIL F1	Silchester flint-tempered ware	68	27.6	1011	17.1	25	17.9
	GRSJ	grog-tempered storage jar	10	4.1	350	5.9	7	5.0
	SIL G1	LIA-ERO grog-tempered	1	0.4	5	0.1	0	0.0
	SIL G4	wheelmade C1 grog-tempered	3	1.2	42	0.7	10	7.1
	SIL SF	mixed grit	1	0.4	24	0.4	7	5.0
UNKNOWN	GYF	fine grey wares	6	2.4	96	1.6	0	0.0
	OXIDF	oxidised fine ware	3	1.2	30	0.5	0	0.0
	OXID3	oxidised ware fabric 3	6	2.4	204	3.5	12	8.6
	OXID4	oxidised ware fabric 4	3	1.2	12	0.2	0	0.0
	WSOXID	white-slipped oxidised ware	2	0.8	29	0.5	0	0.0
	WSOXMIC	white-slipped micaceous oxid ware	2	0.8	32	0.5	0	0.0
	WW	miscellaneous whiteware	1	0.4	3	0.1	0	0.0
TOTAL			246	100.0	5911	100	140	100.0

Period 3 Layers

Object 701	Code	Description	No.	No. %	Wt	Wt %	Eve	Eve%
IMPORTS	SG SAM	South Gaulish samian (apts)	121	1.0	726	0.4	339	2.3
	CGSAM	Central Gaulish samian	630	5.0	5857	3.2	1191	8.0
	EGSAM	East Gaulish samian	2	0.0	3	0.0	0	0.0
	ARG CC	Argonne colour-coat	88	0.7	350	0.2	177	1.2
	CAM PR1	Pompeian redware fabric 1	1	0.0	16	0.0	0	0.0
	CNG BS	Central Gaulish black slip	4	0.0	23	0.0	10	0.1
	CNG CC	Central Gaulish colour-coat	18	0.1	78	0.0	14	0.1
	CNG GL1	St Remy green glazed ware	1	0.0	7	0.0	0	0.0
	CNG WS	Central Gaulish white slip	8	0.1	125	0.1	0	0.0
	CNG MS	Central Gaulish mica-slipped	1	0.0	2	0.0	0	0.0
	EGGSH	eggshell ware	1	0.0	1	0.0	0	0.0
	GAB TN	Gallo-Belgic Terra Nigra	2	0.0	22	0.0	7	0.0
	GAB TR1A	Gallo-Belgic Terra Rubra	1	0.0	2	0.0	0	0.0
	GAB TR1C	Gallo-Belgic Terra Rubra	1	0.0	6	0.0	0	0.0
	GAB TR2	Gallo-Belgic Terra Rubra	3	0.0	21	0.0	0	0.0
	GABTR3	Gallo-Belgic Terra Rubra	1	0.0	2	0.0	0	0.0
	IMP WH	imported whiteware	1	0.0	16	0.0	0	0.0
	ITA WH	Italian whiteware	2	0.0	25	0.0	0	0.0
	KOL CC	Cologne colour-coat	56	0.4	428	0.2	130	0.9
	LYO CC	Lyon colour-coated ware	8	0.1	24	0.0	19	0.1
	NOG WH	North Gaulish whiteware	4	0.0	24	0.0	0	0.0
	SOG CC	South Gaulish colour-coat?	1	0.0	3	0.0	13	0.1
mortaria	NOG WHM	North Gaulish mortaria	16	0.1	636	0.3	11	0.1
	RHL WH	Rhineland whiteware mortaria	2	0.0	194	0.1	0	0.0
amphorae	ASM AM	E Mediterranean amphora	1	0.0	48	0.0	0	0.0
	BAT AM	Baetican amphora	174	1.4	14662	8.0	44	0.3
	BAT AM	Haltern 70	6	0.0	482	0.3	0	0.0
	CAD AM	Cadiz amphora	23	0.2	1569	0.9	0	0.0
	Dressel 2-4	Dressel 2-4 amphora	47	0.4	1793	1.0	28	0.2
	?Dressel 14	S Spanish/ Portuguese amphora	1	0.0	20	0.0	0	0.0
	GAL AM	Gallic amphora	58	0.5	1374.5	0.8	0	0.0

Period 3 Layers

Object 701	Code	Description	No.	No. %	Wt	Wt %	Eve	Eve%
	AMPLID	amphora lids	4	0.0	14	0.0	62	0.4
	AMP	unassigned amphora	20	0.2	829	0.5	0	0.0
REGIONAL	ABN OX	Abingdon oxid butt beaker	6	0.0	20	0.0	0	0.0
	CAR RS	Caerleon mortaria	4	0.0	156	0.1	21	0.1
	COL CC	Colchester colour-coated ware	1	0.0	32	0.0	0	0.0
	DOR BB1	Dorset black-burnished ware	385	3.1	7117	3.9	1562	10.5
	HAM GT	Hampshire grog-tempered	48	0.4	544	0.3	70	0.5
	LNV CC	Lower Nene Valley colour-coat	1	0.0	10	0.0	8	0.1
	OXF WH	Oxfordshire whiteware	254	2.0	2318	1.3	558	3.8
	OXF WHM	Oxon whiteware mortaria	75	0.6	2965	1.6	118	0.8
	SAV GT	?Savernake grog-tempered	1	0.0	55	0.0	6	0.0
	SOW WS	South-West white-slipped	1	0.0	14	0.0	0	0.0
	VER WH	Verulamium whiteware	44	0.3	1017	0.6	83	0.6
	VERWH M	Verulamium whiteware mortaria	14	0.1	5647	3.1	111	0.7
LOCAL	ALH RE	Alice Holt/ reduced wares	6843	54.4	68772	37.6	6001	40.5
	F1	Silchester flint-tempered ware	555	4.4	12917	7.1	276	1.9
	GRSJ	grog-tempered storage jar	711	5.7	29164	16.0	349	2.4
	G1	LIA-ERO grog-tempered	4	0.0	74	0.0	6	0.0
	G4	wheelmade C1 grog-tempered	2	0.0	14	0.0	10	0.1
	GROG	misc. grog-tempered	41	0.3	789	0.4	42	0.3
	SF/GF1	mixed grit	25	0.2	251	0.1	55	0.4
UNKNOWN	BUFF/PALE	misc. buff/ cream wares	196	1.6	1640	0.9	101	0.7
	BWF	fine black ware	8	0.1	120	0.1	18	0.1
	BWFMIC	fine black micaceous ware	11	0.1	77	0.0	16	0.1
	CC	miscellaneous colour-coat	21	0.2	95	0.1	30	0.2
	GYF	fine grey wares	828	6.6	5789.5	3.2	1601	10.8
	GREY	misc. grey/black wares	49	0.4	363	0.2	124	0.8
	GYBSLIP	black-slipped grey ware	8	0.1	64	0.0	51	0.3
	GYMIC	grey micaceous ware	5	0.0	57	0.0	15	0.1
	MICAOX	mica-slipped oxidised ware	43	0.3	673	0.4	14	0.1
	MORT	unknown oxidised mortaria	4	0.0	121	0.1	13	0.1

Period 3 Layers

Object 701	Code	Description	No.	No. %	Wt	Wt %	Eve	Eve%
	OXIDF	oxidised fine ware	30	0.2	371.5	0.2	85	0.6
	OXID	miscellaneous fine-med oxid sandy	433	3.4	4667	2.6	641	4.3
	OXID1	oxidised ware	5	0.0	57	0.0	0	0.0
	OXID2	oxidised ware fabric 2	2	0.0	16	0.0	0	0.0
	OXID3	oxidised ware fabric 3	105	0.8	1932	1.1	360	2.4
	OXID4	oxidised ware fabric 4	2	0.0	176	0.1	68	0.5
	OXID6	micaceous oxidised ware	50	0.4	628	0.3	46	0.3
	WSGREY	white-slipped grey ware	3	0.0	23	0.0	0	0.0
	WSOXIDF	white-slipped fine oxidised ware	50	0.4	528	0.3	38	0.3
	WSOXID	white-slipped oxidised ware	65	0.5	564.5	0.3	145	1.0
		white-slip micaceous oxid ware	7	0.1	122	0.1	25	0.2
	WSOXID3	white-slip oxidised ware fabric 3	159	1.3	1805	1.0	26	0.2
	WW	miscellaneous whiteware	28	0.2	278.5	0.2	19	0.1
	WW3	whiteware fabric 3	8	0.1	107	0.1	49	0.3
	WW4	whiteware fabric 4 -granular	95	0.8	854	0.5	13	0.1
	WWF	fine whiteware	40	0.3	335.5	0.2	12	0.1
	CRUMBS	small unidentified crumbs	2	0.0	4	0.0	0	0.0
TOTAL			12579	100	182727	100	14831	100.0

TABLE 42. SUMMARY OF SAMIAN FABRICS FROM PERIOD 3 LAYERS, OBJECT 701

fabric	sum(no.)	sum(eve)	sum(wt)
?	1	0	2
cg	596	1687	5470
cg.mv	14	32	57
cg?	3	14	8
eg	1	0	1
eg.tr	1	0	2
sg	98	177	455
sg.mo	1	0	6
Total	715	1910	6001

TABLE 43. QUANTIFIED SUMMARY OF POTTERY ASSEMBLAGE FROM PERIOD 4

Period 4	Code	Description	PITS & WELLS				LAYERS (700)				HOUSE 1			
			No.	No. %	Wt	Wt %	No.	No. %	Wt	Wt %	No.	No. %	Wt	Wt %
IMPORTS	SG SAM	South Gaulish samian	19	0.8	126	0.3	32	0.5	374	0.4	171	2.8	979	1.4
	CGSAM	Central Gaulish samian	104	4.3	1266	2.8	413	5.9	4999	4.9	186	3.1	1230	1.7
	EGSAM	East Gaulish samian	0	0.0	0	0.0	10	0.1	295	0.3	0	0.0	0	0.0
	ARG CC	Argonne colour-coat	12	0.5	44	0.1	36	0.5	143.5	0.1	12	0.2	29	0.0
	CNG BS	Central Gaulish black slip	43	1.8	222	0.5	59	0.8	208.5	0.2	6	0.1	30	0.0
	CNG CC1/2	Central Gaulish colour-coat	1	0.0	2	0.0	1	0.0	6	0.0	53	0.9	235	0.3
	CNG TN	Central Gaulish Terra Nigra	0	0.0	0	0.0	1	0.0	14	0.0	0	0.0	0	0.0
	CNG WS	Central Gaulish white slip	0	0.0	0	0.0	0	0.0	0	0.0	2	0.0	19	0.0
	EGGSH	eggshell ware	0	0.0	0	0.0	2	0.0	11.5	0.0	1	0.0	1	0.0
	GAB TN	Gallo-Belgic Terra Nigra	3	0.1	47	0.1	2	0.0	8	0.0	7	0.1	64	0.1
	GAB TR1A	Gallo-Belgic Terra Rubra	0	0.0	0	0.0	0	0.0	0	0.0	1	0.0	4	0.0
	GAB TR2	Gallo-Belgic Terra Rubra	0	0.0	0	0.0	0	0.0	0	0.0	0	0.0	0	0.0
	GAB TR3	Gallo-Belgic Terra Rubra	0	0.0	0	0.0	0	0.0	0	0.0	2	0.0	7	0.0
	IMP WH	imported whiteware	3	0.1	52	0.1	0	0.0	0	0.0	8	0.1	65	0.1
	KOL CC	Cologne colour-coat	12	0.5	41	0.1	55	0.8	515	0.5	40	0.7	165	0.2
	LYO CC	Lyon colour-coated ware	0	0.0	0	0.0	0	0.0	0	0.0	12	0.2	41	0.1
	MOS BS	Moselle black slipped ware	22	0.9	126	0.3	1	0.0	6	0.0	0	0.0	0	0.0
	NOG WH	North Gaulish whiteware	6	0.2	36	0.1	0	0.0	0	0.0	10	0.2	120	0.2
	SOG CC	South Gaulish colour-coat	0	0.0	0	0.0	1	0.0	3	0.0	0	0.0	0	0.0
coarsewares	CAM PR1	Pompeian redware fabric 1	0	0.0	0	0.0	1	0.0	9	0.0	0	0.0	0	0.0
	ITA CW	Campanian coarseware	0	0.0	0	0.0	0	0.0	0	0.0	1	0.0	10	0.0
mortaria	GLX OX	Central Gaulish mortaria	0	0.0	0	0.0	0	0.0	0	0.0	8	0.1	168	0.2
	NOG WHM	North Gaulish mortaria	0	0.0	0	0.0	3	0.0	74	0.1	5	0.1	164	0.2
	RHL WH	Rhenish mortaria	0	0.0	0	0.0	2	0.0	194	0.2	0	0.0	0	0.0
amphorae	ALM 50	Almagro 50	1	0.0	275	0.6	0	0.0	0	0.0	0	0.0	0	0.0
	BAT AM	Baetican amphora	31	1.3	4040	9.1	108	1.5	9912	9.7	58	1.0	3672	5.2
	BAT AM	Haltern 70	0	0.0	0	0.0	2	0.0	117	0.1	3	0.0	230	0.3
	CAD AM	Cadiz amphora	0	0.0	0	0.0	3	0.0	207	0.2	2	0.0	206	0.3
	GAL AM	Gallic amphora	7	0.3	161	0.4	21	0.3	419	0.4	20	0.3	556	0.8
	PAL AM	Palestinian amphora (Cam 189)	0	0.0	0	0.0	1	0.0	20	0.0	2	0.0	21	0.0
	AMPLID	amphora lid	2	0.1	119	0.3	1	0.0	5	0.0	0	0.0	0	0.0

Period 4	Code	Description	PITS & WELLS				LAYERS (700)				HOUSE 1			
			No.	No. %	Wt	Wt %	No.	No. %	Wt	Wt %	No.	No. %	Wt	Wt %
REGIONAL	AMP	unassigned amphora	3	0.0	0	0.0	2	0.0	88	0.0	20	0.3	1906	2.7
	ABN OX	Abingdon oxid butt beaker	1	0.0	1	0.0	1	0.0	20	0.0	18	0.3	81	0.1
	CAR RS	Caerleon red-slipped mortaria	0	0.0	0	0.0	1	0.0	32	0.0	0	0.0	0	0.0
	COL CC	Colchester colour-coated ware	0	0.0	0	0.0	2	0.0	11	0.0	2	0.0	4	0.0
	COL WH?	Colchester mortarium	0	0.0	0	0.0	1	0.0	92	0.1	0	0.0	0	0.0
	PUL SAM	Aldgate-Pulborough samian	1	0.0	26	0.1	0	0.0	0	0.0	1	0.0	24	0.0
	DOR BB1	Dorset black-burnished ware	325	13.3	8247	18.5	445	6.4	8029	7.8	92	1.5	1596	2.2
	HAM GT	Hampshire grog-tempered	15	0.6	218	0.5	0	0.0	0	0.0	5	0.1	108	0.2
	LNV CC	Lower Nene Valley colour-coat	19	0.8	686	1.5	13	0.2	107	0.1	0	0.0	0	0.0
	NFO CC	New Forest colour-coat	6	0.2	63	0.1	4	0.1	25	0.0	8	0.1	52	0.1
	NFO PA	New Forest parchment ware	0	0.0	0	0.0	0	0.0	0	0.0	2	0.0	47	0.1
	OXF RE	Oxfordshire reduced ware	0	0.0	0	0.0	1	0.0	36	0.0	0	0.0	0	0.0
	OXF WH	Oxfordshire whiteware	54	2.2	669	1.5	176	2.5	1328	1.3	75	1.2	504	0.7
	OXF WHM	Oxon whiteware mortaria	15	0.6	581	1.3	81	1.2	3027	3.0	31	0.5	882	1.2
	OXF RS	Oxon colour-coated ware	0	0.0	0	0.0	13	0.2	86	0.1	11	0.2	61	0.1
	OXF WS	Oxon white-slipped mortarium	0	0.0	0	0.0	3	0.0	91	0.1	1	0.0	2	0.0
	OVW WH	Overwey whiteware	1	0.0	10	0.0	1	0.0	16	0.0	0	0.0	0	0.0
	SOW BB1	South-west BB1	2	0.1	40	0.1	0	0.0	0	0.0	0	0.0	0	0.0
	SOW WS	South-west white-slipped ware	0	0.0	0	0.0	2	0.0	13	0.0	0	0.0	0	0.0
	VER WH	Verulamium whiteware	9	0.4	89	0.2	7	0.1	120	0.1	49	0.8	655	0.9
	VERWH M	Verulamium whiteware mortaria	2	0.1	135	0.3	2	0.0	70	0.1	22	0.4	891	1.3
LOCAL	ALH RE	Alice Holt/ reduced wares	1178	48.3	16324	36.6	4347	62.1	50008	48.8	3558	58.4	31855	44.8
	GRSJ	grog-tempered storage jar	75	3.1	3279	7.4	246	3.5	13660	13.3	302	5.0	10302	14.5
	F1	Silchester flint-tempered ware	79	3.2	2194	4.9	56	0.8	1465	1.4	354	5.8	6773	9.5
	F2	finer flint-tempered	0	0.0	0	0.0	0	0.0	0	0.0	27	0.4	334	0.5
	G1	LIA-ERO grog-tempered	1	0.0	26	0.1	1	0.0	4	0.0	11	0.2	81	0.1
	G4	wheelmade C1 grog-tempered	3	0.1	15	0.0	2	0.0	13	0.0	9	0.1	74	0.1
	GROG	misc. grog-tempered	5	0.2	118	0.3	11	0.2	294	0.3	12	0.2	204	0.3
	SF/GF1	mixed grit	11	0.5	149	0.3	18	0.3	123	0.1	44	0.7	421	0.6
	BB1 COPY	BB1 wheelmade copies	37	1.5	502	1.1	0	0.0	0	0.0	0	0.0	0	0.0
UNKNOWN	BUFF	misc. buff/ cream wares	17	0.7	257	0.6	133	1.9	772	0.8	28	0.5	156	0.2
	BWF	fine black ware	3	0.1	17	0.0	0	0.0	0	0.0	4	0.1	87	0.1

Code	Description	Count	%	Count	%	Count	%	Count	%	Count	%	Count	%
BWFMIC	fine black micaceous ware	1	0.0	5	0.0	6	0.1	70	0.1	2	0.0	19	0.0
BWMIC	black micaceous ware	1	0.0	2	0.0	0	0.0	0	0.0	2	0.0	7	0.0
CC	miscellaneous colour-coat	7	0.3	58	0.1	5	0.1	62	0.1	7	0.1	43	0.1
GYF	fine grey wares	81	3.3	609	1.4	433	6.2	2427	2.4	171	2.8	1044	1.5
GREY	misc. grey wares	16	0.7	1009	2.3	3	0.0	129	0.1	20	0.3	111	0.2
GYBSLIP	black-slipped grey ware	3	0.1	115	0.3	1	0.0	46	0.0	0	0.0	0	0.0
MICAOX	mica-slipped oxidised ware	9	0.4	300	0.7	9	0.1	48	0.0	106	1.7	575	0.8
MORT	unknown mortaria	0	0.0	0	0.0	7	0.1	180	0.2	7	0.1	411	0.6
OXID	oxidised ware	21	0.9	185	0.4	26	0.4	297	0.3	121	2.0	787	1.1
OXIDF	oxidised fine ware	14	0.6	47	0.1	59	0.8	286	0.3	89	1.5	880	1.2
OXIDFMIC	mica-slipped fine oxidised ware	0	0.0	0	0.0	0	0.0	0	0.0	0	0.0	0	0.0
OXID2	oxidised ware fabric 2	0	0.0	0	0.0	1	0.0	10	0.0	0	0.0	0	0.0
OXID3	oxidised ware fabric 3	17	0.7	613	1.4	48	0.7	907	0.9	176	2.9	1778	2.5
OXID4	oxidised ware fabric 4	29	1.2	293	0.7	0	0.0	0	0.0	11	0.2	397	0.6
OXID5	oxidised ware fabric 5	10	0.4	84	0.2	0	0.0	0	0.0	0	0.0	0	0.0
OXID6	micaceous oxidised ware	4	0.2	99	0.2	12	0.2	175	0.2	0	0.0	0	0.0
OXIDBS	black-slipped oxidised ware	0	0.0	0	0.0	1	0.0	6	0.0	0	0.0	0	0.0
OXIDMIC3	mica-slipped oxid fabric 3	6	0.2	218	0.5	0	0.0	0	0.0	0	0.0	0	0.0
SHELL	shelly ware	2	0.1	10	0.0	3	0.0	52	0.1	1	0.0	33	0.0
SOB GL	Southern British glazed ware	0	0.0	0	0.0	1	0.0	7	0.0	1	0.0	14	0.0
WSGREY	white-slipped grey ware	0	0.0	0	0.0	1	0.0	4	0.0	10	0.2	83	0.1
WSOXIDF	white-slipped fine oxidised ware	0	0.0	0	0.0	5	0.1	30	0.0	7	0.1	81	0.1
WSOXID	white-slipped oxidised ware	1	0.0	13	0.0	31	0.4	328	0.3	43	0.7	528	0.7
WSOXIDMIC	white slip micaceous oxid ware	3	0.1	114	0.3	0	0.0	0	0.0	0	0.0	0	0.0
WSOXID1	white-slip oxidised ware fabric 1	1	0.0	15	0.0	0	0.0	0	0.0	0	0.0	0	0.0
WSOXID3	white-slip oxidised ware fabric 3	7	0.3	73	0.2	3	0.0	20	0.0	3	0.0	44	0.1
WSOXID4	white-slip oxidised ware fabric 4	1	0.0	2	0.0	0	0.0	0	0.0	0	0.0	0	0.0
WW	miscellaneous whiteware	16	0.7	477	1.1	12	0.2	255	0.2	18	0.3	97	0.1
WWF	fine whiteware	0	0.0	0	0.0	1	0.0	6	0.0	2	0.0	5	0.0
MISC	unidentified miscellaneous	4	0.2	34	0.1	0	0.0	0	0.0	0	0.0	0	0.0
CRUMBS	small unidentified crumbs	75	3.1	95	0.2	13	0.2	10	0.0	0	0.0	0	0.0
TOTAL		2438	99.8	44547	100.0	7005	100.0	102426	99.9	6093	97.2	71074	100.0

TABLE 44. QUANTIFIED SUMMARY OF POTTERY FROM PERIOD 4 PIT 3406 (OBJECT 500033)

	Code	Object 500033	No.	No. %	Wt	Wt %	Eve	Eve%
IMPORTS	SG SAM	South Gaulish samian	4	0.7	7	0.0	5	0.4
	CGSAM	Central Gaulish samian	17	2.9	174	1.2	52	4.0
	CNG CC	Central Gaulish colour-coat	4	0.7	10	0.1	0	0.0
	KOL CC	Cologne colour-coat	2	0.3	1	0.0	0	0.0
	BAT AM	Baetican amphora	10	1.7	2129	14.8	0	0.0
	ALM 50	Almagro 50	1	0.2	275	1.9	16	1.2
	AMP	South Spanish amphora (misc.)	2	0.3	72	0.5	0	0.0
REGIONAL	DOR BB1	Dorset black-burnished ware	113	19.2	2417	16.8	329	25.5
	LNV CC	Lower Nene Valley colour-coat	5	0.8	527	3.7	100	7.8
	OXF WH	Oxfordshire whiteware	23	3.9	336	2.3	100	7.8
	OXF WH(M)	Oxon whiteware mortaria	8	1.4	314	2.2	12	0.9
	VER WH	Verulamium whiteware	5	0.8	69	0.5	0	0.0
LOCAL	ALH RE	Alice Holt/ reduced wares	233	39.5	4951	34.4	408	31.7
	SIL F1	Silchester flint-tempered ware	14	2.4	723	5.0	22	1.7
	GRSJ	grog-tempered storage jar	7	1.2	300	2.1	6	0.5
	HAM GT	Hampshire grog-tempered	6	1.0	126	0.9	10	0.8
	SIL SF	mixed grit	5	0.8	17	0.1	5	0.4
UNKNOWN	BB1 copy	black wheelmade BB1 copies	37	6.3	502	3.5	59	4.6
	CC	miscellaneous colour-coat	6	1.0	51	0.4	50	3.9
	GYF	fine grey wares	27	4.6	260	1.8	27	2.1
	GYBSLIP	black-slipped grey ware	1	0.2	104	0.7	0	0.0
	MICASL	mica-slipped ware	2	0.3	80	0.6	0	0.0
	OXIDF	fine oxidised ware	12	2.0	31	0.2	0	0.0
	OXID3	oxidised ware fabric 3	13	2.2	559	3.9	88	6.8
	OXID4	oxidised ware fabric 4	25	4.2	267	1.9	0	0.0
	PALE	misc. buff/ cream wares	1	0.2	26	0.2	0	0.0
	SHELL	shelly ware	1	0.2	6	0.0	0	0.0
	WSOXMIC	white-slipped micaceous oxidised ware	1	0.2	13	0.1	0	0.0
	WW	misc. whiteware	1	0.2	14	0.1	0	0.0
	MISC	misc. unclassified wares	4	0.7	34	0.2	0	0.0
TOTAL			590	100.0	14395	100.0	1289	100.0

TABLE 45. QUANTIFIED SUMMARY OF POTTERY FROM PERIOD 4 PIT 3102 (OBJECT 500034)

	Code	Object 500034	No.	No. %	Wt	Wt %	Eve	Eve%
IMPORTS	SG SAM	South Gaulish samian	1	0.2	1	0.0	0	0.0
	CGSAM	Central Gaulish samian	38	6.3	374	4.1	1085	60.0
	ARG CC	Argonne colour-coat	8	1.3	23	0.3	23	1.3
	CNG CC	Central Gaulish colour-coat	2	0.3	4	0.0	0	0.0
	KOL CC	Cologne colour-coat	5	0.8	22	0.2	0	0.0
	BAT AM	Baetican amphora	10	1.7	576	6.4	0	0.0
	GALAM	Gallic amphorae	1	0.2	29	0.3	0	0.0
REGIONAL	DOR BB1	Dorset black-burnished ware	88	14.6	1685	18.6	329	18.2
	NFO CC	New Forest colour-coat	4	0.7	42	0.5	0	0.0
	OXF WH	Oxfordshire whiteware	6	1.0	30	0.3	0	0.0
	OXF WHM	Oxon whiteware mortaria	2	0.3	65	0.7	5	0.3
	SOW BB1	South-west black-burnished ware	3	0.5	40	0.4	1	0.1
	VER WHM	Verulamium whiteware mortaria	1	0.2	51	0.6	0	0.0
LOCAL	ALH RE	Alice Holt/ reduced wares	354	58.7	3879	42.8	210	11.6
	SIL F1	Silchester flint-tempered ware	5	0.8	313	3.5	15	0.8
	GRSJ	grog-tempered storage jar	21	3.5	1138	12.6	20	1.1
	SIL G4	wheelmade C1 grog-tempered	2	0.3	13	0.1	5	0.3
UNKNOWN	BWF	fine black ware	1	0.2	6	0.1	0	0.0
	BWFMIC	fine black micaceous ware	1	0.2	5	0.1	3	0.2
	GYF	fine grey wares	7	1.2	30	0.3	3	0.2
	OXID	oxidised ware	5	0.8	38	0.4	0	0.0
	PALE	misc. buff/ cream wares	11	1.8	198	2.2	0	0.0
	WSOXID3	white-slipped oxidised ware fabric 3	1	0.2	9	0.1	0	0.0
	WSOXMIC	white-slipped micaceous oxidised	1	0.2	36	0.4	0	0.0
	WW	miscellaneous whiteware	9	1.5	438	4.8	110	6.1
	CRUMBS	small crumbs	16	2.7	10	0.1	0	0.0
TOTAL			603	100.0	9055	100.0	1809	100.0

TABLE 46. QUANTIFIED SUMMARY OF POTTERY FROM PERIOD 4 WELL 5735 (OBJECT 500037)

	Code	Object 500037	No.	No. %	Wt	Wt %	Eve	Eve%
IMPORTS	SG SAM	South Gaulish samian	15	2.5	101	1.1	27	2.4
	CGSAM	Central Gaulish samian	24	4.0	297	3.2	147	13.0
	ARG CC	Argonne colour-coat	3	0.5	7	0.1	0	0.0
	CNG CC	Central Gaulish colour-coat	30	5.0	177	1.9	42	3.7
	GAB TN	Gallo-Belgic Terra Nigra	1	0.2	11	0.1	6	0.5
	KOL CC	Cologne colour-coat	1	0.2	2	0.0	0	0.0
	MOS BS	Moselle black-slipped ware	14	2.3	120	1.3	72	6.4
	NOG WH	North Gaulish whiteware (Cam.113)	6	1.0	32	0.3	17	1.5
	BAT AM	Baetican amphora	3	0.5	147	1.6	0	0.0
	GALAM	Gallic amphorae	6	1.0	132	1.4	0	0.0
	AMP SS	South Spanish amphora	1	0.2	134	1.4	0	0.0
	AMPLID	amphora lid	2	0.3	119	1.3	17	1.5
REGIONAL	ABN OX	Abingdon oxidised ware	1	0.2	1	0.0	0	0.0
	DOR BB1	Dorset black-burnished ware	115	19.1	1878	20.1	246	21.8
	LNV CC	Lower Nene Valley colour-coat	3	0.5	34	0.4	0	0.0
	NFO CC	New Forest colour-coat	1	0.2	11	0.1	0	0.0
	OXF WH	Oxfordshire whiteware	17	2.8	233	2.5	0	0.0
	OXF WHM	Oxon whiteware mortaria	1	0.2	28	0.3	0	0.0
	VER WH	Verulamium whiteware	2	0.3	14	0.1	0	0.0
LOCAL	ALH RE	Alice Holt/ reduced wares	240	39.9	3668	39.3	355	31.4
	SIL F1	Silchester flint-tempered ware	29	4.8	496	5.3	30	2.7
	GRSJ	grog-tempered storage jar	17	2.8	980	10.5	12	1.1
	GROG	other grog-tempered	1	0.2	67	0.7	0	0.0
	SIL SF	mixed grit	6	1.0	132	1.4	10	0.9
UNKNOWN	CC	miscellaneous colour-coat	1	0.2	7	0.1	12	1.1
	GREY	grey sandy ware	1	0.2	40	0.4	0	0.0
	GYF	fine grey wares	36	6.0	244	2.6	34	3.0
	OXID	oxidised ware	2	0.3	7	0.1	2	0.2
	OXIDF	oxidised fine ware	1	0.2	14	0.1	0	0.0
	OXID5	oxidised ware fabric 5	10	1.7	84	0.9	0	0.0
	PALE	misc. buff/ cream wares	5	0.8	33	0.4	0	0.0
	WSOXID4	white-slipped oxidised ware fabric 4	1	0.2	2	0.0	0	0.0
	WSOXMIC	white-slipped micaceous oxidised ware	1	0.2	64	0.7	100	8.9
	WW	miscellaneous whiteware	5	0.8	19	0.2	0	0.0
TOTAL			602	100.0	9335	100.0	1129	100.0

TABLE 47. QUANTIFIED SUMMARY OF POTTERY FROM PERIOD 4 WELL 1750 (OBJECT 500020)

	Code	Object 500020	No.	No. %	Wt	Wt %	Eve	Eve%
IMPORTS	MOS BS	Moselle black-slipped	4	8.0	3	0.4	9	40.9
	BAT AM	Baetican amphora	1	2.0	350	50.3	0	0.0
REGIONAL	DOR BB1	Dorset black-burnished ware	2	4.0	13	1.9	0	0.0
LOCAL	ALH RE	Alice Holt/ reduced wares	33	66.0	237	34.1	8	36.4
	SIL F1	Silchester flint-tempered ware	2	4.0	15	2.2	5	22.7
	GRSJ	grog-tempered storage jar	2	4.0	46	6.6	0	0.0
UNKNOWN	BWMIC	black micaceous ware	1	2.0	2	0.3	0	0.0
	OXID4	oxidised ware fabric 4	4	8.0	26	3.7	0	0.0
	SHELL	shelly ware	1	2.0	4	0.6	0	0.0
TOTAL			50	100.0	696	100.0	22	100.0

TABLE 48. QUANTIFIED SUMMARY OF POTTERY FROM PERIOD 4 PIT 2434 (OBJECT 500031)

	Code	Object 500031	No.	No. %	Wt	Wt %	Eve	Eve%
IMPORTS	SG SAM	South Gaulish samian (apts)	3	1.0	13	0.3	9	2.1
	CGSAM	Central Gaulish samian	12	3.9	222	4.8	40	9.2
	ARG CC	Argonne colour-coat	1	0.3	14	0.3	12	2.8
	CNG CC	Central Gaulish colour-coat	2	0.7	30	0.7	0	0.0
	KOL CC	Cologne colour-coat	3	1.0	6	0.1	0	0.0
	MOS BS	Moselle black-slipped ware	1	0.3	3	0.1	0	0.0
	NOG WH	North Gaulish whiteware (Cam.113)	3	1.0	56	1.2	0	0.0
	BAT AM	Baetican amphora	4	1.3	766	16.6	0	0.0
REGIONAL	PUL SA	Pulborough samian	1	0.3	26	0.6	0	0.0
	DOR BB1	Dorset black-burnished ware	47	15.4	1059	23.0	140	32.3
	HAM GT	Hampshire grog-tempered	9	3.0	92	2.0	0	0.0
	LNV CC	Lower Nene Valley colour-coat	11	3.6	125	2.7	50	11.5
	NFO CC	New Forest colour-coat	1	0.3	10	0.2	0	0.0
	OXF WH	Oxfordshire whiteware	5	1.6	21	0.5	0	0.0
	OXF WH(M)	Oxon whiteware mortaria	3	1.0	155	3.4	14	3.2
	SOW BB1	South-West black-burnished ware	3	1.0	84	1.8	20	4.6
	VER WH	Verulamium whiteware	2	0.7	6	0.1	0	0.0
	VER WH(M)	Verulamium whiteware mortaria	1	0.3	84	1.8	0	0.0
LOCAL	ALH RE	Alice Holt/ reduced wares	124	40.7	1450	31.5	86	19.9
	SIL F1	Silchester flint-tempered ware	5	1.6	94	2.0	7	1.6
	GRSJ	grog-tempered storage jar	7	2.3	101	2.2	0	0.0
	SIL G1	LIA-ERO grog-tempered	1	0.3	26	0.6	9	2.1
	SIL G4	wheelmade C1 grog-tempered	1	0.3	2	0.0	0	0.0
	OVW WH	Overwey whiteware	1	0.3	10	0.2	12	2.8
UNKNOWN	GYF	fine grey wares	9	3.0	63	1.4	31	7.2
	MICAOX	mica-slipped oxidised ware	1	0.3	2	0.0	0	0.0
	OXID	oxidised ware	1	0.3	3	0.1	0	0.0
	OXIDF	oxidised fine ware	1	0.3	2	0.0	0	0.0
	OXID3	oxidised ware fabric 3	2	0.7	31	0.7	3	0.7
	WSOXMIC	white-slipped micaceous oxidised ware	1	0.3	14	0.3	0	0.0
	CRUMBS	small unidentified crumbs	39	12.8	40	0.9	0	0.0
TOTAL			305	100.0	4610	100.0	433	100.0

TABLE 49. QUANTIFIED SUMMARY OF POTTERY FROM PERIOD 4 PIT 2601 (OBJECT 500032)

	Code	Object 500032	No.	No. %	Wt	Wt %	Eve	Eve%
IMPORTS	CGSAM	Central Gaulish samian	14	3.8	200	3.5	51	12.0
	CNG BS	Central Gaulish colour-coat	1	0.3	3	0.1	0	0.0
	GAB TN	Gallo-Belgic Terra Nigra	2	0.5	36	0.6	9	2.1
	KOL CC	Cologne colour-coat	1	0.3	10	0.2	0	0.0
	MOS BS	Moselle black-slipped ware	1	0.3	2	0.0	0	0.0
	BAT AM	Baetican amphora	3	0.8	72	1.3	0	0.0
REGIONAL	DOR BB1	Dorset black-burnished ware	57	15.6	1111	19.5	98	23.1
	OXF WH	Oxfordshire whiteware	3	0.8	49	0.9	100	23.6
	OXF WH(M)	Oxon whiteware mortaria	1	0.3	19	0.3	0	0.0
LOCAL	ALH RE	Alice Holt/ reduced wares	208	56.8	2497	43.8	100	23.6
	SIL F1	Silchester flint-tempered ware	24	6.6	553	9.7	10	2.4
	GRSJ	grog-tempered storage jar	21	5.7	714	12.5	0	0.0
	GROG	grog-tempered	4	1.1	51	0.9	5	1.2
UNKNOWN	BWF	fine black ware	2	0.5	11	0.2	3	0.7
	BSLIPGYF	fine grey ware black-slipped	2	0.5	11	0.2	12	2.8
	GYF	fine grey wares	4	1.1	23	0.4	0	0.0
	OXMIC3	mica-slipped oxidised ware fabric 3	6	1.6	218	3.8	31	7.3
	OXID	oxidised ware	1	0.3	10	0.2	5	1.2
	OXID3	oxidised ware fabric 3	3	0.8	23	0.4	0	0.0
	WSOXID1	white-slipped oxidised ware fabric 1	1	0.3	15	0.3	0	0.0
	WSOXID3	white-slipped oxidised ware fabric 3	6	1.6	65	1.1	0	0.0
	WW	miscellaneous whiteware	1	0.3	6	0.1	0	0.0
TOTAL			366	100.0	5699	100.0	424	100.0

TABLE 50. BREAKDOWN OF FORMS (EXPRESSED AS % EVE) ACROSS THE PITS AND WELLS OF
PERIODS 3 AND 4

	FORM	South-east pits					Northern pits			
		500035	44008	500033	500034	500037	500031	500032	41016	500028
		%	%	%	%	%	%	%	%	%
Fineware	platter	0.0	0.8	0.0	0.0	0.0	1.4	2.1	10.8	0.9
	dish	0.0	0.9	2.6	2.7	7.3	4.8	0.0	1.2	7.0
	bowl	0.0	0.8	0.0	0.5	2.0	0.0	0.0	0.0	2.2
	cup	0.0	2.9	1.5	4.8	6.1	4.1	12.2	1.7	0.9
	jar	0.0	0.0	0.0	0.0	0.0	0.0	0.0	0.0	0.0
Coarseware	platter	0.0	0.0	0.0	0.0	0.0	2.1	0.0	0.0	0.0
	dish	9.4	4.7	14.6	10.8	1.6	5.0	11.5	1.0	3.1
	bowl	13.0	15.6	4.0	16.2	6.0	9.6	3.4	3.1	42.7
	mortaria	1.0	1.2	8.1	0.5	0.0	4.6	1.1	1.9	0.0
	jar	45.3	46.2	39.0	44.0	47.4	46.5	37.6	27.6	30.0
	flagon	20.9	11.8	5.4	11.9	8.9	0.0	0.0	47.0	0.0
	flask	0.0	0.0	7.2	0.0	0.0	0.0	22.9	0.0	0.0
	jug	0.0	0.0	0.7	0.0	0.0	0.0	0.0	0.0	0.0
	beaker	0.0	5.3	5.2	4.6	15.9	16.9	5.0	2.4	4.4
	mug	0.0	0.0	0.0	1.4	0.0	4.6	0.0	0.0	0.0
	storage jar	4.1	0.8	2.0	2.0	1.7	0.0	4.1	2.1	3.1
	dolium	0.0	0.0	0.0	0.0	0.0	0.0	0.0	0.0	0.0
	amphorae	0.0	0.0	1.2	0.0	0.0	0.0	0.0	0.0	0.0
	lid	6.4	8.9	8.6	0.5	3.0	0.7	0.0	1.2	5.7
TOTAL		100.0	100.0	100.0	100.0	100.0	100.0	100.0	100.0	100.0

TABLE 51. SUMMARY OF SAMIAN FABRICS FROM OBJECT 700

fabric	sum(no.)	sum(eve)	sum(wt)
cg	404	1400.5	4829
cg.mv	9	19	170
co/ar	1	5.5	10
eg	7	24	247
eg.ar	1	0	13
eg.rz	2	18	35
sg	24	64	291
sg.mo	8	16.5	83
Total	456	1547.5	5678

TABLE 52. SUMMARY OF POTTERY FROM PERIOD 4 LAYERS, OBJECT 700 (NO./WT/EVE)

Period 4							LAYERS	
Object 700	Code	Description	No.	No. %	Wt	Wt %	Eve	Eve%
IMPORTS	SG SAM	South Gaulish samian	32	0.5	374	0.4	80.5	0.7
	CGSAM	Central Gaulish samian	413	5.9	4999	4.9	1420	11.5
	EGSAM	East Gaulish samian	10	0.1	295	0.3	42	0.3
	ARG CC	Argonne colour-coat	36	0.5	143.5	0.1	52	0.4
	CAM PR1	Pompeian redware fabric 1	1	0.0	9	0.0	0	0.0
	CNG BS	Central Gaulish black slip	59	0.8	208.5	0.2	54	0.4
	CNG CC2	Central Gaulish cream fabric	1	0.0	6	0.0	0	0.0
	CNG TN	Central Gaulish Terra Nigra	1	0.0	14	0.0	7	0.1
	EGGSH	eggshell ware	2	0.0	11.5	0.0	0	0.0
	GAB TN	Gallo-Belgic Terra Nigra	2	0.0	8	0.0	0	0.0
	KOL CC	Cologne colour-coat	55	0.8	515	0.5	95	0.8
	MOS BS	Moselle black-slipped ware	1	0.0	6	0.0	0	0.0
	SOG CC	South Gaulish colour-coat	1	0.0	3	0.0	13	0.1
Mortaria	NOG WHM	North Gaulish mortaria	3	0.0	74	0.1	5	0.0
	RHL WH	Rhineland mortaria	2	0.0	194	0.2	0	0.0
Amphorae	BAT AM	Baetican amphora	108	1.5	9912	9.7	3	0.0
	BAT AM	Haltern 70	2	0.0	117	0.1	28	0.2
	CAD AM	Cadiz amphora	3	0.0	207	0.2	0	0.0
	GALAM	Gallic amphora	21	0.3	419	0.4	0	0.0
	PAL AM	Palestinian amphora (Cam. 189)	1	0.0	20	0.0	0	0.0
	AMPLID	amphora lid	1	0.0	5	0.0	10	0.1
	AMP	unassigncd amphora	2	0.0	88	0.1	10	0.1
REGIONAL	ABN OX	Abingdon oxid butt beaker	1	0.0	20	0.0	0	0.0
	CAR RS	Caerleon red-slip mortaria	1	0.0	32	0.0	0	0.0
	COL CC	?Colchester colour-coat	2	0.0	11	0.0	0	0.0
	COL WHM	?Colchester mortaria	1	0.0	92	0.1	12	0.1
	DOR BB1	Dorset black-burnished ware	445	6.4	8029	7.8	1815	14.8
	LNV CC	Lower Nene Valley colour-coat	13	0.2	107	0.1	17	0.1
	NFO CC	New Forest colour-coat	4	0.1	25	0.0	20	0.2
	OXF RE	Oxfordshire grey ware	1	0.0	36	0.0	0	0.0
	OXF WH	Oxfordshire whiteware	176	2.5	1328	1.3	489	4.0
	OXF WHM	Oxon whiteware mortaria	81	1.2	3027	3.0	149	1.2
	OXF RS	Oxon colour-coated ware	13	0.2	86	0.1	18	0.1
	OXF WS	Oxon white-slipped mortarium	3	0.0	91	0.1	0	0.0
	OVW WH	Overwey whiteware	1	0.0	16	0.0	8	0.1
	SOW WS	South-west white-slipped	2	0.0	13	0.0	0	0.0
	VER WH	Verulamium whiteware	7	0.1	120	0.1	23	0.2
	VERWH M	Verulamium whiteware mortaria	2	0.0	70	0.1	0	0.0
LOCAL	ALH RE	Alice Holt/ reduced wares	4347	62.1	50008	48.8	6412	52.1
	GRSJ	grog-tempered storage jar	246	3.5	13660	13.3	116	0.9
	F1	Silchester flint-tempered ware	56	0.8	1465	1.4	115	0.9
	G1	LIA-ERO grog-tempered	1	0.0	4	0.0	0	0.0
	G4	wheelmade C1 grog-tempered	2	0.0	13	0.0	10	0.1
	GROG	misc. grog-tempered	11	0.2	294	0.3	15	0.1
	SF/GF1	mixed grit	18	0.3	123	0.1	40	0.3
UNKNOWN	BUFF	misc. buff/ cream wares	133	1.9	772	0.8	53	0.4
	BWFMIC	fine black micaceous ware	6	0.1	70	0.1	22	0.2
	CC	miscellaneous colour-coat	5	0.1	62	0.1	28	0.2

GYF	fine grey wares	433	6.2	2427	2.4	820	6.7
GREY	misc. grey wares	3	0.0	129	0.1	8	0.1
GYBSLIP	black-slipped grey ware	1	0.0	46	0.0	12	0.1
MICAOX	mica-slipped oxidised ware	9	0.1	48	0.0	0	0.0
MORT	unknown mortaria	7	0.1	180	0.2	6	0.0
OXID	oxidised ware	26	0.4	297	0.3	39	0.3
OXIDF	oxidised fine ware	59	0.8	286	0.3	66	0.5
OXID2	oxidised ware fabric 2	1	0.0	10	0.0	0	0.0
OXID3	oxidised ware fabric 3	48	0.7	907	0.9	88	0.7
OXID6	oxidised, sandy, micaceous ware	12	0.2	175	0.2	31	0.3
OXIDBS	black-slipped oxidised ware	1	0.0	6	0.0	0	0.0
SHELL	shelly ware	3	0.0	52	0.1	0	0.0
SOB GL	Southern British glazed ware	1	0.0	7	0.0	0	0.0
WSGREY	white-slipped grey ware	1	0.0	4	0.0	0	0.0
WSOXIDF	white-slipped fine oxidised ware	5	0.1	30	0.0	5	0.0
WSOXID	white-slipped oxidised ware	31	0.4	328	0.3	7	0.1
WSOXID3	white-slipped oxidised ware fabric 3	3	0.0	20	0.0	0	0.0
WW	miscellaneous whiteware	12	0.2	255	0.2	36	0.3
WWF	fine whiteware	1	0.0	6	0.0	0	0.0
MISC	unidentified miscellaneous	0	0.0	0	0.0	0	0.0
CRUMBS	small unidentified crumbs	13	0.2	10	0.0	0	0.0
TOTAL		**7005**	**99.99**	**102426**	**99.96**	**12300**	**99.98**

TABLE 53. SUMMARY OF THE REPRESENTATION OF FORMS (% EVE) FROM PERIOD 3 PITS & WELLS AND SOUTH-EAST LAYERS

		Layers		SE pits		N pits	
Period 3	Object	701	ALL PITS	500035	44008	41016	500028
	FORM	%	%	%	%	%	%
Fineware	platter	0.1	3.0	0.0	0.8	10.8	0.9
	dish	13.2	1.3	0.0	0.9	1.2	7.0
	bowl	2.1	0.5	0.0	0.8	0.0	2.2
	cup	24.7	1.6	0.0	2.9	1.7	0.9
	jar	0.1	0.0	0.0	0.0	0.0	0.0
Coarseware	platter	0.2	0.0	0.0	0.0	0.0	0.0
	dish	3.5	5.0	9.4	4.7	1.0	3.1
	bowl	9.4	14.3	13.0	15.6	3.1	42.7
	mortaria	0.9	1.2	1.0	1.2	1.9	0.0
	jar	25.7	39.8	45.3	46.2	27.6	30.0
	flagon	2.8	22.0	20.9	11.8	47.0	0.0
	flask	1.6	0.0	0.0	0.0	0.0	0.0
	jug	0.0	0.0	0.0	0.0	0.0	0.0
	beaker	7.7	2.9	0.0	5.3	2.4	4.4
	mug	0.0	0.0	0.0	0.0	0.0	0.0
	storage jar	1.9	2.3	4.1	0.8	2.1	3.1
	dolium	0.1	0.0	0.0	0.0	0.0	0.0
	amphorae	0.2	0.0	0.0	0.0	0.0	0.0
	box	0.0	0.0	0.0	0.0	0.0	0
	lid	5.5	6.0	6.4	8.9	1.2	5.7
	lamp	0.3	0.0	0.0	0.0	0	0.0
TOTAL		**100.0**	**100.0**	**100.0**	**100.0**	**100.0**	**100.0**

TABLE 54. SUMMARY OF THE REPRESENTATION OF FORMS (% EVE) FROM PERIOD 4 PITS & WELLS AND SOUTH-EAST LAYERS

Period 4			Layers	SE pits			N pits	
	Object	All pits	700	500033	500034	500037	500031	500032
	FORM	% EVE	% EVE	%	%	%	%	%
Fineware	platter	0.4	0.1	0.0	0.0	0.0	1.4	2.1
	dish	3.9	6.5	2.6	3.0	7.3	4.8	0.0
	bowl	0.7	2.5	0.0	0.6	2.0	0.0	0.0
	cup	4.9	5.2	1.5	5.3	6.1	4.1	12.2
Coarseware	platter	0.2	0.0	0.0	0.0	0.0	2.1	0.0
	dish	9.3	5.2	14.6	12.2	1.6	5.0	11.5
	bowl	7.8	16.7	4.0	18.2	6.0	9.6	3.4
	mortaria	3.4	1.7	8.1	0.6	0.0	4.6	1.1
	jar	41.5	41.8	39.0	37.2	47.4	46.5	37.6
	flagon	6.8	3.4	5.4	13.4	8.9	0.0	0.0
	flask	4.8	6.6	7.2	0.0	0.0	0.0	22.9
	jug	0.2	0.0	0.7	0.0	0.0	0.0	0.0
	beaker	9.2	4.3	5.2	5.1	15.9	16.9	5.0
	mug	0.8	0.0	0.0	1.6	0.0	4.6	0.0
	storage jar	2.0	1.6	2.0	2.2	1.7	0.0	4.1
	amphorae	0.4	0.3	1.2	0.0	0.0	0.0	0.0
	lid	3.8	4.2	8.6	0.6	3.0	0.7	0.0
TOTAL		100.0	100.0	100.0	100.0	100.0	100.0	100.0

TABLE 55. COMPARISON OF THE REPRESENTATION OF THE MAIN WARE GROUPS BETWEEN THE PITS & WELLS OF PERIODS 3 AND 4 AND THE 4TH–5TH CENTURY (FULFORD ET AL. 2006)

		No. %	No. %	No. %
		Late pits	Period 4	Period 3
Imports	samian	4.9	6.0	5.0
	other imported finewares	6.7	2.7	1.6
	imported mortaria	0.0	0.1	0.2
	amphorae	2.4	1.8	2.1
Regional	Dorset black-burnished ware	11.1	5.5	1.8
	Lower Nene Valley wares	0.6	0.2	0.0
	New Forest wares	2.3	0.1	0.0
	Oxfordshire wares	3.3	3.0	1.6
	Verulamium-type wares	0.6	0.6	1.1
	Other regional imports	0.8	0.2	0.3
Local	Alice Holt wares	53.9	58.4	50.6
	C1 residual coarsewares	9.2	4.1	13.0
	grog-tempered storage jar	2.3	4.0	5.1
	Hampshire wares grog/white	1.0	0.1	0.2
	Tilford ware	0.6	0.0	0.0
Unknown	miscellaneous oxidised wares	2.8	4.1	6.0
	misc. fine grey wares	1.4	4.4	5.5
	miscellaneous grey wares	5.9	0.5	0.3
	other unprovenanced	4.2	4.0	5.8
TOTAL		100.0	100.0	100.0

APPENDIX 5

CERAMIC BUILDING MATERIAL

By Peter Warry

TABLE 56. *TEGULAE*: CONTEXT ASSEMBLAGES

Context	Assemblage	Type	Context	Assemblage	Type
1750	A	A	3827	C	C
4331	A	A	3849	B,3C	C
5340	A	A	3858	C	C
7347	A	A	3911	C	C
3375	B	B	4020	A,2C	C
3544	B	B	4035	C	C
3597	B	B	4098	C	C
3746	B	B	4151	C	C
4275	B	B	4152	A,C	C
2	C	C	4170	3C	C
53	B,2C	C	4197	B,C	C
223	B,C	C	4243	C	C
374	C	C	4265	12A,B,42C	C
492	C	C	4281	A,2C	C
1003	2C	C	4307	2C	C
1006	C	C	4426	C	C
1140	C	C	4454	2A,2B,5C	C
1141	2B,2C	C	4459	A,B,2C	C
1151	B,2C	C	4477	C	C
1173	C	C	4514	C	C
1263	C	C	4528	C	C
1656	C	C	4549	C	C
2310	C	C	4559	2C	C
2452	C	C	4563	C	C
3175	C	C	4592	C	C
3178	C	C	4751	C	C
3200	2C	C	4758	4A,B,10C	C
3300	C	C	4803	4C	C
3407	C	C	4819	C	C
3463	B,C	C	4862	C	C
3467	C	C	5003	C	C
3560	A,B,C	C	5007	C	C
3595	C	C	5040	C	C
3611	2C	C	5054	2C	C
3663	C	C	5071	C	C
3669	C	C	5073	C	C
3688	C	C	5087	2C	C
3693	C	C	5149	C	C
3804	2C	C	5222	C	C

Context	Assemblage	Type	Context	Assemblage	Type
5252	C	C	7106	C	C
5501	C	C	7125	C	C
5547	C	C	7247	C	C
5654	2C	C	7252	C	C
5696	C	C	7256	C	C
5700	C	C	7270	7C	C
5723	C	C	7287	C	C
5790	C	C	7318	C	C
5816	C	C	7341	C	C
5867	C	C	8012	C	C
5915	A,C	C	8119	C	C
6020	2C	C	8155	C	C
6110	C	C	8171	C	C
6156	2C	C	8180	C	C
6213	C	C	67	D	D
6228	C	C	1390	D	D
6368	2C	C	1752	D	D
6370	3C	C	2579	B,D	D
6377	C	C	2639	D	D
6436	C	C	3024	D	D
6474	C	C	3101	2D	D
7011	C	C	3821	B,5D	D
7040	C	C	6243	D	D
7062	2C	C			

APPENDIX 6

THE ANIMAL BONE

By Claire Ingrem

TABLE 57. TAXA REPRESENTATION ACCORDING TO RECOVERY METHOD (NISP)

(a) In hand-collected material

	Period								Total
	3				4				
	SE Layers		House 1		SE Layers		House 1		n
	n	%	n	%	n	%	n	%	
Horse	14	<1	6	<1	11	<1	8	1	39
Cattle	860	16	288	18	1432	19	142	13	2722
Sheep	62	1	6	<1	59	1	58	5	185
Goat			1	<1					1
Sheep/goat	595	11	204	12	712	9	118	11	1629
Pig	757	14	208	13	518	7	119	11	1602
Dog	143	3	27	2	315	4	18	2	503
Capreolus capreolus	19	<1	15	1	8	<1	3	<1	45
Cervus elaphus	24	<1			15	<1			39
Lepus europaeus	14	<1	10	1	10	<1	1	<1	35
Meles meles		<1			15	<1			15
Rattus rattus		<1			1	<1			1
Rodent	1	<1			4	<1			5
Anser anser	3	<1			4	<1			7
Anser spp.	1	<1			2	<1			3
Anas/Aythya spp.	19	<1	4	<1	5	<1	1	<1	29
Galliformes	90	2	14	1	105	1	8	1	217
Scolopax rusticola	6	<1	3	<1	8	<1	3	<1	20
Scolopacidae spp.					1	<1			1
Columba spp.	3	<1	1	<1	1	<1			5
Corvus corax			3	<1	19	<1			22
Corvus frugilegus/ corone	1	<1							1
Corvidae spp.	1	<1			1	<1			2
Turdidae spp.	1	<1							1
Bird	71	1	15	1	35	<1	14	1	135
Salmonidae spp.	2	<1			1	<1			3
Flatfish					1	<1			1
Fish	2	<1							2
?Anser spp.	1	<1							1
?Anas/Aythya spp.	3	<1	1	<1					4
?Galliform	41	1	5	<1	29	<1	5	<1	80

	3 SE Layers n	%	House 1 n	%	4 SE Layers n	%	House 1 n	%	Total n
?Gallinago spp.					2	<1			2
?Columba spp.	1								1
?Corvus corax	1								1
?Corvidae spp.	1								1
Large mammal	1783	33	596	36	3699	49	432	40	6510
Medium mammal	805	15	227	14	583	8	138	13	1753
Small mammal	9	<1	1	<1	30	<1	4	<1	44
Unidentifiable	3507		1713		5189		914		11323
Total	8841		3348		12815		1986		26990
Total identifiable	5334		1635		7626		1072		15667
% identifiable	60		49		60		54		58

(b) In sieved sample

	Period								Total
	3				4				
	SE Layers		House 1		SE Layers		House 1		n
	n	%	*n*	%	n	%	*n*	%	
Cattle	5	*4*	*2*	*13*	6	*3*	*1*	*7*	14
Sheep	1	*1*			2	*1*			3
Sheep/goat	9	*6*	*4*	*27*	23	*11*			36
Pig	21	*15*			52	*26*	*5*	*33*	78
Lepus europaeus							*1*	*7*	1
Apodemus sylvaticus	2	*1*							2
Rodent	2	*1*	*1*	*7*	2	*1*	*2*	*13*	7
Large mammal	33	*23*	*2*	*13*	30	*15*			65
Medium mammal	9	*6*	*5*	*33*	26	*13*	*5*	*33*	45
Small mammal	5	*4*			8	*4*	*1*	*7*	14
Galliform	3	*2*			3	*1*			6
?Galliform	1	*1*	*1*	*7*	2	*1*			4
Scolopax rusticola	3	*2*			1	*<1*			4
Corvidae spp.					1	*<!*			1
Bird	29	*21*			17	*8*			46
Cyprinidae spp.	4	*3*							4
Anguilla anguilla	7	*5*			3	*1*			10
?Trachurus trachurus	1	*1*							1
Sparidae spp.					1	*<1*			1
?Muglidae spp.	1	*1*							1
Flat fish	1	*1*							1
Fish	4	*3*			5	*2*			9
Rana temporaria					2	*1*			2
Amphibian					17	*8*			17
Unidentifiable	1966		*248*		2503	1245	228		4945
Total	2107		*263*		2704		*243*		5317
Total identifiable	141		15		201		15		372
% identifiable	7		6		7		6		7

TABLE 58. SOUTH-EAST LAYERS: NUMBER OF PAIRED AND ARTICULATED SPECIMENS (NISP)

(a) Period 3

	Matching sides	Articulation
Horse		2
Cattle	2	2
Sheep	4	
Pig	2	
Cervus elaphus		9
Total	**8**	**13**

(b) Period 4

	Matching sides	Partial skeleton
Cattle	2	
Pig	6	12
Meles meles		15
Galliform	2	
Corvus corax	6	5
Medium mammal		33
Total	**14**	**65**

TABLE 59A. SOUTH-EAST LAYERS: MINIMUM NUMBER OF ELEMENTS AND INDIVIDUALS

(i) Period 3

	Horse Left	Horse Right	Cattle Left	Cattle Right	Sheep/goat Left	Sheep/goat Right	Pig Left	Pig Right	C. capreolus Left	C. capreolus Right	C. elaphus Left	C. elaphus Right
Mandible			13	11	17	21	17	12	3	1		
Scapula			14	11	10	11	9	11	1	1		
Humerus			14	9	11	9	19	15				
Radius		1	15	16	24	12	7	9				
Ulna			8	9	7	4	17	22				
Pelvis			14	8	6	9	6	10				1
Femur			7	10	6	6	9	16				
Tibia			9	11	24	21	19	24				
Calcaneum			10	7	3	4	10	14				
Astragalus			10	8	4	1	4	6				
Metacarpal			7	11	21	12			3		1	
Metatarsal	1		13	12	13	10			1			1
MNE	2		257		266		256		10		3	
MNI	1		16		24		24		3		1	

(ii) Period 4

	Horse Left	Horse Right	Cattle Left	Cattle Right	Sheep/goat Left	Sheep/goat Right	Pig Left	Pig Right	C. capreolus Left	C. capreolus Right	C. elaphus Left	C. elaphus Right
Mandible	1		9	11	22	18	9	8	1	1		
Scapula			33	20	10	9	7	8			1	
Humerus		1	20	23	15	13	15	17				
Radius	1		37	26	19	10	8	9				
Ulna	1		14	17	2	5	7	12				
Pelvis			16	13	7	5	8	7				1

	Horse		Cattle		Sheep/goat		Pig		*C. capreolus*		*C. elaphus*	
	Left	Right	Left	Right	Left	Right	Left	Right	Left	Right	Left	Right
Femur			22	18	6	9	10	7				
Tibia	1		29	25	25	19	21	19			2	
Calcaneum			14	11	5	2	7	5				
Astragalus			15	11	1	2	3	2				
Metacarpal			11	13	17	15			1			
Metatarsal			10	16	19	18			1	1		1
MNE		5		434		273		189		5		5
MNI		1		37		25		21		1		1

TABLE 59B. 'HOUSE 1' SEQUENCE: MINIMUM NUMBER OF ELEMENTS AND INDIVIDUALS

(i) Period 3

	Cattle		Sheep/goat		Pig	
	Left	Right	Left	Right	Left	Right
Mandible	3	2	3	5	3	3
Scapula	1	3	2	2	3	2
Humerus	3	4	2	4	3	4
Radius	4	5	6	2	2	5
Ulna	5				6	8
Pelvis	3	4	5	2	3	3
Femur	1	1		2	3	3
Tibia	2		3	5	3	7
Astragalus	2	6	1	1		1
Calcaneum	4	8	1	1	1	7
Metacarpal	4	4	3	3		
Metatarsal	2	6	5	2		
Metapodial						18
MNI		8		6		8

(ii) Period 4

	Cattle		Sheep/goat		Pig	
	Left	Right	Left	Right	Left	Right
Mandible	2	2	2	4	2	5
Scapula	3	2	1	1	2	2
Humerus	2	2	1	3	4	1
Radius		4	7	3	1	1
Ulna		1	1	1	2	
Pelvis	2	2	2	3	2	5
Femur				2		1
Tibia	2	3	1	5	3	2
Astragalus	1	1		1	1	1
Calcaneum	3	2	1	3	4	
Metacarpal	1	1	4	4		
Metatarsal	4	3	2	1		
Metapodial						7
MNI		4		7		5

TABLE 60. ANATOMICAL REPRESENTATION OF SELECTED TAXA (NISP)

(a) Period 3

	Horse			Cattle			Sheep/goat			Pig			*C. capreolus*			*C. elaphus*			*L. europaeus*			Lge. mammal			Med. mammal			Total		
	S.E.L	H1	Total	S.E.L	H1	Total	S.E.L	H1	Total	S.E.L	H1	Total	S.E.L	H1	Total	S.E.L	H1	Total	S.E.L	H1	Total	S.E.L	H1	Total	S.E.L	H1	Total	S.E.L	H1	Total
Antler														2	2	2		2										8	2	10
Horn core				16	4	20		1																				41	5	46
Frontal				1		1																						7		7
Zygomatic				7		7																						17		17
Occipital condyle				4		4	3		3	3	2	5																21	2	23
Premaxilla				4		4		1	1	1		1																11	1	12
Tooth	8	1	9	84	43	127	117	64	181	90	32	122				11		11										310	140	450
Maxilla				4		4	5		5	25	8	33																84	8	92
Mandible				58	18	76	73	16	89	66	17	83	5	2	7				1	2	3	20	3	23	12		12	574	58	632
Hyoid				2		2	1		1																			6		6
Atlas				2	2	4	1		1	1		1																12	2	14
Axis				2		2																	2	2				8	2	10
Scapula	1		1	48	7	55	38	7	45	35	6	41	2	2	4							15	10	25	6	3	9	351	36	387
Humerus	1		1	37	12	49	33	9	42	55	11	66		1	1					2	2	63	9	72	13	7	20	486	52	538
Radius	1	1	2	66	18	84	60	18	78	22	13	35							3	2	5	15	1	16	4		4	444	53	497
Ulna				27	6	33	20		20	52	14	66							1		1	11	1	12				264	21	285
Pelvis				53	12	65	30	13	43	32	10	42							4		4	12	3	15	1		1	341	38	379
Femur				36	3	39	33	5	38	43	9	52				1		1	1	1	2	22	1	23	28	3	31	339	22	361
Patella				1	1	2	1		1																			6	1	7
Tibia				46	7	53	80	20	100	75	17	92							1	3	4	43	9	52	15	8	23	625	64	689
Fibula										22	1	23																46	1	47
Distal fibula				1		1																						2		2
Carpal	1		1	7	5	12	5	2	7	2		2				2		2				2	3	5	1		1	45	8	53
Astragalus				24	9	33	7	2	9	11	1	12																104	12	116
Calcaneum	1		1	23	19	42	7	2	9	25	10	35														1	1	174	33	207
Navicular cuboid				12	2	14										1		1				1		1				32	2	34
Sesamoid																									2		2	2		2
Metacarpal				46	20	66	57	12	69				3	3	6	1		1				1		1	1		1	287	35	322
Metatarsal	1		1	53	17	70	42	8	50				7	3	10	1		1				1		1				266	29	295
Metapodial	1		1	11	4	15	3	3	6	76	25	101				1		1	3		3	2	4	6	1		1	267	36	303
Lateral Metapodial										57	9	66																132	9	141

	Horse			Cattle			Sheep/goat			Pig			C. capreolus			C. elaphus			L. europaeus			Lge. mammal			Med. mammal			Total		
	S.E.L.	H 1	Total	S.E.L.	H 1	Total	S.E.L.	H 1	Total	S.E.L.	H 1	Total	S.E.L.	H 1	Total	S.E.L.	H 1	Total	S.E.L.	H 1	Total	S.E.L.	H 1	Total	S.E.L.	H 1	Total	S.E.L.	H 1	Total
1st Phalanx	2		2	85	34	119	19	8	27	26	11	37	1	1	2	3		3							2		2	382	54	436
2nd Phalanx				30	13	43	6	2	8	12	1	13				1		1							1	1	2	131	17	148
3rd Phalanx				42	10	52	1		1	7	1	8																122	11	133
Cervical vertebra																						6	1	7	4	3	7	21	4	25
Thoracic vertebra																						12		12	7	1	8	31	1	32
Lumbar vertebra																						1	1	2	4	1	5	9	2	11
Sacrum								1	1													1		1				4	1	5
Caudal vertebra																									1		1	1		1
Rib																						39	16	55	45	6	51	161	22	183
Tooth frag.	1		1	30	24	54	22	22	46	22	5	27										1		1				258	52	310
Skull frag.				3		3	1		1	17	5	22		1	1							38	3	41	5	3	8	144	12	156
Limb bone fragment																						223	54	277	261	96	357	911	150	1061
Rib frag.																						543	117	660	372	74	446	1766	191	1957
Vertebra frag.																						126	31	157	25	20	45	359	51	410
Total	14	6	20	865	290	1155	667	214	869	778	208	985	18	15	33	24	0	24	14	10	24	1197	270	1467	811	227	1026	9612	1240	10852

Note:
S.E.L. = south-east layers
H1 = House 1

(b) Period 4

Element	Horse			Cattle			Sheep/goat			Pig			*C. capreolus*			*C. elaphus*			*L. europaeus*			Lge mammal			Med. mammal			Total		
	S.E.L.	H1	Total	S.E.L.	H1	Total	S.E.L.	H1	Total	S.E.L.	H1	Total	S.E.L.	H1	Total	S.E.L.	H1	Total	S.E.L.	H1	Total	S.E.L.	H1	Total	S.E.L.	H1	Total	S.E.L.	H1	Total
Antler													1		1	9		9										10		10
Horn core				27	3	30																						27	3	30
Frontal				2		2	4		4																			6		6
Zygomatic				12		12	3		3																			15		15
Nasal																						1		1				1		1
Occipital condyle				8		8	1		1													1		1		1	1	10	1	11
Premaxilla				5		5	2		2	3		3																10		10
Tooth	2	2	4	69	20	89	153	31	184	75	23	98																299	76	375
Maxilla				14		14	10	1	11	22	4	26																46	5	51
Mandible	1		1	76	8	84	90	9	99	34	15	49	2	1	3							5	6	11	1	1	2	209	40	249
Hyoid				1		1	2		2																			3		3
Atlas				11		11		1	1		1	1										1		1				12	2	14
Axis				7		7	2		2													2	1	3				11	1	12
Scapula				109	7	116	35	4	39	26	6	32				1		1	1		1	23	5	28	2	4	6	197	26	223
Humerus	2		2	83	7	90	42	6	48	41	8	49							1		1	180	13	193	8		8	357	34	391
Radius	1	2	3	187	5	192	60	11	71	23	2	25							3		3	65	1	66	1		1	340	21	361
Ulna	1		1	71	2	73	10	2	12	23	2	25										17		17				122	6	128
Pelvis				94	9	103	22	7	29	37	10	47				1		1	2		2	12	2	14				168	28	196
Femur				105	1	106	31	5	36	39	4	43										56	2	58	14	5	19	245	17	262
Patella					1	1																						0	1	1
Tibia	1	1	2	123	9	132	83	10	93	64	8	72				2		2	3		3	107	5	112	13	4	17	396	37	433
Fibula										26	1	27																26	1	27
Carpal	1		1	20	1	21	1		1													5		5				26	2	28
Astragalus				47	3	50	18	1	19	5	2	7																70	6	76
Calcaneum				46	5	51	7	4	11	15	4	19								1	1							68	14	82
Navicular							1		1																			1		1
Navicular cuboid				16	1	17																						16	1	17
Cuboid										1		1																1		1
Sesamoid																						1	1	2	1		1	2	1	3

	Horse			Cattle			Sheep/goat			Pig			C. capreolus			C. elaphus			L. europaeus			Lge mammal			Med. mammal			Total		
	S.E.L	H1	Total	S.E.L	H1	Total	S.E.L	H1	Total	S.E.L	H1	Total	S.E.L	H1	Total	S.E.L	H1	Total	S.E.L	H1	Total	S.E.L	H1	Total	S.E.L	H1	Total	S.E.L	H1	Total
Metacarpal				53	3	56	69	13	82				1		1													123	16	139
Metatarsal				63	16	79	76	5	81				4	2	6	1		1										145	23	168
Metapodial	2		2	23	4	27	7	1	8	40	7	47										3	1	4	2		2	77	13	90
Lateral Metapodial										33	10	43																33	10	43
1st Phalanx	1	1	2	83	12	95	11	8	19	20	2	22													2		2	117	23	140
2nd Phalanx				36	5	41		4	4	8	6	14				1		1										45	15	60
3rd Phalanx				32	3	35		2	2	5	1	6																37	6	43
Cervical vertebra																						15	1	16	4		4	19	1	20
Thoracic vertebra								1	1													18	1	19	9	6	15	27	8	35
Lumbar vertebra								5	5													6		6	5	4	9	11	9	20
Caudal vertebra																									2		2	2		2
Rib								3	3													38	5	43	70	17	87	108	25	133
Tooth frag.	1		1	9	18	27	56	29	85	10	6	16														45	45	75	99	174
Skull frag.				6		6	1		1	17	2	19										127	1	128	6	2	8	157	5	162
Limb bone fragment																						1043	30	1073	178	46	224	1221	76	1297
Rib frag.							1	5	6													520	67	587	266	8	274	787	80	867
Vertebra frag.								8	8													161	28	189	24		24	185	36	221
Total	11	8	19	1438	143	1581	796	176	972	570	124	694	8	3	11	15	0	15	10	1	11	2407	170	2577	608	143	751	5863	768	6631

Note
S.E.L. = south-east layers
H1 = House 1

TABLE 61. SOUTH-EAST LAYERS: ANATOMICAL REPRESENTATION OF BIRDS (NISP)

(a) Period 3

	A. anser	Anser spp.	Anas/Aythya spp.	Galliform	S. rusticola	Columba spp.	C.frugilegus/ corone	Corvidae spp.	Turdidae spp.	Total
Furcula	1		1	2						4
Sternum				6						6
Coracoid			3	8						11
Mandible										0
Scapula			3	6						9
Humerus	2		4	10	1			1		18
Radius				5	1	1				7
Ulna		1		9	3	1	1		1	16
Carpometacarpus			2	3	1	1				7
Pelvis			2							2
Femur				10						10
Tibiotarsal			3	12						15
Tarsometatarsal			1	22	3					26
Total	3	1	18	71	6	3	1	1	1	105
%	*3*	*1*	*17*	*68*	*6*	*3*	*1*	*1*	*1*	*100*

(b) Period 4

	A. anser	Anser spp.	Anas/Aythya spp.	Galliform	S. rusticola	Scolopacidae spp.	Columba spp.	C. corax	Corvidae spp.	Total
Furcula				1						1
Sternum				7						7
Coracoid			1	13	1		1	1		17
Scapula				6	1			1		8
Humerus	1			13	1			4		19
Radius		1		8	1			1		11
Ulna			2	16	1			4	1	24
Carpometacarpus				7	1			1	1	10
Pelvis				1				1		2
Femur	1			7	1			2		11
Foot phalanx	1			1						2
Synsacrum				1						1
Tibiotarsal		1		8	1	1		2		13
Tarsometatarsal	1		2	19				1		23
Skull frag.								1		1
Total	4	2	5	108	8	1	1	19	2	150
%	3	1	3	72	5	1	1	13	1	100

TABLE 62. INCIDENCE OF GNAWING (NISP)

(a) South-east layers

	Canid	Period 3 Rodent	Total n	%	Period 4 Canid n	%
Cattle	41		41	*4*	73	*5*
Sheep/goat	12		12	*2*	38	*5*
Pig	47		47	*6*	48	*8*
Large mammal	16		16	*1*	27	*1*
Medium mammal	1	1	2	*<1*	2	*<1*
?Gallinago spp.					1	*50*
Total	117	1	118	**2*	189	**3*

★ % of identifiable assemblage

(b) 'House 1' sequence

	Period 3 n	%	Period 4 n	%
Cattle	8	*3*	6	*4*
Sheep/goat	2	*1*	3	*3*
Pig	8	*4*	3	*2*
Large mammal	2	*<1*	4	*1*
Medium mammal	1	*<1*		
Total	21	*1*	16	*1*

TABLE 63. INCIDENCE OF BUTCHERY (NISP)

(a) South-east layers

	Period 3 Cut n	Chop n	Sawn n	Sliced n	Total n	%	Period 4 Cut n	Chop n	Sawn n	Sliced n	Total n	%
Cattle	37	57	1	12	107	*12*	60	64		44	168	*12*
Sheep/goat	8	12		2	22	*4*	9	9			18	*2*
Pig	12	14		2	28	*3*	13	14			27	*5*
Cervus elaphus									2		2	*13*
Large mammal	58	21	1	17	97	*5*	78	53		51	182	*5*
Medium mammal	13	4		1	18	*2*	18	2			20	*3*
Total	128	108	2	34	272	**5*	178	142	2	95	417	**6*

(b) 'House 1' sequence

	Period 3 Chop n	Chop/cut n	Cut n	Total n	%	Period 4 Chop n	Cut n	Total n	%
Cattle	8	1	8	17	*6*	1	3	4	*3*
Sheep/goat			3	3	*1*	1	1	2	*2*
Pig	1	1	3	5	*2*	2	1	3	*2*
Capreolus capreolus			1	1	*7*				
Cervus elaphus									
Large mammal	4		12	16	*3*	1	5	6	*1*
Medium mammal	2		3	5	*2*		1	1	*1*
Total	15	2	30	47	** 3*	5	11	16	** 1*

★ = % of identifiable assemblage

TABLE 64. SOUTH-EAST LAYERS: EVIDENCE FOR DELIBERATE BREAKAGE IN OBJECT 701 (NISP)

	Smashed diaphysis		Split epiphysis	
	n	%	n	%
Cattle	58	6	36	4
Sheep/goat	50	7		
Pig	36	4	4	<1
Capreolus capreolus	1	5		
Large mammal	8	<1	10	1
Total	153	⋆3	50	⋆1

TABLE 65. INCIDENCE OF BURNING (NISP)

(a) South-east layers

		Period 3					Period 4			
	Brown	Calcined	Charred	Total		Calcined	Charred	Total		
				n	%				n	%
Cattle		1	1	2	<1					
Sheep/goat		2	2	4	<1					
Pig	1			1	<1	2	1	3	<1	
Large mammal	1	1	4	6	<1	3	3	6	<1	
Medium mammal		1	1	2	<1	4		4	<1	
Total	2	5	8	15	⋆<1	9	4	13	⋆<1	

(b) 'House 1' sequence

		Period 3				Period 4			
	Calcined	Charred	Total		Calcined	Charred	Total		
	n	n	n	%	n	n	n	%	
Sheep/goat									
Large mammal									
Medium mammal	2		2	1	1	4	5	3	
Small mammal					1		1	25	
Total	2		2	⋆<1	2	4	6	⋆<1	

⋆ = % of identifiable assemblage

TABLE 66. ESTIMATE OF WITHERS HEIGHT (MM)

(a) Sheep

	Period	GL	Factor	Withers height
Metacarpal	3	115.8	4.89	566
	3	124.7	4.89	610
	4	122.2	4.89	598
	4	131.2	4.89	642
	4	120.7	4.89	590
Metatarsal	4	143	4.54	649
	4	144.6	4.54	656
	4	127.2	4.54	577
	4	143.9	4.54	653

⋆ (after Teichert, in Boessneck and von den Dreisch 1974)

(b) Cattle

	Period	GL	Sex	Factor	Withers height
Metacarpal	3	*190*	male	6.33	1203
	3	182	female	6.05	1101
	3	177	female	6.05	1071
Metatarsal	3	204	female	5.28	1077

⋆ (after Matolsci 1970, in Boessneck and von den Driesch 1974)

TABLE 67. SOUTH-EAST LAYERS: TAXA REPRESENTATION ACCORDING TO OBJECT (NISP)

(a) Period 3

	701		41016		44008		500028		500035		Total	
	n	%	n	%	n	%	n	%	n	%	n	%
Horse	13	<1			1	<1					14	
Cattle	731	16	51	44	19	8	42	24	22	9	865	16
Sheep/goat	581	13	4	3	30	13	27	15	25	11	667	13
Pig	673	15	4	3	26	11	31	18	44	19	778	15
Capreolus capreolus	15	<1			1	<1	1	1	2	1	19	<1
Cervus elaphus	24	1									24	<1
Lepus europaeus	12	<1			1	<1			1	<1	14	<1
Apodemus sylvaticus							2	1			2	<1
Rodent	1	<1			1	<1	1	1			3	<1
Large mammal	1576	34	48	42	79	33	43	24	71	31	1817	34
Medium mammal	696	15	3	3	56	24	18	10	41	18	814	15
Small mammal	6	<1			3	1			5	2	14	<1
Anser anser	4	<1									4	<1
Anser spp.									1	<1	1	<1
Anas platyrhyncos												
Anas/Aythya spp.	19	<1									19	<1
Galliform	87	2			3	1	2	1	1	<1	93	2
Scolopax rusticola	4	<1	2	2	3	1			1	<1	10	<1
Columba spp.	3	<1									3	<1
Corvus frugilegus	1	<1									1	<1
Corvidae spp.	1	<1									1	<1
Turdidae spp	1	<1									1	<1
Bird	119	3	2	2	10	4	10	6	8	3	149	3
Salmonidae spp.	2	<1									2	<1
Cyprinidae spp.					1	<1			3	1	4	<1
Anguilla anguilla	1	<1							6	3	7	<1
Fish	4	<1	1	1	3	1			1	<1	9	<1
Total	4574		115		237		177		232		5335	
%	86		2		4		3		4		100	

(b) Period 4

	700 n	700 %	500020 n	500020 %	500031 n	500031 %	500032 n	500032 %	500033 n	500033 %	500034 n	500034 %	500037 n	500037 %	Total n	Total %
Horse	10	<1									1				11	<1
Cattle	1089	19	10	16	36	13	28	13	68	18	122	22	85	28	1438	19
Sheep/goat	634	11	4	6	26	9	24	11	27	7	55	10	26	8	796	11
Pig	408	7	7	11	22	8	29	13	34	9	47	8	24	8	571	8
Capreolus capreolus	8	<1													8	<1
Cervus elaphus	4	<1	1	2	3	1	2	1			3	1	2	1	15	<1
Lepus europaeus	9	<1	1	2			1	<1					1	<1	10	<1
Meles meles					18	7									15	<1
Rattus rattus							1	<1							1	<1
Rodent							3	1	1	<1			2	1	6	<1
Large mammal	2995	52	22	34	73	26	78	36	167	45	271	48	122	40	3728	50
Medium mammal	409	7	2	3	68	25	22	10	40	11	54	10	13	4	608	8
Small mammal	21	<1			5	2	3	1	3	1	5	1	2	1	38	1
Anser anser	2	<1													2	<1
Anser. Spp	1	<1			1	<1			1	<1			1	<1	4	<1
Anas/Aythya spp.	5	<1													5	<1
Galliform	63	1			6	2	14	6	23	6	1	<1			107	1
Scolopax rusticola	2	<1	1	2	2	1			2	1	1	<1			8	<1
Scolopacidae spp.	1	<1													1	<1
Columba spp.	1	<1													1	<1
Corvus corax	2	<1	12	19			5	2							19	<1
Corvidae spp.	5	<1					1	<1	1	<1					2	<1
Bird	49	1	4	6	16	6	5	2	4	1	3	1	5	2	86	1
Salmonidae spp.	1	<1													1	<1
Anguilla anguilla	1	<1											2	1	3	<1
Sparidae spp.									1	<1					1	<1
Flatfish									1	<1					1	<1
Fish	1	<1					1	<1					3	1	5	<1
Rana temporaria													2	1	2	<1
Amphibian													17	6	17	<1
Total	5716		64		276		217		373		563		307		7510	
%	76		1		4		3		5		7		4			

TABLE 68. PERIOD 4. TAXA REPRESENTATION IN EPHEMERAL HOUSES IN OBJECT 700 (% NISP)

	N. building	S. building	Other layers
Horse		<1	<1
Cattle	18	19	19
Sheep/goat	33	12	11
Pig	2	9	7
Lepus europaeus		<1	<1
Large mammal	35	46	54
Medium mammal	9	9	7
Small mammal		<1	<1
Anser anser		<1	<1
Galliform	1	2	1
?Galliform		<1	<1
Bird	1	1	<1

TABLE 69. SOUTH-EAST LAYERS: ESTIMATED AGE ACCORDING TO DENTAL DATA
(after Levine 1982; Legge 1991; Payne 1973; O' Connor 1988)

(a) Period 3

(i) horse

	P3	P4	M1	M2	M3	Estimated age
Maxillary				66.3		5.5-8 years
Maxillary					>65.8	6.5-7.75 years
Mandibular				43.2		8-11 years
Maxillary		41.1				9-11.75 years
Maxillary	35.7					11-15 years
Maxillary				23.4		14+ years

(ii) cattle

P4	M1	M2	M3	Estimated age	%
(c)				1-3 months	3
(k)				15-26 months	7
(k)				15-26 months	
(l)	k	g	b	26-36 months	
E	k	g	d	26-36 months	
E	j	g		26-36 months	
c	j	g	c	26-36 months	
c	j	g	d	26-36 months	
	j	g		26-36 months	38
	j			26-36 months	
f				26-36 months	
		e		26-36 months	
		e		26-36 months	
		f		26-36 months	
g	l	k		3-6 years	
		k	g	3-6 years	14
		k	g	3-6 years	
		k	g	3-6 years	
			g	3-8 years	3

P4	M1	M2	M3	Estimated age	%
		l	g	6-8 years	
g	l	l	h	6-8 years	
			j	6-8 years	
g	l	k	k	6-8 years	
	k	k	k	6-8 years	31
			k	6-8 years	
g	m	l	l	6-8 years	
	m		l	6-8 years	
		l		6-8 years	
	o	m		8-10 years	3

(iii) sheep/goat

P4	M1	M2	M3	Estimated age	%
(b)				2-6 months	
(b)				2-6 months	8
(e)				2-6 months	
(e)				2-6 months	
(h)				6-12 months	2
(h)	f	d		12-24 months	
	g	d		12-24 months	
	f	e		12-24 months	
e	f	e		12-24 months	
	f	e		12-24 months	
g	f	f		12-24 months	23
e	f			12-24 months	
e	f			12-24 months	
f	f			12-24 months	
	g	f		12-24 months	
(n)	g	f	V	12-24 months	
			a	2-3 years	
			a	2-3 years	
	g	f	b	2-3 years	
			b	2-3 years	
			b	2-3 years	
f	g	f	c	2-3 years	23
f	g	f	c	2-3 years	
e	g	f	c	2-3 years	
e		f	c	2-3 years	
g	g	g	c	2-3 years	
			c	2-3 years	
f	g	f	d	3-4 years	
	g	g	d	3-4 years	
			d	3-4 years	
			d	3-4 years	
			d	3-4 years	
f	f	f	e	3-4 years	
g	g	f	e	3-4 years	
h	g	f	e	3-4 years	31
h	j	g	e	3-4 years	
			e	3-4 years	
			e	3-4 years	
			e	3-4 years	
f	f	f	f	3-4 years	
			f	3-4 years	
l	h	g		3-4 years	

P4	M1	M2	M3	Estimated age	%
h	l	g	g	4-6 years	2
			g	4-8 years	
			g	4-8 years	6
			g	4-8 years	
j	m	k	g	6-8 years	4
j	m	k	g	6-8 years	

(iv) pig

P4	M1	M2	M3	Estimated age	%
(a)				Immature	
(b)				Immature	
(c)	a			Immature	
(c)	c			Immature	
(d)				Immature	27
(d)				Immature	
(d)				Immature	
(g)	c	E		Immature	
	c	E		Immature	
E	d	E		Immature	
E	b	a		Subadult	
E	e			Subadult	
b		c		Subadult	
	g	c	E	Subadult	
a		c	E	Subadult	24
		d	E	Subadult	
	h	e	E	Subadult	
b	k	f	E	Subadult	
			E	Subadult	
			b	Adult	
			b	Adult	
		e		Adult	
	h	f		Adult	
d				Adult	
c	k	f	c	Adult	
c	l	f	c	Adult	
e	k	g	c	Adult	
e				Adult	
		g	c	Adult	49
			c	Adult	
			c	Adult	
f	m	h	d	Adult	
		h	d	Adult	
f	n	j	d	Adult	
f	n			Adult	
f				Adult	
			d	Adult	
			d	Adult	

TABLE 69 (CONT.). SOUTH-EAST LAYERS: ESTIMATED AGE ACCORDING TO DENTAL DATA

(b) Period 4

(i) cattle

P4	M1	M2	M3	Estimated age	%
(b)				1-3 months	
(b)				1-3 months	
(b)				1-3 months	
(b)				1-3 months	23
(c)				1-3 months	
(d)				1-3 months	
(k)				15-26 months	8
		f	E	15-26 months	
(l)				15-36 months	4
	j	g	d	26-36 months	8
c	k	j	f	26-36 months	
b				3-6 years	
		j	g	3-6 years	15
f	l	k	g	3-6 years	
	l	k	g	3-6 years	
			g	3-8 years	8
			g	3-8 years	
e	l	k	j	6-8 years	
			j	6-8 years	
			j	6-8 years	
	l	k	k	6-8 years	
g	l	k	k	6-8 ycars	35
g	l			6-8 years	
f	l	k		6-8 years	
			k	6-8 years	
	l		l	6-8 years	

(ii) sheep/goat

P4	M1	M2	M3	Estimated age	%
(b)				2-6 months	3
(f)	E			2-6 months	
(g)				6-12 months	
(g)	f	E		6-12 months	5
(h)	f	E		6-12 months	
e	f			12-24 months	2
(j)				2-3 years	
h	g			2-3 years	
	g	f	b	2-3 years	
			b	2-3 years	
			b	2-3 years	
			b	2-3 years	
e	g	e	c	2-3 years	
e	g	f	c	2-3 years	
e	g	f	c	2-3 years	25
e	g	g	c	2-3 years	
			c	2-3 years	
			c	2-3 years	
			c	2-3 years	
			c	2-3 years	
			c	2-3 years	
			c	2-3 years	

P4	M1	M2	M3	Estimated age	%
(m)	f	e	d	3-4 years	
	f	e		3-4 years	
	f	e		3-4 years	
	g	e		3-4 years	
f	g	f	d	3-4 years	
		f	d	3-4 years	
			d	3-4 years	
			d	3-4 years	
			d	3-4 years	
			d	3-4 years	
g	g	f		3-4 years	
g	g	f		3-4 years	
f	g	f		3-4 years	
g	f	e	e	3-4 years	
e	f	e	e	3-4 years	
f	f	f	e	3-4 years	
f	g	f	e	3-4 years	56
f	g	f	e	3-4 years	
h	g	f	e	3-4 years	
			e	3-4 years	
			e	3-4 years	
			e	3-4 years	
			e	3-4 years	
			e	3-4 years	
			e	3-4 years	
			e	3-4 years	
	g	f	f	3-4 years	
h	j			3-4 years	
	j	g	f	3-4 years	
		g	f	3-4 years	
f	g	g		3-4 years	
			f	3-4 years	
			f	3-4 years	
			f	3-4 years	
h	j	g	g	4-6 years	
	k	g	g	4-6 years	5
j	m	g	g	4-6 years	
			g	4-8 years	3
			g	4-8 years	
j	m	j	g	8-10 years	2

(iii) pig

P4	M1	M2	M3	Estimated age	%
(b)				Juvenile	
(b)				Juvenile	
(d)				Juvenile	
(e)				Juvenile	44
c	g	d	E	Juvenile	
			E	Juvenile	
			E	Juvenile	
			I/2	Juvenile	

P4	M1	M2	M3	Estimated age	%
	d	a		Subadult	
b	e	c		Subadult	
a	e			Subadult	
	f	d		Subadult	
a	f			Subadult	44
		d		Subadult	
		e		Subadult	
b	g			Subadult	
	j			Adult	
			c	Adult	11

TABLE 70. 'HOUSE 1' SEQUENCE: ESTIMATED AGE ACCORDING TO TOOTH ERUPTION AND WEAR
(after Levine 1982; Legge 1991; Payne 1973; O' Connor 1988)

(a) Period 3

	P3	P4	M1	M2	M3	Estimated age
Horse				10.4mm		over 18 years
Cattle		(k)	g	f		15-26 months
Cattle					a	15-36 months
Cattle					b	26-36 months
Cattle					g	over 26 months
Cattle					k	6-8 years
Cattle		h	>p	n	m	over 8 years
Sheep		(d)				2-6 months
Sheep		(g)	d			6-12 months
Sheep		(h)				6-12 months
Sheep/goat					a	2-3 years
Sheep/goat					a	2-3 years
Sheep/goat					b	2-3 years
Sheep/goat					c	2-3 years
Sheep/goat					c	2-3 years
Sheep/goat					c	2-3 years
Sheep/goat					e	3-4 years
Sheep/goat					e	3-4 years
Sheep/goat				f	e	3-4 years
Sheep/goat					f	3-4 years
Sheep/goat					f	3-4 years
Sheep/goat		f	g			4-6 years
Sheep/goat					g	4-8 years
Sheep/goat		g	g	j		over 6 years
Pig			a	E		Immature
Pig					a	Subadult
Pig			g	d		Adult
Pig					b	Adult
Pig				e	c	Adult
Pig					c	Adult
Pig				g	c	Adult

(b) Period 4

	P3	P4	M1	M2	M3	Estimated age
Horse		60.5mm				6-7.75 years
Cattle					a	15-36 months
Cattle					e	26-36 months
Cattle			l	k	g	3-6 years
Cattle					k	6-8 years
Cattle					k	6-8 years
Cattle				l	k	6-8 years
Sheep		(g)	d			12-24 months
Sheep		(l)				12-24 months
Sheep/goat					e	3-4 years
Sheep/goat					e	3-4 years
Sheep/goat		f	g	f	e	3-4 years
Sheep/goat			g	f		2-4 years
Sheep/goat		f	g	g	g	4-6 years
Sheep/goat					g	4-6 years
Sheep/goat					g	4-6 years
Sheep/goat		j	m	l	l	over 10 years
Pig				e	b	Adult
Pig				e		Adult
Pig					c	Adult
Pig				j	d	Adult

TABLE 71. ESTIMATED AGE ACCORDING TO EPIPHYSEAL FUSION (NISP)

(a) Period 3

(i) Cattle

		Fused	Unfused	% unfused
7-10 months	Scapula	13		
	Pelvis	11		
<1yr		**24**		**0**
12-15 months	Radius,p	42		
15-18 months	Phalanx II	32		
15-20 months	Humerus,d	17		
20-24 months	Phalanx I	82	2	
<2yrs		**173**	**2**	**1**
24-30 months	Tibia,d	19	5	
	Metacarpal	16	1	
	Metatarsal	21	2	
<3yrs		**56**	**8**	**13**
36 months	Calcaneus	2	7	
36-42 months	Femur,p	8	2	
42-48 months	Humerus,p			
	Radius,d	4	6	
	Ulna,p	1	1	
	Femur,d		3	
	Tibia,p	1		
<4yrs		**16**	**19**	**54**

(ii) Sheep/goat

		Fused	Unfused	% unfused
3-4 months	Humerus,d	5	1	
	Radius,p	11		

		Fused	Unfused	% unfused
5 months	Scapula	11		
	Pelvis	3	1	
5-7 months	Phalanx II	3	3	
7-10 months	Phalanx I	16	5	
<1yr		**49**	**10**	**17**
15-20 months	Tibia,d	27	3	
20-24 months	Metacarpal	5	3	
	Metatarsal	1	3	
<2yrs		**33**	**9**	**21**
36 months	Calcaneus	4	3	
<3yrs		**4**	**3**	**43**
36-42 months	Femur,p	2	3	
42 months	Humerus,p			
	Radius,d		5	
	Ulna,p	1		
	Femur,d	3	3	
	Tibia,p		2	
<3.5yrs		**6**	**13**	**79**

(iii) Pig

		Fused	Unfused	% unfused
12 months	Scapula	8	2	
	Humerus,d	2	4	
	Radius,p	8	2	
	Pelvis	8		
	Phalanx II	6	6	
<1yr		**32**	**14**	**30**
24 months	Tibia,d	5	20	
	Metapodial	14	24	
	Phalanx I	12	12	
<2yrs		**31**	**56**	**64**
24-30 months	Calcaneus		10	
<3yrs			**10**	**100**
36-42 months	Ulna,p		4	
	Femur,p	1	3	
42 months	Humerus,p		4	
	Radius,d		4	
	Femur,d		7	
	Tibia,p		4	
<3.5yrs		**1**	**26**	**96**

(b) Period 4

(i) Cattle

		Fused	Unfused	% unfused
7-10 months	Scapula	28		
	Pelvis	4		
Subtotal<1yr		**32**		**0**
12-15 months	Radius,p	86	2	
15-18 months	Phalanx II	35		
15-20 months	Humerus,d	30	2	
20-24 months	Phalanx I	75	1	
Subtotal<2yrs		**226**	**5**	**2**
24-30 months	Tibia,d	33	9	
	Metacarpal	13	1	

		Fused	Unfused	% unfused
	Metatarsal	24	4	
Subtotal<3yrs		70	14	17
36 months	Calcaneus	4	1	
36-42 months	Femur,p	2	10	
42-48 months	Humerus,p			
	Radius,d	13	20	
	Ulna,p	1	3	
	Femur,d	1	2	
	Tibia,p	1	1	
Subtotal<4yrs		22	37	63

(ii) Sheep/goat

		Fused	Unfused	% unfused
3-4 months	Humerus,d	8	2	
	Radius,p	6	1	
5 months	Scapula	4	2	
	Pelvis	8		
5-7 months	Phalanx II			
7-10 months	Phalanx I	7	3	
Subtotal<1yr		33	8	20
15-20 months	Tibia,d	19	5	
20-24 months	Metacarpal	6	1	
	Metatarsal	5	2	
Subtotal<2yrs		30	8	21
36 months	Calcaneus	3	1	
Subtotal<3yrs		3	1	25
36-42 months	Femur,p		1	
42 months	Humerus,p	1	1	
	Radius,d		2	
	Ulna,p			
	Femur,d		1	
	Tibia,p	1	2	
Subtotal<3.5yrs		2	7	78

(iii) Pig

		Fused	Unfused	% unfused
12 months	Scapula	9		
	Humerus,d	4	8	
	Radius,p	13		
	Pelvis	7	4	
	Phalanx II	3	5	
Subtotal<1yr		36	17	32
24 months	Tibia,d	1	19	
	Metapodial	4	14	
	Phalanx I	3	15	
Subtotal<2yrs		8	48	86
24-30 months	Calcaneus		3	
Subtotal<3yrs			3	100
36-42 months	Ulna,p		5	
	Femur,p		3	
42 months	Humerus,p		3	
	Radius,d		1	
	Femur,d		1	
	Tibia,p		4	
Subtotal<3.5yrs		0	17	100

TABLE 72. 'HOUSE I' SEQUENCE: ESTIMATED AGE ACCORDING TO EPIPHYSEAL FUSION

(a) Period 3

(i) Cattle

		Fused	Unfused	% unfused
7-10 months	Scapula	3		
	Pelvis	1		
Subtotal<1yr		**4**		**0**
12-15 months	Radius,p	11		
15-18 months	Phalanx II	11		
15-20 months	Humerus,d	7		
20-24 months	Phalanx I	23	1	
Subtotal<2yrs		**52**	**1**	**2**
24-30 months	Tibia,d	3		
	Metacarpal	5	1	
	Metatarsal	4	2	
Subtotal<3yrs		**12**	**3**	**20**
36 months	Calcaneus	7		
36-42 months	Femur,p		1	
42-48 months	Humerus,p			
	Radius,d	4		
	Ulna,p	2		
	Femur,d			
	Tibia,p	2		
Subtotal<4yrs		**15**	**1**	**6**

(ii) Sheep/goat

		Fused	Unfused	% unfused
3-4 months	Humerus,d	1	2	
	Radius,p	4		
5 months	Scapula			
	Pelvis	5		
5-7 months	Phalanx II	2		
7-10 months	Phalanx I	5	1	
Subtotal<1yr		**17**	**3**	**15**
15-20 months	Tibia,d	4	2	
20-24 months	Metacarpal		1	
	Metatarsal			
Subtotal<2yrs		**4**	**3**	**43**
36 months	Calcaneus		1	
Subtotal<3yrs			**1**	**100**
36-42 months	Femur,p			
42 months	Humerus,p		1	
	Radius,d	1		
	Ulna,p			
	Femur,d		2	
	Tibia,p	1	1	
Subtotal<3.5yrs		**2**	**4**	**67**

(iii) Pig

		Fused	Unfused	% unfused
12 months	Scapula	2	1	
	Humerus,d	2	1	
	Radius,p	6		
	Pelvis	3		
	Phalanx II	1		
Subtotal<1yr		**14**	**2**	**13**

		Fused	Unfused	% unfused
24 months	Tibia,d		7	
	Metapodial	2	12	
	Phalanx I	2	8	
Subtotal<2yrs		**4**	**27**	**87**
24-30 months	Calcaneus		5	
Subtotal<3yrs		**0**	**5**	**100**
36-42 months	Ulna,p		2	
	Femur,p			
42 months	Humerus,p		3	
	Radius,d			
	Femur,d		2	
	Tibia,p		1	
Subtotal<3.5yrs			**8**	**100**

(b) Period 4

(i) Cattle

		Fused	Unfused	% unfused
7-10 months	Scapula	3		
	Pelvis	1		
Subtotal<1yr		**4**		**0**
12-15 months	Radius,p	4		
15-18 months	Phalanx II	4		
15-20 months	Humerus,d	3		
20-24 months	Phalanx I	10		
Subtotal<2yrs		**21**		**0**
24-30 months	Tibia,d	7		
	Metacarpal	1		
	Metatarsal	6	2	
Subtotal<3yrs		**14**	**2**	**13**
36 months	Calcaneus	1		
36-42 months	Femur,p			
42-48 months	Humerus,p			
	Radius,d			
	Ulna,p			
	Femur,d			
	Tibia,p			
Subtotal<4yrs		**1**		**0**

(ii) Sheep/goat

		Fused	Unfused	% unfused
3-4 months	Humerus,d	1		
	Radius,p	3		
5 months	Scapula			
	Pelvis	1	1	
5-7 months	Phalanx II	1	3	
7-10 months	Phalanx I	1	6	
Subtotal<1yr		**7**	**10**	**59**
15-20 months	Tibia,d	1	1	
20-24 months	Metacarpal	1	3	
	Metatarsal		2	
Subtotal<2yrs		**2**	**6**	**75**
36 months	Calcaneus	2	2	
Subtotal<3yrs		**2**	**2**	**50**
36-42 months	Femur,p			

		Fused	Unfused	% unfused
42 months	Humerus,p			
	Radius,d	1	3	
	Ulna,p		1	
	Femur,d		1	
	Tibia,p		2	
Subtotal<3.5yrs		**1**	**7**	**88**

(iii) Pig

		Fused	Unfused	% unfused
12 months	Scapula			
	Humerus,d	1		
	Radius,p	1		
	Pelvis	4	1	
	Phalanx II	2	1	
Subtotal<1yr		**8**	**2**	**20**
24 months	Tibia,d		2	
	Metapodial		2	
	Phalanx I	1	1	
Subtotal<2yrs		**1**	**5**	**83**
24-30 months	Calcaneus		3	
Subtotal<3yrs			**3**	**100**
36-42 months	Ulna,p			
	Femur,p			
42 months	Humerus,p			
	Radius,d		1	
	Femur,d			
	Tibia,p			
Subtotal<3.5yrs			**1**	**100**

TABLE 73. METRICAL DATA FOR MAMMALS: SOUTH-EAST LAYERS

Period	Taxa	Element	Max	45	46	Measurement	ABMAP range
4	*Cervus elaphus*	Antler	60.7				
			47	*45*	*46*		
3	Cattle	Horn core	135	44.9	31.6		
3	Cattle	Horn core		68.2	41.7		
3	Cattle	Horn core					
3	Cattle	Horn core		53.2	41.7		
3	Cattle	Horn core		52.8	39.4		
4	Cattle	Horn core		65.1	43.8		
4	Cattle	Horn core		38.7	31		
4	Cattle	Horn core		65.6	44.5		
4	Cattle	Horn core	143	55.3	34.9		
4	Cattle	Horn core		68.9	54.2		
4	Cattle	Horn core			27.2		
4	Cattle	Horn core		48.3	38.5		
4	Cattle	Horn core		65	44.1		
4	Cattle	Horn core		44.5	33.3		
4	Cattle	Horn core		67.7	44.6		
4	Cattle	Horn core		45.7	36		
		Element	*GL*				
3	Pig	Lower third molar	31.4				
3	Pig	Lower third molar	32.6				
4	Pig	Lower third molar	36.2				
3	Pig	Lower third molar	31.3				
3	Pig	Upper third molar	30.8				
4	Pig	Upper third molar	34.4				

Period	Taxa	Element	Measurement				ABMAP range
			GLP	BG	LG	SLC	
3	Cattle	Scapula	81.3	56.6	68	62	
3	Cattle	Scapula		43.5	51.5	44.3	0.2
3	Cattle	Scapula		33.5			35.3–57.3
3	Cattle	Scapula			51.2	41.3	
3	Cattle	Scapula				43.2	
3	Cattle	Scapula		53.9			
3	Cattle	Scapula		43.7	48		
3	Cattle	Scapula		52.4			
3	Cattle	Scapula				36	
3	Cattle	Scapula		42.8	51.2	46	
4	Cattle	Scapula				46.4	
4	Cattle	Scapula		43.4		50.9	
4	Cattle	Scapula				38.9	
4	Cattle	Scapula				48.1	
3	Sheep/goat	Scapula		18.7		18.4	
3	Sheep/goat	Scapula		15.1			
3	Sheep/goat	Scapula	29.7	19.9	24.5	17.6	
3	Sheep/goat	Scapula	30	18.4	22.3	17.7	
3	Sheep/goat	Scapula				20.3	
3	Sheep/goat	Scapula		20.7		19.3	
3	Sheep/goat	Scapula				17	
3	Sheep/goat	Scapula		18		16.7	
3	Sheep/goat	Scapula					
4	Sheep/goat	Scapula	32.3	22.1	25.1	18.9	
4	Sheep/goat	Scapula		22.1	26.2	17.8	
3	Pig	Scapula	35.8	24.8	28.4	21.8	
3	Pig	Scapula		24.1			
3	Pig	Scapula				25.2	
3	Pig	Scapula	35.2	24.5	28.3		
4	Pig	Scapula	31	22.6	25.9	19.2	
4	Pig	Scapula				22.5	

	Taxon	Element	SD	Bd	BT	HT	HTC	
4	Pig	Scapula	37.5		29.2	26.1		1.5
4	Pig	Scapula	35.8	26	26.9			
4	Pig	Scapula	34	25	28	23		
4	Pig	Scapula	34	E26.1	E30.1	22.4		
4	Pig	Scapula	33.5	25	29.5			
3	Capreolus capreolus	Scapula		19.4	21.5			
			SD	*Bd*	*BT*	*HT*	*HTC*	
3	Cattle	Humerus				39.1	28.6	
3	Cattle	Humerus			58.4	41.8	31.1	
3	Cattle	Humerus	39.4				33.9	
3	Cattle	Humerus		59.5	55.5	44	32	61-94
3	Cattle	Humerus				36.1		
3	Cattle	Humerus		65	62.2	40.3	31	
3	Cattle	Humerus	26					
4	Cattle	Humerus			74.5	46.3	32.9	
4	Cattle	Humerus				35.8	26.9	
4	Cattle	Humerus				34.7	25.3	
3	Sheep/goat	Humerus	14.5		29.8	19.4	13.3	
3	Sheep/goat	Humerus	15		29	19	13.6	
3	Sheep/goat	Humerus			27.6	17.5	13.2	
3	Sheep/goat	Humerus		30.4	29	19.2	13.5	
3	Sheep/goat	Humerus	12.5					
4	Sheep/goat	Humerus	13	26.6	25.6	17.2	13	
4	Sheep/goat	Humerus		29.9	28.8	18	14.4	
4	Sheep/goat	Humerus	13.3					
4	Sheep/goat	Humerus				19		
4	Sheep/goat	Humerus				17.4		
3	Pig	Humerus		35.4	29.3	26.5	17.6	
3	Pig	Humerus	16.9					
3	Pig	Humerus		44.6	35.7	32.7	22.3	
3	Pig	Humerus			34.1	28.9	20.7	

Period	Taxa	Element	Measurement					ABMAP range	
			Bp	*BFp*	*SD*	*Bd*	*BFd*		
4	Pig	Humerus	16.6		31.9	26.5	18.7		
4	Pig	Humerus		38	29.2	27.9	20.2		
4	Pig	Humerus	18.5					11.2-16.9	1.6
3	Horse	Radius	74.7	68.2					
3	Cattle	Radius	75.5	68.4		59.8	51.5		
3	Cattle	Radius	75.1	68.5					
3	Cattle	Radius	67.1	63.3					
3	Cattle	Radius		67.5					
4	Cattle	Radius					45.3	46.1-73.8	0.8
4	Cattle	Radius					59.2		
4	Cattle	Radius	78	69.7					
4	Cattle	Radius	80.6	73					
4	Cattle	Radius	68.7	53.3				54.5-83	1.2
4	Cattle	Radius	83	76.9					
3	Sheep/goat	Radius	28.1	26.6					
3	Sheep/goat	Radius	27.2	25.1	13.3				
3	Sheep/goat	Radius	30.5	28.2	14.8				
3	Sheep/goat	Radius	28.9	25.9	13.3				
3	Sheep/goat	Radius	32	30.3					
3	Sheep/goat	Radius	32.2	30.4					
4	Sheep/goat	Radius	30.9	28.8					
3	Sheep/goat	Radius			15.1				
3	Sheep/goat	Radius			15.1				
3	Sheep/goat	Radius			14.8				
3	Sheep/goat	Radius			13.8				
3	Sheep/goat	Radius			15.3				
3	Sheep/goat	Radius			15.5				
3	Sheep/goat	Radius			14				
4	Sheep/goat	Radius	27.7	24.3					

#	Species	Element					
4	Sheep/goat	Radius			12.5		
4	Sheep/goat	Radius			13		
4	Sheep/goat	Radius			16.7		
3	Pig	Radius	30				
3	Pig	Radius	27.8				
3	Pig	Radius	26		16.4	27–33.2	1
3	Pig	Radius	29.6				
4	Pig	Radius	31.1				
4	Pig	Radius	27.4				
4	Pig	Radius	26.7			27–33.2	0.3
4	Pig	Radius	36.1				
4	Pig	Radius	31.4				
4	Pig	Radius	27.3				
4	Pig	Radius	29				
4	Pig	Radius	25.8			27–33.2	1.2
3	*Lepus europaeus*	Radius	9.1				
3	*Lepus europaeus*	Radius	8.8	6.1			
4	*Lepus europaeus*	Radius	9.6	6.2			
			LA				
3	Cattle	Pelvis	67.8				
3	Cattle	Pelvis	61.5				
3	Cattle	Pelvis	72				
4	Cattle	Pelvis	60.9				
4	Cattle	Pelvis	55.2				
3	Sheep/goat	Pelvis	27.3				
3	Sheep/goat	Pelvis	27				
4	Sheep/goat	Pelvis	26.7				
4	Sheep/goat	Pelvis	27.8				
4	Sheep/goat	Pelvis	25.8				
4	Sheep/goat	Pelvis	26.4				

Pelvis

Period	Taxa	Element	Measurement	ABMAP range
4	Sheep/goat	Pelvis	24.3	
3	Pig	Pelvis	30	
3	Pig	Pelvis	31.9	
3	Pig	Pelvis	36.5	
3	Pig	Pelvis	38.6	
4	Pig	Pelvis	32.5	
4	Pig	Pelvis	32.5	
4	Pig	Pelvis	38	
4	Pig	Pelvis	33	
4	Pig	Pelvis	36.8	
3	*Lepus europaeus*	Pelvis	13.3	
4	*Lepus europaeus*	Pelvis	12.1	

Femur

Period	Taxa	Element	Bp	DC	SD	Bd	ABMAP range
3	Cattle	Femur			33.6		
4	Cattle	Femur	42				
4	Cattle	Femur			30.7		
4	Cattle	Femur			31.2		
3	Sheep/goat	Femur			12.2		
3	Sheep/goat	Femur				26.8	
3	Sheep/goat	Femur	45.1	19.5			35.6–44.8
4	Sheep/goat	Femur			17.2		
3	Pig	Femur			18.5		
3	Pig	Femur			18.2		
4	Pig	Femur			17.7		0.3

Tibia

Period	Taxa	Element	Bp	Dp	SD	Bd	Dd	ABMAP range
3	Cattle	Tibia			36.1	E59.9	45.7	
3	Cattle	Tibia				56.2	42.7	
3	Cattle	Tibia				55.2	38.6	39–56
3	Cattle	Tibia				E62.4	49.1	
3	Cattle	Tibia			64			0.4

3	Cattle	Tibia				62.8		
3	Cattle	Tibia				61.7	44.3	
3	Sheep/goat	Tibia				25.2	18	
3	Sheep/goat	Tibia			11.8	20.7	16.4	
3	Sheep/goat	Tibia				23.9	18.5	
3	Sheep/goat	Tibia				25.3	19.1	
3	Sheep/goat	Tibia				24.4	19	
3	Sheep/goat	Tibia				28.7	21.6	
3	Sheep/goat	Tibia				24.2	19.2	
3	Sheep/goat	Tibia	27.3			24.4	18.5	
3	Sheep/goat	Tibia				27.2	21.9	
3	Sheep/goat	Tibia				27.2	21.6	
3	Sheep/goat	Tibia				25.5	20.4	
3	Sheep/goat	Tibia				26.2	21	
3	Sheep/goat	Tibia				23	18.4	
3	Sheep/goat	Tibia				25.2	18.6	
3	Sheep/goat	Tibia				26.9	22	
3	Sheep/goat	Tibia				27.7	20	
3	Sheep/goat	Tibia				26.6	21.2	
3	Sheep/goat	Tibia				27.1	19.5	
3	Sheep/goat	Tibia				26.7	19.9	
4	Sheep/goat	Tibia				22.4		
4	Sheep/goat	Tibia				26.9		
4	Sheep/goat	Tibia		21.5		22.7	16.8	16–22.4
4	Sheep/goat	Tibia				23	26.8	
4	Sheep/goat	Tibia				27.4	19.1	
4	Sheep/goat	Tibia				26.3	20.4	
4	Sheep/goat	Tibia				26.8	20.5	
4	Sheep/goat	Tibia				26.7	20.8	
4	Sheep/goat	Tibia				26.9	21.3	
4	Sheep/goat	Tibia				23.1	18.2	

Period	Taxa	Element	Measurement			GL	GLM	ABMAP range
4	Sheep/goat	Tibia		25.5	20.4			
4	Sheep/goat	Tibia		21.6	17.1			
3	Sheep/goat	Tibia		25.9				
3	Sheep/goat	Tibia		23.4				
3	Sheep/goat	Tibia		25.5	19.4			
4	Sheep/goat	Tibia		26.2	21.2			
4	Sheep/goat	Tibia		E29.2	22.6			
4	Sheep/goat	Tibia	13.5	24.7	20			
3	Pig	Tibia	18.4					
3	Pig	Tibia		27.6	24.3			
3	Pig	Tibia	19.3		24.9			
3	Pig	Tibia		24.8	21.4			
3	Pig	Tibia		34.1	29			
4	Pig	Tibia		29	25.7			
4	Pig	Tibia						
4	Pig	Tibia	18.6					
3	Cattle	Astragalus				64.2	58.8	
3	Cattle	Astragalus				62.6	58.5	
3	Cattle	Astragalus				62.4	55.8	
3	Cattle	Astragalus				61.1	57.8	
3	Cattle	Astragalus				68.2	62.8	
3	Cattle	Astragalus				56.7	50.8	
3	Cattle	Astragalus				58.8	52.6	
3	Cattle	Astragalus				54.2		
3	Cattle	Astragalus				62	61.7	
3	Cattle	Astragalus				54.3	51	
4	Cattle	Astragalus				56		
4	Cattle	Astragalus				58.8		
4	Cattle	Astragalus				73.5	66.4	
4	Cattle	Astragalus				63	57.1	

			GL	GLM
4	Cattle	Astragalus	56.1	50.9
4	Cattle	Astragalus	64.8	57.1
4	Cattle	Astragalus	60.3	55.5
4	Cattle	Astragalus	69.6	63.9
4	Cattle	Astragalus	61.2	57.2
4	Sheep/goat	Astragalus	26.5	25.2
3	Sheep/goat	Astragalus	27.1	25.9
3	Sheep/goat	Astragalus	26.6	
3	Sheep/goat	Astragalus	23.9	23.3
4	Sheep/goat	Astragalus	28.7	
3	Pig	Astragalus	38.7	37
3	Pig	Astragalus	44.7	41
3	Pig	Astragalus	43.6	42.8
4	Pig	Astragalus	39.1	37.1
4	Pig	Astragalus	43.1	40.1
4	Pig	Astragalus	42	40
4	Pig	Astragalus	49.2	45.7

			GL	
3	Cattle	Calcaneum	114.7	
3	Cattle	Calcaneum	116.1	
3	Sheep/goat	Calcaneum	48	
3	Sheep/goat	Calcaneum	53.6	
4	Sheep/goat	Calcaneum	58.6	
3	Sheep/goat	Calcaneum	55.8	
4	Pig	Calcaneum	34.8	

			GL	Bp	Dp	SD	Bd		m	f
3	Cattle	Metacarpal	190	64.1	40.2	36.1	66.1			
3	Cattle	Metacarpal	182	45.8	29.7	23.8	48.9	24.7–41	0.9	
3	Cattle	Metacarpal		48.3	27.2		57.7			
3	Cattle	Metacarpal								

Period	Taxa	Element	Measurement				ABMAP range
3	Cattle	Metacarpal		54.4			
3	Cattle	Metacarpal					53
3	Cattle	Metacarpal					50.7
3	Cattle	Metacarpal					55
3	Cattle	Metacarpal	177	50.4	30.5	28	53
3	Cattle	Metacarpal		48.6			
3	Cattle	Metacarpal		53.5	33.2		
3	Cattle	Metacarpal					50.6
3	Cattle	Metacarpal					60.7
3	Cattle	Metacarpal					74.2
3	Cattle	Metacarpal		55.7	33.3		
3	Cattle	Metacarpal		61	36.2		
3	Cattle	Metacarpal		52.2	31.2		
3	Cattle	Metacarpal		57	34.4		
3	Cattle	Metacarpal		54	31.7		
3	Cattle	Metacarpal		54.2	33		
3	Cattle	Metacarpal					50.7
3	Cattle	Metacarpal		52.2	33.8		
3	Cattle	Metacarpal					
3	Cattle	Metacarpal					52.9
3	Cattle	Metacarpal					
4	Cattle	Metacarpal		54.2	33.5		
4	Cattle	Metacarpal					55.6
4	Cattle	Metacarpal		53.1	30.2		
4	Cattle	Metacarpal		51.2	33.2		
4	Cattle	Metacarpal					51.8
4	Cattle	Metacarpal					52.4
4	Cattle	Metacarpal		49.9			
4	Cattle	Metacarpal		58	33.8		
4	Cattle	Metacarpal			32.3		
4	Cattle	Metacarpal					53.6
4	Cattle	Metacarpal		49.5	30.1		

4	Cattle	Metacarpal		60.7	37.8				
4	Cattle	Metacarpal		52.5	33.5				
4	Cattle	Metacarpal		52.6	33.8				
4	Cattle	Metacarpal					64.4		
4	Cattle	Metacarpal					53.7		
4	Cattle	Metacarpal		53.1	33.3				
4	Cattle	Metacarpal		51.9	31.1				
4	Cattle	Metacarpal							
4	Cattle	Metacarpal		59.7	36.1				
4	Cattle	Metacarpal		51.3	30.1				
4	Cattle	Metacarpal		55	50.8				
4	Cattle	Metacarpal		53.2	33.9				
4	Cattle	Metacarpal					54.6		
4	Cattle	Metacarpal					56.7		
4	Cattle	Metacarpal					76.8	46–76	0.8
4	Cattle	Metacarpal					57.3		
4	Cattle	Metacarpal		54.2					
3	Sheep/goat	Metacarpal	115.8			11.8	21.6		
3	Sheep/goat	Metacarpal		19.9	14.7	11.1	21.7		
3	Sheep/goat	Metacarpal					26		
3	Sheep/goat	Metacarpal		20.2	15.4	11.4			
3	Sheep/goat	Metacarpal		20.4	15.4	11.5			
3	Sheep/goat	Metacarpal	124.7				22.6		
3	Sheep/goat	Metacarpal		21.7	15.1	13.2	25.5		
3	Sheep/goat	Metacarpal				11.4			
3	Sheep/goat	Metacarpal		19.4	14.9				
3	Sheep/goat	Metacarpal		21.4	15.5	13			
3	Sheep/goat	Metacarpal		23.3	16.2				
3	Sheep/goat	Metacarpal				15.3			
3	Sheep/goat	Metacarpal		21.3	15.5	13.8			
3	Sheep/goat	Metacarpal		22.5	16.3	13.6			
3	Sheep/goat	Metacarpal		22.3	17				

Period	Taxa	Element	Measurement					ABMAP range
			GL	Bp	Dp	SD	Bd	
3	Sheep/goat	Metacarpal		24.1	17.7			
3	Sheep/goat	Metacarpal		20.2	15.8			
3	Sheep/goat	Metacarpal				13		
3	Sheep/goat	Metacarpal		20.3	15.8	11.8		
3	Sheep/goat	Metacarpal		19.6	14.8	11.2		
3	Sheep/goat	Metacarpal		24.2	18.4	12.4		
3	Sheep/goat	Metacarpal				14.7	21.5	
3	Sheep/goat	Metacarpal				12.1	23.8	
4	Sheep/goat	Metacarpal					25.3	
4	Sheep/goat	Metacarpal					24.3	
4	Sheep/goat	Metacarpal	122.2	21.7	16.8	12.7	22.8	
4	Sheep/goat	Metacarpal	131.2	23.1	17.2	13.5	25	
4	Sheep/goat	Metacarpal	120.7	20.5	15.4	12	22	
4	Sheep/goat	Metacarpal		22.1	17.3	14.4		
4	Sheep/goat	Metacarpal		21.6	16.6			
4	Sheep/goat	Metacarpal		20.5	14.4	11.6		
4	Sheep/goat	Metacarpal		26.2	20.1		11.3	
4	Sheep/goat	Metacarpal				13.6		
4	Sheep/goat	Metacarpal				14.2		
4	Sheep/goat	Metacarpal		24.1	17		22.4	
4	Sheep/goat	Metacarpal		22.4	16.6			
4	Sheep/goat	Metacarpal		21.6	16.4			
4	Sheep/goat	Metacarpal		22.7	16			
4	Sheep/goat	Metacarpal		19.7	16			
4	Sheep/goat	Metacarpal		23	17.6			
4	Sheep/goat	Metacarpal		E22.8	17.2			
3	*Capreolus capreolus*	Metacarpal					21.5	
3	Horse	Metatarsal		48.8	40.4			.

No.	Species	Element	GL	Bp	Dp	SD	Bd	WH	(index)	Note
3	Cattle	Metatarsal	211	51.9	46.2	26.95	57.3			?
3	Cattle	Metatarsal					51.1			
3	Cattle	Metatarsal					47.2			
3	Cattle	Metatarsal		55.6	53.1		54.4	36.5–52.5	3.1	
3	Cattle	Metatarsal					49.3			
3	Cattle	Metatarsal					48.3			
3	Cattle	Metatarsal					51.7			
3	Cattle	Metatarsal		45.1	46.8					
3	Cattle	Metatarsal	204	44	43.4	22.2	47			f
3	Cattle	Metatarsal		43.2	38.2					
3	Cattle	Metatarsal		45.3	45.7					
3	Cattle	Metatarsal		46.3	46.2					
3	Cattle	Metatarsal					51			
3	Cattle	Metatarsal					63			
3	Cattle	Metatarsal		49.1	49.1					
3	Cattle	Metatarsal		47.5	43.5					
3	Cattle	Metatarsal					60.5			
3	Cattle	Metatarsal					59.5			
3	Cattle	Metatarsal		46.4	45.7					
3	Cattle	Metatarsal					47.8			
3	Cattle	Metatarsal					52.8			
3	Cattle	Metatarsal					50.2			
3	Cattle	Metatarsal		37.2	35.5			36.2–49.3	0.7	
4	Cattle	Metatarsal					52.2			
4	Cattle	Metatarsal					57.2			
4	Cattle	Metatarsal					56.9			
4	Cattle	Metatarsal					48.5			
4	Cattle	Metatarsal					49.6			
4	Cattle	Metatarsal					49.7			
4	Cattle	Metatarsal					47.1			

Period	Taxa	Element	Measurement			ABMAP range	
4	Cattle	Metatarsal			49.6		
4	Cattle	Metatarsal	41.7	41.6	48.4		
4	Cattle	Metatarsal			49.3		
4	Cattle	Metatarsal			52		
4	Cattle	Metatarsal			54.5		
4	Cattle	Metatarsal	49.4	44.2	48.2		
4	Cattle	Metatarsal			45.2		
4	Cattle	Metatarsal	44.8	44.5	49.1		
4	Cattle	Metatarsal			46.5		
4	Cattle	Metatarsal	52	54.1	49.3	36.2-49.3	4.8
4	Cattle	Metatarsal			49.3		
4	Cattle	Metatarsal			56.8		
4	Cattle	Metatarsal	45.4	44.1			
4	Cattle	Metatarsal	49.2	49.7	27.3		
4	Cattle	Metatarsal	53.4	53.3		36.5-52.5; 36.2-49.3	0.9; 4
4	Cattle	Metatarsal	46.5	44.2	48.5		
4	Cattle	Metatarsal	42.5	42			
4	Cattle	Metatarsal	55	52.2		36.5-52.5; 36.2-49.3	2.5; 2.9
4	Cattle	Metatarsal			62.5		
4	Cattle	Metatarsal		47.6			
4	Cattle	Metatarsal	E44.8	45.1			
4	Cattle	Metatarsal	43.3	41.4			
4	Cattle	Metatarsal			49		
4	Cattle	Metatarsal	46.3				
3	Sheep/goat	Metatarsal	18.1	19.2	11.4		
3	Sheep/goat	Metatarsal	19.7	20.2	10.8		

3	Sheep/goat	Metatarsal		19.5	19.5	10.5			
3	Sheep/goat	Metatarsal		21.5	22.3				
3	Sheep/goat	Metatarsal		19.9	20.4	9.9			
3	Sheep/goat	Metatarsal				11.4			
3	Sheep/goat	Metatarsal				12.4			
3	Sheep/goat	Metatarsal		18.9	19.8		22		
3	Sheep/goat	Metatarsal		18.5	19.5	9.8			
3	Sheep/goat	Metatarsal		18.4	19.7	9.8			
3	Sheep/goat	Metatarsal				9.8			
3	Sheep/goat	Metatarsal	143	21.9	22.1	12.3	25.3	15.7-22.1	0.1
3	Sheep/goat	Metatarsal					23.2		
4	Sheep/goat	Metatarsal	144.6	20	21.4	11	23.9		
4	Sheep/goat	Metatarsal	127.2	20.6	22.2	11.9	25.2		
4	Sheep/goat	Metatarsal	143.9	19.4	19.9	12.9	25		
4	Sheep/goat	Metatarsal		21.1	20.2	11.8			
4	Sheep/goat	Metatarsal		21.7	21.2	11.6			
4	Sheep/goat	Metatarsal		17.4					
4	Sheep/goat	Metatarsal		19.9	20.3	11.8			
4	Sheep/goat	Metatarsal		20	20.1	8.5			
4	Sheep/goat	Metatarsal		20	20				
4	Sheep/goat	Metatarsal		20.7					
4	Sheep/goat	Metatarsal		20.8	22.5	11.6		15.7-22.1	0.4
4	Sheep/goat	Metatarsal		25.7	20.7				
3	*Cervus elaphus*	Metatarsal					41		

TABLE 74. METRICAL DATA FOR MAMMALS: 'HOUSE 1' SEQUENCE

Period	Taxa	Element	Measurement type				
			GL	*Max*	*Min*	*SLC*	
4	Cattle	Horn core					
4	Cattle	Horn core	123	50.5	34.3		
				40.7	28		
			GL				
4	Pig	Lower M3	31.2				
4	Pig	Upper M3	29.5				
			GLP	*BG*	*LG*	*SLC*	
3	Cattle	Scapula	72.2	52	62.8	55.5	
3	Pig	Scapula	35.6				
4	Pig	Scapula				24.5	
3	*Capreolus capreolus*	Scapula	25.4	19.4	21	16.7	
3	*Capreolus capreolus*	Scapula	29	20.5	22.5		
			Bd	*BT*	*HT*	*Htc*	
3	Horse	Humerus	92	82.4	47.5	37.9	
4	Pig	Humerus	38.8		30.4	23	
4	Dog	Humerus	20.5	14.6	9.9	8.3	
4	Dog	Humerus		13.1			
4	Dog	Humerus			14	9.7	
4	Dog	Humerus	17.4	13.8	10	16.6	
3	*Capreolus capreolus*	Humerus	26.1		18.7	13.5	
			Bp	*BFp*	*SD*	*Bd*	*BFd*
3	Horse	Radius	e82.8	77.8	43.9	65.5	49.8
3	Cattle	Radius	e68.2	63.6			
3	Cattle	Radius					
3	Cattle	Radius					48.8

3	Cattle	Radius				70.5	49.2
3	Sheep/goat	Radius	30.9	27.9			
3	Sheep/goat	Radius				28.6	24.5
4	Sheep	Radius	28.6	26.3			
4	Sheep/goat	Radius				26.3	22
4	Sheep/goat	Radius					
3	Pig	Radius	28.8				
3	Pig	Radius	29.3				
3	*Lepus europaeus*	Radius	8.5		13		
			LA				
3	Cattle	Pelvis	58.3				
3	Sheep/goat	Pelvis	22.6				
3	Sheep/goat	Pelvis	24.5				
3	Pig	Pelvis	33.5				
4	Pig	Pelvis	39.6				
4	Pig	Pelvis	34.6				
			SD	*Bd*	*Dd*		
			SD				
4	Horse	Tibia		60.4	35.8		
4	Cattle	Tibia		49.7			
4	Sheep	Tibia		23.2	18		
3	Sheep/goat	Tibia		23.2			
3	Dog	Tibia	9.4	12.6	11.1		
4	Dog	Tibia	8.6				
4	Dog	Tibia	8.3				
4	Dog	Tibia					
			Gl	*GLM*			
3	Cattle	Astragalus	65.2				
3	Cattle	Astragalus	68.8	62.1e			
3	Cattle	Astragalus		59.6			

Period	Taxa	Element	GL	Bp	Dp	SD	Bd	Bf	b	a
3	Cattle	Astragalus	57.5							
3	Cattle	Astragalus	e70							
3	Sheep	Astragalus	24.7	23.8						
4	Sheep	Astragalus	25	24.1						
4	Pig	Astragalus	38.3							
4	Pig	Astragalus	36.9							
			GL							
4	*Lepus europaeus*	Calcaneus	31.9							
			GL	Bp	Dp	SD	Bd	Bf		
3	Cattle	Metacarpal					59.2	52		
3	Cattle	Metacarpal					43.6	42		
3	Cattle	Metacarpal					56.9	51.7		
3	Cattle	Metacarpal		50.9	32.3					
3	Cattle	Metacarpal		49.9	29.6					
3	Cattle	Metacarpal		54.8	32.9					
3	Cattle	Metacarpal					51	48.4		
3	Cattle	Metacarpal					59.7	e54		
4	Cattle	Metacarpal					55	50.3		
4	Cattle	Metacarpal		51.7	32.8					
3	Sheep/goat	Metacarpal		17.2	13.1					
3	Sheep/goat	Metacarpal		18.8	13.3					
3	Sheep/goat	Metacarpal		22	15.9					
3	Sheep/goat	Metacarpal		25.4	17.7					
4	Sheep/goat	Metacarpal				14.7				
4	Sheep/goat	Metacarpal					22.6	22.5		
4	Sheep/goat	Metacarpal				12.4				
4	Sheep/goat	Metacarpal		19.6	14.7					
3	Cattle	Metatarsal		38.5e	37.2e					
3	Cattle	Metatarsal		51.5			e56.5	51.5		

	Species	Element				
3	Cattle	Metatarsal			52.5	50
4	Cattle	Metatarsal			60.2	54.4
4	Cattle	Metatarsal			59.5	54.2
4	Cattle	Metatarsal			57.3	51
3	Sheep/goat	Metatarsal		11		
3	Sheep/goat	Metatarsal		11.4		
3	Sheep/goat	Metatarsal		11.2		
3	Sheep/goat	Metatarsal	18.9			
4	Sheep/goat	Metatarsal	19.2	10.1		

TABLE 75. METRICAL DATA FOR BIRDS

(a) South-east layers

Period	Taxa	Element	GL	Dic
			GL	*Dic*
3	Anas/Aythya spp.	Scapula		11.5
3	Anas/Aythya spp.	Scapula		10.8
3	Anas/Aythya spp.	Scapula		11.3
3	Galliform	Scapula		10.8
3	Galliform	Scapula		9.3
3	Galliform	Scapula		12.2
4	Galliform	Scapula		11.7
4	Galliform	Scapula		11.7
4	Galliform	Scapula		12.2
4	Galliform	Scapula	70.2	13.3
4	Galliform	Scapula		13
4	Scolopax rusticola	Scapula		8.2
4	Corvus corax	Scapula		17.1

Period	Taxa	Element	GL	Bb	Bf
			GL	*Bb*	*Bf*
3	Anas/Aythya spp.	Coracoid	53.5	50.7	
4	Anas/Aythya spp.	Coracoid	56.6	53.1	20.5
4	Columba spp.	Coracoid		33.8	
3	Galliform	Coracoid	47.2	45.4	10.7
3	Galliform	Coracoid	49.8	47.4	10.3
3	Galliform	Coracoid	42.9		
4	Galliform	Coracoid		51.2	
4	Galliform	Coracoid	54	51	11.4
4	Galliform	Coracoid	49.1	46.7	10.5
4	Galliform	Coracoid	49.1	46.2	10.8
4	Galliform	Coracoid	50	47.9	13.2
4	Galliform	Coracoid		45	
4	Galliform	Coracoid	54.8	53.7	12
4	Galliform	Coracoid	54.5	52.6	11.6

Period	Taxa	Element	GL	Bp	SC	Bd
			GL	*Bp*	*SC*	*Bd*
3	Anas/Aythya spp.	Humerus	92.7		7.7	14.8
3	Anas/Aythya spp.	Humerus				14.4
3	Anas/Aythya spp.	Humerus				13.5
3	Anser anser	Humerus			10.3	
4	Anser anser	Humerus				22.5
3	Galliform	Humerus		18.2		
3	Galliform	Humerus				14
3	Galliform	Humerus		17.5		
3	Galliform	Humerus				15.5
3	Galliform	Humerus	71.6	19.1	17.1	15.2
4	Galliform	Humerus	61.7	16.5	6.1	13.3
4	Galliform	Humerus				13.7
4	Galliform	Humerus	68.7		6.5	14.1
4	Galliform	Humerus	64.5	17	6.4	13.4
4	Galliform	Humerus			6.8	15.3

Period	Taxa	Element	Measurement			
4	Galliform	Humerus	75.8	21.6	7.3	16.6
4	Galliform	Humerus	63.9	17.3	5.8	13.6
4	Galliform	Humerus				15.9
4	Galliform	Humerus	66.3	18.2	6.8	14.4
4	Galliform	Humerus	72.6	19.4	7.2	15.5
4	Galliform	Humerus	72.6	19.2	7.7	15.6
3	Scolopax rusticola	Humerus			4.5	10.3
4	Corvus corax	Humerus	96.8	28.2	9.1	20.4
4	Corvus corax	Humerus			8.6	21.8
4	Corvus corax	Humerus			8.6	21.5
4	Corvus corax	Humerus				19
3	Corvidae spp.	Humerus	45.4	13.4	4.1	

Period	Taxa	Element	GL	Bp	Did
3	Anas/Aythya spp.	Carpometacarpus	56	12.2	6.9
3	Columba spp.	Carpometacarpus	33.1	9.7	5.8
3	Galliform	Carpometacarpus	37.3	12.2	7.2
3	Galliform	Carpometacarpus	37.2	10	7
3	Galliform	Carpometacarpus	32.6	9.4	6.4
4	Galliform	Carpometacarpus	32.3	9.5	6.2
4	Galliform	Carpometacarpus	40.5	11.2	8.1
4	Galliform	Carpometacarpus	34.4	10.5	6.7
4	Galliform	Carpometacarpus	38.9		7
4	Galliform	Carpometacarpus	35.8	10.7	6.5
4	Galliform	Carpometacarpus		10.5	
3	Scolopax rusticola	Carpometacarpus	35.1		
4	Scolopax rusticola	Carpometacarpus	37	8.5	4.5

Period	Taxa	Element	GL	SC	Dd
3	Anas/Aythya spp.	Tibiotarsus			8.8
4	Anser anser	Tibiotarsus		9.1	14.8
3	Galliform	Tibiotarsus			12.8
3	Galliform	Tibiotarsus			11.1
3	Galliform	Tibiotarsus		5.3	10.7
3	Galliform	Tibiotarsus			12.9
3	Galliform	Tibiotarsus			10.5
3	Galliform	Tibiotarsus			10.2
3	Galliform	Tibiotarsus			10.3
4	Galliform	Tibiotarsus			11.8
4	Galliform	Tibiotarsus			13.2
4	Galliform	Tibiotarsus			11.2
4	Galliform	Tibiotarsus	114.8	6.5	12.2
4	Galliform	Tibiotarsus			12.2

Period	Taxa	Element	GL	Bp	Dp/GLP	SC	Bd/LG	Dd
4	Anser anser	Femur				21	14.1	
3	Galliform	Femur					13.6	11.1
3	Galliform	Femur		13.7	11.3			
3	Galliform	Femur		15.3	10.6			

Period	Taxa	Element	Measurement						
3	Galliform	Femur						14.1	12.3
3	Galliform	Femur		13.4					
3	Galliform	Femur						14.6	14.2
3	Galliform	Femur						16.8	12.5
3	Galliform	Femur						13.7	10.6
4	Galliform	Femur						13.8	12
4	Galliform	Femur						12.8	12.2
4	Galliform	Femur		13.9	9.2				
4	Galliform	Femur	69.1	12.8	9.7	5.6		13.1	15.7
4	Galliform	Femur	80.4	16.5	12.8	6.9		15.7	15
4	Galliform	Femur	80.7	16.8	12.8	6.8		15.8	14.7
4	Galliform	Femur	67.8	14.1	10.1	5.7		12.9	12
4	Corvus corax	Femur	65.8	14.9		6.6		15	12.1
4	Corvus corax	Femur	66.6	15.1		6.4		15.1	11.8
			GL	*Bp*	*SC*	*Bd/LG*	*Spur*		
4	Anser spp.	Tarsometatarsus	91.4	19.8	8.9	19.2			
4	Anas/Aythya spp.	Tarsometatarsus	44	9.1	4.2	9.2			
4	Anas/Aythya spp.	Tarsometatarsus		8.9					
3	Galliform	Tarsometatarsus	69.8	11.1	5.5				
3	Galliform	Tarsometatarsus	67.9	11.6	5.5	11.5			
3	Galliform	Tarsometatarsus	71.5	13.6	6.7	13.4			
3	Galliform	Tarsometatarsus	56.5	11.3	4.8	10.1			
3	Galliform	Tarsometatarsus				10.1			
3	Galliform	Tarsometatarsus	82.2	14.1	7.1	13.6	23.3		
3	Galliform	Tarsometatarsus				10.6			
3	Galliform	Tarsometatarsus		13.3	6.3	12.2			
3	Galliform	Tarsometatarsus		10.7					
3	Galliform	Tarsometatarsus	63.9	11	5.2	10.3			
3	Galliform	Tarsometatarsus		11.2					
3	Galliform	Tarsometatarsus		11.5					
3	Galliform	Tarsometatarsus				11.2			
3	Galliform	Tarsometatarsus	69.2	10.5	5.7	11.7			
3	Galliform	Tarsometatarsus	61.5	10.8	5.4	10.5			
4	Galliform	Tarsometatarsus		13.3					
4	Galliform	Tarsometatarsus		11.3					
4	Galliform	Tarsometatarsus	68.4	11.7	5.4				
4	Galliform	Tarsometatarsus		13.4	16.9	14.1	20		
4	Galliform	Tarsometatarsus		10.5					
4	Galliform	Tarsometatarsus		11.3	6				
4	Galliform	Tarsometatarsus				10.9			
4	Galliform	Tarsometatarsus					24		
3	Galliform	Tarsometatarsus				10.7			
4	Galliform	Tarsometatarsus	74.3	13.8	6.6	13			
4	Galliform	Tarsometatarsus	66.4	12.2	6	11.9			
4	Galliform	Tarsometatarsus	76.8	12.5	6.1	11.6	11.5		
4	Galliform	Tarsometatarsus				12.5	23.7		
4	Galliform	Tarsometatarsus		13.6	17		22.2		
3	Scolopax rusticola	Tarsometatarsus		6.6					
4	Corvus corax	Tarsometatarsus			4.9	9.8			

(b). 'House 1' sequence

Phase	Taxa	Element	Measurement type				
			GL	*Dic*			
3	Galliform	Scapula	66.4	11.7			
			GL	*Bp*	*SC*	*Bd*	
2	Galliform	Humerus	72	19.9	7		
			GL	*Bp*	*Dip*	*SC*	*Did*
1	Galliform	Ulna	56.4	8.1	11.1	3.7	7.4
1	Galliform	Ulna					8.8
2	Galliform	Ulna		10.1			
			GL	*L*	*Bp*	*Did*	
1	Galliform	Carpometacarpus	33.2	30.6	10.8	6.4	
1	Galliform	Carpometacarpus	37.4				
2	Galliform	Carpometacarpus			7.9		
2	Galliform	Carpometacarpus				6.9	
			Bp	*Dp*	*SC*	*Bd*	*Dd*
1	Galliform	Femur	13.2	8.3			
1	Galliform	Femur				14.3	14.1
2	Galliform	Femur	13.6	10			
2	Galliform	Femur				13.6	11.8
2	Galliform	Femur			5.6		
2	Galliform	Femur	14.1	10.4			
			SC	*Dd*			
1	Galliform	Tibiotarsus		10.5			
1	Galliform	Tibiotarsus		9.6			
2	Galliform	Tibiotarsus	5.2				
			GL	*Bp*	*SC*	*Bd*	*Spur*
1	Galliform	Tarsometatarsus		11			
2	Galliform	Tarsometatarsus			5.5	10.5	
3	Galliform	Tarsometatarsus				11.6	
3	Galliform	Tarsometatarsus		11.5	6.2		16.4
3	Galliform	Tarsometatarsus	69.9	12.3	6.1	11.8	

APPENDIX 7

THE DOG ASSEMBLAGE

By Kate Clark

TABLE 76. DOG TOOTH WEAR

Mandibular

Period	Deposit	Canine	P1	P2	P3	P4	M1	M2	M3
3	Accumulation					0	0	0	
	Accumulation	2							
	Dump			0	0	0	1	0	
4	Pit								0
	Pit			0	0	0	0	0	
	Pit			0	0	0	0	0	
	Pit			0	0	0	0	0	
	Bldg make-up					1		1	
	Bldg make-up					2	2	2	
	Bldg make-up		0	0	0	1	1	0	
	Bldg make-up						0	0	
	Occupation			0	0	0	0	0	

Maxillary

Period	Deposit	Canine	P1	P2	P3	P4	M1	M2
3	Pit			0				0
	Accumulation			1				0
	Accumulation			0	0	0	0	0
	Accumulation							0
	Silt					0	2	
4	Pit			1	1	1	1	1
	Pit			0	0	0	0	0
	Pit					0	0	
	Bldg make-up					1	0	0
	Occupation					0		0

0 = unworn

1 = slight wear

2 = moderate wear

TABLE 77. DOG MEASUREMENTS: SKULL. PERIOD 3 OBJECT 500028 PIT 4835 (5867)

von den Driesch	Measurement	mm
1	Akrokranion-Prosthion	144.9
2	Condylobasal length	
7	Akrokranion-frontal midpoint	71.2
8	Nasion-prosthion	
9	Frontal midpoint-prosthion	
12	Snout length	61.5
15	Length cheektooth row	48.6
16	Length molar row	14.8
17	Length premolar row	36.6
19	Length carnassial alveolus	15
20	Length M1 (alveolus)	9.4
21	Length M2 (alveolus)	5.1
23	Greatest mastoid breadth	
25	Greatest breadth occipital condyles	
27	Greatest breadth foramen magnum	
29	Greatest breadth braincase	49.8
30	Zygomatic breadth	160.8
31	Breadth at postorbital constriction	31.6
32	Frontal breadth	37.5
33	Least breadth between orbits	27.7
34	Greatest palatal breadth	49.1
35	Least palatal breadth	24.5
36	Breadth at canine alveoli	27.1
37	Inner height orbit	25.1
39	Skull height	
40	Akrokranion-basion	

TABLE 78. DOG MEASUREMENTS: AXIAL AND APPENDICULAR. PERIOD 3 PITS

Object	Pit/Well	Context	Element	Side	Measurement	mm
44008	5039	4549	Metatarsal II	L	Greatest length	43.8
500035	5693	6300	Metatarsal IV	L	Greatest length	63.8
500028	4835	5835	Metacarpal II	R	Greatest length	37.4
			Metacarpal V	R	Greatest length	35.9
			Metatarsal II	L	Greatest length	42.5

TABLE 79. DOG MEASUREMENTS: SKULL. PERIOD 3 OBJECT 701

von den Driesch	Measurement	Accum 3469 mm	Accum 5698 mm	Accum 5698 mm
1	Akrokranion-Prosthion			175.7
2	Condylobasal length			
7	Akrokranion-frontal midpoint		69.1	77.4

von den Driesch	Measurement	Accum 3469 mm	Accum 5698 mm	Accum 5698 mm
8	Nasion-prosthion			80.2
9	Frontal midpoint-prosthion			95.6
12	Snout length			68.1
15	Length cheektooth row	57.4	50	52
16	Length molar row	19	14.2	15.9
17	Length premolar row	45	40	39.3
19	Length carnassial alveolus	15.8	15.6	16.8
20	Length M1 (alveolus)	10.6	4.4	10.6
21	Length M2 (alveolus)	6.8	3.3	5
23	Greatest mastoid breadth		50.7	
25	Greatest breadth occipital condyles			
27	Greatest breadth foramen magnum		17.3	
29	Greatest breadth braincase		50.2	
30	Zygomatic breadth			
31	Breadth at postorbital constriction		33.9	33.5
32	Frontal breadth		37.9	46.4
33	Least breadth between orbits		27.3	32.4
34	Greatest palatal breadth		52.9	56.7
35	Least palatal breadth		26.5	29.9
36	Breadth at canine alveoli			32.6
37	Inner height orbit		26.4	
39	Skull height		48.1	
40	Akrokranion-basion			

TABLE 80. DOG MEASUREMENTS: MANDIBLE. PERIOD 3 OBJECT 701

von den Driesch	Measurement	Accum 4309 mm	Dump 4254 mm	Accum 5698 mm	Accum 5698 mm	Accum 5698 mm	Accum 5698 mm
4	Condyle process to aboral border of canine		113.6	101.3	97.1	99.8	
5	Angular process to aboral border of canine		117.8	102.5	98	100.7	
6	Indent between condyle & angular process to aboral border canine		109.8	96.2	94	94.8	
7	Aboral M3-aboral canine alveolus		76	66.8	68	66	
8	Length cheektooth row M3-P1		66.9	62.3	66	62	
9	Length M3-P2		62.9	58.7	61.8	58.3	
10	Length molar row		33.9	31.5	34.8	31.1	
11	Length premolar row P1-P4		35		33.4	30.7	33.9
12	Length P2-P4		32.1		28.7	27.6	29.6
14	Length carnassial alveolus	21	20.7	18.6	20.9	18.8	
17	Thickness below M1	12.1	11.9	9.7	11.2	9.1	11.2
18	Height vertical ramus		49.7	44	42.9		
19	Height behind M1		24		19.5	19.5	
20	Height between P2 & P3		19.5		18	16.2	17.7

TABLE 81. DOG MEASUREMENTS: AXIAL AND APPENDICULAR. PERIOD 3 OBJECT 701

Deposit	Context	Element	Side	Measurement	mm
accum	6290	Humerus	L	Greatest length	131.6
				Greatest length to caput	128.3
				Proximal depth	30
				Min shaft diameter	9.6
				Distal breadth	25.8
		Humerus	R	Greatest length	131.1
				Greatest length to caput	128.5
				Proximal depth	28.2
				Min shaft diameter	9.4
				Distal breadth	25.3
		Metacarpal III	R	Greatest length	48.1
		Metacarpal IV	R	Greatest length	47.1
		Metacarpal V	R	Greatest length	38.6
		Metatarsal II	R	Greatest length	46.1
		Metatarsal III	R	Greatest length	52.5
		Metatarsal IV	L	Greatest length	55.1
		Metatarsal V	L	Greatest length	49
occup	4469	Metacarpal II	R	Greatest length	37.4
bldg m/u	3435	Metatarsal V	L	Greatest length	42.9
occup	3490	Metacarpal II	L	Greatest length	40

TABLE 82. DOG MEASUREMENTS: SKULL. PERIOD 4 PITS

von den Driesch	Measurement	Obj 500032 Pit 2601 2622 mm	Obj 5000031 Pit 2434 2774 mm	Obj 5000031 Pit 2434 2774 mm
15	Length cheektooth row	60.6		56
16	Length molar row	15.6		17
17	Length premolar row	47.2		41.9
19	Length carnassial alveolus	18.1		17.9
20	Length M1 (alveolus)	9.9		10.7
21	Length M2 (alveolus)	7.3		6.9
23	Greatest mastoid breadth	61.6		
25	Greatest breadth occipital condyles	35.1	30.7	
27	Greatest breadth foramen magnum	17.7	16.4	
29	Greatest breadth braincase	56.6	56.6	
30	Zygomatic breadth			
31	Breadth at postorbital constriction	38.8		
32	Frontal breadth	47.6		
33	Least breadth between orbits	33.1		

von den Driesch	Measurement	mm	mm	mm
34	Greatest palatal breadth			
35	Least palatal breadth			
36	Breadth at canine alveoli			
37	Inner height orbit			
39	Skull height			

TABLE 83. DOG MEASUREMENTS: MANDIBLE. PERIOD 4 PITS

von den Driesch	Measurement	Obj 500031 Pit 2434 2774 mm	Obj 500031 Pit 2434 2776 mm	Obj 500032 Pit 2601 2622 mm
1	Condylar process to infradentale			130.4
2	Angular process to infradentale			132.8
3	Indent between condyle & angular process to infradentale			127.8
4	Condyle process to aboral border of canine			111.7
5	Angular process to aboral border of canine			108.3
6	Indent between condyle & angular process to aboral border canine			113
7	Aboral M3-aboral canine alveolus	72.7		74
8	Length cheektooth row M3-P1	69.2	63.7	71.6
9	Length M3-P2	58.7	60	67.7
10	Length molar row	32.8	32.2	34.9
11	Length premolar row P1-P4	41.4	31.9	39
12	Length P2-P4	36.6	27.9	34.5
14	Length carnassial alveolus	20.5	18.6	20.1
17	Thickness below M1	9.9	9.5	11.4
18	Height vertical ramus			49
19	Height behind M1	17.7	19.8	21.1
20	Height between P2 & P3	16.2	15.4	17.9

TABLE 84. DOG MEASUREMENTS: AXIAL AND APPENDICULAR. PERIOD 4 PITS

Object	Pit/Well	Context	Element	Side	Measurement	mm
500032	2601	2622	Metatarsal II	L	Greatest length	57.1
			Metatarsal II	L	Greatest length	54.4
			Metatarsal III	L	Greatest length	64.1
			Metatarsal III	R	Greatest length	59.9
			Metatarsal IV	L	Greatest length	65.1
			Metatarsal V	L	Greatest length	56.1
			Metatarsal V	R	Greatest length	55
			Radius	R	Greatest length	147.5
					Proximal breadth	16.3
					Min shaft diameter	10
					Distal breadth	20.6
500031	2434	2774	Metatarsal III	L	Greatest length	63.8
			Metatarsal IV	L	Greatest length	66

Object	Pit/Well	Context	Element	Side	Measurement	mm
			Metatarsal V	L	Greatest length	56.8
			Humerus	L	Greatest length	146.8
					Greatest length to caput	143.8
					Proximal depth	35.9
					Min shaft diameter	10.6
					Distal breadth	29.7
		2776	Metatarsal II	L	Greatest length	43.6
			Metatarsal IV	L	Greatest length	50.6
			Metatarsal V	L	Greatest length	44.7
		2602	Metacarpal II	L	Greatest length	52.3
		2605	Metacarpal II	L	Greatest length	52
			Metacarpal IV	L	Greatest length	59.1
			Radius	L	Greatest length	145
					Proximal breadth	15.7
					Min shaft diameter	9.7
					Distal breadth	21
			Tibia	R	Greatest length	110.3
					Proximal breadth	26.8
					Proximal depth	28.8
					Min shaft diameter	11.4
					Distal breadth	18.2
					Distal depth	13.3
500070	1750	2767	Femur	L	Greatest length	138.3
					Depth caput	13.7
					Proximal breadth	27.1
					Min shaft diameter	9.1
					Distal breadth	22.7
			Tibia	L	Greatest length	132.1
					Proximal breadth	24.5
					Proximal depth	25.5
					Min shaft diameter	9.6
					Distal breadth	16.1
					Distal depth	11.1
500037	5735	6294	Metacarpal V	L	Greatest length	44.9
		6430	Metacarpal IV	R	Greatest length	55.9
500033	3406	3826	Humerus	R	Greatest length	97.1
					Greatest length to caput	93.1
					Proximal depth	26.4
					Min shaft diameter	8.2
					Distal breadth	21.5
500034	3827	3102	Metatarsal IV	R	Greatest length	51.6

TABLE 85. DOG MEASUREMENTS: MANDIBLE. PERIOD 4 OBJECT 700

von den Driesch	Measurement	Bldg m/u 3468 mm	Bldg m/u 3468 mm	Bldg m/u 3468 mm	Bldg m/u 2916 mm	Bldg m/u 2497 mm	Bldg m/u 3912 mm	Bldg m/u 3836 mm	Occup 3911 mm
1	Condylar process to infradentale								
2	Angular process to infradentale								
3	Indent between condyle & angular process to infradentale								
4	Condyle process to aboral border of canine								108.2
5	Angular process to aboral border of canine	105.8							103.1
6	Indent between condyle & angular process to aboral border canine								106.2
7	Aboral M3-aboral canine alveolus	74	73.2						70.6
8	Length cheektooth row M3-P1	71.2	66.4			62.7			67.6
9	Length M3-P2	67.1	64.1			58.2			62.7
10	Length molar row	35.8	33.1		31.5	30.4			32.1
11	Length premolar row P1-P4	39.1	36.8	31.8		33.2			36.2
12	Length P2-P4	33.9	32.7	28.2		28.9			31.4
14	Length carnassial alveolus	23.7	18.2		19.2	20.3		19.6	18.8
17	Thickness below M1	11	9.8	9.2	10	10.2	11.2	9.7	10.2
18	Height vertical ramus	47.4						43.1	45.2
19	Height behind M1	21.5	19.6		21.4	22.3	21.4	19.5	
20	Height between P2 & P3	19.4	17.7			18			14.8

TABLE 86. DOG MEASUREMENTS: AXIAL AND APPENDICULAR. PERIOD 4 OBJECT 700

Deposit	Context	Element	Side	Measurement	mm
occup	3849	Metacarpal II	L	Greatest length	41.6
bldg m/u	3468	Humerus	L	Greatest length	139.1
				Greatest length to caput	136.1
				Proximal depth	34.1
				Min shaft diameter	12.2
				Distal breadth	28.3
		Femur	R	Greatest length	119.6
				Depth caput	11.9
				Proximal breadth	24.1
				Min shaft diameter	9
				Distal breadth	21.9
		Metacarpal II	L	Greatest length	46.8
		Metacarpal II	L	Greatest length	40.1
		Metacarpal IV	L	Greatest length	38.5
		Metatarsal IV	R	Greatest length	45.7
	3836	Tibia	R	Greatest length	142.5
				Proximal breadth	27.5
				Min shaft diameter	10.8
				Distal breadth	18.3
				Distal depth	13.4
	3498	Metacarpal II	L	Greatest length	48.5
p/h	2670	Metacarpal II	R	Greatest length	46
		Metatarsal IV	R	Greatest length	56.3
	2651	Femur	R	Greatest length	146.4
				Min shaft diameter	11.8
				Distal breadth	26.7
	2658	Metatarsal II	R	Greatest length	48.9

TABLE 87. DOG: ESTIMATED SHOULDER HEIGHT

	height (cm)		height (cm)		height (cm)
Period 3		*Period 4*		Building make-up	30
Pit 5039	32	Pit 2601	44		
Pit 5693	45		49		36
Accumulation	37	Pit 2434	47		44
	42		35	Post-holes	35
Occupation	34	Pit 3102	36		40
	36	Pit 3406	31		45
Building make-up	34	Pit 5735	43		
		Well 1750	40		
		Occupation	37		

TABLE 88. DOG: CUT MARKS. PERIOD 3

Object	Deposit	Context	Element	Proximal	Mid shaft	Distal	Anterior	Post	Med	Lat	Dorsal	Ventral	Buccal	Lingual
44008	Pit 5039	4535	Tibia			★		★						
		4549	Metatarsal II	★					★					
500035	Pit 5693	6300	Tibia		★			★						
701	Occupation	4469	Femur		★				★					
		4277	Scapula						★			★		
	Dump	4308	Humerus			★	★		★					
		4308	Humerus		★		★			★				
		4254	Mandible						★					★
	Silt	4307	Mandible						★					★
	Accumulation	3225	Mandible										★	

TABLE 89. DOG: CUT MARKS. PERIOD 4

Object	Deposit	Context	Element	Proximal	Mid shaft	Distal	Anterior	Posterior	Medial	Lateral	Dorsal	Ventral	Buccal	Lingual
500033	Pit 3406	3829	Tibia			★	★							
		3826	Humerus	★	★				★	★				
500037	Well 5735	6436	Scapula							★	★			
700	Bldg make up	3468	Femur			★			★					
		3468	Femur	★					★					
		3468	Femur	★					★					
		3468	Humerus				★		★					
		3468	Humerus			★			★					
		3912	Humerus				★	★	★					
		3912	Humerus				★	★	★					
		3468	Mandible						★				★	
		3468	Mandible						★				★	
		3468	Mandible								★			
		2497	Mandible						★					★
		2916	Mandible						★					★
		3468	Radius				★	★						
		3468	Radius				★	★						
		3468	Radius		★			★						
		3469	Tibia				★	★						
		3468	Tibia	★					★					
		3444	Tibia			★			★					
		3424	Tibia	★					★					
		3424	Tibia	★					★					
		2916	Tibia	★					★					
		2916	Tibia		★			★			★			
		3912	Tibia		★		★							

Object	Deposit	Context	Element	Proximal	Mid shaft	Distal	Anterior	Posterior	Medial	Lateral	Dorsal	Ventral	Buccal	Lingual
		3912	Tibia		★		★			★				
	Levelling	2467	Maxilla							★				
	Occupation	3911	Mandible							★		★		
		3849	Mandible		★				★					
	Posthole	2658	Humerus		★				★					
	Posthole	2650	Tibia		★				★					

TABLE 90. DOG: CUT MARKS SUMMARY

Period	Deposit type	No. elements examined	No. elements cut	% cut
Limb bones & metapodia				
3	Pits	16	2	12.5
	Layers	29	3	10.3
4	Pits	45	2	4.4
	Layers	47	21	44.7
Mandibles				
3	Pits	1	0	0
	Layers	9	0	0
4	Pits	7	0	0
	Layers	15	7	47

TABLE 91. PERIOD 4 PIT 2601: COMPARATIVE DOG MEASUREMENTS

Skull von den Driesch	Measurement	Obj 500032 Pit 2601 2622 mm	Modern crossbred Staff terrier
15	Length cheektooth row	60.6	61.9
16	Length molar row	15.6	16.6
17	Length premolar row	47.2	49
19	Length carnassial alveolus	18.1	17.6
20	Length M1 (alveolus)	9.9	9.7
21	Length M2 (alveolus)	7.3	7.1
23	Greatest mastoid breadth	61.6	60.7
25	Greatest breadth occipital condyles	35.1	31.3
27	Greatest breadth foramen magnum	17.7	16.4
29	Greatest breadth braincase	56.6	57.3
31	Breadth at postorbital constriction	38.8	39.1
32	Frontal breadth	47.6	48.9
33	Least breadth between orbits	33.1	32.3
Mandible			
4	Condyle process to aboral border of canine	111.7	111.6
5	Angular process to aboral border of canine	113	107.7

von den Driesch	Measurement	mm	
6	Indent between condyle & angular process to aboral border canine	108.3	103.4
7	Aboral M3-aboral canine alveolus	74	73.5
8	Length cheektooth row M3-P1	71.6	70.7
9	Length M3-P2	67.7	66.4
10	Length molar row	34.9	33.7
11	Length premolar row P1-P4	39	38.3
12	Length P2-P4	34.5	34.3
14	Length carnassial alveolus	20.1	20.4
17	Thickness below M1	11.4	9.7
18	Height vertical ramus	49	49.8
19	Height behind M1	21.1	20.2
20	Height between P2 & P3	17.9	18.1

APPENDIX 8

THE MACROSCOPIC PLANT AND INVERTEBRATE REMAINS

By Mark Robinson

TABLE 92. PLANT TAXA IDENTIFIED FROM MID-ROMAN SILCHESTER, INSULA IX
(seeds unless stated)

		Means of preservation
Bryophyta indet. - stem with leaves	moss	w m
Pteridium aquilinum (L.) Kuhn - frond frags	bracken	w m
Ranunculus cf. *acris* L.	meadow buttercup	w
R. cf. *repens* L.	creeping buttercup	w
R. sardous Crantz	hairy buttercup	w
R. S. Ranunculus sp.	buttercup	c m
R. flammula L.	lesser spearwort	w
Thalictrum flavum L.	meadow-rue	w
Papaver somniferum L.	opium poppy	m
Papaver sp. (not *somniferum*)	poppy	m
Morus nigra L.	black mulberry	m
Ficus carica L.	fig	w m
Urtica dioica L.	stinging nettle	w m
U. urens L.	small nettle	w m
Juglans regia L.	walnut	w
Corylus avellana L.	hazel	w
Chenopodium rubrum L.	red goosefoot	w
C. polyspermum L.	many-seeded goosefoot	w
C. album L.	fat hen	w
Chenopodium sp.	goosefoot	c m
Atriplex sp.	orache	w m
Stellaria media gp.	chickweed	w m
S. graminea L.	stitchwort	c
Cerastium sp.	mouse-ear chickweed	w
Agrostemma githago L.	corn cockle	w m
Silene cf. *latifolia* Poir.	white campion	w
Polygonum aviculare agg.	knotgrass	w c m
Fallopia convolvulus (L.) Löv.	black bindweed	w c
Rumex S. Acetosella sp.	sheep's sorrel	w c m
R. crispus L.	curled dock	w
R. conglomeratus Mur.	sharp dock	w
R. obtusifolius L.	broad-leaved dock	w
Rumex sp. (not *Acetosella*)	dock	c m
Rumex sp. - stem	dock	w
Rumex sp.	dock	c m
Malva sp.	mallow	w

		Means of preservation
Viola S. *Melanium* sp.	pansy	w
Capsella bursa-pastoris (L.) Medik.	shepherd's purse	w
Coronopus squamatus (Forsk.) Asch.	swine cress	w
Brassica nigra L.	black mustard	w
Brassica or *Sinapis* sp.	mustard etc.	m
Raphanus raphanistrum L.	wild radish	w
Reseda luteola L.	weld	m
cf. *Anagallis arvensis* L.	pimpernel	w
Filipendula ulmaria (L.)	meadow sweet	w
Rubus cf. *idaeus* L.	raspberry	w
R. fruticosus agg.	blackberry	w c
Potentilla cf. *erecta* (L.) Raeusch.	tormentil	w m
Potentilla sp.	cinquefoil	m
Aphanes arvensis L.	parsley piert	w
Prunus spinosa L.	sloe	w
P. domestica L. ssp. *domestica*	plum	w
P. domestica L. ssp. *insititia* (L.) B.& L.	bullace, damson	w
P. domestica L.	plum etc.	w m
P. cf. *domestica*	plum etc.	m
P. cf. *avium* L.	cherry	m
Prunus sp.	sloe, plum etc.	m
Malus sp. - endocarp	apple	w
cf. *Pyrus* or *Malus* sp.	pear or apple	m
Vicia faba L.	field or Celtic bean	m
Vicia or *Lathyrus* sp.	vetch or tare	c
cf. *Vicia* or *Lathyrus* sp. - pod	vetch or tare	w
Lens culinaris L.	lentil	m
cf. *Lens culinaris* L.	lentil	m
Pisum sativum L.	pea	m
cf. *P. sativum* L.	pea	m
large legume indet.	pea, bean etc.	c m
cf. *Medicago lupulina* L.	black medick	c
cf. *Medicago* sp.	medick	m
Trifolium sp. - flower and calyx	clover	w
cf. *Trifolium* sp.	clover	c
small legume indet.	medick, clover etc.	m
Ilex aquifolium L. - leaf	holly	w
Buxus sempervirens L. - leaf	box	w
Vitis vinifera L.	grape	w m
Linum usitatissimum L.	flax	m
L. catharticum L.	fairy flax	w c
Coriandrum sativum L.	coriander	w m
cf. *C. sativum* L.	coriander	m
Oenanthe pimpinelloides gp.	water dropwort	w
Anethum graveolens L.	dill	w m
cf. *Anethum graveolens* L.	dill	w m
Conium maculatum L.	hemlock	w m
Apium graveolens L.	celery	w m
cf. *Ap. graveolens* L.	celery	w m
Daucus carota L.	(wild) carrot	w
Apiaceae indet.		m
Hyoscyamus niger L.	henbane	w
Lithospermum arvense L.	corn gromwell	m

		Means of preservation
Solanum nigrum L.	black nightshade	w
S. dulcamara L.	woody nightshade	w
cf. Solanaceae indet.	nightshade	m
Ballota nigra L.	black horehound	w
Lamium sp.	dead-nettle	w
Prunella vulgaris L.	selfheal	w c
Satureja hortensis L.	summer savory	m
Mentha cf. *aquatica* L.	water mint	w
Mentha sp.	mint	m
Lamiaceae indet.		m
Plantago major L.	great plantain	w
P. lanceolata L.	ribwort plantain	c
cf. *P. lanceolata* L.	ribwort plantain	m
Galium aparine L.	goosegrass	c m
Sambucus nigra L.	elder	w
Carduus sp.	thistle	w
cf. *Carduus* or *Cirsium* sp.	thistle	m
Centaurea nigra L.	knapweed	w c
Hypochoeris sp.	cat's ear	w
Leontodon sp.	hawkbit	w
Sonchus asper (L.) Hill	sow-thistle	w
Taraxacum sp.	dandelion	w
Leucanthemum vulgare Lam.	oxeye daisy	c
Asteraceae indet.		m
Juncus articulatus gp.	rush	w
J. effusus gp.	tussock rush	w
Luzula sp.	wood-rush	w
Eleocharis palustris (L.) R. & S. or *uniglumis* (Link) Schul.	spike-rush	w c
Carex sp.	sedge	w c m
Cyperaceae indet.	sedge etc.	c
Bromus cf. *secalinus* L.	rye brome	w m
Triticum spelta L. - grain	spelt wheat	c
T. spelta L. - spikelet	spelt wheat	w m
T. spelta L. - glume	spelt wheat	w c
T. cf. *spelta* L. - grain	spelt wheat	m
T. dicoccum Schübl. or *spelta* L. - grain	emmer or spelt wheat	c
T. dicoccum Schübl. or *spelta* L. - double grain spikelet	emmer or spelt wheat	m
T. dicoccum Schübl. or *spelta* L. - single grain spikelet	emmer or spelt wheat	m
T. dicoccum Schübl. or *spelta* L. - glume	emmer or spelt wheat	c
Triticum sp. - short grain	wheat	c
Triticum sp. - grain	wheat	m
Hordeum vulgare L. - hulled lateral grain	six-row hulled barley	c m
Hordeum sp. - hulled median grain	hulled barley	c
Hordeum sp. - hulled grain	hulled barley	c m
Hordeum sp. - grain	barley	c
Avena sp. - grain	oats	c m
cf. *Avena* sp. - grain	oats	c
cereal indet. - hulled grain		m
cereal indet. - grain		c m
cereal indet. - bran		w m
Poaceae indet.	grass	w c m
cf. fruit seed indet.		m
weed seed indet.		c m

	Means of preservation
leaf frag. indet.	m
plant stem indet.	m
wood frag. indet.	w c m
bud scale	w
leaf abscission pad	w

KEY: m mineralised, w waterlogged, c charred

TABLE 93. WATERLOGGED SEEDS FROM MID-ROMAN SILCHESTER, INSULA IX

	Sample	1715	1646	1581	386
	Context	6960	6436	6436	2778
		P4	P4	P4	P4
		well	well	well	well
		5735	5735	5735	1750
	Sample volume (litres)	18.5	5.0	17.5	6.0
Ranunculus cf. *acris*	meadow buttercup	2	4	-	2
R. cf. *repens* L.	creeping buttercup	4	15	5	9
R. sardous Crantz	hairy buttercup	-	2	-	-
R. S. Ranunculus sp.	buttercup	3	16	5	7
R. flammula L.	lesser spearwort	1	4	1	2
Thalictrum flavum L.	meadow rue	-	3	-	5
Ficus carica L.	fig	-	5	7	-
Urtica dioica L.	stinging nettle	47	26	120	-
U. urens L.	small nettle	75	35	1	1
Juglans regia L.	walnut	-	1	-	-
Corylus avellana L.	hazel	-	1	-	1
Chenopodium rubrum L.	red goosefoot	2	4	-	2
C. polyspermum L.	many-seeded goosefoot	2	-	2	-
C. album L.	fat hen	-	12	1	86
Atriplex sp.	orache	1	14	5	14
Stellaria media gp.	chickweed	174	61	1	12
S. graminea L.	lesser stitchwort	-	2	1	-
Cerastium sp.	mouse-ear chickweed	1	1	-	-
Agrostemma githago L.	corn cockle	-	1	-	-
Silene cf. *latifolia* Poir	white campion	-	1	-	2
Polygonum aviculare agg.	knotgrass	3	17	2	10
Fallopia convolvulus (L.) Löv.	black bindweed	-	-	-	1
Rumex S. Acetosella sp.	sheep's sorrel	4	10	2	3
R. crispus L.	curled dock	-	3	-	-
R. conglomeratus Mur.	sharp dock	-	-	1	-
R. obtusifolius L.	broad-leaved dock	-	41	1	4
Rumex sp. (not *Acetosella*)	dock	3	61	27	8
Malvaceae indet.	mallow	-	1	-	-
Viola S. Melanium sp.	wild pansy	-	1	-	-
Capsella bursa-pastoris (L.) Medik.	shepherd's purse	3	1	-	-
Coronopus squamatus (Forsk.) Asch.	swine cress	-	1	-	-
Brassica nigra (L.) Koch	black mustard	4	2	-	-
Raphanus raphanistrum L.	wild radish	-	-	-	1
cf. *Anagallis arvensis* L.	pimpernel	1	-	-	-
Filipendula ulmaria (L.)	meadow sweet	1	2	-	-
Rubus fruticosus agg.	blackberry	1	9	29	2
Potentilla cf. *erecta* (L.) Raeusch	tormentil	-	13	-	10

		Sample	1715	1646	1581	386
		Context	6960	6436	6436	2778
			P4	P4	P4	P4
			well	well	well	well
			5735	5735	5735	1750
		Sample volume (litres)	18.5	5.0	17.5	6.0
Agrimonia eupatoria L.	agrimony		-	-	-	1
Aphanes arvensis L.	parsley piert		-	2	-	-
Prunus domestica L. ssp. *domestica*	plum		-	1	-	-
P. domestica L. ssp. *insititia* (L.) B. & L.	bullace, damson		-	1	-	-
P. domestica L.	plum etc.		-	1	-	-
Vitis vinifera L.	grape		-	1	-	-
Linum catharticum L.	fairy flax		-	2	-	-
Coriandrum sativum L.	coriander		-	1	-	1
Oenanthe pimpinelloides gp.	water dropwort		-	-	1	-
Anethum graveolens L.	dill		-	5	-	-
cf. *Anethum graveolens* L.	dill		-	6	-	-
Conium maculatum L.	hemlock		2	10	2	1
Apium graveolens L.	celery		1	1	-	-
cf. *Apium graveolens* L.	celery		1	1	-	-
Daucus carota L.	(wild) carrot		1	1	-	1
Hyoscyamus niger L.	henbane		1	2	11	-
Solanum nigrum L.	black nightshade		-	10	1	-
S. cf. *dulcamara* L.	woody nightshade		-	1	-	-
Ballota nigra L.	black horehound		-	1	34	-
Lamium sp.	dead-nettle		1	2	3	-
Prunella vulgaris L.	selfheal		2	8	-	-
Mentha cf. *aquatica* L.	water mint		-	3	2	-
Plantago major L.	great plantain		-	1	-	-
Sambucus nigra L.	elder		3	20	128	2
Carduus sp.	thistle		1	-	-	-
Centaurea nigra L.	knapweed		-	1	-	-
Hypochoeris sp.	cat's ear		2	4	-	-
Leontodon sp.	hawkbit		-	1	-	1
Sonchus asper (L.) Hill	sow-thistle		1	5	-	-
Taraxacum sp.	dandelion		-	-	1	-
Juncus articulatus gp.	rush		1	20	60	-
J. effusus gp.	tussock rush		-	-	20	-
Luzula sp.	woodrush		1	-	-	-
Eleocharis palustris (L.) R. & S. or *uniglumis* (Link) Schul.	spike-rush		5	31	10	7
Carex sp.	sedge		3	53	16	4
Bromus cf. *secalinus* L.	rye brome		1	-	-	-
cereal indet. - bran			+	+	-	-
Poaceae indet.	grain		7	11	-	-
Total			366	577	500	200

Key: + present

TABLE 94. OTHER WATERLOGGED PLANT REMAINS FROM MID-ROMAN SILCHESTER, INSULA IX

		Sample	1715	1646	1581	386
		Context	6960	6436	6436	2778
			P4	P4	P4	P4
			well	well	well	well
			5735	5735	5735	1750
		Sample volume (litres)	18.5	5.0	17.5	6.0
Bryophyta indet. - stem with leaves	moss		+	+	-	+
Pteridium aquilinum (L.) Kuhn - frond fragment	bracken		-	13	-	-
Rumex sp. - stem	dock		-	1	-	1
Malus sp. - endocarp (core)	apple		-	2	-	2
cf. *Vicia* or *Lathyrus* sp. - pod	vetch or tare		1	2	-	-
Trifolium sp. - flower	clover		1	10	-	-
Trifolium sp. - calyx	clover		-	3	-	-
Ilex aquifolium L. - leaf frag.	holly		1	-	-	-
Buxus sempervirens L. - leaf frag.	box		1	-	-	-
bud scales			13	4	-	16
leaf abscission pad			-	1	1	-
Triticum spelta L. - spikelet	spelt wheat		-	1	-	-
T. spelta L. - glume	spelt wheat		-	3	-	-

Key: + present

TABLE 95. COLEOPTERA FROM MID-ROMAN SILCHESTER, INSULA IX

	Minimum number of individuals		
Sample	1715	1646	
Context	6960	6436	
	P4	P4	
	well	well	
	5735	5735	
Sample volume (litres)	18.5	5.0	Species Group
Nebria brevicollis (F.)	1	-	
Notiophilus sp.	1	-	
Trechus obtusus Er. or *quadristriatus* (Schr.)	2	1	
Bembidion tetracolum Say	1	-	
Pterostichus longicollis (Duft.)	1	-	
P. melanarius (Ill.)	2	1	
P. cupreus (L.) or *versicolor* (Sturm)	-	2	
Synuchus nivalis (Pz.)	-	1	
Agonum dorsale (Pont.)	-	1	6a
Amara bifrons (Gyl.)	1	-	6b
Amara sp.	1	1	
Harpalus S. *Ophonus* sp.	1	-	
Agabus bipustulatus (L.)	-	1	1
Helophorus aquaticus or *grandis* Ill.	-	1	1
Helophorus sp. (*brevipalpis* size)	-	1	1
Sphaeridium bipustulatum F.	1	-	
Cercyon analis (Pk.)	1	-	7

	Minimum number of individuals		
Sample	1715	1646	
Context	6960	6436	
	P4	P4	
	well	well	
	5735	5735	
Sample volume (litres)	18.5	5.0	Species Group
C. haemorrhoidalis (F.)	1	1	7
C. pygmaeus (L.)	1	-	7
C. unipunctatus (L.)	-	1	7
Megasternum obscurum (Marsh.)	2	1	7
Ochthebius sp.	3	-	1
Choleva or *Catops* sp.	1	-	
Lesteva longoelytrata (Gz.)	6	2	
Anotylus rugosus (F.)	1	1	7
A. sculpturatus gp.	-	1	7
Stenus cf. *comma* LeCon.	1	-	
Stenus sp. (not *comma*)	1	-	
Gyrohypnus fracticornis (Müll.) or *punctulatus* (Pk.)	1	-	
Xantholinus linearis (Ol.)	-	1	
Philonthus sp.	2	1	
Tachinus sp.	2	-	
Aleocharinae indet.	1	2	
Aphodius contaminatus (Hbst.)	-	1	2
A. cf. *foetens* (F.)	-	1	2
A. granarius (L.)	2	4	2
A. cf. *sphacelatus* (Pz.)	1	1	2
Aphodius spp.	1	1	2
Oxyomus sylvestris (Scop.)	-	1	
Onthophagus sp. (not *ovatus*)	-	1	2
Athous haemorrhoidalis (F.)	-	1	11
Anobium punctatum (Deg.)	5	4	10
Tipnus unicolor (P. & M.)	1	-	9a
Ptinus fur (L.)	2	3	9a
Lyctus linearis (Gz.)	-	1	10
Brachypterus urticae (F.)	2	-	
Atomaria sp.	-	1	
Lathridius minutus sp.	-	1	8
Enicmus transversus (Ol.)	1	-	8
Corticariinae indet.	1	-	8
Phyllotreta nigripes (F.)	-	2	
Longitarsus sp.	1	-	
Chaetocnema concinna (Marsh.)	1	1	
Chaetocnema sp. (not *concinna*)	1	-	
Apion sp.	1	1	3
Barynotus sp.	-	1	
Ceuthorhynchidius horridus (Pz.)	-	1	
Ceuthorhynchinae indet.	1	-	
Total	57	48	

TABLE 96. OTHER INSECTS FROM MID-ROMAN SILCHESTER, INSULA IX

	Minimum number of individuals	
Sample	1715	1646
Context	6960	6436
	P4	P4
	well	well
	5735	5735
	18.5	5.0
Sample volume (litres)		
Forficula auricularia L.	-	1
Aphrodes bicinctus (Schr.)	-	1
Aphidoidea indet.	-	1
Homoptera indet.	1	-
Apis mellifera L. - worker	-	2
Musca domestica L. - puparium	-	1
Stomoxys calcitrans (L.) - puparium	-	1
Diptera indet. - puparium	5	19

TABLE 97. CHARRED PLANT REMAINS FROM MID-ROMAN SILCHESTER, INSULA IX

		Sample	856	324	643	847
		Context	5324	2320	4041	5545
			P2	P3	P4	P2
			pit	well	pit	layer
			5251	2234	3406	
		Sample volume (litres)	10	6	18	29
CEREAL GRAIN						
Triticum spelta L.	spelt wheat		2	-	-	1
T. dicoccum Schübl. or *spelta* L.	emmer or spelt wheat		1	-	-	-
Triticum sp. - short grain	wheat		1	-	-	2
Triticum sp.	wheat		1	-	-	-
Hordeum vulgare L. - hulled lateral	six-row hulled barley		-	1	-	1
Hordeum sp. - hulled median	hulled barley		-	-	-	1
Hordeum sp. - hulled	hulled barley		3	-	-	-
Hordeum sp.	barley		-	-	-	3
cereal indet.			12	-	-	4
Total cereal grain			20	1	0	12
CEREAL CHAFF						
Triticum spelta L. - glume	spelt wheat		-	6	-	-
T. dicoccum Schübl. or *spelta* L. - glumes	emmer or spelt wheat		-	5	-	-
cereal culm node			-	4	-	-
Total cereal chaff			0	15	0	0

		856	324	643	847
Sample		856	324	643	847
Context		5324	2320	4041	5545
		P2	P3	P4	P2
		pit	well	pit	layer
		5251	2234	3406	
Sample volume (litres)		10	6	18	29

WEED SEEDS					
Ranunculus sect. *Ranunculus* sp.	buttercup	-	6	-	-
Stellaria graminea L.	lesser stitchwort	-	-	-	1
Rumex S. *Acetosella* sp.	sheep's sorrel	-	1	-	-
Rumex sp. (not *Acetosella*)	dock	4	3	-	2
cf. *Medicago lupulina* L.	black medick	1	-	-	-
cf. *Trifolium* sp.	clover	-	2	6	-
Linum catharticum L.	fairy flax	-	1	-	-
Prunella vulgaris L.	selfheal	-	1	-	-
Galium aparine L.	goosegrass	-	-	1	-
Leucanthemum vulgare Lam.	ox-eye daisy	-	-	1	-
Eleocharis palustris (L.) R.&S. or *uniglumis* (Link) Schul.	spike rush	5	3	-	6
Carex sp.	sedge	-	10	2	-
Cyperaceae indet.	sedge etc.	-	3	-	18
Poaceae indet.	grass	2	2	-	4
Weed seeds indet.		3	7	10	12
Total weed seeds		15	39	20	43
No. of items per litre		3.50	9.17	1.11	1.90

TABLE 98. MINERALISED PLANT REMAINS FROM MID-ROMAN SILCHESTER, INSULA IX
(seeds unless stated)

		857	855.3	852.3	792	804
Sample		857	855.3	852.3	792	804
Context		5276	5276	5276	5276	5303
		P2	P2	P2	P2	P2
		pit	pit	pit	pit	pit
		5251	5251	5251	5251	5251
Sample volume (litres)		4	1	1	4	19

Bryophyta indet. - stem with leaves	moss	-	-	-	1	-
Pteridium aquilinum (L.) Kuhn - frond fragment	bracken	1	-	-	1	-
Ranunculus S. *Ranunculus* sp.	buttercup	2	1	-	6	-
Papaver somniferum L.	opium poppy	-	2	-	3	1
Papaver sp.	poppy	-	1	-	1	-
Morus nigra L.	black mulberry	-	-	-	14	-
Ficus carica L.	fig	55	9	2	84	-
Urtica dioica L.	stinging nettle	-	1	-	2	29
U. urens L.	small nettle	4	1	-	5	2
Chenopodium sp.	goosefoot etc.	1	-	-	2	2
Atriplex sp.	orache	-	1	-	1	-

		Sample	857	855.3	852.3	792	804
		Context	5276	5276	5276	5276	5303
			P2	P2	P2	P2	P2
			pit	pit	pit	pit	pit
			5251	5251	5251	5251	5251
		Sample volume (litres)	4	1	1	4	19
Chenopodiaceae indet.		goosefoot etc.	-	3	-	4	-
Stellaria media gp.		chickweed	1	-	-	-	-
Agrostemma githago L.		corn cockle	1	-	-	-	-
Polygonum aviculare agg.		knotgrass	-	-	2	-	1
Rumex S. *Acetosella* sp.		sheep's sorrel	-	-	-	-	1
Rumex sp. (not *Acetosella*)		dock	-	-	-	-	8
Rumex sp.		dock	4	2	-	14	-
Brassica or *Sinapis* sp.		mustard etc.	2	-	-	-	-
Reseda luteola L.		weld	-	1	-	-	-
Rubus fruticosus agg.		blackberry	4	3	2	18	-
cf. *R. fruticosus* agg.		blackberry	17	6	2	27	-
Potentilla sp.		cinquefoil	-	-	-	1	1
Prunus domestica L.		plum etc.	-	-	-	1	-
P. cf. *domestica* L.		plum etc.	-	-	-	1	-
P. cf. *avium* (L.) L.		cherry	1	-	-	-	-
Prunus sp.		small plum etc.	46	6	5	70	1
cf. *Pyrus* or *Malus* sp.		pear or apple	-	-	1	2	-
Vicia faba L.		field or Celtic bean	-	-	-	1	-
Lens culinaris L.		lentil	1	-	-	1	-
cf. *Lens culinaris* L.		lentil	1	-	-	-	-
Pisum sativum L.		pea	6	-	-	1	-
cf. *Pisum sativum* L.		pea	56	-	-	3	-
cf. *Medicago* sp.		medick	1	-	-	-	-
small legume etc		medick, clover etc.	-	1	-	-	-
Vitis vinifera L.		grape	3	-	-	2	-
Linum usitatissimum L.		flax	-	1	-	-	-
Coriandrum sativum L.		coriander	6	-	-	2	-
cf. *C. sativum* L.		coriander	4	1	-	6	-
Anethum graveolens L.		dill	5	-	-	8	-
cf. *Anethum graveolens* L.		dill	23	3	-	7	-
Conium maculatum L.		hemlock	1	1	-	3	1
Apium graveolens L.		celery	1	2	-	1	-
cf. *A. graveolens* L.		celery	1	5	1	14	-
Apiaceae indet.			104	18	5	42	-
cf. Solanaceae indet.		nightshade	-	-	-	1	-
Lithospermum arvense L.		corn gromwell	-	1	-	-	-
Galium aparine L.		goosegrass	2	-	-	-	-
Prunella vulgaris L.		selfheal	-	-	-	1	-
Satureja hortensis L.		summer savory	-	-	-	1	-
Mentha sp.		mint	-	-	-	3	-
Lamiaceae indet.			-	1	-	-	-
cf. *Plantago lanceolata* L.		ribwort plantain	-	-	-	1	-
cf. *Carduus* or *Cirsium* sp.		thistle	32	4	3	32	-
Asteraceae indet.			-	-	-	-	1
Carex sp.		sedge	1	1	2	2	1
Bromus cf. *secalinus* L.		rye brome	2	-	1	-	-
Triticum spelta L. - spikelet		spelt wheat	2	-	1	-	-

		Sample	857	855.3	852.3	792	804
		Context	5276	5276	5276	5276	5303
			P2	P2	P2	P2	P2
			pit	pit	pit	pit	pit
			5251	5251	5251	5251	5251
		Sample volume (litres)	4	1	1	4	19
T. cf. *spelta* L.		spelt wheat	4	-	-	-	-
T. dicoccum Schübl. or *spelta* L. - double grain spikelet		emmer or spelt wheat	2	-	-	1	-
T. dicoccum Schübl. or *spelta* L. - single grain spikelet		emmer or spelt wheat	-	-	-	2	-
Triticum sp.		wheat	5	-	-	-	-
Hordeum vulgare L. - hulled lateral grain		six-row hulled barley	1	-	-	-	-
Hordeum sp. - hulled grain		hulled barley	1	-	-	-	-
Avena sp. - hulled grain		oats	1	-	-	-	-
cereal indet. - hulled grain			56	-	-	-	-
cereal indet.			21	-	2	3	-
cereal bran			+	+	-	+	-
Poaceae indet.		grass	2	5	-	9	1
cf. fruit seed / peas etc indet.			311	14	4	84	-
cf. weed seeds indet.			49	22	10	58	94
plant stem indet.			+	+	-	+	-
wood frag. indet.			+	+	-	-	-
Total number of quantified items			844	117	43	547	144

+ present

TABLE 99. MINERALISED INSECT AND OTHER ARTHROPOD REMAINS FROM MID-ROMAN SILCHESTER, INSULA IX
(adult unless stated)

			Minimum number of individuals				
		Sample	857	855.3	852.3	792	804
		Context	5276	5276	5276	5276	5303
			P2	P2	P2	P2	P2
			pit	pit	pit	pit	pit
			5251	5251	5251	5251	5251
INSECTS - Diptera (flies)							
Psychoda alternata Say	- pupa	trickling filter fly	2	6	-	20	-
Sphaeroceridae indet.	- puparium	sewage fly	5	3	-	5	5
Fannia sp.	- puparium	latrine fly	20	1	-	3	-
Diptera indet.	- puparium		9	6	2	12	13
OTHER ARTHROPODS							
Diploda indet.		millepede	2	1	-	11	-
Isopoda indet.		woodlouse	1	1	-	4	-
Total number of individuals			39	18	2	55	18

TABLE 100. WATERLOGGED SEEDS FROM THE MID-ROMAN LATRINES,
SILCHESTER, INSULA IX

	Sample	857	855.3	852.3	792
	Context	5276	5276	5276	5276
		P2	P2	P2	P2
		pit	pit	pit	pit
		5251	5251	5251	5251
Rubus cf. *idaeus* L.	raspberry	2	-	-	-
R. fruticosus agg.	blackberry	1511	186	2	179
Prunus spinosa L.	sloe	1	-	-	-
P. domestica cf. ssp. *domestica* L.	plum	1	-	-	-
P. domestica L. cf. ssp. *insititia* L.	bullace, damson	8	-	-	-
P. cf. *domestica* L.	plum etc.	5	1	-	1
Prunus sp.	plum etc.	17	3	-	5
Conium maculatum L.	hemlock	1	-	-	-
Sambucus nigra L.	elderberry	3	1	-	5
Juncus sp.	rush	1	3	-	2

BIBLIOGRAPHY

Adam, J.P. 1994: *Roman Building*, translated A. Mathews, London

Alexander, J. and Pullinger, J. 1999: *Roman Cambridge, Excavations on Castle Hill 1956–1988, Proceedings of the Cambridge Antiquarian Society* 88, Cambridge

Allen, D. 2002: 'Roman window glass', in M. Aldhouse-Green and P. Webster (eds), *Artefacts and Archaeology. Aspects of the Celtic and Roman World*, Cardiff, 102–11

Allen, D. 2007: 'The glass', in Clarke *et al.* 2007, http://intarch.ac.uk/journal/issue21/4/finds_glass.htm

Allen, D. and Price, J. 2000: 'The glass', in Fulford and Timby 2000, 312–21

Allen, J.R.L. 1987: 'Interpretation of some Romano-British smithing slag from Awre in Gloucestershire', *Journal of the Historical Metallurgy Society* 20 (2), 97–105

Allen, J.R.L. 2006: 'The slag basins', in Fulford *et al.* 2006, 160–3

Allen, J.R.L. 2008: 'Romano-British iron-making on the Severn Estuary Levels: toward a metallurgical landscape', *Archaeology in the Severn Estuary* 19, 71–119

Allen, J.R.L. 2009: 'The geology of early Roman mosaics and opus sectile in southernmost Britain: a summary', *Mosaic* 36, 5–10

Allen, J.R.L. and Fulford, M.G. 1987: 'Romano-British settlement and industry on the Wetlands of the Severn Estuary', *Antiquaries Journal* 67, 237–89

Allen, J.R.L. and Fulford, M.G. 2004: 'Early Roman mosaic materials in southern Britain with particular reference to Silchester (*Calleva Atrebatum*): a regional geological perspective', *Britannia* 35, 9–38

Allen, J.R.L, Fulford, M.G. and Todd, J.A. 2007: 'Burnt Kimmeridgian shale at early Roman Silchester, south-east England, and the Roman Poole-Purbeck complex-agglomerated geomaterials industry', *Oxford Journal of Archaeology* 26 (2), 167–91

Amsden, A.F. and Boon, G.C. 1975: 'C.O. Waterhouse's list of insects from Silchester (with a note on early identifications of insects in archaeological contexts)', *Journal of Archaeological Science* 2, 129–36

Andersen, S.T. 1979: 'Identification of wild grass and cereal pollen', *Danmarks Geologiske Undersøgelse Arbok* 1978, 69–92

Anderson, A.S., Wacher, J.S. and Fitzpatrick, A.P. 2001: *The Romano-British 'Small Town' at Wanborough, Wiltshire: Excavations 1966–1976*, Britannia Monograph 19, London

Annelay, G. 2008: *Liss Roman Villa, Liss Hampshire*, Liss Archaeological Group

Arkell, W.J. 1933: *Jurassic System in Great Britain*, Oxford

Arkell, W.J. 1947: *The Geology of the Country around Weymouth, Swanage, Corfe & Lulworth*, Memoir of the Geological Survey of Great Britain, Sheets 341, 342, 343 with small portions of 327, 328 and 329 (England and Wales), London

Armitage, P., West, B. and Steedman, K. 1984: 'New evidence of black rat in Roman London', *London Archaeologist* 4 (14), 375–83

Ashdown, R. and Evans, C. 1981: 'Mammalian bones', in C. Partridge (ed.), *Skeleton Green: a Late Iron Age and Romano-British Site*, Britannia Monograph 2, London, 205–35

Aston, M. and Gerrard, C. 1999: '"Unique, traditional and charming": the Shapwick project, Somerset', *Antiquaries Journal* 79, 1–58

Aston, M., Martin, M.H. and Jackson, A.W. 1998a: 'The use of heavy metal soil analysis for archaeological surveying', *Chemosphere* 37 (3), 465–77

Aston, M., Martin, M.H. and Jackson, A.W. 1998b: 'The potential for heavy metal soil analysis on low status archaeological sites at Shapwick, Somerset', *Antiquity* 72, 838–47

Atkinson, D. 1914: 'A hoard of Samian ware from Pompeii', *Journal of Roman Studies* 4, 27–64

Atkinson, R.J.C. 1941: 'A Romano-British potters' field at Cowley, Oxon', *Oxoniensia* 6, 9–21

Ball, J.W. and Kelsay, R.G. 1992: 'Prehistoric intrasettlement land use and residual soil phosphate levels in the upper Belize Valley, Central America', in T.W. Killion (ed.), *Gardens of Prehistory: The Archaeology of Settlement Agriculture in Greater Mesoamerica*, Tuscaloosa, 234–62

Barker, G. 1983: 'The animal bones', in J. Collis, 'Excavations at Silchester, Hampshire, 1968', *Proceedings of the Hampshire Field Club and Archaeological Society* 39, 67

Bartosiewicz, L., Van Neer, N. and Lentacker, A. 1993: 'Metapodial asymmetry in draft cattle', *International Journal of Osteoarchaeology* 3 (2), 69–75

Beckman, G.G. and Smith, K.J. 1974: 'Micromorphological changes in surface soils following wetting, drying and trampling', *Soil Microscopy: Proceedings of the Fourth International Working-meeting on Soil Micromorphology*, Ontario, 832–45

Beer, R.J.S. 1976: 'The relationship between *Trichuris trichiura* (Linnaeus 1758) of Man and *Trichuris suis* (Schrank 1788) of the pig', *Research in Veterinary Science* 20, 47–54

Bell, A. 1983: *Dung Fungi: an Illustrated Guide to Coprophilous Fungi*, Wellington

Bémont, C. 1977: *Moules de gobelets ornés de la Gaule centrale au Musée des antiquités nationales*, Supplément à Gallia 33, Paris

Bennett, K.D., Whittington, G. and Edwards, K.J. 1994: 'Recent plant nomenclatural changes and pollen morphology in the British Isles', *Quaternary Newsletter* 73, 1–6

Berglund, B.E. and Ralska-Jasiewiczowa, M. 1986: 'Pollen analysis and pollen diagrams', in B.E. Berglund (ed.), *Handbook of Holocene Palaeoecology and Palaeohydrology*, Chichester, 455–84

Bersu, G. 1940: 'Excavations at Little Woodbury, Wiltshire', *Proceedings of the Prehistoric Society* 6, 30–111

Bertrand, I. 1999: 'Fouilles du Parking Vaulabelle à Auxerre (Yonne): les objets de tabletterie', *Revue Archéologique de l'Est* 48, 287–96

Bertrand, I. 2003: *Objets de parure et de soins du corps d'époque romaine dans l'Est picton (Deux-Sèvres, Vienne)*, Mémoire de l'Association des Publications Chauvinoises 23, Chauvigny

Bet, P. and Delage, R. 2000: 'Du nouveau sur le centre de production de céramique sigillée de Lubié (Allier): étude préliminaire du mobilier issu d'un sondage récent', in L. Rivet (ed.), *SFECAG, Actes du Congrès de Libourne*, Marseille, 441–59

Bethell, P.H. and Máté, I. 1989: 'The use of soil phosphate analysis in archaeology: a critique', in J. Henderson (ed.), *Scientific Analysis in Archaeology*, Oxford University Committee for Archaeology Monograph 19, Oxford, 1–29

Betts, I., Black, E.W. and Gower, J. 1997: *A Corpus of Relief-Patterned Tiles in Roman Britain* (= *Journal of Roman Pottery Studies* No. 7)

Bewley, R. and Fulford, M. 1996: 'Aerial photography and the plan of Silchester', *Britannia* 27, 387–9

Bidwell, P.T. 1985: *The Roman Fort of Vindolanda at Chesterholm, Northumberland*, HBMC Archaeological Report 1, London

Bidwell, P.T. 1996: 'The exterior decoration of Roman buildings in Britain', in P. Johnson and I. Hayes (eds), *Architecture in Roman Britain*, CBA Research Report 94, York, 19–29

Biel, J. 1985: *Der Keltenfürst von Hochdorf. Methoden und Ergebnisse der Landesarchäologie*, Stuttgart

Bird, J. 1986: 'Samian wares', in L. Miller, J. Schofield and M. Rhodes, *The Roman Quay at St. Magnus House, London: Excavations at New Fresh Wharf, Lower Thames Street, London 1974–78*, London and Middlesex Archaeological Society Special Paper 8, London, 139–85

Bird, J. 2007: 'Catalogue of Iron Age and Roman artefacts discovered before 1995', in R. Poulton, 'Farley Heath Roman Temple', *Surrey Archaeological Collections* 93, 1–147

Bird, J. forthcoming: 'Decorated samian', in J. Hill and P. Rowsome (eds), *Excavations at 1 Poultry: The Roman Sequence*, Vol. 1, London

Black, E. 2008: 'Pagan religion in rural south-east Britain: contexts, deities and belief', in D. Rudling (ed.), *Ritual Landscapes of Roman South-East Britain*, Great Danham & Oxford, 1–25

Blake, J.H. 1903: *The Geology of the Country around Reading*. Memoir of the Geological Survey of Great Britain (Old Series Sheet 268), London

Boessneck, J. 1969: 'Osteological differences between Sheep (Ovis aries Linné) and Goat (Capra hircus Linné)', in D. Brothwell, E. Higgs and G. Clark (eds), *Science in Archaeology* (2nd edn), London, 331–58

Boesterd, M.H.P. den 1956: *Description of the Collections in the Rijksmuseum G.M. Kam at Nijmegen, 5: The Bronze Vessels*, Nijmegen

Bonnet, C., Batigne Vallet, C., Delage, R., Desbat, A., Lemaître, S., Marquié, S. and Silvino, T. 2003: 'Mobilier céramique du IIIe siècle à Lyon. Le cas de trois sites de la ville basse: place des Célestins, rue de la République/rue Bellecordière et place Tolozan', *SFECAG, Actes du Congrès de Saint-Romain-en-Gal*, Marseille, 145–81

Boon, G.C. 1974: *Silchester: The Roman Town of Calleva*, Newton Abbott

Boon, G.C. 1991: '*Tonsor humanus*: razor and toilet-knife in antiquity', *Britannia* 22, 21–32

Boon, G.C. 2000: 'The other objects of copper alloy', in Fulford and Timby 2000, 338–57

Booth, P., Clark, K.M. and Powell, A. 1996: 'A dog skin from Asthall', *International Journal of Osteoarchaeology* 6 (4), 382–7

Bowman, A. and Thomas, D. 1983: *Vindolanda: the Latin Writing-Tablets*, Britannia Monograph 4, London

Brain, C.K. 1969: 'The contribution of Namib Desert Hottentots to an understanding of australopithecine bone accumulations', *Scientific Papers of the Namib Desert Research Station* 39, 13–22

Brewer, R. and Guest, P. forthcoming: *Caerwent – Venta Silurum: Forum-Basilica*

Brigham, T. 1990: 'A reassessment of the second basilica in London, A.D. 100–400: excavations at Leadenhall Court, 1984–86', *Britannia* 21, 53–97

Brigham, T. and Hillam, J. 1990: 'The late Roman waterfront in London', *Britannia* 21, 99–183

Brigham, T., Goodburn, D., Tyers, I. with Dillon, J. 1995: 'A Roman timber building on the Southwark waterfront, London', *Archaeological Journal* 152, 1–72

Brodribb, G. 1987: *Roman Brick and Tile*, Gloucester

Brodribb, G., McWhirr, A. and Darling, M. 1977: 'Notes: Romano-British chimney pots and finials', *Antiquaries Journal* 57, 314–16

Bull, G. and Payne, S. 1982: 'Tooth eruption and epiphysial fusion in pigs and wild boar', in W. Wilson, C. Grigson and S. Payne (eds), *Ageing and Sexing Animal Bones from Archaeological Sites*, BAR British Series 109, Oxford, 55–71

Bullock, P., Fedoroff, N., Jongerius, A., Stoops, G. and Tursina, T. 1985: *Handbook for Thin Section Description*, Wolverhampton

Burnham, B., Collis, J., Dobinson, C., Haselgrove, C. and Jones, M. 2001: 'Themes for urban research, c. 100 BC to AD 200', in S. James and M. Millett (eds), *Britons and Romans: Advancing an Archaeological Agenda*, CBA Research Report 125, York, 67–76

Burnham, B.C., Keppie, L. J. F., Esmonde-Cleary, A.S., Hassall, M.W.C. and Tomlin, R.S.O. 1994: 'Roman Britain in 1993', *Britannia* 25, 245–314

Callender, M.H. 1965: *Roman Amphorae: with Index of Stamps*, University of Durham Publications, London

Canti, M.G. and Linford, N. 2000: 'The effects of fire on archaeological soils and sediments: temperature and colour relationships', *Proceedings of the Prehistoric Society* 66, 385–95

Charlesworth, D. 1972: 'The glass', in Frere 1972, 196–215

Clark, K.M. 1996: 'The later prehistoric and protohistoric dog: the emergence of canine diversity', *Archaeozoologia* 7 (2), 9–32

Clark, K.M. 2000: 'Dogged persistence: the phenomenon of canine skeletal uniformity in British prehistory', in S.J. Crockford (ed.), *Dogs through Time: An Archaeological Perspective. Proceedings of the 1st ICAZ Symposium on the History of the Domestic Dog*, British Archaeological Reports International Series 889, Oxford, 163–70

Clark, K. 2006: 'The dog assemblage', in Fulford *et al.* 2006, 189–95

Clarke, A., Fulford, M.G., Rains, M. and Shaffrey, R. 2001: 'The Victorian Excavations of 1893', *Silchester Roman Town – The Insula IX Town Life Project*, <http://www.silchester.reading.ac.uk/victorians>

Clarke, A. and Fulford, M.G. 2002: 'The excavation of Insula IX, Silchester: the first five years of the "Town Life" Project, 1997–2001', *Britannia* 33, 129–66

Clarke, A., Eckardt, H., Fulford, M.G., Rains, M. and Tootell, K. 2005: 'Silchester Roman Town: The Insula IX Town Life Project: the Late Roman Archaeology', <http://www.silchester.reading.ac.uk/later>

Clarke, A., Fulford, M.G., Rains, M. and Tootell, K. 2007: 'Silchester Roman Town Insula IX: the development of an urban property c. AD 40–50 – c. AD 250', *Internet Archaeology*, <http://intarch.ac.uk/journal/issue21/4/index.html>

Clarke, G. 1979: *The Roman Cemetery at Lankhills*, Winchester Studies 3, Oxford

Cohen, A. and Serjeantson, D. 1996: *Manual for the Identification of Bird Bones from Archaeological Sites*, London

Conway, J.S. 1983: 'An investigation of soil phosphorus distribution within occupation deposits from a Romano-British hut group', *Journal of Archaeological Science* 10, 117–28

Cook, S.R., Clarke, A. and Fulford, M.G. 2005: 'Soil geochemistry and detection of early Roman precious metal and copper alloy working in the Roman town of Calleva Atrebatum (Silchester, Hampshire, UK)', *Journal of Archaeological Science* 32 (5), 805–12

Cool, H.E.M. 1990: 'Roman metal hair pins from southern Britain', *Archaeological Journal* 147, 148–82

Cool, H.E.M. and Price, J. 1995: *Roman Glass Vessels in Colchester 1971–85*, Colchester Archaeological Reports 8, Colchester

Corney, M. 2000: 'The brooches', in Fulford and Timby 2000, 322–38

Courty, M.A., Goldberg, P. and Macphail, R. 1989: *Soils and Micromorphology in Archaeology*, Cambridge Manuals in Archaeology, Cambridge

Coy, J. 1984: 'The bird bones', in Cunliffe 1984, 527–31

Coy, J. 1987: 'Animal bones and marine molluscs', in N. Sunter and P.J. Woodward, *Romano-British Industries in Purbeck*, DNHAS Monograph 6, Dorchester, 178–9

Crummy, N. 1983: *The Roman Small Finds from Excavations in Colchester 1971–9*, Colchester Archaeological Report 2, Colchester

Crummy, N. 1992a: 'The Roman small finds from the Culver Street site', in P. Crummy 1992, 140–205

Crummy, N. 1992b: 'The Roman small finds from the Gilberd School site', in P. Crummy 1992, 206–44

Crummy, N. 2001: 'Bone-working in Roman Britain: a model for itinerant craftsmen?' in M. Polfer (ed.), *L'artisanat romain: évolutions, continuités et ruptures (Italie et provinces occidentales)*, Monographies Instrumentum 20, Montagnac, 97–109

Crummy, N. 2006a: 'The small finds', in Fulford, Clarke and Eckardt 2006, 120–32

Crummy, N. 2006b: 'Worshipping Mercury on Balkerne Hill, Colchester', in P. Ottaway (ed.), *A Victory Celebration: Papers on the Archaeology of Colchester and Late Iron Age–Roman Britain Presented to Philip Crummy*, Colchester, 55–68

Crummy, N. 2006c: 'A jug handle from Silchester', *Lucerna, Roman Finds Group Newsletter* 32, 4–6

Crummy, N. 2007: 'The small finds', in Clarke *et al.*, http://intarch.ac.uk/journal/issue21/4/finds_sf.htm

Crummy, N., Crummy, P. and Crossan, C. 1993: *Excavations of Roman and Later Cemeteries, Churches and Monastic Sites in Colchester, 1971–1988*, Colchester Archaeological Report 9, Colchester

Crummy, N. and Eckardt, H. 2003: 'Regional identities and technologies of the self: nail-cleaners in Roman Britain', *Archaeological Journal* 160, 44–69

Crummy, N. with Pohl, C. 2008: 'Small toilet instruments from London: a review of the evidence', in J. Clark, J. Cotton, J. Hall, R. Sherris and H. Swain (eds), *Londinium and Beyond: Essays on Roman London and its Hinterland for Harvey Sheldon*, CBA Research Report 156, York, 212–25

Crummy, P. 1984: *Excavations at Lion Walk, Balkerne Lane, and Middleborough, Colchester, Essex*, Colchester Archaeological Report 3, Colchester

Crummy, P. 1992: *Excavations at Culver Street, The Gilberd School, and Other Sites in Colchester, 1971–85*, Colchester Archaeological Report 6, Colchester

Crummy, P., Benfield, S., Crummy, N., Rigby, V. and Shimmin, D. 2007: *Stanway: An Elite Burial Site at Camulodunum*, Britannia Monograph 24, London

Cunliffe, B. 1975: *Excavations at Portchester Castle. Vol. 1: Roman*, Report Research Committee Society of Antiquaries of London 32, London

Cunliffe, B. 1984: *Danebury: An Iron Age Hillfort in Hampshire*, CBA Research Report 52, London

Cunliffe, B.W. 1986: *Danebury: Anatomy of an Iron Age Hillfort*, London

Cunliffe, B. 1995: *Danebury: An Iron Age Hillfort in Hampshire. Vol. 6. A Hillfort Community in Perspective*, CBA Research Report 102, York

Cunliffe, B.W. and Poole, C. 1991: *Danebury: An Iron Age Hillfort in Hampshire (England). Vol. 5. The Excavations, 1979–88: The Finds*, CBA Research Report 73, London

Cushing, E.J. 1967: 'Evidence for differential pollen preservation in late Quaternary sediments in Minnesota', *Review of Palaeobotany and Palynology* 4, 87–101

Dannell, G.B., Dickinson, B.M., Hartley, B.R., Mees, A.W., Polak, M., Vernhet, A. and Webster, P.V. 2003: *Gestempelte südgallische Reliefsigillata (Drag. 29) aus den Werkstätten von La Graufesenque: gesammelt von der Association Pegasus Recherches Européennes sur La Graufesenque*, Römisch-Germanisches Zentralmuseum, Forschungsinstitut für Vor- und Frühgeschichte. Kataloge Vor- und Frühgeschichtlicher Altertümer, Band 34 A (13 vols), Mainz

Davies, B., Richardson, B. and Tomber, R. 1994: *A Dated Corpus of Early Roman Pottery from the City of London*, CBA Research Report 98, Archaeology of Roman London 5, London

Déchelette, J. 1904: *Les vases céramiques ornés de la Gaule Romaine (Narbonnaise, Aquitaine et Lyonnaise)*, Paris

Degen, R. 1984: 'Eine römische Kleinplastik: der Schafhirt von Cham-Hagendorn', *Helvetia Archaeologica* 15, 169–84

Delage, R. 2003: 'Les sigillées du centre de la Gaule peuvent-elles contribuer à la datation des niveaux du IIIe s.?' in L. Rivet (ed.), *SFECAG, Actes du Congrès de Saint-Romain-en-Gal*, Marseille, 183–90

Deyts, S. 1976: *Dijon, Musée Archéologique: sculptures gallo-romaines mythologiques et religieuses*, Paris

Dickinson, B.M. 1999: 'Samian stamps', in R.P. Symonds and S. Wade, *Roman Pottery from Excavations in Colchester, 1971–86*, Colchester Archaeological Report 10, Colchester, 120–36

Dickson, C. and Dickson, J. 2000: *Plants and People in Ancient Scotland*, Stroud

Dobney, K. 2001: 'A place at the table: the role of vertebrate zooarchaeology within a Roman research agenda for Britain', in S. James and M. Millett (eds), *Britons and Romans: Advancing an Archaeological Agenda*, CBA Report 125, York, 36–45

Dobney, K., Hall, A. and Kenward, H. 1999: 'It's all garbage … a review of bioarchaeology in the four English *colonia* towns', in H. Hurst (ed.), *The Coloniae of Roman Britain: New Studies and a Review. Papers of the Conference held at Gloucester on 5–6 July, 1997*, JRA Supplementary Series 36, Portsmouth, R.I., 15–35

Down, A. 1979: *Chichester Excavations IV: the Roman Villas at Chilgrove and Upmarden*, Chichester

Drew, C.D. and Selby, K.C.C. 1939: 'Colliton Park excavations: first interim report', *Proceedings Dorset Natural History and Archaeological Society* 59, 1–14

Driesch, A. von den 1976: *A Guide to the Measurement of Animal Bones from Archaeological Sites*, Peabody Museum Bulletin 1, Cambridge, Mass.

Driesch, A. von den and Boessneck, J. 1974: 'Kritische Anmerkungen zur Widerrist-höhenberechnung aus Langenmassen vor- und frühgeschichtlicher Tierknochen', *Säugetierkundliche Mitteilungen erlagsgesellshaft München* 40(4), 325–48

Drummond-Murray, J. and Thompson, P. 2002: *Settlement in Roman Southwark: Archaeological Excavations (1991–8) for the London Underground Limited Jubilee Line Extension Project*, MoLAS Monograph 12, London

Dungworth, D. 1997a: 'Roman copper alloys: analysis of artifacts from northern Britain', *Journal of Archaeological Science* 24 (10), 901–10

Dungworth, D. 1997b: 'Iron-age and Roman copper alloys from northern Britain', *Internet Archaeology*, <http://intarch.ac.uk/journal/issue2/dungworth_toc.html>

Dzwiza, K. 2004: 'Ein Depotfund reliefverzierter südgallischer Terra Sigillata-Schüsseln aus Pompeji', *Jahrbuch des Römisch-Germanischen Zentralmuseums Mainz* 51 (2), 381–587

Eastham, A. 1975: 'The bird bones', in Cunliffe 1975, 409–15

Eckardt, H. 2002: *Illuminating Roman Britain*, Monographies Instrumentum 23, Montagnac

Eckardt, H. 2006: 'The character, chronology and use of the late Roman pits: the Silchester finds assemblage', in Fulford, Clarke and Eckardt 2006, 221–45

Eckardt, H. and Crummy, N. 2002: 'Ivory folding-knife handle from Silchester', *Instrumentum Bulletin* 15, 11

Eckardt, H. and Crummy, N. 2008: *Styling the Body in Late Iron Age and Roman Britain. A Contextual Approach to Toilet Instruments*, Monographies Instrumentum 36, Montagnac

Eggers, H.J. 1966: 'Römische Bronzegefässe in Britannien', *Jahrbuch des Römisch-Germanischen Zentralmuseums Mainz* 13, 67–164

Entwistle, J.A., Abrahams, P.W. and Dodgshon, R.A. 2000: 'The geoarchaeological significance and spatial variability of a range of physical and chemical soil properties from a former habitation site, Isle of Skye', *Journal of Archaeological Science* 27 (4), 287–303

Evans, J. 2001: 'The pottery', in P.M. Booth, J. Evans and J. Hiller (eds), *Excavations in the Extramural Settlement of Roman Alchester, Oxfordshire, 1991*, Oxford Archaeology Monograph 1, Oxford, 263–383

Faiers, J. 2000: 'The Period 2 pottery', P. Ellis (ed.), *The Forum Baths and Macellum at Wroxeter: Excavations by Graham Webster 1955–85*, English Heritage Archaeological Report 9, London, 263–73

Fell, V., Peacock, Z. and Watson, J. 2008: 'Groundwell Ridge, Wiltshire: investigative conservation of finds recovered during excavation 2003–5', *Research Department Report Series*, 60-2008, English Heritage, Portsmouth

Firth, J. 2000: 'The human bones', in Fulford and Timby 2000, 501–5

Flower, B. and Rosenbaum, E. 1958: *Apicius: The Roman Cookery Book*, London

Forbes, R.J. 1964a: *Studies in Ancient Technology*, VI, Leiden

Forbes, R.J. 1964b: *Studies in Ancient Technology*, VIII, Leiden

Forster, R.H. and Knowles, W.H. 1913: 'Corstopitum: report on the excavations in 1912', *Archaeologia Aeliana* 9 (3rd Series), 230–80

Fowler, E. 1960: 'The origins and development of the penannular brooch in Europe', *Proceedings of the Prehistoric Society* 26, 149–77

Fox, G.E. 1895: 'Excavations on the site of the Roman City at Silchester, Hants, in 1894', *Archaeologia* 54 (2), 439–94

Frere, S.S. 1972: *Verulamium Excavations I*, Reports of the Research Committee of the Society of Antiquaries of London 28, London

Frere, S.S. 1983: *Verulamium Excavations II*, Reports of the Research Committee of the Society of Antiquaries of London 41, London

Fulford, M.G. 1975: *New Forest Roman Pottery: Manufacture and Distribution, with a Corpus of the Pottery Types*, BAR 17, Oxford

Fulford, M.G. 1984: *Silchester: Excavations on the Defences 1974–80*, Britannia Monograph 5, London

Fulford, M.G. 1989a: *The Silchester Amphitheatre: Excavations of 1979–85*, Britannia Monograph 10, London

Fulford, M.G. 1989b: 'The economy of Roman Britain', in M. Todd (ed.), *Research on Roman Britain 1960–89*, Britannia Monograph 11, London, 175–201

Fulford, M.G. 1991: 'Britain and the Roman Empire: the evidence for regional and long distance trade', in R.F.J. Jones (ed.), *Roman Britain: Recent Trends*, Sheffield, 35–47

Fulford, M.G. 2000: 'Synthesis', in Fulford and Timby 2000, 545–81

Fulford, M.G. 2001: 'Links with the past: pervasive "ritual" behaviour in Roman Britain', *Britannia* 32, 199–218

Fulford, M.G. 2008: 'Nero and Britain: the palace of the client-king at *Calleva* and imperial policy towards the province after Boudicca', *Britannia* 39, 1–14

Fulford, M.G. and Clarke, A. 2002: 'Victorian excavation methodology: the Society of Antiquaries at Silchester in 1893', *Antiquaries Journal* 82, 285–306

Fulford, M.G. and Timby, J. 2000: *Late Iron Age and Roman Silchester. Excavations on the Site of the Forum-Basilica 1977, 1980–86*, Britannia Monograph 15, London

Fulford, M.G. and Timby, J. 2001: 'Timing devices, fermentation vessels, "ritual piercings"? A consideration of deliberately "holed pots" from Silchester and elsewhere', *Britannia* 32, 293–7

Fulford, M.G., Clarke, A. and Eckardt, H. 2006: *Life and Labour in Late Roman Silchester. Excavations in Insula IX since 1997*, Britannia Monograph 22, London

Fulford, M.G., Handley, M. and Clarke, A. 2000: 'An early date for Ogham: the Silchester Ogham Stone rehabilitated', *Medieval Archaeology* 44, 1–23

Fulford, M.G., Rippon, S., Ford, S., Timby, J. and Williams, B. 1997: 'Silchester: excavations at the North Gate, on the north walls, and in the northern suburbs 1988 and 1991–3', *Britannia* 28, 87–168

Gale, R. and Cutler, D. 2000: *Plants in Archaeology*, Otley, West Yorkshire

Galimberti, M., Bronk Ramsey, C. and Manning, S.W. 2004: 'Wiggle-match dating of tree-ring sequences', *Radiocarbon* 46 (2), 917–24

Gé, T., Courty, M.A., Matthews, W. and Wattez, J. 1993: 'Sedimentary formation processes of occupation surfaces', in P. Goldberg, D.T. Nash and M.D. Petraglia (eds), *Formation Processes in Archaeological Context*, Monographs in World Archaeology 17, Madison, 149–64

Germ. Rom. 1924–30: *Germania Romana: ein Bilder-Atlas*, 5 vols, Bamberg

Getty, R. 1975: *Sisson and Grossman's The Anatomy of the Domestic Animals* (5th edn), Philadelphia

Gifford, D.P. 1978: 'Ethnoarchaeological observations of natural processes affecting cultural materials', in R.A. Gould (ed.), *Explorations in Ethnoarchaeology*, Albuquerque, 77–101

Gifford-Gonzalez, D.P., Damrosch, D.B., Damrosch, D.R., Pryor, J. and Thunen, R.L. 1985: 'The third dimension in site structure: an experiment in trampling and vertical dispersal', *American Antiquity* 50 (4), 803–18

Going, C.J. 1987: *The Mansio and Other Sites in the South-Eastern Sector of Caesaromagus: the Roman Pottery*, Chelmsford Archaeological Trust Report 3.2, CBA Research Report 62, London

Goldberg, P. and Macphail, R. 2006: *Practical and Theoretical Geoarchaeology*, Oxford

Goodburn, R. and Grew, F. 1984: 'Miscellaneous objects of clay', in S.S. Frere, *Verulamium Excavations Vol. III*, Oxford University Committee for Archaeology Monograph 1, Oxford, 107–12

Gowland, W. 1900: 'Remains of a Roman silver refinery at Silchester', *Archaeologia* 57, 113–24

Grant, A. 1971: 'The animal bones', in B. Cunliffe (ed.), *Excavations at Fishbourne 1961–1969. Vol. 2: The Finds*, Society of Antiquaries Research Report 27, London, 377–88

Grant, A. 1982: 'The use of tooth wear as a guide to the age of domestic ungulates', in W. Wilson, C. Grigson and S. Payne (eds), *Ageing and Sexing Animal Bones from Archaeological Sites*, BAR British Series 109, Oxford, 91–108

Grant, A. 1984: 'Animal husbandry', in B. Cunliffe (ed.), *Danebury: An Iron Age Hillfort in Hampshire. Vol. 2, The Excavations 1969–1978: the Finds*, CBA Research Report 52, London, 496–548

Grant, A. 1991: 'Animal husbandry', in Cunliffe and Poole 1991, 447–87

Grant, A. 2000: 'Diet, economy and ritual: evidence from the faunal remains', in Fulford and Timby 2000, 425–84

Grant, A. 2002: 'Food, status and social hierarchy', in P. Miracle and N. Milner (eds), *Consuming Passions and Patterns of Consumption*, Cambridge, 17–23

Grant, A., Rush, C. and Serjeantson, D. 1991: 'Animal husbandry', in B. Cunliffe and C. Poole (eds), *Danebury: An Iron Age Hillfort in Hampshire. Vol. 5, The Excavations 1979–1988: the Finds*, CBA Research Report 73, London, 447–87

Grapin, C. and Sivignon, J. 1994: 'Un couteau signé Siacni aux Bolards, Nuits-Saint-Georges (Côte-d'Or)', *Revue Archéologique de l'Est et du Centre-Est* 45 (1), 203–9

Green, M. 1989: *Symbol and Image in Celtic Religious Art*, London & New York

Green, M. 1992: *Animals in Celtic Life and Myth*, London

Green, M. 1997: *Celtic Goddesses: Warriors, Virgins and Mothers*, London

Greig, J. 1994: 'Pollen analyses of latrine fills from archaeological sites in Britain; results and future potential', *AASP Contributions Series* 29, 101–14

Grimm, J. 2007: 'A dog's life: animal bone from a Romano-British ritual shaft at Springhead, Kent (UK)', in N. Benecke (ed.), *Beiträge zur Archäozoologie und Prähistorischen Anthropologie*, Band VI, Langenweißbach, 54–75

Guido, M. 1979: 'Catalogue of beads', in Clarke 1979, 297–300

Guido, M. and Mills, J.M. 1993: 'Beads (jet, glass, crystal and coral)', in D.E. Farwell and T.L. Molleson, *Excavations at Poundbury 1966–80. Vol. 2: The Cemeteries*, Dorchester, 100–2

Hall, A.R. and Kenward, H.K. 1990: *Environmental Evidence from the Colonia: General Accident and Rougier Street*, Archaeology of York 14/6, York

Hall, A.R., Jones, A.K.G. and Kenward, H. 1983: 'Cereal bran and human faecal remains – some preliminary observations', in B. Proudfoot (ed.), *Site Environment and Economy*, BAR International Series 173, Oxford, 85–104

Hall, A.R., Kenward, H.K. and Williams, D. 1980: *Environmental Evidence from Roman Deposits in Skeldergate*, Archaeology of York 14, The Past Environment of York 3, York

Hamilton-Dyer, S. 1993: 'Animal bones', in R.J.C. Smith (ed.), *Excavations at County Hall, Colliton Park, Dorchester, Dorset, 1988*, Wessex Archaeology Report 4, Salisbury, 77–82

Hamilton-Dyer, S. 1997: 'The animal bones', in Fulford *et al.* 1997, 131–5

Hamshaw-Thomas, J. 2000: 'When in Britain do as the Britons: dietary identity in early Roman Britain', in P. Rowley-Conwy (ed.), *Animal Bones, Human Societies*, Oxford, 166–9

Hands, A.R. 1993: *The Romano-British Roadside Settlement at Wilcote, Oxfordshire I: Excavations 1990–92*, BAR British Series 232, Oxford

Hands, A.R. 1998: *The Romano-British Roadside Settlement at Wilcote, Oxfordshire II: Excavations 1993–96*, BAR British Series 265, Oxford

Harcourt, R.A. 1974: 'The dog in prehistoric and early historic Britain', *Journal of Archaeological Science* 1, 151–75

Hartley, K.F. 1984: 'The mortarium stamps', in S.S. Frere, *Verulamium Excavations III*, Oxford University Committee for Archaeology Monograph 1, Oxford, 280–91

Hartley, K.F. 1991: 'Mortaria', in Holbrook and Bidwell 1991, 189–215

Hather, J. 2000: *The Identification of the Northern European Woods*, London

Hattatt, R.A. 1987: *Brooches of Antiquity*, Oxford

Hayward, K. 2007: 'Building Materials: The Stone', in Clarke *et al.* 2007, http://intarch.ac.uk/journal/issue21/4/finds_stone_house_1.htm; http://intarch.ac.uk/journal/issue21/4/finds_stone_link_room.htm

Hayward, K.M.J. 2009: *Roman Quarrying and Stone Supply on the Periphery – Southern England. A Geological Study of First Century Funerary Monuments and Monumental Architecture*, BAR 500, Oxford

Henig, M. 1977: 'Death and the maiden: funerary symbolism in daily life', in J. Munby and M. Henig (eds), *Roman Life and Art in Britain: A Celebration in Honour of the Eightieth Birthday of Jocelyn Toynbee*, BAR British Series 41, Oxford, 347–66

Henig, M. 1984: 'Amber amulets', *Britannia* 15, 244–6

Henig, M. and Wickenden, N.P. 1988: 'A hoard of jet and shale', in P.J. Drury, *The Mansio and Other Sites in the South-Eastern Sector of Caesaromagus*, Chelmsford Archaeological Trust Report 3.1, CBA Research Report 66, London, 107–10

Hermet, F. 1934: *La Graufesenque (Condatomago)*, 2 vols, Paris

Hill, J.D. 1995: *Ritual and Rubbish in the Iron Age of Wessex: a Study on the Formation of a Specific Archaeological Record*, BAR British Series 242, Oxford

Hodder, I. 1987: 'The meaning of discard: ash and domestic space in Baringo', in S. Kent (ed.), *Method and Theory for Activity Area Research: An Ethnoarchaeological Approach*, New York, 424–8

Holbrook, N. and Bidwell, P. 1991: *Roman Finds from Exeter*, Exeter Archaeological Report 4, Exeter

Hope, W.H. St John 1906: 'Excavations on the site of the Roman city at Silchester, Hants, in 1905', *Archaeologia* 60 (1), 149–68

Hope, W.H. St John 1907: 'Excavations on the site of the Roman city at Silchester, Hants, in 1906', *Archaeologia* 60 (2), 431–50

Hope, W.H. St John 1909: 'Excavations on the site of the Roman city at Silchester, Hants, in 1908', *Archaeologia* 61 (2), 473–86

Houben, H. and Guillaud, H. 1994: *Earth Construction: A Comprehensive Guide*, Encyclopaedia of Earth Construction 1, London

Hull, M.R. 1968: 'The Nor'nour brooches', in D. Dudley, 'Excavations on Nor'nour, Isles of Scilly, 1962–6', *Archaeological Journal* 124, 1–64

Hull, M.R. forthcoming: 'Brooches in pre-Roman and Roman Britain', in G.M. Simpson, N. Crummy and B. Blance (eds), Oxford

Hurrell, H. 1904: 'Roman vessels found at Hauxton Mill', *Proceedings of the Cambridge Antiquarian Society* 10, 496

Ingrem, C. 2006: 'The animal bone. The late pits and wells', in Fulford, Clarke and Eckardt 2006, 167–84

Ingrem, C. 2007: 'The animal bone from early and mid-Roman deposits in the House 1 sequence', in Clarke *et al.* 2007

Jackson, R. 1986: 'A set of Roman medical instruments from Italy', *Britannia* 17, 119–67

Jackson, R. 2007: 'The surgical instruments', in P. Crummy *et al.* 2007, 236–52

Jackson, R. and Friendship-Taylor, R. 2003: 'The Piddington gladiator clasp-knife', *Lucerna, Roman Finds Group Newsletter* 25, 9–11

James, P. 1999: 'Soil variability in the area of an archaeological site near Sparta, Greece', *Journal of Archaeological Science* 26, 1273–88

Jarvis, R.A. 1968: *Soils of the Reading District*, Memoirs of the Soil Survey of Great Britain: England and Wales, Harpenden

Jenkins, F. 1957: 'The role of the dog in Romano-Gaulish religion', *Latomus* 16, 60–76

Johnson, P. and Hayes, I. (eds) 1996: *Architecture in Roman Britain*, CBA Research Report 94, York

Johnston, D.E. 1972: 'A Roman building at Chalk, near Gravesend', *Britannia* 3, 112–48

Jones, A.K.G. and Hutchinson, A.R. 1991: 'The parasitological evidence', in M.R. McCarthy, *The Structural Sequence and Environmental Remains from Castle Street, Carlisle: Excavations 1981–2*, Kendal, 65–72

Jones, J. 1991: 'Conservation of the Carlisle Roman writing tablets', *Ancient Monuments Laboratory Report Series* 24/1991, English Heritage, London

Jones, M. 1978: 'The plant remains', in M. Parrington, *The Excavation of an Iron Age Settlement, Bronze Age Ring-Ditches and Roman Features at Ashville Trading Estate, Abingdon, (Oxfordshire), 1974–76*, Oxford Archaeology Unit Report 1, CBA Research Report 28, London, 93–110

Keay, S.J. and Williams, D.F. 2005: 'Roman Amphorae: a digital resource', <http://ads.ahds.ac.uk/catalogue/archive/amphora_ahrb_2005>

Keefe, L. 2005: *Earth Building: Methods and Materials, Repair and Conservation*, London

Keepax, C. 1975: 'St Thomas Street, Southwark, wooden writing tablets', *Ancient Monuments Laboratory Report* 1924, English Heritage, London

Keevill, G.D. 1996: 'The reconstruction of the Romano-British villa at Redlands Farm, Northamptonshire', in Johnson and Hayes 1996, 44–55

Keith-Lucas, D.M. 1984: 'Analysis of the pollen from the South-East Gate', in Fulford 1984, 215–21

Kellaway, G.A. and Welch, F.B.A. 1993: *Geology of the Bristol District*. Memoir for 1:63 360 geological special sheet (England and Wales), London

Keys, L. 2002: 'Iron smithing', in Drummond-Murray and Thompson 2002, 240–2

King, A. 1991: 'Food production and consumption – meat', in R.F.J. Jones (ed.), *Roman Britain: Recent Trends*, Sheffield, 15–20

King, A. with Crummy, S. 1996: 'The south-east façade of Meonstoke aisled building', in Johnson and Hayes 1996, 56–69

Kloet, G.S. and Hincks, W.D. 1977: 'A checklist of British insects: Coleoptera and Strepsiptera', *Handbook for the Identification of British Insects 11 (3)* (2nd revised edn), London

Knight, B.A., Dickson, C.A, Dickson, J.H. and Breeze, D.J. 1983: 'Evidence concerning the Roman military diet at Bearsden, Scotland, in the 2nd century AD', *Journal of Archaeological Science* 10, 139–52

Lambrick, G.H. and Robinson, M.A. 1979: *Iron Age and Roman Riverside Settlements at Farmoor, Oxfordshire*, Oxfordshire Archaeological Unit Report 2, CBA Research Report 32, Oxford and London

LaMotta, V.M. and Schiffer, M.B. 1999: 'Formation processes of house floor assemblages', in P. Allison (ed.), *The Archaeology of Household Activities*, London, 19–29

Lauwerier, R.C.G.M. 1999: 'Eating horsemeat: the evidence in the Roman Netherlands', *Archaeofauna* 8, 101–13

Lawson, A.J. 1976: 'Shale and jet objects from Silchester', *Archaeologia* 105, 241–75

Legge, A.J. 1981: 'The agricultural economy', in R.J. Mercer (ed.), *Grimes Graves, Norfolk: Excavations 1971–72, Volume 1*, London, 79–103

Letts, J.B. 1999: *Smoke Blackened Thatch: a Unique Source of Late Medieval Plant Remains from Southern England*, London

Levine, M.A. 1982: 'The use of crown height measurements and eruption-wear sequences to age horse teeth', in W. Wilson, C. Grigson and S. Payne (eds), *Ageing and Sexing Animal Bones from Archaeological Sites*, BAR British Series 109, Oxford, 223–50

Ling, R. 1992: 'A collapsed building façade at Carsington, Derbyshire', *Britannia* 23, 233–6

Lippi, R.D. 1988: 'Paleotopography and phosphate analysis of a buried jungle site in Ecuador', *Journal of Field Archaeology* 15, 85–97

Liversidge, J. 1958: 'Roman discoveries from Hauxton', *Proceedings of the Cambridge Antiquarian Society* 51, 7–17

Lloyd-Morgan, G. 1981: *Description of the Collections in the Rijksmuseum G.M. Kam at Nijmegen, 9: The Mirrors*, Nijmegen

Locker, A. 2007: 'In piscibus diversis; the bone evidence for fish consumption in Roman Britain', *Britannia* 38, 141–80

Lowther, A.W.G. 1934: 'The Roman chimney pots from Ashtead, and parallel examples from other sites', *Surrey Archaeological Collections* 42, 61–6

Lowther, A.W.G. 1972: 'The ventilator', in Johnston 1972, 146–7

Lowther, A.W.G. 1976: 'Romano-British chimney pots and finials', *Antiquaries Journal* 56, 35–48

Luff, R.M. 1982: *A Zooarchaeological Study of the Roman North-Western Provinces*, BAR International Series 137, Oxford

Lyne, M.A.B. and Jefferies, R.S. 1979: *The Alice Holt/Farnham Roman Pottery Industry*, CBA Research Report 30, London

MacGregor, A., Mainman, A.J. and Rogers, N.S.H. 1999: *Craft, Industry and Everyday Life: Bone, Antler, Ivory and Horn from Anglo-Scandinavian and Medieval York*, The Archaeology of York 17/12, York

Mackenzie, W.S. and Adams, A.E. 1994: *A Colour Atlas of Rocks and Minerals in Thin Section*, London

Major, H.J. and Eddy, M.R. 1986: 'Four lead objects of possible Christian significance from East Anglia', *Britannia* 17, 355–8

Maloney, C. 1991: review of Wilmott 1991 in *Transactions London and Middlesex Archaeological Society* 42, 122–3

Maltby, M. 1979: *Faunal Studies on Urban Sites: The Animal Bones from Exeter 1971–1975*, Exeter Archaeological Reports 2, Sheffield

Maltby, M. 1981: 'Iron Age, Romano-British and Anglo-Saxon animal husbandry – A review of the faunal evidence', in M. Jones and G. Dimbleby (eds), *The Environment of Man: the Iron Age to the Anglo-Saxon Period*, BAR British Series 87, Oxford, 155–203

Maltby, M. 1984: 'The animal bones from the 1974, 1975 and 1978 excavations', in Fulford 1984, 199–207

Maltby, M. 1985a: 'Patterns in faunal assemblage variability', in G. Barker and C. Gamble (eds), *Beyond Domestication in Prehistoric Europe*, London, 33–74

Maltby, M. 1985b: 'The animal bones', in P.J. Fasham (ed.), *The Prehistoric Settlement at Winnall Down, Winchester: Excavations of MARC3 Site R17 in 1976 and 1977*, Hampshire Field Club and Archaeological Society Monograph 2, M3 Archaeological Rescue Committee Vol. 8, Winchester, 97–112

Maltby, M. 1987a: 'The animal bones from the excavations at Owslebury, Hampshire: an Iron Age and early Romano-British settlement', *Ancient Monuments Laboratory Report 6/87*

Maltby, M. 1987b: 'The animal bones from Brighton Hill South (trenches B, C and K), Farleigh Wallop, Hampshire', *Ancient Monuments Laboratory Report 155/87*

Maltby, M. 1993: 'Animal bones', in P.J. Woodward, S.M. Davies and A.H. Graham (eds), *Excavations at the Old Methodist Chapel and Greyhound Yard, Dorchester, 1981–1984*, DNHAS Monograph 12, Dorchester, 315–45

Maltby, M. 1994: 'The meat supply in Roman Dorchester and Winchester', in A.R. Hall and H.K. Kenward (eds), *Urban-Rural Connexions: Perspectives from Environmental Archaeology*, Symposia of the Association for Environmental Archaeology No. 12, Oxbow Monograph 47, Oxford, 85–103

Maltby, M. 1995: 'Animal bones', in G.J. Wainwright and S.M. Davies (eds), *Balksbury Camp, Hampshire: Excavations 1973 and 1981*, Archaeological Report 4, London, 83–7

Manning, W.H. 1985: *Catalogue of the Romano-British Iron Tools, Fittings and Weapons in the British Museum*, London

Marsden, P.R.V. 1967: *A Ship of the Roman Period: from Blackfriars, in the City of London*, London

Marshall, J.D. 1982: 'Isotopic composition of displacive fibrous calcite veins', *Journal of Sedimentary Petrology* 52, 615–30

Mathers, S.J. and Smith, N.J.P. 2000: *Geology of the Reading District: a Brief Explanation of the Geological Map Sheet 268 Reading*, London

Mathews, C.L. and members of the Manshead Archaeological Society of Dunstable 1981: 'A Romano-British inhumation cemetery at Dunstable', *Bedfordshire Archaeological Journal* 15, 1–73

Matthews, W. 1995: 'Micromorphological characterisation and interpretation of occupation deposits and microstratigraphic sequences at Abu Salabikh, Southern Iraq', in A.J. Barnham and R. Macphail (eds), *Archaeological Sediments and Soils: Analysis, Interpretation and Management*, London, 41–76

Matthews, W. 2000: 'Micromorphological analysis of occupational sequences', *Contextual Analysis of the Use of Space at Two Near Eastern Bronze Age Sites*, <http://ads.ahds.ac.uk/catalogue/resources.html?tellbrak>

Matthews, W., Postgate, J.N., Payne, S., Charles, M.P. and Dobney, K. 1994: 'The imprint of living in an early Mesopotamian city: questions and answers', in R.M. Luff and P. Rowley-Conwy (eds), *Whither Environmental Archaeology?* Oxbow Monograph 38, Oxford, 171–212

May, T. 1916: *The Pottery Found at Silchester: A Descriptive Account of the Pottery Recovered during the Excavations on the Site of the Romano-British City of Calleva Atrebatum at Silchester, Hants., and Deposited in the Reading Museum*, Reading

Mees, A.W. 1995: *Modelsignierte Dekorationen auf südgallischer Terra Sigillata*, Forschungen und Berichte zur Vor- und Frühgeschichte in Baden-Württemberg, Band 54, Stuttgart

Mensch, P.J.A. van 1974: 'A Roman soup-kitchen at Zwammerdam?' *Berichten van de Rijksdienst voor het Oudheidkundig Bodemonderzoek* 24, 159–65

Mercklin, E. von 1940: 'Römische Klappmessergriffe', *Serta Hoffilleriana: Commentationes Gratulatorias Victori Hoffiller Sexagenario Obtulerunt Collegae Amici Discipuli Ad XI Kal Mar MCMXXXVII*, Vjesnika Hrvatskoga Archeoloskoga Drustva new ser. 18–21, Zagreb, 339–52

Merrifield, R. 1965: *The Roman City of London*, London

Merrifield, R. 1987: *The Archaeology of Ritual and Magic*, London

Merrifield, R. 1995: 'Roman metalwork from the Walbrook – rubbish, ritual or redundancy', *Transactions London and Middlesex Archaeological Society* 46, 27–44

Mikler, H. 1997: *Die römischen Funde aus Bein im Landesmuseum Mainz*, Monographies Instrumentum 1, Montagnac

Millett, M. 2001: 'Approaches to urban societies', in S. James and M. Millett (eds), *Britons and Romans: Advancing an Archaeological Agenda*, CBA Research Report 125, York, 60–6

Millett, M. with James, S. 1983: 'Excavations at Cowdery's Down, Basingstoke, Hampshire, 1978–81', *Archaeological Journal* 140, 151–279

Moffett, L., Robinson, M.A. and Straker, V. 1989: 'Cereals, fruit and nuts: charred plant remains from Neolithic sites in England and Wales and the Neolithic economy', in A. Milles, D. Williams and N. Gardener (eds), *The Beginnings of Agriculture*, BAR International Series 496, Oxford, 243–61

Moore, P.D., Webb, J.A. and Collinson, M.E. 1991: *Pollen Analysis* (2nd edn), Oxford

Morgan, G.C. 2000: 'Mortar analysis', in Fulford and Timby 2000, 114–15

Morley, G. and Wilson, P. forthcoming: *Groundwell Ridge Roman Villa in Swindon, Wilts. Excavations in the Bath Suite and Wider Area, 1996–2005*, English Heritage Research Department Report

MoLAS 2002: *A Research Framework for London Archaeology*, London

Moore, H.L. 1982: 'The interpretation of spatial patterning in settlement residues', in I. Hodder (ed.), *Symbolic and Structural Archaeology*, Cambridge, 74–9

Murphy, P. 1984: 'Carbonised fruits from building 5', in P. Crummy *et al.*, *Excavations at Lion Walk, Balkerne Lane, and Middlesborough, Colchester, Essex*, Colchester, 40

Neal, D.S. 1996: 'Upper storeys in Romano-British villas', in P. Johnson and I. Hayes (eds), *Architecture in Roman Britain*, CBA Research Report 94, York, 33–43

Needham, S. and Bowman, S. 2005: 'Flesh-hooks, technological complexity and the Atlantic Bronze Age feasting complex', *European Journal of Archaeology* 8.2, 93–136

Nenova-Merdjanova, R. 1998: 'The bronze jugs decorated with a human foot from the Roman provinces Moesia and Thracia', *Archaeologia Bulgarica* 2 (3), 68–76

Neville-George, T. 1970: *British Regional Geology. South Wales* (3rd edn), London

Northover, J.P. and Palk, N. 2000: 'Metallurgical debris: catalogue and analysis', in Fulford and Timby 2000, 395–420

Norton, J. 1997: *Building with Earth: A Handbook* (2nd edn), London

O'Connor, T.P. 1988: *Bones from the General Accident Site, Tanner Row*, The Archaeology of York 15/2, London

Ohlson, M. and Tryterud, E. 2000: 'Interpretation of the charcoal record in forest soils: forest fires and their production and deposition of macroscopic charcoal', *The Holocene* 10 (4), 519–25

Osborne, P.J. 1971a: 'An insect fauna from the Roman site at Alcester, Warwickshire', *Britannia* 2, 156–65

Osborne, P.J. 1971b: 'The insect fauna from the Roman harbour', in B. Cunliffe (ed.), *Excavations at Fishbourne, 1961–1969*, Research Reports of the Society of Antiquaries of London 27, 2, London, 393–6

Osborne White, H.J. 1909: *The Geology of the Country around Basingstoke*, Memoirs of the Geological Survey of Great Britain, London

Oswald, F. 1936–37: *Index of Figure-Types on Terra Sigillata ('Samian Ware')*, Annals of Archaeology and Anthropology Supplement 23.1–4, 24.1–4, Liverpool

Parker, A.J. 1988: 'The birds of Roman Britain', *Oxford Journal of Archaeology* 7(2), 197–226

Payne, S. 1973: 'Kill-off patterns in sheep and goats: the mandibles from Aşvan Kale', *Anatolian Studies* 23, 281–303

Payne, S. 1985: 'Morphological distinctions between the mandibular teeth of young sheep, ovis, and goats, capra', *Journal of Archaeological Science* 12, 139–47

Payne, S. and Bull, G. 1982: 'Tooth eruption and epiphyseal fusion in pigs and wild boar', in W. Wilson, C. Grigson and S. Payne (eds), *Ageing and Sexing Animal Bones from Archaeological Sites*, BAR British Series 109, Oxford, 55–71

Peacock, D.P.S. 1987: 'Iron Age and Roman quern production at Lodsworth, West Sussex', *Antiquaries Journal* 67, 61–85

Peacock, D.P.S. and Williams, D.F. 1986: *Amphorae and the Roman Economy: An Introductory Guide*, London

Perrin, R. 1999: *Roman Pottery from Excavations at and near to the Roman Small Town of Durobrivae, Water Newton, Cambridgeshire, 1956–8 = Journal of Roman Pottery Studies* 8

Perring, D. 1987: 'Domestic buildings in Romano-British towns', in J. Schofield and R. Leech (eds), *Urban Archaeology in Britain*, CBA Research Report 61, London, 147–55

Perring, D. 1991: *Roman London*, London

Perring, D. 2002: *The Roman House in Britain*, London

Pirling, R. 1993: 'Ein Trierer Spruchbecher mit ungewöhnlicher Inschrift aus Krefeld-Gellep', *Germania* 71 (2), 387–404

Pliny: *Natural History*, trans. H. Rackham 1968, 2nd edn, Loeb Classical Library (Vol. 5), Cambridge, Mass.

Powell, A., Smith, P., Clark, K. and Serjeantson, D. 2006: 'Animal bone', in M.G. Fulford, A.B. Powell, R. Entwistle and F. Raymond (eds), *Iron Age and Romano-British Settlements and Landscapes of Salisbury Plain*, Wessex Archaeology Report 20, Salisbury, 163–95

Price, J. 1987: 'Glass from Felmongers, Harlow in Essex. A dated deposit of vessel glass found in an Antonine pit', *Annales du 10e Congrès de l'Association Internationale pour l'Histoire du Verre*, 185–206

Price, J. and Cottam, S. 1998: *Romano-British Glass Vessels: A Handbook*, CBA Practical Handbook in Archaeology 14, York

Radnóti, A. 1938: *Die römischen Bronzegefässe von Pannonien*, Dissertationes Pannonicae Series 2, 6

Rawes, B. and Gander, E.D. 1978: 'Ancient quarry at Manless Town', *Transactions Bristol and Gloucestershire Archaeological Society* 96, 79–82

Rayner, L. and Seeley, F. 2002: 'The Roman pottery', in J. Drummond-Murray and P. Thomson with C. Cowan, *Settlement in Roman Southwark. Archaeological Excavations (1991–8) for the London Underground Limited Jubilee Line Extension Project*, MoLAS Monograph 12, London, 162–212

Reece, R. 1991: *Roman Coins from 140 Sites in Britain*, Cotswold Studies 4, Cirencester

Reece, R. 2002: *The Coinage of Roman Britain*, Stroud

Rees. H., Crummy, N., Ottaway, P.J. and Dunn, G. 2008: *Artefacts and Society in Roman and Medieval Winchester: Small Finds from the Suburbs and Defences, 1971–86*, Winchester

Reid, C. 1901: 'Notes on the plant remains of Roman Silchester', in G.E. Fox and W.H. St John Hope, 'Excavations on the site of the Roman city at Silchester, Hants, in 1900', *Archaeologia* 57 (2), 252–6

Reid, C. 1902: 'Notes on the plant remains of Roman Silchester', in W.H. St John Hope, 'Excavations on the site of the Roman city at Silchester, Hants, in 1901', *Archaeologia* 58 (1), 34–6

Reid, C. 1903: 'Notes on the plant remains of Roman Silchester', in W.H. St John Hope, 'Excavations on the site of the Roman city at Silchester, Hants, in 1902', *Archaeologia* 58 (2), 425–8

Reid, C. 1905: 'Notes on the plant remains of Roman Silchester', in W.H. St John Hope, 'Excavations on the site of the Roman city at Silchester, Hants, in 1903 and 1904', *Archaeologia* 59 (2), 367

Reid, C. 1906: 'Notes on the plant remains of Roman Silchester', in Hope 1906, 164

Reid, C. 1907: 'Notes on the plant remains of Roman Silchester', in Hope 1907, 449

Reid, C. 1908: 'Notes on the plant remains of Roman Silchester', in W.H. St John Hope, 'Excavations on the site of the Roman city at Silchester, Hants, 1907', *Archaeologia* 61 (1), 210

Reid, C. 1909: 'Notes on the plant remains of Roman Silchester', in Hope 1909, 485

Reinach, S. 1894: *Bronzes figurés de la Gaule romaine*, Antiquités nationales, Paris

Richards, D. 2000: 'Iron-working and other miscellaneous metal-working residues', in Fulford and Timby 2000, 421–2

Richardson, B. 1986: 'Pottery', in L. Miller, J. Schofield and M. Rhodes, *The Roman Quay at St Magnus House, London. Excavations at New Fresh Wharf, Lower Thames Street, London 1974–78*, London and Middlesex Archaeological Society, Special Paper 8, London, 96–138

Ricken, H. 1934: 'Die Bilderschüsseln der Kastelle Saalburg und Zugmantel', *Saalburg Jahrbuch* 8, 130–82

Riha, E. 1986: *Römisches Toilettgerät und medizinische Instrumente aus Augst und Kaiseraugst*, Forschungen in Augst 6, Augst

Riha, E. 1990: *Der römische Schmuck aus Augst und Kaiseraugst*, Forschungen in Augst 10, Augst

Riha, E. 2001: *Kästchen, Truhen, Tische – Möbelteile aus Augusta Raurica*, Forschungen in Augst 31, Augst

Rippon, S.J., Martin, M.H. and Jackson, A.W. 2001: 'The use of soil analysis in the interpretation of an early historic landscape at Puxton in Somerset', *Landscape History* 23, 27–38

Robinson, M.A. 1991: 'The Neolithic and late Bronze Age insect assemblages', in S.P. Needham (ed.), *Excavation and Salvage at Runnymede Bridge, 1978: the Late Bronze Age Waterfront Site*, London, 277–326

Robinson, M.A. 2006: 'The macroscopic plant remains', in Fulford, Clarke and Eckardt 2006, 206–20

Robinson, M.A. 2007: 'Environmental archaeology of the Cotswold Water Park', in D. Miles, S. Palmer, A. Smith and G.P. Jones (eds), *Iron Age and Roman Settlement in the Upper Thames Valley. Excavations at Claydon Pike and Other Sites within the Cotswold Water Park*, Oxford Archaeology Thames Valley Landscapes Monograph 26, Oxford, 355–64

Robinson, M. and Hubbard, R.N.L.B. 1977: 'The transport of pollen in the bracts of hulled cereals', *Journal of Archaeological Science* 4, 197–9

Rodet-Belarbi, I. and Dieudonné-Glad, N. 2008: 'Os, bois de cerf et ivoire à Rom (Deux-Sèvres). Quelques éléments de réflexion sur l'approvisionnement en matière première et la distribution des objets dans l'agglomération', in I. Bertrand (ed.), *Le travail de l'os, du bois de cerf et de la corne à l'époque romaine: un artisanat en marge? Actes de la table-ronde Instrumentum de Chauvigny (Vienne, F), 8–9 décembre 2005*, Monographies Instrumentum 34, Montagnac, 145–63

Rogers, G.B. 1974: *Poteries sigillées de la Gaule centrale, I — les motifs non figurés*, Gallia Supplement 28, Paris

Rogers, G.B. 1999: *Poteries sigillées de la Gaule centrale, II — les potiers*, Le Cahiers du Centre Archéologique de Lezoux 1, Revue archéologique Sites. Hors série 40, Lezoux

Ross, A. 1967: *Pagan Celtic Britain*, London

Ross, A. 1968: 'Shafts, pits and wells – sanctuaries of the Belgic Britons?', in J.M. Coles and D.D.A. Simpson (eds), *Studies in Ancient Europe*, Leicester, 255–85

Sadler, P. 1991: 'The use of tarsometatarsi in sexing and ageing domestic fowl (Gallus gallus L.) and recognising five toed breeds in archaeological material', *Circaea* 8 (1), 41–8

Sarris, A., Galaty, M.L., Yerkes, R.W., Parkinson, W.A., Gyucha, A., Billingsley, D.M. and Tate, R. 2004: 'Geophysical prospection and soil chemistry at the Early Copper Age settlement of Vésztő-Bikeri, Southeastern Hungary', *Journal of Archaeological Science* 31, 927–39

Schädler, U. 2007: 'The Doctor's game – new light on the history of ancient board games', in P. Crummy *et al.* 2007, 359–75

Scheuer, L. and Black, S. 2000: *Developmental Juvenile Osteology*, London

Schiffer, M.B. 1987: *Formation Processes of the Archaeological Record*, Albuquerque

Schmidt, E. 1968: 'Knochendrechsler, Hornschnitzer und Leimsieder in römischer Augst', in E. Schmid (ed.), *Provincialia. Festschrift für Rudolf Laur-Belart*, Basel, 185–97

Schmidt, E. 1972: *Atlas of Animal Bones: For Prehistorians, Archaeologists and Quaternary Geologists*, Amsterdam

Schrüfer-Kolb, I. 2004: *Roman Iron Production in Britain. Technological and Socio-economic Landscape Development along the Jurassic Ridge*, BAR British Series 380, Oxford

Schweingruber, F.H. 1990: *Anatomy of European Woods*, Berne & Stuttgart

Scobie, G.D., Zant, J.M. and Whinney, R. 1991: *The Brooks, Winchester. A Preliminary Report on the Excavations, 1987–88*, Winchester Museums Service, Archaeology Report 1, Winchester

Scott, S. and Duncan, C.J. 1999: 'Malnutrition, pregnancy and infant mortality: a biometric model', *Journal of Interdisciplinary History* 30 (1), 37–60

Seager-Smith, R.H. and Davies, S.M. 1993: 'Roman pottery', in P.J. Woodward, S.M. Davies and A.H. Graham, *Excavations at the Old Methodist Chapel and Greyhound Yard, Dorchester, 1981–1984*, DNHAS Monograph 12, Dorchester, 202–89

Sedlmayer, H. 1999: *Die römischen Bronzegefässe in Noricum*, Monographies Instrumentum 10, Montagnac

Seeley, F. and Drummond-Murray, J. 2005: *Roman Pottery Production in the Walbrook Valley: Excavations at 20–28 Moorgate, City of London, 1998–2000*, MoLAS Monograph 25, London

Sellwood, B. 1984: 'The rock types represented by the town walls of Silchester', in Fulford 1984, 224–30

Serjeantson, D. 1989: 'Animal remains and the tanning trade', in D. Serjeantson and T. Waldron (eds), *Diet and Crafts in Towns: the Evidence of Animal Remains from the Roman to the Post-Medieval Periods*, BAR British Series 199, Oxford, 129–46

Serjeantson, D. 1991: 'The bird bones', in Cunliffe and Poole 1991, 479–81

Serjeantson, D. 1996: 'The animal bones', in S.P. Needham and T. Spence (eds), *Runnymede Bridge Research Excavations, Volume 2. Refuse and Disposal at Area 16 East Runnymede*, London, 194–223

Serjeantson, D. 2000: 'The bird bones', in Fulford and Timby 2000, 484–500

Shaffrey, R. 2003: 'The rotary querns from the Society of Antiquaries' excavations at Silchester, 1890–1909', *Britannia* 34, 143–74

Shaffrey, R. 2006a: 'The worked stone', in Fulford, Clarke and Eckardt 2006, 133–4

Shaffrey, R. 2006b: *Grinding and Milling: A Study of Romano-British Rotary Querns and Millstones made from Old Red Sandstone*, BAR British Series 409, Oxford

Sillar, B. 2000: 'Dung by preference: the choice of fuel as an example of how Andean pottery production is embedded within wider technical, social and economic practices', *Archaeometry* 42 (1), 43–60

Silver, I.A. 1969: 'The ageing of domestic animals', in D. Brothwell and E. Higgs (eds), *Science in Archaeology*, London, 250–68

Sim, D. 1998: *Beyond the Bloom. Bloom Refining and Iron Artefact Production in the Roman World*, BAR International Series 725, Oxford

Simpson, G. 1957: 'Metallic black slip vases from central Gaul with applied and moulded decoration', *Antiquaries Journal* 37, 29–42

Simpson, G. 1973: 'More black slip vases from central Gaul with applied and moulded decoration in Britain', *Antiquaries Journal* 53, 42–51

Simpson, I. 1998: 'Early land management at Tofts Ness, Sanday, Orkney: the evidence of thin section micromorphology', in C.M. Mills and G. Coles (eds), *Life on The Edge: Human Settlement and Marginality*, Oxford

Smith, J.T. 1978: 'Villas as a key to social structure', in M. Todd (ed.), *Studies in the Romano-British Villa*, Leicester, 149–85

Smith, J.T. 1997: *Roman Villas: A Study in Social Structure*, London

Smith, W. 2002: 'A review of archaeological wood analyses in southern England', *Centre for Archaeology Report Series* 75/2002, English Heritage, Portsmouth

Somerville, E.M. 1997: 'The oysters', in Fulford *et al.* 1997, 135–9

Somerville, E.M. 2006: 'The marine shell', in J. Manley and D. Rudkin, 'More buildings facing the Palace at Fishbourne', *Sussex Archaeological Collections* 144, 69–133

Stace, C. 1991: *New Flora of the British Isles*, Cambridge

Stace, C. 1997: *New Flora of the British Isles* (2nd edn), Cambridge

Stanfield, J.A. and Simpson, G. 1958: *Central Gaulish Potters*, University of Durham Publications, London

Starley, D. 2003: 'Analysis of ferrous metalworking evidence', in F. Hammer, *Industry in North-West Roman Southwark: Excavations 1984–8*, MoLAS Monograph 17, London, 131–40

Stead, I.M. 1967: 'A La Tène III burial at Welwyn Garden City', *Archaeologia* 101, 1–62

Stokes, P.R.G. 2000: 'The butcher, the cook and the archaeologist', in J.P. Huntley and S. Stallibrass (eds), *Taphonomy and Interpretation*, Symposia of the Association for Environmental Archaeology 14, Oxford, 65–70

Straker, V. 2000: 'The charcoal', in Fulford and Timby 2000, 512–23

Sumner-Smith, G. 1966: 'Observations on epiphyseal fusion of the canine appendicular skeleton', *Journal of Small Animal Practice* 7 (4), 303–11

Symonds, R.P. and Tomber, R. 1991: 'Late Roman London: an assessment of the ceramic evidence from the City of London', *Transactions of the London and Middlesex Archaeological Society* 42, 59–99

Szabó, K. 1981: 'Emberi lábfejjel díszített füles bronzkorsók Pannoniából', *Archæologiai értesítő* 108, 52–64

Szabó, K. 1983: 'Pot à anse, en bronze, ornée d'un pied humain, provenant de Pannonie', *Antiquités Nationales* 14/15 (1982–83), 86–96

Szynkiewicz, S. 1990: 'Sheep bone as a sign of human descent: tibial symbolism among the Mongols', in R. Willis (ed.), *Signifying Animals: Human Meaning in the Natural World*, One World Archaeology 16, London, 74–84

Tambiah, S.J. 1969: 'Animals are good to think and good to prohibit', *Ethnology* 8 (4), 423–59

Tassinari, S. 1973: 'Pots avec une anse dont l'attache inférieure figure un pied humain', *Collection de la Bibliothèque des Hautes Études* Section 4, 3.5, 127–40

Tassinari, S. 1975: *La vaisselle de bronze romaine et provinciale, au Musée des Antiquités Nationales*, Gallia supplement 29, Paris

Thienpont, D., Rochette, F. and Vanparijs, O.F.J. 1979: *Diagnosing Helminthiasis by Coprological Examination*, Beerse

Timby, J. 1989: 'The pottery', in M.G. Fulford, *The Silchester Amphitheatre: Excavations of 1979–85*, Britannia Monograph 10, London, 80–110

Timby, J. 1991: 'The Berkeley Street pottery kiln, Gloucester', *Journal Roman Pottery Studies* 4, 19–32

Timby, J. 2000a: 'The ceramic tile', in Fulford and Timby 2000, 116–22

Timby, J. 2000b: 'The pottery', in Fulford and Timby 2000, 180–312

Timby, J. 2006: 'The pottery', in Fulford, Clarke and Eckardt 2006, 86–115

Timby, J. 2007: 'The pottery', in Clarke *et al.* 2007

Timby, J., Booth, P. and Allen, T.G. 1997: 'A new early Roman fineware industry in the Upper Thames Valley', Unpublished report

Tomber, R. and Dore, J. 1998: *The National Roman Fabric Reference Collection: A Handbook*, MoLAS Monograph 2, London

Tootell, K. 2006: 'Ironmaking and ironworking: the archaeological context', in Fulford, Clarke and Eckardt 2006, 145–59

Toynbee, J.M.C. 1973: *Animals in Roman Life and Art*, London

Trickett, S. 1999: *The Relevance of Phytosociology to Environmental Archaeology: Archaeobotanical Remains from the Late Bronze Age to the Roman Period in the Lower Thames Valley*, Unpublished BA Diss., University of Oxford

Tyers, P. 1996: *Roman Pottery in Britain*, London

Tylecote, R.F. 1986: *The Prehistory of Metallurgy in the British Isles*, London

Ulrich, R.B. 2007: *Roman Woodworking*, New Haven & London

Vanderhoven, A. and Ervynck, A. 2007: 'Not in my backyard! The industry of secondary animal products within the Roman civitas capital of Tongeren (Belgium)', in R. Hingley and S. Willis (eds), *Roman Finds: Context and Theory. Proceedings of a Conference held at the University of Durham, July 2002*, Oxford, 156–75

Vanvinckenroye, W. 1984: *De Romeinse Zuidwest-begraafplaats van Tongeren: opgravingen 1972–1981*, Publikaties van het Provinciaal Gallo-Romeins Museum te Tongeren 29, Tongeren

Varro: *On Agriculture*, trans. H.B. Ash 1934, Loeb Classical Library 283, Cambridge, Mass.

Veen, M. van der, Livarda, A. and Hill, A. 2008: 'New plant foods in Roman Britain – dispersal and social access', *Environmental Archaeology* 13 (1), 11–36

Venturi, L. 1926: *La Collezione Gualino*, Turin & Rome

Wait, G.A. 1985: *Ritual and Religion in Iron Age Britain*, British Archaeological Report 149, Oxford

Walton Rogers, P. 1997: *Textile Production at 16–22 Coppergate*, Archaeology of York 17/11, York

Warry, P. 2006: *Tegulae: Manufacture, Typology and Use in Roman Britain*, BAR British Series 417, Oxford

Watson, J. 1987: 'Mineral preserved organic material from the Corbridge Hoard', *Ancient Monument Laboratory Reports* 158/87, English Heritage, London

Watson, J. 2008: 'Silchester, Hampshire. Conservation of a Wooden Writing Tablet. Archaeological Conservation Report', *English Heritage Research Department Report Series* no. 54-2008, Portsmouth

Wattez, J. and Courty, M.A. 1987: 'Morphology of ash of some plant remains', in N. Federoff, L.M. Bresson and M.A. Courty (eds), *Micromorphologie des sols — Soil Micromorphology*, Paris, 677–83

Wattez, J., Courty, M.A. and Macphail, R. 1990: 'Burnt organo-mineral deposits related to animal and human activities in prehistoric caves', in L.A. Douglas (ed.), *Soil Micromorphology: A Basic and Applied Science. Proceedings of the VIIIth International Working Meeting of Soil Micromorphology, San Antonio, Texas, July 1988*, Developments in Soil Sciences 19, New York

Waugh, H. and Goodburn, R. 1972: 'The non-ferrous metal objects', in Frere 1972, 114–62

Wedlake, W.J. 1982: *The Excavation of the Shrine of Apollo at Nettleton, Wiltshire, 1956–71*, Report of the Research Committee of the Society of Antiquaries of London 40, London

Welch, F.B.A. and Trotter, F.M. 1961: *Geology of the Country around Monmouth and Chepstow*. Sheets 233 and 250. Memoir of the Geological Survey of Great Britain, London

Wheeler, R.E.M. 1930: *London in Roman Times*, London Museum Catalogues 3, London

Wheeler, R.E.M. and Wheeler, T.V. 1932: *Report on the Excavation of the Prehistoric, Roman and Post-Roman Site in Lydney Park, Gloucestershire*, Report of the Research Committee of the Society of Antiquaries of London 9, London

Wheeler, R.E.M. and Wheeler, T.V. 1936: *Verulamium. A Belgic and two Roman Cities*. Report of the Research Committee of the Society of Antiquaries of London 11, Oxford

White, K.D. 1970: *Roman Farming*, London

Wilkinson, I.P., Williams, M., Young, J.R., Fulford, M.G. and Lott, G.K. 2008: 'The application of microfossils in assessing the provenance of chalk used in the manufacture of Roman mosaics at Silchester', *Journal of Archaeological Science* 35, 2415–22

Williams, D.F. 2002: 'Purbeck marble in Roman and medieval Britain', in D.A. Hinton (ed.), *Purbeck Papers*, Oxford, 126–31

Williams, S. 2006: 'The oyster shells', in Fulford, Clarke and Eckardt 2006, 196–9

Williams, S. 2007: 'The snails', in Clarke *et al.* 2007 http://intarch.ac.uk/journal/issue21/4/finds_nails.htm

Wilmott, T. 1991: *Excavations in the Middle Walbrook Valley*, London & Middlesex Archaeological Society/ Surrey Archaeological Society Special Paper 13, London

Wilson, B. 1992: 'Considerations for the identification of ritual deposits of animal bones in Iron Age pits', *International Journal of Osteoarchaeology* 2, 341–9

Wilson, B. 1996: *Spatial Patterning among the Animal Bones in Settlement Archaeology: An English Regional Exploration*, Oxford

Wilson, B. 1999: 'Displayed or concealed? Cross cultural evidence for symbolic and ritual activity depositing Iron Age animal bones', *Oxford Journal of Archaeology* 18 (3), 297–305

Woelfle, E. 1967: *Vergleichend morphologische Untersuchungen an Einzelknochen des postcranialen Skelettes in Mitteleuropa vorkommender Enten, Halbgänse und Säger*, Unpublished Diss., Universität München

Wooders, J. 2000: 'The stone', in Fulford and Timby 2000, 83–100

Woodward, P. and Woodward, A. 2004: 'Dedicating the town: urban foundation deposits in Roman Britain', *World Archaeology* 36 (1), 68–86

Worrell, S. 2006: 'Roman Britain in 2005. II. Finds reported under the Portable Antiquities Scheme', *Britannia* 37, 429–66

Young, C.J. 1977: *Oxfordshire Roman Pottery*, BAR British Series 43, Oxford

INDEX